PROFESSIONAL
DEVELOPER'S GUIDE
TO

DOMINO®

PROFESSIONAL DEVELOPER'S GUIDE TO
DOMINO®

Jane Calabria and Rob Kirkland

with Susan Trost and Adam Kornak

Professional Developer's Guide to Domino®

Copyright© 1997 by Que® Corporation.

Library of Congress Catalog No.: 97-69960

ISBN: 0-7897-1195-8

99 98 97   6 5 4 3 2 1

Interpretation of the printing code: The rightmost double-digit number is the year of the book's printing; the rightmost single-digit number, the number of the book's printing. For example, a printing code of 97-1 shows that the first printing of the book occurred in 1997.

Screen reproductions in this book were created using Collage Plus from Inner Media, Inc., Hollis, NH.

Credits

President
Roland Elgey

Publisher
Stacy Hiquet

Director of Marketing
Lynn E. Zingraf

Editorial Services Director
Elizabeth Keaffaber

Title Manager
Bryan Gambrel

Project Director
Al Valvano

Production Editor
Matthew B. Cox

Editors
Elizabeth Barrett
Lisa M. Gebken
Kate Givens
Patricia R. Kinyon
Mike La Bonne
Juliet MacLean
Caroline D. Roop
Nick Zafran

Aquisitions Editor
Al Valvano

Product Marketing Manager
Kris Ankney

Assistant Product Marketing Manager
Christy M. Miller

Technical Editors
Steve Kern
Debbie Lynd

Technical Specialist
Nadeem Muhammed

Acquisitions Coordinator
Carmen Krikorian

Operations Coordinator
Patricia J. Brooks
Susan Gallagher

Editorial Assistant
Andrea Duvall

Book Designer
Ruth Harvey

Cover Designer
Glenn Larsen

Production Team
Jason Carr
Julie Geeting
DiMonique Ford
Trey Frank
Brian Grossman

Composed in *Goudy, Helvetica Condensed, MCPdigital, Stone Serif, Symbol, Utopia,* and *Zapf Dingbats* by Que Corporation.

Dedication

Jane and Rob: To Deena Whitfield—We are thinking of you and deeply saddened by your loss. We hope that soon the sun will shine upon you so that you can shine upon us all with your loving memories of Patrick.

Adam Kornak: This book is dedicated to all my family and friends, and especially to Julie, my loving bride-to-be.

Acknowledgments

Jane Calabria and Rob Kirkland: We would like to acknowledge that we are still married. We would also like to acknowledge that we are even still in love, still *like* each other, and hope that it will stay that way forever. To many who know us (and perhaps to ourselves), these are amazing facts considering this book. Writing through several beta releases of software, during the holidays, all the while purchasing a new home, selling an old one, moving, and lastly, perhaps most importantly, during Lotusphere 97, had our friends betting we'd never make it. Well, we did and are thrilled with the results (of the book and our relationship!).

What were the last few months like? Separate offices on separate floors (I smoked, he hated it) with network cabling running through the living room and dining room, draped over half-packed moving boxes. Unopened mail and bills piling on the dining room table. Rubber-banded newspapers lying in the hallway. Empty refrigerators and fast food places who delivered and never needed to ask our address—they recognized our voices on the phone! Clocks whose batteries had run down and dark rooms in need of light bulbs with no one to shop for supplies. Books, release notes, technical publications, white papers, CDs, unlabeled disks on every horizontal surface in the house (and some vertical). Bathroom scales that refused to stay at one number and shrinking clothes with 4 A.M. coffee stains. And then there was that night, just a few days before Lotusphere, lying in bed together, all snuggled up, that Rob read to me in bed. It was about 3 A.M. I interrupted him and asked if he really thought that *any* other couple in *any* other place in the country, no, in the *world* was doing exactly the same thing at that very moment. "Reading in bed? Sure, what's so strange about that?" he replied. I asked, "Really? Reading *Lotus Release Notes* in bed at 3 A.M.?"

So, you see? It is a rather amazing fact that we survived this. That said, and now that we've made it sound as if we wrote this book on our very own, we'd like to share with you our gratitude and highest regard and respect for the team of people, without whom we would still be reading *Release Notes* at 3 A.M. It is this very team of people who are responsible for the success of this project and its timely delivery to the bookshelves.

We count them among our friends, and our blessings, and they are the Lotus Notes professionals and the Que editors you will find in the preceding pages. Please take the time to read their credits.

We would also like to thank our Dad, Weymouth Kirkland, who made it financially possible for us to take the time away from our clients to write this book (and many others over the past few months) and still be able to afford the new house! We love you always and thank you for your love, support, and belief in our efforts. Now, please, you and Jean pack your bags and come and see us!

Next, we'd like to acknowledge the great developers at Lotus Development and Iris Associates for presenting important, valuable, and timely information at Lotusphere 97. This was the best Lotusphere yet and, Ned Batchelder, we voted your Domino presentation Best-in-Show! May we borrow your wizard hat sometime?

Our love and thanks to Patience Rockey, President, Rockey and Associates, Malvern, PA, who shares us with our publisher and who is always waiting with open arms and a ticker tape "task list" for our return.

A special thanks to Ken Adams of InterFusion for developing and bringing up **www. planetdomino.net** as a resource site for this book and a great place for developers to hang out. Please visit this site. You can read about Ken's efforts in Chapter 18. Ken, you still owe us for the hat we had made at Lotusphere—$35!

We'd also like to thank Cate Richards, our friend, for allowing us to participate in her best-selling *Special Edition Lotus Notes and Domino 4.5* and for her invaluable advice during the development of this book. We were proud to wear (though it was weird, Cate) her name upon our left breast pockets during author signing. Be sure to obtain a copy of Cate's book to learn even more about Lotus Notes!

To the folks at Bay Resources, we send our sincere thanks for enabling our book "workshop" to be held at PSR in Orlando, Florida, after Lotusphere. It was a great opportunity to test-drive the book content. Thanks to Amy Draeger, CLI at PSR, for a flawless setup and to the "guys" from NextAge (Norwalk, CT), Doug Campbell and David Frieman, for their contributions to the class.

Personal thanks to Dorothy Burke, who has been an integral part of every Notes writing project we've undertaken. And to Debbie Lynd who is always a close friend, great business partner, a walking Notes knowledge base, and great technical editor. To Christina Rockey, "Ms. ActiveX," who never ceases to amaze us with her editing, writing, and research. We send with you our hearts as you return to Seattle. We will miss you.

Our eternal thanks to Martha O'Sullivan and Lynn Zingraf for allowing us to juggle schedules and see this project in on time.

Most importantly, our sincere gratitude to Al Valvano at Que who started this project as an Acquisitions Editor and ended it as a Title Manager. Congratulations on your well-deserved promotion! Al presented us with this opportunity and worked hard and diligently educating us every step along the way. His rare combination of knowledge, experience, professionalism, and humor has spoiled us completely. If every author in the world were guaranteed the opportunity to work with Al, there would be only authors in the world as no one would want any other job whatsoever! Al, we thank you for this opportunity and for your invaluable guidance. We know that you have an incredible career ahead of you and we hope you remember us "when."

Adam Kornak: Thanks to Al Valvano at Que for giving me the opportunity to contribute to this book. Also, special thanks to Jane and Rob who were an inspiration to write with. Finally, thanks to all my friends at TSG-Chicago, who are a great team to work with.

Adam Kornak: **akornak@swspectrum.com**

About the Authors

Jane "JC" Calabria and Rob Kirkland are husband and wife Lotus Notes Professionals. Jane is Director of Corporate Accounts and Rob is a Senior Systems Analyst for Rockey and Associates, a Lotus Premium Business Partner and Lotus Authorized Education Center located in Malvern, PA, just outside of Philadelphia. Jane's primary responsibilities are Notes rollout and education and Rob is chief geek and Notes guru. Both are Certified Lotus Professionals and Rob is also a Certified Lotus Instructor, Certified NetWare Engineer, and Microsoft Certified Product Specialist in Windows NT. If they passed their beta tests at Lotusphere this year (results aren't known at this writing), Jane will also be a Certified Principal Application Developer and Rob will have the distinction of both Principal Application Developer and Principal System Administrator.

Together, they deliver seminars, classes, and workshops all around the country on Lotus Notes, Domino, and the Internet. They are featured in two Lotus Notes training video series; *Notes Application Development I* and *Domino Essentials* produced by LearnKey Inc. in St. George, UT. LearnKey (1-800-865-0165) features nationally recognized trainers and professionals in their certification and development series of videos and interactive CD-ROMs. In the past year they have authored or have been contributing authors of 13 Que books including *Lotus Notes 4.5 and the Internet 6 in 1, 10 Minute Guide to Lotus Notes Mail 4.5, 10 Minute Guide to Lotus Notes 4.5 Web Navigator,* and Cate Richards' *Special Edition, Using Lotus Notes and Domino 4.5.*

In her spare time, Jane is a correspondent for Philadelphia's KYW News Radio 1060 AM where she broadcasts weekly as "JC on PCs" with her computer news and tips. In his spare time, Rob picked up a law degree from Chicago-Kent College of Law. You can reach them at **74754.3360@compuserve.com**.

Adam Kornak is a consultant and freelance writer currently residing in the Windy City of Chicago. He has been certified with Lotus as a Notes Developer and Administrator through Release 4, as well as becoming a cc:Mail Certified Specialist. He is also working toward becoming an MCSE with Microsoft in the coming months. Adam specializes in managing Notes infrastructures and engineering large networks. He has worked in the computer industry for the last seven years after graduating from Northern Illinois University. Adam has also worked as a technical editor on Que's *Using SmartSuite 97* and *Using 1-2-3.* In his spare time, Adam enjoys writing music on guitar and practicing the martial arts. Adam can be reached via the Internet at **harvinova@aol.com**.

We'd Like to Hear from You!

As part of our continuing effort to produce books of the highest possible quality, Que would like to hear your comments. To stay competitive, we *really* want you to let us know what you like or dislike most about this book or other Que products.

Please send your comments, ideas, and suggestions for improvement to:

The Expert User Team
E-mail: **euteam@que.mcp.com**
CompuServe: **105527,745**
Fax: (317) 581-4663

Our mailing address is:

Expert User Team
Que Corporation
201 West 103rd Street
Indianapolis, IN 46290-1097

You can also visit our team's home page on the World Wide Web at:

http://www.quecorp.com/developer_expert

Thank you in advance. Your comments will help us to continue publishing the best books available in today's market.

Thank you,

The Expert User Team

Contents at a Glance

Contents

7 Designing Forms for an Interactive Web Site   175

8 Building Views for Domino Web Applications   193

9 Preparing to Go Public   211

III Advanced Domino Application Design Techniques for the Web   223

10 Using Special Web Fields and Forms   225

11 Automating Web Applications with Agents   245

16   Using Advanced Administration Techniques   337

V   Building a Domino Site   373

17   Building a Domino Web Site in One Day with Domino Action   375

18 Building a Domino Web Site from Scratch   415

19 Migrating R3 Notes Applications to Domino 447

20 Preparing Existing Applications for the Web   467

VI Implementing and Using Domino's Other Internet Services   489

21 Domino Server Internet Mail Features   491

Introduction

When Lotus released version 4.5 of Notes, it renamed the Notes server. While the Notes client is still called *Lotus Notes*, the server is now called *Lotus Domino, powered by Notes* or simply *Lotus Domino*. Lotus's goal in renaming the server was to highlight the extent to which it has become not merely a Notes server but also an HTTP server, a Web server—indeed, the premier Web server of them all. If it seems like we keep switching back and forth between referring to our subject as Notes and Domino, it is because sometimes we are referring to the Notes client, other times to the Domino server. Since even the Domino server comes with a Notes client interface, sometimes it may seem like we are referring to the server as Notes, not Domino. That is, hopefully, because we are really talking about the server's Notes client, not the server itself. However, we have spent years referring to the server as the Notes server. Sometimes we may revert to old, calcified habits and refer mistakenly to the Domino server as the Notes server. For that, and whatever confusion results either from our error or Lotus's brashness in renaming the server at this late date, we apologize. Take comfort, if you can, that it has been as hard for us, as old Notes hands, to twist our old brains around to this new nomenclature as it is for you to follow the jumps from one name to the other.

Lotus Domino is an extraordinary Web server. It can easily do things that other Web servers can do not at all or only with the application of prodigious feats of programming. When you compare what a Domino Web server can do to the capabilities of a standard Web server, Domino will take your breath away. The reason is that Domino is "powered by Notes"; it applies the fundamental design of Notes and all of Notes's services to the Web server function.

What is a Web Server?

A Web server is basically a file server. Web browsers and other programs can communicate with it using a set of commands known by the collective name of Hyper Text Transfer Protocol; hence Web servers are also known as HTTP servers. You send a file name to a Web server and it sends you back the file. You send the file name in the form of an URL, which identifies not only the name of the file, but the server on which it resides and its location on that server. The Web server sends the file back to you in the form of a MIME-encoded file. The file is usually encoded as a text file in a special text format called HTML, HyperText Markup Language. HTML is a "rich" text format that allows you to embed "tags" in the text that a Web browser can interpret as formatting information, so that the document appears in the browser not as just plain text but as formatted text.

One kind of tag you can embed in an HTML document is special. It is the *hyperlink* tag, and it is largely this that has made the World Wide Web so exciting. It is special because it appears in the browser as highlighted text or as a picture that, when you point at it with your mouse, causes the pointer to change to a special shape, usually that of a pointing hand, and when you click on it, causes the browser to send out, to some Web server somewhere, another URL, which in turn causes that Web server to send yet another file to your browser.

What is special about this is that authors of HTML documents can use it to link them to other documents on other servers all over the world. It enables a new kind of information gathering, one that proceeds by a combination of goal-seeking and serendipity, as the person seeking information has the constantly repeated opportunity to either continue toward the original goal or to change that goal in response to the new document that has just now appeared on the screen, containing new and, perhaps, surprising information that, perhaps, suggests whole new avenues of research.

This new, serendipitous research paradigm has caught the imagination of the world and has actually caused the World Wide Web itself to veer off in directions other than its inventors originally imagined. Initially intended as what we just described—a new and different research tool—the World Wide Web has become many other things. Because the syntax of the URL allows the Web browser to send other types of information than just file names to the Web server, and because the Web server can send out any kind of file defined by the MIME standard, not just HTML files, the Web has evolved and become a platform on which you can build many kinds of tools, not just a new and cool research tool. So, thanks to the infinite cleverness of computer programmers, the Web browser has become the universal tool for accessing not only Web servers but many other kinds of Internet servers, from Archie to FTP to Gopher to WAIS servers. The Web browser is evolving into the universal user interface, the user's access to every kind of program, database, and server. Every kind of program has gained or is being transformed by its creators into either a Web server or a Web browser or both.

But at bottom, the Web server is just a file server. It is that very simplicity of the Web model, in fact, that has propelled it past so many other, more sophisticated information management models, including the most sophisticated of them all, Notes itself, to the front of the pack. On the other hand, it is that very simplicity that, when you compare it to Notes's own information model, makes Domino such an extraordinary Web server. The Web model is not really well suited to all the other uses the world wants to put it to, and it has become festooned, like a Christmas tree, with add-ons—CGI, plug-ins, ActiveX and Java add-ins, and specialized, adjunct servers. The Web model was not originally imagined as the all-purpose vehicle that it has become, so most powerful Web server implementations have a kludginess to them. Domino, the most powerful Web server implementation of all, is sleek and elegant by comparison.

Domino—a Perfect Web Server

Notes was imagined from its inception, and developed from the ground up as a tool to do all the things that people want the Web to do. Notes is the hypertext research medium that the Web was originally designed to be. Notes is a messaging environment. A discussion forum. A project tracking tool. A programming environment. A computer medium in which to model, reproduce, improve, and automate the workflows that occur within groups of people working together. Notes provides an information storage model and an array of information management services that naturally lend themselves to the information publication functions that a Web server provides as well as the many other functions that programmers have envisioned for the Web server of the future. It is these design features and services, applied to Domino's Web server function, that make Domino so much better than other Web servers.

Notes is built on an information storage model that Lotus calls the NSF object store. (NSF stands for Notes Storage Facility). The NSF file is an object storage facility. That is, it is a method of storing, in a single file, any number of information objects of any imaginable kind, from text to formatted text, to numbers, to time and dates, to graphics, sound, and video, to embedded programs and pointers to other objects. That is, the information in the object store can be structured any old way you want. Not only do you store the information in the object store, but you store the *meta*-information as well, that is, the information about the target information. Located in one file are a data object along with various kinds of information about the object, such as what kind of object it is, where it is located in the file, how much space it takes up in the file, and one or more indexes that give quick access to the object.

On top of this foundation Lotus has built the Notes document model and a number of powerful services. In the Notes document model, a *document* exists not as a single entity but has a composite of elements that exist independently of each other. The content of the document is located in one or more *data notes*, the formatting and composition in one or more *design notes*, such as *forms, subforms,* and *shared fields.* The designer of a Notes application determines exactly how a given *document* will appear and what information it will reveal to any given user and how much control the user will have over the document under any given run-time circumstances.

With *Notes views*, Lotus has refined the document model even further. A Note view consists of data pulled from any number of data notes and presented in a table format that s controlled by the designer of the application *or* the user. Views provide a method f access to the data in a Notes database and of organizing and managing data that is revolutionary on the Web. With views, Domino can present content from multiple sources n any number of summary tables, automatically categorized and sorted, without any intervention by the Webmaster. What other Web server can do such a thin?

Notes security is comprehensive and granular. The designer of a Notes application can define at any level—database, view, form, document, or field—who can create, alter, or view the data in a Notes database. This type of control is essential not only to the creation of sophisticated, interactive Web sites in which the Web users participate in the creation of the content, it is also an invaluable feature of any content-authoring system. Even to create a simple Web site that *merely* presents static data to its audience, you have to decide who will create the content, who approve the content for publication, and what will become of the data as it ages. The tools to control these things are an integral part of Notes; they permit you to use Notes itself as the content authoring, editing, and management system. Designers of other Web delivery systems have to build such controls from scratch.

Notes also incorporates comprehensive and pervasive programming capability. Start with the Notes @function language, which anyone who has created a spreadsheet will find familiar, but which, with functions like @dbcolumn, @dblookup, @GetDocField, @SetDocField, and many more, is very powerful. Continue with LotusScript, a full programming language with loops, variables, arrays, access to DLLs, LSXes, the Notes API, compliant with ANSI BASIC, but with object extensions, and built right into the Notes client. Add APIs for Visual BASIC programmers, C and C++ programmers, CGI scriptwriters, and Java programmers.

You need not learn a whole new programming language—CGI, Perl, Java, or whatever—to apply Notes and its power to the Web—unless you want to. Notes will permit you to apply whatever programming capability you already have, starting with your spreadsheet programming experience and building from there.

Replication is another cornerstone of Notes that makes easy what is extremely difficult with other Web servers. Replication provides Notes users with local, easily accessible copies of Notes databases that maintain more or less identical data sets with other replica copies. Replication provides Webmasters with Web site portability unthinkable with any other Web server product. Notes replication permits easy setup of true mirror Web sites, firewalls between a company's public Web site and its internal, "staging" servers. With standard, simple Web technology doing any of these things is onerously difficult or impossible. With Domino Web technology, these things are all but automatic.

Notes messaging is the first thing people think of when they hear the mention of Notes. It provides Notes with its e-mail system, workflow capabilities, and much of its manageability. It provides an alternative to the replication system, so that a database can deliver a document to another database either by replication or mail delivery, depending on the intent of the designer of the Notes application. Whether you need or want to apply Notes messaging capabilities to a Web application is not a question of whether or not you can, but rather a question of how best to design a Web application. Like replication and other Notes services, Notes messaging is a service intended originally to enhance native Notes functionality that naturally lends itself to the enhancement of Web functionality.

Notes's enterprise integration provides access from within Notes to other data storage and management systems of all types, and provides access to Notes data from them. The number and variety of tools for connecting Notes to outside data sources is large and growing. So if your goal it to provide Web users with access to back-end or legacy data, located anywhere from PC-based spreadsheets or relational database systems to mainframe-based data systems, don't think you have to fall back on CGI. Note provides built-in tools for connecting to OLE objects and ODBC-compliant data sources. Use NotesPump, MQSeries, or any number of other tools to connect to other data sources.

Finally, Notes provides comprehensive integration with the Web. Where Notes and HTML have analogous functionality, Domino converts Notes features to their Web analogs transparently. Where HTML provides a function unknown to Notes—for example, horizontal rules—or where Domino does not yet directly support a function—for example, embedding Java applets—Domino gives the Notes application designer and, for that matter, the Notes or Web user the ability to insert HTML tags into Notes forms or into Notes text fields and rich text fields. The Domino extensions to URL syntax and vocabulary effectively provide another API into Notes data. The Web user can extract data from Notes databases using Domino URLs. The Domino application developer can use the Domino URLs to accomplish tricks that would be otherwise impossible, with or without Domino.

Taken all together, the Domino Web server, powered by Notes and all its capabilities, is a Web server in a class by itself. That is the essence of what this book is about. We examine Lotus Domino 4.5 primarily from the point-of-view of the Web developer wanting to employ it to create the perfect Web site. We also focus on the Web site management aspects of Domino, because we don't feel it is possible to create a perfect Web site with Domino if you do not also build in the management functions available to Notes developers. Finally, for the sake of completeness, we look at the other Internet integration features of the Domino 4.5 server—the built-in Web browser functions, the SMTP and POP3 mail functions, and the Web application building tools, Domino Action. Our hope is that this book will help you to gain an in-depth understanding of Web applications you can build and manage with Domino and a complete overview of other Internet capabilities of Domino.

Who Should Use This Book?

This book is written for the Notes application developer who needs to learn how to develop Notes applications for the Web. The developer will learn which design features and functions of Lotus Notes 4.5 will perform well and learn considerations to take when developing applications which will be viewed through a Web browser. The developer will also learn some undocumented trips and tricks for obtaining ultimate performance of their applications as they are delivered to the Web, or the company intranet.

This books is also written for the Notes systems administrator who will learn how to run and manage the HTTP server task, control Web access to Notes applications and manage registration of Web users at the site. Administrators will also learn about Notes other Internet services, such as mail.

Developers and WebMasters who have worked in other products will learn how Domino differs from other Web servers and the details of its ease of use and secure environment. This book is also for those who wish to learn more about Domino's performance on the Web. Managers and business owners who are considering Domino as their Web server will gain insight into Dominos capabilities.

The CD-ROM that accompanies this book contains the *Special Edition, Using HTML* and the *Special Edition Using Java*, important tools for Notes developers who are new to application development for the Web.

How To Use This Book

This book is divided into five parts. The first part of the book provides an introduction to Domino and Notes applications on the Internet and the Web. Even if you are an experienced Domino WebMaster be sure to read Part I to review Web design fundamentals and Web and Internet Tools. Parts II through V concentrate on the implementation of many of the tools discussed in Part I. In addition, these parts cover more advanced development and administration topics and techniques. Finally, Part VI discusses Domino Internet services that extend beyond building a Domino Web site, such as Internet mail features and the Web Navigators.

Part I   Introducing the Domino Server

Part I discusses:

In Chapter 1, "An Introduction To Domino 4.5 and the Internet" you are introduced to Lotus Notes applications, the Domino server, intranets, the Internet and how Domino has developed into a development tool for the Internet.

In Chapter 2, "Setting Up the Domino Server," you learn the system requirements for Domino and how to deploy Domino in your organization.

Chapter 3, "Working with Your Domino Web Site," provides you with the basic skills for navigating the unaltered Domino site.

Chapter 4, "Understanding Web Fundamentals," takes the mystery out of Web terms. In this chapter, you learn about Java, ActiveX and even learn how to create HTML pages.

Part II   Developing New Applications for the Web

In Part II, you learn the basic building blocks used in creating or redesigning a Notes database application for the Web. This part of the book discusses interactive forms, views and the steps you take to present your Notes applications to Web users.

In Chapter 5, "Building a Web Database" you learn how to set up a test environment for building Web applications using Domino and Notes. Here, you will learn which Notes features and functions perform well on the Web and which don't. You also learn options for linking documents.

Chapter 6, "Designing Forms to Display Documents on the Web," teaches you the basics of form design for the Web. You learn how to hide information from Web users, how to use HTML in Notes forms and how to create subforms for use as site navigators.

To make your site interactive, Chapter 7, "Designing Forms for an Interactive Web Site," provides the skills you need for creating input forms for Web users. Here, you learn how to provide access to forms, how to use CGI variables and how to create customized responses to Web users when they submit a form.

Chapter 8, "Building Domino Views for Web Applications" explains how View design considerations may differ for Notes users versus Web users. You learn how to use GIFs in Notes views, how to open documents by key, and how to use Actions in Views designed for the Web browser.

Chapter 9, "Preparing to Go Public," provides you with step-by-step instructions and considerations you need to take as you prepare to release your Notes application to the Web.

Part III   Advanced Domino Application Design

Part III covers advanced design techniques for Notes Web applications. In this section, we explore design techniques, agents and special function databases that give a "Web-look" to Notes applications . Here, you can find the answers to your "how'd they do that?" questions about the Lotus Domino site, **www.domino.lotus.com**.

Chapter 10, "Using Special Web Fields and Forms," defines Domino fields and forms reserved for Web use. You learn how to create customized view, navigator, and search templates. You also learn how to create a Home page form, enabling fields, subforms, and navigators to be incorporated in your Home page.

In Chapter 11, "Automating Web Applications with Agents," you learn how to write and use agents that help to keep your Web site functioning smoothly and efficiently.

Chapter 12, "Applying a 'Web Look' to Notes Applications," teaches you how to incorporate other Web tools into your Notes applications such as frames and java applets. You also learn how to bring your site to life with multimedia.

If you'd like to learn some of the techniques used at **www.domino.lotus.com**, Chapter 13, "Examining Special Function Databases for the Web," is a must-read! Here, we investigate the Domino discussion database and other special function Web databases, and teach you how the Lotus Domino developers designed such great views and forms.

Part IV   Using Advanced Administration Features

Security is of prime interest and importance to companies who are building Web presence. In this section of the book, we delve deep into securing the Domino Web server as well as some of the more advanced administration topics, such as multi-homing the server.

In Chapter 14, "Securing the Domino Web Server," you learn how to control access to your Domino server and request authentication by Notes or Web users. You also learn how to control access to views, folders, forms, and documents.

Chapter 15, "Using Secure Sockets Layer (SSL) with Domino," introduces you to the Internet security protocol, Secure Sockets Layer, and illustrates how Domino implements SSL with the Domino SSL Administration Application.

Learn how to multi-home a Domino site in Chapter 16, "Using Advanced Administration Techniques." In this chapter, you will also learn how to create a scaleable site with Domino Server Clusters.

Part V   Building a Domino Site

Part V discusses building a Domino site, not just a database. Here, you find how other companies designed and built their Domino sites as well as how to build your own site in one day. You also learn how to convert existing Notes applications to Web applications.

Chapter 17, "Building a Domino Web Site in One Day with Domino Action," gives you step-by-step instructions to building an interactive Web site, complete with user registration, discussion database, and a feedback area (to name a few) in a single day.

In Chapter 18 "Building a Domino Web Site from Scratch," we reveal the real life case history of **www.planetdomino.net**. You will understand how this site was planned, developed, designed, and delivered as well as some tips and techniques used by the developers.

In Chapter 19, "Migrating R3 Notes Applications to Domino," you learn how your R3 applications can be prepared and converted to Web applications.

Chapter 20 "Preparing Existing Applications for the Web," provides the information you will need to deliver existing R4x Notes applications to the Web.

Part VI Implementing and Using Dominos other Internet Services

Domino offers more than HTTP services. The Domino server can be your gateway to the Internet. Release 4.5 of Notes also introduces the new Server and Personal Web Navigators, allowing you to surf the Net as you convert Web pages to Notes documents. Part VI covers these additional Internet services in detail.

In Chapter 21, " Domino Server Internet Mail Features," you learn how to install and configure the Lotus SMTP/MIME MTA as well as how to use Domino as a POP3 Mail server.

Chapter 22 "Using the Server Web Navigator" introduces you to Domino's web browser and teaches you how to configure, use, program, and customize the browser for your environment.

Chapter 23, "Using the Personal Web Navigator," discusses this new feature of Notes 4.5. Here, you learn how to set up and configure the Navigator as well as how to take advantage of some advanced features, such as Web Ahead and Page Minder.

Chapter 24 is titled, "Using the InterNotes Web Publisher."

Appendixes

You will also find information in the appendixes and on the enclosed CD-ROM to further facilitate your understanding of Web design. The appendixes provides additional reference information on many of the features and functions used throughout this book.

Appendix A, "Domino URLs," provides you with information on the Domino URL syntax and use.

Appendix B, "$$ Web Forms and Fields," lists the special reserved Domino Web fields and forms, their values, and their application."

Appendix C, "Domino Resources," Provides Web addresses for essential Domino support and information sites.

Appendix D, "Installing Windows NT Server 4.0."

Appendix E, "Lotus Add In Products," describes additional templates available from Lotus that extend Notes capabilities to the Web. These templates include such features as electronic commerce and database connectivity.

Appendix F, "InterNotes News," describes Lotus UseNet News Group services, one of the earliest Lotus products that connects Notes to the Internet.

Appendix G, "Domino Service Provider Applications," provides you with a brief insight into the contents of the enclosed CD and instructions on how to access the information.

Conventions Used in This Book

Que has over a decade of experience writing and developing the most successful computer books available. With that experience, we've learned what special features help readers the most. Look for these special features throughout the book to enhance your learning experience.

Several type and font conventions are used in this book to help make reading easier:

▶ *Italic type* is used to emphasize the author's points or to introduce new terms.

▶ Screen messages, code listings, and command samples appear in `monospace typeface`.

▶ Anything you are asked to type appears in **boldface**.

 Tip

Tips present short advice on a quick or often overlooked procedure. These include shortcuts that can save you time.

 Note

Notes provide additional information that may help you avoid problems, or offers advice that relates to the topic.

 Caution

Cautions warn you about potential problems that a procedure may cause, unexpected results, and mistakes to avoid.

Sidebar

Longer discussions not integral to the flow of the chapter are set aside as sidebars. Look for these sidebars to find out even more information.

Introducing the Domino Server

## chapter 1

An Introduction to Domino 4.5 and the Internet

1

In this chapter

◆ **What Lotus Notes is—an overview**
This is a quick review of the basic features and benefits of Notes.

◆ **What the Internet is—an overview**
If you don't know what the Internet is, the significance of the Notes Internet enhancements will escape you. We present a brief history and overview of the Internet to provide context for the discussion of Notes' Internet enhancements.

◆ **Significant Internet protocols**
The Internet and its protocols are inseparable. You can't fully appreciate the one without knowing something about the other.

◆ **Significant Internet tools**
You may have heard of some of the tools that people use on the Internet. Here, we introduce you to some of the more common Internet tools and their uses.

◆ **The World Wide Web**
This is the part of the Internet that everyone is excited about, so we'll look at it a little more closely than the other parts of the Internet.

◆ **Intranets and extranets**
Intranets and extranets are the latest craze, after the Internet. Here, you learn what they are and how they relate to the Internet.

◆ **Lotus' Internet strategy**
Along with the rise in popularity of the Internet came predictions that it would spell the demise of Notes. Lotus has proven otherwise. Here is Lotus' strategy for integrating Notes with the Internet instead of pitting Notes against the Internet.

◆ **Notes' Internet enhancements—an overview**
This is an overview and brief description of Lotus' Internet products and Notes'/Domino's Internet features.

In the last few years, the long-simmering, slowly growing Internet reached a critical mass and then exploded in popularity. This phenomenon has radically altered the world of software developers. Developers have been scrambling to maintain the success of existing products in the radically changing computing environment and to capitalize on the fantastic new opportunities that the Internet represents.

Lotus Notes has been particularly threatened by the Internet. Many computer pundits have predicted that the Internet would render Notes irrelevant and obsolete. The developers at Lotus, however, preferred to adopt the more positive attitude that Notes and the Internet represent a natural and synergistic pairing, and they proceeded to enhance Notes with all sorts of Internet hooks and to turn Notes from a closed, proprietary system into a powerful platform for developing not just Notes applications but rather Internet applications. Lotus has tied Notes so closely to the Internet, in fact, they decided that, for Notes Release 4.5, which went on sale in December 1996, the Notes server should be renamed for the HTTP service that was formerly an add-in to the server. The server half of Lotus Notes is no longer the *Lotus Notes Server*, but is now the *Lotus Domino Server, Powered by Notes*.

This book is about the Internet enhancements to Lotus Notes/Domino. It is about creating a meaningful, data-rich Web site in a relatively short period of time that is easy to maintain because, to some extent, Notes maintains it automatically. The Notes IDE provides the developer with the ability to create dynamic, interactive Web sites with such impressive features as built-in calendaring and scheduling, support for uploading file attachments, and integrating Java applets.

This chapter provides an overall description of Notes/Domino and its Internet enhancements. For the reader who is not familiar with the Internet, this chapter provides an overview of the Internet.

A Brief Overview of Lotus Notes/Domino

Ask three people what groupware is and you are likely to get three different answers, at least one of which is "e-mail." The problem is groupware is defined as any software that helps people work together more effectively and efficiently. A lot of products fit that definition almost by accident. The Internet is groupware by that definition. Most "groupware" products facilitate workgroups only in a limited fashion. When asked what groupware is, then, most people will grope around for an answer, and reply with the piece of it they have used, usually e-mail.

Lotus Notes is virtually the paradigm of groupware. It is perhaps the only product that was developed to embody a *comprehensive* definition of groupware. It includes messaging, shared databases, and a powerful set of integrated programming tools designed for rapid development and deployment of customized groupware applications. There are numerous third-party products available, including end-user applications, application development tools, and server-enhancing add-ins. Typical Notes applications include electronic mail, information repositories, discussion databases, reference and broadcast databases of the type seen on the World Wide Web, project tracking applications, and automation of workflows.

Lotus Notes combines three key ingredients. It starts with sharable, distributed, document-oriented databases. It adds messaging in the form of fourth-generation (hypertext-enabled) electronic mail and the capability of Notes databases to pass messages to one another. It finishes up with a rich, integrated, easy-to-master set of programming tools with which Notes users can combine the first two features into flexible solutions to their business problems.

▶ *Shared document databases.* The heart of Notes is its shared document database technology. Notes databases consist of collections of documents contributed by Notes users or added automatically by the system in response to various events. Notes databases are sharable in the sense that multiple users can add to and access them simultaneously.

▶ *Messaging.* All Notes databases can be mail enabled, meaning they can be made to send documents to one another via Notes' built-in store-and-forward messaging capability. A by-product of this is Notes Mail, which is Notes' built-in e-mail system. Notes users can communicate with one another by Notes Mail and with non-Notes users through mail gateways.

▶ *Development tools.* In addition to its document databases and messaging capability, Notes provides a rich programming environment that offers you a selection of programming languages, from simple (the Notes @function language) to more powerful and complex (LotusScript™, an ANSI BASIC-compliant language similar to Visual BASIC™ but including object extensions; the Lotus Notes API, a library of C/C++ functions; HiTest Tools™ for Visual BASIC™; numerous third-party programming tools; and, due to be available in the summer of 1997, an implementation of Java™).

Types of Notes Applications

These three features of Notes combine to permit the quick creation and customization of Notes databases (applications) to accomplish a variety of purposes, including publication of information, tracking of projects, and workflow. Notes databases can be classified as follows:

▶ *Broadcast databases and reference libraries.* Notes is an ideal vehicle for storing masses of information that need to be available to masses of users. Notes documents can store virtually any type of information, including embedded files created in other applications. Notes provides powerful tools for locating information in its databases. These include multiple easily defined, user-customizable views of databases and a full-text indexing and search engine. These databases might be populated by people adding individual documents or by Notes programming that converts incoming data from, say, a newsfeed into Notes documents. In this capacity, Notes duplicates the capabilities of World Wide Web servers.

▶ *Discussion databases.* Notes documents can be defined as main documents or responses. As a result, one type of Notes database is the discussion database, in which one person starts a discussion by creating a main document and other people continue the discussion by creating responses. The responses appear in Notes views indented beneath the documents to which they respond, making it easy for the reader to follow a discussion thread. In this capacity, Notes duplicates the functions of bulletin board systems, discussion forums in CompuServe, and UseNet newsgroups and List Servers on the Internet.

▶ *Tracking databases and workflow applications.* This is where Notes stands out from the groupware crowd. In a tracking database, a group of people collaborating on a project add documents describing their activities. Every member of the group can keep track of the progress of the project by referring to the database. In a workflow application, programming and messaging are added to the tracking database so that the members of the group can be notified by Notes when they have to perform some activity crucial to the project.

Notes workflow applications typically incorporate both messaging and shared database features to accomplish their goals. An example of a simple workflow application is an expense-reporting application. At the end of a sales trip, a salesman fills out an expense report form in his Notes mail database. When the salesman saves and closes the expense report, Notes mails it automatically to an expense-tracking database on a Notes server, and mails a message to the appropriate manager notifying her that the expense report requires her review and approval.

The message received by the manager includes a link to the expense report in the tracking database. By double-clicking the link, the manager opens the expense report. The manager approves the report by placing an X in a box marked approved. When she saves the expense report, Notes affixes her signature to it, and then generates another message and mails it to the accounting clerk responsible for paying the expenses, and so the cycle continues.

If either the manager or the accounting clerk neglects a pending task, Notes can be programmed to send a reminder. If the person designated to complete a task is unavailable for any reason, Notes might automatically send the notice to a substitute.

Because all of the evolving information is stored in a central tracking database, anyone involved in the transaction can see its status simply by looking there. Form-routing programs typically mail the expense report successively to the manager and then to the clerk. In such a system, the salesperson who submitted the expense report has no way of checking the status of his expense check other than to track down and ask his manager and the accounting clerk if they have processed it yet. In Notes, he merely opens the expense report in the tracking database. If his manager has approved it, the report will reflect that fact. If the clerk has not issued the check, the report will reflect that fact as well.

Architecture of Notes Databases

Lotus Notes databases bear only the most superficial resemblance to standard computer databases. They do have records and fields in them, as do standard databases, but the resemblance ends right about there. In a standard database, all records in a table have the same set of fields and each field is the same fixed length, whether it contains data or not. This makes for quick retrieval of records because the database management software only has to calculate the offset from a specific memory location to locate any record or field. It also makes for a rigid database design and is best suited to data in which all records are uniform in character, that is, in which all records hold the same amount and type of data.

Notes records, known as *documents* or *notes*, look and feel more like word processor documents than database records. Notes fields do not have a fixed length and the length of any one field varies from document to document depending on the field's actual contents. No two documents in a database need incorporate the same array of fields. Document A might have fields one, two, and three, while document B has fields one, two, and four. And a document might acquire fields one and two when created, and then have fields three and four added at a later date. This characteristic of Notes databases makes them suitable for tracking extremely diverse pools of data, such as the types of data that office workers typically generate.

When you create, edit, or read a Notes document, you do so using a template known as a *form*. Forms define what fields can be added to a document when it is created or edited. They define what fields may be seen when reading the document. They also define how the document is formatted.

You may use one form to create a document and another to read it. Or I may read a document with Form A while you read it with Form B. The result might be that I, the salesperson, would see some fields and you, the manager, would see others. Notes databases typically have multiple forms.

To find information in a Notes database, you can either browse Notes views or you could use Notes' full text search engine to locate documents. A Notes view is a tabular listing of documents. The documents appear in rows, and information from the documents appears in columns. Most Notes databases include multiple views, allowing you to use the one most suited to your current need. For example, in a training department database, you might view course offerings by date in one view and by subject in another view. A third view might show only a subset of documents. For example, a view might show only the classes scheduled for this week.

Other Features of Notes

Standing alone, the features listed previously make powerful tools available to small groups of people—all of whom have constant computer access to the same database server. Several other features of Notes combine to make these capabilities available to groups of hundreds or thousands of people who may be located all over the world. Some of them may be only occasionally or never connected to the company LAN. Others may not be employed by our company at all, but instead may work for our customers or suppliers or business partners.

▶ *Client/server technology.* Notes is a client/server system. Notes servers store Notes databases, provide multiple levels of security, and make information in the databases available to people and other servers according to their access rights.

People use the Notes client to access the data on the servers. The Notes client can access Notes servers via network connections or remotely by modem. Notes Release 4 makes connection to servers a no-brainer for the user by allowing Notes administrators to predefine connection procedures from different locations.

For example, if a salesman is in the office, he connects to the LAN, tells Notes he is in the office, and Notes automatically uses the LAN to connect to the server. Then the salesman goes on the road, arrives in a hotel room, connects his modem to a telephone line and tells Notes he is located in a hotel. Notes automatically calls the server using the modem and a standard hotel phone system dialing sequence. All the user had to know was how to tell Notes his current location. The location profile, predefined by the Notes administrator, did all the hard work of reconfiguring Notes to connect properly using the available mode of connection.

▶ *Distributed data.* Notes databases can be fully replicated, meaning that full copies of them can be maintained in multiple locations, either on Notes servers or on Notes clients. Workers located in offices scattered all over the world may access copies of a database located on their local Notes servers. They don't have to suffer slow response times by accessing remote databases over narrow-bandwidth links in real time. The company does not have to bear the expense of high-bandwidth wide area network connections.

1

Users use the local copy of the database, adding documents, editing existing documents, and reviewing others. Periodically—hourly, daily, or weekly, depending on the nature of the application—the servers replicate with one another. All changes in each copy of the database are replicated with the other copies of the database so that, over time, the workers see not only their local changes but also those made by remote workers.

Likewise, home-based workers or workers who are on the move, flying or driving from appointment to appointment, can carry replica copies of relevant databases on their laptops. They can work locally, reviewing project status and adding new documents to reflect their own activities. From time to time, they can connect to a Notes server by modem or by connecting to the network and replicate their copy of the database with the server copy, sending their changes and receiving those made by their coworkers.

▶ *Connectivity.* Notes was designed from the ground up to work with whatever other software tools you may use. You can pull information into Notes documents from all of your desktop productivity applications as well as from databases located on PCs and mainframes. You can also export information to your back-end databases. Also, Notes runs on a variety of platforms including Windows, Windows 95, Windows NT, Macintosh, OS/2, NetWare, and several varieties of UNIX. It can use all major networking protocols including TCP/IP, SPX/IPX, NetBEUI, NetBIOS, AppleTalk, and Banyan VINES.

A Brief Overview of the Internet

Over the last few years, the Internet has become an inescapable presence in our world. It has been around, in one form or another, since the late sixties, growing slowly over most of that time. But, in the last few years, it has caught the imagination of the general public; and its growth has become explosive as the number of people using the Internet has doubled, redoubled, and redoubled again in a very short period of time. Now you can barely turn on the television or open a magazine without seeing advertisers' Internet addresses plastered across the screen or page.

What became the Internet started out as an experimental network sponsored by the Defense Department. The original purpose of the Internet was to encourage communication and collaboration among people doing government research and, later, general academic research. Over most of its duration, the Internet was a ho-hum, text-only medium. Early on, the tools available for using it were hard to master. These things limited the audience and the appeal of the Internet.

As time passed, the usefulness of the Internet for long-distance communication and collaboration caught the attention of more and more people. Users of the Internet added new and better tools and protocols to the tool set. Computer technology became widely and cheaply available.

A few years ago, these trends converged to fuel the Internet's present explosive growth. Programmers at CERN (European Laboratory for Particle Physics) in Switzerland developed a new kind of research tool that involved rich text documents with links to related documents embedded right in the body of a document. This tool became the World Wide Web. The documents were not just plain text. They were formatted text and they could include embedded objects, such as pictures.

Later, programmers at the National Center for Supercomputing Applications (NCSA) in Urbana, Illinois, created a graphical tool for viewing documents on the World Wide Web. They called this new tool *Mosaic*, and they distributed it for free to anyone who wanted to use it and further develop it.

Mosaic allowed the user to see not only the text of a Web document on-screen, but also the embedded objects—the pictures, the animations, the video clips, and the sound bites (well, you could only hear the sound bites). Mosaic turned the World Wide Web into a multimedia version of the Internet. By the time this happened, computers that could use Mosaic—Macintoshes, PCs running Windows, and computers running graphical versions of UNIX—were sitting on millions of desks in universities, offices, and homes, all over the world. The computers were the tinder. Mosaic was the flint. Together, they sparked the phenomenon that the Internet is today—a fire that consumes the imagination of marketers, programmers, computer makers, and users all over the world.

Mosaic and the World Wide Web are not the sole catalysts that fueled the growth of the Internet. UseNet newsgroups, Internet Relay Chat, and Internet-based sound and video transmission have all contributed new ways to use the Internet. Along with the Web, these new technologies have turned the Internet into not merely a handy communication medium and research library, but rather a marketplace, a playground, and a hotbed of experimentation in new ways to use networked computers.

Furthermore, the growth of networking in general has fed the popularity of the Internet. At bottom, the Internet is simply a computer network based on standard network communication protocols. Even if you don't have a use for all the newfangled communication and research tools that have been popping up, you can still connect two computers, say two Notes servers, to the Internet, and they will communicate with each other the same as if they were both connected to the *local area network* (LAN) in your office. Would you like to establish replication and mail routing between your Notes server and those of, say, your customers? One way to do it would be to connect them to the Internet. The servers could then communicate with each other in the same way they would were they on the same office LAN.

To companies in the computer industry, the Internet is a huge opportunity, a huge risk, and a threat to their livelihoods. Someone will make a lot of money selling products that power the Internet, many people will lose a lot of money trying, and many others will wake up one morning to discover that their products no longer have a market because they don't work with the Internet.

Thus, we are witness to the browser wars. The programmers who wrote Mosaic later left the NCSA and formed a company, Netscape, where they wrote and released Netscape Navigator, an enhanced version of the Mosaic Web browser. Netscape Navigator (commonly referred to as just "Netscape") quickly gained a dominant market position of maybe 80 percent penetration.

Microsoft woke up one day and realized the Internet boat was about to leave the dock without them. Microsoft has managed, through its monopoly on the PC operating system market, to become dominant in all of the desktop software markets. When they realized they were about to be stranded on the DOS/Windows island as the whole world embarked for the "new world" of the Internet, Microsoft transformed themselves overnight into an Internet products vendor and hopped on board. Microsoft has since made it its goal to knock Netscape off its perch. As a result, throughout 1996, Netscape and Microsoft released new versions of their Web browsers—Netscape Navigator and Microsoft Internet Explorer—every three months or so, adding bells and whistles at a furious pace, and all but giving the products away.

The Internet—What It Is

The Internet is the King Kong of all internetworks. Its defining characteristic is the TCP/IP suite. But wait. Let's back up and define a few networking terms. People who work with computer networks define them as follows:

▶ **Local area network (LAN).** Two or more computers connected to each other on a single, shared segment of cable, through which they communicate with each other, constitute a *local area network* or *LAN*. Computers on LANs have to take turns sending data out over the single cable that they share with each other. If too many computers try to send too many messages over a single LAN, the traffic tends to bog down just as it does on an urban highway at rush hour.

▶ **Internetwork.** Two or more LANs connected to each other by an internetworking device such as a *bridge* or a *router* constitute an *internetwork*. Internetworking devices *filter* the data that comes into them from the network cable. Say a router connects

LAN A and LAN B. If a message arrives at a router from LAN A and it is addressed to a computer on LAN B, the router will pass the message through to LAN B. If the message is addressed to another computer on LAN A, then the router does not pass the message through. In this way, internetworking devices serve to keep network traffic localized, which in turn tends to keep it moving along at an acceptably fast rate.

▶ **Wide area network (WAN).** If two LANs are so physically distant from each other that you could not practically wire them to each other directly, and you resort to the resources of the telephone company (leased telephone lines or ISDN services) to connect them, the resulting internetwork constitutes a *wide area network (WAN)*.

▶ **Backbone network.** Any network that exists primarily so that other networks can connect to it is a *backbone* network. Every time a packet of data has to hop from one network to another across an internetworking device, its progress slows down as the router or bridge analyzes it to determine whether to pass it on to the next network or not. In general, the fewer the hops, the better. Backbone networks tend to minimize the number of hops any one packet must take, because the local networks all connect to the backbone, and any one packet needs only to hop onto the backbone, then off, for a maximum total of two hops. Contrast this with a daisy chain of, say, five LANs in which a packet must hop four times to get from LAN A to LAN E. Large internetworks almost always consist of one or more backbone networks. The larger the internetwork, the more backbones.

Fig. 1.1

Data sent from Computer 1 to Computer 2 in the daisy-chained internetwork takes four hops. On a backbone internetwork, the same data takes only two hops.

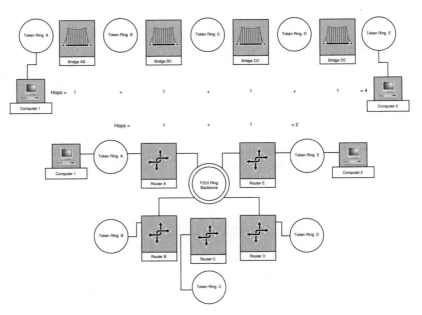

The Internet, then, is thousands of LANs, all over the world, connected to one another primarily through the telephone networks, which constitute backbone networks. The Internet in the United States, for example, consists of continent-wide backbones, the principal one of which is known as NSFNet, to which are connected regional backbones, to which are connected yet smaller backbones, and so on down to the local area networks. All computers on the Internet communicate with one another using a suite of protocols known as the TCP/IP protocol suites. But wait. It's time to define some more terms:

▶ **Computer Networking Protocol.** A *protocol* is a set of rules that defines how a process will take place. A *computer networking protocol* defines how computers on a network will communicate with one another.

▶ **Protocol Suite.** A *protocol suite* is a set of protocols that are related to one another and build on one another.

There are many protocol suites, including TCP/IP, IPX/SPX, NetBEUI, SNA, AppleTalk, and others. Most protocol suites were developed by corporate enterprises and are, therefore, proprietary. The evolution of the Internet from the Defense Department experiment included, among other things, the development of the TCP/IP protocol suite; therefore, TCP/IP is not proprietary.

For any computer to be considered to be "on the Internet," it must use TCP/IP. If your computer does not use TCP/IP, it can still communicate, via a *proxy server*, with computers on the Internet; but your computer is not itself *on the Internet* if it does not itself use TCP/IP.

The TCP/IP suite includes scores of protocols, most of which are acronyms like TCP and IP, but some of which are more cleverly named, like *gopher*. Some of the Internet protocols that are important in your understanding of Notes and its relationship to the Internet include the following:

▶ **Internet Protocol (IP)**—This is the basic communication protocol that computers use when they transfer information back and forth. All the other Internet protocols rely and build on IP.

Among other things, IP defines Internet addressing. Every computer on the Internet must have a unique address. IP addresses consist of 32 bits of information that is usually presented in dotted-decimal format—that is, as a series of four decimal numbers, separated from one another by periods. Each number may be from one to 254. So, an IP address might look like this: 123.123.123.123

▶ **Serial Line Internet Protocol (SLIP) and Point-to-Point Protocol (PPP)—** These are the versions of IP that you will use if your computer is not connected to a LAN and you have to connect to the Internet by dial-up telephone. You will use one or the other, not both. PPP is a later, more powerful version of SLIP.

▶ **Transmission Control Protocol (TCP)**—Adds reliability to IP data transmissions, among other things. Notes uses TCP, not just IP, to transfer data to other Notes computers.

▶ **Domain Name Service (DNS)**—Since most human beings (not including system administrators) don't want to bother with remembering numeric computer addresses (see previous IP addressing bullet), the Internet also permits you to give your computer a host name under the Domain Name system.

Under this system, every computer (or host) belongs to a predefined Internet super domain, which may be one of the three-letter domains, which define a type of organization, or one of the two-letter domains, which define the country in which an organization is located. The three-letter, organization-type domains are: **gov** (government), **mil** (military), **edu** (educational institution), **org** (nonprofit organization), or **com** (commercial enterprise). Examples of the two-letter, country domains are: **us** (United States), **uk** (United Kingdom), **jp** (Japan), **au** (Australia)—the list goes on.

Within the super domain, your computer belongs to a private domain, which may in turn have sub-domains defined. Thus, a computer named **www.lotus.com** has host name **www**. That's the computer's own name. It is a member of the **lotus** domain, which is in turn part of the **com** super-domain. When sending information to that computer, you can address its ***host.domain*** name instead of its IP address. Domain name servers that exist in each domain work together to resolve the host name of each computer to its IP address.

▶ **Hyper Text Transfer Protocol (HTTP)**—World Wide Web servers and browsers communicate with one another and transfer files to one another using this protocol. It, too, builds and relies on IP. A Domino server understands both HTTP and Notes' proprietary method of transferring data to Notes clients and other Notes servers, so Domino servers can communicate both with Lotus Notes clients and with Web browsers.

▶ **Hyper Text Markup Language (HTML)**—This is the set of codes and syntax rules that define the formatting of documents on the World Wide Web. A document written in HTML is called an *HTML document*. If you look at the document with a Web browser, it appears to be fully formatted. If you look at it with a text editor, you see that it is just plain text with some strange-looking codes (or *tags*) tossed in here and there. The tags are enclosed in angle brackets (< and >). The HTML protocol defines a set of tags and their meanings. For example, the tag <HR> means *insert a horizontal rule here*. A Web browser, when it encounters this tag, would insert a line across your computer screen instead of displaying the tag. HTML also encompasses the embedding of hypertext links into HTML documents. A hypertext link is a tag that is interpreted by the browser as a pointer to another document. It appears on your screen as a graphic symbol or a specially formatted string of text. When you click a hypertext link with your mouse, your Web browser will send an HTTP message to the computer named in the link, requesting the document named in the link.

▶ **Uniform Resource Locators (URLs)**—These are addresses of computers and the files on them. The format of an URL for a computer is ***protocol://hostname. domainname.superdomain*** where ***protocol*** is a protocol that the computer named in the URL should use to interpret the accompanying message, and ***hostname.domainname.superdomain*** are the DNS host name of the target computer.

The format of an URL for a file is ***protocol://hostname.domainname. superdomain/directorypath/filename***, where ***directorypath/filename*** is the location of the file on the target computer.

An example of an URL for a computer would be **http://www.lotus.com**. This indicates that the computer, **www.lotus.com**, should interpret the accompanying message using HTTP. It could do so only if it has Web server or client software running on it.

▶ **File Transfer Protocol (FTP)**—This is the original Internet protocol that defines how files will be transferred from one computer to another. Nowadays, you can transfer files using other protocols as well, including HTTP.

▶ **Simple Message Transfer Protocol (SMTP)**—This protocol defines how e-mail messages will be formatted, addressed, and delivered. SMTP does not provide for rich text messages, attached files, or hypertext links. As such, SMTP is a *first-generation mail system* (where file attachment capability defines a second-generation mail system, rich—or formatted—text defines a third-generation mail system, and hypertext links define a fourth-generation mail system, such as Lotus Notes).

▶ **Multipurpose Internet Mail Extensions (MIME)**—This protocol defines a standard way for a program on one computer to send a file to a program on another computer and identify the type of file to the receiving program, so that the receiving program can process the received file appropriately, usually by calling up another program designed to process files of the given type.

A Web server can embed files of various types in HTML files. A mail program can attach files to mail messages. Because an embedded/attached file is preceded in the HTML file or mail message by a MIME header line that describes the embedded file, the receiving browser or mail program can tell what type of file it has received and either display the file correctly itself or call a helper program that can display or process the file correctly.

▶ **Post Office Protocol, version 3 (POP3)**—If your computer does not remain connected to the Internet around the clock, then a computer that is constantly connected must hold your incoming mail for you until you do connect and then receive your mail. POP3 defines a way for this whole transaction to take place.

▶ **Network News Transfer Protocol (NNTP)**—UseNet news servers use this protocol to transfer data back and forth.

▶ **Gopher**—This protocol defines how Gopher servers store and organize information.

▶ **Secure Sockets Layer (SSL)**— The great promise of the Internet, in particular the World Wide Web, to commercial entities is that it will become a huge marketplace with almost no overhead costs, where you and I will shop for and buy their products. But the Internet is notoriously insecure. Everyone knows that you can't risk sending your credit card information over the Net. Someone may intercept it en route, then use it himself. The stranger that you are sending it to may misuse it.

Various entities have been working on this problem. Several security schemes have been proposed. One, SSL, proposed and implemented by Netscape, seems to be gaining wide acceptance (including an implementation by Lotus in Domino Server) and may become an Internet standard for implementing secure financial transactions. SSL works much like Notes security. You and the party you want to do business with both receive identifying certificates from a trusted third party. That way, no impostor can pretend to be the second party that you think you are dealing with. Then you use public key/private key encryption to authenticate each other and protect your data transmissions from eavesdroppers.

Internet Tools

Since the Internet has from its earliest days served as a medium of communication and research, the first available user tools served those purposes. Over time, Internet users have developed more sophisticated tools but generally still serving the purposes of enabling electronic communication, research, and collaboration. The earliest Internet tools still in use include the following:

▶ **Terminal Emulation**—The **Telnet** protocol allows a person sitting at one computer to control and run programs on a remote computer.

▶ **E-mail**—Electronic messaging, in the form of the Simple Message Transfer Protocol (**SMTP**), allows people remote from each other in time and place to carry on long-term conversations.

▶ **File Transfer**—File transfer, in the form of the File Transfer Protocol (**FTP**), allows collaborators in research projects to more easily work together and share the results of their work with one another.

As time has passed, the original communications and research tools have been augmented with newer and better tools. Some, certainly not all of them, are listed here.

The communication tools are as follows:

- **Internet Mailing Lists**—List servers are computers that maintain mailing lists of people's e-mail addresses. If you are on a mailing list, you can send a message to the list server that maintains it, and the list server will broadcast your message to all the other people on the list. Mailing lists provide a great way to hold ongoing, special interest discussions among people who can't easily get together face-to-face.

- **UseNet Newsgroups**—These are Internet-based discussion groups or bulletin boards. You can post messages, called "articles," on news servers. Others can read and reply to your messages. Everyone can read and follow the resulting conversations. This is another good way to hold discussions among widely dispersed people.

- **Internet Relay Chat (IRC)** —These are "live" discussion rooms. You type a short message and hit Enter. Your message appears on the screens of everyone in your "chatroom." Their messages appear when they hit enter. Live conversation.

- **Internet telephone programs**—This is one-to-one, live voice conversation. Just like real telephones, but cheaper for long-distance calls and much lower voice quality and reliability.

- **CU-SeeMe**—This is one-to-one, live voice conversation with video. You can watch each other as you talk to each other.

- **Internet radio and television**—Live or recorded, this is voice or video transmission via Internet into your computer.

- **PointCast Network**—This is customized newsfeeds via the World Wide Web right to your browser.

The research tools are as follows:

- **Archie Servers**—These servers maintain searchable lists of computer-based documents. Need to find research documents about Elvis sightings? Search for them on Archie servers, which will return lists of documents that meet your search criteria.

- **Wide Area Information Servers (WAIS)** —These are like Archie servers, except they maintain full-text indexes of the documents in their libraries, so you can search the bodies of the documents, not just their titles and keyword lists as with Archie servers.

- **Gopher**—Gopher servers let you browse their contents, and the contents of other Gopher servers, in a menu interface. Choose an item on a Gopher menu. It may open to a submenu or a document. The menu or document that it opens to could be on the same or a different Gopher server. The universe of Gopher servers interconnected in this way is sometimes called *Gopherspace*. You might call the menus *hyper-menus* because they can transport you instantly across space to another server entirely.

▶ **World Wide Web**—This is mostly what has caught the imagination of the world and fueled the phenomenal growth of the Internet. Documents in Web servers are connected to one another with hyperlinks. That is, embedded in one Web document are pointers to other Web documents that relate to the first one contextually. You research a topic by activating the hyperlinks and scrolling down page after page until you find the one(s) that have the information you need.

▶ **Finger**—You can use Finger to find the names of people in a specific domain, so that you can send e-mail to them.

The World Wide Web

The World Wide Web is a system of servers and clients. The Web servers store documents, called *Web pages*, in HTML format, and send them to Web clients on request. The more advanced Web servers, like the Lotus Domino Web Server, may also store pages in database format and convert them to HTML when sending them to requesters. The clients, called Web browsers, request and receive the pages from the servers, format them according to the embedded formatting codes, and display them to you. The browsers request documents from the servers by sending a document's URL to the server. If a browser sends an URL that names only the Web server and not a specific page, then the server sends a default page, known as the *home page*, to the browser. The server sends pages to the browser, or sends a reply if the page is unavailable, using the HTTP protocol.

The most capable Web browsers can do lots more than just request and receive HTML pages from Web servers. They can also retrieve Gopher menus from Gopher servers, directory listings and documents from FTP servers, and articles from news servers. They can send Finger requests. They include a POP3 mail reader. It used to be that you needed different programs to do all of these things. The day is not far off when your Web browser will do it all.

Like Lotus Notes documents, HTML documents can store virtually any kind of information. They consist of plain text plus embedded formatting codes, or *tags*, that look something like this: `<HTMLCODE>`, where `HTMLCODE` is a text string that has a specific meaning to a Web browser. A given code might tell the browser to italicize (`<I>`) the text that follows or to center (`<CENTER>`) the paragraph that follows. It might tell the browser to insert a horizontal rule at this point (`<HR>`). It might tell the browser to retrieve a graphics file from the server and insert it at this location (`<IMG SRC="image.location">`).

That last example is significant. The browser interprets the code to mean that it should retrieve another file. The preceding example specifies a graphics file. But similar codes can specify any kind of file. Among the kinds of files that a browser might retrieve are programs that the browser might execute on the spot. Or, when the file arrives, it might be accompanied by a MIME specification that tells the browser which helper application it should start up that can execute the program properly or otherwise handle the data file correctly. Thus your browser might start up a program that can play an audio or video file. If your browser can execute Java or ActiveX or programs, then you might see an animated graphic right in a Web page displayed on your screen, or a spreadsheet might pop up so that you could calculate, say, a mortgage payment. The possibilities are endless.

Intranets and Extranets

The Internet is a public network, available to anyone who wants to connect to it, virtually anywhere in the world. An intranet is a *private* network that uses Internet protocols. It is private in the sense that only company insiders have access to it.

Many companies have realized how the Internet and the World Wide Web can enhance communication and collaboration in teams of people scattered all over the world. These companies would like to take advantage of the Internet but are afraid of opening their internal computer networks to the lawlessness of the Internet. A popular compromise has been to borrow the technology of the Internet—the IP, HTTP, HTML, FTP, and other protocols—and use them internally but without any connection to the Internet, per se. The result is an intranet. Notes and its Internet extensions work just as well on the Internet or a corporate intranet.

An extranet is an extension of a company's intranet that is accessible to outsiders— business partners, customers, or the public at large. A Web server that sits outside a company's firewall and extends company information to the World Wide Web is part of a company's extranet. A Domino server that business partners can dial into is part of a company's extranet. The Web server in this example is also on the Internet whereas the Domino server is not.

Lotus' Internet Thrust—Toward Total Integration

Like everyone else in the computer industry, Lotus is scrambling to establish its presence and identity in the Internet. For Lotus, the rise of Internet hysteria is an especially great opportunity. In case you haven't noticed, the core purposes of the Internet and of Lotus Notes are nearly the same. Both the Internet and Notes were originally developed to promote communication and collaboration among groups of people who need to work together but who are rarely if ever in the same room at the same time.

It must have been vexing to Lotus to watch the World Wide Web steal Notes' fire, especially since the Web can do many, but not all of the things Notes has been doing for years. On the other hand, Notes is well positioned to become the dominant Internet application. Its elegant, simple architecture—the programmable object store, the replication, message routing, indexing, and directory services, its integration with external data stores, its multilevel security, RSA authentication, automatic document management and linking, full-text search engine, and its powerful programming facilities—all these things taken together make Notes an ideal platform on which to build Internet applications, far better than anything offered by Microsoft, Netscape, Novell, or anyone else.

If Lotus can just play its cards right—if it can properly integrate Notes with the Internet, and if it can get the attention of all the people who are so excited about the potential of the Internet and convince them that Notes is the obvious tool for realizing the Internet's potential—then Lotus could be the dark horse that wins the race for Internet dominance.

Lotus' strategy is to offer Domino as an Internet applications server—that is, a Web server that incorporates Notes functionality. Lotus' two main thrusts in accomplishing this goal have been, first, to integrate core Internet protocols right into Notes and, second, to develop a series of add-on products that enhance the value of Domino as an Internet applications server.

Significant Internet-related features of Notes include the following:

▶ **Built-In Internet Protocols**—For years, Notes servers and clients have been able to communicate with one another using the TCP/IP protocol suite. Beginning with Release 4.0, Lotus began incorporating extended Internet protocols, including HTML/HTTP into Notes. Release 4.5 includes HTML/HTTP, FTP, gopher, MIME, and finger protocols in the Notes client and HTML/HTTP, SMTP/MIME, POP3, and SSL in the Domino server.

▶ **Combined Notes/Web Server**—Domino Server is both a Web and a Notes server. It stores data both in Notes databases and, optionally, as HTML documents in an HTML data directory. It serves up Notes documents to Notes clients and, to Web clients, HTML documents, or Notes documents converted on-the-fly to HTML format.

▶ **Internet Mail Server**—Because the Domino Server complies with the SMTP, MIME, and POP3 protocols, it can serve as a post office for SMTP/MIME mail clients and as an SMTP message transfer agent. Domino Server can also act as a post office for MAPI mail clients. These features come with the server software at no additional charge.

▶ **InterNotes Web Navigator**—This is a Web browser built right into Notes. If a Notes user has access to the Internet (or an intranet), he/she can use Notes to browse Web sites, Gopher sites, and FTP servers. Retrieved pages are stored in the Web Navigator database.

▶ **Domino.Action** is bundled with Domino Server. Use it to bring up a full-service corporate Web site, including home page, corporate information pages, user registration database, discussion/feedback database, and more.

Significant Internet-related add-on Notes products and services include the following:

▶ **Server Clustering**—This is part of **Domino Advanced Services**, which is an extra-cost add-in to the Domino Server. Server clustering permits configuring multiple Domino servers to replicate with one another in *real time* and to appear to the user as a single server. Provides fault-tolerance, load balancing, and fail over.

▶ **Server Partitioning**—This is also part of **Domino Advanced Services**. You can create multiple server partitions on one computer, which causes the computer to appear to users as multiple Domino servers. This is useful if you want to host multiple Web sites on one computer or if you want to host multiple Domino applications on one computer.

▶ **Usage Tracking and Billing**—This is also part of **Domino Advanced Services**. You can track and compile system usage and use the information to bill users or to monitor trends.

▶ **Lotus Weblicator**—This brings Notes functionality, including the Notes object store, replication, and agents, to non-Notes Web browsers. In effect, it turns third-party Web browsers, such as Netscape Navigator and Microsoft Internet Explorer, into "Notes Lite." With Weblicator running alongside them, they can retrieve Web pages into a Notes database on the browser computer. You can then use the browser like a Notes client to view the downloaded Web pages offline. Since they are stored in a Notes database, you can index and search through them; you can sort and categorize them various ways; you can edit them or fill in CGI forms offline. Then you can reconnect to Domino servers and replicate back to them any pages you edited. Or you can reconnect to a third-party Web server any CGI forms you filled in offline. Weblicator also includes agents that will automate the retrieval of Web pages.

▶ **InterNotes Web Publisher**—This is Lotus' first Notes-to-Web product. With it, you can publish selected Notes databases to a third-party Web server and, under some circumstances, retrieve information from Web users back into a Notes database.

▶ **InterNotes News**—This is a gateway between Domino servers and UseNet newsgroups. Since news servers are simply a form of bulletin board or discussion forum, they are analogous to Notes discussion databases. InterNotes News converts selected newsgroups to Notes discussion databases. The articles posted in the newsgroups become Notes documents in the Notes discussion databases. Notes users can then follow the newsgroup discussions without ever having to access the news servers directly. If a Notes user contributes to the discussion, InterNotes News converts the user's contribution to a News article and submits it to the news server.

▶ **Notes Network Information Center (NotesNIC)** —This is a service provided on the Internet by Lotus (actually by its subsidiary Iris Development Corporation, the developers of Notes) to all Notes-using organizations. It is a Notes domain that resides on the Internet. You can set up a Notes server of your own in the NotesNIC domain. It being your server, you control what databases reside on it and all access control lists.

Being in the NotesNIC domain, the server's public address book includes the servers of all other organizations that have joined the NotesNIC domain—in other words, hundreds of other Notes organizations. You can set up easy mail delivery and database replication between your organizations by going through your respective NotesNIC servers.

▶ **Domino.Applications**—To make it as easy as possible for a Notes organization to quickly set up a powerful, Domino-based Web site, Lotus has developed Domino.Applications. These are templates from which you can, by filling in a series of forms, generate a whole, interactive Web application. You don't have to develop the applications or create the databases yourself. Just fill in the forms and the Domino.Application does all the programming for you. The purpose of filling in the forms is so you can customize the resulting applications to your own needs, using your own names, vocabulary, rules, and workflows. The first Domino.Application, Domino.Action, is included with the Domino 4.5 server and is described in the previous bulleted list. Others are described later in this list.

▶ **Notes:Newsstand**, available since January 1996, lets you design and publish electronic newsletters, newspapers, and magazines in short order as pages on your Web site. Notes provides the page design and populates the pages with the content you specify.

▶ **Domino.Merchant** generates a Notes/Web marketing application. It includes a catalog builder, a payment mechanism, and SSL security.

▶ **Domino.Broadcast for PointCast** will use Domino Server and PointCast I-Server software to allow you to set up a newsfeed by which you can pipe company news via PointCast to any PointCast subscriber.

In essence, what Lotus is trying to accomplish here is to make Notes and Domino Server indispensable to anyone who wants to accomplish anything more elaborate on the Web than simple publishing. By marrying Notes technology to Web technology, Lotus gives you the tools to create powerful, interactive Internet applications with ease. Then Lotus makes it even easier by offering application generators that do all the work for you. All you have to do is set up Domino on a server, connect the server to the Internet, and fill out a series of questionnaires. The application generator then creates all the Notes databases for you.

From Here...

Lotus has set forth and implemented a powerful strategy for integrating Notes with the Internet. The rest of the book discusses several Notes Internet features in detail. See the following sections:

▶ Part II, "Developing New Notes Applications for the Web," includes chapters on designing forms, input forms, and views. This section also includes creating a test environment for your Web applications.

▶ Part V, "Building a Domino Site," includes chapters on using Domino.Action, a case history of the design and implementation of a Domino site and a chapter on preparing existing Notes applications for delivery on the Web.

▶ Part VI, "Implementing and Using Domino's other Internet Services," includes a chapter on Domino's Internet mail features as well as chapters on the Server and Personal Web browsers.

## chapter 2

Setting Up the Domino Server

In this chapter

◆ **Notes and Domino licenses**
The Notes client and the Domino server come in many different configurations. Here we set forth the strengths and weaknesses of each license.

◆ **Notes and Domino deployment issues**
Before you set up Notes and Domino in an organization, you have to plan their implementation. Here we set forth and explain some of the important considerations, including Notes named networks, Notes domains, Notes organizations, certification, and authentication.

◆ **Notes and Domino system requirements**
Here we set forth the hardware requirements for Notes clients and Domino servers. What processor platforms and operating systems do they run on? How much memory and hard disk space does Notes require on each platform? What network transport protocols does Notes work with?

◆ **Domino server setup**
This is an overview of the process of installing, configuring, and starting and stopping a Domino server.

◆ **Domino Web server setup and Domino Web browser setup**
The generic Domino server does not automatically provide Web server and browser functions. If you want to implement either one, you have to set it up and configure it.

W hile the main focus of this book is the Domino server as a Web server, we do believe that any Notes user or application developer would benefit from knowing some fundamentals about deploying and administering Notes in an organization. In addition, to achieve Notes certification, a Notes developer must have a good knowledge of System Administration. This chapter introduces some system administration basics.

Understanding Notes and Domino Licenses

Lotus Notes is a client/server software package. This means that there are two parts to it—the server and the client. The server used to be called the Lotus Notes Server. With the advent of Release 4.5, in order to reflect the Notes server's increased integration with the Internet, Lotus renamed it the *Lotus Domino Server, powered by Notes*. The Domino server is the custodian of all shared Notes databases. It enforces all Notes security provisions and provides server and database access only to authorized entities. Domino servers can connect to other Domino servers, as well as servers of other kinds, by network connections and modem connections.

The Notes client is called the Lotus Notes Workstation. Lotus did not change the Notes client's name in Release 4.5. The Notes client is the principal interface through which Notes users interact with Notes. You use the Notes client to connect with Domino servers, either by network or modem. You access the Notes databases stored on Domino servers and either work live with the data on the servers or make replica copies of a database on your workstation. Then you can work with the data offline, and replicate any changes you make back to a server.

While using a Notes client is the preferred way to access Notes data, for some time it has not been the only way. For a couple years now it has been possible for developers using development languages—such as ViP from Revelation Technologies or Visual BASIC and the Lotus HiTest Tools for Notes—to write applications that could access Notes databases independently of the Notes client. Also, ever since the first version of InterNotes Web Publisher arrived over two years ago, one could access Notes data via a Web browser. Now, with the integration of an HTTP server in the Domino server itself, anyone with a Web browser can both read and write to Notes databases on Domino servers. With the pending release of Lotus Weblicator, it will be possible for users to maintain replica Notes databases in their Web browsers.

The Domino server is licensed in single processor and symmetric multi-processor (SMP) versions. The SMP versions are available for SMP-enabled versions of the Windows NT, OS/2, IBM AIX, HP-UX, and Sun Solaris platforms. Also, the Domino server can be enhanced with a separately sold package called Domino Advanced Services. The features of Domino Advanced Services include server clustering, server partitioning, and billing and auditing. Chapter 16, "Using Advanced Administration Techniques," covers Domino Advanced Services in greater detail.

There are four different Notes client licenses: The full Lotus Notes license, the Lotus Notes Desktop license, the Lotus Notes Mail license, and the Domino Mail Access license. The four licenses differ as follows:

▶ The Lotus Notes license includes all Notes functionality and is the license of choice for Notes administrators and application developers.

▶ The Lotus Notes Desktop has had system administration and application development features stripped from it, but otherwise is fully functional, and is designed for use by generic Notes users.

(2)

▶ The Lotus Notes Mail license gives access only to certain databases, including mail databases, document library databases, personal journal databases, discussion databases, the Web Navigator databases, documentation databases, and certain administrative databases. That is, it gives access to what Lotus calls the "communication" and "collaboration" databases, but not to any "coordination" databases (such as tracking or workflow applications). The Lotus Notes Mail license is intended for use by people who can benefit from Notes' connectivity features, but who don't otherwise participate in the office workflows that are automated by Notes tracking and workflow applications.

▶ The Domino Mail Access license allows users of non-Lotus mail clients, specifically SNMP, VIM, and MAPI mail clients, to use the Domino Server as their post office. We look at Notes Internet mail features more closely in Chapter 20, "Preparing Existing Applications for the Web."

Deploying Notes in Your Organization

Notes is a powerful communications tool that can be used by a small workgroup within a larger organization, by a whole enterprise, or by multiple enterprises working as partners. While an organization might start out with a small pilot installation of Notes, the product tends to become pervasive in an organization as its benefits become manifest.

A small Notes installation would consist of a single Domino server and multiple Notes clients accessing the server either on a LAN or by modem. A larger Notes installation might consist of multiple Domino servers serving a larger number of users than could one server. A still larger Notes installation might consist of many servers, each specialized for a particular task; some servers might specialize as mail servers, others as database servers, still others as replication hubs, dial-in/pass-through servers, mail gateways, or Web servers. Finally, more and more we can expect the rise of Notes installations that consist of one or more Domino servers and a mix of Notes and non-Notes clients (including Web browsers—some of them Weblicator-enhanced—mail clients compliant with POP3, IMAP4, VIM, or MAPI mail standards, and who-knows-what else).

Exactly how many Domino servers a particular organization has, how they are configured, and where they are located depends on such factors as how many people will be using Notes and where the people are located. If a company expects that there will be hundreds or thousands of Notes users, all located in one large office complex, then there might be relatively few very powerful servers, each capable of meeting the demands of, say, a thousand or more Notes users. Such a server would typically have multiple processors, hundreds of megabytes of memory, and multiple gigabytes of disk capacity.

Another company might have small groups of Notes users located in widely dispersed offices. This company might have a single vanilla Domino server located in each office. Users would access their local server. The servers would replicate databases with one another and route mail to one another either by modem connection or by wide area network. The wide area network could consist of:

▶ Dedicated, leased phone lines connecting the offices to one another.

▶ Company subscription to a quasi-private WAN, such as a frame relay network run by a service provider.

▶ Connections to the Internet.

This is the physical side of deploying Notes in an organization. From our point of view, that is, from the point of view of an organization wanting to implement the Internet connectivity of Notes, the most important physical consideration is this: Where do we want our Internet-enabled servers to be located? Inside or outside the company's firewall? The short answer to this question is probably that we want our intranet servers inside the firewall and our Internet servers outside the firewall.

There is also the logical side of deploying Notes in an organization. When you set up Notes in an organization, you have to organize it internally so that it reflects the logical structure of your organization in a way that makes sense to you. There are three aspects of this:

▶ Notes named networks

▶ Notes domains

▶ Notes organizations

Notes Named Networks

When you set up a Domino server, you have to specify its membership in one or more Notes named networks. A *Notes named network* is a group of servers that share two characteristics:

▸ They share a common transport protocol. For example, they all use TCP/IP or they all use SPX or they all use NetBEUI/NetBIOS.

▸ They share a constant connection with one another, either by LAN or by WAN.

If two Domino servers meet these conditions, they *can* be in the same Notes named network. If they don't meet one of the conditions, they *cannot* be in the same Notes named network. The significant word here is the word *can*; even though two servers meet both conditions, they *don't have to* be in the same Notes named network. It is up to the Notes administrator.

Another important point is that a server can be in more than one Notes named network. In fact, Domino servers have to be in one Notes named network for each transport protocol that is enabled for the server. So, a multi-protocol server, say one that runs both TCP/IP and SPX, is necessarily in two Notes named networks.

The Notes administrator must decide which Notes named network(s) each server will be in. There are three factors that will influence the administrator's decision:

▸ When users open a database for the first time (by choosing File, Database, Open in the menu), they can view a list of Domino servers, pick a server from that list, then view a list of databases on the chosen server and open any of those databases. It is a well-known fact that, the longer the list of servers the user can pick from, the harder it will be for the user to decide which is the best server. If the list is really long, the user may die of despair before ever actually making the choice. Since the only servers that appear in that list are those in the user's home server's Notes named network, the administrator can make the user's life easier by grouping servers into what might otherwise be considered artificially small Notes named networks.

▸ An administrator can encourage users to use local servers (same LAN) rather than more remote servers (different LAN but same WAN) by placing the servers in different Notes named networks. If only local servers appear in users' lists of servers, they probably won't try to use remote servers, because they would have to manually enter the name of the remote server instead of picking from the list of local servers. This is too much work for most people, especially if they don't know the name of the remote server by heart.

▸ Servers in the same Notes named network route mail to each other automatically, without intervention by the Notes administrator. Servers in different Notes named networks can only route mail to each other if there are Connection documents telling them when and how to do so. Administrators must create and maintain the Connection documents. They can minimize the number of Connection documents they must maintain by minimizing the number of Notes named networks.

While Notes named networks constitute a fundamental aspect of the deployment of Notes in an organization, they are of particular interest mostly to Notes administrators. We reviewed them here for the sake of completeness and because application developers and database managers need to have a basic understanding of them and their significance.

Notes Domains and the Public Address Book

Every Domino server and Notes client is a member of a Notes domain. The Notes domain is defined by the Public Address Book. The *Public Address Book* is the central and indispensable database in Notes. A copy of it resides on every Domino server. The server looks to the Public Address Book for directions as to virtually every move the server makes. A server would be paralyzed without the Public Address Book telling it what to do at every tick of the clock; in fact, if a server could not locate the Public Address Book, it would not even be able to start up.

A Domino server is a member of the domain in whose Public Address Book its Server document appears. All servers whose Server documents appear in a particular Public Address Book share replica copies of that Public Address Book. The servers in a domain all work together as a precision team because they are, in effect, working from the same play book.

The Public Address Book also stores a Person document for everyone for whom a member Domino server maintains a mail database. That would include both Notes mail clients and POP3 mail clients. The Public Address Book also includes Person documents for Notes clients who are members of the Notes organization(s) served by the domain. It may also include Person documents for people—anyone with whom Domain members regular correspond by email; this would make it easier for domain members to address e-mail to those people.

In a small organization using Notes, there is typically only one domain that all servers and users belong to. In a larger organization there may be multiple domains. In general, the fewer domains, the easier life is for both Notes users and Notes administrators. For users, it is more work to address mail to someone outside your domain; you have to enter the mail recipient's name in the form *Joe Doaks @ DomainName* or maybe *Joe Doaks/ OrganizationalUnitName/OrganizationName @ DomainName* instead of just *Joe Doaks* or even just *Joe*.

For administrators, getting mail to route between domains is harder than getting it to route within a domain. As with Notes named networks, mail only routes between two Notes domains if the administrators of the domains define and maintain Connection documents dictating how and when the mail will get from one domain to the other.

To get mail to route between a Notes domain and a non-Notes domain, such as the Internet or a cc:Mail domain, the Notes administrator must also define one or more Domain documents. For example, to set up the Lotus SMTP/MIME Message Transfer Agent on a Domino server, the administrator must set up both a Global Domain document and a Foreign SMTP Domain document. See Chapter 21, "Domino Server Internet Mail Features," for detailed information about setting up e-mail communication between a Notes domain and the Internet.

In any organization, large or small, that uses Notes to communicate with other organizations, either routing mail to outsiders or sharing Notes databases with business partners, there are likely to be at least two Notes domains—an internal domain and an external or "firewall" domain. The internal Notes domain includes all the internal Domino servers and all the company's Notes users. The external Notes domain includes one or more Domino servers that serve solely as gateways to the outside world. These might include an Internet HTTP server, a mail gateway server, or a database server.

Why do you care to isolate your internal servers and users from the outside world? One reason is that you can maintain internal, confidential databases on servers in the internal domain and put just public databases on the firewall servers. Another reason is that your domain Public Address Book includes the names and perhaps office phone numbers of all of your company's key people. (What a great resource for a corporate head-hunter!) If outsiders have access to your internal servers, they have access to your internal Public Address Book. If they only have access to servers in your firewall domain, they only have access to that Public Address Book, which has no actual users in it, just administrative users. What it boils down to is you can use a firewall domain to make public information available to outsiders while insulating confidential information from them.

Notes Organizations: Certification, Authentication, and Distinguished Names

The third logical leg of Notes deployment is the Notes organization. Domino servers are the custodians of Notes databases that frequently hold confidential information. The servers are responsible for withholding confidential information from users not authorized to receive it. The only way a Domino server can fulfill this responsibility is by positively identifying every entity that comes to it requesting access to information. A Domino server identifies a Notes user or server by comparing certificates presented by that Notes user or server with certificates in the server's possession. If any of the certificates presented by the Notes user or server were issued and signed by an entity that issued and signed one of the server's own certificates, or if the server issued a certificate to the Notes user or server itself (as in cross-certification), then the server can use that fact to establish the identity of the supplicant.

The certification scheme just described is a common method of authentication, used not only by Notes but also in other software security implementations. We describe Notes authentication and security in greater detail in Chapter 14, "Securing the Domino Web Server," in the section titled "Notes Authentication." We describe a similar authentication system, Secure Sockets Layer (SSL), in Chapter 15, "Using Secure Sockets Layer (SSL) with Domino."

We introduce all this now, however, because you cannot deploy Notes at all without implementing Notes certification and authentication, and first you have to decide how you are going to set it all up. Once you have deployed Notes, you cannot create new servers or users without plugging them into the certification scheme you dreamed up when first deploying Notes.

It works like this. When you set up your first Domino server, you have to decide what organization it will belong to and come up with an *organization name*. You also have to come up with a name for the server and a name for the first user, who will, at least initially, have all administrative rights in the system. Both the server and the user will be members of the organization. The names of the server and user will be a composite of the names you chose for them plus the name of the organization.

Furthermore, all servers and users that you create in the future will also be members of this organization. Their names too will include an organization component.

For example, in setting up our first Domino server, we call it, say, *Oceania*, and we call the first user *Doctor Notes* and we call the organization *PlanetNotes*. The resulting server's name is *Oceania/PlanetNotes*. The resulting user's name is *Doctor Notes/PlanetNotes*. All future servers and users that you create as members of this same organization end up with similarly compounded names.

 Tip

We like to avoid using spaces in server and organization names; it makes our lives as administrators easier in the future. But there is no rule forbidding us from naming our organization *Planet Notes* instead of *PlanetNotes*.

What actually happens when you generate the first server and user in an organization is that Domino generates three ID files. It also generates the Public Address Book and creates documents describing the new server and user—but that is peripheral to this discussion. The ID files are called cert.id, server.id, and user.id.

Note

The new user's ID file may not have a file name yet. When creating it, the certifier may choose to attach the new ID to the user's Person document. Such an ID won't have a file name until the user detaches it from the Person document.

The ID files (as their name implies) identify the new server, the user, and the third entity, the organization itself, which, by the way, goes by the name */PlanetNotes* in our example. cert.id is called the *certifier ID*, because it is the issuer of the certificates described earlier, which the server and user will later use to establish one another's identity. This particular certifier ID is called the *organization certifier ID*, because it embodies and identifies the organization that we just named and created.

The ID files are binary files. Each contains the following information:

▶ The name of the IDed entity.

▶ An optional (but for certifier IDs and person IDs, highly recommended) password that unlocks the ID file and permits access to its contents.

▶ Information about the type of Notes license issued to the IDed entity.

▶ One or more certificates issued by one or more certifier IDs.

▶ Public and private encryption keys.

▶ Optionally and later, other encryption keys.

The certifier ID includes a certificate issued by itself to itself, signed by itself. The server and user IDs include a signed copy of the certificate issued by the certifier ID to itself, as well as certificates signed by the certifier ID and issued by the certifier ID to the server and user, respectively.

What we have created here is a shallow, hierarchical organization. It is hierarchical but only one level deep (see Figure 2.1), which makes it very flat on an organizational chart. But we don't call it flat because that is a name we use when referring to a non-hierarchical Notes organization, which we could go back and create later if we want. However, non-hierarchical Notes organizations are a bit far afield from the subjects we consider important for the reader of this book to be exposed to. Just remember these three things:

▶ First, prior to Notes Release 3.0, non-hierarchical Notes organizations were the only kind.

▶ Second, hierarchical Notes organizations have so many advantages over non-hierarchical ones that the only non-hierarchical Notes organizations you will ever see are the ones that users of Notes Release 2.x have not bothered to convert to hierarchical.

▶ Third, because hierarchical Notes organizations have so many advantages over non-hierarchical ones, you should not even consider creating a new Notes organization as non-hierarchical; your new Notes organizations will all be hierarchical, and you will be better off for it.

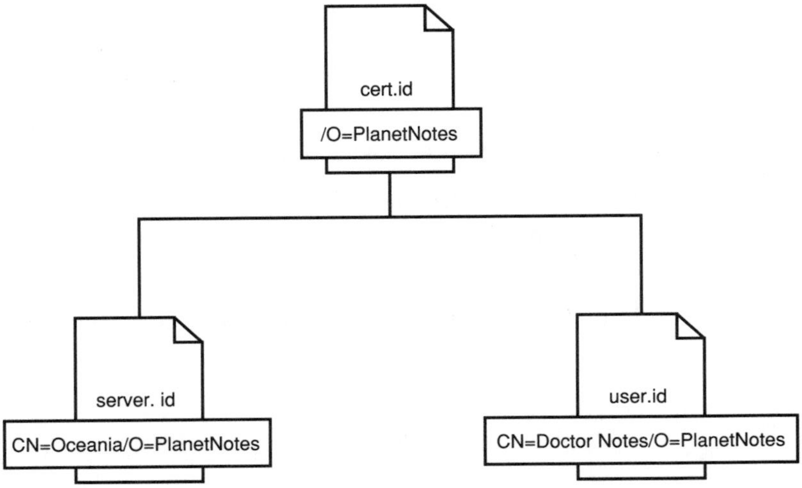

Fig. 2.1

Immediately after setting up our first server, our Notes organization tree looks like a twig with only two leaves on it.

Before you create any more servers or users, you will have to make a fundamental decision about your shallow organization: Will it remain shallow, or will it get deeper? You have the option of creating other certifier IDs with your new organization certifier ID. If you do, they will be *level 1 organizational unit certifier IDs*. They are level 1 because they exist one level down from the organization certifier itself. You will name each one of these that you create, and it will exist as another .id file, just as your organization and first server and user do. Its name, too, will be a composite of the name you give it, plus the organization name.

For example, say we use /PlanetNotes to create a level 1 organizational unit certifier ID called PHL (for Philadelphia, the location of one of our corporate offices). Its ID file name will be phl.id and its Notes name will be /PHL/PlanetNotes. This new certifier ID will contain two certificates: a copy of the certificate that /PlanetNotes issued to itself and a certificate issued by /PlanetNotes to /PHL/PlanetNotes.

Once you have this new certifier ID in hand, you can use either it or /PlanetNotes
to register new servers and users. Any server or user registered by /PlanetNotes will be
named *EntityName/PlanetNotes*. Any user registered by /PHL/PlanetNotes will be
named *EntityName/PHL/PlanetNotes*. Users and servers registered by /PlanetNotes will
exist at the top level of the organization. Users and servers registered by /PHL/
PlanetNotes will exist at the second level of our hierarchical organization.

2

You can, if you want, create an even deeper organization by using the /PHL/PlanetNotes
certifier ID to create yet another certifier ID, this time a *level 2 organizational unit certifier
ID*. If you name is, say, *Sales*, its full name is */Sales/PHL/PlanetNotes*. If you use it to create
a new user, that user's name is *UserName/Sales/PHL/PlanetNotes*.

/Sales/PHL/PlanetNotes will have a copy of the certificate issued by /PlanetNotes to itself,
a copy of the certificate issued by /PlanetNotes to /PHL/PlanetNotes, and a certificate
issued by /PHL/PlanetNotes to /Sales/PHL/PlanetNotes. The new user will have all of
those certificates plus the one issued by /Sales/PHL/PlanetNotes to UserName/Sales/PHL/
PlanetNotes. Our organization chart would look something like that in Figure 2.2.

Fig. 2.2

*After we have created
OU certifiers and
created users and
servers with them, our
Notes organization
tree looks more like a
tree—many branches
and leaves.*

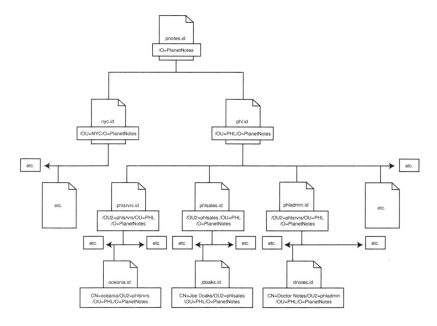

You can also create level 3 and level 4 organization unit certifiers. That, however, is as
deep as Notes will let you go in a Notes organization hierarchy. That's plenty deep,
though. We have never seen an organization that was deeper than two organizational
units. That's good; those long names can get awfully unwieldy.

This type of organization and its naming scheme comply with an internationally recognized standard for directory services called X.500, which was promulgated by the ITU-TS (International Telecommunications Union—Telecommunications Standardization Sector, formerly the Consultative Committee for International Telegraphy and Telephony, or CCITT).

Under X.500, directory information is stored in an inverted tree-structured format. At the top is the root. Branching out from that are one or more top-level structures which could be either Country (C) nodes, which are optional, or Organization (O) nodes. If Country nodes appear, then Organization nodes must appear beneath them. Beneath the Organization nodes may appear one or more levels of Organizational Unit (OU) nodes, which are also optional. C, O, and OU nodes are all known as "container" objects.

Beneath the O and OU nodes you may create "leaf" nodes, which are the actual people or servers in the Notes directory scheme, but might be other types of objects, such as computers, printers, or print queues, in another directory scheme. Leaf objects are referred to by their *common name* (CN).

In our example, Joe Doaks/Sales/PHL/PlanetNotes, *Joe Doaks* is the CN portion, *Sales* and *PHL* are OU portions, and *PlanetNotes* is the O portion. An alternate way of writing out this name is in *canonical* format, in which the type of object is included in the notation, and looks like this: *CN=Joe Doaks/OU2=Sales/OU1=PHL/O=PlanetNotes*. The first way we wrote the name (without the type identifiers) is called *abbreviated* format.

Whichever way we write the name, it is known as a *distinguished name*, because it fully distinguishes this object from any others. For example, there may be another Joe Doaks in our office, but because the second Joe is in the accounting department, his fully distinguished name is CN=Joe Doaks/Acctg/PHL/PlanetNotes. His distinguished name differentiates him automatically from the first Joe Doaks, in Sales, and we don't have to resort to some kludge, like Joe Doaks1 and Joe Doaks2, to distinguish the two Joes.

Just as X.500 permits an optional C node above the O node, so we could have specified a two-letter country code when we set up our first server. Had we done so, say, by specifying US (for United States), then PlanetNotes would have been part of C=US, and its name would have been /PlanetNotes/US. Joe Doaks would have been Joe Doaks/Sales/PHL/PlanetNotes/US.

If this all looks vaguely familiar, it may be because you have seen other X.500-compliant directory systems. Two well-known examples of directories that comply to a greater or lesser degree with X.500 are the Novell Directory Service (NDS) and the Internet's Domain Name System (DNS). Novell's notation for a file server named Atlantis may look something like this: CN=Atlantis.OU=PHL.O=PlanetNotes.

Undoubtedly, you have seen hundreds of examples of the Internet's notation, in the form of URLs that appear everywhere these days. An example of this would be **www.planetnotes.com**, where the host name www is the CN portion, the domain name planetnotes is the O portion, and the superdomain name com is neither an O nor a C node, precisely, but something akin to a C node. We could have had a true C node if we had chosen to register our domain as www.planetnotes.us. But people in the United States typically don't bother with the optional C node, not when setting up Internet domains, NDS directories, or Notes organizations. In other countries the C identifier is more widely used.

The upshot of all of this is that, when you set up Notes in your organization, you will have to come up with a plan of organizing your Domino servers and your users that makes sense for your company or workgroup. As you create new servers and users, you will have to fit them into their proper places in the scheme. Each server will fit into its appropriate Notes named network. Each server or user will fit into its appropriate Notes domain. Each entity will fit into its appropriate organization (O) and organizational unit (OU). If you don't decide how the whole thing should be structured before you start registering servers and users, you will be setting yourself up to do a whole lot of repair work later.

On the other hand, if you are setting up a Domino server strictly as a Web server and you don't intend to deploy Notes in your organization beyond that server and, say, a few Notes clients for administrators and application developers, then you don't have to worry much about organization structure and naming. But watch out; Notes is a compelling and contagious product; you might like it so much that you end up deploying it more widely than you originally intended.

One last point: There does not have to be a one-to-one correspondence between Notes domains and Note organizations. For example, your servers may all exist as part of the Acme organization, but they may exist in different domains. Server1/Servers/Acme may exist in the Acme domain and serve as a mail and database server while Server2/Servers/Acme exists in the AcmeExternal domain and serves as a gateway server. Your Notes topology might look something like Figure 2.3.

Fig. 2.3

Here is a single Notes organization in which one server is in a separate Notes domain from the rest of the servers and the users. The lone server is the gateway to the outside world.

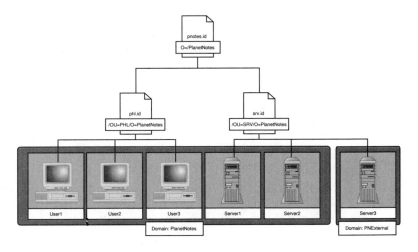

Understanding System Requirements

Notes and Domino are available in versions for a variety of hardware/OS platforms. Each platform has minimum and recommended memory requirements, minimum hard disk space requirements, and specific network infrastructure requirements.

The Domino 4.5 server comes in versions for the operating systems and hardware platforms listed in Table 2.1, below. The Notes 4.5 client comes in versions for operating systems and hardware platforms listed in Table 2.2, below.

Table 2.1   Domino Server System Requirements

Operating System; Processor	RAM, Hard Disk, Disk Swap Space Requirements	SMP Support?	Network Protocols Supported
Windows NT Server, Workstation 3.51, 4.0; Intel, Alpha	Min RAM: 32mb Rec RAM: 48mb Min HDD: 300mb Rec HDD: 500mb Rec Swap: 64mb	Yes	AppleTalk (3.51 only), SPX, NetBIOS/ NetBEUI, TCP/IP, Vines X.PC, X.25, SNA
Windows 95; Intel	Min RAM: 16mb Rec RAM: 24mb Min HDD: 150mb Rec HDD: 300mb Rec Swap: 16mb	No	SPX, NetBIOS/ NetBEUI, TCP/IP, X.PC

Operating System; Processor	RAM, Hard Disk, Disk Swap Space Requirements	SMP Support?	Network Protocols Supported
OS/2 Warp Server 4, Warp Connect; Intel	Min RAM: 32mb Rec RAM: 48mb Min HDD: 300mb Rec HDD: 500mb Rec Swap: 16mb	Yes	AppleTalk (not on SMP), SPX (Warp Connect only), NetBIOS /NetBEUI, TCP/IP, Vines, X.PC, X.25, SNA
NetWare 3.12, 4.1; Intel	Min RAM: 48mb Rec RAM: 96mb Min HDD: 300mb Rec HDD: 500mb Rec Swap: n/a	No	AppleTalk, SPX, TCP/IP, X.PC
AIX 4.1.4, 4.2; PowerPC series	Min RAM: 64mb Rec RAM: 128mb Min HDD: 300mb Rec HDD: 500mb Rec Swap: 128mb	Yes	SPX, TCP/IP, X.PC
HP-UX 10.01; PA-RISC	Min RAM: 64mb Rec RAM: 128mb Min HDD: 300mb Rec HDD: 500mb Rec Swap: 128mb	Yes	SPX, TCP/IP, X.PC
Solaris 2.5, 2.5.1; Intel, SPARC, Ultra SPARC	Min RAM: 64mb Rec RAM: 128mb Min HDD: 300mb Rec HDD: 500mb Rec Swap: 128mb	Yes	SPX, TCP/IP, X.PC

2

Table 2.2   Notes Client System Requirements

Operating System; Processor	RAM, Hard Disk Requirements	Network Protocols Supported
Windows NT Workstation 3.51, 4.0; Intel, Alpha	Min RAM: 16mb Rec RAM: 20mb Min HDD: 30mb Rec HDD: 40mb	SPX, NetBIOS/NetBEUI, TCP/IP, Vines, X.PC
Windows 95; Intel	Min RAM: 8mb Rec RAM: 12mb Min HDD: 30mb Rec HDD: 40mb	SPX, NetBIOS/NetBEUI, TCP/IP, Vines, X.PC
Windows 3.1; Intel	Min RAM: 8mb Rec RAM: 12mb Min HDD: 30mb Rec HDD: 40mb	SPX, NetBIOS/NetBEUI, TCP/IP, Vines, X.PC
OS/2 Warp 3, Warp 4, Warp Connect; Intel	Min RAM: 16mb Rec RAM: 32mb Min HDD: 30mb Rec HDD: 40mb	SPX, NetBIOS/NetBEUI, TCP/IP, Vines, X.PC
Macintosh; 680x0, PowerPC	Min RAM: 12mb 680x0 Min RAM: 16mb PowerPC Rec RAM: 20mb Min HDD: 30mb Rec HDD: 40mb	AppleTalk, TCP/IP, X.PC, MacTCP
AIX 4.1.4, 4.2; PowerPC series	Min RAM: 32mb Rec RAM: 64mb Min HDD: 100mb Rec HDD: 110mb	SPX, TCP/IP, X.PC
HP-UX 10.01; PA-RISC	Min RAM: 32mb Rec RAM: 64mb Min HDD: 100mb Rec HDD: 110mb	SPX, TCP/IP, X.PC
Solaris 2.5, 2.5.1; Intel, SPARC, Ultra SPARC	Min RAM: 32mb Rec RAM: 64mb Min HDD: 100mb Rec HDD: 110mb	SPX, TCP/IP, X.PC

The tables also list the minimum memory requirements as well as the recommended amounts of memory for each system. The numbers represent the amount of memory necessary to run both the operating system and Notes.

Don't be miserly when allocating memory to your Domino servers. While Notes or Domino will *run* on minimally configured systems, Lotus strongly recommends that you treat the recommended memory as the *real* minimums and then add more. If you are going to run the HTTP service, the Web Retriever, or any Message Transfer Agent, consider increasing the amount of server memory by 16M or more. Remember, nobody ever regretted having too much RAM.

Domino servers are scalable. This means that the more memory, processors, and network bandwidth they have, the more clients they can service. A minimally configured Domino server will only be able to service satisfactorily a few simultaneous clients. By *satisfactorily* we mean fast enough so that the human beings driving the client software don't get impatient and frustrated by the long waits for the server to respond. If that happens, they'll hate Notes and refuse to use it. There goes your investment and a great opportunity to streamline your business's workflows with a great software product.

The tables also list minimum and recommended hard disk space requirements. The numbers are the amounts required to install the program and initial data files. Your actual production databases will eventually grow to many times the sizes recommended in the tables, and you should assume that your Domino servers will eventually need gigabytes of disk space.

Finally, the tables list the network protocols supported by each version of Notes or Domino. Notice that Notes supports all the major networking protocols, as well as some minor ones like Vines and AppleTalk. Domino servers and Notes clients are capable of supporting multiple protocols simultaneously, as well. X.PC and X.25 are serial port protocols, for use when computers are communicating by modem. If you plan to use a Domino server as a Web server or as a shared Web browser for your Notes users, it must be configured to use TCP/IP, and it must maintain a constant connection to an intranet or the Internet.

Installing and Configuring Domino 4.5

Once you have put a plan of organization into effect, installing a Domino server (or the Notes client, for that matter) is pretty much a no-brainer. You install the software, then you configure the server or workstation.

You install Domino on the host computer by running an install program and answering a few questions. You can install from a network drive, a CD-ROM, or (if you can't avoid it) floppy disks. The exact sequence of keystrokes and the look of the screens varies according to the underlying platform, but you do the same thing in all cases: specify the target location of the software and the components that are to be installed. Your options are to install a server, a workstation, or individual components (which you would do if you wanted to add a component to an existing server or workstation). When installation is complete, Domino resides (if you accepted the default choices) in a directory called \notes, data files reside in a subdirectory called \notes\data, and other files reside in other subdirectories under the \notes directory. HTTP-specific files reside in a set of directories under \notes\data\domino. The full directory structure, as set up on a Windows NT computer, appears in Figure 2.4.

 Note

When referring to file names, directory locations, and other things specific to a computer's file system, we will use MS-DOS notation. If you are working in a UNIX or Macintosh environment, we hope you will bear with us and translate our syntax into your computer's equivalent.

Fig. 2.4
The Domino installation program sets up the directory structure displayed here.

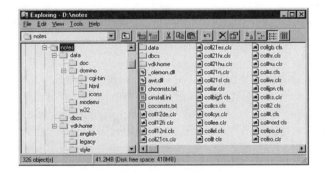

The installation program also creates a Notes configuration file called notes.ini. The file is a text file that begins as an empty shell with just three lines in it. On the Windows platforms, this file appears in the Windows program directory. On all other platforms (except Macintosh) it appears in the Notes program directory. You can put the file anywhere you want it, as long as Notes can find it when Notes starts up. This means that, if you decide to move it from, say, the Windows directory to the Notes directory, you may have to add the Notes directory to the search path.

Next, you configure the installed copy of Notes or Domino by running the workstation software and filling in fields in a series of dialog boxes. Most versions of the Domino server incorporate the workstation software, so that you can either start the server program or the workstation program while sitting at the server itself. The only exception is the NetWare version of the Domino server. Because NetWare file servers do not have a graphical interface, that version of the server includes a Windows version of the workstation software. So you have to configure the NetWare-based Domino server from a workstation. The other servers you can configure either while sitting at the server itself or (depending on what you are configuring) while sitting at another computer running Notes workstation software.

At this stage, if you are setting up the first server in an organization, you enter the name of the organization, the common names of the server and the first user, a password, optionally the domain and Notes named network names, and network and/or modem port information. When you have entered the required information and told Notes to proceed, it generates the first three ID files and certifies them, and it creates a Public Address Book (file name: names.nsf) and populates it with Certificate, Person, and Server documents describing, respectively, the organization certifier, the server, and the user. Notes adds the server's distinguished name to the membership field of the LocalDomainServers group document (which already existed in the Public Address Book at the time it was created). Notes also populates the notes.ini file with variables that it will refer to in the future whenever it starts up and while running.

If you are installing an additional server in an organization, then the configuration process works a little differently. First, you cannot install subsequent servers unless you register them first with a certifier ID. The registration process adds a new server document to the Public Address Book and creates a new server ID, which may be stored in the server document, as a separate file, or in both places.

Having registered the server, you can install the server software, then start the server workstation program. At Notes' prompt, you tell it that you are setting up an additional (not the first) server in the organization. You enter the server's name, the name of an existing server from which the new server can retrieve a replica copy of the Public Address Book as well as the server's ID if it is stored in the Server document in the Public Address Book, and network information, so that the new server can locate the other server. Then the server retrieves its ID file, downloads a replica copy of the Public Address Book, populates its notes.ini file, and takes care of most of the other details of setting itself up.

After you have run a server's workstation program for the first time to complete the server configuration process, you may have to take care of some minor loose ends manually. For example, you may want to configure additional ports for a multi-protocol server. Also, you will have to enter the port names for each of the server's Notes named networks in the Network Configuration section of the Server document. Notes never does that for you during initial system configuration, and the server may not function properly until you add it (see Figure 2.5).

Fig. 2.5

New Domino servers never enter a port name in the Port field of the Server document during initial server configuration. You must add the port name manually.

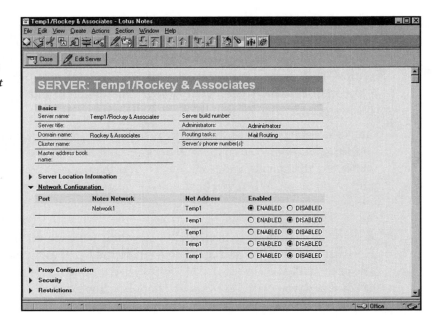

Finally, you are ready to fire up the Domino server. When you do, the server will search for certain databases that it will use in the future for internal purposes. If it does not find those databases (as it probably won't the first time you start up the server) it generates them. These may include (but not necessarily be limited to) the server's Notes Log (log.nsf) and the Administration Requests (admin4.nsf) databases. You may notice that error messages appear on the server console screen at startup. You may particularly see network errors if you have not set up network connections properly.

On the Windows NT version of the server, you will probably see two messages suggesting that you change Registry settings to speed up the Domino server's response times. The two messages are:

▶ KEY_LOCAL_MACHINE\System\CurrentControlSet\Control\Session Manager\Memory Management\LargeSystemCache is currently set to 1. For better server performance, change the setting to 0.

▶ HKEY_LOCAL_MACHINE\System\CurrentControlSet\Control\ PriorityControl\Win32PrioritySeparation is currently set to 2. For better server performance, change the setting to 0.

These messages appear because the Windows NT server is set by default to work best as a file server. You want to reset it to work best as an application server. Setting each of these parameters to 0 does the trick. You can either set the parameters directly in the Windows NT Registry Editor, or set them indirectly by changing settings in two dialog boxes. To run the Registry Editor in Windows NT 3.51, Choose File, Run in the Program Manager, enter regedt32 in the Command Line field, then click OK. To run the Registry Editor in Windows NT 4.0, choose Run in the Start menu, enter regedit in the Open field, then click OK.

In the Registry Editor, double click HKEY_LOCAL_MACHINE to expose its subheadings, then double click System to expose its subheadings, and so on until you reach the dialog box in which you can enter 0 in place of the 1 or 2 that appears there. Make both changes, close the Registry Editor, then reboot the computer for the changes to take effect (see Figure 2.6).

Fig. 2.6

Here, the entry for Win32PrioritySeparation has just been changed from 2 to 0. When we click OK, the value 0x00000002 (2) in the righthand window of the Registry Editor will become 0x00000000 (0).

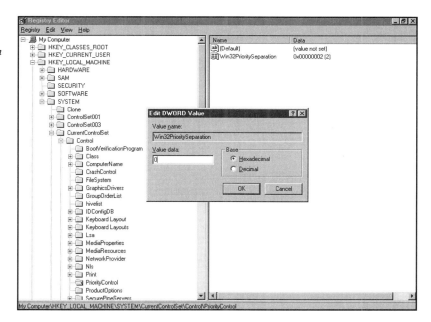

Alternately, you can make changes in two dialog boxes. To change the LargeSystemCache setting, select Maximize Throughput for Network Applications in the Server dialog box. You can open this dialog box by finding the Server service listed in the Network dialog box, which you can open in the Control Panel. This is the case in both Windows NT 3.51 and 4.0, except that, to find the Server listing in 4.0, you have to click the Services tab in the Network dialog box (see Figure 2.7).

Fig. 2.7

By default, server optimization is set to Maximize Throughput for File Sharing. Optimize Domino server by changing it to Maximize Throughput for Network Applications.

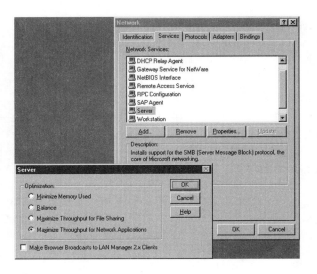

You change the Win32PrioritySeparation setting in Windows NT 3.51 by choosing System in the Control Panel, then clicking the Tasking button, then selecting Foreground and Background Applications Equally Responsive. In Windows NT 4.0, choose System in the Control Panel, click the Performance tab, and then set performance boost for foreground applications to None, as shown in Figure 2.8.

Fig. 2.8

By default, foreground application performance boost is set to Maximum. Optimize Domino server by dragging the slider over to None.

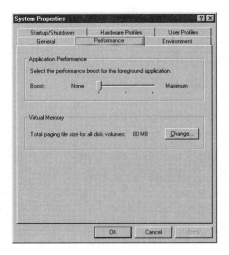

Starting and Stopping Domino

Once you get Domino configured properly, you want to set it up to start automatically whenever the computer starts up. You can always start or stop the server manually. But you don't want to have to babysit the server any more than necessary. On most server platforms, setting up the server to start automatically is a matter of adding its command line to an autoexec.bat file or its equivalent. The program that starts the server running on Windows and OS/2 computers is called nserver.exe.

In Windows NT, you want to set up the Domino server as a service. That way, it will start running when the computer starts, continue running when you log in, and continue running after you log out. Services are the only kind of programs under Windows NT that will behave this way. Set Domino up as a service at install time by choosing Customize Features—Manual Install in the Install Options dialog box, and then selecting Notes Service Install in the Customize dialog box. If the Domino server has already been installed and you want to set it up as a service, you can run the following command at a command prompt:

```
c:\notes\ntsvinst -c
```

If you ever want to remove the Domino server from the list of NT services, run the following command:

```
c:\notes\ntsvinst -d
```

After setting up Notes as a service, you still need to configure it to start automatically. To do this, open Services in the Windows NT Control Panel. Locate and select Lotus Domino Server in the Service field, then click the Startup button. The Service dialog box opens; there, you can set Startup Type to Automatic, click OK, and then click Close.

Setting Up Domino Web Services

When you start up a Domino server for the first time, it is automatically capable of performing standard Notes server tasks like database replication and mail routing with other Domino servers or with Notes workstations. It is *not* automatically capable of performing as a Web server or as a shared Web browser (also known as an InterNotes server). If you intend to use a Domino server in either of these capacities, you must configure it to run these services. The instructions appear in the following sections, but first we remind you that, for a Domino server to function either as a Web server or as a shared Web browser, it must be configured to use TCP/IP and it must be able to maintain a constant connection to either your company's TCP/IP Intranet or the Internet.

Setting Up a Domino Server as a Web Server

To set up a Domino server as a Web server, all you have to do is start the HTTP server task and possibly set a few variables in the Server document. You can start and stop the HTTP service manually whenever you want. Start it with the following command at the server console:

```
load http
```

That's it; that's all you have to do. Domino is now a Web server. To stop the HTTP service manually, enter the following command at the server console:

```
tell http quit
```

Now Domino is no longer a Web server.

If you want the HTTP service to start automatically whenever the server starts, you can edit the ServerTasks variable in the notes.ini file. The services listed in the ServerTasks variable start up automatically when you start up the Domino server. Immediately after server installation, the variable looks as follows:

```
ServerTasks=Replica,Router,Update,Stats,AMgr,Adminp,Sched,CalConn
```

To have the HTTP service start automatically, edit notes.ini and add the word *HTTP* to the ServerTasks variable. You will change the line so it looks like this:

```
ServerTasks=Replica,Router,Update,Stats,AMgr,Adminp,Sched,CalConn,HTTP
```

An alternate way to edit the ServerTasks variable is by entering the following command at the server console:

```
set configuration
"ServerTasks=Replica,Router,Update,Stats,AMgr,Adminp,Sched,CalConn,HTTP"
```

This statement tells Domino itself to insert the quoted text into notes.ini, substituting it for the existing ServerTasks variable. By entering this command, you save yourself the trouble of opening, saving, and closing the notes.ini file. However, we prefer to edit notes.ini directly, because if you mistype a single character of the Set Configuration command, you can really impair the functioning of the server. There is less opportunity for typos if you have to add one word to the end of the statement in a text editor than if you have to re-type the whole, long statement in the Notes server console.

If you do use the *set configuration* command, type carefully and proofread before hitting the Enter key. You can also verify the changed ServerTasks variable with the *show configuration* command. Type the following command at the server console:

```
show configuration ServerTasks
```

Domino will return a line showing the contents of the variable, something like this:

```
ServerTasks=Replica,Router,Update,Stats,AMgr,Adminp,Sched,CalConn,HTTP,Web
```

As we just mentioned, all you normally have to do to start up the Domino Web server function is load the HTTP server task. Verify the proper functioning of Domino as a Web server by trying to contact it from within a Web browser. Enter its host name in the Web browser and press Enter. If all goes well, you should see a screen that looks something like the one shown in Figure 2.9. It displays a list of databases on your Domino server.

Fig. 2.9

If the Domino HTTP service is functioning properly, you should be able to see a list of databases, similar to that pictured here, when you enter your Domino server's host name in a Web browser.

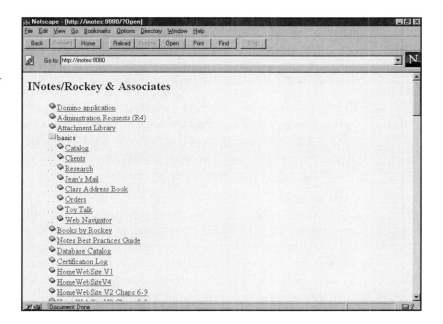

If your Web browser does not succeed in connecting to your Domino server and retrieving a list of databases, then you have to troubleshoot the problem. First determine whether the problem is in the Domino server or the underlying TCP/IP configuration.

Can you *ping* the Domino server from another server? By IP address? By host name? By alias name? If you cannot ping the server at all, then your problem lies in your IP stack configuration or that of your Domain Name Server. If you can ping by IP address but not by host name or alias name, the problem lies in the client computer's hosts or lmhosts file or in your Domain Name Server's configuration.

Using your browser, can you retrieve a list of databases from the Domino server by entering its IP address? By using its host name? If you can ping the Domino server but you cannot retrieve an HTML file from it, the problem lies in Domino's configuration. If you can retrieve a list by using the IP address but not the host name, the problem may reside in the client's hosts or lmhosts file, the Domain Name Server's configuration, or in Domino's configuration.

Can you retrieve a database list using a browser that runs on the Domino server? From a browser running on another computer? If you can retrieve an HTML file using a local browser but not a remote browser, the problem lies outside of Domino's configuration.

Troubleshooting IP connectivity problems is well beyond the scope of this book. For that matter, troubleshooting Domino connectivity problems is beyond the scope of this book. However, if other computers can communicate with your Domino server via TCP/IP, and if other Domino servers or Notes workstations can communicate with this Domino server, but Web browsers cannot find this Domino server, then you should investigate three settings in the Server document: the TCP/IP port number field, the TCP/IP port status field, and the Host name field. These fields are described in the following list:

▸ *TCP/IP port number.* All HTTP servers normally claim port number 80 and Domino's HTTP service is no different. All Web browsers assume that they can address requests to Web servers on port number 80. Problems arise when more than one program tries to claim the same port number, and this might happen if you try to run more than one Web server on one computer.

   If you feel like running multiple Web servers on one computer, you can. But you need to change the port number through which one of the servers communicates, so that both servers don't fight over port 80. This is where you would make the change for your Domino Web server. If you do change the port number, be sure to use a number greater than 1024. Commonly used port numbers other than 80 are 8080 and 8008. Also, if you do change the port number, browsers will have to specify the port number in your URL, like this:

   http://www.planetnotes.com:8008

▸ *TCP/IP port status.* The entry in this field should be *Enabled*. That is the default; but if for any reason the field is set to *Disabled*, that would explain why browsers could not connect to this server.

▸ *Host name.* This field defaults to blank, which means that the HTTP server will return to a browser whatever host name appears in the operating system's TCP/IP stack. If browsers are finding the server, then leave this field blank. If you have registered an alias with your Domain Name Server, enter the alias here. If your server isn't registered in a Domain Name Server, you may enter the Domino server's IP address in this field, in which case Web users will be able to access the server only by typing the IP address.

> **Caution**
> Whenever you make a change in the HTTP Server section of the server document, remember to stop and restart the HTTP server task (if it was running). Otherwise, your changes do not take effect and you will probably feel mildly frustrated.

Setting Up a Domino Server as a Shared Web Browser

In Notes jargon, a Domino server that performs Web browsing services is an *InterNotes* server. Lotus has been retreating from *InterNotes* as a trade name, and some day the term *InterNotes* may disappear entirely from Notes documentation. But it hasn't disappeared yet. It still appears in Server documents and Location documents, where it identifies the server that users of that document should go to for Web browsing services.

A Notes user's home/mail server is the Notes server on which that user's mail database is maintained (if the user is a Notes mail user). It is also the user's *name server*, providing the user with the list of server names that appears in dialog boxes in the user's Notes client program.

To set up shared Web browsing on a Domino server, that is, to set it up as an InterNotes server, you have to perform the following steps:

1. For each home/mail server in your Notes domain, designate an InterNotes server. That is, in the Server document of each Domino server that serves as a home/mail server for one or more users, enter the name of an InterNotes server in the InterNotes server field. The field appears in the *Servers* subsection of the *Server Location Information* section of the Server document. This will establish the *default* InterNotes server for each user of each home/mail server.

   The InterNotes server may or may not be the same server as the home/mail server. For example, if Server1 is to be the InterNotes server for all Notes users whose mail files are on either Server1 or Server2, then the name of Server1 must appear in the *InterNotes server* field of the Server documents of both Server1 and Server2. Got it?

2. If your InterNotes server connects to the Internet via proxy server, enter the proxy server's host name or IP address in the appropriate fields in the Proxy Configuration section of the InterNotes Domino server's Server document.

3. Start the Web Retriever server task on the InterNotes Domino server. Type **load web** at the server console or add the word **web** to the ServerTasks variable in notes.ini and restart the server. See the previous section of this chapter for details of starting and stopping server tasks and editing the ServerTasks variable.

4. Tell your users to start browsing. Assuming they haven't changed any of the Internet settings in their current Location documents, your users should be able browse the Web through the InterNotes Domino server at this time. If a user wants or needs to use a different InterNotes server than the one named in the Server document of his/her home/mail server, he/she can enter the alternate InterNotes server's name in the InterNotes server field of one or more Location documents. When the user uses a Location document that names an InterNotes server, that server selection overrides the default selection that appears in the Server document.

The first time the Web Retriever starts, it creates the Web Navigator database and the Web Navigator Administration document (which is stored in the Web Navigator database), if they don't already exist. It names the new database with the file name that appears in the Web Navigator database field, in the Web Retriever Administration section of the Server document. That file name defaults to web.nsf. If you want to change the database's file name, be sure to enter its new name in this field. Domino creates the new database from a database design template called pubweb45.nsf. This template and the Web Navigator database that springs from it are easily customized to your company's needs. For information about customizing it, and for information about using and administering the Server Web Navigator, see Chapter 22, "Using the Server Web Navigator."

From Here...

Now that your Domino server and the HTTP server task are running, you can set up your Web site. See Chapter 3, "Working with Your Domino Web Site," to learn how the default Domino Web site is structured and how a Web client can get around in it. Also see Part II of this book, "Developing New Notes Applications for the Web," and Part III, "Advanced Domino Application Design Techniques for the Web," to learn how to design Notes applications to take best advantage of Domino's Web capabilities.

For more information on the topics discussed in this chapter, see the following:

▶ Part IV of this book, "Using Advanced Administration Features." There you can find chapters on Notes security and advanced Domino server administration.

▶ *Special Edition Using Lotus Notes and Domino 4.5*, the full text of which is on the CD-ROM that accompanies this book. It covers Domino server setup and administration in much greater detail than we do in this book.

chapter 3

Working with Your Domino Web Site

by Jane Calabria

In this chapter

◆ **How the Domino HTTP server presents its content to the Web client**
HTML pages are created on-the-fly and views, a previously unknown entity in the Web world, are presented in a template with navigational keys. Here, you will see how this all appears to a Web client.

◆ **How to use Domino URL commands to navigate the Domino server**
You can navigate the Domino site with Domino URL commands. These commands are key in designing your Web site as you can use these commands to link and guide users through your site. Here you learn the syntax of the Domino URL commands.

◆ **How the unaltered Notes mail database appears on the Web**
Design and development of your Web site will largely consist of creating access to forms by Web clients. Without a Notes menu, clients have no method of creating content or feedback. Here, we use the mail database as an example of an unaltered Notes database on the Web.

◆ **About the Domino directory structure**
Domino sets up a set of subdirectories just for the Web server. Here we learn what they are, where they are, and their purposes.

As soon as the HTTP server task is running, you can reach the Domino server from a Web Browser. Unless you intend that Web users will have reader access only to your Web site, some design intervention is going to be required at your Domino site. In addition to controlling access to the site and to databases, you'll need to provide a method for Web clients to contribute content. That content might be in the form of contributions to a discussion database, a job posting, or a password-protected registration to allow access to areas of your site. If you want your Notes mail users to have the option of reading their mail over the Internet through a Web browser, they will need an HTTP password in their Person Document in the Public Name and Address Book. But what happens if you start the HTTP server and do *nothing*? This chapter describes the unaltered Domino site.

Understanding the Unaltered Domino site

After you have installed your Domino server (see Chapter 2, "Setting Up the Domino Server"), running the HTTP server process is a simple matter of sending the command "load http" to the server. At that point, the Domino server begins to perform as a Web server. Verify this by entering the host name in a Web browser.

With no further intervention on your part, the server will display a list of databases as shown in Figure 3.1. This is the default "home page" for the HTTP server. It's unlikely that you will want your site to appear to Web clients in this way; you will undoubtedly want to create a "real" site Home page. But it's important to see the result of default settings at the site and understand how to navigate the site as you are developing and designing.

Fig. 3.1

The default settings in the http server serve up a list of databases on the server. Remove the check mark from the box labeled Show in Open Database Dialog from the database properties box, and the database will not appear in this list.

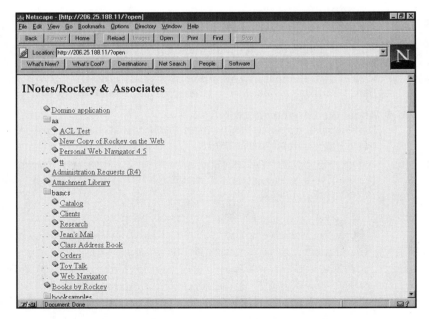

Who can access these databases? The access to the databases on the Web is controlled by the database ACL. If the default ACL is reader, all Web users will have reader access to a database. You will want to control the Web access at the server level. Refer to Chapter 14, "Securing the Domino Web Server," for more information.

Regardless of how the ACL is set, Web clients will see this list of databases unless you design and identify a home page. Additionally, and by default, Web users can browse your site using URLs appended with Domino commands. For example, the default Domino URL, located in the Home URL field of the HTTP Server section of the server document, is

    /?Open

This produces the dynamic creation and delivery of the list of databases shown in Figure 3.1 when users type your Host name or IP address in their Web browsers. Controlling the default view, securing the server, and disabling browsing by Web clients are all described in detail in Chapter 14. Here, we deal with browsing the Domino site under the auspices of the default settings.

Navigating with Domino URL Commands

You can navigate the Domino site by using URLs that include instructions to open a database, a view, and so on. If you disable the ability of Web clients to browse your site, understand that with the name of a file, view, or document, the Web client can still access that file, view or document.

It's important to understand Domino URL commands. You will use these commands when you create links in your Web databases, and when entering commands in your browser to navigate the site. The syntax for the Domino URL command is:

http://Host/NotesObject?Action&Arguments

where *Host* is the host and domain name or IP address of the Domino server, *NotesObject* is a Notes database, view, document, form, navigator, and so forth; *Action* is the operation to be performed on the object such as ?OpenView or ?OpenDocument, and *Arguments* further refines the action such as ?OpenView&10, which will limit the number of rows displayed in a view to 10.

You don't use the Notes server name in Domino URLs. Rather, as with all other URLs, you use the TCP/IP host name or IP address. Of course, if the host name and Notes server name are identical, then you would, coincidentally, also be using the Notes server name.

A *Notes Object* for a database can be the database name or replica ID. A Notes Object for other objects can be the Notes object's name (such as a view name), the universal ID, a NoteID, or a special identifier as described below. In all replica copies of the database, the Notes object's name and universal ID are identical, but the NoteID is likely to differ among replicas. The safest (and easiest) way to identify a Notes Object is to use its name.

Domino URL commands also use special qualifiers to identify default views, default forms, and so forth. Those qualifiers are preceded by a forward slash (/) and are:

```
$defaultView

$defaultForm

$defaultNav

$searchForm

$file

$icon

$about

$Help
```

A Domino URL can include explicit and implicit actions as well as arguments. If you do not specify an action, Domino will default to the ?Open action. For example, the URL

http://inotes

defaults to

http://inotes/?Open.

Actions are preceded by a question mark (?), arguments are separated from the action by an ampersand (&), and separate multiple arguments with an ampersand (&). Explicit actions include, among others, ?OpenServer, ?OpenDatabase, and ?OpenView. Implicit actions include, among others, ?Open, ?Create, ?Edit, and ?Search.

URLs cannot contain spaces. Use a plus sign (+) to replace spaces, such as in the name of a view called By Author. The URL to open the view named "By Author" reads:

http://www.rockey.com/discussion.nsf/By+Author

Separate hierarchical names with forward slashes (/). For example, to open a view named Comments\By Author in a database named Talk to Us (talk.nsf), enter

http://www.rockey.com/talk.nsf/Comments/By+Author

For a complete list of Domino URLs, see Appendix A, "Domino URLs." p. 609

To Open a Database, type the following syntax

http://host/DatabaseName

or

http://host/DatabaseName/?Open

or

http://host/DatabaseName/?OpenDatabase

Figure 3.2 shows the resulting HTML page returned with the URL:

http://206.25.188.11/eagle.nsf/?OpenDatabase

Fig. 3.2

Precede special commands such as ?OpenDatabase with a forward slash. Domino URL commands are not case-sensitive.

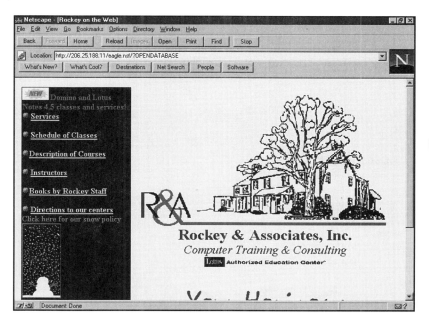

3

To Open the default view of a database :

http://host/DatabaseName/$defaultView

Figure 3.3 shows the resulting page from the following URL:

http://206.25.188.11/internet.nsf/$defaultView

Fig. 3.3

$defaultView opens the default view of the database. By default, all views are collapsed when served to a Web client. Domino generates the view on-the-fly.

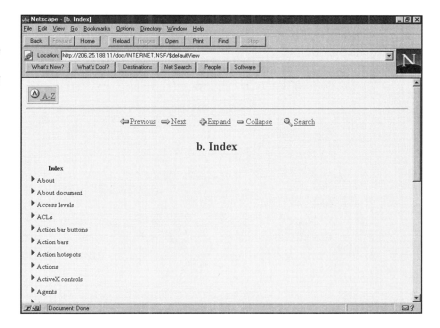

By adding an argument to the URL

http://host/DatabaseName/$defaultView,

you can open a view in expanded mode. Append to the URL by adding
?OpenView&ExpandView. Figure 3.4 shows the results.

Fig. 3.4

*http://206.25.188.11/
doc/INTERNET.NSF/
$defaultView/
?OpenView&ExpandView
opens the default view
of the database in
expanded mode to the
Web client. You can
replace $defaultView
with a view name.*

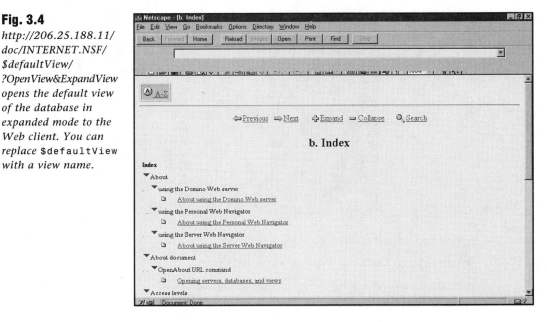

These URL commands are an effective method of guiding Web clients through your site.
You can use them in action hotspots and link hotspots. Chapter 13, "Examining Special
Function Databases for the Web," discusses the use of the Domino Configuration database to redirect URLs so that you can keep HTML files, CGI scripts, and Reference Databases and files in multiple locations or move them without breaking the URL links.

 Tip

If you have a multiple server site, you may wish to keep HTML files, CGI scripts
and graphics in multiple databases. You might also need or want to move these
files and databases. Using the Domino Configuration database, you can redirect
URLs to facilitate multiple locations or moves without breaking the URL links. Refer
to Chapter 13, "Examining Special Function Databases for the Web," for more
information on the Domino Configuration database.

Viewing a Mail Database

For Notes users to access their mail via the Web, at a very minimum they must have an HTTP password provided in their person documents in the Public Name and Address book. After a user provides a password, the user will need to authenticate by providing his/her user name as well as the password. Of course, mail on the Web without any intervention or redesign amounts to read only access. Since Web browsers provide no menu entries for creating or replying to messages, there is no vehicle for users to create new mail. Lotus Development provides an experimental Web mail template available for download at the Lotus site, **www.Lotus.com**. Follow the links to Domino download and you will find the mail template. Also, we have provided a copy of the template on the CD-ROM accompanying this book.

Once you incorporate the Web mail template, Notes clients can create mail from a Web client; however, no copy of Web generated mail is created in the Notes database. It might be prudent to advise users if they want to retain copies of sent mail to include themselves in the To: or cc: field of the memos they send as Web clients.

For more information on the Notes Web mail template, and the mail database on the Web, refer to Chapter 13, "Examining Special Function Databases for the Web."

Figure 3.5 shows the request for authentication sent to the Web client when the Web client requests to open a mail database. Opening the mail database can be done, in the *raw* Domino site, by double clicking the database in the list of the default view for the server (host/?open).

Fig. 3.5

To access mail as a Web client, the Notes user must have an HTTP password provided in the appropriate field of the Person Document in the Public Name and Address book.

Figure 3.6 shows the default view of mail on the Web without the use of the Web mail Template. This view is generated on-the-fly by Domino.

Fig. 3.6

The default view of the mail database lists all available views and folders. Authentication is required to access this view.

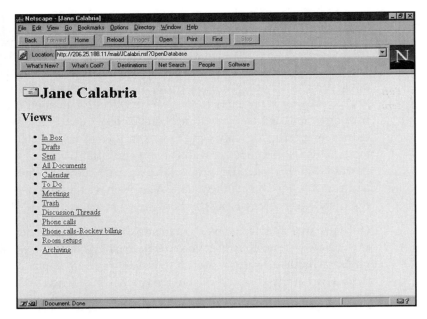

> ⚛ **Tip**
>
> Domino displays all views in the view template shown in Figure 3.6 with navigational directions for previous, next, expand, collapse, and search. This template is generated dynamically by Domino and does not appear in the design view of a given database. You can create your own default view template by creating a form named `$ViewTemplateDefault`. You can also customize or alter the view template shown in Figure 3.6 by downloading the template from the Lotus Web site. For more information on customizing view templates, see Chapter 10, "Using Special Web fields and Functions."

Open the Mail Inbox view and note that there is no method for creating mail. As indicated earlier, Lotus has provided a Web mail template that allows easy access to creating mail on the Web. Read about mail on the Web in Chapter 13.

The default view template contains a search icon. When a Web user selects the search icon, Domino displays a search form as shown in Figure 3.7. When the Web user submits the form, Domino conducts a search of the currently displayed database (but only if the database has been full-text indexed). Domino displays the results using the same view from which the Web user conducted the search.

Fig. 3.7

Enter a query in the search window. Notes returns a list of links to documents in the database that meet the terms of your query.

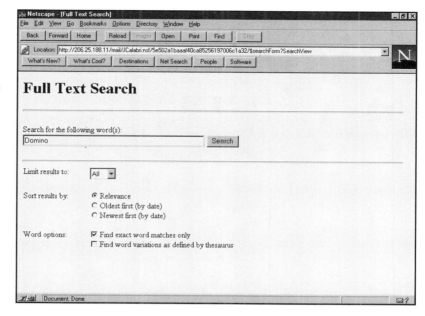

Figure 3.8 displays the search results of a search for "Domino." The search results display on one page. Although you cannot see it in the figure, all 155 documents are listed on this page. The search results are presented as hypertext links.

Fig. 3.8

Search results are presented as hypertext links.

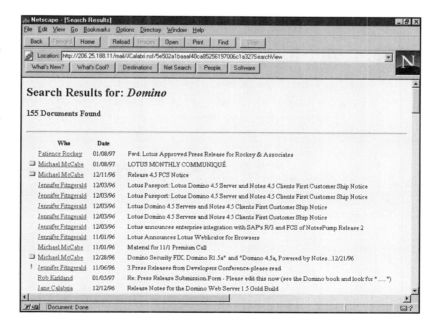

The Calendar view in the Mail database allows you to read calendar entries as shown in Figure 3.9. Note the action bar from the calendar view in *Notes* is served up and Web clients can select from Calendar views that include one day, two weeks, one month and so forth.

Fig. 3.9

The Calendar view as displayed through a Web browser. The Action bar contains no actions enabling calendar entries.

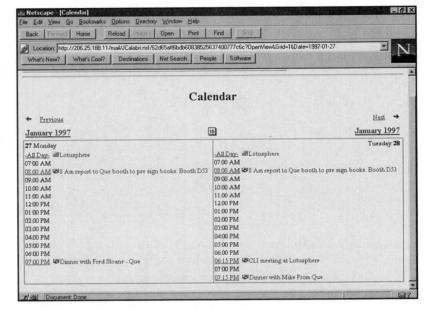

Understanding the Domino Directory Structure

When you install the Domino server for the first time or upgrade a Notes server to Domino 4.5 status, Domino creates a default directory structure for itself, where it will assume files of certain types will go. The default directory structure is as appears in Figure 3.10.

Fig. 3.10

This screen shot displays the default directory structure of a Domino server.

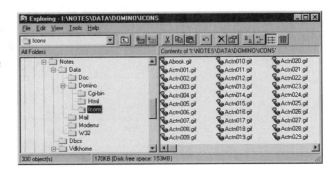

All Notes 4.x servers have the data\doc, data\mail, data\modems, and data\w32 (or its equivalent) directories. All Notes 4.x servers have the dbcs and vdkhome directories. What the others do not have, what are unique to servers running Domino 4.5 or the Domino 1.x HTTP add-in software, are data\domino and its subdirectories, data\domino\cgi-bin, data\domino\html, and data\domino\icons.

In addition to being a Notes server, the Domino 4.5 server is also a full-blown HTTP server. That is, not only can it serve the contents of Notes databases to Web users, but it can also serve HTML files. The data\domino directory is the root data directory for all Web-related data, including HTML files, CGI scripts, and graphics files.

The data\domino\html subdirectory is where Domino stores HTML files. The data\domino\cgi-bin directory is where Domino stores CGI scripts, and the data\domino\icons directory is where Domino stores graphics files. This is true not only because Domino created these directories but also because Domino maps them to standard UNIX settings that Web users are used to looking for them in.

That is, in the Mapping section of the Server document, Domino sets domino\HTML as the root HTML directory. This means that, if a Web user enters http://dominoserverhostname/filename.htm, Domino will look in the domino\HTML directory for the file. The user in this case asks the server for a file called filename.htm in the root HTML directory of the server called dominoserverhostname. See the Mapping section of a Server document in Figure 3.11.

Fig. 3.11

The Mapping section of the Server document defines which physical directory maps to the standard UNIX locations for various Web-related files.

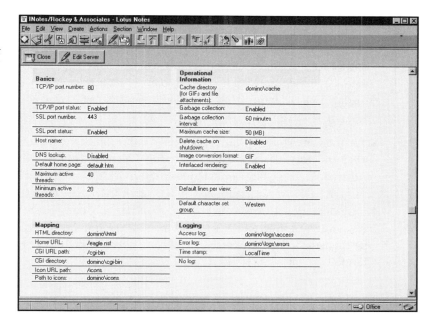

In that same Mapping section, Domino maps the data\domino\cgi-bin directory to /cgi-bin, and the data\domino\icons directory to /icons. This means that, if a Web user asks for a file called http://dominoserverhostname/cgi-bin/filename.exe, Domino will look for the file in the data\domino\cgi-bin directory. If a user asks for a file called http://dominoserverhostname/icons/filename.gif, Domino will look for it in the data\domino\icons directory.

By setting up standard mappings in this way, Domino makes it easy for Web users to find files on it. They don't have to know the actual directory structure of the Domino server. Rather, they simply look for HTML files in what appears to them to be the root directory. They look for cgi scripts in the cgi-bin directory that appears to them to be under to root directory. And they look for graphics files in the icons directory which appears to them to be under the root directory.

There is one last mapping, which we have not mentioned yet, in the Mapping section of the Server document. That is the Home URL. This maps to the default home page of the Domino Web server. That is, when a Web user enters http://dominoserverhostname, Domino retrieves the page named in the Home URL field of the Server document.

By default, the entry in this field is /?Open. This tells Domino to present a list of databases to the user when the user simply enters http://dominoserverhostname. Sure enough, when you first enable http on the Domino server and look at it with a Web browser, you see a list of Notes databases, as shown in Figure 3.1, at the beginning of this chapter.

You will undoubtedly want to change the Home URL setting so it names either an actual HTML document in the HTML directory, or a Notes database. In Figure 3.10, you can see that we have changed the setting to eagle.nsf, which is the file name of our home page Notes database. Eagle.nsf is set to display its About document whenever anyone opens the database. Therefore, the About document of eagle.nsf is the home page for our whole Web site.

The first time you start the HTTP server task, Domino will automatically create yet another directory, the data\domino\cache directory. There it will store copies of GIF files and attachments that people request. This is a time-saving technique. It takes time for Domino to convert bitmaps to GIF format. It takes time to extract attachments from Notes documents, especially because Notes usually compresses attached files. If Domino can store the converted GIFs and extracted attachments in a cache directory, then deliver the cached copies to the second and subsequent requesters of them, Domino can substantially improve its response time.

You can disable caching of bitmaps and attachments by removing the cache directory name from the Cache directory field. However, unless you were absolutely out of disk space, you never would want to disable caching. You can also specify a different directory as a cache directory. You might do this if you wanted to move the cache to another physical disk drive.

Domino will create yet another set of directories if you enable logging of Web events to text files. By default, logging is not enabled. To enable it, you do one of two things. Either you create a database named domlog.nsf to enable logging to that database. Or you enter into the Access log field, the Error log field, or both fields—in the Logging section of the Server document—the names of the directories where Domino should store these two types of text log files. If you set up the second method of logging, Domino creates the directories you specified in the two log fields and stores the log files in them. For more information on logging, see Chapter 16, "Using Advanced Administration Techniques."

Finally, as time goes by, you may decide to create yet other directories. For example, you might create a directory called classes under the HTML directory and designate it for storage of Java .class files. See Chapter 12, "Applying a 'Web Look' to Notes Applications," for information about Domino's support of Java programming.

From Here...

Although Domino converts views, forms and documents, you will need to create access to form for Web clients to make your site more interactive, add graphics and links to make your site more appealing and navigable.

As soon as you enable the HTTP server task, Domino makes your Notes databases available to Web users. It automatically converts views and documents into HTML document. The default Domino site is not, however, either visually appealing or interactive. To create such a site, you will either have to redesign your existing databases or create new ones, using techniques that we describe in later chapters.

For more information, see the following chapters:

▶ Chapter 5, "Building a Web Database," describes the basics of optimizing the design of a Notes database for Web access.

▶ Chapter 6, "Designing Forms to Display Documents on the Web," addresses the issues involved in making Notes documents look great when converted to HTML.

▶ Chapter 7, "Designing Forms for an Interactive Web Site," describes the process of creating Web input forms in Notes.

▶ Chapter 8, "Building Views for Domino Web Applications," discusses the issues involved in building Web-friendly Notes views.

▶ Chapter 10, "Using Special Web Fields and Forms," shows you how to create customized templates as forms which will display on the Web containing views, navigators or search results.

## chapter 4

Understanding Web Fundamentals

4

In this chapter

◆ **The fundamentals of HTML**
Here you get the ABCs of HTML. You learn how an HTML document is struc-tured. You review many of the tags used in HTML documents. You look at some HTML techniques in detail.

◆ **Graphics on the Web**
Although other chapters distinctly address graphics in Notes Web applications, here's a little background to help you understand Web graphics in general.

Please allow us to make one thing perfectly clear: We are Notes developers and systems administrators. We are not Web-heads. Web development called to us when Notes extended its power to the Web. With our Notes skills, we were able to quickly, efficiently, and delightfully design Web applications from Notes applications. That said, in this chapter we introduce you to some Web fundamentals, particu-larly the fundametals of HTML, with a smattering of HTTP fundamentals.

Throughout this book, we show you methods of implementing these tools in Notes applications for the Web. Beyond that, we leave such topics as Java programming and designing Web pages in HTML to the professionals.

Understanding Why Domino is a Great Web Tool

To most Notes application developers, Web applica-tions are a new frontier. After all, if one had a background in Web application development, one would find little or no time to cross over to Lotus Notes development. The market and demand for Web developers has far exceeded the need for Notes application developers. So it's a pretty safe guess that Web development is going to be new to you, just as Domino is new to the World Wide Web. Building Web applications requires Web tools such as HTML editors, site authoring tools, and data access tools, to name a few.

Domino combines these tools and more. Having been called the first real Internet application server, Domino delivers Notes applications—interactive, collaborative applications—to the Web. There is simply nothing else like it. For example, Notes views, the daily bread of Notes applications, are a concept revolutionary to the Web. You can't deliver a dynamic view of a Web server's content to the Web with any tool—except Domino. In addition, Domino brings to the Web:

▶ Collaboration

▶ Workflow

▶ Field Level Access Control

▶ Replication

▶ Access to relational and transactional databases

▶ Messaging

▶ Flexible content navigation

▶ Late binding

▶ Dynamic security

▶ Interactivity

▶ Web user registration in real time

Domino combines Notes features, services, and applications, and adds a dash of Web tools (embedded HTML, site authoring, data access) to earn its increasing reputation as the first true provider of Internet applications.

Understanding HTML

The Domino HTTP server task, once running, dynamically converts Notes views, documents, and forms to HTML as it serves pages to the Web. How much HTML you need to learn is completely at your discretion. Since Domino does 99% of the conversion for you, you could ignore HTML almost completely.

However, there is not a one-to-one correspondence between the features supported by Notes and HTML. Notes does not support all HTML formats. HTML does not support all

Lotus Notes formats. So, at the very least, you need to be aware of those restrictions. Chapter 6, "Designing Forms to Display Documents on the Web", demonstrates how you can use HTML code in Notes documents. In this chapter, you learn about the basics of HTML. When you feel ready to master HTML, be sure to check out the book, *Special Edition Using HTML,* Second Edition, which we have provided on the CD.

HTML stands for *HyperText Mark Up Language.* It is a *page description* language designed to work within the limitations of any computer platform. That is, it is designed to be universal. As its name implies, HTML performs two kinds of functions: linking (hypertext) and formatting (markup).

The word *hypertext* in HTML identifies HTML's linking function. Hypertext is a link or *pointer*, embedded in a file, to another document or file, or to another section within a document or a file. Hypertext links appear as underlined text in a different color than other text on the screen—usually purple or green. When a user clicks a hypertext link, the browser attempts to retrieve the associated document or file. Notes database, document and view links, and Notes link hotspots are Notes's own hypertext links.

The word *markup* in HTML identifies HTML's formatting function. A *markup* language annotates a file, in this case, a text file. The job performed by this annotation is similar to the job performed by the editors at Que—sending messages and instructions for formatting. These instructions include such things as when to start a new paragraph, insert a table, or emphasize a block of text. A mark up language places notes throughout the document. In the case of HTML, these notes are called *tags,* or *tag commands.*

HTML is a relatively new and very quickly evolving protocol. For this reason, it is difficult to say what is or is not true about it, because what is true today may not be true tomorrow. HTML came into existence in 1990 at CERN (Conseil Europeen pour la Recherche Nucleaire) in Switzerland. It is a subset of a larger, more comprehensive markup language called Standard Generalized Markup Language (SGML), which itself is not an Internet standard but rather an ISO (International Organization for Standardization) standard. It also partakes of the Internet Multipurpose Internet Mail Extensions (MIME) protocol.

HTML's creator, Tim Berners-Lee, and other researchers at CERN, the National Center for Supercomputing Applications (NCSA) at the University of Illinois, The World Wide Web Consortium, and elsewhere have quickly and enthusiastically expanded and enriched HTML. In November 1995, Berners-Lee, by then at MIT, and Daniel Connolly submitted a Request for Comment, RFC1866, to the Internet Engineering Task Force (IETF). RFC1866 purported to collect the then-current state of the art of HTML and proposed that it become an Internet Standard known as HTML 2.0 (1.0 being the unstandardized, earlier forms of HTML). For a while compatibility with HTML 2.0 was what all browser developers, including Lotus with InterNotes Web Navigator, aimed to achieve.

4

But HTML 2.0 quickly became obsolete when some of the people at NCSA who had been developing HTML created Netscape Communications Corporation in hopes of capitalizing on the commercial potential of HTML, and created and started marketing the browser called Netscape Navigator. Netscape was an overnight, wild success. It woke up all sorts of sleeping giants, most notably Microsoft, which perceived the rising popularity of the Internet and the World Wide Web as a threat to its monopoly over the personal computer software market, and concluded that it had to compete with Netscape and, if possible, co-opt and dominate the development of the HTML and HTTP standards.

Thus, 1996 became the year of the browser wars as Netscape and Microsoft issued new, improved versions of their browsers every three months, Netscape in an effort to stay as many steps ahead of the 800-pound gorilla as possible, Microsoft in an effort to overtake Netscape. In the process the two companies left all other HTML developers in their dust as they introduced one proprietary (but open) extension of HTML after another. By the end of 1996 the state of the art of HTML was vastly advanced beyond the proposed HTML 2.0.

Berners-Lee and his associates at the World Wide Web Consortium gamely tried to nail down progressive standards. They recommended first HTML 3.0 and then, in January 1997, HTML 3.2. Things had advanced so quickly that they decided to skip over HTML 3.1 entirely. HTML 3.0 and 3.2 have not even been submitted to the IETF as RFCs but are merely, at this writing, recommendations of the authoritative but unofficial World Wide Web Consortium.

However, HTML 3.2 does represent the state of the art of HTML as of the end of 1996 and is supported by Netscape, Microsoft, Lotus, and many other interested software developers. It is the current, de facto standard for HTML, compatibility with which all browser developers, including Lotus, currently aim for—except, of course, Netscape and Microsoft. Those two companies continue to extend HTML as fast as they can in their efforts to win market- and mind-share for their own products.

Domino 1.0 and the Notes 4.0 version of InterNotes Web Navigator were largely (if not entirely) compatible with HTML 2.0. Domino 1.5/4.5 and the Notes 4.5 version of InterNotes Web Navigator (now called simply *Web Navigator*) are largely but not entirely compatible with HTML 3.2. Lotus will undoubtedly continue to enhance Domino and Web Navigator, adapting them to the current state of the art as it develops. But HTML is a fast moving target, so Lotus permits us to use pass-thru HTML and non-Notes-based HTML documents wherever necessary to overcome the inevitable limitations of Domino as a state of the art Web server.

Understanding HTML Tags

HTML tags are always enclosed in angle brackets, so that they look something like this: *<tag>*. A block of text in an HTML file might look something like <I>this</I>, where the tag *<I>* signals the beginning of *italicized* text and the tag *</I>* signals the return to Roman text. Thus, an HTML file is a text file with tags inserted here and there that an HTML formatter will interpret as formatting commands or programming instructions. An unformatted HTML file (as seen through a text editor) looks like a WordPerfect document as seen in Reveal Codes mode.

Empty/Open Tags versus Container Tags

HTML uses two kinds of tags: *empty* or *open tags* and *container tags*. Empty/open tags are instructions that need to be carried out once, as in the insertion of a paragraph break <P>, a line break <BR>, or a horizontal rule <HR>. Container tags, as their name implies, contain text in between two tags—a starting tag and an ending tag. For example, if you want to make a block of text bold, the first container tag, <B>, is followed by the text to be bolded which is then followed by the end bold tag, </B>. Ending container tags match the beginning container tags and are preceded by a forward slash /. Container tags can be nested or overlapped, and they can contain empty tags.

Qualifying Tags with Attributes

Some tags may include *attributes*. An attribute is additional information that appears between the text of the tag and its closing angle bracket, and is separated from the tag text and other attributes by spaces. Attributes qualify a tag in the same way that arguments and flags qualify a DOS command. For example, the <HR> tag tells the browser to display a *horizontal rule* at the point in the document where the tag appears. The <HR> tag may appear by itself or it may appear with one or more attributes appended, as follows:

```
<HR SIZE=4 WIDTH=75% ALIGN=CENTER NOSHADE>.
```

This instructs the browser to display the horizontal rule 4 pixels high, with a length of only 75% of the width of the screen on which it is displayed, centered horizontally on the screen, and without a shadow.

Attributes may be optional, as in the example above of the <HR> tag. Or, they may be mandatory. For example, if you want to embed a graphic image into a document, you can do so with the <IMG> tag. However, standing by itself, the <IMG> tag is meaningless. It *must* include the SRC attribute, which tells the browser the URL of the image to be embedded. Thus, the <IMG> tag will *always* appear something like this:

```
<IMG SRC="URL">
```

Here *URL* is the location and name of the file containing the image. Because the <IMG> tag always includes the SRC attribute, some people call it the <IMG SRC> tag. But that is technically incorrect.

Overriding Tag Settings in a Browser

Using HTML, you, the author of a document, can dictate such things as page and text colors, font sizes, placement and characteristics of tables, placement of line and para-graph breaks, and the overall appearance and formatting of your page. However, the browser receiving the HTML page has ultimate control over the page's appearance and may override many of your instructions with the user's own preferences. For example, Netscape Navigator 3.0 allows the user to set preferences for how hypertext links appear, with choices of underlined, or not underlined. Netscape also allows the user to deter-mine colors for links and followed links, and background colors, and allows the browser to override the HTML code provided in the receiving document. Figure 4.1 shows the Colors tab of the Preferences dialog box in Netscape Navigator 3.0

Fig. 4.1

Browsers such as Netscape allow users to set preferences which can override the incoming HTML code. Some HTML used in your applications will be lost on users who select this option.

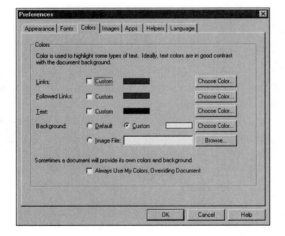

Understanding Domino and HTML

Both Notes documents and HTML documents are *rich text* documents. Notes uses its own, proprietary system of encoding rich text. HTML provides an open, standardized method of encoding rich text. The Domino HTTP service translates between the two systems.

However, the two are not 100% compatible with each other. Notes supports some features that HTML does not, and vice versa. Where there is a one-to-one correspondence between a Notes formatting feature and an HTML formatting feature, Domino automatically translates between them, and you as an author of Notes applications for Web users do not have to concern yourself with the details of the translation. Thus, things like bolded or italicized text and centered paragraphs translate automatically.

Where there is an approximate correspondence between a Notes feature and an HTML feature, Domino translates semi-automatically. That is, Domino lets you override its default methods of translation, but otherwise translates automatically. An example of this is translation between Notes font sizes and HTML <Hn> tags. HTML does not permit definition of precise font sizes as Notes does. Rather, HTML only permits you to define between logical text types such as body text and various types of headings. The browser assigns font sizes to the different logical types of text. So Domino translates between Notes font sizes and HTML heading types according to a table.

Finally, there are features of both Notes and HTML for which there is no corresponding feature in the other system. For example, Notes does not allow you to format text as *blinking*, whereas HTML does. In these circumstances, Domino almost always permits you to embed HTML tags into your Notes forms and documents. Lotus calls these embedded tags *pass-thru HTML*, because they *pass through* the Domino Notes-to-HTML translation process unchanged so that the receiving browser can interpret them correctly.

Since there are only so many things you can do to text on a computer screen, the vast majority of Notes formatting features translate to HTML satisfactorily without any intervention from Notes authors or application designers. This is great because it allows people like us, who have lots of expertise in Notes and little or no expertise in HTML, to make our Notes applications available to Web users without learning a whole new discipline. That is, we can set up Domino-based Web applications without knowing anything about HTML.

However, before you decide to ignore HTML completely and let Domino do all the work for you, understand that you'll benefit greatly from knowing something about HTML. At the very least, you need to know how to create *pass-thru HTML*.

The good news is that HTML is very easy to learn, and pass-thru HTML is very easy to use in Notes applications. Here, we provide you with some basics and background.

Understanding HTML Document Structure

As Domino serves a Notes element, such as a view or document, to the Web, it converts the Notes element to an HTML page. Some browsers let you view the raw HTML code behind an HTML page. For example, if you're using Netscape 3.0, select <u>V</u>iew, Document Source from the menu.

In Figures 4.2 and 4.3, we demonstrate the document structure of the HTML page.

Figure 4.2 shows a page from our publisher's site at **www.mcp.com/que.** The page was not generated by a Domino server, but a Domino server would have generated the page very similarly.

Fig. 4.2

Visiting Que's Web site, we find Special Edition Using HTML, 2nd Edition. This entire book can be found on the CD-ROM included with this book.

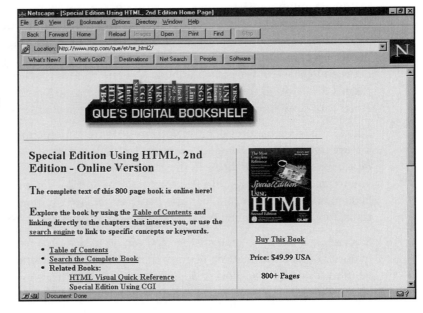

Figure 4.3 shows some of the raw HTML source code for the page in Figure 4.2. The code runs off the right side of the screen and is not completely visible within one screen shot.

The page displayed in Figures 4.2 and 4.3 is a moderately complex page. Its full listing would occupy several pages of this book. Rather than show you the full listing, which would serve no compelling purpose, we show you, below, the portions of the listing that define the structure of the document.

```
<html>

<head>

...

</head>

<body ... >
```

```
...

</body>

</html>
```

As you can see in Figure 4.3 and the previous listing, the HTML page starts and ends with the HTML container tags—<HTML>...</HTML>—as every HTML file must. You can see the <HTML> tag in both the listing above and Figure 4.3. You can see the </HTML> tag only in the listing, not the figure.

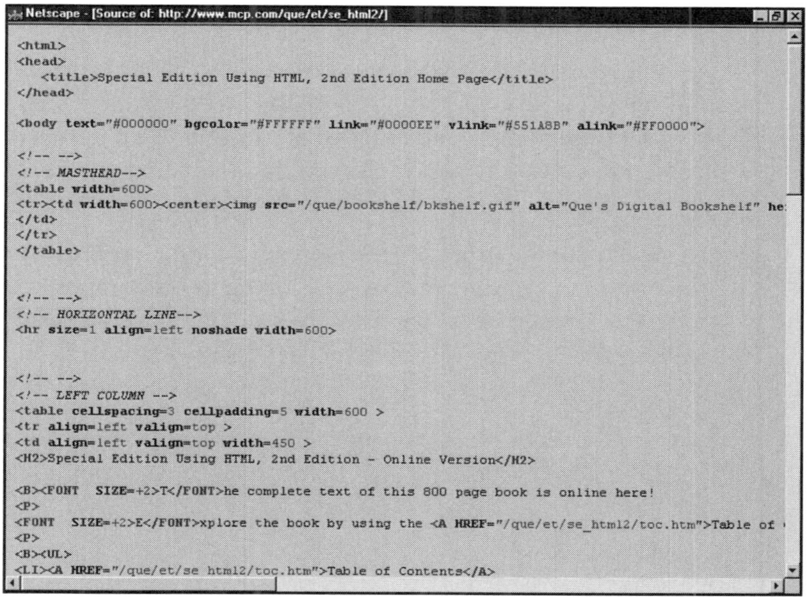

Fig. 4.3

HTML code of the HTML document displayed in Figure 4.2.

As the previous listing shows, the HTML document in Figures 4.2 and 4.3 includes two main sections, the Head and the Body. Each is preceded and closed by container tags— <HEAD>...</HEAD> for the Head and <BODY>...</BODY> for the Body. Most HTML documents follow this pattern, although pages designed to appear in a series of frames on-screen will substitute one or more Frameset sections and possibly a NoFrames section for the Body section.

The Head section contains information about your page and its relationship with other pages at your site, and also contains the URL of your page. Web browsers can use it as sort of a "quick reference" to the page and certain of its characteristics.

The Head section usually contains a title, set off by the <TITLE>...</TITLE> tags. The title contains a short description of the page or site. The source code for the Que page reads:

```
<html>
<head>
<title>Special Edition Using HTML, 2nd Edition Home Page</title>
</head>
Some browsers display the title in the Title Bar of the window in which the page
appears. You can see an example of this in Figures 4.2 and 4.3, above. Browsers also
➥use the title when creating bookmarks and history lists. The title is also used by
➥indexing programs. A title cannot contain colons or backslashes, images, links or
➥formatting.
```

While the page displayed in Figures 4.2 and 4.3 only includes a title in its Head section, other elements that may appear there include *Base*, *Link*, *IsIndex*, and *Meta* elements. Of these, Domino eliminates any need for all but the *Meta* element, since Domino automatically takes care of the problems these elements are designed to address.

Among other things, Web servers use the *Meta* element to send *cookies* to Web browsers, and this is the principle use you will have for the Meta element on a Domino server. If you will be sending cookies to Web browsers, you will have to embed *Meta* tags into Notes forms. See Chapter 13, "Examining Special Function Databases for the Web," for a good example of the use of a cookie in the Domino Discussion database.

The BODY section is usually the next to be found in an HTML page. The BODY section comprises most of the Web page, including tables, formatting, graphics, and text. As a container tag, the <BODY> tag must have an ending tag—</BODY>—and the only tag permitted after the body tag is the closing HTML tag—</HTML>.

In Figure 4.3, you can see that the <BODY> tag may include several optional attributes. You can also see that the body includes HTML tags for tables, alignment, images, bolding, and font sizes. The following section describes some commonly used HTML tags.

Using HTML Tags

While you will rarely *have* to use HTML tags directly in Notes applications, you will have to do so occasionally, and you will probably want to at times, even though you don't strictly have to. To give you an overview of what you can accomplish with HTML tags, we have provided several tables. In Table 4.1, we've listed the tags that can be used in the Head section of an HTML document. In Table 4.2, we've listed the most commonly used tags that can appear in the Body section of an HTML document. In Table 4.3, we've listed the tags that can appear in an HTML input form.

If our overview of HTML is not enough to satisfy your craving for expertise, you'll find that the *Special Edition Using HTML*, Second Edition, included on the CD, is a much more comprehensive treatise on HTML. If that doesn't sate your appetite, see also RFC1866, *HTML 2.0*, (ftp://ds.internic.net/rfc/rfc1866.txt), and the World Wide Web Consortium's recommendation for HTML 3.2 (http://www.w3.org/pub/WWW/TR/REC-html32.HTML).

Finally, see RFC2045 through RFC2049 for the latest developments in the MIME protocol.

Table 4.1   HTML Tags Used in the Head Sections of HTML Documents

Element	Type	Description
BASE	empty	Base context document.
HEAD	container	Document head.
ISINDEX	empty	Inserts a search field in the document.
LINK	empty	Link to other documents. Analogous to <A> in Body section.
META	empty	Additional information about the document.
NEXTID	empty	An obsolete tag that is no longer recommended. Is not listed among the elements of the Head section in the recommended HTML 3.2 standard as published by the World Wide Web Consortium in January 1997.
SCRIPT	container	Not used yet. In the recommended HTML 3.2 standard, this tag is "Reserved for future use with scripting languages."
STYLE	container	Not used yet. In the recommended HTML 3.2 standard, this tag is "Reserved for future use with style sheets."
TITLE	container	Document title.

Table 4.2   HTML Tags Used in the Body Sections of HTML Documents

Tag	Type	Description
A	container	Anchor. Can be either the source or the destination of a hypertext link.
ADDRESS	container	Address, signature, or byline for a document. Usually appears in italics at the bottom of the document.
B	container	Boldface text.
BLOCKQUOTE	container	Quoted paragraph that the browser would usually display indented further than standard paragraphs.
BODY	container	The body of a document.

continues

Table 4.2   Continued

Tag	Type	Description
BR	empty	A line break but not a paragraph break. No white space appears between the lines.
CITE	container	Title of a cited document. Usually appears italicized.
CODE	container	Text of programming code. Usually appears in monospaced font.
DIR	container	Directory list. See LI below.
LI	empty	List item.
DL	container	Definition list or glossary. See DT and DD below.
DT	empty	Defined term. See DL and DD.
DD	empty	Definition of a term. Appears in a Definition List. See DL and DT above.
EM	container	Emphasized text. Usually appears italicized.
H1 through H6	container	Heading paragraph, levels 1 (most general, main headings) through 6 (most specific, sub-headings). Can be used to outline a document. Appear in progressively smaller fonts with progressively less emphasis.
HR	empty	Horizontal rule. A line across the screen. Notes does not provide such a tool, so if you want to use them in Notes documents on the Web, you must use pass-thru HTML.
I	container	Italics.
IMG	empty	Contains the URL of any image or icon to be embedded in an HTML document.
KBD	container	Used to denote any keyboard input to be entered by the user. Usually appears in a monospace font.
LISTING	container	Computer listing. See also Code, above, which would be used for one line of code, whereas LISTING would be used for multiple lines of code. Use the LI tag, above, to delimit the lines of code.
MENU	container	Menu list. Use the LI tag, above, to delimit the menu choices.

Tag	Type	Description
OL	container	Ordered list. Appears as a numbered list. Use the LI tag to delimit the listed items.
UL	container	Unordered list. Appears as a bulleted list. Use the LI tag to delimit the listed items.
P	empty (but optionally can take a </P> tag	Paragraph break. Similar to the tag but tag defines a new paragraph. A line of white space appears between the paragraphs.
PRE	container	Contains *pre*formatted text. Appears as a monospace font. Extra spaces between characters are preserved to maintain column formatting. (Normally HTML removes extra spaces.)
STRONG	container	An alternative to <EM>. Usually displayed in boldface.
TT	container	Typewriter text. Appears in monospace font. Like <PRE>, permits column formatting because extra spaces between characters are preserved.
TABLE	container	Defines an HTML table. This is a feature of HTML 3.2.
TH	container	Defines a header row at the top of a table or header column down the left side of a table.
TR	container	Defines a standard row in a table.
TD	container	TD stands for *Table Data*. Defines a cell in a table row.

4

Table 4.3 HTML Tags Used in HTML Forms

Tag	Type	Description
FORM	container	Defines an input form. Appears within the Body section of an HTML document. The other form tags, listed below, must appear within the <FORM>...</FORM> container.
INPUT	empty	One-line form input field. Can be of types Text, Password, Check box, Radio, Reset, or Submit. Text is the default and appears as a box into which the user can

continues

Table 4.3   Continued

Tag	Type	Description
		enter text. Password is also a text box, but nothing appears on the screen when the user enters text into the field. Check box and Radio both present lists. Reset and Submit both present clickable buttons.
TEXTAREA	empty	Multiline form input field. Defines a rectangular area into which the user can enter lines of text.
SELECT	empty	Pick-list form input field. Appears either as a popup menu or a scrollable list of choices.

Some HTML structures in widespread use are not mentioned in the previous tables. In particular the tags that define frames are missing. Frames are not included in the World Wide Web Consortium's recommended HTML 3.2 standard, but they are a feature of both Netscape Navigator 3.0 and Microsoft Internet Explorer 3.0, and we discuss them later in this chapter.

Understanding Color Attributes in HTML

Many tags permit you to set a color attribute for the affected text. You may be able to set either the text color or the background color. This introduces all sorts of opportunities for fun, creativity, and making your documents more user-friendly. But colors can backfire on you if you choose the wrong ones, because browsers don't all support the same color palette—the same set of colors. You may choose a color that Netscape supports, only to find that Internet Explorer or Mosaic substitutes some other color for the one you chose.

To make sure that all browsers display your pages in the colors you expect, you must choose from a limited range of colors that all browsers support. As it happens, there are 216 of them.

HTML documents are intended to be displayed on computer screens, which define colors in terms of their red, green, and blue components. Therefore, when you choose colors for components of HTML documents, you describe the colors in terms of the amount of red, green, and blue in them. That is, each color is represented by a six-digit hexadecimal number in the form RRGGBB. The first two digits represent the red component, the second two, the green component, and the last two, the blue component. The numbers for each component can range from 00 to FF, that is, from 0 to 255.

If you think about it, 256 red shades, multiplied by 256 green shades, multiplied by 256 blue shades (which represents all the possible combinations of red, green, and blue shades) is an awful lot of colors—16,777,216 colors, to be exact. Which 216 of these 16 million to all the browsers support? Only six of the possible 256 shades of each component: the shades numbered 00h, 33h, 66h, 99h, CCh, and FFh. Six shades of red, multiplied by six shades of green, multiplied by six shades of blue comes to 216 possible colors.

A sample listing of color codes appears in Table 4.4. Some of the listed colors—red, orange, green, blue, black, and white—are available in all browsers. The other listed colors are not available in all browsers, and you should use them advisedly. The color names are taken from Netscape Navigator, in which you can, if you want, assign colors by name instead of by number.

Table 4.4   Hexadecimal Equivalents for Colors (a Small Sample)

Color	Hexadecimal Equivalant
Red	FF0000
Orange	FF9900
Apple Green	CED500
Green	00FF00
Avocado	CECDB4
Blue Green	088D6C
Ocean Blue	0994A6
Blue	0000FF
Dark Blue	06438A
Dark Purple	5B0B5A
Light Purple	940B63
Dark Grey	A7A7A7
Black	000000
White	FFFFFF

A good book on the topic of using color and graphics in Web design is *Designing Web Graphics.2* by Lynda Weinman, New Riders Publishing, Indianapolis, IN, 1996.

Adding a Horizontal Rule

You can add a horizontal rule to your HTML document. The horizontal rule is the only graphic that HTML can produce. Assign attributes to the rule (width, height) with the following:

[<HR SIZE=*n*>]   Sets the height of the horizontal rule in pixels where *n* is the number of pixels (such as 1, 5, 6, and so on) and shows the rule on the Web page.

[<HR WIDTH=*n*>]   Sets the width of the horizontal rule in pixels where *n* is the number of pixels (such as 100, 200, 350, 500, and so on) and shows the rule on the Web page.

[<HR WIDTH=*n*%>]   Sets the width of the horizontal rule as a percentage of the browser screen's width, where n is the percentage (for example, 25%, 75%, or 100%) and shows the rule on the Web page.

[<HR SIZE=n WIDTH=n>]   Sets both the height and width of the horizontal rule where, in both cases, *n* is the number of pixels and shows the rule on the Web page.

Creating Hypertext Links

Creating hypertext links in HTML is a simple matter of inserting an HTML *Anchor* tag pair:

```
<A HREF="URL">URL highlighted text or graphic goes here</A>
```

The <A> tag begins the Anchor. The </A> tag ends it. The text or picture in between is what the Web user clicks to activate the link. If it is text, it will appear in the browser as either underlined text or in a different color than the surrounding text, or perhaps both, depending on how the browser works and how the user has configured the browser. A graphic link won't appear different from any other graphic in the browser. But when the user points at it, the mouse pointer icon will change from an arrow to a pointing hand.

The <A> tag includes an HREF attribute, which is set equal to the name and location (that is, the URL) of the file to which the anchor links.

The previous syntax points to a file, and when a Web user clicks the link, his/her browser retrieves that file, formats it, and displays it to the user with the beginning of the file at the top of the browser's screen. If a given HTML page is many screens in length, you can set up hypertext links to different places on the page. You can do this by inserting anchors with Name attributes on the page at the positions you want to link to and then pointing to those anchors by name.

A Name anchor would look something like this:

```
<A NAME="XYZ">XYZ</A>
```

A hypertext link that points to it would look something like this:

```
<A HREF="#XYZ">Go to XYZ</A>
```

Note that *XYZ* in the HREF is preceded by a pound sign (#). This is the tip-off to the browser that the HREF refers to a named anchor rather than a file, and that the browser should search through the current page for an anchor with NAME="XYZ" as one of its attributes.

If the named anchor is in a different file, use the following syntax:

```
<A HREF=#URL#AnchorName>...</A>
```

For an example of the use of named anchors, take an HTML page that consists of an alphabetical listing of people's names. You could divide it up alphabetically by inserting Name anchors at the beginning of each letter break in the list. At the beginning of the document you could insert a list of pointers to the letters of the alphabet. The user could click a letter in the list at the top of the page; the browser would then jump to that point in the alphabet. The raw HTML might look something like this:

```
<HTML>
<HEAD>
<TITLE>Friends of Bill</TITLE>
</HEAD>
<Body>
<CENTER><H1>Friends of Bill</H1></CENTER><P><P>
Click on a letter below to jump to that part of the alphabet:<P>
<A HREF="#A">A  </A>
<A HREF="#B">B </A>
<A HREF="#C">C </A>
...
<A HREF="#Z">Z </A>
<P><HR><P>
<CENTER><H2><A NAME="A">A</A></H2></CENTER><P>
Aardvark, Alvin<BR>
Abate, Mary<BR>
Accardo, Ricardo<BR>
...
Azzolino, Nina<P><P>
<CENTER><H2><A NAME="B">B</A></H2></CENTER><P>
Babbage, Bob<BR>
...
</BODY>
</HTML>
```

4

Understanding HTML Tables

Notes tables translate very well to HTML, so you will rarely have any need to generate an HTML table using HTML tags. However, there may be times when you will want the results of a formula to display in columns and rows. You can see an example of this in Chapter 13, "Examining Special Function Databases for the Web." There, in the Domino Discussion database, a formula sets up its results in an HTML table. What is especially interesting about the formula is that it appears in a field which itself appears in a cell in a Notes table. The resulting HTML page, then, has a manually built HTML table embedded in the cell of another HTML table that was created automatically by Domino from a Notes table.

HTML table tags include:

<TABLE> </TABLE> starts and ends the table.

<TH> </TH> starts and ends a table header cell. You might want table header cells to run along a row in a table, down a column, or both.

<TR> </TR> starts and ends a table row. You will need one set of <TR></TR> for each row in the table.

<TD> </TD> starts and ends a table cell. Contains the contents of the cell: [<TD>]cell contents[</TD>].

Table attributes can include:

BORDER or BORDER=n places a border around the table, or places a border of a specific thickness (in pixels) around the table. This tag must be contained inside the initial [<TABLE>] tag.

WIDTH=X, HEIGHT=Y sets the size of the entire table when used inside of the initial <TABLE> tag, <TABLE WIDTH=50% HEIGHT=50%> sets X and Y as a percentage of the full window size. X and Y can also be expressed as absolute values (in pixels). This can also be used to set the size of an individual cell when placed inside the <TH> or <TD> tag:

<TH HEIGHT=100 WIDTH=100>CellContents</>TH>

ALIGN=*direction* Sets the horizontal alignment of the contents of a cell where *direction* is either left, center, or right. Can be used within the <TH> or <TD> tags:

```
<TH ALIGN=left>CellContents</TH>
```

VALIGN=*direction*. Sets the vertical alignment of the contents of a cell where *direction* is either top, middle, bottom, or baseline:

```
<TD VALIGN=bottom>
```

Having now learned some basic HTML, let's take another look at the source code of an HTML document. Figure 4.4 shows a Notes form as viewed through a Web browser. This form was created in Notes using Notes tables.

4

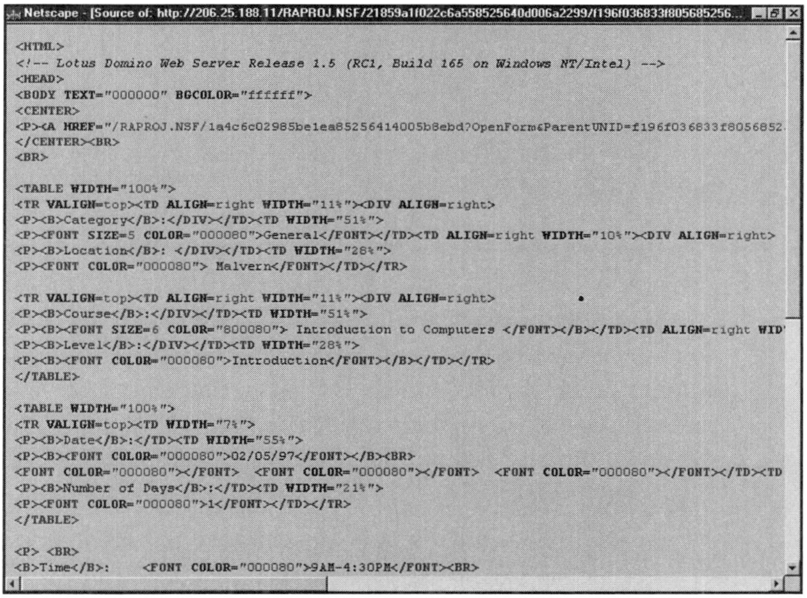

```
Netscape - [Source of: http://206.25.188.11/RAPROJ.NSF/21859a1f022c6a558525640d006a2299/f196f036833f805685256...

<HTML>
<!-- Lotus Domino Web Server Release 1.5 (RC1, Build 165 on Windows NT/Intel) -->
<HEAD>
<BODY TEXT="000000" BGCOLOR="ffffff">
<CENTER>
<P><A HREF="/RAPROJ.NSF/1a4c6c02985be1ea85256414005b8ebd?OpenForm&ParentUNID=f196f036833f8056852
</CENTER><BR>
<BR>

<TABLE WIDTH="100%">
<TR VALIGN=top><TD ALIGN=right WIDTH="11%"><DIV ALIGN=right>
<P><B>Category</B>:</DIV></TD><TD WIDTH="51%">
<P><FONT SIZE=5 COLOR="000080">General</FONT></TD><TD ALIGN=right WIDTH="10%"><DIV ALIGN=right>
<P><B>Location</B>: </DIV></TD><TD WIDTH="28%">
<P><FONT COLOR="000080"> Malvern</FONT></TD></TR>

<TR VALIGN=top><TD ALIGN=right WIDTH="11%"><DIV ALIGN=right>
<P><B>Course</B>:</DIV></TD><TD WIDTH="51%">
<P><B><FONT SIZE=6 COLOR="800080"> Introduction to Computers </FONT></B></TD><TD ALIGN=right WID'
<P><B>Level</B>:</DIV></TD><TD WIDTH="28%">
<P><B><FONT COLOR="000080">Introduction</FONT></B></TD></TR>
</TABLE>

<TABLE WIDTH="100%">
<TR VALIGN=top><TD WIDTH="7%">
<P><B>Date</B>:</TD><TD WIDTH="55%">
<P><B><FONT COLOR="000080">02/05/97</FONT></B><BR>
<FONT COLOR="000080"></FONT>  <FONT COLOR="000080"></FONT>  <FONT COLOR="000080"></FONT></TD><TD
<P><B>Number of Days</B>:</TD><TD WIDTH="21%">
<P><FONT COLOR="000080">1</FONT></TD></TR>
</TABLE>

<P> <BR>
<B>Time</B>:    <FONT COLOR="000080">9AM-4:30PM</FONT><BR>
```

Fig. 4.4
A Notes document viewed through a Web browser. The form used for this document was created in Notes, and tables were used when designing the form.

Using the Web browser to view the source code of this page, Figure 4.5 displays the HTML code. Completely generated on-the-fly, we see the HTML code created by Domino.

Fig. 4.5

Notes tables are converted to HTML tables by Domino. Note the <TABLE> tags as well as the table size attributes (100%).

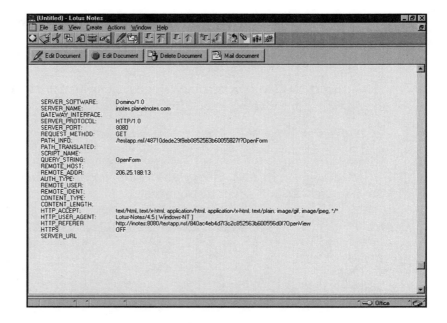

Understanding Graphics on the Web

There are two kinds of computer graphics: vector graphics and bitmap graphics. Vector graphics are pictures made up of mathematically described objects, such as lines, arcs, ellipses, and rectangles. Bitmap graphics are pictures made up of an array of dots of different colors and shades. Notes documents can include both kinds of graphics. Web browsers can only display bitmap graphics and only two types of bitmap graphics:

▶ *GIF (Graphics Interchange Format)*. A compressed bitmap file format first made popular by CompuServe. GIF files use "lossless" compression, in which the compressed version of a file is identical to the precompressed version.

▶ *JPEG*. A compressed bitmap file format developed by the Joint Photographic Experts Group. JPEG uses *lossy* compression, which permits you to compress a file more if you are willing to give up fidelity to the original version. The more fidelity you are willing to lose, the more you can compress the file. Good for photographs.

Domino will automatically convert graphics in Notes documents to .GIF or JPEG. So, in general, you don't have to work very hard to get Notes graphics to appear in translated HTML documents.

However, if a particular graphic image appears in multiple Notes documents, you can speed up the transmission of those documents to a Web browser and save disk space on the Web browser computer by embedding in the Notes documents a pointer to a file containing the graphic image from within Notes documents, rather than embedding the file directly in the Notes documents.

Also, you might want to override Domino's default translation for a particular image. For example, your Domino server may, by default, translate all embedded graphic images to GIF format. If you want to transmit a particular image—a photograph—in JPEG format, then you would have to embed a pointer to the JPEG file in the Notes document, rather than embedding the file itself, which Domino would then translate to GIF.

In other words, there are situations in which you really want to use pass-thru HTML to refer in a Notes document to an external graphics file instead of letting Domino translate the embedded image for you automatically. For more information on Domino's handling of graphics, see the section titled "Graphics Formatting Considerations" in Chapter 5, "Building a Web Database." See also "Using Images in Forms" in Chapter 6, "Designing Forms to Display Documents on the Web."

HTML defines the <IMG> tag for the purpose of embedding images in HTML documents. When Domino translates a Notes document that includes an embedded graphic image, Domino inserts an <IMG> tag in the place of the graphic. When you use pass-thru HTML in a Notes form or document to refer to an external graphic file, you embed an <IMG> tag in your form or document.

The <IMG> tag always takes a SRC attribute in the form SRC="*URL*", where *URL* is the location and name of the graphics file to be inserted. Thus, a minimal <IMG> tag would look something like this:

```
<IMG SRC="http://www.planetnotes.com/filename.gif"
```

Of course, the <IMG> tag can also take other attributes, such as HEIGHT and WIDTH, which define the size of the image on the browser screen.

Understanding Image Maps

An image map is a graphic in which regions of the graphic are linked to a series of URLs. Click this part of the image map, and you retrieve document A; click that part of the image map, and you retrieve document B, instead.

HTML 2.0 defines *server-side* image maps, in which, when a user clicks the image map, the browser sends the coordinates of the pixel on which the user clicked back to the server. The server compares those coordinates to the coordinates of the image map as stored in an Image Map Definition file, maintained on the server, to determine which file those coordinates correspond to. The server then sends the URL of that file back to the browser, which then retrieves the file.

HTML 3.x defines *client-side* image maps, in which the server sends to the browser, along with the image map, a list of files associated with the various regions of the image map. When the user clicks the image map, the browser itself compares the coordinates of the clicked pixel with the list of files, determines which file corresponds to the clicked pixel, then retrieves the file. Except for sending the image map and list of files to the user originally, the server does not participate in the processing. Netscape Navigator 2.0 and Internet Explorer 3.0 support client-side image maps.

The easiest way to create Image Maps for the Web, using Notes, is to created a Notes navigator. Navigators in Notes support hot spots, which can be links to URLs. Domino automatically converts Notes navigators into image maps. For information on creating Notes navigators as image maps, see "Understanding Navigators" in Chapter 5, "Building a Web Database."

To create a server-side image map using pure HTML techniques, you combine an <A> tag with an <IMG> tag, as follows:

```
<A href="/cgi-bin/imagemap.map"><img ismap src="icons.gif"></A>
```

The <A> tag references the image map definition file. The <IMG> tag appears between the <A> and </A> tags. It identifies the graphic image itself and includes a special attribute—ISMAP—that signals the browser that it should treat the image as an image map. When the user clicks the image map, the browser will send the clicked coordinates back to the server.

To create a client-side image map using pure HTML techniques, you create an <IMG> tag with the USEMAP attribute and a <MAP>…</MAP> container. Here is an example, taken from the W3C

```
<img src="navbar.gif" border=0 usemap="#map1">

<map name="map1">
 <area href=guide.html alt="Access Guide" shape=rect coords="0,0,118,28">
 <area href=search.html alt="Search" shape=rect coords="184,0,276,28">
 <area href=shortcut.html alt="Go" shape=rect coords="118,0,184,28">
 <area href=top10.html alt="Top Ten" shape=rect coords="276,0,373,28">
</map>
```

The <IMG> tag identifies the graphic file to be used as the image map. The attribute *usemap="#map1"* identifies a <MAP> element named *map1* that associates specific files with various regions of the image map.

The <MAP> tag includes the NAME attribute, equal to *"map1"*. The MAP container includes several <AREA> elements. Each one includes an HREF attribute, a SHAPE attribute, and a COORDS attribute. The HREF attribute identifies the file that will be retrieved when a user clicks that area of the image map. The SHAPE and COORDS attributes identify the portion of the image map associated with the file. SHAPE can be equal to *rect* for rectangle, *circle*, and *poly* for polygon. The coordinates listed in the COORDS attribute vary according to the SHAPE of the region.

Understanding Web Forms and CGI Script Processing

Web servers are designed primarily to broadcast information to Web clients. However, a Web server can also receive information from Web clients. In fact, every time a user sends a URL to a Web server, the Web server is receiving the URL and acting on it. If a Web application designer wants the server to do more than simply serve up pages to users, then the designer can set up HTML documents that return more than just plain "filename" URLs to the server.

Instead of sending a URL that simply identify static HTML pages, a Web user can send a URL that names a program in a Web server's CGI script directory. When a Web server receives such a URL, it executes the CGI script, then returns the CGI program's output to the Web user.

For example, whenever a Web user performs a simple search of a Web server, the search arrives at the server in the form of an HTTP *Get* command that includes a URL with arguments appended to it. Such a URL might look something like this:

> **http://search.yahoo.com/bin/**
> **search?p=elvis&t=on&u=on&c=on&s=a&w=s&l=100**

In the previous line, *p=elvis* is the search term. The other arguments specify details of how the search results will be presented to the user. The server passes this URL to its search engine (in the example case, a program called *search* located in the *bin* directory). Using the appended arguments, the search engine performs the search, then compiles the results as an HTML document, and the server returns this document to the Web user.

Web users can also submit filled-in Web forms to the server. A Web form is a section of the body of an HTML document. A Web form begins with a <FORM> tag and ends with a </FORM> tag. In between, along with the usual text and formatting tags, one or more data input tags (<INPUT>, <SELECT>, or <TEXTAREA>) appear. These look to the Web user like data entry fields and buttons. Each one includes a NAME attribute and a VALUE attribute. If a <FORM> section has more than one data entry field, it will also have a *Submit* button, which is itself simply an <INPUT> tag of type *submit*.

When a user submits a form to a Web server, the browser usually sends the entered data back to the Web server in the form of an HTTP *Post* command. The Post command returns the user-entered data in the form of a data body that follows the URL but (unlike the arguments in a Get command) is not part of it. The Web server then transmits the data to the CGI program by setting one or more environment variables that the CGI program will read. The data consists of a series of *name=value* pairs, one for each data entry field that the user filled in.

URLs are passed to CGI scripts as command-line arguments on some systems and are therefore limited to 255 characters or less, depending on the limits of the underlying operating system. Therefore, by using the Post command to send the data as an appended body rather than as arguments, the browser can send more information to the server.

A CGI script or program is any program that conforms to the Common Gateway Interface (CGI) specification, which is a standardized way for information servers, such as Web servers, and "gateway" programs to pass data between themselves. A gateway program would be any program or script that would pass information between the Web server and another server, say, a relational database server, or that would simply process the information and return it in some other form. CGI specifies that the Web server can pass information to the gateway program via command-line argument (but only for limited purposes), environment variables that the Web server sets and the gateway program reads, and as MIME-compliant header lines followed by data. The gateway program sends information back to the Web server as a MIME-compliant header followed either by a file or a URL.

Understanding Java Applets and Java

Java is a programming language patterned after C++. Java is fast becoming popular on the Web because it can run on the client, eliminating the round trip taken each time a new page is requested from an HTTP server. Hence, improved performance and speed.

Java is cross-platform and performs well in browsers, unlike LotusScript, which does not work well in browsers.Although Lotus has announced more and more integration with Java, they assure the Lotus community that LotusScript is not going away. Thank goodness! Wouldn't it be a bear to think you took all of those classes for nothing?

Java can bring a Web site to life with animated text, pictures, graphics, and sound. Most Web sites today are still static in nature consisting primarily of text with small bits of real animation, or a few animated GIFs amounting to blinking text or bouncing balls. Java programs can change graphics before your eyes, presenting a number of images of say, the Alps, which scroll on the Web page without user intervention. Java is the most widely used tool in creating advertising on the Web; you see Java in use when you see ad content change continuously.

Java gives you the power to provide more dynamic and interactive Web pages. Java provides interactive Web pages. In the world of Java, there are two types of programs; Java applets and Java applications. Java applets are programs that are downloaded to the client by the server and can execute only in a browser.

Java applets have some security restrictions. For example, they can only talk back to the machine from which they came. Java applications, on the other hand, are stand-alone and run from a disk. They can run in a browser or can include their own User Interface. Java applications have no security restrictions.

You invoke a Java applet in an HTML file with the <OBJECT<...</OBJECT> tag pair. They surround the name of the Java applet to be called. The Java applet file extension identifies its class, and the applet and its class must be stored in the HTML\Classes directory of the Domino server.

For examples on using Java applets in Notes applications for the Web, see "Working with Java" in Chapter 12, "Applying a 'Web Look' to Notes Applications."

On the CD

Everything you ever wanted to know about Java can be found in *Special Edition Using Java* book located on the CD.

Understanding ActiveX and OLE

Object Linking and Embedding, or *OLE*, was developed by Microsoft to enable the creation of *compound* objects made up of objects created in multiple applications. ActiveX was developed to make it easy for any developer to create Windows applications made up of OLE objects. It consists of four essential components:

▶ *ActiveX controls*. These are similar to Java Applets, in that they are programs that you embed in data files. There are over 2,000 ActiveX controls available, including buttons, spreadsheets, and image controls.

▶ *ActiveX scripting*. ActiveX scripting gives you the ability to create a bridge or exchange between two more complex objects, without having to resort to a more advanced programming language such as C/C++.

▶ *ActiveX documents*. These allow you to develop Web pages that reference groups of documents, such as consultant bios, without having to convert the documents themselves to HTML.

▶ *ActiveX conferencing*. This gives you the power to let users do real-time conferencing and data exchange and share applications on the Web.

The use of ActiveX controls is growing rapidly. While dynamic, ActiveX has a more sized-down infrastructure than OLE, so it can enable multiple controls within a Web page to communicate without taking up much space, or dramatically slowing down loading time.

Like Java applets, ActiveX controls are reusable components that can stand alone as applications or be included in Web pages. Parallels are often drawn between Java applets and ActiveX controls, but don't think that they are mutually exclusive. They can happily coexist on a Web page, and may combine to make a great page. In fact, ActiveX may increase the power of your Java applets, by providing the infrastructure for the applets to communicate with other objects in other languages in the same page.

There are, however, two significant differences between Java applets and ActiveX controls that you should keep in mind when deciding which to use:

▶ ActiveX controls currently run on Windows platforms only. Microsoft is working with other vendors to develop versions for Macintosh and UNIX.

▶ Unlike Java applets, ActiveX controls can be written in virtually any language including Visual C++, Borland C++, and Delphi.

You can insert an ActiveX control with an HTML <OBJECT>...</OBJECT> tag pair, between which you insert the name of the ActiveX component to be activated. For more information on using and creating ActiveX controls, visit Microsoft's Web site at **http://www.microsoft.com**.

Understanding Plug-Ins

Plug-ins are not just electrical appliances; they are software modules that allow users to unleash the power of non-native data types like video, animation and even virtual reality on the Web. Before plug-ins became available (starting with Netscape Navigator 2.0), you could install Helper applications that would support file types that your browser did not natively support. To use a Helper application, you would have to launch the application from within your browser, and having done that, it was obvious that you were now running another application.

Plug-ins are programs that, well, plug into your browser and scan incoming data types. If the object matches a plug-in type, the plug-in will present it appropriately. All this takes place without any intervention by the user and without any obvious switch-over to another program. The plug-in runs within the context of the Browser window itself.

Plug-ins support file types that are otherwise not supported by HTML. Many Web users do not have full video and sound playback capabilities on their desktop. However, with plug-ins an object is seamlessly launched on the Web page.

An example of the use of plug-ins is to provide a Freelance presentation at your site. With plug-ins, visitors could see the presentation without having to launch a copy of Freelance, not knowing, not owning, and not having to care about the presentation's native software. Another example: Plug-ins allow Web users to view a video or listen to audio without additional software. To the user, the video or audio appears as if part of the Web page itself, and he may never be aware that additional software is playing it. The most advanced plug-ins include specialized encoding techniques that can handle massive files. These plug-ins produce almost immediate output and shorter download time without losing quality.

When you embed a media file in your Web page, it has a MIME Content-Type header field which tells the browser how it should be handled, for example, which plug-in or external application it requires for presentation. The media type could be a file extension or a descriptive header within the file itself that the browser reads and interprets.

4

Plug-ins are available for most media types including GIF, JPEG, AU, MPEG, MIDI, and EPS, and you can even create your own. When a plug-in launches an object, it can appear to the user in one of three ways (depending on what you, the developer, choose to do):

- ▶ In the background
- ▶ Embedded within the frame of the page
- ▶ As a full-screen presentation

As a developer, you will want to keep in mind the following considerations when using plug-ins:

- ▶ Plug-ins were originally developed by Netscape to enhance the power of their Web browser. However, the popularity of plug-ins is growing rapidly and more and more third-party plug-ins are available to Web users. So, while many plug-ins can be downloaded from the Web, you do not want to make your users run all over to find what they need. It is very helpful if you provide the necessary plug-in software right on your page, or include a link to a site where they can download it. There is nothing more frustrating for a user than getting to a site and not being able to access all the information.

  (See the Netscape Web page that lists registered plug-ins and plug-in developers at **http://home.netscape.com/comprodproducts/navigator/ version_2.0plugins/index.html**.)

- ▶ Not everyone has the system capabilities to produce quality sound. If sound quality is integral to your site, realize that others may not hear the quality you do.

- ▶ If the Web client doesn't have the proper plug-in needed for your site, your plug-in may not appear at all through their browser—or, (and much worse) could appear as placeholder. Some browsers will notify the user of the needed Plug-In and prompt them to retrieve it from Netscape's site.

▶ An alternative to providing the plug-in software is putting an aside near the top of your page that notifies users that there is an object in the page and what its function is. Then, even if they can't present it, they know what it contains.

You can invoke plug-ins by using the <EMBED> tag. The tag might look something like this:

```
<EMBED SRC="video.avi" WIDTH=100 HEIGHT=100 AUTOSTART=TRUE LOOP=TRUE
```

The browser would automatically invoke the plug-in that runs *.avi* files. The Plug-In would play this file repeatedly in a window 100 pixels square, embedded in the host HTML page.

Cookies

Web servers are stateless. That means that, after a server has delivered a requested document to a Web user, the server closes the session and forgets the Web user ever existed. If the Web user requests another document, the server is unaware that the user is a repeat customer. Web servers also transfer only one document at a time to a user. These two facts combine to make Web servers poor platforms from which to stage transactions that involve more than a single step.

Cookies are one of several patches that have been applied in an effort to maintain information about the state of a conversation between a Web server and user between sessions. Others include:

▶ <INPUT> tags of type HIDDEN
▶ The Internet Server Application Programming Interface (ISAPI)
▶ Java applications

We only discuss cookies here, since they have gained widespread usage, including usage in Domino applications.

A cookie is a chunk of information—any information, but usually information about the current state of the relationship between the server and the client—that the server sends to the browser. The browser saves the information/cookie to disk. The next time the browser connects to the server, the browser sends the cookie back to the server, along with its initial URL. The cookie tells the server the state of its relationship with the browser as of the date of their last transaction. As a result, the server is no longer "stateless."

You send a cookie to a browser by inserting a <META> tag into the <HEAD> section of an HTML document. A cookie would look something like this:

```
<META HTTP-EQUIV="Set-Cookie" CONTENT="prefs=dbl; path=/; expires=Thu, 01-Jan-2009
12:00:00 GMT">
```

In the previous example, *HTTP-EQUIV="Set-Cookie"* is the part that tells the browser that it should store a cookie. *CONTENT="..."* sets forth the actual cookie that the browser will store. In this case, the cookie consists of several *name=value* pairs: *prefs=dbl*; *path=/*; and *expires=Thu 01 Jan 2009 12:00:00 GMT*. The browser will save these pairs to disk, then send them back to the server the next time the browser contacts the server. This example is an actual cookie used by Lotus on its domino.lotus.com Web site in its discussion database. See "Running Discussion Databases on the Web" in Chapter 13, "Using Special Function Databases for the Web," for more information about what this cookie accomplishes.

From Here...

This chapter was intended to give you an overview of HTML and a general idea how it works. Domino automatically takes care of most of the details of using HTML, so this chapter was of largely academic interest to Domino/Web application developers. The rest of the book deals with the actual building of Web applications in Notes. Virtually every chapter includes information about using HTML tags in Notes applications.

Some chapters include information of special interest:

▶ Chapter 12, "Applying a 'Web Look' to Notes Applications," includes information on working with HTML frames, Java applets, and ActiveX controls in Notes applications.

▶ Chapter 13, "Examining Special Function Databases for the Web," includes examples of the use of HTML tables and cookies in Notes applications.

Developing New Notes Applications for the Web

## chapter 5

Building a Web Database

In this chapter

◆ **How to set up a test environment**
Once your Notes databases are converted to HTML by Domino, their appearance may change due to restrictions of HTML or elements of Notes. Here, you learn how to set up a testing environment so that you can view your Notes databases through a Web browser during your design process.

◆ **How to create and identify a database or site home page**
With Domino, you may have a home page for a database as well as a home page for your site. Here, you will learn how to design a home page. You'll also learn which of the Notes elements is best for home pages.

◆ **How to allow Web users to navigate through your Web site or database**
An important consideration in designing a Web site is to provide ways to navigate through the site. Here, you will learn ways to link documents, views, databases, and URLs through the use of Notes links: Hotspots, URLs, and HTML.

◆ **How Domino translates Notes Navigators**
As Domino delivers Notes Navigators to Web clients, it converts them to image maps. You will learn the steps necessary to enable Navigators as image maps on the Web.

Designing a Notes database for Web clients is not much different from designing a database intended for Notes clients. However, the generic Notes database does not make for especially exciting viewing in a browser. It makes the information available, but does not send shockwaves out over the Internet. What you really want is to grab your reader's attention and maybe hold it for a while.

You can design your databases and your site so that, instead of seeing an undifferentiated list of database names and exploring them at random, the Web user can see an attractive and informative home page that focuses his attention on the things you want him to see. Instead of browsing your site more or less aimlessly, the user can see on the home page what is available, what is interesting, and how to get there. Your user doesn't waste time getting the information he needs, and he is less likely to try to get into databases you don't want him in.

Configuring a Test Environment

In order to create Domino-based Web applications efficiently, you have to be able to see the results of your design efforts immediately. When designing a PONDB (plain old Notes database), this is usually not a problem; you can just save your design, then test it right there on your workstation. However, when designing a Web application, you have to be able to see your results through a Web browser.

That means that you must have available to you, as you design your application, not only your Notes workstation but also a Domino server running the HTTP service and at least one Web browser. Of course, you also have to be running the TCP/IP protocol, preferably on both the server and the workstation.

You could get by with TCP/IP running on just the server if you use the Server Web Navigator as your browser. When you browse with the Server Web Navigator, you can communicate with the server using any old communications protocol.

But you really do want to run TCP/IP on your workstation, too, if only because future visitors to your Web site will be using a variety of Web browsers, and what you really want is to be able to test your design results with more than one browser. Different browsers have different feature sets, and a really cute design trick may work great when viewed with Netscape Navigator 3.x but be a dog when viewed with, say, Internet Explorer 2.x.

Scenario One: Domino Server and Notes Workstation both Running on One Computer

You could set all this up on one computer. That is, you could do your work at a Domino server. The server would be running in the background, and it would be running the HTTP server task. If you plan to view your work with the Server Web Navigator, then Domino should also be running the Web Retriever server task. You could work in the server's Notes workstation program and optionally hold one or more Web browsers in memory while you work, switching back and forth as needed.

And whether you view your design results with the Server Web Navigator or a third-party browser, you need to be running the TCP/IP protocol suite on your computer, even though you are doing all of your testing without ever going out over a LAN. That is because the browser and the Domino Web server will pass data to each other by going through the TCP/IP stack running beneath them in your computer's memory. If TCP/IP is not running, the Server Web Navigator will report ironically that it cannot locate the Web server, even though they reside together in memory as sister server tasks.

One last point about running all this software on one computer: you will need lots of memory. Or, to put it another way, you finally have a legitimate excuse to buy all that RAM you always wanted. If you are running on, say, a Windows NT workstation, you should have at least 48M RAM, preferably 64M. The Windows NT operating system, Domino server with HTTP and Web Retriever, and Notes client software should all run okay in 32M RAM, since this isn't a production server. Add RAM for each third-party Web browser and any other programs you might want to run—say, for example, one or more graphics programs—and it all adds up to a hefty RAM requirement.

You could minimize Domino's RAM requirements by shutting down the server tasks you won't actually be using. Assuming you are running on a test system (please tell me you aren't trying to do this on a production Domino server), this would include every server task except the indexer, the HTTP service, and maybe the Web retriever. You can unload the replicator, the mail router, the administration process, the statistics collection process, the schedule manager, the calendar connector, the statistics reporter, and the event dispatcher, if they are running. Your *servertasks* variable, in the notes.ini file, could look like this:

```
SERVERTASKS=index,HTTP,Web
```

Pretty neat, huh? That's one lean, mean, fightin' Domino machine. You do want to keep that indexer running, because it maintains your view indexes and full-text indexes.

Scenario Two: Domino Server and Notes Workstation Running on Different Computers

Alternately, you could work in a Notes workstation running on one computer and the Domino server running on a second computer. The two computers would have to be connected to each other. You *could* connect them by phone, communicating via PPP or SLIP. But you want to avoid that if you can, because you will grow old and die waiting for the data to move back and forth between the computers over the phone line.

Note

You *should* set up the computers to communicate by TCP/IP; however, this is not absolutely necessary. If you use the Server Web Navigator as your only Web viewer during the testing process, you could get by with any old communications protocol between the two computers. As long as the Notes client and the Domino server could communicate with each other, you would only need TCP/IP on the server so that the Web Retriever and the Domino HTTP service could use it to communicate with each other. As mentioned previously, you really want to view your design in more than one browser. So you might as well set up TCP/IP on both computers.

On the server computer, you would run only the Domino server software. As mentioned previously, if your test server is not a production server (which would be acceptable in this scenario), you could strip the server down to running just three server tasks: the indexer, the HTTP service and, optionally, the Web Retriever. Finally, you should arrange to have access to the server's file system. Typically, users do not have access to the file system of a Domino server, as it represents a breach of security. But you will be needing to put GIF and JPEG files in the Domino data directories, so you should either have the server nearby, so you can walk over to it and log in, or you should arrange to be able to log in remotely and have read/write access to at least the /notes/data/domino directory and its subdirectories.

On your workstation you would run Notes and, optionally, one or more third-party Web browsers. If you have plenty of RAM (you can never have too much RAM, right?), you could run other programs as well, such as graphics programs. Your workstation can run whatever operating system you prefer. Windows NT, Windows 95, Windows 3.11, Macintosh, OS/2, and UNIX systems should all work well as workstations.

Setting Up a Quick and Dirty TCP/IP Network

If you are working for a big company and have a lot of network experts handy, then you could skip this part, because chances are TCP/IP is either already in place on your LAN or you can get one of the network techies to set it up for you. But if you work for a small company, where you are expected to do it all yourself, or if you want to set yourself up at home, then you need to know how to set up TCP/IP on your computer/LAN. This section is intended to give you an overview of that process. We can't get too detailed here because that's not what this book is about. Besides, you could be working in a Windows, OS/2, Macintosh, or UNIX environment and, frankly, we haven't tried to set up TCP/IP in all of them.

We have set this up in a Windows environment and we can tell you this: if you are running Windows 3.1*x*, do yourself a favor and upgrade to Windows 95 or Windows NT 4.*x*. TCP/IP is a comparative breeze to set up under those operating systems. In fact, it is the default communications protocol under Windows 95 and Windows NT versions 3.51 and later; Windows will offer to set it up when you enable networking on the computer.

Also, we recommend that you run Domino over Windows NT. You could run it over several other operating systems, of course, (see Chapter 2, "Setting Up the Domino Server") and if you are an OS/2 or UNIX expert then, by all means, stay with your favorite operating system. But Lotus writes all the new Internet features for the NT version of Domino first, so with that version you will have earliest access to the latest bells and whistles. You could run Domino over Windows 95, but our experience is that NT is a much more stable and faster operating system than Window 95.

Your hardware requirement is that your computers be connected to a local area network. In fact, even if you intend to work in a single-computer test environment, as described previously, you will have to be connected to a LAN. If your LAN adapter is a 10BaseT Ethernet adapter (the most common kind), it will have to be connected to an Ethernet hub. There may be no other computers connected to the hub, but your computer must be attached to it.

You have to be set up this way because you will not be able to set up TCP/IP on your computer without first installing a LAN adapter driver for TCP/IP to bind to. You will not be able to set up such a driver without having a functioning LAN adapter for it to drive. Even if you could install all these programs without the network, they would never actually run without a functioning LAN adapter, and the LAN adapter won't function properly if it is not connected to a properly terminated LAN.

Look at it this way: Now you have a perfect excuse to install that home LAN that you always dreamed about. Aren't you glad you read this chapter? So far, we've given you ammunition to argue for more RAM *and* a home LAN. Actually, if you think about it, we've given you ammo to argue for a whole new computer too because you can't reasonably be expected to do all this work on that underpowered old 486 you have sitting at home, now, can you? Here's what you do: Buy a new, Pentium-based computer with lots of RAM. Connect it by Ethernet LAN to the old 486, and use the 486 as a file server. Either put 48M or more RAM in the new computer and use it in the single-computer test environment, described previously, or put 32M RAM in the new computer and boost the RAM on the 486 enough to run Windows NT Workstation and a stripped down Domino server on it. 32M RAM should be enough, since this server is just for test purposes; a production server, of course, would demand more RAM.

To set up either a Windows 95- or a Windows NT-based computer up to run TCP/IP, you have to follow these steps:

1. Install the LAN adapter and connect to the LAN. When installing the LAN adapter, you may have to select an interrupt number, a shared memory address, a port address, a slot number, or some combination of the four. The trick here is to select numbers that aren't in use by some other device already installed in the computer. Follow closely the directions that came with the LAN adapter to make sure you don't set up a conflict with another device.

2. Open the Control Panel, then the Network dialog box. How the dialog box appears depends on what operating system and version you are running. But, however it looks, you will follow a certain order of activities in it. First you will install the LAN adapter driver, then you will install the TCP/IP protocol, finally (if Windows didn't do it for you automatically during the protocol installation), you will install client and maybe server software.

3. You will install the driver software for the LAN adapter by choosing the adapter's name from a list. If its name doesn't appear on the list provided by Windows, then you will either choose Other or Unlisted in the list, or you will click Have Disk, which is a button that you will see. Then you will insert a diskette that came with the adapter, and your adapter's name will magically appear; you will choose it, and Windows will copy its driver into the appropriate Windows subdirectory. When installing the driver software, you may have to enter the interrupt, address, port, and slot numbers that you chose when you installed the LAN adapter.

4. You will install the TCP/IP protocol by choosing it from a list of available protocols. When installing the TCP/IP protocol, you will have to enter a host name, a domain name, an IP address, and a subnet address. The host name can be any short word without spaces. If a computer's full name is www.planetnotes.com, the host name is the first part, www. The domain name is the second and third parts, planetnotes.com. When referring to the server from within a browser in your test environment, you may refer to the computer by its host name alone, www, if you want.

   The IP address is a 4-byte decimal number that looks something like this: 123.123.123.123. If you are setting up on a LAN that already has IP running on it, you should find out from the LAN administrator what numbers to enter; while you're at it, get the administrator to tell you what goes in the other fields, too. If you are setting up your own LAN at home or if you are setting up on your office LAN and all the other computers on it use some other protocol like NetBEUI or IPX/SPX, and the LAN is not connected to the Internet, then you can pick any numbers you want for the IP address as long as no other computer on your LAN uses that number, and with the following restrictions: each part of the number must be a number from 1 to 254. So, for example, if you were setting up a two computer network at home, you could number them 123.123.123.10 and 123.123.123.20. Why those numbers? No good reason. Any numbers between 1 and 254 will do. Enter 255.255.255.0 in the Subnet address field, and leave the Gateway address field blank.

In Windows NT Workstation, Enter IP address information in the TCP/IP Properties dialog box. Get here from the Control Panel by choosing Network, Protocols, TCP/IP Protocol, Properties.

5. When you are finished installing the network programs and you click OK, Windows will have you restart the computer. When it restarts, the network programs will load into memory—first the adapter driver, then the protocol driver, finally the client and server software and any other services that installed themselves automatically. If any of them fail to load properly—because of an interrupt, port, or memory conflict—Windows will warn you and instruct you how to proceed. It will offer to pop up the network troubleshooting section of the online Windows help. Go with it. Follow the directions in the Network Troubleshooter. It will take you on a well-organized, thorough troubleshooting tour and, chances are, it will find the problem and tell you how to fix it.

Having a test setup that allows you to immediately see the results of your programming efforts is essential to writing good, Notes-based web applications. The hardest part of it is getting the networking hardware and software working properly. There was a time when setting up a LAN was a black art—frequently you had to propitiate the gods to get one working. Nowadays, however, with the help of modern operating systems like Windows NT, Windows 95, and OS/2 Warp Connect, setting up a LAN is pretty easy. Even now, though, it can get hairy, and you should be sure to read and follow closely the instructions that come with your networking hardware and software and your operating system.

Understanding the Web Design Process

More important even than making your site inviting is making it interactive. The big advantage that Domino has over standard World Wide Web servers is that it is powered by Notes, and Notes was designed from the bottom up to be interactive. The users both create the data and retrieve it. The World Wide Web started out as a one-way information publishing scheme. To get information from the users back into the vanilla Web server, you have to build what amount to kludges by writing scripts in CGI. Because the Web is not inherently a two-way information tool, browsers don't typically provide tools for users to add, edit, or delete documents on Web servers. To provide that functionality, you have to add those capabilities to the views, forms, and documents in your Notes databases.

After you make the initial choice on this form—Windows or OS/2—and click OK, the form will present you with a second choice, then another choice, intelligently eliciting information from you, until it has all the information it needs.

To make your Domino Web site and databases both more appealing and more interactive, you can do the following:

▶ Designate and create a home page document or home page database containing links to all the other pages and databases you want to make available to Web users.

▶ Add actions to forms and views to enhance interactivity.

▶ Redesign forms to minimize the text formatting limitations of HTML.

▶ Consider the differences in how Notes and HTML handle graphics.

▶ Consider enhancing views, forms, and documents with embedded HTML codes.

▶ Consider enhancing views and forms with special Notes fields designed specifically for Web-enhancing your databases.

▶ Use Notes graphics navigators as HTML image maps.

▶ Add CGI variables to input forms to gather information automatically from Web users.

▶ Use MIME type mappings to inform the Web user's browser what program to open an attached file with.

▶ Use multimedia effects such as sound and movies.

The development process for Web databases may be different from developing applications for Notes clients. When designing databases intended for Notes clients, one normally follows this series of steps:

1. Create the database file.
2. Design forms and fields.
3. Build views and folders.
4. Create actions, agents, and navigators.
5. Build the ACL.
6. Create the About Database and Using documents.
7. Make an icon.
8. Document the database.
9. Generate a design template.

10. Pilot the database, test, debug, and refine.

11. Roll out the database.

The preceding list is a simplified look at the highest level, and testing takes place at every step along the way. Testing views forms, fields, formulas, views and so forth is critical to developing Notes databases and even more critical for Web databases. (Our internal Notes users may forgive a small blemish in design or functionality, but we don't want the *world* to see it.) When you design a view in Notes, you can refresh and populate the view while in design mode to see the results of your formulas and properties. For Web databases, you'll need to see the results of your view through a Web browser. So designing a Web database will require more of your time.

The development stages of a database will change if you are designing for the Web. You have a different set of considerations that may dictate a database design process. For example, do you want to use the About Database document as the home page for the database? If you do, designing the About Database document might move up to step two on your list.

5

We like to design the Home page first, even though the view, navigators, and databases to which the home page will link may not yet exist. The center of your database or site is the home page and by building it first, you can refer back to it as sort of a "table of contents" or "site conductor" when adding the other components or databases to your application.

Considering this, our recommended order for building a database for Web clients is:

1. Create the database file. See "Creating a Database" in this chapter.

2. Create the Home Page for the database or the site, using the About Database document or by creating a graphical navigator. See this chapter, below.

3. Design forms and fields to deliver information to the Web client. See Chapter 6, "Designing Forms to Display Documents on the Web."

4. Design forms and fields to receive information from Web clients. See Chapter 7, "Designing Forms for an Interactive Web Site."

5. Build views and folders. See Chapter 8, "Building Views for Domino Web Applications."

6. Build the ACL, make final preparations, and pilot to test functionality. See Chapter 9, "Preparing to Go Public."

7. Customize form, navigator, and search results templates (optional). See Chapter 10, "Using Special Web Fields and Forms."

8. Create agents. See Chapter 11, "Automating Web Applications with Agents."

9. Give the database a "Web Look" with frames, multimedia, and Java applets (optional). See Chapter 12, "Applying a 'Web Look' to Notes Applications."

10. Refine the ACL. See Chapter 9, "Preparing to Go Public."

11. Document the database. Create initial content. See Chapter 9, "Preparing to Go Public."

12. Generate a design template. See Chapter 9, "Preparing to Go Public."

13. Pilot the database. Establish ongoing content-creation and approval process. Train in-house content-creators and approvers. Train database managers. See Chapter 9, "Preparing to Go Public."

14. Deliver the database to the Web. See Chapter 9, "Preparing to Go Public."

A word about creation of content: In this regard, rolling out a Domino-based Web site is a little different from rolling out a standard, non-Domino Web site. In a non-Domino Web site, you would normally have to generate content for the new Web site manually. You could do it by creating HTML pages or converting documents originally created in other formats to HTML format, then storing the HTML documents in the HTML directory (or subdirectories), and building links between them. Or you could use any of a number of site-building tools that partially automate the process of building the site and generating linked HTML pages.

In a Domino site, if you design your Notes databases correctly, Web content will come into existence naturally, by the simple process of Notes users creating and editing Notes documents, as they always have in the past. Content may already exist in the form of existing Notes databases which you will simply replicate onto the Domino Web server. Perhaps after modifying the databases in some way, and as links in the Notes databases to non-Notes data sources, such as LAN- and mainframe-based relational databases.

You will probably have to create some new content specifically because you have a new Web site; but people will create that content, too, by adding documents to Notes databases. You may designate certain people in the company to create certain kinds of content, and others to approve it for replication to the Domino Web server, all as part of the refinement of ACL rights in the databases. Finally, Web users themselves may create some of the content. For example, you may make a discussion database available to your Web users; their contributions would automatically be available to later readers of the discussion.

Creating a Database

You should sketch out the design of your database on paper. Once you have your application design worked out on paper, you're ready to implement it in Notes by creating the database file. You can create this file in one of three ways:

▶ Create a database using a template.

▶ Copy an existing database.

▶ Create a new database from scratch.

To create a new database choose File, Database, New from the menu, change the default Server selection field to indicate the name of the *Domino Web server* and select it. This is a very different step than one would take in designing Notes applications intended for Notes clients. Standard Notes development practice dictates that databases are designed *locally*, on a workstation, not involving the server until the database is ready to be tested by a pilot group. But the Web application needs to reside on the Domino server during development, so you can see your changes as they are delivered to the Web.

Understanding Home Pages

A home page is the first screen you see when you visit a site on the Internet. Because it introduces the site, a home page should be attractive and useful. It must contain links to other documents, views, databases, or sites, or the Web client will be stuck at a dead end. What makes a Web site exciting is eye-grabbing artwork, color, movement, and content. Visiting a Web site in February of 97 and finding the words "this page was last edited on April 11, 1996" might leave one with the impression either that the site is neglected or that the company has nothing new or interesting to say.

People look for new news on the Home page. The home page should always include information about your site or your company. We get frustrated when we are seeking information on the Web and we come to a Home page that is nothing but a graphic, taking forever to load, and that contains only a logo or a pretty picture with a link that says "Click here to continue." It's a waste of people's time to make them wait for a "nothing" page.

The Domino site allows you two *methods* for creating a home page:

▶ The About Database document

▶ A graphical navigator

The Domino site also allows you two kinds of home pages:

▶ A Site Home Page

▶ Database Home Pages

In presenting these choices, we've given them to you in the order in which we recommend you use them. Use the About Database document for the site home page; a navigator for a database home page. Why? There are distinct advantages to each.

▶ Using the About Database Document: *Advantage*: You need flexibility in your site Home page. Remembering that visitors to your site will be looking for new and updated information, and changing the look and links of the Home page tell them that you have new information to share. The About Database document is one large rich text field, and changes to this document are easy. Simply edit the document to include new graphics or GIFs, new links, new text. *Disadvantage*: The Home page is a *document* and cannot, therefore, contain any fields or navigators (hence, image maps).

▶ Using a Navigator: *Advantage*: Domino converts navigators to image maps, which make really catchy home pages if done well. If you are an accomplished computer graphics artist, or you have someone like that at your disposal, by all means use Navigators for your site home page and all your home pages. *Disadvantage*: When Domino converts the Navigator to an image map, it discards everything except the graphic background and any hotspot rectangles and hotspot polygons. Any pasted artwork or text disappears. This means all graphics and all accompanying text must be part of the background graphic. You will be creating this in a graphics program such as Corel Draw or Adobe PhotoShop. This could be a bear if you aren't very familiar with your graphics program and cannot make changes quickly and easily, or if your taste is all in your mouth. If you're not a computer artist, we recommend that you save navigators for those pages which will have infrequent changes.

In addition to a site home page, you can create a home page for each database, using either the About Database document or a navigator. If you don't create a home page for each database, the Web user's first view of a database will be a list of views, similar to the Folders navigator that Notes users normally see on the left side of the screen when they open a database.

Designing the About Database Document

Essentially one big rich text field, the About Database document can contain graphics, text, HTML code, tables, and color. It's a Notes *document*, not a form, and therefore you can't place fields or subforms on this document.

To create the About Database document, open your database, select *Other* in the navigator pane and double-click the About Database document. It is now open in edit mode.

HTML does not respect horizontal spacing entered in the form of tabs or extra space characters. It closes them up to the width of a single space character. Instead, use one or more tables to control the spacing of the text, graphics, and other components that will appear on the page. It's helpful to have table borders showing while in design mode. You can do this without having to worry about your borders showing up in the Web client, as long as you have no border at the top and left of cell A1. When HTML converts Notes tables to HTML tables, it puts borders around all cells or none of them, based on whether there is a border around cell A1 in the Notes table. You can also select a color for your document background or insert background colors within the cells of a table.

As you design the About Database document, save the document frequently and view it through a Web browser. Since you haven't yet made this About Database document the site home page. you'll need to use a Domino URL to access it through a Web browser. To access your About Database document, use one of the following URLs (for a complete list of Domino URLs, see Appendix A "Domino URLs"). Which one you use will depend on whether you have designated the About document as the *Launch, On Database Open* option (see "Designating the Database Home Page," in Chapter 9, "Preparing to Go Public"). If you have *not*, then open it with this URL:

http://nameofserver/filename/$About

If you *have* designated the About document as the *Launch, On Database Open* option, open it with this URL:

http://nameofserver/filename/?Open

In each of the preceding URLs, *nameofserver* is your Domino Web server's host name, as defined in the Network dialog box of the Control Panel (for example, *inotes or www*), or the server's IP address, and *filename* is the file name of the database (for example, homepage.nsf).

Figure 5.1 shows a Home Page in its initial design stage. It consists of one table with two columns. We have added a background color to cell A1, giving a frame-ish look to the page. Table borders are on in Notes, but no border exists at the top and left of cell A1, so no borders will appear in the resulting Web document. Graphics are bitmap images pasted in from a graphics package. Text is underlined for effect, but no links yet exist.

Using the Domino URL to access this Home page, we now view the page through a browser. It's important to check the results of your work frequently. Our objective is to fit as much as possible into one screen on a browser, without making the page look too cluttered. Figure 5.2 shows that we have accomplished that goal.

Fig. 5.1

This is the About Database document in its initial design stage. Text is underlined for effect, but no links have been created.

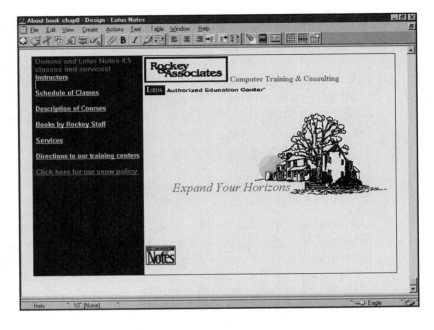

Fig. 5.2

The About Database document in its initial design stage as viewed through a Web browser.

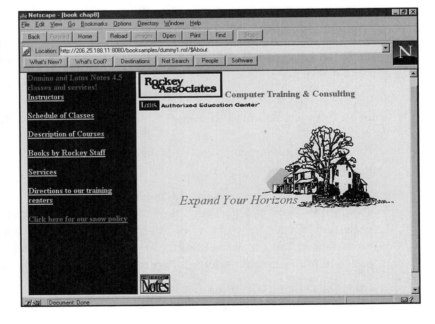

Understanding Notes/HTML Conversion Issues

When designing any form—whether an About Database document that Web users will view as a home page, or a form that will act as template for documents in a database—you need to be aware of the limitations of HTML text formatting. You don't want to use Notes text formatting features that do not translate well into HTML.

Notes text formatting features that *are supported* by HTML include the following:

- Left-aligned, centered, and right-aligned paragraphs
- Inter-paragraph spacing
- Table column alignment (but not column widths)
- Extra space characters (preserved only if using a platform's default monospace font—for example, Courier in Windows)
- Most font styles (bold, italic, underline, strikethrough, subscript, and superscript; but not Shadow, Emboss, or Extrude)
- Font colors
- Bulleted and numbered lists
- Named styles

Notes text formatting features that *are not supported* by HTML include the following:

- Paragraph indentation (whether using tabs or the indentation markers on the ruler)
- Inter-line spacing
- Tab spacing
- Extra space characters (are removed on translation to HTML except when using a platform's default monospace font—for example, Courier in Windows)
- Fully justified and no-wrap paragraphs (they become left-aligned)
- Font sizes (they are mapped to predefined HTML Heading styles, the displayed sizes of which are defined by the target browser)

The upshot here is that HTML eliminates white space from paragraphs, no matter how you insert the white space, except for one way—using tables. Inter-line spacing within a paragraph is reduced to single-spacing. Indents disappear, whether they were created using tabs, spaces, or the indent markers on the ruler. With one exception, white space between words disappears, all but one space, whether put there with spaces or tabs.

On the other hand, centered and right-aligned paragraphs are supported. Inter-paragraph spacing is preserved, whether inserted with carriage returns or by using the Spacing Above/Below fields in the Text Properties Box. Column alignments are preserved in a table. And if you use your computer platform's default monospace font (in Windows that is Courier, not Courier New), then white space inserted using the space bar is preserved.

The Notes formatting features that Domino does support, it supports by inserting equivalent HTML codes into the text at the time it delivers a form or document to the Web user.

Text Tables

If you want to set up text in columns that translate into HTML columns, there are two ways to do it: using HTML tables or using extra spaces with your operating system's default monospace font. Use Notes tables if your Web audience uses graphical browsers that support HTML tables. That includes most of the world. If a large number of the Web users that you cater to (and this should be a dwindlingly small number) use text-based browsers or any browser that does not support HTML tables, you can use manually spaced tables formatted in your computer platform's default monospace font. In Windows, the default monospace font is Courier; it is *not* Courier New.

When you use Notes tables, the border settings of the top, left cell become the border settings of the whole table in HTML. And you can choose whether to have cell borders or not.

Font Sizes

Font sizes in Notes map to HTML header styles as shown in Table 5.1. The HTML header styles in turn map to font sizes on a Web browser according to the browser's configuration. What that boils down to is there is not a one-to-one correlation between the font sizes Notes uses to display a document and the font sizes a Web browser uses to display the same document.

Table 5.1   Notes Font Sizes versus HTML Header Styles

Notes font point sizes less than or equal to	HTML header style
8pt	H1
10pt	H2
12pt	H3
14pt	H4
18pt	H5
24pt	H6
Larger than 24pt	H7

Understanding Links

The World Wide Web is a collection of hyperlinks. It is a *super*-document, made up of lots and lots of documents, all of which are connected to each other by hyperlinks. Notes is *not* merely a collection of hyperlinks; it is certainly a whole lot more. But Notes supports hyperlinks in the form of document links, view links, and database links, as well as various kinds of hotspots that can link you to navigators, views, forms, and documents. Notes and the Web are a natural fit. Domino automatically converts Notes links into Web hyperlinks. It automatically turns lists into lists of hyperlinks. That is, the list of databases that appears as the default home page is really a list of hyperlinks to the databases. The list of views that appears when you click one of the databases is a list of hyperlinks to the listed views. The views are lists of hyperlinks to the listed documents.

The vast majority of links on a Domino server are forged automatically. You only have to create a few of them yourself. If you replace the default home page, you have to add links to your home page by hand. You may also want to add links to other Web sites. You may want to put links in documents that shortcut you back to a view or a home page. Occasionally, you might want to set up a special relationship between two otherwise unlinked documents.

Most of the links you have to create by hand you will do with Notes linking techniques. Some—mostly to pages at other Web sites—you will do with HTML linking techniques. The linking techniques that Domino recognizes include the following:

- ▶ Notes document, view, and database links
- ▶ Link hotspots
- ▶ URL Link hotspots
- ▶ Action hotspots
- ▶ Actions on action bars
- ▶ Passthru HTML

The question arises: When should you choose one type of link instead of another? Here are some rules of thumb:

- ▶ Use links that Notes maintains whenever possible. These include document, view, and database links, and link hotspots. When you use URL Link hotspots, Passthru HTML, or an action bar action or action hotspot with @URLOpen, you enter a static URL. Notes cannot automatically update the URL if the address of the resource that it points to changes; you have to change it manually.
- ▶ Use link hotspots, URL link hotspots, and action hotspots when you want static text or a pasted graphic to appear as a link.

5

▶ Use action bar actions when you want a link to appear as a "button" at the top of a document or view.

▶ You can only use Actions in forms and views. You can only use Action Hotspots in forms. You can use links of all kinds on forms and in rich text fields of documents. You can use passthru HTML as static text in forms or in text fields or rich text fields in documents.

Placing Links on the About Database Document

Considering that the About Database document is a Notes *document*, use of actions is restricted, in that you cannot create an action bar for the About document. The types of links you *can* use in the About document (and, by extension, all Notes documents) and their purposes are listed in Table 5.2.

Table 5.2   Types of Links That Can Be Inserted in the About Document as well as Other Notes Documents

To Link to:	Use:	Comments
A document, view, or folder within the same database	Notes Document Link Link Hotspot	
A form in the current or a different database	Domino URL Passthru HTML Action Hotspot	Use these to permit a Web user to use a form to create a document in a Notes database.
Another database Domino URL Passthru HTML	Notes Database Link	Both databases must reside on the same server. Databases may reside anywhere.
A document, view or folder in another database Domino URL	Notes View Link	Both databases must reside on the same server. Databases may reside anywhere.
The About database document of another database	Domino URL	Use this if the About Database document is not selected as the database launch option. If the database launches the About database document, you can use a Notes database link.

To Link to:	Use:	Comments
Another Web Site	Passthru HTML Link Hotspot Action Hotspot	

Passthru HTML works for all of the links mentioned in Table 5.2. However, Notes links will keep your maintenance down, and are easier to create correctly in that you don't have to type the path. This raises a smaller chance of error when creating your links.

Figure 5.3 shows an example of a Notes Document Link, a Notes Link Hotspot, an HTML Passthru link, a Notes URL Link Hotspot, and an Action Hotspot as seen through a Web browser.

Fig. 5.3

Notes provides lots of tools for creating links between documents.

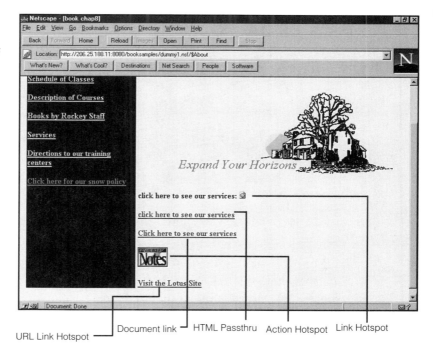

There isn't much difference in the *appearance* of these types of links when viewed through a browser. The document link shows the document icon. The Link Hotspot is underlined and looks like any other hypertext in our browser. The HTML Passthru displays as hypertext. The Hotspot URL link is a graphic but could have been text and would have looked like any other hypertext. The Action Hotspot displays as hypertext.

Notes Links

You can link Notes documents to other Notes documents with Document Links, to Notes views with View Links, or to other Notes databases with Database Links.

When you create a Notes link, the linking mechanism is an Icon. Figure 5.4 shows the representative icons for each type of Notes link as seen through a Web browser.

Fig. 5.4

If you use Notes link icons in your Web database, precede the icons with instructions for the Web client. For example: "To see our list of services, click here."

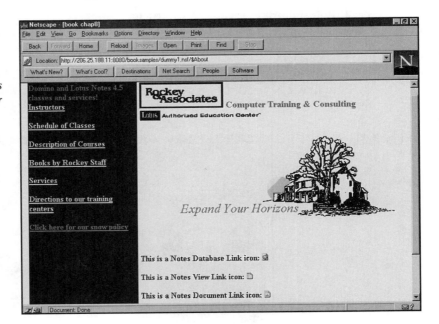

To create Notes Database, View, and Document links, follow these instructions:

Database link. Select the database you wish to link to, either by opening it or clicking once on the database icon on your workspace. Choose <u>E</u>dit, Copy As Li<u>n</u>k, <u>D</u>atabase link from the menu. Switch back to the document in which you are creating the link and paste the icon in its desired position.

View link. Open the database view you wish to link to and choose <u>E</u>dit, Copy as Li<u>n</u>k, <u>V</u>iew link from the menu. Switch back to the database in which you are creating the link and paste the icon in its desired position.

Document link. Open the database you wish to link to and select the document by either highlighting it in a view or opening it. Choose <u>E</u>dit, Copy as li<u>n</u>k, <u>D</u>ocument Link from the menu. Switch back to the database in which you are creating the link and paste the icon in it's desired position.

Link Hotspots

Hotspots act like document, View, and Database Links but look like boxed text in Notes, like hypertext on the Web. A *Link* Hotspot functions the same as a Notes link: it can link to documents, databases, and views. Use a *URL Link* Hotspot to link to another Web site.

 Note

Hotspots: formula pop up, text pop up, and button hotspots are not supported for use on the Web.

To create a *Link Hotspot*, open the database, document, or view you wish to link *to* and choose Edit, Copy as Link. Then select Document, View or Database, whichever is appropriate. Switch to the database in which you are creating the link and highlight the text or graphic that will act as the link. Choose Create, Hotspot, Link Hotspot from the menu. Notes will paste the link and put a border around the text or graphic.

5

 Caution

Do not "paste" Link Hotspots. If you paste, you'll generate a Notes link instead of a Link Hotspot and your text will be replaced with an icon. It's critical that you use the menu commands Create, Hotspot, Link hotspot. If you paste by mistake, undo the paste immediately, then go to the Create menu to create the link.

Figure 5.5 shows a Link Hotspot, which links to a different database. The property box displays the link description, which was entered by Notes when the menu command for creating the hotspot was selected. The link property is editable.

URL Link Hotspots

Creating a URL Link is a slightly different process from the other links we've created so far. In this case, there is nothing to link *from*, only instructions for where to link *to*.

To create a URL Link, highlight the text or graphic that will become a hotspot. Choose Create, Hotspot, URL Link from the menu. The Hotspot Properties box will appear as shown in Figure 5.5.

Fig. 5.5

A Link hotspot. The properties box allows you to change the font, select a style, include a border, or change the link description.

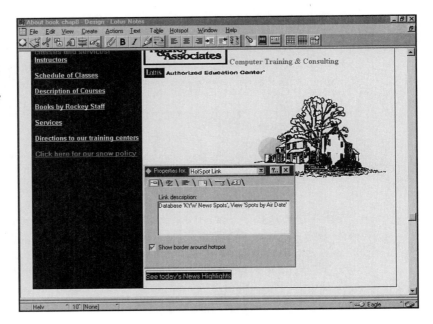

> ## Caution
>
> Be careful when highlighting a graphic versus selecting a graphic. A single click *selects* the graphic. Its corner handles will appear. Any attempt to create a link will be fruitless when a graphic is *merely* selected, and the fact that the link did not take will not be immediately apparent until you view the graphic through a Web browser.
>
> To create a graphics link, you must have the graphic *highlighted*. Hold down the mouse key and drag it across the graphic until the entire image is shaded. Then create the link.

As you add links to Notes documents and forms, be certain to test them in a Web browser.

Using Domino URLs in Links

Just as you can use Domino URLs to navigate a Domino site, you can also use Domino URLs in programming. With Domino URLs you can:

▶ Open objects, including the following:

- Servers
- Databases

- Views
- Forms
- Navigators
- Agents
- Documents
- Image files
- Attachments
- OLE objects

▶ Create search queries

▶ Edit and delete existing documents

Fig. 5.6

The Properties box appears when creating an URL Link. Type the URL in the properties box. You can use Domino URLs here.

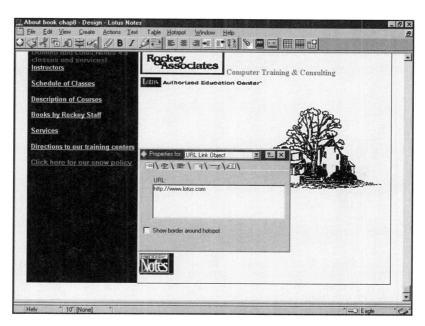

The Domino URL commands have the following syntax:

http://Host/NotesObject?Action&Argument

where *Host* is an IP address or a DNS entry; *NotesObject* is a database view, form, or any of the other objects previously listed; *Action* is the action you wish to take upon the *NotesObject*; and *Argument* is one or more qualifiers of the *Action*.

When using Domino URLs, consider the following guidelines in Table 5.3 and 5.4.

Table 5.3   Guidelines for Using Domino URLs

Guideline	Function
Host	You do not use the Domino *server name* in Domino URLs; rather, you use the DNS *host name* of the computer. Both names may or may not be the same.
NotesObject	Can be a database name or replica ID. For other objects, this can be the object name, UNID, NoteID, or special identifiers (which include $defaultView, $defaultForm, $defaultNav, $file, $icon, and $about). URLs cannot contain spaces. Substitute a plus sign (+) for spaces. For example, when naming a form called By Author, enter By+Author instead.
Action	Examples of actions include ?Open, ?Edit, ?Delete (implicit) and ?OpenView, ?OpenForm, ?EditDocument. If you do not specify an action, Domino defaults to the implicit action ?Open.
Arguments	You may use multiple arguments if the current Action supports them. Separate multiple arguments with ampersands.

Caution
An object's NoteID will change in database replicas. Use the Notes object name or universal ID (UnID) in URLs, since they are identical in all replicas of a database.

Table 5.4   Examples of Domino URLs

Action	Syntax
Open a Domino server	**http://www.planetnotes.com/?open**
Open a Database	**http://www.planetnotes.com/leads.nsf?Open** **http://www.planetnotes.com/sales/** **discussion.nsf?open**
Open a View	**http://www.planetnotes.com/leads.nsf/** **$defaultview?OpenView** **http://www.planetnotes.com/leads.nsf/** **By+Salesperson?OpenView**
Open a View fully expanded	**http://www.planetnotes.com/leads.nsf/** **By+Salesperson?OpenView&Expand**View

Action	Syntax
Open a default view, form, or navigator	**http://www.planetnotes.com/ leads.nsf$defaultview** **http://www.planetnotes.com/ leads.nsf$defaultform** **http://www.planetnotes.com/ leads.nsf$defaultnavigator**
Open the About Database Document	**http://www.planetnotes.com/leads.nsf$About**

> **Note**
>
> When creating Domino URLs, you can address Notes Objects by name. But when viewing the same Domino URLs with a browser, you'll notice that the objects named in the URLs have changed to long hexadecimal numbers. This is a consequence of Domino's generating URLs automatically, linking to the Notes object using its unique ID.

5

To require user authentication so that anonymous Web users are prompted for a name and password to complete tasks, append the login argument. This forces authentication regardless of the ACL. The syntax for the login argument is:

http://Host/?OpenServer&login
http://Host/DatabaseDirectory/DatabaseFileName?OpenDatabase&Login

See "Securing the Domino Server," p.297

To see a complete list of Domino URLs, see Appendix A "Domino URLs."

Action Hotspots

An action hotspot is a block of text—usually surrounded by a box so that it stands out from surrounding text—programmed, when you double-click it, some action takes place. It is a Notes equivalent to a text hotspot in an HTML document, and you can program it to open a form in Compose mode, open a document in Edit mode, delete a document, and all the other things you could do in Notes with the action bar. Of course, a document such as the About Database document cannot contain an action *bar*. Howver, it can contain an action *hotspot* that contains an @Command or @URLOpen. Use an @Command to navigate to a document, view or navigator within the Domino server. Use @URLOpen to navigate to another Web site.

When you view an Action Hotspot in a browser, the hotspot text appears as a standard hypertext link. When you point to it in a browser, the mouse pointer changes to a hand.

To create an Action Hotspot, highlight the text or graphics that will become the hotspot and choose <u>C</u>reate, <u>H</u>otspot, <u>A</u>ction hotspot from the menu. In the Design pane, choose formula and enter a formula for your link. Do not try to use a simple action or write a script in the programming pane. Domino does not support simple actions or scripts when converting pages to HTML, and drops entirely in the conversion process any Action Hotspot based on them.

Some examples of formulas you can use in an Action Hotspot are:

To link outside of the Domino server using @URLOpen:

```
@URLOpen(URL)
```

where URL is the actual URL of the page to which this reference points.

To Open another view with an @Command:

```
@Command([OpenView];"ViewName")
```

where *ViewName* is the actual name of the view.

To Open a navigator with an @Command:

```
@Command ([OpenNavigator]; "NavigatorName")
```

where *NavigatorName* is the actual name of the navigator.

To Open another document with an @Command from within a browser, you must first tell it which document to open. Since you can't select a document in a browser-based view, you have to use a special form of the [OpenView] @Command or the [FileOpenDatabase] @Command, as follows:

```
@Command([OpenView];"ViewName";"key");
@Command([OpenDocument])
```

or

```
@Command([FileOpenDatabase];"":"DatabaseName";ViewName";"key");
@Command([OpenDocument])
```

Here *DatabaseName* is the name of a database, ViewName is the name of a view, and *key* is the contents of the first column of the named view. You can identify a given document in a view with this command. You can open the document by following the first command with the [OpenDocument] command.

Using Pass-Through HTML Links

You can use pass-through HTML links to navigate to another Web site. A pass-through HTML link is an HTML tag that contains a URL and *passes* unchanged *through* the Domino process of converting a Notes document to an HTML document. A pass-through HTML link is text and it can appear anywhere on a form in Design mode, including in a text field or a rich text field.

A Passthru HTML link to another document would look something like this in a Notes document or form:

```
[<A HREF="url.address">clickable text</A>]
```

In the previous reference, *url.address* is the actual URL of the page to which this reference points, and *clickable text* is the text that, in the HTML page as it appears in a Web browser, is highlighted and, when clicked with the mouse, causes the browser to retrieve *url.address*. The letter A in the example stands for Anchor and *anchors* the beginning of the tag. The /A code *anchors* the end of the tag. Finally, HREF stands for Hypertext Reference and identifies to Domino that what follows the equal sign is a URL. To link to the Lotus site, for example, a pass-through HTML link would look like this:

```
[<A HREF="http://www.lotus.com">Click here to visit Lotus</A>]
```

Finally, you can open a form for editing (but not perform any other action) with a pass-through HTML link. The link would appear as follows:

```
[<a href="databasename/formname?OpenForm">click here to create formname </a>]
```

Here `databasename` and `formname` are the names of the database and form to be opened, respectively. `?OpenForm` is the command to open the Notes form. Click here to create `formname` is the text that becomes the hotspot.

Understanding Navigators

In Notes applications as viewed in Notes clients, navigators normally appear in the Navigator Pane, which usually appears on the left side of the screen, next to the currently selected view. The default navigator is called the Folders navigator. You don't have to create it when you create a database, and you can't delete it or edit it. The Folders navigator appears as an outline list of views and folders. You can replace the folders navigator with a graphical navigator or your own.

A graphical navigator is called graphical for two reasons. First, you use a graphics interface to create it. That is, instead of the text interface of the standard Notes form, in which you position objects by inserting tabs, spaces, and hard returns, you place objects in the navigator design screen the way you do in a graphics program, by dragging them to any position on the screen. Second, a graphical navigator consists of one or more graphics objects, such as imported pictures, lines, rectangles, polygons, and ellipses, as well as hotspots, buttons, and text objects.

Creating Navigators as Image Maps

An image map is a graphic image, included in an HTML document, that has hotspot links associated with different parts of it. If you click *this* portion of the image, you are requesting one document; if you click *that* portion of the image, you are requesting another document. Well-designed image maps are attractive and make it easy for a Web user to navigate around in your Web site.

Domino converts graphics navigators in Notes databases into image maps in the resulting HTML documents. Domino-created image maps are both *client-side* and *server-side* image maps, meaning that all browsers support them.

To create an image map, you create a graphic navigator, paste the graphic image you want to use into it as a graphic background, then add hotspots to it that link to other navigators, views, documents, other databases, and so on.

There are two caveats. First, any graphics that you paste onto the navigator as anything other than a graphic background disappear from the image map upon translation to HTML. Second, any text that you add in Notes to the navigator also disappears on translation. Therefore, you need to create the entire graphic image, including all graphical and text components, in a graphics program external to Notes. The only thing you do in Notes is paste the image in the navigator as a graphic background, add the hotspots to it, and program the hotspots.

To create a navigator, follow these steps:

1. Create or open in a paint or drawing program the graphic image that will become the image map.

2. Copy the image (or a portion of it) to the Clipboard. Most programs allow you to do this by selecting the image (or part of it) and then choosing Edit, Copy in the menu. You may also be able to select the image, then press Ctrl+C.

3. Return to Notes. Open the database in which you intend to create the navigator.

4. Create a new navigator by choosing Create, Design, Navigator in the menu. A new navigator design window appears. Or open an existing navigator by clicking—in the Navigator Pane—Design, Navigators. Then, in the View Pane, double-click the name of the navigator you want to work in.

5. If you are creating a new navigator, then in the menu choose Design, Navigator Properties. The Properties for Navigator InfoBox appears. Enter a name for the

navigator in the Name field of the InfoBox. You can give it an alias as well as a name by naming it in the format *Navigator Name\Alias*.

6. Paste the Clipboard image into the navigator by choosing <u>C</u>reate, <u>G</u>raphic Background in the menu. Do not paste the image using <u>E</u>dit, <u>P</u>aste; it won't work properly if you do it that way.

7. Assign URL links to different portions of the image. To learn how, see Creating a Hotspot Rectangle, Creating a Hotspot Polygon, Defining Hotspot Properties, and Assigning a URL to a Hotspot Rectangle or Polygon, later in this chapter.

8. Save and close the navigator.

To define a URL link in a graphical navigator, create a Hotspot Rectangle or Hotspot Polygon and assign the @URLOpen (*"URLname"*) @function to it (see Figure 5.7).

Fig. 5.7
This is a Navigator in Design mode. Note the @URLOpen @function in the formula pane.

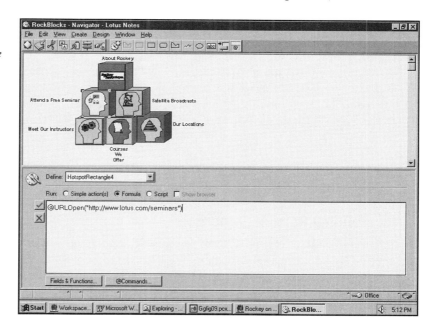

Creating a Hotspot Rectangle

To create a hotspot rectangle, choose <u>C</u>reate, Hotspot <u>R</u>ectangle in the menu; or click the red rectangle icon in the Toolbar. Your mouse pointer becomes a crosshair. Place the crosshair at one corner of the area to be covered by the rectangle, then, holding the mouse button down, drag the crosshair to the opposite corner. You see a black rectangle appear as you draw. When you release the mouse button, it becomes a red rectangle.

If you are not happy with the resulting rectangle, you can resize it by dragging the corner handles. If no corner handles appear, click anywhere on the rectangle to make them appear.

Creating a Hotspot Polygon

Use the hotspot polygon to define a non-rectangular portion of the graphic image. To create a Hotspot Polygon, choose Create, Hotspot Polygon in the menu; or choose the red polygon icon in the toolbar. Your mouse pointer becomes a crosshair.

Place the crosshair at one apex of the area to be defined. Click the mouse button to anchor a line at that point. Move the mouse pointer to an adjacent apex. A line connects the first apex to your mouse pointer.

At the second apex, click the mouse again to anchor the other end of the first line and create an anchor for your next line. Move the mouse pointer to the third apex. Click to create the third line.

Continue until you have reached the last unconnected apex. There you *double-click*, which creates the second-to-last line and the last line between the last apex and the first apex. The secret to using the Hotspot Polygon tool is to remember to double-click the last apex to close the polygon.

When you finish creating the hotspot polygon, the lines turn red, and corner handles appear when the hotspot polygon is selected. If you want to adjust the shape of the polygon, drag the handles.

Defining Hotspot Properties

After you have created a hotspot rectangle or polygon, you can define its properties in the Hotspot Rectangle/Polygon Properties InfoBox. You can rename it in the Name field. You can lock or unlock its size and position. You can define whether the outline of the hotspot appears either when you touch it with the mouse pointer or when you click it. Finally, you can define the weight and color of the outline.

Assigning an URL to a Hotspot Rectangle or Polygon

To assign an URL to a hotspot rectangle or hotspot polygon in a graphic navigator, select the rectangle or polygon while in Design mode. Handles appear at the corners of the object when it is selected. Or, you can select the name of the hotspot from the list in the Define field in the Formula pane of the design window. Then, in the Run field, choose Formula. In the formula pane, enter @URLOpen ("*URLname*"), where *URLname* is the URL of the page that this hotspot should point to.

For example, if the hotspot should point to the Lotus Domino Web site, the formula should read: @URLOpen("http://domino.lotus.com").

Graphics Formatting Considerations

You can transfer graphic images from Notes documents to HTML documents in two ways. First, Domino automatically converts embedded graphics of all kinds into files in either GIF or JPEG format (depending on your choice in the HTTP Server section of the Server document) and sends the resulting graphic file to the Web user along with the HTML document, which has a reference in it to the graphic file.

Second, you can insert *Passthru HTML code* into a form or document. Passthru HTML is a reference to an existing file on your server. When Domino converts the Notes document to HTML and sends it to the user, the reference is passed, unchanged, through to the HTML document. The user receives both the document and the referenced graphics file. A Passthru HTML code looks something like this:

```
[<IMG SRC="http://domino.chestnet.com/filename.gif" WIDTH=240 HEIGHT=120>]
```

In the preceding code, IMG means image, SRC means source, and SRC="http:// www.planetnotes.com/filename.gif" identifies the location of the image file; *filename* is the name of the file, and the WIDTH and HEIGHT commands tell the browser the size of the image in pixels. For absolute fidelity to the original image, use the same width and height sizes as the actual image. If you use different sizes, some browsers resize the image accordingly, others do not.

If you do resize an image, you can avoid distorting it or creating moire patterns in it by increasing it in integral multiples. That is, increase it to 200%, 300%, or 400% of its original size, but not by, say, 110% or 125%. And, whatever you do, don't shrink the image to less than its original size.

The idea here is to resize every pixel equally. Since a pixel is the smallest unit of measurement on an output device such as a computer monitor or printer, it can only be doubled, tripled, or quadrupled. You can't resize a pixel to 1.5 times its original size, because you cannot work in fractions of pixels; there is no such thing as a fraction of a pixel. So, if you try to resize an image to 1.5 times its original size, the computer has no choice but to double the size of one half of the pixels and leave the remaining pixels the original size. As a result, some pixels are twice as big as others, and the image looks odd. Even worse, if you try to shrink an image to, say, 50% of its original size, the computer has to discard half of the pixels entirely.

If the image is a screen shot of, say, a dialog box, you might notice that some of the text strokes have either dropped out altogether if you made the image smaller than its

5

original size, or they have doubled in width if you enlarged the image. If the image is a photograph of, say, a person's face, you may notice a "plaid" effect on the person's face; that would be the moire pattern caused by resizing only some of the pixels.

The problem with telling you not to resize images in small increments is that this is exactly the way you will want to resize an image. You won't want to double its size. Rather, you will want to enlarge or reduce it just a little bit so that it fits esthetically within your overall page design.

If you must resize in small increments, our best advice is to crop the image instead. Start with an image that is larger than the space that it will occupy, open it in a graphics program, and crop it down to the right size. Our second best advice, if you can't crop, is to resize carefully. Resize the image to the size you want it to be, then view the results in a browser. If you don't like the results, resize the image slightly, then view it again. Keep this up until you arrive at an acceptable image quality.

Finally, Domino servers store embedded graphics in two forms, a platform-dependent metafile (Windows Metafile in Windows), and a platform-independent bitmap. When you view the document in Notes, you may be looking at either the metafile or the bitmap (depending on a choice made by the person who embedded the file originally). Notes ships the bitmap, not the metafile, to the Web user. Because the metafile and the bitmap may not look exactly alike, the graphic that Notes users and Web users see might be slightly different.

From Here...

Although Domino handles the Notes/HTML conversion issue, you might want to learn more about or use more HTML code in your Notes documents. You can make your Home page come alive with multimedia, animated icons, and Java applets.

For related information, see the following chapters:

▶ Chapter 4, "Understanding Web Fundamentals," discusses the use of HTML, Java applets, plug-ins, and ActiveX and their roles in Notes Web applications.

▶ Chapter 12, "Applying a 'Web Look' to Notes Applications," provides instructions on adding multimedia to Notes documents.

chapter 6

Designing Forms to Display Documents On the Web

6

by Jane Calabria

In this chapter

◆ **How forms may appear differently to Web clients**
You learn which Notes formatting features don't translate well to HTML. You also learn how to enhance your Notes forms with HTML tags.

◆ **How to use Tables to align database elements**
You learn how to create properly aligned text and graphics through the use of tables.

◆ **What you need to consider when your applications are intended for both Notes and Web clients**
We show you how to hide information from Notes or Web clients, so that you can design one database with multiple audiences.

◆ **How to help Web users navigate your site**
Web users need navigational capabilities. We suggest subforms as one method of providing a roadmap of your site. You learn how to insert subforms intended as roadmaps.

◆ **How to incorporate images into forms**
We show you how to include images in your forms and where to store those images in the Domino File structure as well as in a Notes Database.

When delivering Notes documents to Web clients, you need to know how your documents will appear when viewed through a Web browser. Because a *form* is the framework for the document, your design considerations start here. Will your text formatting convert well? Will fields and formulas function the same for Web users as for Notes users?

The focus of this chapter is on designing forms that will effectively *display* your Notes documents *to* Web users. The basic design concepts offered in this chapter also apply to Chapter 7, "Designing Forms for an Interactive Web Site," which focuses on extending to Web users the ability to *create* Notes documents in their browsers.

Understanding Forms on the Web

The HTTP server task, running in the Domino server, converts Notes forms and subforms to HTML documents and delivers them to Web users. When you create forms intended to display documents to Web clients, consider the following:

▶ Domino converts Notes text formatting features to HTML tags. Not all Notes text formatting survives the translation process. Not all browsers support all of the HTML tags used by Domino.

▶ You can include HTML tags and URLs in your forms and documents. For more information on HTML, see Chapter 4, "Understanding Web Fundamentals."

▶ All buttons embedded in Notes documents disappear entirely when the documents are translated to HTML. Except as described in Chapter 7, "Designing Forms for an Interactive Web Site," regarding Submit buttons, Domino does not support translation of buttons to HTML.

▶ Whatever you define as the Window Title in a Notes form will appear as the Window title on the Web browser. If you do not define a Window Title, the URL of the Notes component will appear in the browser window title.

Inserting Fields

There is little about fields for Notes applications intended for the Web that is different from fields intended for Notes clients. There are, however, some field design features, properties or functions that have exclusion or exception. In the following list, "not supported" means that the listed feature of Notes does not translate to HTML and cannot be used in any document or database intended for translation to HTML.

▶ Names, Readers, and Authors fields: the following options will not function on the Web:

   Use Address dialog for choices

   Use View dialog for choices

   Use Access Control List for choices

▶ Keyword fields: keyword entry helper option is not supported

▶ Default value formulas: cannot reference "selected document in the view"

▶ Compute after validation: not supported

▶ Field Help: not supported

▶ Field-level encryption: not supported

- Give this field default focus: not supported
- Signed fields: not supported

 Tip
Shared fields slow the performance of the Web Server because it has to work harder to produce an HTML document. Try to keep your use of shared fields to a minimum.

@Function Formulas in Web Databases

@Functions that fail in Web applications do so for one of two reasons: they are not supported by the Domino translation, or they do not apply to Web clients.

Those that are not supported are:

@DeleteDocument	@IsDocBeingRecalculated
@DocMark	@URLGetHeader
@GetPortsList	@URLHistory
@IsAgentEnabled	@UserPrivileges
@IsDocBeingMailed	

@Functions that are not applicable to the Web client are:

@Certificate	@MailDbName
@DDEExecute	@MailEncryptSavedPreference
@DDEInitiate	@MailEncryptSendPreference
@DDEPoke	@MailSavePreference
@DDETerminate	@MailSignPreference
@DialogBox	@PickList
@Domain	@Prompt
@Environment	@SetEnvironment
@IsModalHelp	ENVIRONMENT keyword

Lastly, Table 6.1 describes those @Functions which are supported with restrictions.

Table 6.1   @Functions with Exceptions or Limited Application for Web Clients

@Function	Comment
@DbCommand	Restricted: can be used only to create a link to the next/previous page in a view with the following syntax: @DbCommand("Domino"; ViewNextPage") and @DbCommand ("Domino"; "ViewPreviousPage") Not available in any other context.
@DocChildren	Available only for use in view and column formulas. Not available in any other context.
@DocDescendants	
@DocLevel	
@DocNumber	
@DocParentNumber	
@DocSiblings	
@Platform	Returns server's platform only.

@Command Formulas in Web Databases

Most Notes @Commands are designed to perform with the notes client and do not apply to the Web client. However, a limited number of @Commands will be converted to URLs on the Web and are useful in designing your Web applications. Table 6.2 describes these commands.

Table 6.2   @Commands which will be Converted to URLs on the Web

@Command	Remarks/Restrictions
@command([CalendarFormat]) @Command([CalendarGoTo])	
@Command([Compose])	The server argument does not apply
@Command([EditClear])	Not supported for view actions. Use only for forms. Deletes the current document.
@Command([EditDocument])	Not supported for view actions. Use only for forms. Edits the current document.
@Command([EditInsertFileAttachment])	Used with an action hotspot to create a

@Command	Remarks/Restrictions
	field for Web clients to attach files. Works for clients using Netscape Navigator only.
@Command([FileOpenDatabase])	The server argument must be specified as a null string ("").
@Command([FileOpenDatabase]; "":"dbname"; "ViewName"; "key");	This pair of commands allows you to open documents in a non-current database by key.
@Command(([Opendocument])	
@Command([NavigateNext]) @Command([NavigatePrev]) @Command([NavigateNextMain]) @Command([NavigatePrevMain])	Not supported in view actions. Use only for forms.
@Command([OpenNavigator]) @Command(OpenView])	
@Command([OpenView]; "ViewName";"key");	This pair of commands allows you to open documents in the current database by key.
@Command(([Opendocument])	
@Command([ToolsRunMacro])	
@Command([ViewChange])	Operates like OpenView, but you must include the view name.
@Command([ViewExpandAll]) @Command([ViewCollapseAll]) @Command)ViewShowSearchBar])	

Hiding Information from Notes or Web Users

If both Notes users and Web users will be accessing any of your databases, you will want to use different versions of forms, views, and folders for each. One way to use different versions of forms is to use Hide When properties to hide from each type of user the version of the form intended for the other. Using this technique, you can hide paragraphs, fields, and sections from either type of user. To hide a paragraph, field, or section from either type of user, follow these steps:

1. Open a document in Edit mode or a form in Design mode.

2. If hiding a paragraph, put the text cursor anywhere in the paragraph. You need not select the whole paragraph because Hide When properties always affect whole paragraphs, whether you like it or not. If you want to hide more than one paragraph, then you should select at least some part of each paragraph you intend to hide.

   If hiding a field, select the field.

   If hiding a section, select the section title by clicking it. You'll know that you have selected the section title because the word *Section* will appear in the menu.

 Tip

While you can use this technique to hide paragraphs of text, fields, or sections, in actuality you are doing the same thing no matter which type of object you try to hide. In all three cases, you are hiding the text paragraph in which the object resides, That is, if you hide a field, you are actually hiding the paragraph in which the field resides, and if you are hiding a section, you are hiding the paragraph that holds the section.

Where this fact could trip you up is if you have more than one field in a single paragraph. If you try to hide only one of the fields, you will fail. Because you are actually hiding the paragraph itself, you will be able to hide all the fields in the paragraph, or none.

---

3. Open the Text Properties box, the Field Properties box, or the Section Properties box. To open the Text Properties box, choose <u>T</u>ext, Text <u>P</u>roperties. To open the Field Properties box, double-click the field or choose <u>D</u>esign, Field <u>P</u>roperties. To open the Section Properties box, choose <u>S</u>ection, Section <u>P</u>roperties.

4. Click the window shade tab. The Hide-When panel appears.

5. Check the box marked Hide Paragraph if Formula is True.

6. In the Formula Window, enter a formula that evaluates to true for the group that you want to hide the paragraph from. To hide the paragraph from Web users, enter the following formula in formula window:

   ```
   @Contains ( @UserRoles ; "$$WebClient" )
   ```

   or

   ```
   @IsMember ( "$$WebClient" ; @UserRoles )
   ```

7. Close the Text Properties box and save and close the document.

Both formulas in the preceding step 6 work the same:

@UserRoles returns any roles that the current user fills. These are the roles that appear in the database ACL, mostly. However, if a user is coming to the server from the Web, @UserRoles returns $$WebClient as an additional user role.

@IsMember and @Contains work differently from each other, but, as written, they both ask if $$WebClient is a member of the list of roles returned by @UserRoles. If it is a member—as it would be if the user is coming from the Web—then @IsMember returns "1", or true. If it is not a member—as it would not be if the user is coming in from a Notes client—then @IsMember returns "0", or false.

The whole formula taken together is true if the user is a member of $$WebClient. Because the hide when formula hides the paragraph if the formula resolves to true, this formula causes the instruction paragraph to be hidden from that user.

To hide the selected paragraph(s) from Notes users, enter this formula instead:

```
!@Contains ( @UserRoles ; "$$WebClient" ) & !@IsDocBeingEdited
```

or

```
@IsNotMember ( "$$WebClient" ; @UserRoles ) & !@IsDocBeingEdited
```

Again, both formulas work the same.

The exclamation point that precedes @Contains means NOT. It negates the result of @Contain so that the result of the @Contains statement is true if $$WebClient is *not* a member of the list returned by @UserRoles.

You could use the exclamation point with @IsMember, too, except you don't have to because @IsNotMember accomplishes the same thing.

The second condition (!@IsDocBeingEdited) asks if the document is in Edit mode. Because it is preceded by an exclamation point, it returns 0 (false) if the document is being edited. The reason it is included in the formula is so that the hidden paragraph will reappear when the document is in Edit mode. In other words, the document is only hidden from Notes users when in Read mode.

When hiding from a Web user, we did not bother adding *&!@IsDocBeingEdited* because, when you edit a document in a browser, the Hide When conditions are ignored. So we wouldn't have gained by adding that condition.

The two conditions are separated by an ampersand (&), which means they must *both* be true for the whole formula to be true. The user must be a Notes user and the document must be in Read mode for the paragraph to be hidden.

6

The example in Figure 6.1 shows the results of following the earlier steps. You can see that paragraph 2 is hidden in the browser, bottom right, and paragraph 4, formatted with HTML tags, is hidden from Notes in Read mode, bottom left, but revealed in Edit mode, top left. The Text Properties box shows the Hide When formula that hides paragraph four in Notes in Read mode but not in Edit mode.

Fig. 6.1

In Edit mode, all paragraphs appear. In Read mode, the fourth paragraph is hidden. In Netscape, the second paragraph is hidden. The Text Properties box shows the hide when formula for the fourth paragraph.

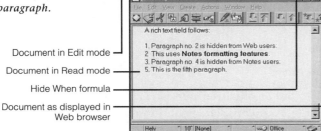
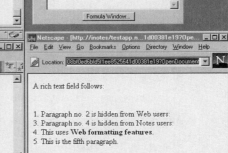

Document in Edit mode

Document in Read mode

Hide When formula

Document as displayed in Web browser

 Note

The hide when formula for paragraph 2, not shown, is @IsMember ("$$WebClient" ; @UserRoles). Please note that parameter one ("$$WebClient") is case sensitive. Also note that you can use @Contains instead of @IsMember.

Caution

When hiding paragraphs in a document rich text field from Notes users, be careful if the paragraph being hidden is the only paragraph in the field. If your formula merely hides the paragraph from Notes users, then the whole field will disappear from view both in Read mode and in Edit mode. This makes it a little awkward either to edit the contents of the field or to remove the Hide When condition. After all, if you can't see the field, you can't edit it. Therefore, consider using the !@IsDocBeingEdited condition to make the hidden paragraph reappear when you open the document in Edit mode.

This problem only occurs when hiding paragraphs in rich text fields in documents. It is not a problem when hiding static text paragraphs in forms, because the hidden paragraphs will always reappear when you open the form in Design mode.

Another technique for hiding parts of forms is to insert subforms in a form. You can use a formula similar to those previously described to insert one subform for Web users, another for Notes users. See "Using Subforms as Site Navigators," p.167

Text Formatting

6

One of the most important considerations in form design for Web clients is text formatting. Your forms will be converted to HTML dynamically by Domino. However, HTML does not support all Notes text formatting features. Therefore, your documents will look different to Web users than they look to Notes users and some of the formatting may disappear entirely in the translated document. For example, interline spacing, indentation, and tabs characters aren't supported by HTML. Neither are multiple space characters in most circumstances. When Notes documents that sport these types of layout formatting are converted to HTML, the text on your forms crowds to the left, extra white space between characters on the line disappears, and extra white space between lines of text is squeezed out. If you typically lay out a form with tab stops, your documents will lose their layout when translated to HTML (see Figure 6.2).

There are two workarounds for this: use the Courier font in all of your forms and use space characters to create white space between fields; or build your forms using Notes tables. Domino will tag all Courier text with the HTML tag <TT>. *TT* means *typewriter text* or *teletype*. Browsers do not remove extra space characters from text tagged <TT>.

However, nobody wants to return to the technology of the typewriter. A more effective way to preserve white space in the HTML versions of Notes documents is to format the Notes forms with Notes tables. Since Domino converts Notes tables to HTML tables, that is clearly the way to go. We use tables for almost all of our Notes forms regardless of the client we think users will be using.

Fig. 6.2

The carefully aligned text and fields in the form (top) are preserved in the resulting Notes document (middle), but lost in the resulting HTML document (bottom).

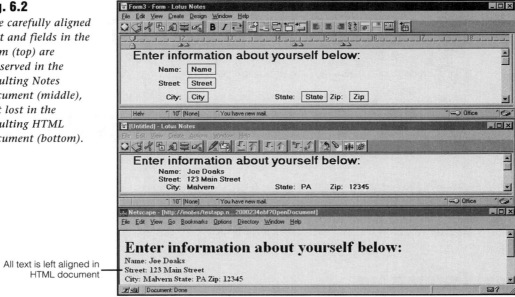

All text is left aligned in HTML document

Text formatting considerations are important and will affect the design of Home Pages, forms, views, and so on. For that reason, and for your convenience, we've repeated some encapsulated information regarding text throughout this book.

Domino does support:

▶ Left, center, and right-aligned paragraphs

▶ Inter-paragraph spacing (but not Inter-line spacing).

▶ Font colors

▶ Typeface styles: Bold, Italics underlining, strikethrough, superscript, subscript

▶ Font Sizes (mapped by Domino to HTML sizes shown previously in Table 6.1)

▶ Bulleted and numbered paragraphs

Domino maps Notes font sizes to HTML headers according to the schedule in Table 6.3.

Table 6.3   Font Size Mapping—Domino to HTML

Notes Font Sizes	Map to HTML Font Size
Less than 8 points	1
Equal to or greater than 8	2

Notes Font Sizes	Map to HTML Font Size
Equal to or greater than 10	3
Equal to or greater than 12	4
Equal to or greater than 14	5
Equal to or greater than 18	6
Equal to or greater than 24	7

Caution

Documentation and help databases provided by Lotus with Lotus Domino 4.5 are in error regarding translation of Notes font sizes to HTML Header numbers. Notes documentation states incorrectly that Notes font sizes up to and including 8 points map to HTML font size 1, which Notes font sizes greater than 8 and less than or equal to 10 map to HTML font size 2, and so on. Our testing indicates that in fact Notes font sizes map as Table 6.3 indicates.

Figure 6.3 illustrates the differences in font sizes between a Notes document and its HTML counterpart.

Fig. 6.3

The Notes document (left), looks different in Netscape (center), because Domino maps font size ranges to HTML Header codes 1 through 7, as revealed in the raw HTML document (right).

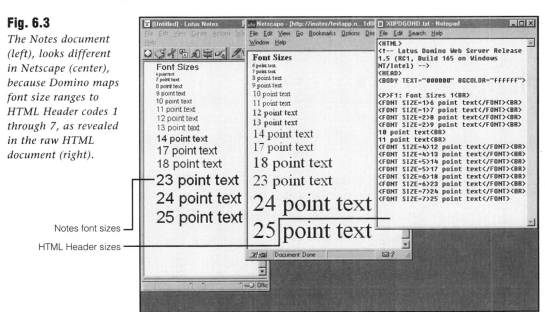

Because display characteristics of HTML documents are controlled by the reader, the actual display sizes of HTML font sizes 1 through 7 depend on what browser you use. Different browsers map the HTML font sizes to different type sizes, according to user preferences set in the browser and platform limitations. Thus, one browser might display <H3> as 10 point text, while another might display H3> as 12 point text. A third browser, being designed to run on a terminal rather than a personal computer, might display all HTML font sizes the same, since the terminal can only display text in one size.

HTML size 3 is usually the default for body text, so you should define the font size of body text in your Notes forms to be equal to or greater than 10 points and less than 12 points. Since the default body text size in Notes documents is 10 points, this is normally not a problem. But if you design a form in which body text is 12 points in size, the resulting HTML documents will display very large body text. If you are catering to an audience of elderly Web surfers, this might be a good thing.

 Note

The illustration in Figure 6.3 shows the font sizes in the Notes document, steadily increasing in size. If you try to re-create that illustration, you may notice that Notes does *not* display the text in steadily increasing sizes, but rather that the sizes seem to jump from 8-point to 10 point, to 12 point, to 14 point, to 18 point, to 24 point. The reason for this is that Notes' default font, Helvetica, is a non-scalable, bitmap font that only comes in those sizes. Switch to a scalable TrueType font, such as Arial, and the text will gradually increase in size.

Placing HTML in Notes Forms

You don't need to use HTML tags in your databases, but they do offer a handy set of tools for improving the look of your databases when viewed in a Web browser. You can add them in the following three ways:

▶ Embed them in formulas that result in textual output, static text in forms, text or rich text fields in documents, or view columns by enclosing them in square brackets.

▶ Place them in a rich text paragraph assigned a paragraph style named HTML

▶ Special case: place HTML documents in a text or rich text field named HTML

Using Bracketed HTML Tags

Because HTML tags are already enclosed in angle brackets, like this: *<HTMLcode>*, when you embed them in a text or rich text field or in static text by enclosing them in square brackets, they end up being double-bracketed, like this: [*<HTMLcode>*] (where *HTMLcode* is the actual code). When Domino translates the document into HTML, it strips off the square brackets and passes the enclosed code, unchanged, through to the HTML document, so that the code appears like this: <u>*<HTMLcode>*</u> in the resulting raw HTML document.

Table 6.4 displays a list of popular HTML codes you can incorporate into your form. See Chapter 4, "Understanding Web Fundamentals," for more detailed information on HTML in Notes databases.

Table 6.4 HTML Tags can be Placed Directly on your Notes Form

To	Use	Remarks
Insert a graphic	`<IMG SRC=path>`	Path is the location of the source file
Make Text Blink	`<BLINK>text</BLINK>`	Cannot use within a window title
Add a horizontal rule	`<HR>`	

6

Remember that Domino will convert Notes components to HTML, so you don't have to. An example of Domino at work appears in Figure 6.4. A document appears in Design mode in Notes. The document includes Notes tables, text formatting, colors, links, sections and centered text. These Notes formatting features are all converted by Domino to HTML.

Figure 6.5 shows the same document as seen in a Web browser. This looks similar to the way the document appeared in Notes. The use of a table preserves text alignment. Text colors were formatted in Notes, and although it's not apparent in this black-and-white representation, the text colors are preserved in the HTML form of the document. Collapsible sections, lose their borders on the Web.

Sometimes it's helpful to see the code behind the Web form created by Domino. This will assist you when you are placing your own code on forms or documents, and also helps you to understand how Domino translates Notes elements to HTML. Using Netscape 3.0 as the browser, the following is the HTML code generated by Domino for this form. You can view the code in Netscape by selecting <u>V</u>iew, Document <u>S</u>ource from the Netscape menu.

Fig. 6.4
HTML code ([<blink>][</blink] used in a Notes document. All other text formatting is Notes text formatting.

HTML tags ——

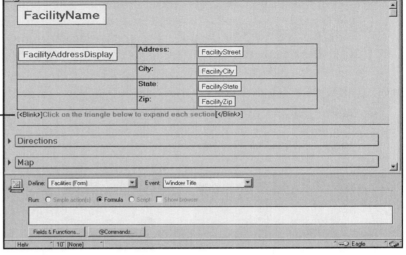

Fig. 6.5
A Notes form as viewed through a Web browser. Notice that the collapsible sections lose their borders.

No borders ——

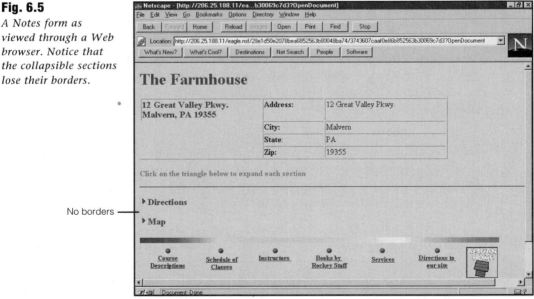

```
<HTML>
<!-- Lotus Domino Web Server Release 1.5 (RC1, Build 165 on Windows NT/Intel) -->
<HEAD>
<BODY TEXT="000000" BGCOLOR="00ffff">
```

```
<P><B><FONT SIZE=6 COLOR="0000ff">The Farmhouse</FONT></B><BR>
<BR>

<TABLE BORDER>
<TR VALIGN=top><TD WIDTH="240">
<P><B><FONT SIZE=4 COLOR="0000ff">12 Great Valley Pkwy.<BR>
Malvern, PA 19355</FONT></B></TD><TD WIDTH="120">
<P><B>Address:</B></TD><TD WIDTH="240">
<P>12 Great Valley Pkwy.</TD></TR>

<TR VALIGN=top><TD WIDTH="240">
<P>      </TD><TD WIDTH="120">
<P><B>City:</B> </TD><TD WIDTH="240">
<P>Malvern</TD></TR>

<TR VALIGN=top><TD WIDTH="240">
<P>      </TD><TD WIDTH="120">
<P><B>State</B>:</TD><TD WIDTH="240">
<P>PA    </TD></TR>

<TR VALIGN=top><TD></TD><TD WIDTH="120">
<P><B>Zip:</B></TD><TD WIDTH="240">
<P>19355</TD></TR>
</TABLE>

<P><Blink><B><FONT COLOR="ff0000">Click on the triangle below to expand each section</
FONT></B></Blink><BR>
<B>_____
➥_____</B><BR>
<BR>
<A NAME="1"></A><A HREF="/eagle.nsf/28e1d50e2078bea6852563b80048ba74/
3743607caaf0e86b852563b30069c7d3?OpenDocument&ExpandSection=1"><IMG SRC="/icons/
expand.gif" BORDER=0></A><B><FONT SIZE=4 COLOR="0000ff">Directions</FONT></B><BR>
<BR>
<A NAME="2"></A><A HREF="/eagle.nsf/28e1d50e2078bea6852563b80048ba74/
3743607caaf0e86b852563b30069c7d3?OpenDocument&ExpandSection=2"><IMG SRC="/icons/
expand.gif" BORDER=0></A><B><FONT SIZE=4 COLOR="0000ff">Map</FONT></B><BR>
<BR>
<IMG SRC="/eagle.nsf/31c40aca6e3ae69085256409001babc6/$Body/
0.2c?OpenElement&FieldElemFormat=gif" WIDTH=719 HEIGHT=11>
<TABLE WIDTH="100%">
<TR VALIGN=top><TD ALIGN=center WIDTH="14%"><CENTER>
<P><B><FONT SIZE=2 COLOR="000080"> <IMG SRC="/icons/ball1.gif"\border=0></FONT></B><A
HREF="/eagle.nsf/3c189102bd94570c85256409000b7685?OpenView"><B><U><FONT SIZE=2
COLOR="000080"><BR>
Course Descriptions</FONT></U></B></A></CENTER></TD><TD ALIGN=center
WIDTH="14%"><CENTER>
<P><B><FONT SIZE=2 COLOR="000080"><IMG SRC="/icons/ball1.gif"\border=0> </FONT></
B><B><U><FONT SIZE=2 COLOR="000080"><BR>
</FONT></U></B><A HREF="/RAPROJ.NSF/
21859a1f022c6a558525640d006a2299?OpenView"><B><U><FONT SIZE=2 COLOR="000080">Schedule
of Classes</FONT></U></B></A></CENTER></TD><TD ALIGN=center WIDTH="14%"><CENTER>
<P><B><FONT SIZE=2 COLOR="000080"><IMG SRC="/icons/ball1.gif"\border=0></FONT></B><A
HREF="/eagle.nsf/4fe41dde4418d1ca852563b80048bbe6?OpenView"><B><U><FONT SIZE=2
COLOR="000080"><BR>
Instructors </FONT></U></B></A></CENTER></TD><TD ALIGN=center WIDTH="14%"><CENTER>
<P><B><FONT SIZE=2 COLOR="000080"><IMG SRC="/icons/ball1.gif"\Border=0></FONT></B><A
```

6

```
HREF="/Books.nsf/$about?OpenAbout"><B><FONT SIZE=2 COLOR="000080"><BR>
Books by <BR>
Rockey Staff</FONT></B></A></CENTER></TD><TD ALIGN=center WIDTH="14%"><CENTER>
<P><B><FONT SIZE=2 COLOR="000080"><IMG SRC="/icons/ball1.gif"\border=0> </FONT></
B><B><U><FONT SIZE=2 COLOR="000080"><BR>
Services</FONT></U></B></CENTER></TD><TD ALIGN=center WIDTH="14%"><CENTER>
<P><B><FONT SIZE=2 COLOR="000080"><IMG SRC="/icons/ball1.gif"\border=0></FONT></B><A
HREF="/eagle.nsf/28e1d50e2078bea6852563b80048ba74?OpenView"><B><U><FONT SIZE=2
COLOR="000080"><BR>
Directions to <BR>
our site</FONT></U></B></A></CENTER></TD><TD WIDTH="14%">
<P><A HREF="/eagle.nsf?OpenDatabase"><B><FONT SIZE=2 COLOR="000080"><IMG SRC="/icons/
returnho.gif"\border=0></FONT></B></A></TD></TR>
</TABLE>

<P><BR>
<BR>
<FONT SIZE=2>Created by:        </FONT><FONT SIZE=2>Dorothy Burke</FONT><FONT SIZE=2>
Date Created:    </FONT><FONT SIZE=2>08/26/96</FONT><BR>
```

You can see that all of the HTML code, with the exception of `<Blink></Blink>` (which is located just above the rule near the middle of the previous page), has been generated by the Domino http server.

Debugging Embedded HTML Tags

If you embed an HTML tag or pair of tags in a form, then discover that they are not working as expected, there are a couple possible causes. One is that the preceding tag itself is formatted differently than the text it is supposed to affect.

For example, your form has the following static text in it:

```
[<blink>]Click the triangles below to expand the collapsed sections[</blink>]
```

This should cause the text between the tags to blink. However, if the initial blink tag is formatted differently than the text that follows it, then when Domino translates documents based on this form, it inserts a `</FONT>` tag immediately following the initial blink code. This has the effect of turning the code off before it has a chance to affect the text that follows it.

You can try fixing this problem in three different ways. Probably the best way is to make sure the tag itself is formatted as `<H3>` (in Notes the tag should be from 10 points up to but less than 12 points in size), and otherwise unformatted; that is, it should be black and devoid of things like bold, italic, and underlining.

Alternatively, you can make sure the initial tag and the text that follows it are formatted alike. Say, both Italicized or both 18 point. But if the tag and text are in a color other than black, this might not work.

Finally, if you are working with a tag pair, you can remove the inner square brackets, as follows:

```
[<blink>Click the triangles below to expand the collapsed sections</blink>]
```

This way, the tagged text itself will be passed through the translation process unchanged. Of course, if you had applied Notes formatting to the tagged text, that formatting will not translate. Thus, the text in the example will only be formatted as blinking. If it were bolded in Notes, the bolding is lost in translation to HTML because the text itself is enclosed in a pair of square brackets.

Remember, the goal here is to convince Domino not to insert that pesky `</FONT>` tag after the initial tag.

On the CD For more information on HTML and a complete list of HTML tags and their proper usage, see the electronic book *Special Edition Using HTML* that appears on the accompanying CD-ROM.

6

Using a Paragraph Style Named HTML

If you have one or more whole paragraphs of text containing multiple HTML tags, you can save yourself a little work by assigning a Notes paragraph style named HTML to the paragraphs in question. The benefit is that you need not use square brackets to enclose any HTML tags that appear in that paragraph. Domino passes the whole paragraph through the translation process untouched.

In effect, the paragraph style called HTML is just an alternative to enclosing codes in a double set of brackets. If you have a lot of HTML codes you want to embed, you can save yourself the hassle of entering all those square brackets (see Figure 6.6).

Fig. 6.6

On the left is a Notes rich text paragraph with the HTML style applied. The embedded HTML tags have no square brackets surrounding them. On the right is how the paragraph looks in a browser.

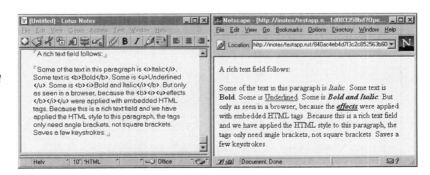

To create a paragraph style in Notes, follow these steps:

1. In Notes, place the text cursor in a rich text field. If you are in a form in Design mode, you can just put your text cursor in the Design pane, since the whole form *is* a rich text field.

   A quick way to get to a rich text field is to compose a mail memo and put the insertion point into the Body field, which is a rich text field. The reason for getting into a rich text field is to make the Text menu item appear in Notes' menu bar.

2. If you were creating any style other than this one, you would format a paragraph of text just the way you want the paragraph style to be. However, since you are creating an HTML style, you don't much care about the Notes formatting, because the purpose of this style is to inform the Domino HTTP service that this paragraph consists of HTML tags which should be passed through the translation process unaltered to the Web client.

3. In the menu, choose Text, Text Properties. The Text Properties InfoBox opens.

4. Click the last tab in the Text Properties Box. The tab looks like a tag with the letter S in it. The paragraph style panel appears (see Figure 6.7).

Fig. 6.7

The Style panel of the Text Properties box contains a list of existing paragraph styles. From here you can assign an existing style to text in your form or document, create new styles, redefine styles, and delete styles.

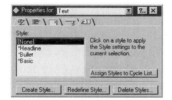

5. Click the Create Style button. The Create Named Style dialog box appears (see Figure 6.8).

Fig. 6.8

Use the Create Named Style dialog box to create a paragraph style called HTML.

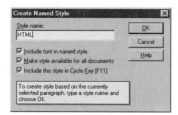

6. Enter **HTML** in the <u>S</u>tyle Name field.

7. Check the boxes in the other three fields according to your own preferences. For most styles, we prefer to check all three boxes. For the HTML style, only the second and third choices are relevant.

> ▶ *<u>I</u>nclude Font in Named Style*. If this box is checked, the font and character style applied to the first character of the selected paragraph will become part of the style. When the style is later applied to paragraphs, the affected paragraphs will take on the style's font and character style, as well as its paragraph formats. If this box is not checked, then only paragraph formatting will be applied to affected paragraphs.

> ▶ *<u>M</u>ake Style Available for All Documents*. If this box is not checked, this style will exist only in the currently selected or open document. If the box is selected, the style will be available to all documents opened from this workstation and the style will appear preceded by an asterisk in all Style lists.

> ▶ *Include this style in the Cycle <u>K</u>ey (F11)*. If you check this box, the new style will be included in the list of styles that you can apply with the F11 key. Pressing the F11 key repeatedly when the text cursor is in a rich text field will cause Notes to cycle through the included styles, applying first one to the currently selected paragraph, then the next, then the next, and so on until you cycle around to the first again.

8. Click OK when you've finished defining the new style. It will hereafter appear in the Style list in the Text Properties box.

The new style appears in the list of available styles in the Text Properties box. Apply the HTML style to a paragraph by placing the insertion point anywhere in the paragraph, then selecting HTML in either style list (the one in the Text Properties Box or the one in the status bar). See the style list in the Status Bar shown in Figure 6.9.

Fig. 6.9

The new paragraph style appears in the status bar list at the bottom of the Notes program window.

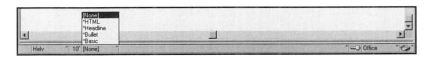

Or, assign the style by cycling to it with repeated presses of the Cycle key (F11). While our goal here is to save ourselves the trouble of entering square brackets around every HTML tag in this paragraph, you might just take note that paragraph styles are also a great, fast, easy way to apply formatting to any Notes paragraph.

Using a Text or Rich Text Field Named HTML

Finally, let's say you have a bunch of existing HTML documents. Maybe they are currently being stored on the third-party Web server that you plan to retire just as soon as you get your Domino Web server running smoothly. You don't want to lose those documents.

Well, you can just move them over to the HTML directory on the Domino server. But then you can't track them with Notes. You still have to manage them manually. What you really want to do is import them into one or more Notes databases. That way, Notes can keep track of them for you.

The question is, how can you take these existing HTML documents and store them in Notes documents in such a way that they pass, entire and unchanged, through Domino's translation process to Web users?

You can create a form that contains a text or rich text field that you name HTML. If the HTML field is rich text, you should also include at least one other text field, so that the document can appear in a view, because rich text fields do not appear in view columns. The form can also include other fields, as many (and of whatever data types) as you want. Next, create documents based on the form, paste or import your HTML documents into the HTML field of each new document, and save the new documents (see Figure 6.10).

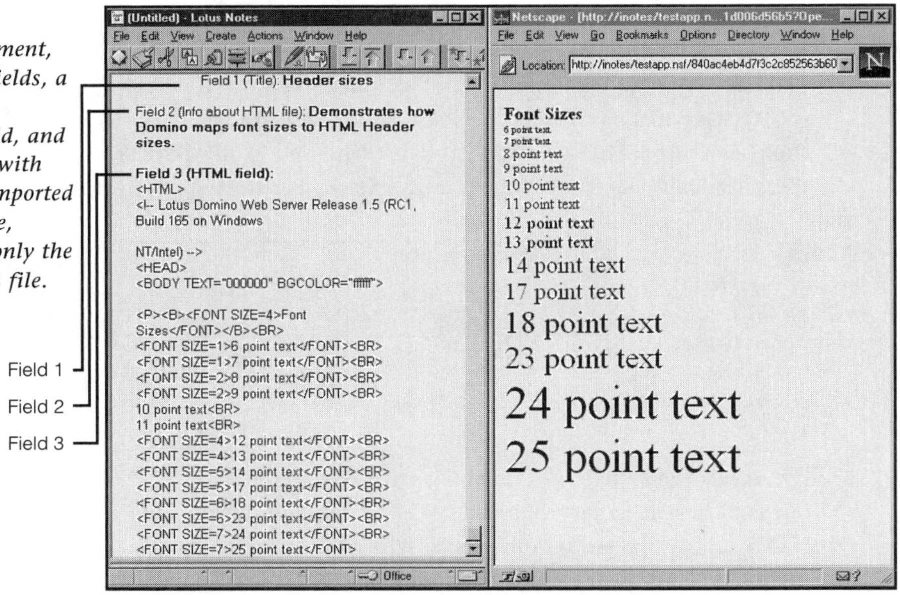

Fig. 6.10

The Notes document, left, has three fields, a Title field, an Information field, and an HTML field with an HTML file imported into it. Netscape, right, displays only the imported HTML file.

Tip

If an HTML field is rich text, you can either import or paste HTML files into it. If the HTML field is text, you can only paste HTML files into it.

The result is the same, whether you import or paste. But importing a file may be more convenient at times, because you don't have to open the file first, select its contents, copy it to the clipboard, then switch back to Notes and paste. Rather, you just pick the file from a list in a dialog box and click the Import button.

Whenever Domino translates such a document, it not only passes the imported HTML document though unaltered to the Web user, but—and this is the cool part—it ignores all other fields in the document. It passes *only* the contents of the HTML field to the Web user.

The other fields are important. They can include all sorts of information about the contents of the HTML field, so that you can classify the document. Most important, a year or two after you have forgotten altogether that the document exists, you can go back and draw some clue from the other fields what the document is all about.

6

Using Tables

As a Notes developer, the framework for your form is undoubtedly a table. HTML does not recognize tab characters or indenting. So Notes tables, which Domino converts to HTML tables, are a critical tool for the proper alignment of components in your documents intended for display on the Web.

 Caution

Some browsers do not support HTML tables. While these browsers are becoming more scarce, consider using the Courier font and extra space characters to align the elements on your pages if you know that your audience will include users of such browsers. Notes tables become HTML tables and will not work with older browsers.

Notes 4.5 introduces some new table features, including the ability to merge cells both horizontally and vertically. Another new table property is color. Tables with merged cells translate properly to HTML. Also, you can color the cells of the entire table, a single cell, a group of cells, a row, or a column. Your cell background colors will also translate properly to HTML.

To add a table to a form, open the form in Design mode. Position your cursor where you want the table to start. Choose Create, Table from the menu and enter your desired number of rows and columns. If you are not sure of the eventual size of your table, don't worry; you can insert, append, or delete rows or columns later. Use the properties box to set size, color, and borders. Figure 6.11 shows a form containing several tables used to align the components (static text, graphics, and fields) of the form. The table shows varying gray shades in some cells as a result of using color in some cells.

Fig. 6.11

This Notes form uses several tables. Some cells are shaded differently than others. Only one table will display borders when viewed in a browser.

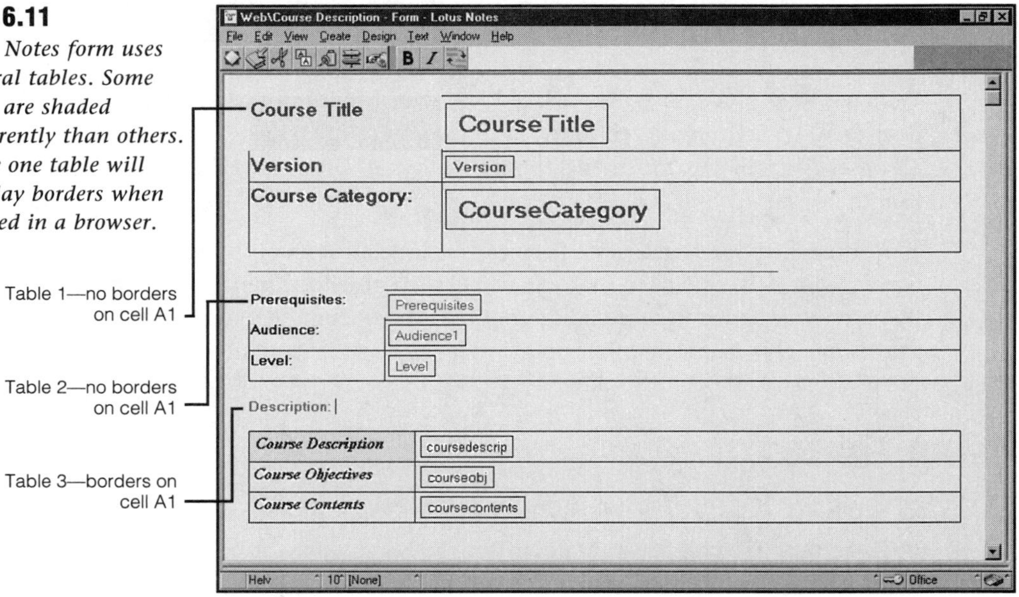

Table 1—no borders on cell A1

Table 2—no borders on cell A1

Table 3—borders on cell A1

If the top-left cell (cell A1) of a table has a border along any one side, the entire table will have a border when viewed on the Web. If there is no border along any side of this cell, no border will appear on the table. Although you can format Notes tables in applications intended for Notes clients to have different and individual borders on cells within a table, the choice for the Web is all or none.

The form shown in Figure 6.11 has three tables, only one of which contains borders (Table 3). Tables 1 and 2 have no borders and might be difficult to identify as tables, but for the cursor position. We've positioned the cursor inside of the table, and the word *Table* appears on the menu. The Table menu is context sensitive, and if we were not positioned inside of a table, no Table menu choice would appear. You can see that borders are turned on for the third table on the form, (Table 3) and that they display in cell A1. Figure 6.12 shows the resulting table borders as seen from a Web client.

Fig. 6.12
Notes tables as viewed through a Web browser.

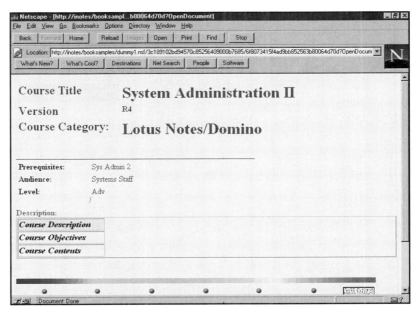

 Tip
For a really good looking form, try right-aligning the field labels in the left column and left-aligning the fields in the right column of a table. This makes a nice break between the end of the static text and the cell containing the field, and nice alignment between column a and column b.

Using Images in Forms

There are several applications for images in forms. You can use images as backgrounds, place graphics (such as company logos), and use GIFs and animated GIFs. The methods for placing images in forms are:

▶ *Background images*: To use a graphical background on a form, copy the image to the clipboard, open the form in design mode, open the Properties box for the form, select the background tab, and click the Paste Graphic button.

▶ *Placing images on forms*: The field offset part of the Domino URL syntax makes it difficult to create URLs for images. The best methods are:

Import or paste a bitmap in place of a reference

Create URL references to image files stored in the file system <[IMG SRC=http://www.planetnotes.com/filename.gif" WIDTH=24- HEIGHT=120>]

Add images as attachments

Store images in a Notes database

See "Graphics Formatting Considerations," p. 141

Domino supports the use of transparent images but they must be imported (not pasted) for the image to keep its transparent setting.

Notes Database to Store Images

Using a Notes database to store images allows the designer to update the Web applications without access to the Domino file server. For example, instead of storing icons in the Domino/Icon directory, storing icons in a database allows for replication and remote maintenance of the graphics used in a Web application.

To facilitate this process,

1. Create a graphics library database (or use a blank template). Create a document with two fields: one rich text field, and one text field called *key*. The text field doesn't actually have to be named *key*, but it will contain a keyword or key phrase that Domino will use to find the image.

2. Create a view, and set the first column to contain the field *key*, sorted in ascending order.

3. Create the documents for the database. Use one document for all of your graphics, attaching them in the rich text field, or create a document for animated gifs, one for background graphics, another for JPEGS, or maybe one for logos, another for product images, and so on. In the "key" field, put the descriptive name of your document, for example, *GIFS, JPEGS, logos*, whatever.

4. Reference the images with the following URL on your Web forms or documents:

[<IMG SRC="http://HostName/DatabaseName.nsf/Viewname/key/$file/filename">]

Where *HostName* is the host name or IP address, *DatabaseName* is the name of the database, *Viewname* is the name of the view, *key* is the text that appears in the first sorted column of the view, *$file* is a Domino instruction to look for an attached file, and file name is the actual name of the attached graphic file and must include the file extension.

Note that you cannot use the About or Using documents to store these images. Also, and this is important, the URL will fail if you delete the carrier document or make a *non-replica* copy the database instead of replicating it.

For more information on opening a document by key, refer to the "Working with Lotus Notes and the Internet" database that is supplied with Domino 4.5.

See "Graphics Formatting Considerations," p. 141

Using Subforms as Site Navigators

Earlier in this chapter we saw how to tailor the look of a form to the needs of users by using the Hide When property of a paragraph, field, or section to selectively hide these objects from either Notes users or Web users. Here we discover another useful technique for customizing forms for our readers. Also we learn how to use one subform for one type of user, say, a Web user, and either another subform or no subform at all for the other type of user.

An important consideration in designing a Web application, is whether users can navigate the Web site easily. You don't want Web clients to be "Lost in Space." You want to provide a roadmap for navigating the site. Subforms are the perfect vehicle for roadmaps. Creating one or two subforms that contain links to important areas of your site is much easier than placing and maintaining links on every form.

Figure 6.13 provides an example of a subform-based roadmap. Figure 6.13 is a split-screen image showing a subform in Design mode in Notes and the same subform (now simply part of a form) as viewed through Netscape Navigator. Images appear in a table on the form. Note that the table options are set for no borders in cell A1, hence no borders appear to the Web client. Hotspots provide the links to other areas of the site. The hotspots can be identified by the border that surrounds them in Notes.

Caution

The use of subforms (and shared fields) probably slows down Domino's performance on the Web. However, no performance benchmarks are available to suggest how much Domino slows down. In any case, the use of subforms—for headers, footers, banners, and "web-ifying" forms—is a widely practiced technique among developers of Domino Web applications.

Fig. 6.13

This subform is designed for use as a site roadmap and will be inserted into all forms used in the Web application. You cannot insert a subform into a document, only into a form or another subform.

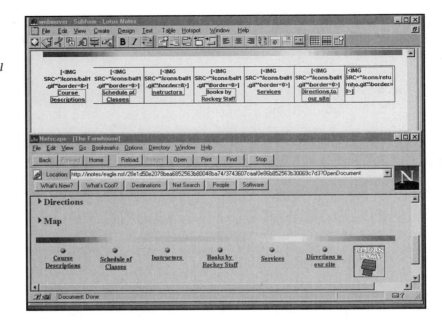

Creating a Subform

To create a subform, open the database in Design mode. Select Create, Design, Subforms from the menu. Treat the subform as if it were a form. That is, place fields, static text, tables, sections, and graphics on it just as you would on a form. Don't try to give the subform a background color or background graphic—you can't. Subforms take the background of their parent form.

When naming a subform, you can give it an alias name if you want, by separating the subform name and its alias name with a vertical bar, as follows:

```
SubFormName [vb] AliasName
```

If you do use an alias, the subform name will appear in dialog boxes and you will use the alias in formulas. This is, of course, no different from the way it works with form and view aliases.

In the Subform Properties box (see Figure 6.14), there are three check boxes that you must consider:

> ▶ *Include in Insert Subform... Dialog.* This box is checked by default. If the subform will never be inserted manually, but rather always as the result of a formula, then you should deselect this box.

> ▶ *Include in New Form... Dialog.* Check this box if you will want the Insert Subform dialog box, with this subform listed, to pop up as soon as you create a new form.

The idea here is that you may intend the subform to appear at the top of every form you create; so you can have it prompt you to do just that as soon as you start to create each new form.

Fig. 6.14

In the Subform Properties box, you only have to name a subform and consider whether to check any of the check boxes.

▶ *Hide Subform from R3 Users.* Check this box if the subform will use features of Notes Release 4.*x* that are not backward-compatible with Release 3. You can use this feature, along with the @Version function, to design applications tailored to the version of Notes the user is running.

Of the three check boxes, the most relevant to our discussion is the first. When designing a subform that you will use, say, in Web versions of documents but not Notes versions, you will probably be inserting the subform in a form or not based on the results of a formula. Therefore, you may decide to deselect the first check box.

Inserting Subforms in Forms

To use subforms, you insert them into forms. You can either insert subforms by name at design time by picking from a list, or you can write a formula that inserts a form at run time, based on the criteria in the formula. Whichever way you choose, you start out the same:

1. Open the host form in Design mode and move the text cursor to the position that the form will occupy.

2. In the menu, choose <u>C</u>reate, Insert S<u>u</u>bform. The Insert Subform dialog box appears (see Figure 6.15).

Fig. 6.15

In the Insert Subform dialog box, either choose a subform from the list or choose to insert a subform on the basis of a formula you will write.

3. Either choose a subform from the Insert Subform list or check the box labeled Insert Subform Based on Formula. Then click OK.

If you choose a subform from the list, the subform will appear immediately, embedded in the form. If you double-click the embedded subform, it will open in Design mode and you can edit it directly.

If you choose to insert a subform based on a formula, the words *<computed subform>* will appear on the host form. If you click the words, a frame appears around them indicating that the computed subform is selected. Also, the words *Computed (Subform)* appear in the Define field of the Design Pane (see Figure 6.16).

Fig. 6.16

When you click the words <computed subform>, a frame appears around them to indicate the computed subform is selected.

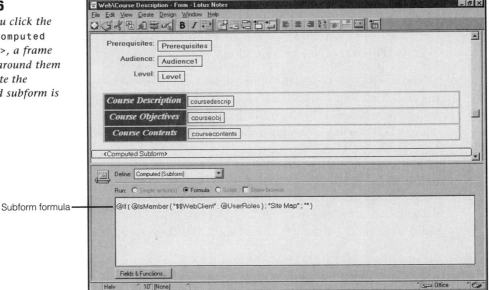

When the computed subform is selected, you can enter a formula in the Design Pane in the bottom half of the Design window. If the Design Pane does not appear, choose View, Design Pane to reveal it. To write a formula that chooses one subform for Web users and another subform for Notes users, write a formula like the following:

```
@IF ( @IsMember ( "$$WebClient" ; @UserRoles ) ; "WebSubForm" ; "NotesSubFormB" )
```

To write a formula that chooses a subform for Web users and no subform at all for Notes users, enter a formula like this:

```
@IF ( @IsMember ( "$$WebClient" ; @UserRoles ) ; "WebSubForm" ; "" )
```

Using Attachments and MIME

If you attach files to Notes documents, they appear in the documents as representative icons. When you double-click the icon in Notes, an Attachment Properties box appears (see Figure 6.17). On the first tab, three buttons appear: View, Launch, and Detach. Clicking View allows you to view the contents of the file, if you have installed a viewer that is compatible with the file in question. Clicking Run causes the program that created the file to run and open the file. Clicking Detach allows you to make a copy of the file on disk.

Fig. 6.17
When you double-click an attachment icon in a Notes document, the Attachment Properties box appears and gives you three options: View the file, Run the program that created the file and open it in that program, or Detach the file and save it to disk.

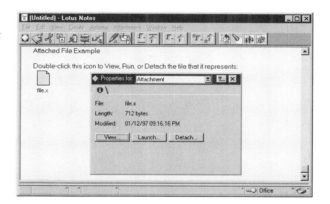

When Domino sends a Notes document with attachments to a Web user, it does two things. First, it copies the attached file to the cache directory, that is, the \notes\data\domino\cache directory. Second, it converts the icon representing the file in the Notes document to a GIF image in the HTML document and turns the GIF image into a link hotspot that points to the location of the file on the Domino server. The code behind the link uses this syntax:

> **http://www.planetnotes.com/*DatabaseName*.nsf/*ViewUNID*/**
> ***DocumentUNID*/Attachments/*CachedFileName*/**
> ***OriginalAttachmentFileName*.ext?OpenElement**

In the preceding code, DatabaseName is the name of the database in which the HTML document originated. ViewUNID is Notes' unique identifier of the view in which the document was located. DocumentUNID is Notes' unique identifier of the original document. CachedFileName is the file name under which Domino stored the cached version of the attached file. OriginalAttachmentFileName.ext is the original file name of the attachment before it was attached to the Notes document. ?OpenElement is the HTTP command to send the attachment to the browser.

If the user clicks the GIF hotspot, the browser retrieves the file from Domino's cache and attempts to view it or run it as a program. If the browser cannot figure out how to do either of those things, it presents the viewer with a dialog box offering the options of either saving the file or telling the browser what helper application it should use to launch or view the file. If the user decides to save the file, the browser offers to use the OriginalAttachmentFileName.ext as the default file name (see Figure 6.18).

Fig. 6.18

If a Web browser does not recognize the MIME type of a file it has retrieved from a Web server, it displays this dialog box so the user can decide what to do with the file.

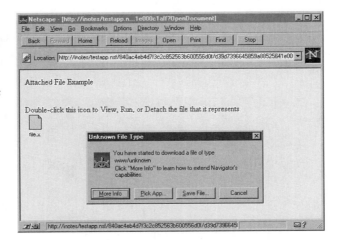

The way the browser figures out how to handle a downloaded file is by referring to a file in the Notes data directory, an HTTP configuration file called HTTPD.CNF, placed there by the installation program when the Domino server was installed (or by the Domino HTTP install program if Domino HTTP service was installed separately from Notes 4.5). HTTPD.CNF is a text file that contains line after line of MIME type mappings as well as lots of other interesting and mystifying lines of text.

MIME is an acronym that stands for Multipurpose Internet Mail Extensions. MIME is an Internet protocol that defines a set of rules for attaching files of all kinds to mail messages, HTML files, and other types of files that computers send to each other across the Net.

The early Internet messaging protocols, such as SMTP (Simple Message Transfer Protocol), defined how to format an e-mail message but did not provide for attaching files to messages. In the early days of the Internet, you didn't attach files to messages. You sent the messages by SMTP and you transferred the files by a separate process called FTP (File Transfer Protocol). As time passed, people came up with various ways to attach files to mail messages, but it was always a chore until MIME established a standard way of doing it, because the sender and receiver had to agree on how to encode/decode the attached message, and probably had encode/decode the attached file manually.

A MIME-type mapping is a line of text that defines a file type and equates its file name extension to a program that can be used to open the file or run the program, if that is what the file is. MIME-compliant programs, such as modern Internet mail programs like

Eudora and modern Web browsers, can receive a file attached to or embedded in another file, and then process the attached/embedded file or hand it off to another program to process. The way a MIME-compliant browser knows how to do this is by obtaining the file type from the HTTPD.CNF file.

If you get in the habit of attaching a particular type of file to your Notes documents, and you would like Web users to be able to process the files automatically, you can add a type-mapping row to the HTTPD.CNF file to represent your file type. When the user downloads a file, Domino sends the information from the type-mapping line to the user along with the file. If the user has the program needed to process the file, the processing takes place automatically.

The syntax for a MIME type mapping line is the following:

```
Addtype .extension type/subtype/ encoding [quality[ character-set]] # Comment
```

Addtype is the MIME keyword identifying this as a type mapping line. Extension is the file extension used to identify the file type. This refers to the same extensions that you are familiar with in DOS; for example, .nsf is a Notes database and .exe is an executable program. Type/subtype identifies the file type. Examples of types are application, audio, image, and text. Encoding tells how the file is encoded. Types of encoding include binary, 7-bit bytes, and 8-bit bytes. Quality and character set, both optional, further refine the definition of the file. The pound sign (#) identifies any text that follows it as a comment.

A sample of type mappings appears in Figure 6.19.

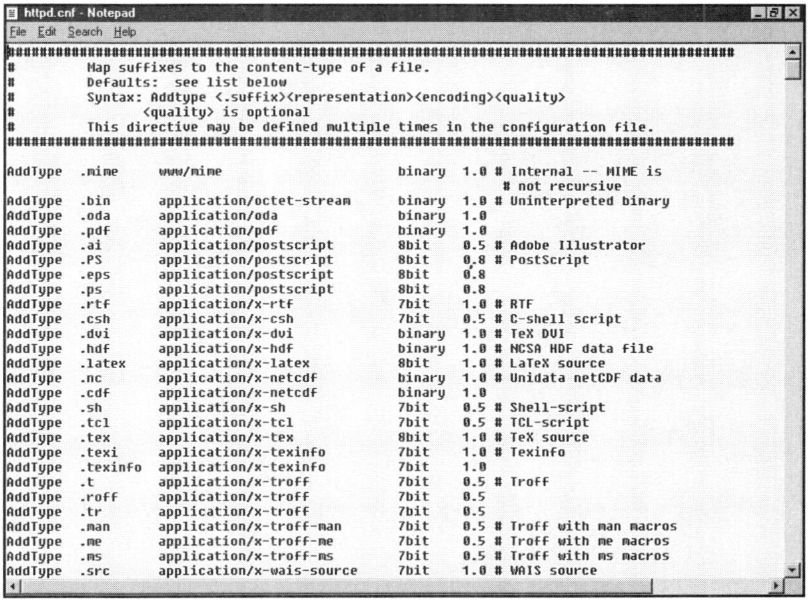

```
httpd.cnf - Notepad
File Edit Search Help
##########################################################################################
#         Map suffixes to the content-type of a file.
#         Defaults:  see list below
#         Syntax: Addtype <.suffix><representation><encoding><quality>
#                <quality> is optional
#         This directive may be defined multiple times in the configuration file.
##########################################################################################

AddType   .mime      www/mime                       binary  1.0 # Internal -- MIME is
                                                                 # not recursive
AddType   .bin       application/octet-stream       binary  1.0 # Uninterpreted binary
AddType   .oda       application/oda                binary  1.0
AddType   .pdf       application/pdf                binary  1.0
AddType   .ai        application/postscript         8bit    0.5 # Adobe Illustrator
AddType   .PS        application/postscript         8bit    0.8 # PostScript
AddType   .eps       application/postscript         8bit    0.8
AddType   .ps        application/postscript         8bit    0.8
AddType   .rtf       application/x-rtf              7bit    1.0 # RTF
AddType   .csh       application/x-csh              7bit    0.5 # C-shell script
AddType   .dvi       application/x-dvi              binary  1.0 # TeX DVI
AddType   .hdf       application/x-hdf              binary  1.0 # NCSA HDF data file
AddType   .latex     application/x-latex            8bit    1.0 # LaTeX source
AddType   .nc        application/x-netcdf           binary  1.0 # Unidata netCDF data
AddType   .cdf       application/x-netcdf           binary  1.0
AddType   .sh        application/x-sh               7bit    0.5 # Shell-script
AddType   .tcl       application/x-tcl              7bit    0.5 # TCL-script
AddType   .tex       application/x-tex              8bit    1.0 # TeX source
AddType   .texi      application/x-texinfo          7bit    1.0 # Texinfo
AddType   .texinfo   application/x-texinfo          7bit    1.0
AddType   .t         application/x-troff            7bit    0.5 # Troff
AddType   .roff      application/x-troff            7bit    0.5
AddType   .tr        application/x-troff            7bit    0.5
AddType   .man       application/x-troff-man        7bit    0.5 # Troff with man macros
AddType   .me        application/x-troff-me         7bit    0.5 # Troff with me macros
AddType   .ms        application/x-troff-ms         7bit    0.5 # Troff with ms macros
AddType   .src       application/x-wais-source      7bit    1.0 # WAIS source
```

Fig. 6.19
The HTTPD.CNF file includes line after line of MIME type mappings.

    ◆ See "Enabling Attachments from the Web," p. 188

From Here...

Building forms for Web clients is as much work as you wish it to be. As you read in this chapter, most of Notes elements, components and functions will perform well on the Web. Alterations that you make will be based upon two considerations; first, is your application going to have dual use; that is, will it be accessed by both Web clients and Notes clients? Second, how much formatting will you need to do to work around the few restrictions involved in the conversion of your Notes documents to HTML?

For more information on forms for the Web, see the following chapters:

    ▶ Chapter 4, "Understanding Web Fundamentals," provides a basic understanding of HTML, Java applets, plug-ins, and Active X.

    ▶ Chapter 12, "Applying a 'Web Look' to Notes Applications," shows how to incorporate Java applets, multimedia, and frames into Notes applications.

    ▶ Chapter 20, "Preparing Existing Applications for the Web," discusses how you retro-fit your Notes applications for optimum performance on the Web.

chapter 7

Designing Forms for an Interactive Web Site

by Jane Calabria

In this chapter

◆ ***How to make input forms available to Web users***
Web users have no menu to access forms. Here you learn how to create Actions and Action Hotspots to facilitate access to forms on the Web.

◆ ***How to control the formatting of input forms***
When Web users fill information into fields, you can control the size of single line fields and the wrap characteristics of rich text fields.

◆ ***How to customize the Submit button***
By default, Domino creates a Submit button for Web forms. Here, you learn how to customize the Submit button label.

◆ ***How to customize Response Messages***
The default response Web users receive from Domino is rather impersonal and forces a Web user to use his back key in a browser to find his way around the site again. Here, you learn how to customize responses and link to another page.

In the last chapter, you learned how to design forms that effectively make information in Notes databases available to Web users. In this chapter, you learn how to design forms that Web users can use to add information to Notes databases and, by extension, to participate in Notes applications.

Making Input Forms Accessible to Web Users

When a Web user needs to create, edit, or delete a Notes document from within a browser, he or she can't just pull down the menu and choose a command. Browsers don't support Notes directly, so you, the database designer, must embed those functions in the HTML documents Domino sends to the Web user. You can make Notes functions available to Web users in one of the following three ways:

▶ As actions on view and form action bars

▶ As action hotspots anywhere in a document or form

▶ As HTML links anywhere in a document or form

These all appear in a browser as HTML hyperlinks—that is, clickable text or graphics hotspots. The user clicks the hotspot to perform the designated function.

For example, the Web user clicks a hotspot for creating a new document. This triggers the browser to retrieve a form from the Domino server and display it in edit mode to the user. The user fills in the fields on the form, clicks the Submit button that appears automatically at the bottom of the form, and the browser sends the form to Domino using standard CGI methods. Domino receives the form, translates it back into Notes format, and stores the resulting Notes document in a Notes database. The arrival of the new document might trigger agents that can then pull the form and the information it contains into Notes workflow applications.

Domino will automatically generate a submit button on all forms accessed by Web clients, so you need not create one yourself. You can customize the label of the submit button if you want, and you can choose its position on your forms. Beyond that, Domino doesn't support buttons in HTML documents, so don't bother to use buttons for any other purpose.

Creating Actions

Actions in Notes are buttons that appear in an action bar at the top of the screen whenever a view or document that has an action bar is present on the screen. When viewed in a Web browser, action bar actions look like cells in a bordered table at the top of the HTML document. The text inside each cell is a link that, when you click it, performs the defined action.

For the most part, actions in Notes allow users to perform the same sorts of tasks by clicking an on-screen button that they would otherwise have to perform by making choices in the Notes menu. That is, actions in Notes are mostly a convenience feature. Notes application designers create them to make an application easier to use. They use actions to streamline the activities that users are most likely to want to perform in a given situation. So, instead of having to pick their way through the menu, users can just click a button at the top of the screen.

While actions are a great enhancement of a regular Notes application, they are *more* than a mere enhancement of a Web application. Because HTTP doesn't inherently support user additions to, edits of, and deletions from the knowledge base, browsers don't include menu choices to do this sort of thing. Actions provide the Web user with his *only* means of doing things like creating a new document, opening an existing document in Edit mode, moving a document to a folder, or deleting a document.

An Action for Creating a New Document

To create an action that creates a new document, you can use `@Command([Compose]; formname)`. The steps for creating such an action are as follows:

1. Open in Design mode the view or form in whose action bar the action should appear. If the user will be creating a main document, you can create a form or view action. If the user will be creating a response document, you must create a form action.

 Tip

Unlike Notes users, Web users cannot select a document in a view. Therefore, they cannot respond to a document while in a view. First, they have to open the document; then they can respond to it.

You, the application designer, can create either view actions or form actions for composing main documents. But for composing responses, you can use only form actions or action hotspots, which are also form-based.

---

2. Make the action pane appear. Choose <u>V</u>iew, <u>A</u>ction Pane in the menu. Or, drag the action pane border out from the right side of the screen. Or, double-click the action pane border. Or, click the action pane SmartIcon (third from the right in a Form window, rightmost in a View window).

    The action pane displays a list of all currently defined actions for the current view or form. There are six Default Actions, recognizable because their names begin with an asterisk (such as *Categorize and *Edit Document).

3. Create another action by choosing <u>C</u>reate, A<u>c</u>tion in the menu. The word `(Untitled)` appears in the action pane. The Properties box for that action appears on the screen (see Figure 7.1).

7

Fig. 7.1

When you choose Create, Action in the menu, a new action, as yet untitled, appears in the Action Pane, right, and the Action Properties box appears. This is true for both View actions and Form actions.

Action Pane icon

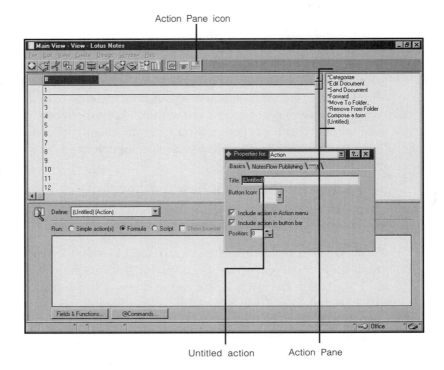

Untitled action   Action Pane

4. Name the new action in the Title field of the Properties box. The name should be descriptive but short, because it will be the text that appears on the action button in both Notes and the browser.

5. Optionally, choose an icon from the array in the Button Icon field. The icon will appear in the action button, to the left of the action's title, both in Notes and the browser. Don't skip this step. Choosing an icon adds a customized look to your action.

6. Check the box labeled Include Action in Button Bar. This is important—if you don't check this box, the action won't be available to Web users.

7. Change the number in the Position field if you want. It indicates the action's horizontal position in the action bar (and its vertical position in the Notes Action Menu). Number one is the leftmost (or topmost) position.

8. If this form is to be used only by Web users, click the window shade icon to open the Hide When panel. Check the box labeled Hide action if formula is true. Enter the following formula in the formula field:

   ```
   @IsNotMember("$$WebClient";@Userroles)
   ```

9. Close the Action Properties Box. Make sure the Design pane appears in the bottom half of the screen. If it does not, open it by doing one of the following: choose

View, <u>D</u>esign Pane in the menu; or drag the Design Pane border up from the bottom of the screen; or double-click the Design Pane border; or click the Design Pane SmartIcon (fourth from right in the Form window, second from right in the View window).

10. In the Design Pane, make sure the Define field says *ActionName*(Action), where *ActionName* is the title of your action. Make sure the Formula radio button is selected. Enter the following formula in the formula window:

```
@Command([Compose]; "FormName")
```

See Figure 7.2 for an example of the Title of the action shown in the Action Properties box.

Fig. 7.2
This action will create a new main topic in a discussion database.

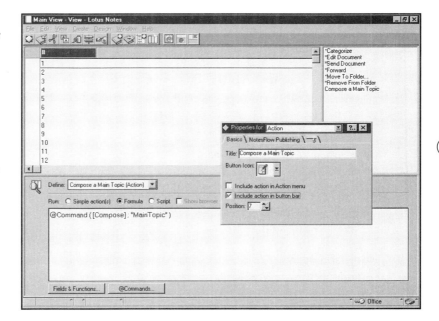

11. Save, close, and test the form.

If you did everything correctly, your new action should appear in the action bar when the view or form to which you added it is open on the screen. If you did not hide the action from Notes users, it should appear when the form or view is open in Notes and when it is open in a browser. If you hid the form from Notes users, then the action should appear only in a Web browser.

In the formula in Step 8 of the previous numbered list, @UserRoles returns a list of roles that the current user fills. These are the roles that appear in the database ACL, mostly. However, if a user is coming in from the Web, @UserRoles also returns $$WebClient as a role.

@IsNotMember asks if $$WebClient is a member of the list of roles returned by @UserRoles. If it is a member, as it would be if the user is coming to the Domino server from the Web, then @IsNotMember returns 0 (false). If it is not a member, as it would not be if the user is coming in from a Notes client, then @IsNotMember returns 1 (true). The whole thing taken together is true if the user is *not* a member of $$WebClient (and is therefore a Notes user, not a Web user), in which case the action is hidden from that user.

The second formula, in Step 10, says compose a form called *FormName*, where *FormName* is the name of the form the user wants to compose. In the example in Figure 7.2, the form is called *MainTopic*.

Other Useful Actions

To create an action that performs, in a Web browser, some act upon an existing document, you have to add an action to the action bar of the form that Domino uses to convert the document to HTML. You cannot put this kind of action in a view action bar because there is no way in a Web browser to tell the action which document in the view it should act upon. The kinds of actions that must appear in form action bars and not view action bars include:

▶ *Compose a response document.* @Command([Compose]; "*formname*") where *formname* is the name of the response form. Domino will automatically treat the open document as the parent of the new response.

▶ *Edit an existing document.* @Command([EditDocument])

▶ *Delete an existing document.* @Command([EditClear])

Interestingly, one of the Default Actions (the ones whose names begin with an asterisk) is Edit Document. You can't use it, however, because Domino does not translate any of the Default Actions to HTML. You have to make your own Edit Document action and use @Command([EditDocument]) in it.

Also, Notes provides a Simple Action that deletes documents. But you can't use that either because Domino does not translate any of the Simple Actions to HTML. You have to use @Command([EditClear]).

You cannot use the default actions or simple actions. What about LotusScript actions? You can't use those either. Domino only translates actions to HTML if they are defined with the @function/@command language. All others do not translate.

Finally, even if you create an action using @functions and @commands, Domino will not translate the action to HTML if it tries to do something that Domino can't make it do. For example, if you add an Edit Document or Delete Document action to a view action bar, Domino won't translate the action to HTML because you simply cannot do those things from a view in a browser.

Creating Action Hotspots

An action hotspot in Notes is a block of text—usually surrounded by a border so that it stands out from surrounding text—or a pasted or imported graphic programmed so that, when you double-click it, some action takes place. It is a Notes equivalent to a text or graphic hotspot in an HTML document, and you can program it to open a form in Compose mode, open a document in Edit mode, delete a document, and all the other things you can do with action bar actions as discussed in the preceding section.

To create an action hotspot, select the block of text or graphic that will be clickable. If selecting a graphic, you must not merely click it, but rather drag across it so that the whole graphic changes color. Then choose Create, Hotspot, Action Hotspot in the menu. The Properties box for the HotSpot Button appears, but you don't have to do anything in it. All you have to do next is, in the Design Pane, choose Formula and enter the appropriate formula for what you want to do. For example, if the hotspot is supposed to trigger the composing of a document, you would use:

```
@Command ( [Compose] ; "formname" )
```

In a browser, hotspot text appears as a standard, differently colored, underlined HTML link. When you point to it, the mouse pointer changes to a hand. A hotspot graphic does not have a special appearance, but when you point to it, the mouse pointer changes to a hand. When you click either hotspot, a new document, based on the Notes form *FormName*, opens in Edit mode.

If you want to perform some other action, just substitute the appropriate @Command.

Creating HTML Links

Finally, you can open a form (but not perform any other action) with an HTML link. This is an HTML tag; that is, it is text and it can appear anywhere on a form in Design mode. You can even add it to a text field in a document. It appears as follows:

```
[<a href="/databasename/formname?OpenForm">Click here to create formname</a>]
```

An HREF is the HTML tag that means "add a hypertext reference." *databasename* and *formname* are the names of the database and form to be opened, respectively. */databasename/formname*?OpenForm is the Domino URL syntax to open the named Notes form in the named Notes database. *Click here to create formname* is the text that becomes the hotspot. </A> denotes the end of the opening <A> reference (<A> and </A> being paired tags).

The resulting link appears and performs as a standard text link in a browser.

Making Input Forms Functional

Notes input forms behave differently in a Web browser than in Notes. For that reason, you may need to redesign a form so that it is usable in a browser. Or, you may decide to create two sets of forms, one for use in Notes, the other for use in Web browsers.

Most of the features of Notes that you apply to forms work the same whether the form appears in a Notes client or a Web browser. For example, Default Value, Input Translation, and Input Validation formulas work the same on both platforms. All types of Computed fields work on both platforms.

All data types are available in Web-based forms, with some limitations. For one, text fields are only one line in height on the Web. If you want multiple lines to appear in the form, you have to use a rich text field instead. Rich text fields also are limited. Web users can only enter plain, monospace text into them. Also, the types of keyword fields that are unique to Layout Regions are not available in Web-based forms, because Layout Regions themselves do not work at all in Web-based forms.

Field inheritance works slightly differently in Web-based forms. Rich text fields cannot inherit from another document. Also, if you compose a document by clicking a view action, no inheritance takes place, because no document was or could have been selected in the Web-based view. You have to compose a document from within another document for inheritance to work.

Forms on the Web have some features that forms in Notes do not. In particular, you can use HTML tags in Web-based forms to control field input.

Controlling the Size of Single-Line Text Fields

You can control the width and maximum characters in a text field by entering a tag similar to the following into the Help Description field of a Field Properties Box: [<size=40 maxlength=50>]. This example sets the width of the field as displayed in a browser at 40 characters, and permits entry of no more than 50 characters into the field (see Figure 7.3).

Controlling the Size and Wrap Characteristics of Rich Text Fields

You can control the size and wrap characteristics of a rich text field with the following tag: [<rows=xx cols=yy wrap=zz>], where xx is a number of text rows, yy is a number of text columns, and zz is virtual, physical, or off. The tag [<rows=6 cols=60 wrap=virtual>] would cause the rich text field to display in the browser as a 6-row by 60-column text entry area, and text will wrap within the confines of this space but be transmitted as long, unbroken lines. wrap=physical is supposed to cause lines to wrap within the defined space and be transmitted with breaks at wrap points. However, in our testing, wrap=physical works no differently than wrap=virtual. Wrap=off turns word wrap off, so that the typist has to press Enter to force wrapping (see Figure 7.4). For an example of how the text in all of the fields wraps when in Read mode, see Figure 7.5.

Fig. 7.3

The entry in the Help Description field is an HTML tag that will control the appearance and behavior of the field to Web users.

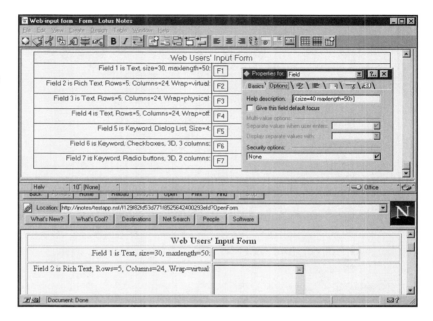

Fig. 7.4

Fields 2 and 3, top and middle, have wrap set to virtual and physical, respectively. Text wraps automatically in both. Field 4, bottom, has wrap set to off. Text scrolls off the edges of the field.

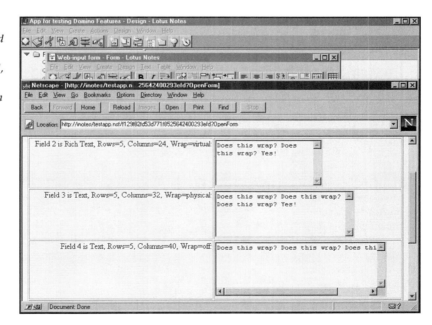

Fig. 7.5
Whether wrap is turned on or off for the person creating the new document, it is on for all readers of the document, whether in Notes or in a browser.

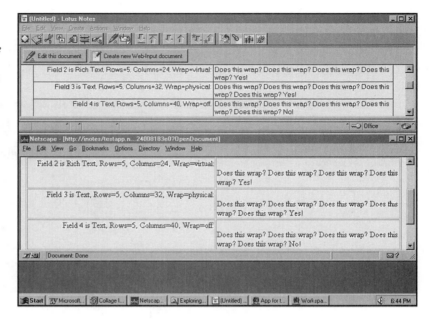

The wrap options were not part of standard HTML until the release of HTML version 3.2. They were introduced by Netscape in Netscape Navigator version 2.0. Whether and exactly how they will work will depend on what browser one uses to submit a form. Before the wrap options existed, text did not automatically wrap within a multiline field, and wrap=off is still the default, so you probably want to add wrap=virtual to all of your rich text fields. It can't do any harm, but it can make your user's experience filling in forms for you much more pleasant.

Controlling the Appearance of Key Word Fields

You can control how many keywords appear in the browser display of a keyword field by putting a tag similar to the following into the Help Description field of the Field Properties Box: [<size=4>]. This tag would cause a scroll bar to appear in the field if more than four keywords are available (see Figure 7.6).

Fig. 7.6
This keyword field is limited to four choices showing in the field. A scroll bar permits viewing of other entries if there are more than four.

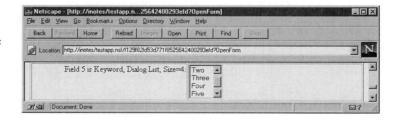

Understanding the Submit Button

Another way Notes forms perform differently on the Web is that they have a Submit button, which the user must click in order to send the form back to the Domino server. The Submit button is HTML's standard method for browsers to submit forms to Web servers. Domino automatically adds a Submit button to the bottom of any form that a Web user opens. The default Submit button has the word Submit on it.

You can move the Submit button or change the words that appear on its face. However, you cannot alter its behavior. To move or change the Submit button that Domino puts on forms, do the following:

1. Open the form in Design mode.
2. Place the text cursor where you want the Submit button to appear.
3. In the menu, choose Create, Hotspot, Button. A button appears on your form and the Button Properties box opens.
4. In the Button Properties box, enter the desired button text into the Button label field. If you leave this blank, the word Submit will appear when Web users open the form.
5. Save and close the form.

Don't bother trying to program an action for the button—Domino ignores your programming. And don't bother to add more than one Notes Submit button. Domino will convert the first one to an HTML Submit button and will ignore any other buttons it encounters.

Other HTML Buttons

That's not to say that you can only have one button on your forms. While you cannot put more than one *Notes* button on a form, and you cannot program that Notes button as anything other than a Submit button, you can use HTML tags to put multiple Submit buttons on a form. You can use an HTML tag to add a *Reset* button that clears all values out of a form on the screen. And, while at this writing Domino doesn't handle it properly, HTML 3.2 supports the ability to add a graphical Submit button to a form; watch for this capability in a future release of Domino.

When Domino converts a Notes input form to HTML and sends it to a Web user, it adds the following tag to the bottom of the form:

```
<INPUT TYPE=submit VALUE="Submit">
```

<input> is an HTML tag that sets up a field on the Web input form in which a Web user can enter information. HTML recognizes several types of <input> tags, including text, password, check box, radio, file, submit, image, and reset. Of these types, three—submit, image, and reset—set up clickable buttons on the input form. The others set up fields into which the user can enter data in various ways and types. As it appears previously, the <input> tag that Domino inserts to become the submit button is of TYPE=submit. This means that, when the user clicks the button, it will trigger the submission of the form to the Domino server. The tag also has VALUE="Submit," which means that the word *Submit* will appear on the face of the button.

When you add a Notes button to a form, Domino interprets that to be the Submit button and puts the <INPUT TYPE=submit VALUE="Submit"> tag at the position of your button instead of at the end of the form. When you enter text into the Button label field in the Button Properties box, Domino substitutes that text for *Submit*. That is, if you enter *Send form to server* in the Button label field, Domino inserts the following tag in place of the button:

```
<INPUT TYPE=submit VALUE="Send form to server">
```

While Domino will not recognize more than one button that you add to a Web input form, it will let you add additional Submit buttons by inserting <INPUT TYPE=submit> statements into your form. Put in as many as you want; put them wherever you want. Notes will convert them to Submit buttons. However, remember that Domino will still add a Submit button of its own in addition to the ones you create this way. It will either substitute one for the first Notes button it encounters on the form or it will add one all the way at the bottom of the form, just as it would have done had you done nothing at all.

While Domino will not recognize any other functions for Notes buttons than Submit, HTML does support a Reset button that clears the values from the fields in an on-screen form. You can add one or more *Reset* buttons by adding the following tag to your input form:

```
<INPUT TYPE=reset>
```

Add a *VALUE=* parameter to this tag if you want the button to say anything other than "Reset."

Finally, HTML 3.2 supports substitution of a graphical image as a Submit button for the standard Submit button. That is, you can insert the following tag into an input form:

```
<INPUT TYPE=image NAME=anyname SRC="pathname">
```

Enter any text string in place of *anyname*. Enter the actual mapped path name of the graphical file you want to use in place of *pathname*. By "mapped path name," we mean the mapped path according to the Domino server's Server document in the Public

Address Book. For more information on mapped path names, see Chapter 16, "Using Advanced Administration Techniques."

An HTML 3.2-compliant browser will display the graphical image in place of this tag. When the user clicks it, the browser will try to submit the form to the Domino server.

The only problem is that Domino 4.5a does not properly support the HTML 3.2 *image* input type, so that, if you try adding this tag, the submission of the form will fail. The browser will display an error message, and Domino will not receive the form. However, Lotus is committed to supporting HTML 3.2 in Notes 4.5. So watch future maintenance releases of Notes (every quarter or so) for a fix of this problem or, more likely, a way of creating this type of button by creating some sort of Hotspot rather than having to hand tool an URL.

Customizing Response Messages with the *$$Return* Field

When a Web user does submit a form back to a Domino server, a default message, "Form processed," appears on the screen. You can customize this response with the $$Return field. For example, you can cause Domino to respond: "Thank you, Rob. One of our representatives will reply to you within one business day."

You do this by adding a computed field to the form that users submit, and naming the field $$Return. In the formula pane, you enter a formula defining the response message. The formula that responds with the preceding example *Thank You* message looks something like this:

```
@Return("<H2>Thank you, " + FirstName + ". One of our representatives will reply to
you within one business day.</H2>")
```

The <H2> and </H2> tags tell the browser to display the text between the tags in a smaller font than the default, which is H3. The rest of this formula is standard Notes programming.

The following formula says, "Thank you, Rob." and displays, on the following line, a hotspot back to the site home page:

```
@Return("<H2>Thank you, " + FirstName + ".</H2><BR><H4><a href=/>Return to Home Page</
a>")
```

The "Thank you" message is in a small typeface, <H2>. The hyperlink, "Return to Home Page", is in a larger typeface, <H4>.

By enclosing an URL in brackets, you can reroute the user upon submitting a form. The following formula skips the "Form processed" or "Thank you" message entirely and simply returns the user to a different Web page. That is, when the user clicks the Submit button, the browser sends the form to the Domino server, then sends out an URL for some other HTML page, and displays it when it receives it.

"[http://www.planetnotes.com]".

You can use the same technique to run a CGI script. Simply enter the URL of the script you want to run, instead of an HTML page:

"[http://inotes/cgi-bin/*cgiscriptname*.ext]"

Enabling Attachments from the Web

If you want Web users to be able to submit files attached to an input form, you can set the form up by creating an action hotspot, as follows:

1. Enter a static text label.
2. Select the text, then choose Create, Hotspot, Action Hotspot.
3. Enter the formula @Command([EditInsertFileAttachment])
4. Save and test the action hotspot.

As a result of this, when Domino generates an HTML document from this form it will insert an <input> tag of type=file. The Web input form should have a field in it that will accept entry of a file name, and a Browse button with which you can pick a file from a list (see Figure 7.7).

Fig. 7.7

The label to the left of the field is the static text that you highlighted when creating the action hotspot. Click the browse button to pick a file from the Windows File Upload dialog box.

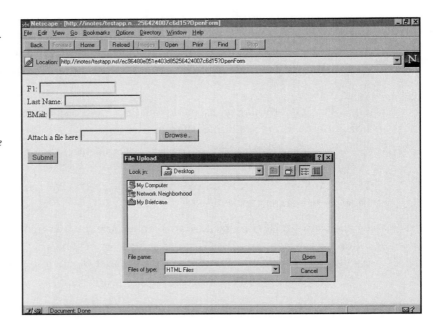

The resulting field lets you attach only one file to the input form. If you want users to be able to attach more than one file, you can repeat the preceding procedure to include more than one file attachment field.

Returning Information with CGI Variables

Finally, there is a set of Notes fields you can put in a form that only have meaning and function in Web-based forms. These are the fields named after CGI variables. CGI variables are a set of standard variables that CGI programmers can use when writing scripts. CGI variables are the vehicle by which a Web client delivers information about itself to CGI scripts running on Web servers. If fields named for CGI variables appear in an input form, the Web browser automatically enters the values of those variables into the fields, and when the Web user submits the form, the included CGI variables are returned along with the user-entered data. Notes could then use the information when processing a form received from a Web user. See Figure 7.8 for an example of each field name and a corresponding value.

Fig. 7.8
These are sample values that would appear in the CGI variable fields of a Web input form.

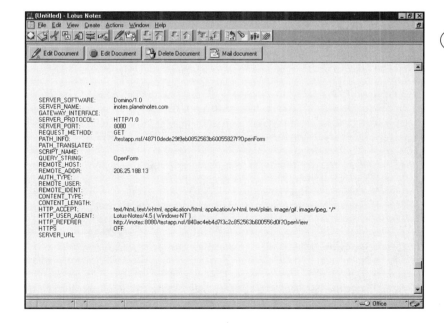

If you add CGI variable fields, they should be text fields. Name them with the CGI variable names whose data you want to collect. Because the user submitting the form will not fill in these fields manually, you should mark them hidden. To do so, open the Field Properties box for each such field. Display the Hide When panel by clicking the window shade tab. Mark the fields Hide When Editing. If the submitted form will later appear as a document on the Web site, you might also want to mark the fields Hide When Reading.

The CGI variable names that Domino recognizes include those in Table 7.1.

Table 7.1   CGI Environment Variables

Variable	Description
Auth_Type	Returns the protocol-specific authentication method used to validate the user, but only if the server supports user authentication and the script is protected.
Content_Length	Returns the length of the content, if and as reported by the browser.
Content_Type	Returns the content type of the data for queries which have attached information, such as PUT and HTTP POST queries.
Gateway_Interface	Returns the server's CGI version number.
HTTP_Accept	Returns the MIME types that the client will accept.
HTTP_Referer	Returns the URL of the page from which the user opened this form.
HTTP_User_Agent	Returns the name and version of the browser used to create this form.
HTTPS	Returns On if the server is running the SSL protocol; otherwise returns Off.
Path_Info	Returns the portion of an URL that trails the name of the HTTP server.
Path_Translated	Returns the same as Path_Info, but in terms of the physical path name, not the virtual path name.
Query_String	Returns the portion of an URL that trails the question mark.
Remote_Addr	Returns the IP address of the browser's host.
Remote_Host	Returns the host name of the browser's host.
Remote_Ident	Returns the user name of the browser's host.
Remote_User	Returns the name by which a Web user authenticated.
Request_Method	Returns the HTTP command the browser used to make the current request.
Script_Name	Returns the virtual path name of the script being executed.
Server_Name	Returns the server's host name or IP address.

Variable	Description
Server_Port	Returns the server's HTTP port number.
Server_Protocol	Returns the name and version number of the protocol being used by the browser to make this request.
Server_Software	Returns the name and version of the HTTP server program.
Server_URL	Returns the version of CGI with which the server complies.

For more information about CGI variables, see *Special Edition Using CGI*, published by Que.

 Tip
If an input form does double-duty—both Notes and Web users use it—you can include the CGI variable fields in a Web-only subform. Insert the subform based on the following formula: @If (@IsMember ("$$WebClient"; @UserRoles); "*subformname*"; ""). *Subformname* is the subform that contains the CGI variable fields. If the current user is a Web user, this formula inserts that subform. If the current user is a Notes user, the formula inserts nothing.

7

From Here...

As you have seen, input forms can serve both Notes and Web users with some customization, and the major consideration to input forms is access. Customized responses to input forms, which include a method of returning the user to the Home page, previous page, or another site, prevent the user from feeling "abandoned" when they supply and submit information to the Domino server.

For related information, see the following chapters:

▶ Chapter 11, "Automating Web Applications with Agents," discusses agents that run based upon information provided in input forms.

▶ Chapter 13, "Examining Special Function Databases for the Web," describes registration databases and discussion databases on the Web, both of which rely on input forms.

## chapter 8

Building Views for Domino Web Applications

8

by Jane Calabria

In this chapter

◆ **How to use Actions in views**
From within a view, you can create actions to open other views. These Actions can help Web users to navigate a site.

◆ **How to use GIFs in views**
Add interest to your views by adding GIFs to notify Web users that documents are newly added to the database.

◆ **How to create frames with the Notes 3 Pane UI**
You can imitate a frame look using the Notes 3 Pane User Interface, which generates scroll bars for Web clients.

Views perform as a table of contents to a Database, listing the documents of a database in a table format to the Notes client. Views perform in the same way on the Web, but are a brand new concept to the Web. Only Domino can create views dynamically—no other HTTP server can perform in this manner. In the Web world, Domino presents a first—the ability for a Web client to create content and see that content listed among other documents upon saving.

Understanding Views

Web view design requires the Notes developer to adapt to a new way of thinking. The primary difference in Notes views versus Web views is the selected document in a view. On the Web, there is no such thing. Yet, it is a common practice for Notes designers to allow documents to inherit value from a selected document in a view.

If you can't inherit from a selected document, how then can you inherit values at all? Inheritance on the Web must be drawn from the document, not the document in a view. Therefore, a document must be composed from within a document. Adding an action to a view to compose a document will, indeed, deliver a new, blank document to the Web client. But, the document will be blank with no inherited values. Adding an action to a document to compose a document will present a new document with inherited values specified by the designer.

If inheritance is not a factor, then by all means provide actions in views to compose documents, such as a new Main Topic in a discussion database. But place the action to compose a *response* document on the action bar of the Main Topic of Response Document.

Beyond this notable difference, Domino supports most of the Notes view functions. Table 8.1 lists view and column properties that are not supported, or that are restricted.

Table 8.1   View and Column Properties Not Supported or Supported with Restrictions on the Web

Notes View and Folder Properties	Comments	Restrictions
Calendar-style views	Web clients can see all calendar entries. Calendar entries are converted to HTML tables by Domino.	The clock, creating new appointments, scrolling through entries on a single day and conflict bars are not supported.
Folders	Supported.	You cannot move documents into a folder using a Web browser.
Multiline column headings and multiline rows	Supported. Consider that column headings might clutter the Web page. Examine their real value. Are they necessary?	
On Open, Go To options	Not supported.	
On Refresh options	Not supported.	

Notes View and Folder Properties	Comments	Restrictions
Show in View menu	"Show in View Menu" in the view properties box has no effect on Web clients.	Deselecting the "Show in View Menu" option does not affect whether or not the view will show in a list of views.
Style options for Unread rows, Alternate row colors, Show selection margin, and Beveled column headings	Not supported.	To prevent line wrap, open the View properties box and specify 1 in the Lines per heading section.
View Indexing options	Not applicable.	
Column Properties		
Click column header to sort	Not supported.	
Collapsed/expanded categories	Supported.	
Resizable column	Not supported.	
"Show twisties" when row is expandable	Not supported; twisties can't be hidden.	

Tip

To remove a view from the folders navigator on the Web, use a hidden view.

Consider that Notes views are expandable and collapsible by Web users, and twisties are converted to triangles on the Web. By default, Notes views will serve to the Web client in collapsed mode. When a Web user clicks an expandable category in a view, the entire view—not just the category—will expand. This is a result of Domino caching. The memory requirements necessary to cache every iteration of a categorized, collapsible view are too large. Therefore, the choices are three: collapse all, expand one, or expand all.

Unless you create a view template (form), Domino uses a default view template to serve views to the Web client. Actually, there are two view templates. The first displays a list of available views in a database as well as the database name and icon shown in Figure 8.1.

Fig. 8.1

Domino presents the available views in a database using a view template that contains the database name, icon, and list of views.

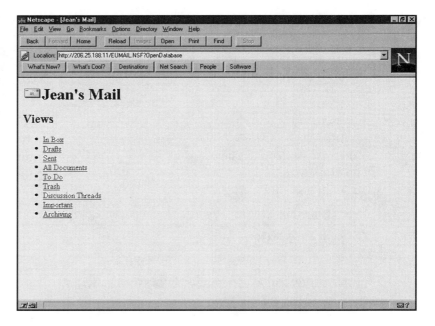

The second template contains the list of documents in a view, converting the first column of a view into hypertext, and adding hotspots to navigate to the previous and next pages of a view, to expand or collapse all sections of the view, and to search the database as shown in Figure 8.2.

Fig. 8.2

This template, named $ViewDefaultTemplate, is generated on-the-fly by Domino. You can replace this template with your own design by naming a form $ViewDefaultTemplate.

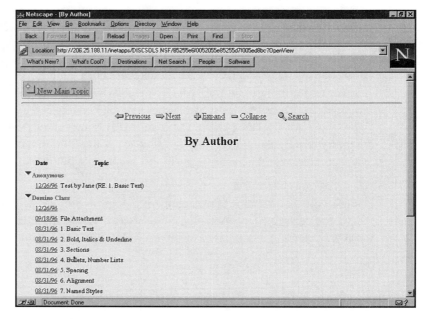

Tip
You can customize View templates or create your own. See Chapter 10, "Using Special $$ Web Fields and Forms," for more information.

Although Chapter 10 covers the view template in more detail, it's good to understand here how they work. Each of the images (the arrows and the plus and minus signs) are followed by text, such as Previous and Next, as shown in Figure 8.2. The image and the word following the image are hotspots containing the following formulas:

Table 8.2   Navigable Icons on the Default Search Template

Icon	Hotspot Formula
Previous	@DbCommand("Domino"; "ViewPreviousPage")
Next	@DbCommand("Domino"; "ViewNextPage")
Expand	@Command([ViewExpandAll])
Collapse	@Command([ViewCollapseAll])
Search	@Command([ViewShowSearchBar])

By default, the leftmost, non-categorized column of a view becomes the anchor to the document on the Web. At this time, Lotus has announced plans to incorporate design control that will allow you to tell Domino which of the columns you want to convert to hypertext links. But, as of this version, the first column is converted to the anchor. This is an important consideration when designing views for Web clients, as the leftmost column of an existing database may be an inappropriate anchor for a Web client.

An example of this can be found in the R4 Discussion template, where the date column is the first non-categorized column found in the views called "All documents" and "By Author." Figure 8.3 displays such a discussion database viewed through a Web browser. Note that the date column becomes the anchor on the Web.

Fig. 8.3
The first non-categorized column in a view becomes the anchor when Domino generates views.

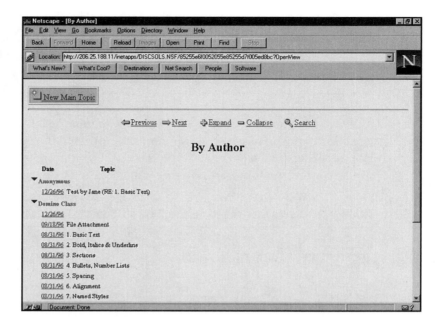

Although there is nothing wrong with this display of documents, and the anchors work properly, it might be more appropriate for Web users to see an anchor on the topic instead of the date field. Reordering the columns and placing the Topic before the date column, the anchor now appears on the document title itself as shown in Figure 8.4.

Fig. 8.4
Be cognizant of the anchor when designing views for Web clients. You may want to reorder columns to present a more logical anchor to the Web visitor.

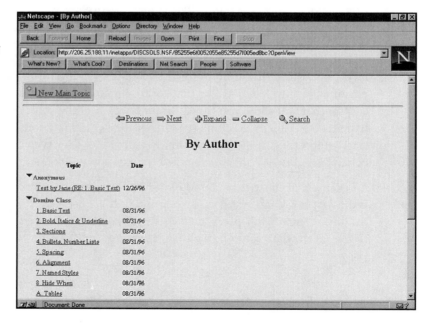

Using Actions in Views

If an existing database has a view which contains actions that display on the action bar, those actions can be converted by Domino and displayed on the Web application. However, simple actions for views are not supported.

Actions in views can assist Web users and Notes users (who are using a Web browser) to navigate your site and work with documents. Depending on your database and its purpose, you might want to provide an action to create a document, or you might want to create an action to help users navigate through other available views.

For example, your views for a document database might include: by author, by date, or by title. When the Web user is looking at the By Author view, actions on the action bar can point him or her to the other views, or to the site home page shown in Figure 8.5.

Fig. 8.5

Actions placed on the action bar will translate well to the Web and can work as navigators throughout your site.

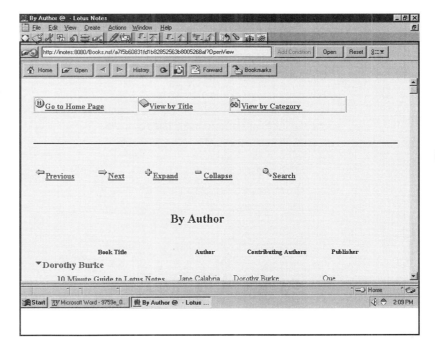

Creating an @URLOpen Action

Domino URL commands can be used in actions and are an efficient way to move Web visitors throughout your site. To create an Action that uses an @URLOpen command to navigate to another view:

1. Open in Design mode the view that will contain the action.

2. Choose **Create**, **Action** from the menu. Click the Action Pane icon in the toolbar. The Action Properties Box appears.

3. Type a title for your action, such as **Home Page**. Remember that the title will appear as a button label. Don't make it too long.

4. (Optional) Select an icon for your action.

5. Check the box labeled Include Action in Button Bar. You don't need to change or select the position of the icon, unless you have more than one action for this form.

6. In the formula pane, select **Formula**.

7. Enter the formula:

   @URLOpen("http://Host/databasename.nsf/?Open")

8. Save and Close the view.

A link to the home page (see Figure 8.6) is a useful and welcomed addition to your views. Web visitors will appreciate easy navigation of your site, eliminating the need to click the Back key. You might consider putting this link in each of your views. You can copy it from view to view as follows:

1. Open the view that contains the action.

2. Click the Action Pane icon in the toolbar.

3. Select the action you want to copy.

4. Select Edit, Copy from the menu (or use Ctrl+C).

5. Open the view you want to copy the action to.

6. Select Edit, Paste from the menu (or use Ctrl+V).

 Tip

As an alternative to creating actions in views, you can provide the actions (links to home page, and so on) in a view template form. Creation of this form is described in Chapter 10, "Using Special Web Fields and Forms."

Creating an Action to Open a View

You'll want to make your site as navigable as possible by the Web visitor. To this end, you can create a view action to navigate a Web user to another view in your database, a different database, or a view within a different database. To create this action:

Fig. 8.6

Providing a link to the home page in each view is one method of providing easy navigation of your site.

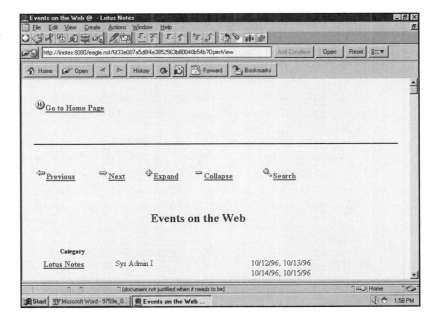

1. Open the view that will contain the Action in Design mode.

2. Choose Create, Action from the menu. Click the Action pane icon in the toolbar.

3. The Action Properties box appears. Type a title for your action such as **View By Category**. Remember that the title will appear as a button label. Don't make it too long.

4. (Optional) Select an icon for your action.

5. Check Include Action in Button Bar. You don't need to change or select the position of the icon, unless you have more than one action for this form.

6. In the formula pane, select Formula.

7. Enter the formula:

    @Command([OpenView];"*By Category*")

    where "*By Category*" is the name of your view.

8. Save and Close the view.

Using GIFs and HTML in Views

GIF files can bring a view to life, acting as flags in a view and notifying Web visitors of documents that are new or updated. In a Notes database, icons are used in a similar fashion. Icons are prevalent in the Mail database, as demonstrated when a mail memo is sent with an attachment (a paper clip icon appears in the view), or with a high priority (which uses a red exclamation mark).

Notes Icons cannot translate to the Web. So the practice of placing icons in Notes views is going to fail when Domino converts the view to HTML. But GIFs can be used in a view in the same manner as icons are used in Notes databases. For example, a column can contain a formula that will display a GIF file labeled new! whenever a new document is displayed in a view.

GIFs can be inserted with the use of *Passthru HTML code* in a formula for a view. Passthru HTML is a reference to a file on your server. When Domino converts the document, or generates the view, the reference is passed through to the resulting HTML page. The formula containing the HTML Passthru might appear something like this:

```
@If(@Now < @Adjust(@Created; 0; 0; 5; 0; 0; 0); "[<img src=/icons/new.gif\ bor-
der=0>]";"")
```

This results in the icon named new.gif to appear in a column if a document is less than five days old, and to have no border around the image.

Animated GIF files can also be used in views, or in documents in Notes. Although you have an option to paste graphics into Notes documents, you will need to reference graphics with HTML code in views.

 Tip
Since views are created on-the-fly by Domino, you won't have the opportunity to paste any graphics into a view, but you can place them there with HTML code. If you decide to build view template forms, keep in mind that graphics will load faster to a Web browser if they are referenced rather than pasted.

Key to the use of GIFs is the location on the Domino server in which they are stored. They must be stored in the path set in the HTTP section of the Server Document, as shown in Figure 8.7. The default directory is the Icons directory which, of course, can be changed in the server document if desired.

If a GIF cannot be located by the Domino server, the resulting HTML page will display a placeholder for the GIF, an unwelcome addition to your Web site. Figure 8.8 shows a Web page as viewed through Netscape Navigator, and the default Navigator image that replaces the unfound GIF or image. In this case, we see a broken page, but this image is generated by the Web browser, not the Domino server, and other browsers will see a different image representing a broken, or not-to-be-found graphic.

Fig. 8.7

The HTTP section of the Server document contains the default directory for icons.

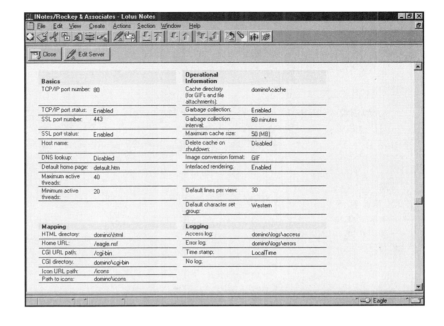

Fig. 8.8

The Web browser generates an icon representing images not found on the HTTP server.

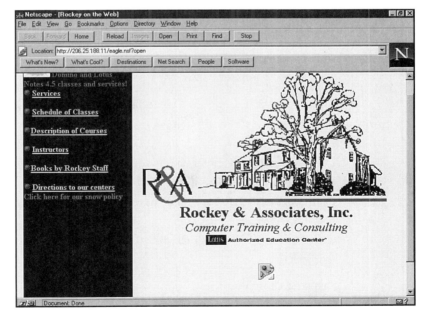

The downside to creating a Web site which requires images to be stored in the Icons directory is accessibility. Either remote access to the file system or presence at the server itself is required when you want to add GIFs to your site. If neither of these conditions is a problem, then there is no downside to storing GIFs in the Icon directory. However, if you want to manage your site remotely through replication, you can create a database to store images, allowing you to make changes in a replica copy. See Chapter 13, "Examining Special Function Databases for the Web," for more information.

That aside, Figure 8.9 shows the resulting HTML page in which the GIF is located by the server, used in a view based upon a formula and passed through to the Web browser.

Fig. 8.9

Using GIF files can help target areas or documents at your site. This New flag assists users in locating new information.

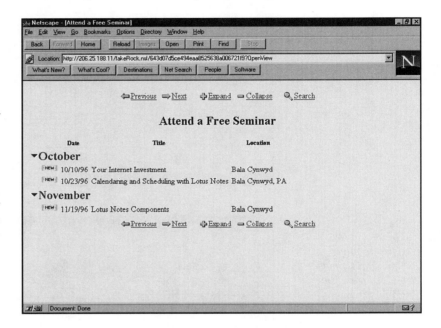

To create this formula:

1. Create or edit the view in which you want to use the .GIF file.

2. Enter a formula in the column where you want the .GIF to appear. In the following example, the .GIF file is called "new" and will appear if the document is less than five days old.

   @If(@Now < @Adjust(@Created; 0; 0; 5; 0; 0; 0); "[<img src=/icons/new.gif\ border=0>]";"")

3. Save and Close your view.

Tip

GIF files are very popular and are found in abundance on the Web. Many are there for your use. Using your browser, search the Web for "animated GIFs" and you'll find lots (maybe hundreds) of sites sponsored by hobbyists, artists, and the like who enjoy spending their time creating GIFs and allowing you to download their files for use at your site.

Using HTML and GIFs in Column Headers

Another method for adding interest to the standard Domino view template involves adding GIFs to a column header in a view. If you have a large number of documents that will display in a view, you might consider a view that contains all documents less than 10 days old. Using this method, your view looks more streamlined than one which contains a *New!* GIF file next to every other document in the view. To further emphasize and remind the Web visitor that these are new documents, you might place the *New!* GIF in a column header, rather than the column itself as shown in Figure 8.10.

Fig. 8.10

Here, the GIF appears in a column title. Column titles are a good place to display company logos. In this way, your company logo can appear on every view page, eliminating the need to create custom view templates.

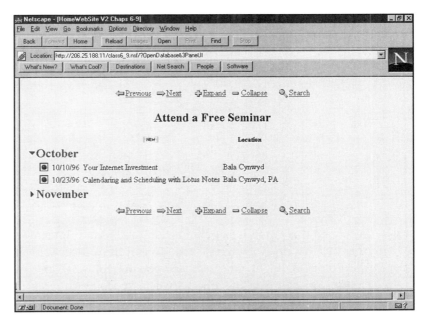

Creating Frames with the Notes 3 Pane UI

You can "imitate" an HTML frame environment by utilizing the Notes R4 3 Pane UI (User Interface). Although we have had success with this, it should be noted that Lotus does not support or recommend the use of the 3 Pane UI on the Web. Rather, their recommendation is to use HTML frames, as described in Chapter 12, "Applying a 'Web Look' to Notes Applications."

The syntax for the Domino URL command is as follows:

http://host/DatabaseName/?OpenDatabase&3PaneUI

Figure 8.11 shows the resulting HTML page when the home page of this site contains an URL link using the ?OpenDatabase&3PaneUI command.

Fig. 8.11

The Notes 3 Pane UI generates scroll bars for Web clients. Windows can be sized by the Web client, and sizing the window is the only way to enlarge a window. Double-clicking a document here has no effect.

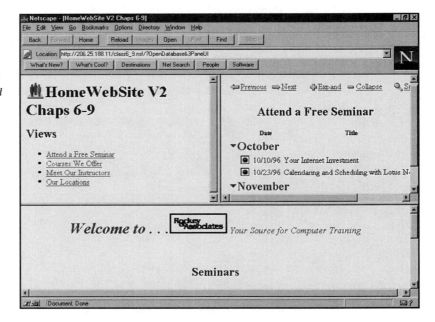

Although this certainly has a frame look and feel, it is not always evident to the Web user which of the views is selected. Note in the top-left pane of Figure 8.8, the current view is neither highlighted nor (and you undoubtedly can't see this in black and white) a different color than the others. By default, Domino does place the name of the view in the view template (upper-right pane); if the user scrolls down past the title, there is no further indication of the selection or name of the current view.

Since background colors can be used in forms and views, your 3 Pane UI can display different colors for the selected view as well as the corresponding document in the view.

In Figure 8.12, the view in the upper-right pane has a background color, and although you cannot see this color in a black and white image, you can see that the view pane is a different shade of gray.

Fig. 8.12

The Notes 3Pane UI with background color in view. A border appears around the bullets in the view, as a result of the absence of "\ border=0" in the HTML code.

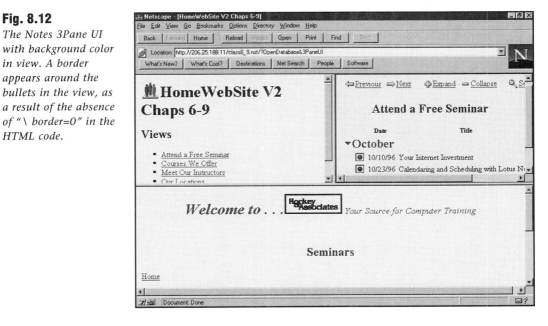

Opening Documents by Key

Creating a view with a key column allows you to use an URL to open a document, or generate a link to a document by key. The benefit here is found in the example of a database used to store images. In such a database, one might have an attached file in each document, using the file name as the key.

To facilitate this, create a sorted view. Sort on the first key column. Then, use the syntax:

http://Host/DatabaseName/View/FileName?OpenFile

where view is the name of the view (use + where spaces are found in the name) and Filename is the key that appears in the first sorted column.

The key is not case-sensitive, and if Domino finds more than one match, the first match found will be returned.

This method can also be used to open documents with the ?Opendocument URL command as follows:

http://Host/DatabaseName/View/DocumentName?OpenDocument

where DocumentName is the key that appears in the first sorted column.

Once you have created a view that uses a key, you can also use @Commands to link to documents. Create an action button or action hotspot that combines two @commands, one to select the document, the other to open it. Use the key argument with the ([OpenView]) or ([FileOpenDatabase]) @commands, and to open or edit the document use the ([Opendocument]) @command. Both of these @commands are required for Domino to generate the URL.

The syntax for this type of @command is:

```
@Command([OpenView];"ViewName";"key");@Command(OpenDocument)
```

where "*ViewName*" is the name of the view and "*key*" is the key that appears in the first sorted column.

Listed as follows are the only @Command combinations that will give the required results in a view action. If you want the document to be opened in edit mode, you must refine the [OpenDocument] argument to "1" to edit and "0" to read. The following examples are the only legal combinations @Command arguments that can be used in this way:

```
@Command([OpenView]); "ViewName"; "key"); @Command ([OpenDocument])
```

or

```
@Command([FileOpenDatabase]);"";"DatabaseName"; "ViewName"; "key"); @Command
([OpenDocument])
```

or

```
@Command([OpenView]); "Registered Users"; @UserName); @Command ([OpenDocument])
```

or

```
@Command([FileOpenDatabase]); "" :  "Register.nsf"; "Registered Users" ;@UserName);
@Command ([OpenDocument])
```

To append the OpenDocument command to open the document in edit mode, add a "1." The default is "0" to read:

```
@Command([OpenView]); "ViewName"; "key"); @Command ([OpenDocument];1)
```

Using Default View Qualifiers

The Domino URL command uses a special qualifier to identify a default view. That qualifier, $defaultView, can include explicit and implicit actions, such as ?OpenView and ?Search. To open the default view of a database, use the following Domino URL:

http://Host/DatabaseName/$DefaultView

You could append this URL with the ?OpenView command, but should you leave it out, Domino defaults to ?Open.

Domino URL commands can include arguments such as the following URL which opens and expands a view:

http://Host/DatabaseName/NameOfView/?OpenView&ExpandView

By default, Domino presents views in a collapsed mode to the Web client. Using a Domino URL with arguments to link to a view is one method of assuring the view will open in Expanded mode. Using a Notes view link will link to the view, but the view will be presented in collapsed mode to the Web client.

From Here...

As you read in this chapter, most of Notes view properties and elements are converted to HTML by Domino. With little or no intervention, Domino provides a consistent look and feel to the views in your databases as it serves them to the Web client. You can further embellish your views with GIF files or by rearranging column titles to provide logical anchors for Web users.

Further, you can customize the view template, or create your own from scratch.

For more information on working with Views on the Web, see the following chapters:

▶ Chapter 3, "Working with Your Domino Web Site," explains in detail the use of Domino URL commands for navigating and linking at your site.

▶ See Chapter 6, "Designing Forms to Display Documents on the Web," for a more comprehensive list of @Commands applicable to Web clients.

▶ See Chapter 10, "Using Special Web Fields and Forms" for information on creating forms (templates) which contain views, navigators, and search results.

▶ See Chapter 13, "Examining Special Function Databases for the Web," to learn more about the use of opening documents by key, and the creation of views that use keys.

## chapter 9

Preparing to Go Public

In this chapter

◆ **Defining the Access Control List**
Access to Notes databases from Web clients is controlled through a list defined in each database of who can or cannot open the database as well as what they are initially able to do once they gain entry to the database. This includes reading, creating, editing, and deleting documents.

◆ **Identifying the Home Page**
There are several options for creating a home Page to guide users through your Web site. Here, you will see what those options are and how to set them.

◆ **Controlling Web access**
You can control whether a database will appear in a list of databases when a Web user uses the ?open command and whether users are permitted to see any list of databases using the ?open or ?openServer commands. In this chapter, we show you how.

◆ **Creating a database template**
Creating a design template allows you to make design changes to your database while working outside of the production copy. Here, we show you the advantages of using a design template and how to create it.

O kay, your Domino server and databases are ready for prime time. Before you unleash your data to the millions of Web users who you anticipate will hit your site, you should determine just how much you want them to see and what types of access they should have to the databases, views, and documents you've prepared. There are definite steps that should be taken to ensure that your site is used appropriately and to provide data to those that should receive it. These steps should also provide the database developer with an easy method of making and applying changes to the database design.

Defining the Access Control List

Each Notes database contains its own Access Control List (ACL) that determines who can access the database and what impact they can have on the data once accessed. The names contained in the ACL can be the names of individual Notes users with valid Notes ID's, or Web users who have had their name and a password registered in the Public Address Book. Names specified in the Access Control List can also include group names which have been defined in the Public Address Book, as well as one of several predefined "group" names that the Domino server is aware of and prepared to handle. For additional information on the registration process, see Chapter 13, "Examining Special Function Databases for the Web."

The name "Anonymous" is available as a predefined name to define the "group" of all Web users that are not registered in the Public Address Book. If "Anonymous" is not defined in the ACL, the access level given to the "Default" entry is used instead. There are seven levels of database access available within each database ACL. They are:

▶ *Manager*. This level of access is not appropriate for Web browsers. A database manager can perform any of the tasks that any of the lower levels are able to perform, but in addition, can define the ACL settings for the database. Only a Notes client can make changes to the ACL.

▶ *Designer*. This level of access is not appropriate for Web browsers. A database designer can perform any of the tasks that any of the lower levels are able to perform, but, in addition, can create and change the design elements of the database. Only a Notes client can make design changes.

▶ *Editor*. This level of access provides users with the ability to create pages and edit all pages in the database. Although this level of access is appropriate for Web users, you should be cautious in assigning Editor access. This is because everyone with this level of access can change any page in the database that they want including those that they have not created.

▶ *Author*. This level of access provides users with the ability to create page content and edit the pages they have created. This is appropriate access for most databases where user interaction is required. Discussion databases are usually set this way.

▶ *Reader*. This level of access provides users with the ability to read documents in the database but not create or edit documents.

▶ *Depositor*. This level of access provides users with the ability to create documents, but, once created, users cannot see the document they have created or any other document in the database.

▶ *No Access*. This level of access prevents users from opening the database.

The Editor, Author, Reader, Depositor, and No Access levels are appropriate for defining what a Web user can and can't do with a Notes Database.

Some examples of ACL's for databases are:

A highly restricted database that requires Notes user identification (authentication):

Default	No Access
Anonymous	No Access
Readers Group	Reader
Authors Group	Author
Data Managers Group	Editor

For a database that is published for reader access by web users:

Default	Reader

Or

Anonymous	Reader
Notes Readers	Reader
Authors Group	Author
Editors Group	Editor

For a database that is available for "discussion" purposes to Web users:

Default	Author
Anonymous	Author
Editors Group	Editor

9

There are a few other considerations to setting the ACL on a database. One is the Maximum Internet browser access allowed. This is set in the Advanced section of the Access Control List screen. This setting determines the highest level of access for any Web client, which means that if the name Anonymous is set to Editor, but the Maximum Internet browser access is set to Reader, the Web clients would be restricted to Reader access. By default this setting is "Editor" but may be set lower if you want to restrict access to all Web clients to a lower level of access.

The second consideration is on the Basics screen for the Access Control List under the Access option. The two settings that can be controlled from here are Create documents and Delete documents. After the Access level has been determined for an entry, such as Author access, the restrictions for creating and deleting pages can be set.

Additional security features are available for Notes databases on the Web and are covered in more detail in Chapter 14, "Securing the Domino Web Server," and Chapter 15, "Using Secure Sockets Layer (SSL) with Domino."

In general:

For any database that will be accessible by all Web users for reading only, set an ACL entry for "Anonymous" and set the access level at Reader.

If a database is available to Web users for entering information, set an ACL entry for "Anonymous" and set the access level at Author.

Authenticating Registered Web Users

To require a Web user to enter a registered name and password to gain access to a database, set up an ACL entry for "Anonymous" and set the access level at No Access. This will cause any Web user who tries to gain entry to be prompted for their user name and password. This method is used in conjunction with the Domino Registration Application as discussed in Chapter 13.

You can also create a Domino URL which requires authentication regardless of how the access control list is set. In this way, any anonymous Web users who entered the site without authentication would be required to supply a name and password to access other databases, views, and areas of the site, or to complete tasks which require authentication.

Append the Login argument to any Domino URL. Add this argument to the Home URL field in the Server Document or as a link from the home page to a restricted database. The syntax for this URL and argument is:

> **http://host/OpenServer&Login**
> **http://host/DatabaseDirectory/DatabaseName?OpenDatabase&login**

To set basic authentication for Web users allowing them individual database access, you need to create a person document or use a registration database. See Chapter 14, "Securing the Domino Web Server," for information on registering Web Users. See also Chapter 13, "Examining Special Function Databases for the Web," which explains the details of a registration database.

Identifying the Home Page

If your database or application contains the site home page, you need to identify the home page in the server document by providing the Domino URL as explained later. The site home page is, of course, the first page a Web user will come across when visiting your site.

Each database can also have its own home page. You might want to launch a navigator for some databases, the About Database document for others. Identifying the database home page is a simple task and is described in the next section.

You can also create a *form* that can serve as the site or as a database home page. Using a form allows you to include fields and even views and navigators on the form. This method is described in Chapter 10, "Using Special Web Fields and Forms."

Designating The Database Home Page

To identify the About Database document as the home page for a database, highlight the database icon, and then from the Notes menu, choose File, Database Properties. Click the Launch tab as shown in Figure 9.1.

Fig. 9.1

If a database uses the About Database Document as the home page and is going to be used by both Notes and Web clients, consider using a Domino URL command instead of launching the About Database document on open. Then, your Notes clients will not have to view the About Database document every time they access the database.

9

In this tab, the fields On Database Open and Navigator define what will be displayed to a user as the home page when the database is accessed.

In the field On Database Open, all options are supported on the Web except for Launch 1st attachment in "About Database." The remainder are interpreted by the Web as described in Table 9.1.

Table 9.1   On Database Open Options

Option	Result on the Web
Restore as last viewed by user	Displays the database Show folders navigator
Open Designated Navigator	Opens the named navigator in its own window
Open Designated Navigator in its own window	Opens the named navigator in its own window
Launch 1st doclink in "About Database"	Opens the document linked in the about document

Designating the Site Home Page

After you have designed the home page that will act as the gateway to the rest of your Web site, you must define it as the default page for all Web users to access. This will provide the same consistent starting point for your site, even if a Web user is accessing your server by its site or host name. To set up the site home page, you must modify the server document in the Public Address Book for the Domino server that will host your site. To modify the server document, open the address book to the servers view, then open the appropriate server document by highlighting the document in the view and selecting the Edit action from the action bar.

The information you are looking for is in the HTTP server section. Once open, look at the information under the heading Mapping as shown in Figure 9.2.

The field that must be set is the home URL. This should reflect the name of the database that contains the home page for the site. You can use one of the following URLs or Domino URL commands if you have set the database default to open to the About Database Document:

```
/DataBaseName
/DatabaseDirectory\DatabaseName
/DatabaseName/?Open
```

Alternatively, the URL syntax could be:

http://Host/Database/$about?OpenAbout

Fig. 9.2

The Mapping section of the Server Document sets defaults for the site home page. If the database containing the home page is located in the server default data directory, it is not necessary to include the path.

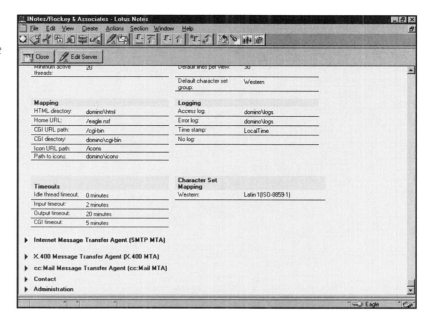

Controlling Web Access

Although the Access Control List determines who can access a database, there are additional settings that can determine whether a database can be accessed by a Web user or what portions of a database can be accessed by the Web user.

If a database on the Web server should not be accessed by curious Web browsers, there are two settings that can be deselected to accomplish this. You can control:

▶ If a database appears in the list of databases when a Web user uses the ?open command.

▶ If Web users are permitted to see *any* list of databases at all, using the ?open or ?OpenServer commands.

Figure 9.3 shows the resulting HTML page when a Web user types the Domino URL command:

http:/Host/?Open

Fig. 9.3

*Browsing a Domino
server, access to the list
of databases can be
achieved with the
?Open or ?OpenServer
commands.*

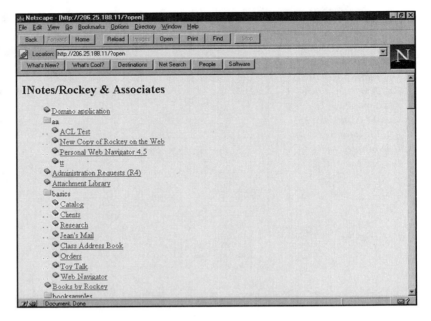

To keep a database from displaying in the list of databases on the server (you might want
to do this for your Public Address Book), open the Database properties dialog box, and
choose the Design tab. In the Options List in Database Catalog, deselect Show in Open
Database dialog. When deselected, this will prevent the datatabase from appearing in the
list shown in Figure 9.3. Figure 9.4 shows the database properties design tab. This will
also prevent Notes users from seeing the database in the File Database Open dialog box.

Fig. 9.4

*Deselect Show in
'Open Database'
Dialog to prevent
databases from
appearing in your list
of databases when
users type the Domino
?Open command.*

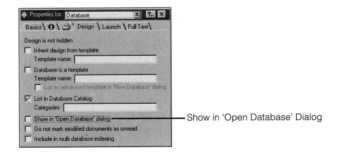

To keep a Web user from browsing your site with the Domino ?open command, open the
Server Document, expand the Security Section (see Figure 9.5) and set Allow HTTP Clients to Browse Databases to No. This disallows the use of the following commands:

http://Host/?OpenServer

and

http://Host/?Open

Fig. 9.5

Although you can prevent Web users from using the //Host/?Open or //Host?OpenServer commands success-fully, you are effec-tively only denying access to a list of databases. If the user knows the specific names of files, forms, views, and so forth, they can still browse the site with such commands as //Host/DatabaseName/?Open.

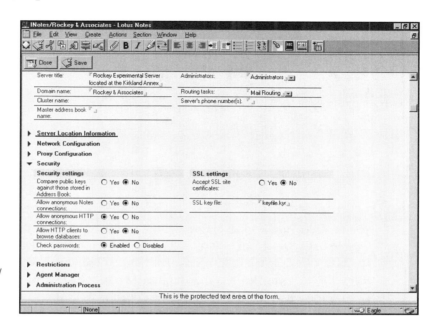

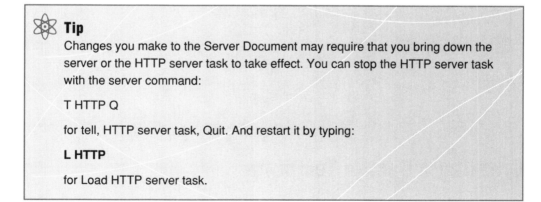

Tip

Changes you make to the Server Document may require that you bring down the server or the HTTP server task to take effect. You can stop the HTTP server task with the server command:

T HTTP Q

for tell, HTTP server task, Quit. And restart it by typing:

L HTTP

for Load HTTP server task.

Keeping Documents from Web Users

To restrict *document* access within the database, access lists can be set for reading docu-ments in a view and for creating documents and reading documents created with a spe-cific form.

To restrict access to documents within a *view*, a view access list is maintained. To assign users to a view access list, open the view in Design mode and right-click the mouse to choose the View Properties dialog box. Then click the key tab to reveal the view access list. To restrict access to documents in the view, deselect the box for May Be Used by All Readers and Above, and select from the list of names provided those who may access the documents in that view (see Figure 9.6).

Fig. 9.6
The Key Tab of the View Properties dialog box allows you to set access to the view.

Restrict access to documents through the *form* used to create that document, open the form in design mode and right-click the mouse to choose the Form Properties dialog box. Then click the Key tab to reveal the Form access options. To restrict read access or create access for the form, deselect the appropriate box and select from the list of names provided those who may read or create the documents, as shown in Figure 9.7.

Fig. 9.7
The Key Tab of the Form Property Box allows you to set who can read and who can create documents using the form.

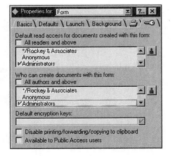

Creating a Design Template

A design template is a copy of a Notes database that contains the design elements of the database without the data. When a database is available on the Web or placed into production, design changes to the database should not be made to the live database. Therefore, it is important to know how to create a database design template that can be used to refresh the design of the production database when changes must be applied.

Design templates have unique characteristics that make them easily recognizable. They use a filename extension of .NTF and they have a separate template name that is defined in the database properties. The template name is used to associate the template with the database that inherits its design from the template.

To Create a design template from a live database:

1. Highlight the database icon and choose File, Database, New Copy. Figure 9.8 shows the Copy database dialog box.

2. Choose the Domino server as the server on which to place the new database.

Fig. 9.8

The Copy Database dialog box. Give your design template as the production copy of the database, to facilitate easy identification between the two databases.

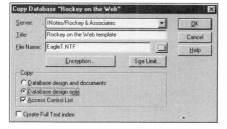

3. Enter the filename for the template, making sure the extension is NTF and that the file will be stored in the default data directory. It is important that the template be available to the server process that runs at night to update the database designs. This process looks for template files on the server in the default data directory.

4. Choose Database Design Only under the copy heading.

5. Click OK to create the template file.

9

When created, you must assign a template name to the file. To do this, highlight the template icon, choose File, Database Properties, then choose the Design tab. Within the Design tab, check the box next to Database is a Design Template and then type in a name for the template below in the Template Name field, as shown in Figure 9.9.

Fig. 9.9

A template name must be assigned to the file. The Design tab provides the field in which you supply the template name.

The template is now complete. Next, you must assign the template to the database to ensure automatic updates will occur. To do this, highlight the production database icon, choose File, Database Properties, then choose the Design tab. Within the Design tab, check the box next to Inherits its Design From and then type the name you gave to the template in the Template Name field.

This completes the template design creation and definition. Whenever a design change is made to the template, the live database will be refreshed at night.

Caution
Once a design template has been assigned to a database, do not make design changes directly in the database, because they will be overwritten when the design is refreshed by the server process. At this point all changes should be made through the design template.

From Here...

As you can see, creating a design template is an effective way to make changes to the database design. Using this template, you can test the result of your changes prior to affecting the production copy of the database. Templates are commonly used through Notes application design. For other template information see the following chapters:

▶ Chapter 13, "Examining Special Function Databases for the Web," describes registration and discussion database templates available for Web applications.

Advanced Domino Application Design Techniques for the Web

## chapter 10

Using Special Web Fields and Forms

10

by Jane Calabria

In this chapter

- ◆ **How to use special reserved fields such as $$ViewBody**
- ◆ **How to create view templates with $$ViewTemplateDefault and $$ViewList forms and fields**
- ◆ **How to create navigator templates using a form named $$NavigatorTemplate**

Domino provides you with the opportunity to customize your views, navigators, and searches by embedding special reserved fields into specially named forms. Here, we show you.

Customizing Database Elements for Viewing on the Web

When you access an unaltered Notes database through a Web browser, Domino displays the database's views in a *template*. This template and the list of views are generated dynamically. As you see in Figure 10.1, each view in the list appears as an HTML hyperlink. Domino created the template on-the-fly with no customization by a developer.

Fig. 10.1

The default view list template accessed by links or by the Domino URL: **http://host/ DatabaseName/ ?open**.

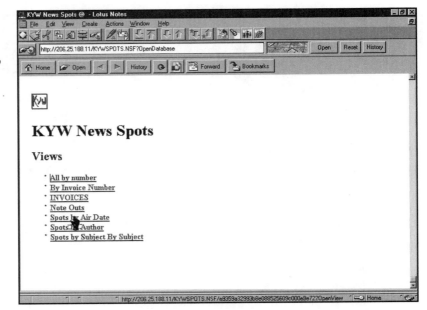

Not only does Domino create a template to display view lists, when the user clicks a view link, Domino will also create a template to display the documents in the view. Figure 10.2 shows all the documents in the Spots by Air Date view as well as i cons for navigating to the previous and next documents, for expanding and collapsing categories, and for searching that part of the default template.

Fig. 10.2

The default view template displaying the documents as well as navigation icons and the action bar.

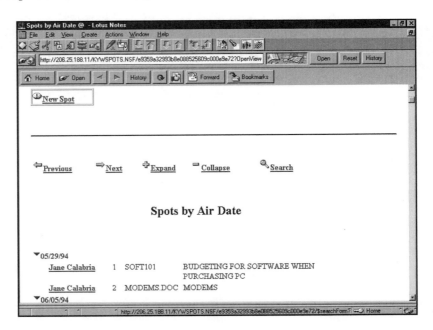

When Domino generates the template that displays a list of views, it is actually creating a *form* named $$ViewTemplateDefault. Search as you may, you will not find the $$ViewTemplateDefault form in the Notes database. The form is generated dynamically by the Domino server and contains a reserved and required field name, $$ViewList, which distinguishes it from other Notes forms.

If a database was designed to display a graphic navigator or About database document when opened, the navigator or About document appears instead of the list of views. If the database has not been reengineered for the Web, the browser goes no further since no links appear to direct the user.

If you want to create your own form for displaying views, it is simple to do. Create a new form, place the reserved field $$ViewList where you want the list to appear, and name the form $$ViewTemplateDefault. This new form will automatically replace the default Domino form and be accessed by browsers. Figure 10.3 shows a customized form named $$ViewTemplateDefault.

Fig. 10.3

This customized view template includes navigators for the view as well as links for navigating the site contained in a subform.

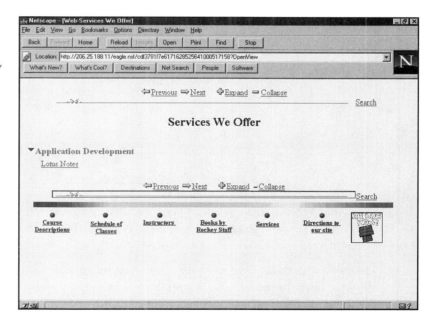

10

Domino also uses a reserved field called $$ViewBody, which contains a view, rather than a list of views. With this field, you can create a view template for individual views, by naming each view *$$ViewTemplate for viewname*. These procedures are explained here in this chapter.

Domino also generates, on-the-fly, a template to deliver search results on the Web. That template is called $$SearchTemplateDefault and contains the reserved field, $$ViewBody. In this case, the $$ViewBody displays the search results.

Fig. 10.4

The default search results view Domino returns if no $$SearchTemplateDefault form is created in the database.

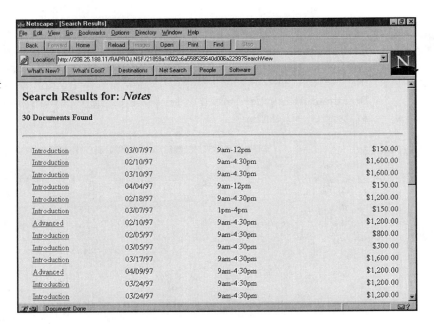

You might wish to display a navigator *and* a list of views in the same HTML document. Or, you might want to customize the search results page to include pointers to other areas of your site, such as the home page.

Notes provides a series of tools that allow you to enhance Notes databases so that lists of views, lists of documents, navigators, and search results appear as elements on a page, along with other text and graphics elements. In effect, you can merge views, navigators, and search results with forms. You can then name those forms with special template names, resulting in a consistent and customized look to your views.

This merger of tools is done within the design of the Notes *form*. Keep in mind that the About Database Document, often used as a Site Home Page, is a single rich-text field and therefore cannot contain fields that result in the display of lists of views, documents, navigators, or search results.

By creating forms that act as templates for views, navigators, or search results, the user sees a resulting page that includes textual and graphic enhancements that normally appear only on forms.

There are two approaches to using these tools and the difference is quite subtle. The first approach enhances *forms* (therefore documents) by embedding views, view lists, and navigators in them.

The second approach enhances *views*, *navigators*, and *search* results with elements that normally appear only on forms.

Understanding $$ Reserved Field Names

Domino reserves certain field names for Web applications. You can embed a list of views, a view, or a navigator in a form by creating fields using the following reserved field names:

- **$$ViewList**—returns a list of available views and folders in the database. They appear as they do in the standard Folders navigator.

- **$$ViewBody**—returns the contents of a specific view in the database. You may use only one $$ViewBody field per form. Search results are displayed in a view; therefore this field can also be used in creating search result templates.

- **$$NavigatorBody** or **$$NavigatorBody_n**—returns a specific navigator in the database. You may use more than one $$NavigatorBody field in a form; if you do use more than one, name them $$NavigatorBody_1, $$NavigatorBody_2, and so on.

These fields may be Editable, Computed, Computed for display, or Computed when composed. They should be of data type *text*. $$ViewBody and $$NavigatorBody field definitions must include a string value equal to the name of a view or navigator; or they must include a formula that resolves to the name of a view or navigator. $$ViewList field definitions need not include any value; in fact any value you supply will be ignored by Domino.

Create these fields where you want the element to appear on a form. You may place these fields in collapsible sections or in tables. These fields have no effect when viewing the resulting document from within Notes; they affect only documents seen from a Web browser. Figure 10.5 shows a navigator and a list of views displayed on the same form.

10

Fig. 10.5

In this form, named $$ViewNavigator For RockBlocks (the navigator name), the $$NavigatorBody field is placed in cell A1 of a table. Cell A2 contains the $$ViewList field.

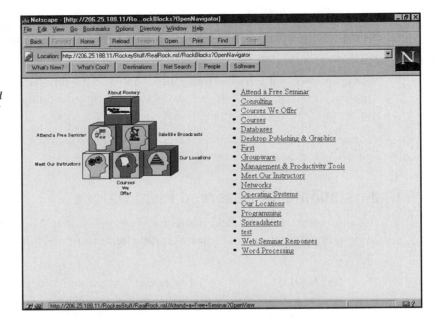

Understanding $$ Reserved Form Names

Domino reserves certain form names for use in Web applications. You may create custom views, navigators, or search results pages by creating forms that use the following, reserved form names:

▶ **$$ViewTemplate for *viewname***—where *viewname* is the alias or name of a view. This form must include a $$ViewBody field for *viewname*.

▶ **$$ViewTemplateDefault**—All views not associated with a specific form using $$ViewTemplate for *viewname* will be displayed using this form.

▶ **$$NavigatorTemplate for *navigatorname***—where *navigatorname* is the alias or name of a navigator. This form must include a $$NavigatorBody field for *navigatorname*.

▶ **$$NavigatorTemplateDefault**—All navigators not associated with a specific form using $$ViewTemplate for *navigatorname* will be displayed using this form.

▶ **$$SearchTemplate for *viewname***—where *viewname* is the alias or name of a view. This form must include a $$ViewBody field for *viewname*; the search results will appear in the $$ViewBody field.

▶ **$$SearchTemplateDefault**—All search results from views not associated with a specific search results form using $$SearchTemplate for *viewname* will be displayed using this form.

▶ **$$SearchSiteTemplate**—If you create this form in a *site search database*, all re-
sults of all site searches from this database will display using this form. For more
information, see Domino Site Searches later in this chapter.

The effect of creating these forms is that whenever someone opens a view or navigator
that is associated with the form, the view or navigator will appear on-screen framed in
the form. Thus, the forms act as templates and you tend to refer to them as such. When-
ever someone conducts a search that is affected by one of these templates, the search
results will appear framed by the form. So, you can include custom text, graphic ele-
ments, anything you want in these forms; the resulting Web pages will look customized,
not generic.

If you do not generate these templates yourself, Domino creates the templates when it
serves the view, navigator, or search page to the Web client.

To understand the templates, and layout of a template, it helps to see the resulting
HTML code after Domino generates the default templates. Below is the HTML code
generated by Domino. You can use your browser to view source code.

In Listing 10.1, you can see where Domino places title information, opens a view
(?OpenView&Start=1), sets the default at no wrap for the view (NOWRAP), and places
the expand, collapse, next, previous, and search icons on the view. Note the Domino
URLs used for expanding and collapsing views.

Listing 10.1   Domino-Generated HTML Code

```
<HTML>
<!-- Lotus Domino Web Server Release 1.5 (RC1, Build 165 on Windows NT/Intel) -->
<HEAD>
<TITLE>Attend a Free Seminar</TITLE><BODY TEXT="000000" BGCOLOR="ffffff">
<CENTER>
<TABLE CELLSPACING=2 CELLPADDING=2>
<TR VALIGN=top><TD><A
HREF="/fakeRock.nsf/643d07d5ce494eaa8525638a006721f9?OpenView&Start=1"><IMG
SRC="/icons/prevview.gif" BORDER=0 ALIGN=top>Previous</A></TD><TD><A
HREF="/fakeRock.nsf/643d07d5ce494eaa8525638a006721f9?OpenView&Start=2.1"><IMG
SRC="/icons/nextview.gif" BORDER=0 ALIGN=top>Next</A></TD><TD><A
HREF="/fakeRock.nsf/643d07d5ce494eaa8525638a006721f9?OpenView&ExpandView"><IMG
SRC="/icons/expview.gif" BORDER=0 ALIGN=top>Expand</A></TD><TD><A
HREF="/fakeRock.nsf/643d07d5ce494eaa8525638a006721f9?OpenView&CollapseView"><IMG
SRC="/icons/colview.gif" BORDER=0 ALIGN=top>Collapse</A></TD><TD><A
HREF="/fakeRock.nsf/643d07d5ce494eaa8525638a006721f9/$searchForm?SearchView"><IMG
SRC="/icons/schview.gif" BORDER=0 ALIGN=top>Search</A></TD></TR>
</TABLE>
</CENTER><CENTER><H2>Attend a Free Seminar</H2></CENTER>
<TABLE>
<TR>
<TH NOWRAP><B><FONT SIZE=2></FONT></B></TH>
```

continues

10

Listing 10.1   Continued

```
<TH NOWRAP><B><FONT SIZE=2></FONT></B></TH>

<TH NOWRAP><B><FONT SIZE=2>Date</FONT></B></TH>

<TH NOWRAP><B><FONT SIZE=2>Title</FONT></B></TH>

<TH NOWRAP><B><FONT SIZE=2>Location</FONT></B></TH>
</TR>

<TR VALIGN=top><TD COLSPAN=5 NOWRAP><A
HREF="/fakeRock.nsf 643d07d5ce494eaa8525638a006721f9?OpenView&Start=1&Count=30&Col
➡lapse=1#1"><IMG SRC="/icons/collapse.gif" BORDER=0 ALT="- "></A><B><FONT SIZE=5
COLOR="0000ff">October</FONT></B></TD></TR>

<TR VALIGN=top><TD NOWRAP></TD><TD NOWRAP><A><IMG SRC="/icons/ecblank.gif"
BORDER=0 ALT="  "></A><A
HREF="/fakeRock.nsf/643d07d5ce494eaa8525638a006721f9/c0e1a98f2a61198e8525638a00684
➡ef0?OpenDocument"><img src=/icons/new.gif  BORDER=0></A></TD><TD
NOWRAP>10/10/96</TD><TD NOWRAP>Your Internet Investment</TD><TD NOWRAP>Bala
Cynwyd</TD></TR>

<TR VALIGN=top><TD NOWRAP></TD><TD NOWRAP><A><IMG SRC="/icons/ecblank.gif"
BORDER=0 ALT="  "></A><A
HREF="/fakeRock.nsf/643d07d5ce494eaa8525638a006721f9/c430da84cb4c97098525638a00066f
➡3fd?OpenDocument"><img src=/icons/new.gif  BORDER=0></A></TD><TD
NOWRAP>10/23/96</TD><TD NOWRAP>Calendaring and Scheduling with Lotus Notes</TD><TD
NOWRAP>Bala Cynwyd, PA</TD></TR>

<TR VALIGN=top><TD COLSPAN=5 NOWRAP><A
HREF="/fakeRock.nsf/643d07d5ce494eaa8525638a006721f9?OpenView&Start=1&Count=30&Col
➡lapse=2#2"><IMG SRC="/icons/collapse.gif" BORDER=0 ALT="- "></A><B><FONT SIZE=5
COLOR="0000ff">November</FONT></B></TD></TR>

<TR VALIGN=top><TD NOWRAP></TD><TD NOWRAP><A><IMG SRC="/icons/ecblank.gif"
BORDER=0 ALT="  "></A><A
HREF="/fakeRock.nsf/643d07d5ce494eaa8525638a006721f9/6bb07ac9e1846c7e8525638a00689
➡37c?OpenDocument"><img src=/icons/new.gif  BORDER=0></A></TD><TD
NOWRAP>11/19/96</TD><TD NOWRAP>Lotus Notes Components</TD><TD NOWRAP>Bala
Cynwyd</TD></TR>
</TABLE>
<CENTER>
<TABLE CELLSPACING=2 CELLPADDING=2>
<TR VALIGN=top><TD><A
HREF="/fakeRock.nsf/643d07d5ce494eaa8525638a006721f9?OpenView&Start=1"><IMG
SRC="/icons/prevview.gif" BORDER=0 ALIGN=top>Previous</A></TD><TD><A
HREF="/fakeRock.nsf/643d07d5ce494eaa8525638a006721f9?OpenView&Start=2.1"><IMG
SRC="/icons/nextview.gif" BORDER=0 ALIGN=top>Next</A></TD><TD><A
HREF="/fakeRock.nsf/643d07d5ce494eaa8525638a006721f9?OpenView&ExpandView"><IMG
SRC="/icons/expview.gif" BORDER=0 ALIGN=top>Expand</A></TD><TD><A
HREF="/fakeRock.nsf/643d07d5ce494eaa8525638a006721f9?OpenView&CollapseView"><IMG
SRC="/icons/colview.gif" BORDER=0 ALIGN=top>Collapse</A></TD><TD><A
HREF="/fakeRock.nsf/643d07d5ce494eaa8525638a006721f9/$searchForm?SearchView"><IMG
SRC="/icons/schview.gif" BORDER=0 ALIGN=top>Search</A></TD></TR>
</TABLE>
</CENTER>
```

By now, you know that you don't have to create this code yourself. Domino will do it for you. But, we are hoping you are interested enough in the Notes to HTML conversion to want to explore some HTML pages created by Domino to better understand Domino's interpretations.

You won't have to create customized templates yourself, either. Well, at least not from scratch. Lotus has always been generous with its Notes information, databases, techniques, and design "secrets," and Web templates are no exception.

Creating Custom Views, Navigators, and Search Templates

The easiest way to create custom templates is to base your templates on those provided by Lotus at the Domino Web site (**www.Domino.Lotus.com**) in several databases you can download. Those databases include:

▶ View Template Samples, *Stdvwtmo.nsf*

contains two sample view templates.

▶ Navigator Samples, *Navsamp.nsf*

contains a home page image map sample. Copy this into a form and name it $$ViewNavigatorDefault, then customize it.

▶ Domino Samples: Discussion, *DomDisc.nsf*

contains a form named $$ViewTemplateDefault, which displays a list of views with the currently selected view highlighted in a list of views. A bullet also appears next to the current view.

The Domino site is updated frequently. You should visit the download area of the site often to take advantage of the databases and samples that Lotus makes available.

10

Customized View Templates

The View Template Samples database includes two sample view templates you can copy into your database and customize as you wish.

The first template (or form) contains hotspots with @commands that navigate the user to the next and previous pages of the view. It also contains hotspots for expanding and collapsing the view as well as a search icon. Figure 10.6 shows this template in design mode. This template also contains the field $$ViewBody which displays a view in the database. It contains a formula that results to the name of that view.

Fig. 10.6

$$ViewTemplateDefault in design mode in Notes. This template includes a $$ViewBody field to display the view contents and a field to display the view title.

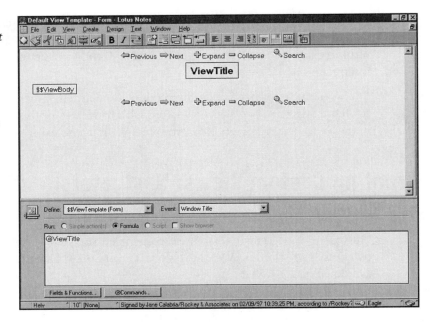

Copy this form into your database and you can customize it. In Figure 10.7, an animated GIF has been added to the form, as well as a subform that acts as a navigational footer.

Fig. 10.7

This custom view template includes navigators for the view as well as navigators for the site.

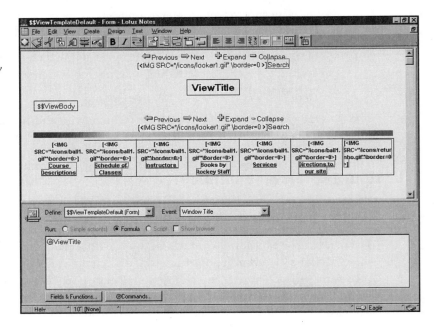

In design mode you can see that the GIF is inserted into the page using HTML passthru. A table is used to align images (bullets) and hypertext links to other areas of the site. Figure 10.8 shows this view template as seen through a Web browser.

Fig. 10.8

The bottom of this form includes a table with hypertext links and GIFs. Borders are turned off in the table and the text for the links is centered in each cell.

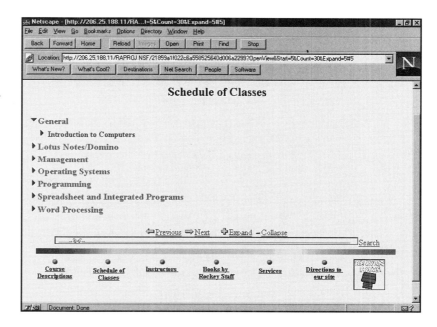

Embedding Views, View Lists, and Navigators in Forms

Another way to make your Web site look different from other Domino Web sites is to define a Notes form as a frame for a Notes view or navigator. In this case, whenever a Web user retrieves the view or navigator, it will appear within the defined form. When you retrieve a view or navigator, it appears "framed" in a form; that is, it has custom text and graphics above and below it. Does this sound very close to embedding a view, view list, or navigator in a form? The difference is that, with embedding, when you retrieve a document, it appears with a view, view list, or one or more navigators embedded in it.

To create a special form that Domino will use to frame a view or navigator when a Web user retrieves that view or navigator, you take the two following special steps when creating the form:

1. Name the form with one of the following special names:

> $$ViewTemplate for *viewname*, where *viewname* is the name or alias of a view

> $$ViewTemplateDefault

10

$$NavigatorTemplate for *navigatorrname*, where *navigatorrname* is the name or alias of a navigator

$$NavigatorTemplateDefault

Use $$ViewTemplate for *viewname* and $$NavigatorTemplate for *navigatorname* for a form that should be used only with one view or navigator.

Use $$ViewTemplateDefault or $$NavigatorTemplateDefault for a form that should be used with all views or navigators that are not otherwise associated with another view or navigator template form.

2. Insert a $$ViewBody field or $$ViewNavigator field in the form where you want the view(s) or navigator(s) to appear. See the previous section of this lesson for instructions regarding these two fields.

Examine the Lotus approach to this. Here, we dissect the Domino Discussion database made available for download at the Domino site. This database, named *domdisc.nsf*, is examined again in Chapter 13, "Examining Special Function Databases for the Web," but here, we investigate their interesting $$ViewTemplate form.

The view template for this database, as shown in Figure 10.9, contains actions for creating documents, searching, navigating, and a list of available views. This cool list of views stays active at all times; this is the default view template. What's different about this template is that the currently selected view is *highlighted* and *bulleted*.

Fig. 10.9

HTML Code is added to a viewtemplate formula to highlight and bullet the current view. This view uses URLs instead of actions on an action bar to create new topics.

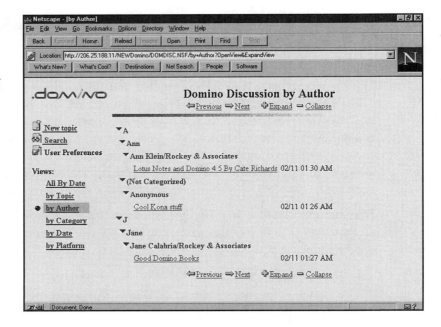

How'd they do that? Examining the form $$ViewTemplateDefault in design mode in Figure 10.10, you can see that the form contains only a few fields.

Fig. 10.10

This view contains a field whose value is a list of views, and a formula in the Views field to display the list of views in the template.

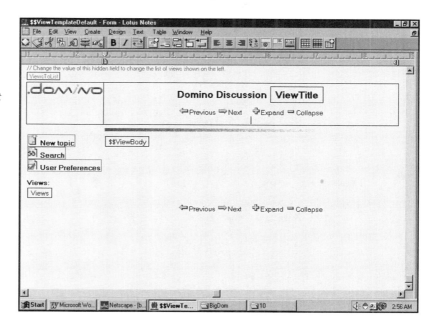

The ViewsToList field formula contains a list of all of the views in the database. The formula is simple:

"All By Date":

"by Topic":

"by Author":

"by Category":

"by Date":

"by Platform":

It is a text field, computed for display. It is a hidden field, as shown in Figure 10.11.

Fig. 10.11

The Properties box for the field "Field" shows that it is hidden, and that its formula lists the available views in the menu.

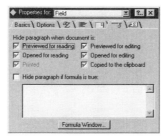

The *Views* field in Listing 10.2 contains the formula that places a bullet next to the active view (vwicn118). It also places gray highlighting around the active link by putting a color in the cell of the table containing the active link </td><td bgcolor=\"c0c0c0\">.

Listing 10.2   Views Field Formula

```
views := ViewsToList;
xs :=
"x":"x":"x":"x":"x":"x":"x":"x":"x":"x":"x":"x":"x":"x":"x":"x":"x":"x":"x":"x":"x":"x":"x":"x":"x":"x":"x":"x":"x":"x";
ncurr := @Member(@LowerCase(@ViewTitle); @LowerCase(views));
vmask := @Explode(@Implode(@If(
                          ncurr = 0;   @Subset(xs; @Elements(views));
                               @If( ncurr > 1; @Subset(xs; ncurr-1); "") :
                               "y":
                               @If( ncurr < @Elements(views); @Subset(xs;
@Elements(views) - ncurr); "")))));

anchors := " <a href=\"/" + @ReplaceSubstring(@Subset(@DbName; -1); "\\"; "/") +
"/" + @ReplaceSubstring(views; " "; "+") + "\"><b>" + views + "</b></a> ";

xrow := "<tr><td></td><td>";
yrow := "<tr><td><img src=\"/icons/vwicn118\"></td><td bgcolor=\"c0c0c0\">";

rows := @Replace(vmask; "x":"y"; xrow:yrow) + anchors + "</td></tr>";

"[<table>" + @Implode(rows; "") + "</table>]"
```

To change the value of the color-coded highlight, change the hexadecimal color value. The following example changes the highlight to yellow:

```
yrow := "<tr><td><img src=\"/icons/vwicn118\"></td><td bgcolor=\"F9C60F\">";
```

To change the bullet, simply replace the name of the file in the same line of the formula. The following replaces the bullet *vwicn118* with the animated GIF file called *reminder* as shown in Figure 10.12

```
yrow := "<tr><td><img src=\"/icons/reminder.gif\"></td><td bgcolor=\"F9C60F\">";
```

Caution

Before you replace your discussion database with this domdisc.nsf, read the "using" document provided with the database. This database uses agents and cookies, and you will need to make changes to the database prior to using it. Chapter 13, "Examining Special Function Databases for the Web," discusses this database in detail. At a minimum, read and follow the instructions provided in the *Using* document of the database.

Fig. 10.12
Because cell A1 contains a border (any border—on any side of the table), the entire table will display with a border on the Web. Here, an icon and highlight appear near and around the currently selected view.

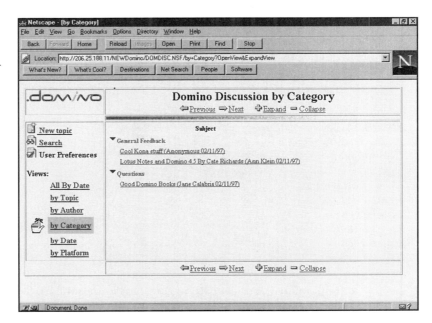

This template is obviously designed for a discussion database template. But the Views and ViewsToList field can be useful in your own database, and can be easily modified to suit your $$ViewTemplateDefault for any database by following the steps that follow. Note that in the example, we first copied the $$ViewTemplateDefault form from the Lotus database, View Template Samples, *Stdvwtmo.nsf*. We then copied the fields *$ViewsToList* and *Views* from the Domino Discussion Database, *domdisc.nsf*, as described in step 1 as follows.

1. Copy the field *$ViewsToList* from domdisc.nsf into the $$ViewTemplateDefault form of your database.
2. Change the value of the $ViewsToList field to include the names of the views you wish to show to Web users. In the formula box, list your views in quotes and separated by a colon as shown in Figure 10.13.

Fig. 10.13
The ViewsToList field is a computed-for-display text field whose value is a list of available views.

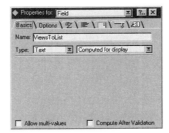

3. Copy the field *Views* from domdisc.nsf into the $$ViewTemplateDefault form of your database. You need not change any values in this field unless you want to change the color of the highlighted text or the icon (bullet) that appears next to the active view (as described in steps 4 and 5, as follows). Figure 10.14 shows the HTML code indicating the color of the highlighted text.

Fig. 10.14

A color is added to the cell containing the field "Views." Since "Views" also has an HTML table and color associated with it, we are essentially creating a nested cell.

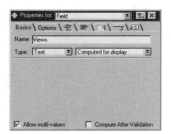

4. (Optional) The bullet used in the Lotus form (vwicon118) is located in the /icons directory of Domino, so you are in good shape and Domino should find the icon. If you are storing icons in another directory and have changed the default icon directory in the server document, you need to be certain that this icon is in the proper directory. Alternatively, if you wish to use a different icon, be certain that you have placed the icon in the appropriate directory on the Domino Web server.

5. (Optional) To change the highlight color, change the value for the color as described earlier.

6. Make certain that your $$ViewTemplateDefault form contains the field $$ViewBody and the field $ViewTitle. Figure 10.15 shows the $ViewTemplateDefault created using these steps as viewed through a Web browser.

 Tip

To prevent line wrap in your *view* on the Web, specify 1 in the Lines Per Heading and Lines Per Row fields on the Options tab of the View Properties Box.

Consider the size of your view. If you place the $$ViewBody field in a table (as seen in Figure 10.15), the default setting for tables is *Fit Table Width to Window*. This may cause wrapping in your $ViewBody field, as well as the *View* field, if they are contained in the same table.

Adjust the view font and the information or number of columns in the view so that the information displayed by the $$ViewBody field actually fits in the table. Alternatively, disable *Fit Table Width to Window* on the Layout tab of the Table Properties box to allow your view to scroll off the right side of the browser window.

Fig. 10.15
As seen through a Web browser, a highlighted view (the current view) is displayed within a Notes table which has a colored cell.

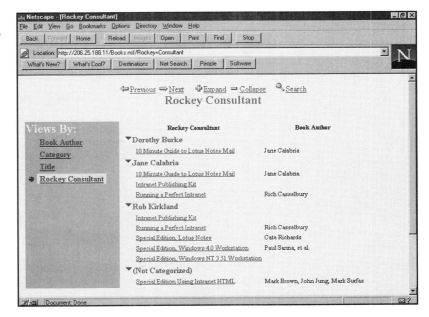

Creating Custom Search and Search Result Pages

When a user selects an URL containing a $SearchForm object, Domino will search the database for a form (or alias) named $$Search. If no such form exists, Domino displays the default search.htm file located in the icons directory as shown in Figure 10.16.

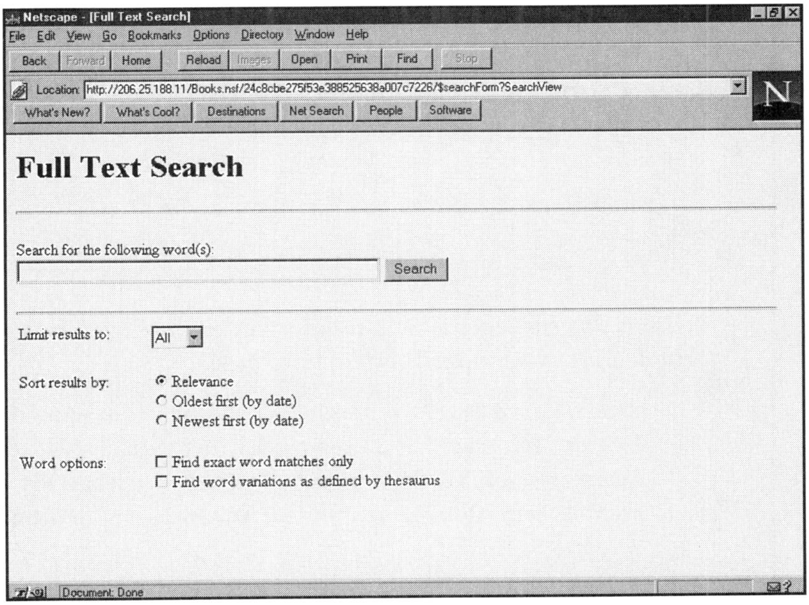

Fig. 10.16
Search.htm is the default form used by Domino when a search is requested. This form can be customized and is located in the /icons directory on Domino.

10

If Domino finds the form $$Search, it serves that form to the browser.

The Search Site database includes an advanced and a simple search form that you can paste into your database or site search database and customize. If you wish, you can also customize the search.htm form. Figure 10.17 shows the uncustomized simple search form and Figure 10.18 shows the uncustomized advanced search form as seen through a Web browser.

Fig. 10.17

This Domino simple search form is available in the Search Site database. This form can be copied into your database and customized.

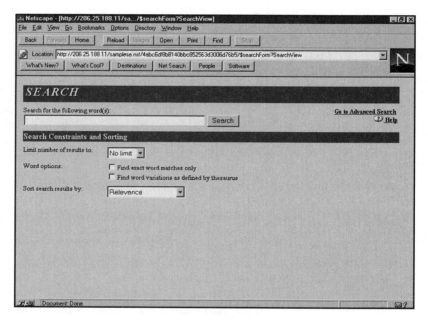

<table>
<tr><td>

> ## Caution
>
> Although you can create a custom search results page, you cannot include all of the features of Domino's default search results. The count for the number of documents found, the restate ability for the query, and the reset bar cannot be recreated on a default search results page.

</td></tr>
</table>

You can also customize search result pages in a way similar to when you created View Templates. To customize a search result page:

1. Create a form that includes the field $$ViewBody. Name the form $$SearchTemplateDefault to identify this form as your search results default form. Any search results that are not associated with a specific view will be returned using this form. Domino ignores any values placed in the $$ViewBody field.

Fig. 10.18

This Domino advanced search form is available in the Search Site database. This form contains links to return to the simple search form, as shown in Figure 10.17, or to request help with the search as shown in Figure 10.19.

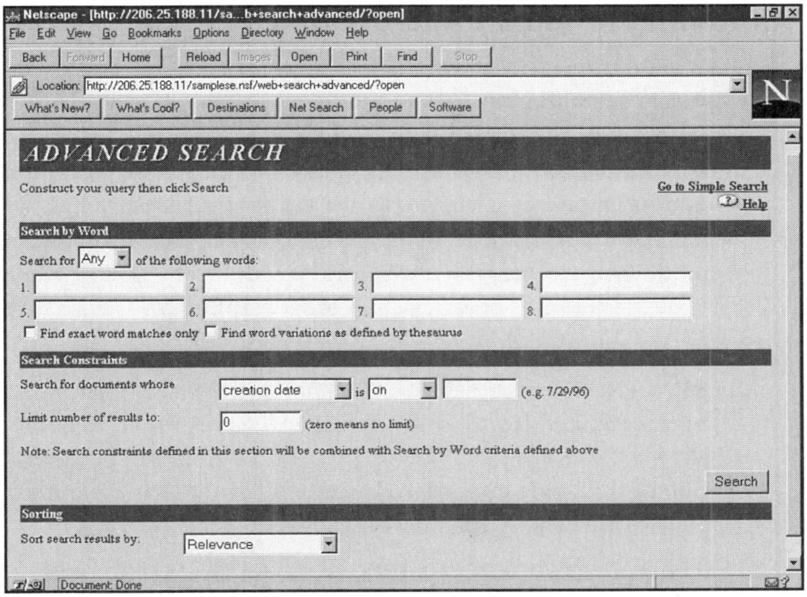

Fig. 10.19

Domino Search Help. From this page, you can return to the advanced or simple.

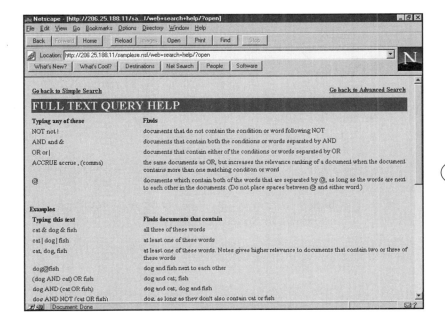

2. (Optional) Name the form $$SearchTemplateDefault for *viewname* where viewname is the alias (preferred) or the name of a view. Include the $$ViewBody field. Domino ignores any values placed in this field.

Creating a Home Page Form

You can use a *form* as your home page, for your site, or for a database, giving you greater design capability than using the About Database Document or a navigator. The about Database document is limited in that it is a document, not a form, and therefore cannot contain fields. A navigator has limitations in that all parts of the navigator must originate as graphics pasted into Notes as a graphic background. This means changes to the navigator, and changes to textual parts of the navigator, must be made in the software used when creating the navigator. Wouldn't it be great if you could have a navigator, text, the contents of a view, and other graphics on one single page? Yes!

Accomplish this by creating a form, using fields such as $$ViewBody and or $$ViewNavigator as described in *"Embedding Views, View, Lists and Navigators in Forms"* in this chapter. If you want this form to serve as the site home page, you need to change the server document. Type the URL for the form in the *Home URL* field of the HTTP section of the server document. Be certain to include the Domino URL command ?open or ?openForm. The syntax for this URL is:

> **http://Host/DatabaseName/FormName/?Open**

If you wish to make this form the home page for a *database*, simply provide links to the form from other areas in your site using the same syntax for the URL.

From Here...

Customized view, navigators and search templates are a great way to polish your site and give it a different look than the standard Notes look.

For related information, see the following chapters:

▶ Chapter 4, "Understanding Web Fundamentals," which discusses the use of HTML, Java applets, and plug-ins and their roles in Notes Web applications.

▶ Chapter 12, "Applying a 'Web Look' to Notes Applications," to learn about adding multimedia to Notes documents.

chapter 11

Automating Web Applications with Agents

by Jane Calabria

In this chapter

◆ **Using the registration database to help automate user requests**
Learn how to simplify the task of registering users for your Domino Web site by using a registration database. In addition, see how easy automating Web registration with Notes agents is.

◆ **Maintaining user requests**
Learn how the Handle Requests and Send Problem Mail agents can help you maintain Web user requests.

◆ **Using the Archive Old Successful Requests and Archive Old Unsuccessful Requests Agents**
See how two very powerful Notes agents can help you manage your registration database.

Now that you've had a chance to design some really great Web applications for your Domino site, you might be wondering how your users can get to this information quickly and easily, and without having to do too much work. For instance, you might want to automate some of the day-to-day Web administration tasks such as registering your Web users to give them access to your Domino site. Even better would be to enable your Web users to register themselves—let the user do the work for a change! Well, the whole process isn't quite as simple as that, but this chapter should give you a good head start.

As any Notes developer knows, agents, formerly known as macros, are great tools for speeding up everyday Notes tasks. For example, you might create an agent to update certain documents in a database that adds reader names fields for additional security in your documents. You might also want to create a scheduled agent to run during non-working hours that will delete old data from a database. The possibilities for using agents in Notes are virtually endless.

As you'll see, agents also help you automate everyday Web development and administration tasks.

Using the Registration Database to Process Requests

Securing your Domino Web site from wandering Web clients is a major concern for any Notes developer/administrator. After your site is released to the Internet community, anyone with a simple Web browser will be able to browse your site. One way to keep your databases secure is to change the default ACL (Access Control List) on each database to No Access and force the Web users to obtain an account and password by registering with your Domino server. The registration process requires the user to input her name, company, password, and other personal information in the registration document. Notes then takes this document and creates a person document in the Domino server's Name and Address book that contains the user's information and password. Notes also automatically adds that user to a Domino Users group, which is given access through the ACL. As soon as registration is complete, the Domino Web user will receive proper access to the requested databases.

Now take a closer look at the registration database and how it works. The Domino sample registration database can be found on the CD-ROM at the back of this book or can be downloaded from the **www.domino.lotus** Web site.

Understanding the Design of the Domino Registration Database

When you first open the Domino sample registration database, you should see the About Database document, which is shown in Figure 11.1.

Notice that this document contains two hotspots: one for requesting a new account and one for examining existing accounts. Additionally, the document contains some HTML tags, which are represented by <h2> and </h2> and are used for highlighting the text. When a user hits the Request a New Account hotspot, Notes runs the formula:

```
@Command([Compose];"New Account")
```

The next thing the users see is a registration form with fields of information that they are required to complete. Note that some fields are required fields and some are not required (see Figure 11.2).

Fig. 11.1

The About Database document is the first screen the user will see when opening the Domino Site Registration database.

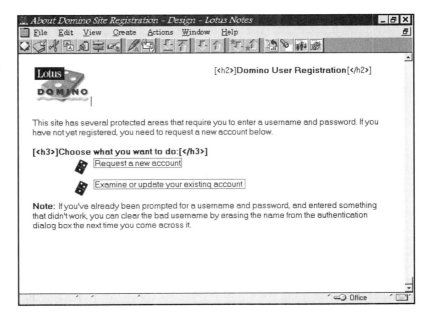

Fig. 11.2

The User Registration Form requires that the new user completes the required fields before accessing any Notes databases on the Domino server.

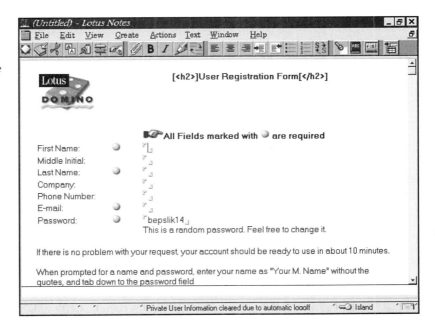

You'll find that most of these fields contain very basic Notes design that can be edited in any way to suit your own needs. See Table 11.1 for a brief explanation of the key formulas used in these fields.

Table 11.1　New User Registration Form Fields and Formulas

Field	Formulas and Description
FieldName	This is a required field that includes the basic @if and @failure functions, but also the following: @Explode("<x>x{x}x[x]x?x!x#x-x=x+x*x(x)x&x^x%x$x@x/x\\x\""; "x")), which actually looks for any unwanted characters in the name field and converts them to a text list.
MiddleInitial	This field uses the basic input translation formula: @trim(MiddleInitial), which removes any extra spaces or special characters.
LastName	This field is required and uses the same basic formulas that the FirstName field uses.
Company	This field uses a similar input translation formula that is used in the MiddleInitial field: @trim(Company).
OfficePhoneNumber	This is basically just a static text field, not using any formulas.
EMail	This field uses three very important checks to determine if an e-mail address is valid: @Contains(Email; "@")¦ @Length(domain) < 2 ¦ @Length(domain) >3¦ (@Length(domain) = 3 & @Member(@LowerCase(domain);com":"edu":"org":"net":"gov":"mil":"int") = 0). These formulas together will check for the "@" symbol and that the length of the domain is two or three characters; if 3, then the characters must agree with the ones listed in the formula. If any of these conditions are not met, an error message prompts the user to correct the field.
NewPassword	Initially this field will display a random password, using a default formula (see Figure 11.3). If the user chooses to input a different password, the input translation formula nchars := 3;FIELD NPProblem := @If(@Length(@Trim(NewPassword)) < nchars; "Your password must be at least " + @Text(nchars) + " characters long. Please go back to the form and correct your password."; ""); is used to check for the correct number of characters in the field.

Keep in mind that the Domino registration database and all of the forms and views that come with it use *open architecture*, meaning that any Notes developer can modify the design to his own company's standards.

Fig. 11.3

The NewPassword field uses a default formula to randomly select a password for the Domino user account.

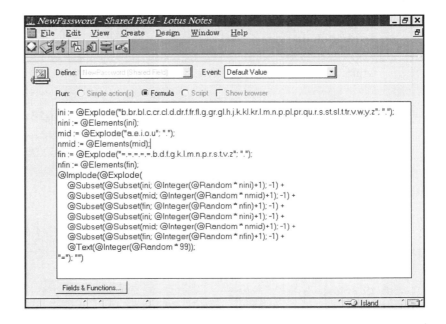

Registration Database Administration

Now that you've got a good handle on the design of the registration database, you need to know a few things about the administration side before you release the database to your Web users. Because the registration process involves reading and writing documents to your public address book, it is important to know the proper access levels to initiate certain tasks. The administration processes that you need to be concerned with are:

▶ Setting the proper ACL in all of the databases

▶ Modifying the server document in the Public Address Book

▶ Customizing the agents within the registration application

Setting the Proper ACL in All the Databases

Making sure that unwanted users cannot get into your Domino site is a major concern. But making sure that you, the developer/administrator, have the proper access is equally important. Because the registration process creates person and group documents to your public address book and writes data to the Domino registration application, you'll need to make sure that everyone is given the proper ACL. Additionally, before your registration application is tested, make sure that at least one database has an ACL set to No Access. Otherwise, any user with reader access or higher will have the capability to access

11

your Notes databases. You will also need to be specified as Manager in the ACL of the registration database as well as make sure that you are a member of the {UserManager} role. The person documents in the registration database include a reader names field, which you cannot see unless you are a member of that role.

Modify the Server Document in the Public Address Book

In addition to setting the proper access control, you'll also need to make sure that you will be able to have the registration database run restricted LotusScript agents. You can change your access under the Agent Manager section in the server document, as shown in Figure 11.4.

Fig. 11.4

Edit the Agent Manager section in the server document of the public address book on the Domino server to give yourself access to run restricted LotusScript agents.

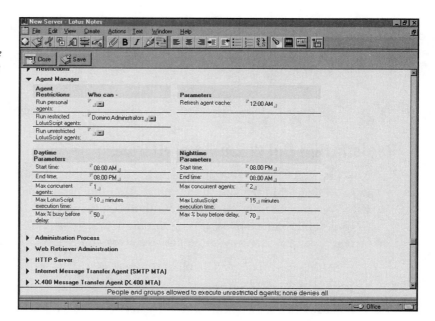

Customization of the Agents Within the Registration Application

You will need to customize the Send Problem Mail agent and the Handle Requests agent for your own specifications. These agents are covered in the next section of this chapter.

Maintaining User Requests

After you've edited or created your registration database and are ready to put it in production, you need to consider two agents that will help your process run smoothly.

These two agents, which accompany the sample registration database, are key factors to the success of your Domino server's registration process. The two agents are:

▶ Handle Requests agent

▶ Send Problem Mail agent

It will be necessary for you to edit these agents appropriately for your registration process to function effectively. Dissect each of these agents and get a better idea of what each of them does in the registration database.

The Handle Requests Agent

The Handle Requests agent comes stored with the sample registration database that you've been working with throughout this chapter. Basically, the Handle Requests agent will process all of your Web user's requests for access to your Domino Web site. It makes perfect sense, then, that this agent runs automatically when a document has been created or modified in the database.

From the Handle Requests agent's view within the registration database, you should see two agents: Handle Requests and Send Problem Mail. Double-click the Handle Requests agent shown in Figure 11.5.

Fig. 11.5

The Handle Requests Agent runs automatically when a document is added or modified in the Domino Registration database.

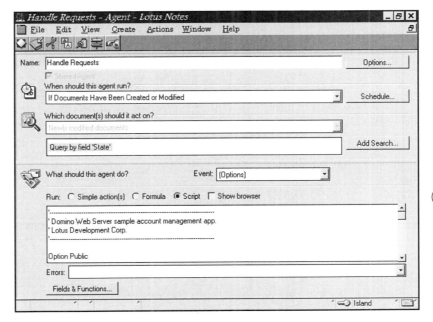

You also can see that the agent runs on documents that contain the field State, which is actually a hidden field on the New Account form in the registration database. As you can see in Figure 11.6, the field State is a keyword field listed in a sub-form included in the New Account form. The default keyword is P for pending, which represents a pending request.

Fig. 11.6

The New Account form in the registration database uses several hidden fields in its design. One key hidden field used in the formulas is the State field.

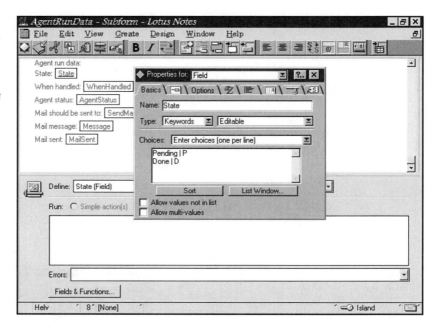

As soon as a Web user makes a new request to have an account on your Domino server, this agent will run and handle the request. Now delve a bit deeper and look at the LotusScript code used in the agent. The following is the main subroutine in the Handle Requests agent:

```
Sub Initialize

    Set s = New NotesSession
    Set db = s.CurrentDatabase

    Set nabPeople = New NotesDatabase( "", nabPeoplePath$ )
    Set nabGroups = New NotesDatabase( "", nabGroupsPath$ )

    ' Get the collection of all documents this agent should run against
    ' (Those that have been newly modified or created)

    Dim coll As NotesDocumentCollection
    Set coll = db.UnprocessedDocuments

    Dim doc As NotesDocument
    Dim i As Integer
```

```
' Loop over the documents to handle.

For i = 1 To coll.Count
    Set doc = coll.GetNthDocument( i )

    ' Handle Change Password Requests
    If ( doc.Form(0) = "ChPw" And doc.State(0) = "P" ) Then
        Call HandleChangePassword( doc )
    End If

    ' Handle New Account Requests
    If ( doc.Form(0) = "NewAcc" And doc.State(0) = "P" ) Then
        Call HandleNewAccount( doc )
    End If

    ' UpdateProcessedDoc makes sure the agent won't run on this
    ' document again.

    Call s.UpdateProcessedDoc( doc )
Next

End Sub
```

The three primary variables in this code are:

▶ s = New NotesSession, which gives access to the current Notes Session

▶ db = s.CurrentDatabase, which gives access to the Notes database

▶ coll = db.UnprocessedDocuments, which is all the unprocessed documents

The next half of the code questions if an unprocessed document has a request to change a password—hence, the subroutine HandleChangePassword is called—or if this is simply a new account request that runs the HandleNewAccount subroutine. Both of these statements depend upon the State and Form fields, as seen in the following:

```
' Handle Change Password Requests
        If ( doc.Form(0) = "ChPw" And doc.State(0) = "P" ) Then
            Call HandleChangePassword( doc )
        End If

' Handle New Account Requests
        If ( doc.Form(0) = "NewAcc" And doc.State(0) = "P" ) Then
            Call HandleNewAccount( doc )
        End If
```

The portion of the Handling Requests agent that needs to be customized for your site is under the (Declarations) event in the design pane (see Figure 11.7).

You'll need to edit the fields for the path of your public name and address book. As soon as you make the changes, save the agent. You will also need to edit the Send Problem Mail agent, which you'll learn how to do next.

Fig. 11.7

The Handle Requests Agent must be customized for use with your Domino site.

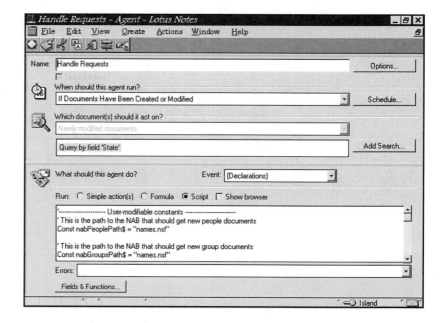

The Send Problem Mail Agent

There might be times when a new user request results in an error or problems occur with a request. The Send Problem Mail agent will send a message to the administrator of the Notes server to notify him of the problem. This agent is also part of the Domino registration database. Listing 11.1 is the main subroutine from the Send Problem Mail agent:

Listing 11.1 LotusScript Code Subroutine from the Send Problem Mail Agent

```
' This sub creates a mail message and sends it, but does not save it anywhere.

Sub SendProblemMail ( req As NotesDocument )
    Dim email As NotesDocument

    Set email = New NotesDocument( db )

    email.Form = "Memo"
    email.SendTo = req.SendMailTo
    email.Subject = "Problem with request: " & req.AgentStatus(0)
    email.SaveMessageOnSend = False


    Dim bodyItem As NotesRichTextItem
    Set bodyItem = email.CreateRichTextItem( "Body" )

    Call bodyItem.AppendText( "There was a problem with your " & req.Form(0) & "
    ➥request: " & req.AgentStatus(0) & "." )
```

```
        Call bodyItem.AddNewLine( 2 )
        If req.Message(0) <> "" Then
            Call bodyItem.AppendText( req.Message(0) )
            Call bodyItem.AddNewLine( 2 )
        End If
        Call bodyItem.AppendText( "If you need help, send mail to " & helpEmail$ & ".
Include the text of this message, and the problems you are experiencing." )
        Call bodyItem.AddNewLine( 1 )

        email.Send( False )

        req.MailSent = "Y"
        Call req.Save( False, True )

    End Sub
```

The Send Problem Mail agent will also run on any new or modified document in the registration database. You will also need to edit the Send Problem Mail agent in the same way as you did the Handle Requests agent. You will need to select the (Declarations) event in the design pane, as shown in Figure 11.8.

Fig. 11.8

The Send Problem Mail agent will send an e-mail to the recipient specified in the (Declarations) events in the design of the agent.

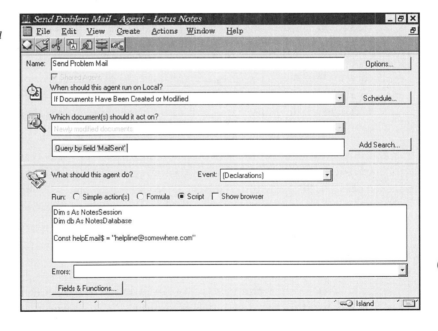

11

The line that states:

```
    Const helpEmail$ = "helpline@somewhere.com"
```

must be edited to reflect the e-mail address to which you would like help requests to be sent. This could be, for example, a Notes administrator or possibly a Notes support person.

Creating Agents to Help Manage Domino Web Sites

Much of what you've learned so far in this chapter has covered the nitty gritty of agents and how they can help you manage your Domino site. Let's take a step back now and look at some other agents that you can use to help you manage your Domino server.

Three very powerful tools to help you manage your Domino Web documents are:

▶ The Archive Old Successful Requests agent

▶ The Archive Old Unsuccessful Requests agent

▶ The Purge agent

Let's take a look at each of these agents in detail.

Getting Acquainted with Using the Archive Old Successful Requests Agent

As you saw in the beginning of this chapter, the registration database can be a very useful tool to help you automate the process of registering a new Domino Web user for your Domino server. You saw that as each new user attempts to access a database that they are not authorized to read, they are presented with the option to register with your Domino server. Once registered, they are given the proper authority to browse the database. Behind the scenes, Domino takes the registration document and creates a person document for them in the public name and address book as well as registering a user document in the registration database.

But what if some of these users decide they only want to access your Domino server once, or maybe twice? Eventually, your registration database becomes a home for the forgotten. You may find that registered users are stored in your registration database that haven't accessed Domino for months. To keep your registration database from getting too large, deleting the "dead weight" might be a good idea.

The Archive Old Successful Requests agent will help you manage the size of your database by doing the following:

1. Check your Domino server's registration database for registered Domino users and when they registered their account.

2. Perform a query search by Change Password form, by the default State, and by the AgentStatus field.

3. If a Domino Web user's account has not been accessed for more than four months (or longer) his or her registration document will be archived to another database or deleted for good.

4. A message will be sent to the administrator's e-mail address informing them of the deletions and requesting them to delete the user's person document.

Let's get started and take a look at each of these functions in detail so you can see the makeup of this very useful agent. Believe it or not, this agent is made up purely of simple actions.

You'll need to be in the sample registration database which you used from the beginning of this chapter. Once you get into the agent design mode of the database, double-click the Archive Old Successful Requests agent (see Figure 11.9).

Fig. 11.9

The basic design of the Archive Old Successful Requests agent consists of simple actions only.

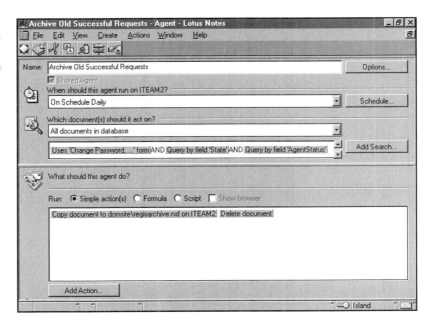

The concept behind the agent is actually very simple and a bit of a change compared to the previous agents you were presented with earlier. As you can see, this agent starts out running as a daily scheduled task and is a shared agent. Remember that a shared agent can be executed by on the server by anyone given access to run agents. Additionally, the task of running this agent daily can easily be changed to weekly, monthly, or any other schedule that fits your server's needs.

As you'll see, the agent performs several queries next to determine what documents the agent will run on as well as several other determining factors. The Archive Old Successful Requests agent performs the following four queries:

1. Selects the Change Password form from the registration database.

2. Searches for the field state.

3. Searches for the field `AgentStatus`.

4. Looks for a specific date which the form was modified.

As shown in Figure 11.10, the first search performed looks at the condition By Form Used and selects the Change Password form from the registration database.

Fig. 11.10

The first query selects the Change Password form used in the registration process.

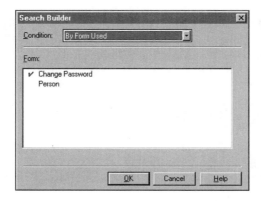

The next query searches on the hidden field state in the Change Request form. The query also searches for the letter "D" which is synonymous with the term Done. It's probably a little easier to understand if you look at Figure 11.11.

Fig. 11.11

The second search looks for the hidden field State and checks to see if the document status is Pending or Done.

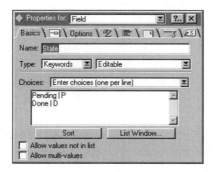

The Query by State field is extremely important to the success of this agent since you want to concentrate on requests that have been completed and not pending. You'll see in the next section how the opposite is true for the Unsuccessful Requests agent.

The next query performs a search on the field `AgentStatus` to determine if the agent ran successfully. As you can see in Figure 11.12, the design of this field is set to a default value of not run yet. Once the agent completes, the status is changed to successful.

Fig. 11.12

The hidden field, AgentStatus, defaults to not run yet and changes to successful when the agent is complete.

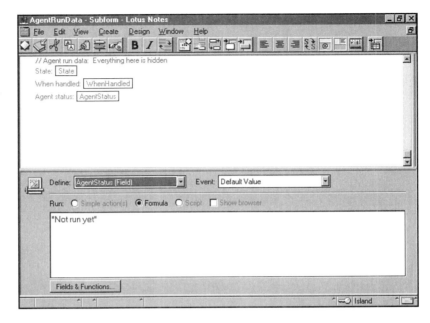

Finally, the agent searches for modified documents older than 90 days, or whatever the designer specifies (see Figure 11.13). Once the all the queries are completed the agent runs a simple action to archive the documents to a database and subsequently deletes them from the original database.

Fig. 11.13

The query search By Date finds modified documents older than 90 days.

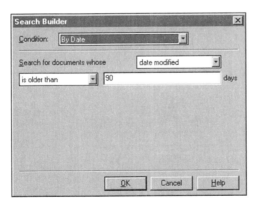

As you can see, the whole process from start to finish is quite simple and can easily be edited to your own specifications. You'll see that the Archive Old Unsuccessful Requests agent, which is covered next, is very similar in most features.

The Archive Old Unsuccessful Requests Agent

As you saw in the previous section, archiving requests from users which have been completed properly and approved successfully by Notes does not have to be a chore. The process is actually quite simple and uses very few complex formulas in its design.

But what happens to all those documents that end up with errors or don't get successfully approved in the registration process? The documents end up crowding your database which could be used for more productive work. An easy solution would be to use the Archive Old Unsuccessful Requests agent, which happens to be the kissing cousin of the Archive Old Successful Requests agent covered in the previous section.

The two agents are basically the same, with the exception of one key point—the query which checks for the completion of the agent is missing (see Figure 11.14).

Fig. 11.14

The Archive Old Unsuccessful Requests omits the query search on the AgentStatus field.

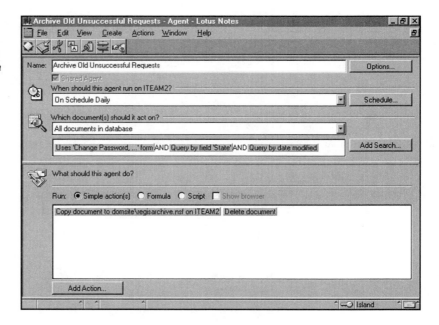

If you recall from the previous section, you saw that the query on the AgentStatus field had a default value of not run yet. This means that there is no need to create a query to search on a status field when we already know by default that nothing has been run. This is an easy way to determine if a request was successful or not.

As you can see if Figure 11.14, the rest of the queries are exactly the same as the Archive Successful Requests agent performs. Just like before, the form used is the Change Password form. The next search looks for the "D" character in the State field. The final query search for documents modified which are older than 90 days is also performed. Finally, once the agent finds all the documents required, it archives them and deletes them.

As you can see, the archiving agents can be very useful tools in helping you manage your Domino databases. Another agent that can help you with your Domino administration is the Purge agent.

Running the Purge Agent

Anyone whose job it is to manage Domino databases knows that it can be quite a challenge to keep track of their sizes and amount of use. One database in particular, the Server Web Navigator, or web.nsf, can get quite big if not monitored closely. Because Notes clients are constantly adding their own Web pages to the database mix, it can become larger than life in almost no time. A very useful tool developed to help you manage the size of your database is the Purge agent, which is included in the Server Web Navigator 4.5.

The Purge agent is a scheduled agent that runs on a daily basis on all of the documents in your Server Web Navigator database. Specifications are set from the Document Management section of the Administration document in the database (see Figure 11.15).

Fig. 11.15

Edit the Document Management section of the Administration document in the Server Web Navigator Database 4.5.

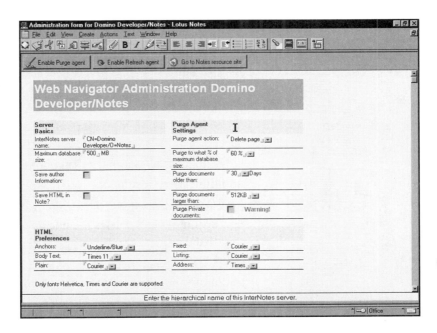

You will have to edit the following criteria:

▶ Deletion of expired documents

▶ Age of expired documents that are to be deleted

▶ Size of expired documents set for deletion

▶ The maximum size of the database at purge time

▶ Deletion of private documents

▶ Deletion of recommended documents

▶ Number of days following which the recommended documents should be removed

▶ Refresh of documents

To better understand the logic behind this agent, take a look at Table 11.2 for a brief explanation of the subroutines in the LotusScript design.

Table 11.2   Purge Agent Subroutines

Subroutine	Description
Initialize	As in most LotusScript code, the Initialize subroutine does a bulk of the work in the agent. As usual, the first step is initializing the variables. Next, it checks for the name of the InterNotes server, followed by a check of the variables from the Administration document. After that, the subroutine runs and loops several times to determine the size of the database and which documents should be deleted. After they are deleted, the $All view is refreshed and information is sent to the Notes log before the database is closed.
ReduceToLink	Reduces the Web page to a link as opposed to deleting the whole page.
SetQuota	Determines the size of the database from the field entered in the Administration document.
DeleteExpired	Checks the "Delete Expired Documents" field in the Administration document and deletes the documents that are older than the specified days.
DeleteBySize	Checks the "Expire documents older than" field of the Administration document and deletes the document if it exceeds that limit.
ReadAdminValues	Reads the fields in the Administration document and records their values.

From Here...

This chapter provides an in-depth look at a sample registration database used to register new Web users for your Domino site. You also saw what agents are used in the registration process to help automate day-to-day tasks. For related information, please see:

▶ Chapter 12, "Applying a 'Web Look' to Notes Applications," for details on some more advanced Domino design features, including Frames, Java, Multi-Media, and Active X.

11

Applying a "Web Look" to Notes Applications

In this chapter

◆ **How HTML frames work**
First, we take an overview of HTML frames. Then we walk through several samples of their use, starting with a very simple application and continuing with more and more complex examples.

◆ **How to use HTML frames in your Domino Web applications**
We learn how to make HTML frames available through HTML documents attached to Notes documents.

◆ **About the &3PaneUI argument**
We learn about the shortcut to emulating the Notes 3 Pane User Interface on the Web.

For the most part, Domino does not support HTML frames directly. You can accomplish frame-like effects using a view template like the one in the discussion databases on the Lotus Web sites. You can also use frames indirectly in your Domino Web applications, using the techniques discussed in this chapter.

Working with Frames

Frames present multiple HTML pages to the Web browser at one time. Each frame holds its own HTML page or image file. The frames are tiled on the screen per the designer's specification. Between tiled pages there can be borders or no borders, scroll bars or no scroll bars. Frames can be resized by the user (unless the designer programs otherwise) and the designer determines the size of the frames in the browser. Chapter 4, "Understanding Web Fundamentals," also discusses frames however, here we learn how to *construct* frames.

Frames first appeared in Netscape Navigator 1.0 and were further enhanced in Netscape Navigator 3.0. Microsoft has adopted frames in Internet Explorer 3.0, but slightly differently than in Netscape Navigator. Frames do not work in Lotus Web Navigator.

Since frames are supported by the two browser market leaders, you might think they would become a part of the HTML standard (if HTML ever stands still long enough for a standard to crystallize out of it), but the proposed HTML 3.2 standard, published by the World Wide Web Consortium, the nearest thing to a standard-setting body for HTML, makes no mention of frames, probably because there is no agreement as to exactly how they should be implemented. In fact, Netscape doesn't even follow its own published rules regarding implementation of frames. So the precise status and future of frames is unclear. Therefore, use them with care. Test your implementations of frames in both Netscape Navigator and Internet Explorer, as well as one or more browsers that don't recognize frames, to make sure your pages will display properly to everyone who may see them.

With a minor exception, Domino does not support frames directly. The exception is the *&3PaneUI argument* which, when appended to an URL sent to a Domino server, causes the server to return an HTML page that has three panes, á la Notes interface. A list of views appears in one pane, a view in the second pane, and a document in the third view. However, the &3PaneUI argument is an unsupported, undocumented feature of Domino which Lotus claims will not work in future releases of Domino. So you should hesitate to use it.

Not only does Domino not support frames directly, but because of the way Domino converts Notes documents to HTML, Domino doesn't even support the embedding of frames into Notes forms as passthru HTML. When Domino translates a Notes document into an HTML document, it places the visible contents of your Notes document, including all passthru HTML, within the BODY section of an HTML document. Frames are implemented in their own section—FRAMESET—which is independent of the BODY section. In fact, neither Netscape Navigator nor Internet Explorer will display both a FRAMESET and a BODY section of a document. Netscape Navigator will display whichever one it encounters first. Internet Explorer will ignore the BODY section entirely if a document also includes a FRAMESET section.

Since Notes would put any frame-related tags you embed in a Notes form inside a BODY section of the HTML document that it creates, both browsers will ignore your frame-related tags altogether. In fact, frames are the only HTML feature we know of that cannot be incorporated into Notes documents in this way. Therefore, to use frames in Domino applications, you have to save the frame code in a separate HTML document (which could be attached to a Notes document) and refer to it with a pointer.

Table 12.1 lists frame-related tags and attributes commonly used with frames.

Table 12.1 HTML Frame Tags and Attributes

Tag or Attribute	Description	Comments
FRAMESET... FRAMESET	Container Tag that displays multiple windows.	Within the FRAMESET tag, the only other tags that can be used are the FRAME tag, another—nested—FRAMESET container, or a NOFRAMES container.

ROWS
COLS
	ROWS is the attribute that defines a row of frames within a FRAMESET. It defines the number and height of frames within the row. COLS is the attribute that defines a column of frames within a FRAMESET. It defines the number and width of frames within the column.	Use: ROWS=*n* and/or COLS=*m* where *n* and *m* are the absolute value in pixels, or a percentage of the entire FRAMESET, or an integer followed by an asterisk, which represents a proportional amount of screen space. A FRAMESET must contain more than one row *or* more than one column. Otherwise the browser will ignore the FRAMESET. A FRAMESET *may* include multiple rows *and* multiple columns. Separate values in each list (*n, m*) with commas and, optionally, surround each list with quotes. Examples:
		`FRAMESET ROWS="25%, 25%, 50%"`
		sets three rows.
		`FRAMESET ROWS="1*, 2*, 1*"` sets three rows of exactly the same height as the first example.
		`FRAMESET ROWS="256, 2*, 1*"`
		`COLS="50%, 50%` sets three rows

continues

12

Table 12.1 Continued

Tag or Attribute	Description	Comments
		and two columns. The first row is 256 pixels high. The second and third rows take up 2/3 and 1/3, respectively, of the remaining screen height. The columns each occupy half of the screen width.
<FRAME>	Empty tag that identifies a single frame or window.	You may have one FRAME tag or one nested FRAMESET container for each window you have defined in a FRAMESET tag. The browser assigns FRAME references to defined frames first left-to-right, then top-down. If a FRAMESET defines more frames than there are FRAME or nested FRAMESET tags, the unused frames are left empty.
SRC	The attribute of FRAME that identifies the source file to be displayed in the frame.	Use: `FRAME SRC="URL"` or `FRAME SRC="filename.HTM"` or `FRAME SRC="URL/FileName.HTM"` The quotation marks are optional.
NAME	The attribute of FRAME that assigns a name to a frame. This name can be used in links to the frame.	`FRAME NAME = "SERVICES"`
TARGET	The attribute of HREF used to reference a named frame.	`A HREF="http://www.PlanetDomino.net" TARGET="SERVICES">Click here for our Services</A`
MARGINWIDTH MARGINHEIGHT	The amount of white space between a frame's left and right or top and bottom borders and the contents of the frame.	Measured in pixels.

Tag or Attribute	Description	Comments
SCROLLING	Permits the designer to turn off scroll bars that would otherwise appear automatically in a frame smaller than its contents.	Set it equal to Yes, No, or Auto. Default is Auto, which means that scroll bars appear only if they are useful. Yes means scroll bars appear whether they are useful or not. No means scrollbars do not appear, whether useful or not.
NORESIZE	Permits the designer to disable the otherwise automatically available resizing of a row or column by dragging its borders.	Boolean. Takes no parameters. If NORESIZE is present in the FRAME tag, the frame will not be resizable.
NOFRAMES... /NOFRAMES	Permits display of alternate content by browsers that do not support frames.	This is an optional container, sort of like the BODY container. It can contain any tags the BODY container can. Place it within your outermost FRAMESET container.

Everything you ever wanted to know about frames, HTML and more can be found in the *Special Edition Using HTML* book found on the CD-ROM, in this book. We encourage you to check it out!

 Tip

Frames can't have background images or background colors. Those attributes work only within the BODY tag.

Let's take a look at some examples. Following is an HTML document that splits the screen in half horizontally. It inserts the contents of two HTML files in the two windows. The file *frame1.htm* displays the words "Frame 1". The file *frame2.htm* displays the words "Frame 2".

```
<HTML>
<HEAD>
<TITLE>Frame Example 1</TITLE>
</HEAD>
<FRAMESET rows="50%, 50%">
     <FRAME SRC=frame1.htm>
     <FRAME SRC=frame2.htm>
```

12

```
</FRAMESET>
</HTML>
```

Figure 12.1, as follows, shows how the preceding document appears in Netscape's browser.

Fig. 12.1

This is how the code titled Frame Example 1 appears in a browser that supports frames.

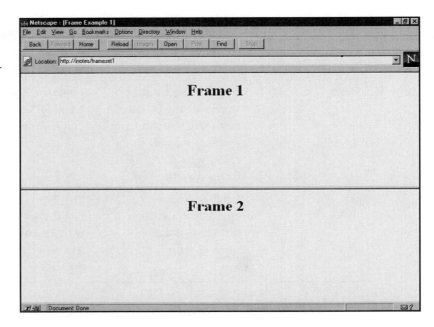

Next, let's modify the preceding example as follows:

```
<HTML>
<HEAD>
<TITLE>Frame Example 2</TITLE>
</HEAD>
<FRAMESET rows="50%, 50%" COLS="50%, 50%">
        <FRAME SRC=frame1.htm>
        <FRAME SRC=frame2.htm>
        <FRAME SRC=frame3.htm>
        <FRAME SRC=frame4.htm>
</FRAMESET>
</HTML>
```

We added a COLS attribute to the opening FRAMESET tag and two more FRAME references. Figure 12.2, as follows, shows how this document looks in a Web browser.

Now let's nest one FRAMESET within another, as follows:

```
<TITLE>Frame Example 3</TITLE>
</HEAD>
<FRAMESET rows="1*, 1*">
<FRAMESET cols="2*, 1*">
        <FRAME SRC=frame1.htm>
```

```
        <FRAME SRC=frame2.htm>
</FRAMESET>
        <FRAME SRC=frame3.htm>
</FRAMESET>
</HTML>
```

Fig. 12.2

This is how the code titled Frame Example 2 appears in a browser that supports frames.

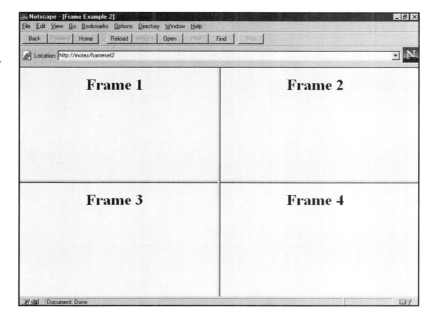

Notice also that, in the COLS and ROWS attributes, we substituted "1*, 1*" and "2*, 1*" for the percentages that appeared in the previous examples. "1*, 1*" means the same thing as "50%, 50%" meant in the previous examples. "2*, 1*" means the first window should occupy 2/3 of the available space and the second window should occupy 1/3 of the available space. Figure 12.3, as follows, shows how this page looks in a browser.

Let's take our example one step further. We'll nest two FRAMESETs within another. We'll add a NOFRAMES section. And we'll leave one frame empty. The code looks like this:

```
<TITLE>Frame Example 4</TITLE>
</HEAD>
<FRAMESET rows="1*, 2*, 1*">
        <FRAMESET cols="256, *">
                <FRAME SRC=frame1.htm>
                <FRAME SRC=frame2.htm>
        </FRAMESET>
        <FRAME SRC=frame3.htm>
        <FRAMESET cols="40%, 60%">
                <FRAME SRC=frame4.htm>
                <FRAME>
        </FRAMESET>
```

12

```
<NOFRAMES>
     <H2>This page only works in a browser that supports frames. <BR>So
     ➥whatzamatta witchew? Buy our browser or go away!</H2>
</NOFRAMES>
</FRAMESET>
</HTML>
```

Fig. 12.3

This is how a
FRAMESET *nested*
within another
FRAMESET *appears in*
a browser.

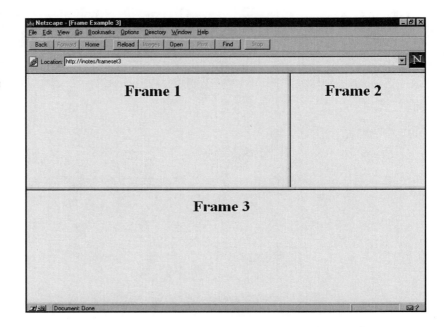

Notice the text that appears in the NOFRAMES section. It's more blunt, maybe, but no more rude than any other Web site that refuses to cater to the needs of people whose browsers don't skate on the cutting edge. Don't be like that. Design your pages so that less fortunate people than you can read them.

Notice also that the heights of the rows in the first FRAMESET are 1/4, 1/2, and 1/4, respectively, of the screen height. The width of the first column in the second FRAMESET is fixed at 256 pixels, and the second column, showing an asterisk only, takes up all the remaining horizontal space. The widths of the columns in the third FRAMESET are 40% and 60%, respectively, of the screen width.

Figure 12.4 shows how this page looks in a browser that supports frames.

Fig. 12.4

This page has three rows resulting from the main FRAMESET *section. The top and bottom rows each have two columns, resulting from two nested* FRAMESET *sections.*

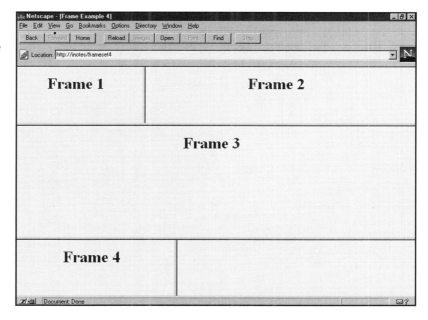

Figure 12.5, as follows, shows how the above page looks in a browser that does not support frames.

Fig. 12.5

The NOFRAMES *section displays alternate content to users whose browsers don't support frames.*

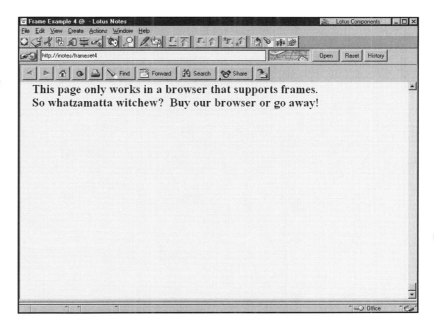

By the way, a NOFRAMES section can contain BODY…/BODY tags. Here is an example of a page in which this is the case. We found this page on one of the Lotus Web sites. It is the Virtual Lotusphere Web page.

```
<HTML>
<!-- Lotus Domino Web Server Release 1.5 (RC1, Build 165 on AIX) -->
<HEAD>
<HTML>
<HEAD>
    <TITLE>Welcome to Virtual Lotusphere</TITLE>
</HEAD>
<FRAMESET cols="125,1*" frameborder="0" framespacing="0" border=0>
<NOFRAMES><BODY BGCOLOR="#ffffff">
<P>This web s±,e requires a browser that supports frames.</P>
</BODY>
</NOFRAMES>
<FRAME SRC=/home.nsf/names/nv1 name="nv1" NORESIZE scrolling="no" marginwidth=0
marginheight=0 border=0>
    <FRAME SRC=/home.nsf/names/nv2 name="nv2" scrolling="no" marginwidth=10
marginheight=0 border=0>
</FRAMESET>
</HTML>
```

Figure 12.6 shows the resulting page as seen through a Web browser.

Fig. 12.6
www.Lotusphere.com
uses Frames on their
Virtual Lotusphere
Page.

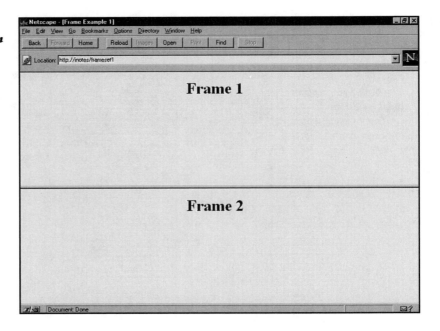

Creating Frames

For Domino to successfully use your frames, you must create the frames definition and save and store it in a separate HTML file. This file can be attached to a Notes document or stored in the HTML directory on the Domino server. It can also be stored in the server directory structure. Use a Domino URL to reference the file and you've got frames!

We like to store our GIFs, images and HTML files in a database. This allows us to more easily maintain our Web site remotely. We store our frame definition files in this database and use URLs with the following syntax to open the files:

```
<A HREF="/DatabaseName/ViewName/Key/$File/FileName.htm"> Click here to see a
➥frame-based page</A>
```

This anchor reference includes the Domino URL for opening documents in a view by a key name. If your frame definition is to be your home page, you can place this URL in the server document, under the HTTP section in the field called *Home URL*.

Using the Notes 3PaneUI Argument

You can use the &3PaneUI argument in URLs to reproduce the Notes 3-Pane User Interface in Web browsers. In fact, if you look at the source code of the Domino URL: **http://host/DatabaseName/?OpenDatabase&3PaneUI**, you can see that Domino creates a FRAMESET when it converts the 3PaneUI. This doesn't look much different than if you created the frame definition yourself. Figure 12.7 shows the resulting page as viewed through a browser when we enter the following URL: **http://206.25.188.11/eagle.nsf?opendatabase&3PaneUI**.

12

Fig. 12.7
This is the PlanetNotes Web site, retrieved with the &3PaneUI argument.

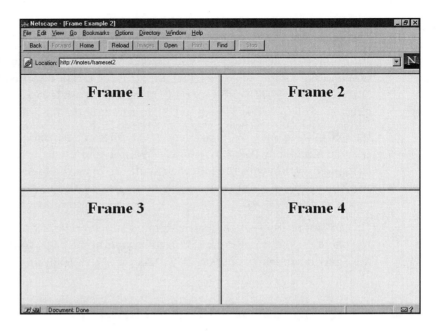

Figure 12.8 shows the resulting source code as viewed through a browser.

Fig. 12.8
This is the raw HTML code produced by Domino in response to an URL with the &3PaneUI argument appended.

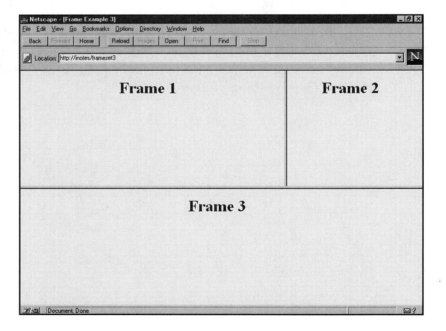

CAUTION
Lotus has indicated that the &3PaneUI argument on the Web is not supported.
They do not recommend that you use this method for creating frames, since they
do not intend to continue implementing the &3PaneUI argument in future releases
of Domino.

From Here...

HTML frames make for interesting Web sites. But they do put a lot of the work of creating a Web site back into the process, after Domino removed it. To learn more, see the following:

▶ To learn how to use a view template to accomplish the same sort of functionality that frames give us, see *Using the Domino Discussion Database* in Chapter 13, *"Examining Special Function Databases for the Web."*

▶ To learn more about frames in general, go to the Netscape and Microsoft Web sites, **www.netscape.com** and **www.microsoft.com**.

▶ To learn more about HTML in general, go to the Web site of the World Wide Web Consortium **(www.w3c.com)**.

12

Examining Special Function Databases for the Web

In this chapter

◆ **Understanding the Domino discussion database**
Examine the powerful features that Lotus has written into its discussion database for the Web.

◆ **A user registration database**
Look at Lotus's own registration database.

◆ **A file download database**
Consider another Lotus database, this one with a context-sensitive input form.

◆ **An image repository database**
Examine the benefit and technique of storing files in a database instead of the file system.

D omino affords us many techniques for automating the process of setting up, authoring, and maintaining a Web site. Some of these techniques involve special purpose databases. This chapter presents several special purpose databases. We explain what they can do for you and how they work. We have even included copies of them on the CD-ROM that accompanies this book.

Understanding the Domino Discussion Database

The Domino Discussion database is, of course, intended to be used as a Web-based discussion forum, and several enhancements have been made to make it more effective as one. First, it uses a view template that employs some sophisticated programming to display a very rich set of options to the user. You will want to borrow the techniques used to create this view template, for use in your own view designs. Second, it employs a Lotuscript agent to display, at the end of every displayed message, the message's place within the discussion thread. Finally, it demonstrates the use of a cookie by a Domino application to retain user preferences from session to session.

This database works together with a *preferences* database to set the cookie, and both databases are available on the CD-ROM, as well as from Lotus's Domino Web site, **domino.lotus.com**. Also, Lotus has given you permission to reuse any code in these databases in your own applications, so don't be shy.

A Very Powerful View Template

When you open the Domino Discussion database in your browser, you see a view of the database similar to that shown in Figure 13.1.

Fig. 13.1

The list of views appears on the left, and the selected view appears on the right.

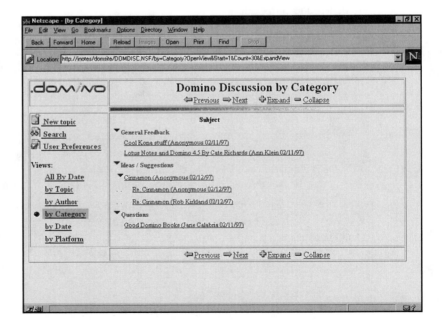

The layout that you see in Figure 13.1 results from a view template named $$ViewTemplateDefault, which forms the backdrop for every view in the database (except for one, *Plain by Date*, which has its own view template). Across the top you see the Domino logo (substitute your own logo here), the title of the view you are currently looking at, and the standard set of view actions that appear at the top of all views on the Web. Next you see a series of user actions on the left side of the screen—New Topic, Search, and User Preferences. Below that is a list of available views. One of the views has a different background than the others and a bullet to its left.

To the right of the list of views appear the contents of the currently selected view. It is a standard Web-based view. Finally, across the bottom, as across the bottom of any Web-based view, you see a repeat of the action buttons that appear at the top of the screen.

The remarkable aspect of this view template that we want to examine first is the fact that on the left side of the view you can see selected what is on the right. Also, the views listed on the left are selectable HTML hotspots.

A close look at the design of the view template reveals how the designer created it (see Figure 13.2).

Fig. 13.2
In Design Mode is the form that, in Figure 13.1, appeared in a Web browser.

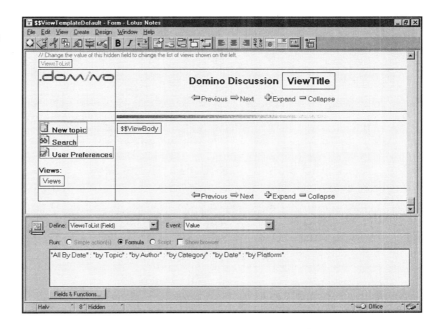

First you see a hidden field at the top of the form, ViewsToList. The value of the field is a list of views, as appears in the formula window at the bottom of the screen. The comment at the top of the screen reveals that the list of views in this field appears to the

13

Web user. We also see that the field named Views appears to produce the list of views that the Web user sees and from which the user can select a view.

In Figure 13.3 you see the value of the field Views. The last line of the formula in Figure 13.3 reveals that the list of views is an HTML table. This is an HTML table inside the cell of a Notes table—very powerful. The rest of the formula primarily sets the position in the list of the currently selected view, and then formats the members of the list in cells in the HTML table.

Fig. 13.3

Notice the last line of this formula. The list of views is an HTML table, embedded in your Notes table.

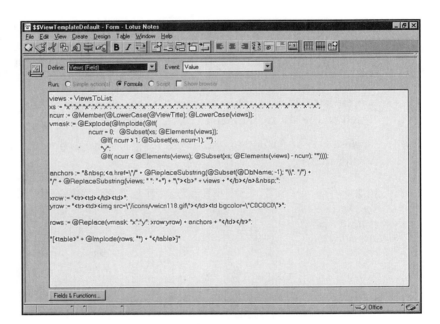

You can borrow this whole view template if you want and just use it as is or make minor changes in it. But all that you actually need to use from the view template, to gain a Web page similar to that produced by this view template, are the ViewsToList field, in which you will insert the list of views from your own database, and the Views field, which creates the table of views to choose from. Of course, you will also need a $$ViewBody field that will list the members of the chosen view.

Storing User Preferences in a Cookie

Another interesting feature of the view template is what happens when the Web user chooses User Preferences, one of the choices on the left side of the view template. The form in Figure 13.4 appears. There the user can choose to receive from the server either pretty pages or fast pages. In other words, either the server will send pages with eye-catching graphics that will take a little more time to arrive, or the server will send plain text pages that will arrive faster.

Fig. 13.4

Choose either pretty or fast pages in this form, and then click the Change my Preferences button.

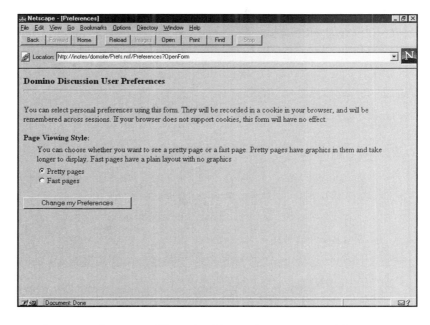

Figure 13.5 illustrates the pages that you will receive if you choose pages with eye-catching graphics, whereas Figure 13.6 illustrates plain pages that require less time to transmit.

Fig. 13.5

If you choose pretty pages, the server sends you pages that look like this—lots of graphics.

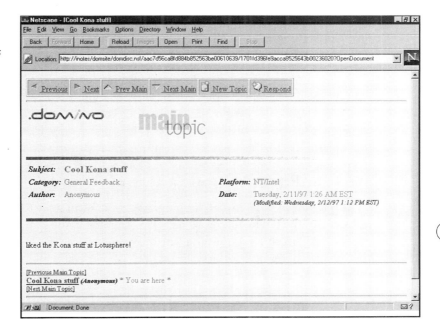

13

Fig. 13.6

If you choose fast pages, the server sends you pages that look like this—no graphics.

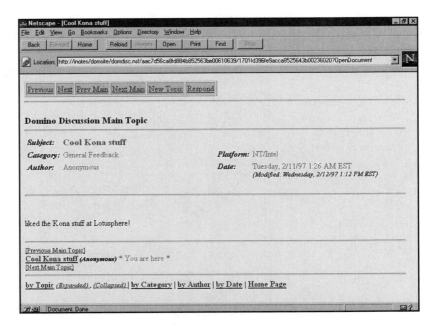

It is interesting and convenient that the server remembers your preferences, and the next time you return to it, this server will send you the correct type of pages. Web servers do not retain information about you after they respond to an URL received from you. That is to say, they are "stateless."

Some other types of servers (Domino servers, for example, when they are communicating with Notes clients) establish a "session" with a client and remember, for the duration of the session, the "state" of the conversation with the client. They can hold a back-and-forth conversation with a client. They can conduct a multi-step transaction with a client. They recall what has transpired previously in the conversation and perhaps anticipate what the client will do or say next.

But HTTP does not provide for such "stateful" relationships between server and client. With HTTP, each request a client makes of a server is, as far as the server is concerned, the first request it has ever received from the client. This makes sense if you consider that, at its outset, the World Wide Web was intended not to be a sales transaction server or workflow server but merely an information repository, a research library. There is little point in such a server retaining information about you or about its past transactions with you.

However, people keep envisioning new and wonderful ways to use the World Wide Web. But some of these new functions imply an ongoing conversation between server and client, which in turn requires that the server client keep track of the state of their conversation. Although HTTP servers cannot do this, many browsers (including current versions of Netscape Navigator, Microsoft Internet Explorer, and Notes' integrated browser) *can* track the state of your relationship with individual Web servers. The way this works is that the server can ask your browser to retain information about the state of their relationship. Your browser stores the requested information on disk. This stored information is known, whimsically, as a "cookie." The next time you send an URL to the server, your browser can append the cookie (the stored information) to the URL. When the server receives the cookie, it effectively "remembers" the state of its previous relationship with you.

Netscape Navigator stores the cookies in a file called cookies.txt. Microsoft Internet Explorer stores the files as separate text files in a subdirectory called cookies.

Regarding the discussion database, the cookie tells the server to send either a graphics-rich version of each document or a graphics-poor version.

That the discussion database sets and reads cookies is of particular value to us because we can see how the programmer accomplished it, and then use the same technique to have our own servers set and read cookies.

The way this works in general is as follows:

1. The HTTP server asks the browser to save a cookie by including a <META> tag in the <HEAD> section of an HTML document. The tag uses the following syntax:

   ```
   <META HTTP-EQUIV="Set-Cookie" CONTENT="name=value; [[name=value]...]">
   ```

   where name=value is any name/value pair. If one of the name=value pairs is expires=date, where date looks like Thu, 01-Jan-2009 12:00:00 GMT, the cookie will be written to disk. If no such pair exists, the browser will not write the cookie to disk and the cookie will expire when the user exits from the browser.

2. The browser, if it recognizes cookies, stores the name=value pairs on disk or in memory (depending on the presence of an expires=date value pair), then returns them to the server with its next page request, that is, appended to the next URL it sends to the server.

The way it works in the discussion database is as follows:

1. The user clicks the User Preferences hotspot in the view template of the discussion database. This retrieves the Preferences form from the Preferences database. (The reason it retrieves a form in a second database is so that the discussion database can have a default access of Reader. This forces anyone who wants to contribute to the discussion database to register and log in. Anonymous users can read the discussion database and can author a preferences form without registering.)

13

2. The user chooses either "fast" or "pretty" in a radio button field on the Preferences form, then submits the form. This sets the value of a field named Bandwidth to either dbh or dbl, which stand for "high bandwidth" connection with speedy page retrieval or "low bandwidth" connection with slow page retrieval. The $$Return field in the form includes the following formula:

```
cookie := Bandwidth;
"<head>" +
"<META HTTP-EQUIV=\"Set-Cookie\" CONTENT=\"prefs=" + cookie + "; path=/;
➥expires=Thu, 01-Jan-2009 12:00:00 GMT\">" +
"<title>Preferences</title>" +
"</head><body>Thanks! Your new preferences are now set. <a href=\"" + ReturnTo +
➥"\">Return to discussion</a>."
```

which (if the user chose "fast") sends the following HTML page back to the browser:

```
<head><META HTTP-EQUIV="Set-Cookie" CONTENT= "prefs=dbl; path=/; expires=Thu,
➥01-Jan-2009 12:00:00 GMT"><title>Preferences</title></head><body>Thanks! Your
➥new preferences are now set. <a href="URL">Return to discussion</a>
```

where URL is the URL of the view template in which the user clicked the User Preferences hotspot in the first place.

3. Thereafter, when the user clicks the name of a document, his browser sends, along with the URL of the clicked document, the value of the cookie. In the example, this would be a name=value pair of HTTP COOKIE="prefs=dbl path=/". This becomes an environment variable in the Domino server's memory, which the server then inserts into the HTTP_COOKIE field on the form on which the requested document is based.

4. Domino sends the requested document to the Web user. The user sees non-graphical actions in the action bar because the document's form included a computed subform which chose either the subform with a graphical action bar or the subform with a text-only action bar, depending on the value of prefs in the HTTP_COOKIE field. The user does not see the graphics embedded in the form because hide when formulas hide them when the value of prefs in the HTTP_COOKIE field is dbl.

Using the Domino Registration Database

The Domino Registration database is designed to automate the process of registering anonymous Web users, that is, to obtain identity information from them so that you can later authenticate them and include them in access control lists and workflows. To authenticate a Web user, Domino elicits a user name and password from him or her. Domino compares the name and password received with the contents of the User name field and HTTP password field in the Person documents in the Public Address Book. If a match appears, then Domino assumes that the anonymous user is the user named in the Person document and extends to that user all access rights.

The User name field for a Notes user typically has at least two entries in it, a fully distinguished hierarchical name and a common name, normally appearing in that order. When a Notes user tries to authenticate as a Web user, Domino will accept only the form of the user's name that appears first in the User name field.

The HTTP Password field for a Notes user by default has no entry. Until an entry appears there, a Notes user will not be able to authenticate from the Web. Web authentication does not permit authentication without a password by anyone.

You can create a Person document for a Web user any way that you want, including manually. However, the nature of the Web is that there are or, for any given Web site, soon will be far more users who might potentially want to register than there are people available to create Person documents for them. So an automated way of processing registrations is much to be desired. Lotus offers its own user registration database for free use by all to use as needed. You can use it as is, alter it, or borrow pieces of programming from it and embed them in your own applications. A copy of the Lotus user registration database is on the CD-ROM enclosed with this book. You can also download the latest version of it from the Lotus Web site at **www.lotus.com**.

The Lotus user registration database works by accepting an information form from the Web user. An agent then creates a Person document in the Public Address Book based on the information in the form. If it does not already exist, a Group document called Domino Web Users is also created by the agent and added to that group. The name of the group is configurable. Also, the agent that adds names to the group ensures that the group does not automatically grow larger than the maximum size (about 15,000 bytes in the Members field) for a group in the Public Address Book. The information form that the user submits appears in Figure 13.7.

The Registration database refuses to accept the submitted form from the user if certain required fields are not properly completed. The required fields include:

▶ First Name *field*   Contains an input translation formula that verifies that alphabetical characters were entered.

▶ Last Name *field*   Contains an input translation formula that verifies that alphabetical characters were entered.

▶ E-mail *field*   Contains an input translation formula that assures that the e-mail address is syntactically correct (if not an actual e-mail address).

▶ Password *field*   Contains a default value formula that enters a random password, which the user can then change.

13

But the centerpiece of this database is the Lotuscript agent that generates a `Person` document for the new registrant and adds his or her name to the appropriate `Group` document. In its original version, this was a scheduled agent. However, Lotus discovered that people would register, go off and do something else while waiting for their registration to take effect, and then lose interest while waiting and never return. So for this version of the database, Lotus has rewritten the agent so that it runs as soon as the user hits the submit button.

Fig. 13.7

Here is the Web user's submission form, as seen in a Web browser.

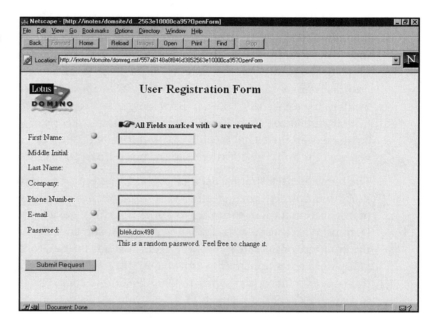

Lotus has achieved this by including a hidden field called `$$QuerySaveAgent`, which is a `Computed for Display` field. The value of this field is `Handle New Account Request`, which is the name of the agent that generates the new `Person` document. Hitting the Submit button on the Registration form triggers the running of the agent named in this field.

The agent itself, `Handle New Account Request`, is quite complex. Although the code resides mostly in the agent, it calls a series of functions that themselves reside in script libraries or in a .dll file in the Notes program directory. If you are a student of Lotuscript, you will find a study of this agent and its supporting functions a valuable exercise.

The user cannot only register with this database, but can also later examine and change her password. The user can first examine her password, and then choose to change it. The form that displays the user information has `Readers` and `Authors` fields in it that resolve to the names of the authenticated user and the Role of User Manager so that unauthorized people cannot examine user personal information. The form on which the user enters a new password, like the New Account form, has a $$QuerySaveAgent field, so the change request is processed immediately.

Using the Domino Download Database

This database was developed by Lotus to manage the process of file downloads by customers. The Webmasters at **lotus.com** realized that they needed a sophisticated download application soon after their site went up, at which time they were running InterNotes Web Publisher. As the number of downloadable Domino kits increased, they realized that they had a potential nightmare on their hands as some kits were available on all platforms, some were not, some were available in many languages, and others were not. They realized that customers would be disappointed if they were permitted to download software that didn't exist—say, for example, the German version of Foobar 1.5, which, of course, exists only in Japanese.

So the wizards at Lotus came up with the Domino Kits database. This database includes a KitMap document, which is a lookup table that includes every major version number, build number, platform, and language with which Lotus creates any Domino kit that it makes available for download from its Web site. The Domino Kits database includes a Kit document for every available kit. The Kit document includes the actual kit as an attachment.

Finally, the Domino Kits database includes the *pièce de résistance*, a self-updating form for Web users to complete. When this form first appears on the Web, it offers the user one choice: Which platform do you want Domino software for? After this, you pick from a list that includes the only available platforms. If there is only one available platform, however, then you never have to make this choice at all but are automatically moved instead to the next step.

Assuming, though, that you could choose a computer platform, the initial version of the input form looks something like that in Figure 13.8.

You choose a platform and click OK. Next, one of two things happens. If you clicked OK without choosing a platform, the form re-presents itself but this time with a big, red reminder on it that you must make a choice before clicking OK, as shown in Figure 13.9.

When you finally do make a choice and click OK, the form re-presents itself showing the platform choice and a list of available versions to choose from (see Figure 13.10).

You continue making choices, and the form continues updating itself and presenting the next set of choices until you have narrowed the field to a single kit. At that point, the form presents you with a legal agreement. If you click the Agree button, the form presents you with the actual kit to download.

13

Fig. 13.8

Here is the first iteration of the input form.

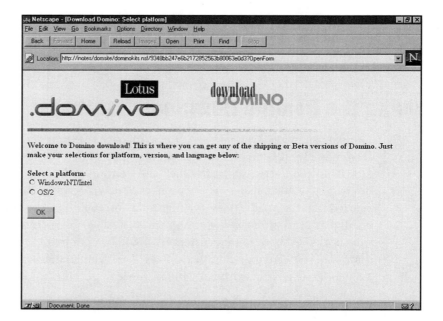

Fig. 13.9

If the user clicks OK without making a choice, the form reappears with a big, red help message.

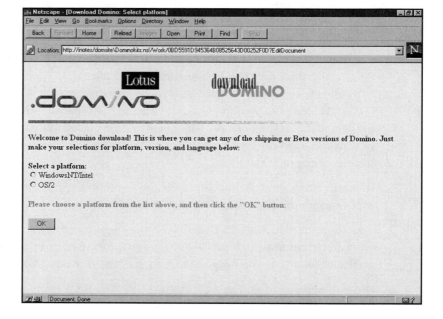

Fig. 13.10

Now that the user finally made a choice, the form reappears with a second choice to make.

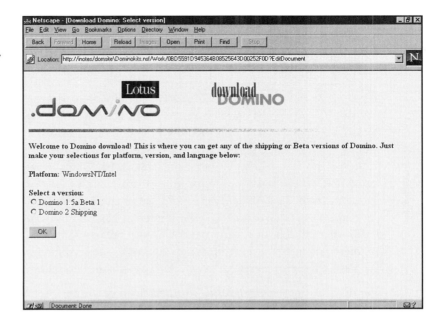

The interesting things that this form does are:

▶ It presents choices that are represented only in actual kits.

▶ It re-presents itself in an updated state whenever you click OK, without stopping at an intermediate state to tell you what it is going to do next.

▶ It skips over the process of choosing when there is only one available choice.

▶ It presents explicit, on-screen help if you make a mistake.

Here's how the process of choosing, always from an accurate list of choices, works. Whenever a new kit becomes available for download, the App Manager creates a kit document that describes the kit in terms of version, platform, language, and so on, and that includes a copy of the kit in the form of an attachment. Then the App Manager runs a Lotuscript agent that updates the Kit Map document by adding a series of fields to it that contain the actual available choices of kits.

Whenever a user is presented with a list of choices, the list includes only the available choices because the Download document receives the choices from the Kit Map document. The field PlatformChoices in the Download document receives the initial choices from the Kit Map document with the following formula: @GetDocField(KitMapUNID; "Choices"). Later, the field VersionChoices receives a valid set of version choices from the Kit Map with the

13

formula: `@GetDocField(KitMapUNID; "Choices" + Platform)`, which pulls the list of available versions of the already chosen platform. Yet later it goes through a similar process to come up with the valid list of languages available for the already chosen platform and version.

Here's how the self-updating form works. There is a field called `State`, which starts out in state 1, and then is updated as you progress through the series of choices. When it reaches state 5, you are presented with the download software. The field has a series of subforms in which the choices and the Submit button appear. The first subform displays the first choice—which platform to choose. After you have successfully chosen a platform and clicked the Submit button, the form updates the `State` field and then re-presents itself. The updated `State` field causes the form to hide the first subform that it presented to you, with the first set of choices in it and to display instead a subform that shows the chosen item; it then displays a second subform that presents the second set of choices and a Submit button. When you make the second choice, it goes through this process again and then again until you have made all the choices.

If you click the Submit button without making a proper choice, the form detects that fact and sets a field called `ShowFieldHelp` to `Y`. This in turn causes the red help text paragraph to unhide itself the next time the form reappears, because the paragraph has a hide-when formula that says hide when `ShowFieldHelp != Y`. Since the second time around it *is* equal to `Y`, the paragraph magically appears.

Finally, if you look at the `$$Return` field on the `Download` form, you see that the formula there resolves to the URL of the `Download` form itself. If the user has made all required choices, however, the formula resolves to the URL of the `kit` document, and you then see the attach kit, ready for download. The actual formula in the `$$Return` field is:

```
"[/" + @Subset(@DbName; -1) +
   @If(
      State < "x5D";
         "/Work/" + @Text(@DocumentUniqueID) + "?EditDocument";
         "/Kits/" + KitUNID + "?OpenDocument&Color=" + Color
   ) +
"]"
```

This resolves to:

```
[/databasename/Work/DocUNID?OpenDocument]
```

or to:

```
[/databasename/Kits/KitUNID?OpenDocument&Color=SomeColor],
```

where `DocUNID` is the Download form and `KitUNID` is the chosen kit document.

Creating a Database to Manage Files

If you ever have to manage a remote Domino server, you will appreciate this next database, which is a repository of images and files. Recall that you can make an image available to Web users in several ways. One way is to embed the image in a Notes document. This becomes a problem if the image is embedded in a form rather than a document. For example, if the image is your logo and you want it to appear everywhere, embedding it in all of your forms means that every time a Web user retrieves any document, she will retrieve and cache yet another copy of the same logo. This is very wasteful of time, bandwidth, and disk space.

You can avoid this problem in one of two ways. First, you can copy the image into a subdirectory of your Domino data directory, say, into the icons directory. Then you can replace the embedded copy of the image with an URL that points to the image in the icons directory. The URL would look something like this:

```
[<img src=domino/icons/filename.gif.}
```

This works fine as long as the server you are managing is nearby. You just walk up to it and copy the file to the subdirectory. But what if the server is remote, say, at your ISP rather than at your own office? Now you have to traipse down there to copy the file into the subdirectory, send the file over and beg someone else to copy the file for you, or set up a remote access service, dial in, log in to the server remotely, and then copy the file remotely.

Here's a better way to manage attached files. Create a database that acts as a repository of images. Attach the image to a document. Set up a view in which the first sorted column is a keyword column that enables you to select any document by referring to the unique keyword for the document that appears in the column. Then, use the following URL to extract the document from the document at runtime.

```
[<img src = "/DatabaseName.nsf/ViewName/Keyname/$File/Filename.gif">]
```

That is, instead of an URL pointing to the location of the image in the file system, set up an URL that points to the image in a named document in a named database. Then replicate the database over to the remote server and sit back with your feet up. You can also retrieve any other kind of file this way, such as, for example, Java .class files.

On the CD-ROM you'll find a database called source.nsf. It is a simple file repository database put together by our friend David Freiman, a Certified Lotus Instructor, of Norwalk, Connecticut. He gave it to you, the readers of this book, with his compliments. You'll find that it includes several graphics files which, as far as we know, do not include any copyrighted files.

13

From Here...

The databases listed here are available at **http://domino.lotus.com**. However, they are not the only sample database available from Lotus.

▶ At the time of this writing, there was a sample mail template that extended the functionality of the Notes mail database to mail users who open their mail databases from within a browser.

▶ Also, there was a sample home page database, a sample Software Problem Reports database, and a database in which Lotus from time to time adds sample agents.

Using Advanced Administration Features

## chapter 14

Securing the Domino Web Server

In this chapter

◆ **About Domino security features as they apply to Notes users**
Learn about network security, authentication, server access lists, database access control lists, view and form access lists, document access restrictions, section access lists, and field-level security.

◆ **About Domino security features as they apply to Web users**
Learn how all those Notes security features apply to Web users.

◆ **Learn what steps you can take to protect information in Notes databases from Web users while making it available to Notes users**
What are the specific steps you can take to protect confidential data from unauthorized access from the Web?

Domino Security Features

An amazing thing happens when you start up the HTTP server for the first time. A server that previously would have guarded its databases with all the zeal of a mother bear protecting her cubs suddenly lets almost anyone in the world have entry to them (the databases, not the cubs). Lotus Notes is renowned for its robust security. The typical Domino server requires positive identification of anyone coming to it with a request for data. Even after you identify yourself, you may be turned away or given only the most proscribed access to the data you seek.

Every Notes administrator knows that you *can* disable the authentication function in Lotus Notes. But they know that you have to do so positively, by changing a field in the server document. Now comes along this server task that, by the mere act of loading it, disables the requirement of authentication. If you're new to Notes, you may be thinking right about now, "Okay, so what?" But people who have spent some time with traditional Notes servers tend to react to this discovery with shock. The really ironic part is that, while loading the HTTP service into memory opens the Domino server's secrets up to any old total stranger of a Web surfer who wants to come poking around, the Domino server continues to jealously protect that same data whenever a legitimate Notes user comes around. Notes users have to authenticate with the server, while mere Web users can have anonymous access. Makes us light-headed just to think about it.

If this still doesn't make *you* light-headed, let's step back and examine Domino's security features from the ground up.

Understanding Domino Security Features as Applied to the Notes User

To gain access to databases on a standard (non-HTTP) Domino server, a Notes user must first *authenticate* with the server, then must survive the server's access list, then get past a layered series of access lists in each database—view access lists, form access lists, document access lists, section access lists, and encrypted fields. One roadblock anywhere along the way, and the user is stopped cold.

Notes Authentication

In the authentication process, both the user and the server have to prove to each other that they are members of *trusted* organizations and they have to prove their identities. This involves a series of encryptions and decryptions of information using public and private keys.

To understand how Notes authentication works and why it is very effective, you must understand how public key, private key encryption works. Notes generates a pair of encryption keys for every Notes entity, including certifiers, servers, and users, at the time the entity is created. The keys are stored in the .id file of the entity. A copy of the public key is stored in the entity's document in the Public Address Book—in Certifier document for each certifier, Server document for each server, and Person document for each user. You can see the public key in each of these documents by opening it in Edit mode and scrolling to the bottom of the document (see Figure 14.1).

Fig. 14.1

You can see this certifier's public key by opening the Certifier document in Edit mode. The key is a very large hexadecimal number.

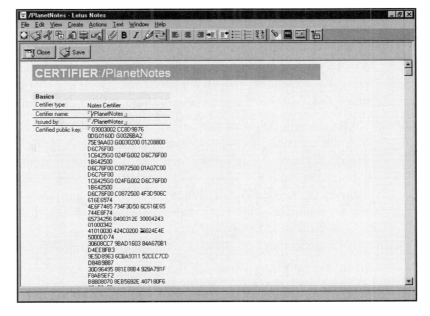

Each pair of public and private keys is related to each other. You can derive each one from the other. The derivation is what is known as a one-way algorithm because it is relatively easy to derive the public key from the private key but extremely difficult to derive the private key from the public key. Other examples of one-way algorithms include multiplication, division and taking powers and roots. It is easy to multiply two numbers, harder to divide two numbers. It is easy to square a number, harder to find a number's square root. It is vastly more difficult to calculate a private key knowing its public key counterpart than it is to find a square root.

The algorithm Notes uses to generate the key pairs is called the RSA cryptosystem. It is named after its inventors, three mathematicians at MIT, Rivest, Shamir, and Adelman. Many other encryption systems use the RSA cryptosystem; one example is the Secure Sockets Layer (SSL) security system used by Domino servers can optionally use to secure communications between itself and Web clients. SSL is covered in the next chapter.

Dual-Key Encryption

The way dual-key encryption systems work is that you can encrypt information with either the public key or the private key. Whichever key you use, you can only use the other key to decrypt. You can encrypt with the public key, then decrypt with the private key, or you can encrypt with the private, then decrypt with the public.

If I want to send you a message for your eyes only, I can encrypt it with your public key. Since only you have a copy of your private key, only you can decrypt it. If I want to send you a message with assurance that it came from me, I can encrypt it (or some portion of it) with my private key. Since I have the only copy of my private key, the fact that you can decrypt the message with my public key assures you that it must have been me who encrypted it. In effect, I signed the message in a way that nobody else could have.

Notes (like other software that uses dual-key encryption) uses this feature for encryption and identification purposes. Notes uses it for mail encryption, signatures, and authentication. Of course, Notes automates the encryption/decryption process so that it is transparent to you and me. When sending a message, we just choose Encrypt or Sign in the Delivery Options dialog box. When we try to open a database on a Domino server, we just enter our password. Notes does all the hard work of retrieving keys, encrypting, and decrypting behind the scenes.

Single-Key Encryption

You could contrast dual-key encryption with single-key encryption, which Notes uses for field encryption. With single-key encryption, one encryption key both encrypts and decrypts data. Dual-key encryption is preferred for encrypting information that I will send to you because we don't both have to have copies of the same key in dual-key encryption. If we used single-key encryption, we would both somehow have to acquire copies of the same key. Either one of us could generate the encryption key, then send it to the other. However, this would compromise the key's security, since someone could intercept it en route and make a clandestine copy, then use it to read our supposedly secure communications. We could meet personally to exchange a copy of the key, but that would be a big hassle.

With dual-key encryption, the problem of securely and conveniently exchanging encryption keys is eliminated by the fact that we never have to exchange the private key at all, just the public key, and we don't care who grabs a copy of that, since it can't be used to decrypt anything encrypted by it. In fact, we want our public keys to be as widely, publicly, and conveniently available as possible, so that anyone, even a total stranger, could obtain a copy of it and send us an encrypted message if they want. So Notes automatically puts a copy of every public key that it generates in the Public Address Book.

Mail Encryption in Notes 4.x

Actually, Notes 4.x encrypts mail slightly differently than described above. Because Notes 4.x supports shared mail storage, it can't simply encrypt messages with public keys. On any Domino server on which shared mail is enabled, only one copy of the body of each mail message is stored, no matter how many people it was sent to. If I send a message to you with copies to two other people, as long as the mail databases of you and the other recipients are all on the same shared-mail-enabled Domino server, only one copy of the body of the message is maintained. It is stored in the shared mail database. When you or the other recipients read the message, you are reading from the same, shared copy of the body of the message.

If mail encryption caused the body of the message to be encrypted with the public key of each recipient, then each body would be different from the others, and Domino could not retain a single copy of the message body. Instead, what Notes does is this rather clever workaround. When I tell it to encrypt the mail message to you and the others, Notes generates a single-key encryption key. It encrypts the body of the message with that key, then encrypts one copy of that key with the public key of each of the recipients. Domino then delivers the encrypted message body to the shared mail database and the message headers, each with the appropriately encrypted encryption key attached, to each of the recipients. When each of you goes to read the message, Notes decrypts the encryption key with your private key, then decrypts the message body with the decrypted encryption key.

Signatures

What is really elegant is that the dual-key system can also be used to identify us to each other. When you receive a message from me, you assume that it is from me because it says I am the author. But if I wanted to, I could easily alter the way my mail database works, so that it would allow me to enter any name in the From field. Then I could send you a message that purports to be from, say, Bill Gates. Being the gullible type, you would, of course, fall hook, line, and sinker for my ruse, right? Well, maybe I could be more subtle and enter the name of someone from whom you actually receive mail on a regular basis (like Bill Clinton, maybe), and I could cause all sorts of grief between the two of you.

To assure you that the mail you receive is really from me (or Bill, or whomever), the sender could sign it by affixing to it a block of data that was encrypted with the sender's private key. When you receive the message, you could try decrypting the signature with the sender's public key. If you succeed in decrypting it, you can rest reasonably assured that the sender is who he/she purports to be, because presumably the only copy of the private key in existence is the one in the sender's .id file, protected from use by others by a password which the sender jealously refuses to share with anyone. (That's the theory, anyway; if people fail to protect their passwords, well, that's another issue.)

14

The Authentication Process

Authentication also uses the public key, private key system, even more elegantly than mail encryption and signatures do. Domino servers are charged with the responsibility of releasing data only to users who are authorized to see it, and accepting data only from those authorized to add it. Domino servers can only fulfill this responsibility if they know who they are dealing with. You can identify yourself to a Domino server by sending it something signed by you. It can verify with your public key that the signed object is signed by you, not some impostor. However, how can the Domino server know that the public key, private key pair it is using really identifies you?

In other words, why couldn't I, Doctor Notes, generate a pair of keys that purport to identify me as, say, Bill Gates. The fact is that I very well could. When I come to the server, hat in hand, requesting entrance to the sanctuary within, I not only present the server with my signed certificate, but I also provide the server with the public key it will use to decrypt my signature.

The server could refuse to accept the public key I offer it, using the copy of my public key stored in the Public Address Book instead, but there are difficulties with that. Principally, I may be from another domain and the server may not have my public key in its public address book. Because of this, Domino servers normally do accept and use the public key offered to them by the users themselves.

So, how does the server verify that the public key I offer it really does identify the *real* Doctor Notes, and not some impostor? It relies on the certification process, that's how. If you and I were introduced to each other at a party by a mutual friend, we would automatically trust that the other was really the person identified, because we believe our mutual fried. If I showed up on your doorstep with a letter of introduction signed with a signature that you know to be that of your trusted friend, you would be inclined to assume that I really am the person identified in the letter of introduction, even though you had never before seen or heard of me. Domino servers do it the same way.

Our Notes ID files have in them not only our encryption keys but also one or more certificates that identify us. The certificate says something like "The holder of this certificate is Doctor Notes/Admin/PHL/PlanetNotes. Signed: /Admin/PHL/PlanetNotes." The certificates are issued by the certifier IDs in our organization. That is, Doctor Notes's ID file has the following certificates in it:

▶ A certificate issued to Doctor Notes by /Admin/PHL/PlanetNotes;

▶ A copy of the certificate issued to /Admin/PHL/PlanetNotes by /PHL/PlanetNotes;

▶ A copy of the certificate issued to /PHL/PlanetNotes by /PlanetNotes;

▶ A copy of the certificate issued to /PlanetNotes by itself.

Each of these certificates is signed by its issuer, and I can verify that fact because the public keys of the issuers are in the Certifier documents in the Public Address Book. When I come to a Domino server asking for access to data, before it asks me to identify myself, it asks what certificates I hold, and I tell it. If it also holds a certificate issued by the issuer of one of my certificates, then it can assume that I am really Doctor Notes. It can verify from the public keys held in the Public Address Book that at least one of my certificates really is signed by the issuer of one of its own certificates. Because the certifier that certified the server (or one of the certifiers in its chain of certification) also certified me (or one of the certifiers in my chain of certification), the server can assume that the public key that I offer really is the public key of Doctor Notes, and as long as I also possess the companion private key, the server can assume I really am Doctor Notes. It has authenticated me. Now the server and I reverse the process, so that I can authenticate the server and rest easy in the sure knowledge that the data I am about to work with really is in (or going into) the custody of the Domino server that I thought I was dealing with.

Anonymous Notes Clients

In Notes Release 4.x, you can relax Notes security by allowing unauthenticated users to access a given server and its databases. An unauthenticated user is one whose identity the server has not ascertained and who, therefore, is essentially *anonymous* to the server. You permit anonymous access by setting the Allow Anonymous Notes Connections field to Yes, which appears in the Security section of the Server document in the Public Address Book; the field defaults to No. You can control the degree of access such users have to given databases by adding Anonymous to each database's Access Control List and specifying the degree of access that Anonymous should have. If you don't add Anonymous to a database Access Control List, anonymous users are granted Default access.

Server Access Lists

Now that the Domino server has authenticated me, the server can still refuse me access to its databases if I am listed in the Not Access Server field or *not* listed in the Access Server field in the server's Server document in the Public Address Book (see Figure 14.2). Actually, if I am not listed in the Access Server field, it will only refuse me access if the field is not empty. If I want to create a new database or a replica database, the server will only permit it if I am listed in the appropriate field. Same if I want to pass through the server to get to another server or reach this server by pass-through. I either am listed individually in the appropriate field or I am a member of a group that is so listed.

Database Access Control Lists

Fig. 14.2

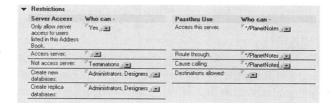

The Domino server permits or restricts access to its databases according to the entries in the fields in the Restrictions section of its Server document.

If I get past the server access lists, the server will now consider any request I might make to access a database. The server now consults the database's Access Control List, where the I may be listed, either individually or as a member of a group, as having Manager access, Designer access, Editor access, Author access, Reader access, Depositor access, or No access. Or I may not be listed at all, in which case the server will grant me the Default level of access, which could be any of the listed levels. The rights that each access level grants are in Table 14.1.

Table 14.1　Lotus Notes Database Access Rights

Access Level	Activities Allowed
Manager	The database manager can do anything in a database, including change the Access Control List.
Designer	Database designers can do anything in a database, including making changes in the database design, but excluding making changes in the Access Control List.
Editor	Database editors can add data documents to a database and can make changes in any data document in the database, regardless of the document's authorship. Editors *cannot* change database design or the Access Control List.
Author	Database authors can create new data documents. They cannot edit documents, including those authored by themselves, unless they are named in the document in a field of Authors data type. If they are so named, they can edit the document whether they originally authored it or not. Also, users with Author access cannot make changes in the database design or Access Control List.
Reader	Database readers can read data documents and views but cannot make changes of any kind in the database.

Access Level	Activities Allowed
Depositor	Database depositors can create and save new data documents, but they cannot read any document, including their own after they close it; nor can they make changes of any kind in the database.
No Access	Users with no access are not allowed to open a database at all.

Access Restrictions within a Database

Assuming a user has some degree of access that allows him or her to at least read documents, the user may further be restricted by the following:

▶ **View access lists**, which forbid the use of a particular view to see what documents are in the database.

▶ **Form create access lists**, which forbid the use of a particular form to create documents.

▶ **Readers fields** and **$Readers fields** (generated by **Form** and **Document Reader Access Lists**), which can forbid the viewing of a particular document.

▶ **Authors** fields, which can grant to an ACL Author the power to edit a particular document.

▶ **Section access lists**, which can restrict who can edit a section of a document.

▶ **Encrypted fields**, which can forbid the reading of those fields in a document.

▶ **Signed fields**, which can positively identify the last person to have entered data into a field or the fields within a given section of a document.

Web Users and Domino Security

When you load the HTTP server task into the Domino server's memory, you permit (by default) unauthenticated Web users to access your server and its databases. As a result, whether you like it or not, Web users now have access to your databases. They have Anonymous access to any database in which Anonymous appears in the database's Access Control List. They have Default access to all other databases.

You can tighten up the security of the databases on your Domino Web server in the following several ways:

▶ Remove from the Domino Web server any databases that don't need to be there.

▶ Altogether deny Web users anonymous access to your server, just the way the server denies access to unauthenticated Notes users, by resetting a field in the Security section of the server document.

▶ Hide all or individual databases from view by resetting fields in the server document or each database's Properties InfoBox.

▶ Lower the maximum access permitted to any database from a Web browser in the Advanced panel of the Access Control List dialog box.

▶ Review the Access Control List of every database on the server and insure either that there is an entry in it for Anonymous, with the appropriate degree of access assigned, or that the degree of access assigned to Default is appropriate for unauthenticated Web users.

▶ Deny anonymous access to a given database, then require Web users who want access to it to register with you. This is known as basic authentication. It is a standard Web authentication technique, and it gives a Web user *individualized* access to your site. That is, after registering with you, they are no longer anonymous. They tell you their name and password, then you give them access based on their identities—just like Notes users.

▶ Activate Secure Sockets Layer (SSL) security for Web-based transactions. This provides a level of security akin to Notes authentication, because SSL authentication requires certification and signature identification, just as Notes does.

Limiting Web Access at the Server Level

The Security section of the Server document has several fields that apply to Web security. By default, they permit wide open access to your Notes server. The fields are as follows:

▶ *Allow anonymous HTTP connections*—Defaults to Yes. Setting it to No allows only authenticated Web users to access the databases on your site. All Web users, when they request a document from your site, must first enter their name and password in a dialog box. The server denies access if the name and password submitted do not match those in a Person document in the Public Address Book.

▶ *Allow HTTP clients to browse databases*—Defaults to Yes. By default, any Web user who can access your site can retrieve a list of databases there by entering either the ?Open or ?OpenServer command. That is, they could enter something like this: **http://domino.chestnet.com/?OpenServer**. Setting this field to No disables this capability. Web users will be blocked from retrieving a list of databases on the server.

This last restriction, disablement of browsing, will only keep casual Web users out of databases. If you know the name of a database, you can still use ?OpenDatabase to get into that database. A savvy Notes user could easily get around the browse restriction by simply opening the Notes Catalog, catalog.nsf, which resides on every server by default. From there you could obtain the file names of every database on the Domino server. Then you could simply use the ?OpenDatabase command to open each database by name.

Limiting Web Access at the Database Level

The fields described in the preceding section limit the types of access that Web users can gain to your server. You can also limit access to individual databases. You can make it difficult for a Web user to locate a database on your server by changing two settings in the Properties for Database InfoBox. You can control the types of things a Web user can do in a database by adding a user named Anonymous to the database's Access Control List.

You may not want to altogether disallow browsing with the ?open command. Instead, you can stop a database from appearing in the list that the ?open command procures. You do this in that database's Properties InfoBox, in the Design panel. Remove the check mark from the box labeled Show in 'Open Database' dialog box (see Figure 14.3). You can also make sure the check box labeled List in Database Catalog is not checked, so that a user cannot browse in the Database Catalog database for the database you are trying to hide. However, watch out for unintended consequences: Notes users will no longer be able to find the database by browsing either.

Fig. 14.3

Two fields in the Database Properties Box affect people's ability to find databases on the Domino server: List in Database Catalog and Show in 'Open Database' dialog box.

However, even if you hide a file so that a user cannot discover it by browsing and cannot discover its name in the Database Catalog, the user can still open any database whose file name he knows with the following command:

http://www.planetnotes.com/dbfilename.nsf/?OpenDatabase

14

Anonymous Web Users and the Database Access Control List

Ultimately, you control user access to databases with the Database Access Control List (ACL). Domino controls anonymous access to databases with two ACL entries: Anonymous and Default. If you add the name Anonymous to a database's ACL, anonymous users have the level of access that you assign to Anonymous. This includes both anonymous Web users and anonymous Notes users. If you don't want anonymous Web users poking around in, say, your Public Address Book, gathering the names and phone numbers of your most valued employees, add Anonymous to the ACL and assign No Access.

If you neglect to add Anonymous to the ACL of a database, not to worry. Anonymous users still only get the level of access assigned to Default. Assign No Access to Default in the ACLs of your most sensitive databases, and only users who are named in the ACL or who are members of groups named in the ACL will be able to open them.

Controlling Web User Access to Views, Folders, Forms, and Documents

You can further control user access to views, forms, and documents. Every view, form, and document in a database has an Access List, located in the object's Properties InfoBox, which defaults to permitting use by everyone with appropriate ACL access. You can limit the membership of any Reader Access List. Notes documents can include Readers or Authors fields. If a user with Author ACL access is included in an Authors field, that user can edit the document even though he did not create it. If a user with Reader ACL access is excluded from a Readers field, he is not able to read the document. Anonymous users may be included in or excluded from any of these Access Lists or fields. Anonymous users may be members of groups which are, in turn, included in or excluded from any of these Access Lists.

View and Folder Access Lists

Every Notes view and folder includes an access list that, by default, permits every user with Reader access to the database to use the view. The access list is located on the "key" panel of the View Properties box, and can be opened when the view is open in Design mode (see Figure 14.4). The designer of the view can designate which users can use the view by deselecting the All readers and above checkbox and selecting individual users, servers, groups, roles, or resources from the scrollable list that appears. The designer can also click the Person icon to the right of the user list to bring up a Names dialog. From there the designer can choose any user, server, group, role, or resource that may appear in any available address book. Because Web users are identified as Anonymous by Notes, they will not be able to read this view or even see it in a list of views if you don't select Anonymous in the view access list.

Fig. 14.4

You can render a view unusable by Web users by excluding Anonymous users in the view access list. Here every user is checked except Anonymous.

The view access list is not really a security feature when used to exclude Notes users, since Notes users can create their own private views and folders and could define them to display the exact same information about the exact same subset of Notes documents as a restricted view displays. When used to exclude Notes users, view access lists are more of a convenience feature—they reduce the clutter on the Notes user's screen by making views that are of little use to a user disappear entirely from the user's view lists.

However, when used to exclude Web users, the view access list really is a security feature (well, almost), because Web users cannot create private views or folders. When you exclude Anonymous from a view access list, the view disappears from the list of views that an anonymous Web user can retrieve from your Domino server. On the other hand, the data that you want to hide is stored in documents, not views. Hiding a view does not block user access to the documents listed in it; it just forces the user to get at the documents some other way, say, by finding them in another view or by using a Domino URL to retrieve a Notes document directly. Of course, in a well-designed database there may not be another view that lists a given document, and retrieving documents directly using Domino URLs is no easy task, since you have to identify them by their unique ID, a thirty-two digit, hexadecimal number that is generated more or less randomly by Domino or Notes.

The long and short of it is that the view access list can be an effective way of keeping Web users from poking around in the parts of databases where you don't want them. An even better way, however, would be to keep confidential documents out of the database altogether and, better yet, off the Web server entirely.

Form Access Lists

Every Notes form includes two access lists: a read access list and a create access list. They appear on the "key" panel of the Form Properties box, which you can open when the Form is open in Design mode (see Figure 14.5).

Fig. 14.5

Forms have two access lists: a read access list that may limit who can read documents created with the form; and a create access list that may limit who can create documents with the form.

The read access list sets default read access for documents created with the form. Its function corresponds to several document access mechanisms. Therefore we discuss the form read access list with them, below.

The form create access list specifies who can use a form to create new documents. By default anyone can use the form, but the form designer can restrict use of the form to create documents by selecting users, groups, roles, and the rest, from the list in the *Who can create documents with this form* section of the Form Properties box. This feature would block use by anonymous Web users if Anonymous is not selected in the list.

It could also be used to create a form exclusively for use by Web users. All you would have to do is deselect all users except Web users. That is, select Anonymous if you want anonymous Web users to use the form. First, however, you better add Anonymous to the database Access Control List; otherwise Anonymous won't appear in the create access list at all. And be sure to give Anonymous at least Author access to the database; the create access list only refines the database ACL; it does not override it.

Document Access Lists

Access to individual documents is controlled by three different mechanisms: the $Readers field, fields of Readers data type, and fields of Authors data type. Authors fields expand the list of users who can edit a document. All three field types combine to restrict who can read a document. That is, anyone named in an Authors field, a Readers field, or the $Readers field can read a document. If there are no Readers field and there is no $Readers field, all users with Reader access to the database can read the document.

Form and Document Read Access Lists and the *$Readers* Field

The $Readers field may or may not exist in a given document. If it does exist, only the users listed in it will be able to read the document. The $Readers field will exist only under certain circumstances. First, if the designer of a form limits readership in the Form read access list (refer to Figure 14.5), Notes will create a $Readers field in every document created with the form and populate the field with the names of the entities listed in the form read access list. This constitutes the designer's opportunity to define a default read access list, because the designer's choices will show up in the Document read access list when a user creates a new document using the form.

The document read access list appears in the Document Properties box, which is available when a document is selected in a view or opened. It appears on the "key" panel (see Figure 14.6).

Fig. 14.6

The Document read access list appears in the Document Properties box. The choices in it are set initially by the designer of the form used to create the document, but can be altered by the author of the document.

If the form designer didn't restrict read access in the Form read access list, the author of a new document can do so in the Document read access list. This also will cause Notes to create a $Readers field. If neither the form designer nor the document author restricts readership in a read access list, then no $Readers field will appear in the new document. However, a reader can later restrict read access, whereupon Notes would create a $Readers field at that time. Or a reader could remove the read restrictions, in which case Notes would remove the $Readers field.

In any event, the existence of a $Readers field will restrict who can read a document and that restriction is effective against users on the Web. The effect it will have is that Web users will not see the document in any views, and will generate an error if they try to retrieve such a document with a Domino URL.

Readers Fields

A form designer can add one or more fields of Readers data type to a form. Readers fields hold the names of Notes users, groups, roles, and servers. If a Readers field exists in a document and is not empty, it governs who can read that document. That is, the entities allowed to read the document will include only those listed in that Readers field, plus anyone listed in other Readers fields in the document, plus anyone listed in the $Readers field, if it exists, plus anyone listed in any Authors fields if they exist. If no $Readers field exists and if all Readers fields, if they exist, are empty, then anyone with Reader access to the database can read the document.

Readers fields, like the $Readers field, are effective against both Notes users and Web users. Like $Readers fields, Readers fields have the effect of making the affected documents disappear entirely from the database when viewed by someone not authorized to read them.

Authors Fields

A form designer can also add one or more fields of Authors data type to a form. Authors fields hold the names of Notes users, groups, roles, and servers. Authors fields permit users who have Author access in the database ACL to edit the document. Normally, only users with Editor access in the database ACL can edit a document. Authors fields expand that privilege to users with Authors access whose names appear in the Authors field or who are members of groups or roles that appear in the Authors field.

Authors fields extend their benefits to Web users as well as Notes user. That is, if Anonymous appears in an Authors field, then, if Anonymous has Author access in the database ACL, anonymous Web users will be able to edit the document in question.

Web Users and Notes Field-Level Security

The field-level security features of Notes do not function the same for Web users as for Notes users. These include controlled-access sections and signed and encrypted fields. None of them have any effect in documents sent to Web users.

Notes users can be restricted from editing fields in a controlled-access section. But that access control does not extend to Web users. When a Web user opens a document in Edit mode, he has access to all non-hidden, editable fields, even those in controlled-access sections.

Finally, field signatures and field encryption do not function when Web users view a document. Be clear about this. Web users will be able to see the contents of all encrypted fields in any documents that they can read.

Caution
Field encryption does not function when Web users view a document. They will be able to see the contents of all encrypted fields, even though they possess no encryption keys.

Setting Up Basic Authentication for Web Users

You can give a Web user *individualized* database access if you create a Person document for that user and enter data in at least two of the fields. First, you must enter the user's name in the User Name field. Second, you must enter a password into the HTTP Password field. The password is encrypted as soon as you save the Person document, so that readers of the Person document cannot read the password.

 Note

If you don't feel like personally creating a Person document for every Web user who wants access to your restricted databases, you can set up a Notes registration application that allows Web users to register themselves.

Lotus provides a sample registration database at domino.lotus.com. A Web user fills in a Web form and submits it, then a LotusScript agent creates a Person document for him in the Public Address Book and adds him to a group in the Public Address Book called Domino Users. This is a really cool application! Lotus uses it to register users at its own Web sites.

Download it. Use it as is, customize it, or borrow pieces of it and create your own registration application. Better yet, look for it on the CD-ROM in the back of this book. The application is called Domino Registration Application.

For yet another automated user registration application from Lotus, check out Domino.Action, which Lotus ships with the Domino 4.5 server. See Chapter 17, "Building a Domino Web Site in One Day with Domino Action," for more information about Domino Action.

After a Person document exists for a Web user, you can treat the user individually in database ACLs. You can set the access level of Anonymous in a database to No Access, and the access level of the registered user—or more realistically, of a group to which the registered user belongs—to Reader or some higher access level. When the registered Web user tries to access the database, Domino presents a dialog box asking the user to identify himself by name and password (see Figure 14.7). Notes verifies the information entered against the information in the Public Address Book, then gives appropriate access to the database.

Fig. 14.7

If an anonymous Web user tries to do something forbidden to anonymous users, Domino offers to authenticate the user with this dialog box.

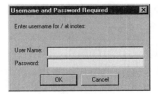

Here's another example: In a database ACL, you can give Reader access to Anonymous and Author access to your registered user (or a group of which he is a member). When the registered but as yet unauthenticated user opens the database, Notes goes along and opens it. When the user tries to add a document to the database, then Domino asks the user to identify himself.

You can also give your registered Notes users Web access to the server by adding a password to the HTTP Password field in their Person documents. Actually, if Default access in the Public Address Book ACL is set to Author, then your users can do this for themselves. Thereafter, your Notes users are able to access the Notes server using either their Notes client or their Web browser.

There's one little catch here, though. Your users have to enter their fully-distinguished names when prompted by their Web browser for name and password. The reason for this is that each Notes user's fully-distinguished name appears first in the Full Name field of his/her Person document. You can remedy this by re-ordering the versions of each user's name in the Full Name field of his/her Person document, so that the user's common name (first name, optional middle initial, and last name only) appears first, on a line by itself. The resulting entry in the field looks like this:

```
User name:      Bob Dobbs
                Bob Dobbs/Sales/AcmeCorp
```

Thereafter, your users will be able to enter their common names when prompted by their Web browsers.

There is yet another safeguard in the ACL of each database that applies to Web users. On the Advanced panel of the database ACL, the *Maximum Internet browser access* field defaults to Editor access. You can set it to any ACL access level. It defines the maximum level of access that any non-Notes user will have to that database, no matter what access is shown for the user (or for Anonymous) on the Basics panel. For example, if *Maximum Internet browser access* is set to Author, and a Web user is a member of a group that has Editor access on the Basics panel, the Web user still only has Author access. The ACL access level in *Maximum Internet browser access* prevails over any higher access level granted on the Basics panel. While this field lets you choose any ACL degree of access, the highest practical level of access that you can give to Web users is Editor, because there is no way for Web users to actually affect the design or ACL of a database, even though you give them Designer or Manager access.

From Here...

In this chapter, you learned about basic Domino security features as they apply to both Notes and Web users who seek access to databases on Domino servers.

▶ To learn about advanced Domino security as it applies to Web users, that is, about Secure Sockets Layer security, read the following chapter.

▶ You can read about the security features of the Personal Web Navigator and Server Web Navigator in Chapters 22 and 23 of this book.

▶ You can learn about Notes security features in general by reading *Special Edition Using Lotus Notes 4.5*, published by Que.

## chapter 15

Using Secure Sockets Layer (SSL) with Domino

In this chapter

◆ **How to issue a self-signed certificate**
You will learn the procedure for creating a key ring file and self-signed certificate.

◆ **How to apply for a commercially signed certificate and merge it into a key ring file**
We will review the whole process of creating a key ring file for, applying for, and merging a commercially issued certificate (by VeriSign) into the key ring file.

◆ **How to become a Certificate Authority for internal purposes, and how, as an internal Certificate Authority, to administer the whole process of requesting, issuing, and merging certificates into key ring files**
We will review the whole process of creating key ring files, requests to an internal CA for certificates, creation of certificates, merging certificates into key ring files, and the administration process in general.

Lotus Notes has always maintained robust security internally. Now that Web users can directly access Notes databases, the issue of external security arises. That is, Domino servers protect resident databases from unauthorized access by Notes users by requiring that Notes users authenticate their identity before gaining access to the databases; how will Domino servers protect those same databases from unauthorized access by Web users?

Lotus addresses that issue with two layers of security features. First, Domino servers recognize Web authentication, which we covered in the previous chapter. Second, Domino servers recognize a Web-based form of authentication known as Secure Sockets Layer, or simply SSL, which is the subject of this chapter.

Overview of Security Issue

Domino servers are charged with the responsibility of giving users—Notes users and Web users—access to databases in the servers' care, but only the degree of access that each individual user has been granted by the manager of each database. Thus, some users may only read the contents of databases, while others may add data to them, and still others may edit some or all of the existing data. In order to carry out this responsibility, Domino servers must first ascertain the identity of each user.

At the same time, you and I approach Domino servers with the intention of either pulling information from them or adding information to them. We desire that the information we receive be reliable, and that the information we give be properly protected and not misused. By this we mean that we need to know that the information is really being received from or delivered to the server we think we are dealing with, and not some impostor, and that nobody sitting between us and the server can intercept the information flowing back and forth and misuse it.

Note users are almost always dealing with proprietary information, so Notes security is very strong by default. Web servers, on the other hand, typically maintain information of a public nature, so default Web security—Web authentication, if any security is maintained at all—is correspondingly weak. But there has been ongoing, increasing demand for stronger Web-based security and for stronger Internet security in general. The world has visions of an electronic marketplace, in which people can buy and sell goods over the Internet. But as long as strangers can listen in on our electronic conversations or pose as someone they are not (and how can we tell who they really are when all we know about them is what they tell us), that dream will never become reality. That is, I can put up a Web site called www.well-known-retailer.com, even though I am not really well-known-retailer. Or I can simply listen in on your electronic conversation with well-known-retailer. How can you know that I am not really well-known-retailer? How can you confidently send credit card information to well-known-retailer if you can't ascertain that, one, you are really talking to well-known-retailer and, two, someone with bad intentions isn't listening in.

You can't. For that reason, a lot of people are looking for solutions to the problem. Web authentication isn't the answer. Under the Web authentication scheme, you send your name and password to a Web server. If the name and password show up together in the same record of a database the Web server maintains, it assumes you are the person whose name you typed in. The server doesn't know if someone else figured out your password. Someone else could easily do so, since you are sending your password to the server over the Internet. You don't know if the server really is the server it claims to be; someone could have set up an impostor server to gather information from you.

The solution to these problems lies in any one of a number of security schemes all of which work very similarly to Notes' own security scheme. That is, the answer lies in public key/private key security schemes. Several such schemes exist, both proprietary (for example, Lotus Notes security) and standards-based (such as those offered to the public as Internet standards).

Among those available publicly, Secure Sockets Layer (SSL) stands out because it appears to be gaining widespread acceptance. Netscape proposed it and supports it in its products. Domino supports it for communications between Web users and Domino servers.

Overview of SSL

SSL supports the following features:

▶ Encryption of data transferred between the Domino server and Web clients

▶ Validation that messages between the Domino server and Web clients were not tampered with en route

▶ Digital signatures, from which arises the possibility of server authentication

This support, in turn, permits you to establish true user/server authentication between Web users and your Domino Web server, not just the pale imitation that basic Web authentication represents. Domino 4.5 supports SSL 2.0. This means that only server authentication takes place, not user authentication. SSL 3.0, due to be added to Domino in the next release, will support both server and user authentication.

The SSL system works like other public/private key systems, such as Notes' own security system. In fact, both Notes and SSL use the RSA cryptosystem to create their public and private keys. The RSA cryptosystem is a public key/private key encryption system invented by three mathematicians, Ron Rivest, Leonard Adlemen, and Adi Shamir, who then formed a company, RSA Data Security, Inc., to market their encryption system. The company has since been acquired by another company. RSA has been very successful, in that the RSA cryptosystem is by far the most widespread encryption system in use today.

In an RSA-based system, each user and server possesses both a private key and a public key. The user or server then makes the public key available to the world and keeps the private key to themselves.

Only the private key can decrypt data that was encrypted with the public key. Only the public key can decrypt data that was encrypted with the private key. If I want to encrypt a message to you, I do so with your public key. Only you have possession of your private key, so only you can decrypt the message. If I want to assure you that a message is really from me and not some impostor, I can sign the message with my private key. If you can decrypt the signature with my public key, you can assume it came from me, because (presumably) nobody but me has access to my private key.

The weakness of public/private key encryption systems is that I can send you a public key and tell you it is from anyone in the world—say, for example, Bill Clinton. Then I can send out all sorts of politically damaging statements, sign them with Bill Clinton's private key, and you might say, "I know Bill Clinton said these things because he signed his name to them!"

How do you verify that the public key I send you really isn't from Bill Clinton at all? You establish positive identification of me, that's how. Either you have to get the public key from me personally, satisfying yourself at that time that I am who I say I am. Or you have to get someone that you trust to vouch for me and the public key I am offering you. In SSL parlance, this trusted third party is a Certification Authority (CA). It is the equivalent of the Certifier in Notes.

The CA establishes who I am and issues me a certificate, signed by the CA, declaring that I am who I say I am. The CA does the same for you. (Under SSL, we store our certificates, along with our private and public keys, in a password-protected file called a *key ring* file. In Notes we store our certificates in our ID files.) When you and I, total strangers until now, want to establish a confidential relationship, we can establish each other's identity by presenting to each other the certificate issued to us by the CA. We can trust each other's certificate because both your certificate and my own were signed using the same private key (that belonging to the CA). We each know the third-degree (or lack thereof) we had to undergo to get the certificate; we assume the other had to go through the same ordeal (or breezed through as easily as we did).

Or, instead of assuming, we can find out from the CA exactly what its requirements are for issuing a certificate to the type of entity (corporation, person, and so on) that we are dealing with. Each of us has the assurance of the CA that the other is the person the CA certifies him to be. If the CA made the other walk over coals to get the certificate, then we have relatively high assurance. If the CA only made the other cross his/her heart and hope to die, then we have relatively low assurance. In fact, CAs may issue different types of certificates, depending on how much evidence one can produce of one's identity. So that a given corporation might have a highly assured certificate and another might have a less assured certificate.

In the future, any time we want to communicate with each other, we can reestablish each other's identity the same way. We never have to worry that we are talking to an impostor (unless someone stole one of our private keys).

15

Notes' implementation of SSL allows great flexibility in establishing a certification scheme. If you only care about encrypting transmissions but not about authentication, you can issue a self-signed certificate to your Domino server. Alternatively, if you do care about authentication but your users are all internal users, say, because you are running on an intranet, you can become a CA in your own right and issue certificates to your Domino server and your users. For example, if you want to set up secure transactions within your own intranet, you can set yourself up as the company CA. Your office issues the certificates to your Domino server and to all of the secured users.

Finally, you can apply to a commercial CA for issuance of a certificate to your Web server. If you want to set up secure transactions outside your company—say, to conduct sales on the Internet—you can contract with a commercial CA, such as VeriSign (**www.verisign.com**), to certify you and all users who want to do business with you.

Unfortunately, at this writing the first two certification schemes are more or less academic, since there is no secure, documented way to add non-commercial certificates to today's browsers. That is, Netscape Navigator will let you request and add a certificate from Verisign, but from no other CA. Internet Explorer won't let you add any certificates at all to the narrow list of commercial CAs it supports.

In our tests, both browsers rejected our server outright when it presented a self-signed certificate to them. Then we set ourselves up as a private CA and signed a certificate on behalf of our server. Internet Explorer rejected this certificate as well (see Figure 15.1).

Fig. 15.1

Internet Explorer refuses to have any intercourse with a secure site if it does not recognize the signer of the site's certificate. Nor does it provide a way to add a certificate.

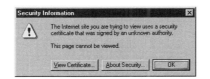

Netscape Navigator, through a series of dialog boxes that were part of an assistant, offered us the choice of accepting this certificate for its life, accepting it for the current session only, or rejecting it. We chose to accept for the current session and were then permitted to browse the site, presumably securely (see Figure 15.2).

Fig. 15.2
This was the first of several screens in which Netscape Navigator guided us, with warnings of dire consequences should we guess wrong, through a series of decisions whether to accept our server's certificate as genuine.

Working with the Domino SSL Administration Application

The Domino server comes with a Notes application, Domino SSL Administration, that automates the establishment of SSL security. It guides you through the processes of either self-certifying or submitting a request for a certificate to either your own internal CA or VeriSign. It also guides you through the process of merging the resulting certificate into your key ring file. Finally, if you want to become a CA yourself, it guides you through that process as well as the process of issuing certificates to others. In short, it holds your hand through all phases of SSL administration and makes the whole process pretty easy.

Caution
You can only perform SSL administration when working locally at the Domino server. If you attempt to administer SSL remotely, you will receive repeated warnings to turn back. Look around the database if you want. But go to the server if you actually want to perform the procedures in the SSL Administration database.

Open the SSL Administration database as follows:

1. At the Domino server that will be the Web-enabled server, run the Notes workstation software. This is important. You can open the SSL Administration database from a workstation, but you cannot do any actual administration from there. To do actual administration, you have to be working locally at the server itself.

2. In the Notes menu, choose File, Database, Open. The Open Database dialog box will appear.

3. In the Open Database dialog box, leave the Server field set to Local. Choose Domino SSL Administration from the Database list. The file name ssladmin.nsf will appear in the Filename field when Domino SSL Administration is selected in the Database field. Click Open. The database will open and an icon for it will appear on the current page of the workspace of the computer you are using.

Each time you open the Domino SSL Administration database, the About document appears. If you are opening from the Domino server, you will see an icon that looks like a set of keys and the message Click here to set up and manage SSL on your site (see Figure 15.3).

Fig. 15.3

The message Click here to set up and manage SSL on your site *appears if you are sitting at the server, using the local copy of the database.*

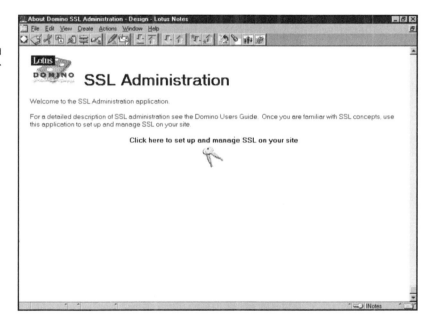

If you are opening from a workstation, or from the Domino server but not a "local" copy of the database, you will see the message, This application should be run locally at the server, rather than from a remote client. If you see that message, start over from the server, with Local selected in the Server field (see Figure 15.4). Likewise, if you open the SSL Administration document directly from a workstation, you will see a similar warning message. On the other hand, if your workstation is remote and disconnected from any Notes server, the warning message will not appear. However, while we have not tested it, we believe that the various procedures that the database performs will not work properly if you try to run them on a remote, disconnected workstation.

Fig. 15.4

The message This application should be run locally at the server, rather than from a remote client, *appears if you are sitting at the server, using the local copy of the database.*

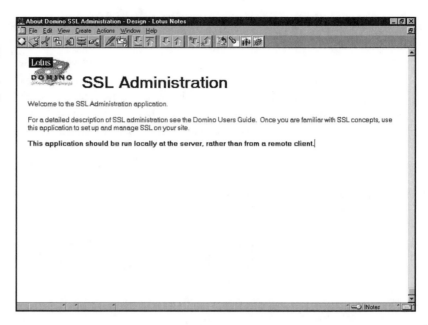

When you click the keys icon, the SSL Administration document opens. It consists of five collapsible sections:

▶ Create Key Ring - Self-Certification

▶ Create Key Ring - Commercial Certification

▶ Create Key Ring - Internal Certification

▶ Certificate Authority - Create Certificate Authority Key Ring

▶ Certificate Authority - Certify Certificate Request

Each section consists of an explanation of its purpose and uses and includes one or more buttons to click to actually perform the processes involved (see Figure 15.5).

Self-Certification with Domino SSL

Self-certification does not at this time work with any mainstream browser, including Note's own Web Navigator. You receive error messages from the browser indicating that the certificate it is receiving is corrupted or unreadable. A self-certified key ring is, in fact, a key ring that holds a certificate signed by the server itself. The effect of using such a certificate should be to defeat any effort by a browser to authenticate the server, but to allow a secure session to take place if the user at the browser decides to trust the certificate anyway and proceed.

Fig. 15.5

The first section of the SSL Administration document explains the purpose of the procedure and provides a button for initiating the procedure.

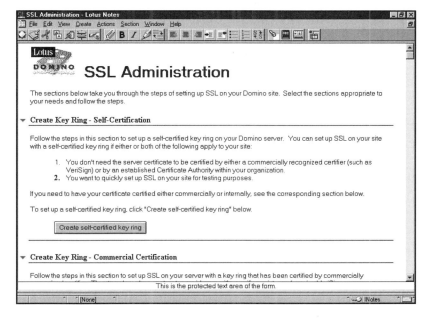

However, creating a self-certified key ring does not work this way. We know of no reason why browsers would not accept such a certificate in the same spirit they accept any other certificate signed by an unknown CA. We expect that, as time passes and the SSL standard matures, future browsers will be able to accept self-signed certificates.

We describe the process of creating a self-signed certificate below because, even though the process does not result at this time in a useable key ring file, it is the simplest of all the operations you can perform with SSL Administration, and what happens is representative of what happens during each of the other operations performable in the SSL Administration document.

Clicking the button labeled *Create self-certified key ring* opens a dialog box, as pictured in Figure 15.6, which follows. Fill in the details of the dialog box, then click OK. The fields in this dialog box are mostly self-explanatory with the following exceptions:

▶ **Common name field:** Enter the fully qualified host name of your server. If your server is registered with a Domain Name Server, its fully qualified name is its full host.domain name, such as www.planetnotes.com. If your server is on an intranet that does not use DNS, your server's common name is just that—its host name alone. For example, the test server on which we tested SSL is called INotes. Its name is a relic of the days when we used it to test InterNotes Web Publisher. It is not in any Internet domain. So its common name for purposes of this dialog box is just its host name.

▶ **State or Province field:** Since the standard two-letter State abbreviations are not acceptable here, Domino documentation recommends you use the full name of the State if you are in the United States.

▶ **Key name field:** This is a case-sensitive, descriptive name the purpose of which is to identify the purpose or owner of the key ring file later, after you have not looked at it for a while and you have forgotten what it is.

▶ **Password field:** This is a case-sensitive phrase of at least six characters' length. The password protects the key ring from unauthorized use and is analogous to the password you use to unlock your Notes ID file.

Fig. 15.6

Fill in the details of the Create Self-Certified Key Ring dialog box, then click OK. If a field is not marked optional, it is required.

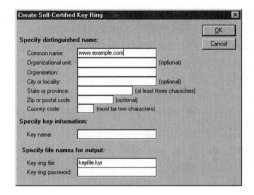

What you are actually doing here is filling in a Notes form that consists of a layout area contained within a dialog box generated by a script contained in the button. When you finish filling in the dialog box and click OK, the field validation formulas check that you have entered acceptable data in the fields, then the script carries out a series of actions. In this case, the script does not actually create a Notes document but rather creates a key ring file with a certificate in it signed by your server. When it finishes, the script displays a dialog box informing you of the fact (see Figure 15.7).

Fig. 15.7

This dialog box appears, letting you know Domino has completed the action you asked it to perform.

Obtaining a Certificate from a Commercial Certificate Authority

15

Obtaining a certificate from a commercial CA is important if your Domino Web server is on the Internet and you want to conduct secure transactions across the Internet. For example, you may set up a Web site from which you sell products directly to Web users. They submit payment in the form of credit card information and you ship the product in response. Web users will not want to submit sensitive information such as credit card number and expiration date if they have no assurance that the server they are sending the information to is really your company's server and not that of some pretender. They will not want to send that data if they fear that an interloper could intercept the data en route.

If you can present a certificate signed by a commercial CA from which the user also has a certificate, then you can provide both assurances. The commercial CA—VeriSign, for example—provides the assurance of your server's authenticity in the form of the certificate issued to the server. The customer knows the certificate was really issued by VeriSign because the customer has their own certificate issued by VeriSign, and can compare the signatures on the two certificates and verify that they are the same. The automatic encryption of the subsequent dialog between the two computers provides the second assurance—that the credit card information (among other sensitive bits of information) won't be stolen by an interloper, because the interloper will not be able to decipher the encrypted information.

The Domino SSL Administration database provides a three-step procedure for obtaining a certificate in favor of the server from Verisign or any other commercial CA. The three steps are:

1. Create a key ring and a request for a certificate.
2. Send the request for certificate to the commercial CA.
3. When you receive the requested certificate from the CA, merge it into the key ring created in step 1.

If you visit the VeriSign Web site, specifically to the following URL:

http://www.verisign.com/lotus/index.shtml

you will discover that the three steps previously listed are not the whole story. Verisign will require you to perform two other steps:

1. Enroll with VeriSign.
2. Pay VeriSign

VeriSign's two steps are really steps 1 and 2, and the SSL Administration's three steps are really steps 3, 4, and 5. Taking them in that order, the details of each step are as follows.

Steps 1 and 2: Enrolling with and Paying VeriSign

In a Web browser, retrieve the following document:

http://www.verisign.com/lotus/index.shtml

This document describes (among other useful things) the process of obtaining a server certificate from VeriSign and includes links to other important documents, including the price schedule and the enrollment form. You must complete and submit the enrollment form and pay the correct fee according to the current price schedule.

You can complete the form online and submit it by clicking the button at its end. In the enrollment form you will supply the same information about your server that the dialog box in Figure 15.6 requested for the self-certification process. That is, you must provide the following information:

▶ **The fully qualified domain name (FQDN) of your Web server**—That is, something in the form *www.domainname.xxx*. This will become, in the certificate that you will later receive, the Common Name portion of your server's fully distinguished name.

▶ **Organization name**—They want your company's or organization's legal name, as it appears in your incorporation papers, organization charter, or partnership agreement. If you are a sole proprietor, this would presumably be your own name, though you might want to verify this with VeriSign. No abbreviations, please.

▶ **Organizational Unit name**—This is optional and could be a department, region, whatever you want it to be. If you are a sole proprietor, this could be the name you are *doing business as*, that is, your *fictitious* name.

▶ **City/Locality**—This is optional unless you are registered only locally. If your company is registered locally only, for example by having a business license registered with a City Clerk, the Locality/City field must contain the name of the city where registered. Again, no abbreviations, please.

▶ **State/Province**—This is required. The name mustn't be abbreviated. It should be where you do business, not necessarily where you are incorporated.

▶ **Country**—This is also required and should be the 2-letter ISO code, for example, US for United States, CA for Canada.

The form also requests information about company contacts—a technical contact and a billing contact. It asks you to identify your Web server software. It gathers payment information. And it requests your DUNS number. This last expedites verification of your company's identity, since VeriSign checks with Dun & Bradstreet, among other things.

If your company has not existed for long and, therefore, is unknown to Dun & Bradstreet, VeriSign will seek other evidence that your organization exists in good standing with the local government where you are located. If you know that your company fits this profile, you might just go ahead and send such evidence—Articles of Incorporation, Partnership Agreement, and so on—to VeriSign up front.

You can pay VeriSign by check, credit card, or purchase order. The cost (at this writing) is $295 for the initial certification of the first server in your organization, $95 for each additional server, and $75 per year to renew certificates.

Step 3: Requesting a Certificate

Step 3 (SSL Administration database Step 1) is virtually identical to the procedure described in the earlier section of this chapter regarding self-certifying. You start off by clicking the Step 1 button, "Create key ring and certificate request." When you click the button, a dialog box appears that is *almost* identical to the one pictured in Figure 15.6, and you fill in this dialog box exactly as you filled in the one in Figure 15.6. That is to say, you enter the some of the same information you entered in the VeriSign enrollment form, described previously: server name, organization name, optional organizational unit name, optional city/locality name, state/province name, and country code.

There are two differences between this dialog box and the one in Figure 15.6: First, the title of this dialog box is simply *Create Key Ring*. Second, there is one additional field in this dialog box: *Certificate Request*. Enter here the file name of the request that Domino will generate. By default the file name is *certreq.txt* but you can name it anything you want.

The certificate request is an encrypted text file. It includes the information you provided in the fields of the dialog box. The CA will compile that information into a distinguished name for your server. However, you can't tell this from looking at the file, because it is encrypted. It looks in a text editor like random gibberish (see Figure 15.8).

Fig. 15.8

A certificate request, as pictured here, is unreadable by the casual reader because it is encrypted.

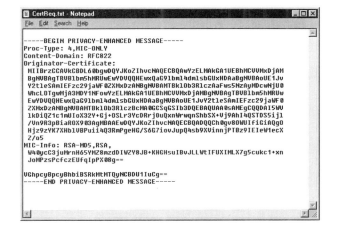

Step 4: E-mailing the Certificate Request to VeriSign

In VeriSign Step 4 (SSL Administration database Step 2) (in which you send the certificate request to the CA), if the CA is VeriSign, you can click the Step 2 button, "Create mail message for VeriSign." If the CA is a company other than VeriSign, you will have to follow a manual procedure which the CA will provide. In the case of VeriSign, clicking the button displays a dialog box, as pictured in Figure 15.9.

Fig. 15.9

When you click OK in this dialog box, Domino will generate an e-mail message to VeriSign with the certificate request pictured in Figure 15.8 attached.

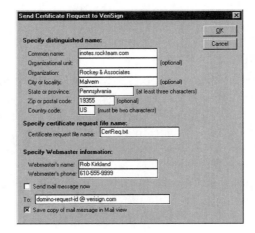

Note that the preceding dialog box has the same set of fields as the dialog box that appeared in Figure 15.6, in addition to some new fields. The new fields include information about the WebMaster of the server, VeriSign's e-mail address, and the choice whether to send the e-mail immediately or save it in the SSL Administration database for mailing out later.

When you click OK, Domino generates an e-mail message addressed to VeriSign. The message looks like the one in Figure 15.10.

If you chose to save the e-mail message for mailing later, Domino saves it in the SSL Administration database, in the Mail Backup view.

Step 5: Merging the Certificate with the Server's Key Ring

After VeriSign receives the enrollment form, payment, and certificate request from you, they verify the identity and existence of your organization, then issue your certificate and e-mail it back to the "WebMaster" named in Step 4. When you, the WebMaster, receive the requested certificate from VeriSign (or another commercial CA) you will perform SSL Administration database Step 3, *Merge certified certificate into key ring*. This itself is a two-step operation.

Fig. 15.10

This e-mail message contains the request to VeriSign for a certificate in favor of the server inotes.rockteam.com.

First, you will export the certificate from the e-mail message. The certificate looks exactly like the request you sent earlier (see Figure 15.8), only it is longer. It is longer primarily because they sent back not one but at least two certificates—the one they are issuing to your server, and one issued to VeriSign. This is exactly what your Notes ID has in it—a certificate issued to you, and a certificate issued to your certifier. You can select the certificate portion of the e-mail message, then export it to a text file.

Finally, you will click the button called *Merge certificate into key ring*. A dialog box will pop up, as in Figure 15.11.

Fig. 15.11

The first field of the Merge Certificate dialog box is the name of the file you created when you exported your server's new certificate from the VeriSign e-mail. The other two fields are the file name and password of the key ring file.

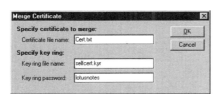

Enter the file name of the exported certificate, the file name of the key ring file created in Step 3, and the password of the key ring file, then click OK. Domino will automatically merge the new certificate into the key ring file. Thereafter, if anyone sends a URL to your server beginning with the protocol *http://*, your server will respond properly. It will send its certificate to the requesting party, so the requester can authenticate it. When authentication is complete, the two computers will establish an encryption key known only to themselves. Then, until Domino closes the session, all communications between them will be encrypted.

Becoming a Certification Authority and Issuing Certificates

If your Domino Web server will operate strictly within your company's intranet, there will be no need for third-party assurance of its authenticity. A certificate issued by a CA within your company should be adequate. Even if the server will operate on the Internet, a privately issued certificate should be satisfactory if the only visitors (or the only secure visitors) are people otherwise well-known to you—your employees, customers, and business partners, for example.

The last three sections of the SSL Administration database provide for this situation. These three sections lead you through the processes of:

1. Generating an internal certification key ring for your server.
2. Generating a Certificate Authority key ring for yourself or whoever will be in charge of issuing certificates.
3. Issuing certificates—to your server(s) and your users.

The SSL Administration database presents the procedures for these three activities in the order they appear. However, we present the following procedure for number 2 first, then number 1, finally number 3.

Issuing a Certificate Authority Key Ring

First you must create a key ring for the certificate authority. This is where the CA will store its own certificates—that issued by itself to itself or (in future releases of SSL and Domino) those issued to it by higher certificate authorities, a la Notes' multi-level certifiers.

Create this key ring by clicking the button labeled *Create Certificate Authority key ring*, then completing the dialog box that appears. Like the other dialog boxes we've seen for creating key ring files (see Figure 15.6), this dialog asks for information from which Domino will generate a distinguished name for the CA. It asks for a descriptive key name, a file name and password for the key ring file, and file name for the separate certificate text file that it will create. You will need the certificate text file when fulfilling requests for certificates.

When you click OK, Domino will generate the key ring file containing a new CA certificate and, if you entered a file name in the Certificate Authority certificate file field, a file containing a text version of the CA certificate. Keep this key ring secure. It is valuable in the same way your Notes certifier IDs are valuable. If you lose it, you have given away the keys to the kingdom. Your whole security scheme is compromised and the only way to re-secure is to issue a whole new set of keys—not fun.

Issuing a Key Ring for Internal Certification and a Certificate Request

Now you can issue a key ring for your Domino Web server, along with a request to the internal company CA for a certificate for the server. We have described this process twice already—once when generating the self-signed certificate, and once when requesting a certificate from a commercial CA. The procedure here is not much different from that for requesting a certificate from a commercial CA. You don't have to enroll or pay a fee—necessarily. But you do have to create the key ring, generate a certificate request, then e-mail the certificate request to the internal CA (who is probably yourself, in which case maybe you won't actually *e-mail* the request). Since we have described these procedures before, we won't describe them again here, except to say click the buttons, fill in the dialog boxes, and follow the instructions.

After receiving the certificate from the CA (or, if you are the CA, after creating the certificate), you will have to merge the resulting certificate into your key ring file. This is Step 3 of the process described in the *Create Key Ring - Internal Certification* section of the SSL Administration document. Follow the numbered steps in that document. Notice that you will need not one but *two* certificates (just as you did in the earlier described procedure when we merged a commercial certificate into a key ring (see *Step 5: Merging the Certificate with the Server's Key Ring*). You need the server's own certificate and the CA's certificate. They will both be merged into the key ring. If you received an e-mail from your company's CA (or from yourself, if you are the CA), both certificates will be attached to it.

The steps are:

1. Detach the server's certificate from the CA's e-mail message. Save it as a .txt file.

2. Detach the CA's certificate from the e-mail message. Save it, too, as a .txt file.

3. Merge both certificates into the server's key ring (created when you created the certificate request) by clicking the *Merge certificate into key ring* button, filling in the fields in the dialog box that appears, and clicking OK. This is the same process that we followed and described earlier in *Step 5: Merging the Certificate with the Server's Key Ring*, so we need not describe it in detail again.

This section omitted one very important step—the actual creation of the certificate that we first requested, then merged. That part is handled by the SSL Administration document in its last section, rather awkwardly titled *Certificate Authority - Certify Certificate Request*. We describe that process in our next section (elegantly titled *Issuing Certificates*).

Issuing Certificates

As a CA, you will issue certificates to servers and users, just as a Notes certifier does. In fact, you still need to finish the process described in the previous section by issuing the certificate for your Web server. This is either a one- or three-part process, depending on how you came into possession of the certificate request. Either you have to extract the certificate request from the e-mail in which it arrived, issue the certificate, then e-mail it back to the requester. Or, if you generated the certificate request yourself, you don't have to extract it from an e-mail or e-mail it back to yourself. Just issue the certificate.

You issue the certificate by clicking the button called *Certify certificate request*. The dialog box titled Sign Certificate Request appears (see Figure 15.12).

Fig. 15.12

Complete the Sign Certificate Request dialog box to create a new certificate.

Fill in the fields in this dialog box as follows:

▶ **Certificate request file name**— Enter the file name of the certificate request. If you don't know the file name, you probably skipped the first step of detaching the certificate request from the e-mail message in which it arrived.

▶ **Validity period (days)**—Enter the number of days before the certificate expires. It defaults to 365 days.

▶ **CA key ring file name**—This is the file name of your CA key ring file.

▶ **CA key ring password**—This is the password of your CA key ring file. You won't be able to issue a certificate if you do not know this password.

▶ **Certificate file name**—This is the file name of the new certificate that Domino creates when you click OK.

Now either attach the new certificate to an e-mail message and send it back to the requester or, if you generated the certificate request yourself, merge the newly created certificate file into the waiting key ring (see *Step 5: Merging the Certificate with the Server's Key Ring*).

Putting it All Together as an Internal CA

The whole process of issuing certificates involves creating a key ring, generating a certificate request, generating the certificate, then merging the certificate into the key ring. Technically, the certificate owner—the server or user—is supposed to create the key ring and certificate request, then send the certificate request to you, the CA. You, for your par, are supposed to issue the certificate, then return it along with a copy of your own certificate to the requester/owner. The requester/owner is supposed to complete the process by merging the two certificates into the waiting key ring file.

Practically speaking, you will probably end up performing this whole process yourself. The SSL standard is still too immature to support a realistic hope that users will be able to perform the tasks assigned to them. Browsers either don't support the process of requesting/merging privately issued certificates at all. Or they don't provide a sufficiently automated process for it.

In the unlikely event you do receive an encrypted certificate request in the form we ourselves generated earlier in the chapter (see Figures 15.8 and 15.10), you can assume the requester has already generated a key ring file and will know how to merge the certificate into it when you send it back. All you have to do (as the instructions in the SSL Administration database state) is extract the certificate request from the e-mail message in which it arrived, create the certificate by pressing a button on the SSL Administration document and filling in the fields in the dialog box that appears, then send the certificate to the requester as an e-mail attachment.

But let's assume you will have to do all the work yourself. You will perform the following steps in the following order:

1. Generate a key ring and certificate request.
2. Use the resulting certification request file to generate a certificate.
3. Merge the resulting certificate file, along with your own CA certificate file (created earlier and kept in a handy place just for this purpose), into the key ring file created in step 1.
4. Deliver the key ring file to the user or server.

Because you are doing all the steps yourself, you can omit the e-mailing hassle—that's some consolation. On the other hand, when the certificates begin to expire, you will have to get the old key ring file back from the user and go through the whole process again. If you ever want to examine a certificate to find out such things as who issued it, when, to whom, for what purpose, or when it expires, you will discover that the SSL Administration database provides no way to do view the contents of key ring files.

Presumably the whole SSL "standard" will mature, the procedures will become widely and uniformly supported, and the next release of the SSL Administration database will provide more administration tools. Until then, SSL as implemented in Domino is useable but sort of rough. You might reasonably conclude that implementing it, at least for internal use—intranet or Extranet—is not worth the effort. On the other hand, SSL does offer positive benefits with little administrative effort if you want to use it to implement secure conversations on a public Web site, and the major Web browsers—Netscape Navigator 3.0 and Microsoft Internet Explorer 3.0, and successor—do support SSL when used for that purpose.

From Here...

In this chapter, you learned how to use Domino's support of SSL to permit secure conversations between your Domino server and Web users across the Internet or your company's intranet or extranet. For more information on the security features of Domino, see the following chapters:

▶ Chapter 2, "Setting Up the Domino Server"

▶ Chapter 14, "Securing the Domino Web Server"

For more information on SSL and Internet security in general, see the following Web sites:

▶ **www.rsa.com**

▶ **www.netscape.com**

▶ **www.verisign.com**

▶ **www.w3.org.**

For more information about Domino's implementation of SSL, see also the Notes and the Internet database that comes with the Domino server. Search for SSL.

## chapter 16

Using Advanced Administration Techniques

In this chapter

◆ **Server Document Variables**
We review all of the settings in the Server document that relate to the HTTP server task.

◆ **Server Logging**
We learn how to enable logging of Web-related server activity.

◆ **Multi-homing and scaling a Domino Web server with the Domino Configuration database**
We explore several different uses for the Domino Configuration database, including one way to scale up a Domino Web server when it starts getting really popular.

◆ **Site Search databases**
We learn how to set up multiple database searches and how to make multi-database searching available to Web users.

◆ **Domino Advanced Services**
We learn what Domino Advanced Services are. We focus primarily on the Server Clustering feature, which gives us an even more powerful way to scale up a Domino server when it gets popular.

I n this chapter, we look at the configuration of the Domino server and seek ways to fine-tune its performance. We see how to set up server logging. We look at the Domino Configuration database and see how to use it to set up either a multi-homed Web site or a scaleable Web site. We also look at the Site Search database template to see how to set up multi-database searches. Finally, we take a brief look at Domino Advanced Services, which provide further possibilities for scaling a Web site and for billing your clients for usage of your Web site. Much of the material in this chapter is of only peripheral interest to Notes application developers. But read it anyway; we discover some really powerful tools and techniques in this chapter that will be really useful to you when your Web site starts getting really popular.

Fine-Tuning Domino's Configuration

In this section, we look at all of the variables in the Server document that affect the performance of the Domino server. Elsewhere in the book, we further discuss many of these variables in other contexts. This section brings all of those discussions together in one place to provide you with a reference source.

Server Document Variables

Two sections of the Server document control the actions of the HTTP service: HTTP Server and Security. You look at HTTP Server in this chapter. We examined Security in the Chapter 14, "Securing the Domino Web Server."

The HTTP Server section of the Server document has six parts: Basics, Mapping, Timeouts, Operational Information, Logging, and Character Set Mapping. Initially, you have to make only a few decisions. Later you can go back and perhaps fine-tune Domino's settings. The fields you must first look at include those in Table 16.1.

Table 16.1   Essential HTTP Server Settings

Review These Fields Before Running Domino for the First Time

Part	Field	Description
Basics	TCP/IP port number	The default port is 80. You need to change it only if you are running a third-party Web server on the same computer, so that both servers don't try to use the same port.
	Host name	Default is blank, which means that the HTTP server will get the host name from the TCP/IP stack in the server's memory. If you have registered an alias with your Domain Name Server, enter the alias here. Or enter the server's IP address, so that Web users can access the server by typing the IP address.

Part	Field	Description
Mapping	Home URL	Default is /?Open, which causes the server to send a list of Notes databases as the site home page. If you want to create a real home page, enter its file name here. If you want to designate a home page database, enter its file name here. If the home page file is not in the root HTML directory or the home page database is not in the root Domino data directory, you should enter its relative path name, not just its file name.

Caution

Whenever you make a change in the HTTP Server section of the server document, remember to stop and restart the HTTP server task (if it was running). Otherwise, your changes do not take effect and you might feel mildly frustrated.

The rest of the fields are listed in the following section, grouped by subsection. Many of them you should never have to change. You may be able to improve the performance of your server by changing some of them; see especially the fields on DNS lookup, port status, time-outs, garbage collection, cache size and deletion, and server logging.

HTTP Server Basics

This is the first subsection of the HTTP Server part of the Server document. It covers items that effect whether the Web server will function at all (see Figure 16.1).

▶ *TCP/IP port number*—The default is 80, which is the standard HTTP port. You need to change it only if you are running more than one HTTP server on this computer—that is, you are running some other HTTP server in addition to Domino. If you do have to change it, you must change it to a port number greater than 1024, and you might prefer to change it to 8008 or 8080, which are commonly used as alternative HTTP port numbers. If you use a port number other than 80, users have to enter it as part of your URL, in the form **http://domino.chestnet.com:8080**.

▶ *TCP/IP port status*—The default is Enabled. You disable this only if you want to force users to use the SSL (Secure Sockets Layer) port. If both ports are disabled, the HTTP service will not function properly. For more information on SSL, see Chapter 15, "Using Secure Sockets Layer (SSL) with Domino."

▶ SSL port number—The default is 443, which is the standard SSL port. Only change it if you are running more than one SSL server on this computer.

▶ SSL port status—The default is Enabled. If you will not be using SSL, you can gain a slight server performance boost if you disable this port.

▶ *Host name*—By default, this field is blank, which means that Domino will get the host name from the TCP/IP stack in the server's memory. If you have registered an alias with your Domain Name Server, you can enter the alias here. Or, if the server is not registered with a Domain Name Server, enter the server's IP address, which enables users to access the server by typing the IP address in the form **http:// 192.192.192.11**.

▶ *DNS lookup*—This is disabled by default. If enabled, Domino attempts to retrieve the host name of all requesting clients. If disabled, Domino gets only the client's IP address. Because enabling this function requires the server to do more work, it degrades overall server performance. If the server obtains clients' host names, they will be recorded in the Domino log files and filter.

▶ *Default home page*—This defaults to default.htm. If you want to use an HTML file as your home page, rather than a component of a Notes database, save the file to the HTML directory, enter its name here, and blank out the Home URL field. If the file does not exist, Domino will serve up an error message to the visiting user, so be careful to enter the file name correctly here, and test afterwards to ensure that the server is serving up the intended home page.

▶ *Maximum active threads* and *Minimum active threads*—These default to 40 and 20, respectively. Domino always keeps at least the minimum number of threads open, even when idling. If it reaches the maximum number, it puts any additional requests on hold until threads become free. The more RAM your server has, the higher you should set these values. If your computer seems to spend a lot of time and effort swapping memory to disk, reduce these values.

Mapping

The fields in this subsection of the Server document specify the physical and mapped locations of Domino's data directories (see Figure 16.2). The mapped values are shorthand values that conform to UNIX/URL syntax rules (meaning that they use forward instead of back slashes). Web users enter the mapped locations. The server uses the entries in these fields to translate from the mapped to the actual locations of these directories. As long as you do not change the default setup of the server, you need not change most of these values. If you do decide to designate data directories other than the system defaults, you must change the entries in the path fields in this section.

Fig. 16.1

The Basics section of the HTTP Server section of the Server document covers—you guessed it— the basics of HTTP server task configuration.

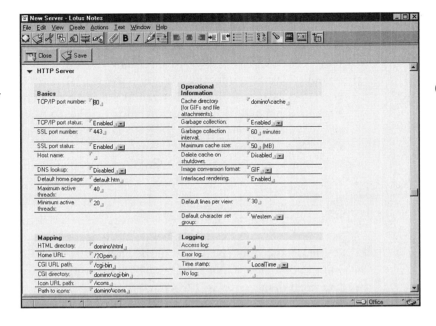

16

Fig. 16.2

Set the locations of Web-related files in the Mapping section of the Server document.

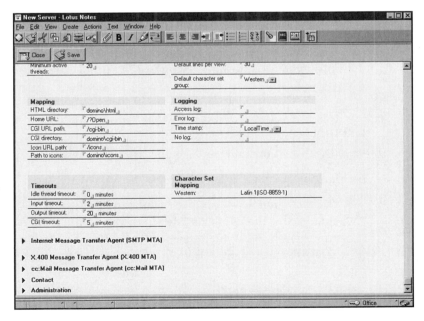

The default data directories, being subdirectories of the Notes data directory, are designated by their relative path names. If you move the data directories out of the Notes data subdirectory tree, enter full versions of the new path names.

The fields in the Mapping subsection are as follows:

▶ *HTML directory*—By default, it is set to domino\html. If the Notes data directory path is c:\notes\data, then this partial path name translates to c:\notes\data\domino\html. If you move the HTML data files to, say, c:\domino\html, then you change this field to c:\domino\html. There is no corresponding mapped path for this directory, because to users seeking static HTML pages from the Domino server, this is the root data directory. That is, if a user asks for **http://domino.chestnet.com/pagename.htm**, the Domino server translates that to c:\notes\data\domino\html\pagename.htm.

▶ *Home URL*—This defaults to /?Open, which causes the server to send a list of Notes databases as the site home page (sort of like when a Notes user chooses File, Database, Open from the menu. If you want to create a static home page that the users see when they enter your host name, put it in the HTML directory, enter its name in the Default home page field in the Basics subsection, and clear this field. If you want to designate a home page database that the users will open when they enter your host name, enter its file name here.

▶ *CGI URL path* and *CGI directory*—The CGI URL path is the name users enter to reach the actual directory identified in the CGI directory field. This is where CGI scripts are located.

▶ *Icon URL path* and *Path to icons*—The Icon URL path is the name users enter to reach the directory identified in the Path to Icons field. These are the graphics files that Domino substitutes for the actual icons when translating from Notes to HTML file format.

Timeouts

All of the system timeout variables appear in this subsection (see Figure 16.3).

The timeout variables are as follows:

▶ *Idle thread timeout*—This is the same thread referred to in the Maximum and Minimum active threads fields listed in the preceding HTTP Server Basics section. As used here, a thread is an independent process that the server maintains to serve up requested documents. Multiple threads are available so that the server can service multiple simultaneous requests. Upon startup Domino creates the number of threads set in the Minimum active threads field. If enough simultaneous page requests come in that the server needs to activate more threads, it will do so on an as-needed basis. Under no circumstances, however, will Domino open more threads than the number in the Maximum active threads field.

16

It takes some time and effort for the computer to establish a new thread, so there is some benefit to keeping inactive threads alive even though there is no work for them to do. On the other hand, they use up memory and processor time, so there is also benefit to killing inactive threads. This field dictates how long after it finishes servicing a request a thread will hang around idle before dying. The default setting of zero minutes means that it never dies. In effect, the number of threads ratchets up, never dropping back down. This favors performance over memory conservation.

▶ *Input timeout*—When one computer transfers a file to another computer, the computers typically establish a *session* or *connection* with each other and maintain that session/connection until the transaction is complete. Some types of servers maintain the connection for a long period of time even though there is no activity with the client. Web servers, impatient beings that they are, and in eager anticipation of receiving requests from large numbers of strangers, typically drop connections after very short periods of inactivity. Domino is configurable in this regard. This field (which defaults to two minutes) dictates how long the server waits for a request after a client first connects. If no request is forthcoming within the time limit, the server drops the connection.

▶ *Output timeout*—This field dictates how much time Domino has to fulfill a request before it drops the connection with the requester. The default is 20 minutes, which means, in effect, that Domino is never able to deliver anything that takes longer than that to download. It also ensures that a malfunctioning delivery does not hang forever. If Web users will be downloading large files from your server, files that, in the real world of congested Internet pathways, might take more than 20 minutes to transfer to a user through the user's 14.4kbps modem, then maybe you should increase the value of this field.

▶ *CGI timeout*—This determines the maximum amount of time (defaulting to five minutes) that any CGI script has to get its job done. Among other things, this kills a program that has gotten trapped in a perpetual loop.

Fig. 16.3

The timeout variables serve a variety of purposes, from ending malfunctioning processes to limiting the size of downloads.

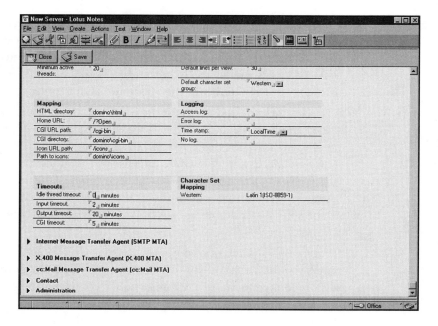

Operation Information

When Domino receives a request for a Notes document that includes embedded images or attached files, Domino converts the images to GIF-formatted files and delivers these and the attached files to the requester. It stores copies of both the newly created GIF files and the attachment files in a cache directory. When Domino receives another request for the same document, it is able to deliver it faster the second time because it does not have to regenerate the GIFs or re-detach (and decompress) the attached files; it retrieves them from the cache, instead. This increases performance at the expense of disk space.

The fields in this subsection determine how, where, and for how long Domino stores these cached files. You can also set default graphics file settings and HTML output settings here (see Figure 16.4).

> ▶ *Cache directory (for GIFs and file attachments)*—This is the location on disk of the file cache directory. It defaults to domino\cache. Domino creates this directory the first time it runs.

> ▶ *Garbage collection*—This is the process Domino uses to delete cached files in order to keep the size of the cache directory within its maximum size (see Maximum cache size, two bullets down). Domino deletes least-accessed files first. Disable this *only if you also disable caching.* If you disable garbage collection without also disabling caching, the cache is able to grow beyond its maximum size, eventually to take over all of the server's disk space.

Fig. 16.4

The parameters in the Operational Information section of the Server document determine how Domino will handle graphics files and attachments to Notes documents.

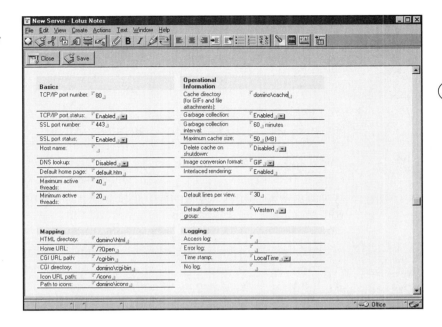

▶ *Garbage collection interval*—Specifies how often the garbage collection process runs, and defaults to every 60 minutes. If the size of the cache exceeds its maximum, garbage collection does not wait until the next scheduled runtime, but runs immediately.

▶ *Maximum cache size*—This is the maximum amount of disk space the files in the cache directory are permitted to occupy. By default, this is set to 50M. If you have lots of free disk space, consider increasing this number. The benefit is faster delivery of documents to requesters.

▶ *Delete cache on shutdown*—This is disabled by default. If you enable it, Domino deletes all files from the cache directory whenever you shut down Domino.

▶ *Image conversion format*—By default, Domino converts images embedded in Notes documents to GIF files. Here, you can change that to JPEG, if you want. If you are not sure which image format to use here, read the following Sidebar, titled *GIF versus JPEG*.

▶ *Interlaced rendering*—This field appears in the server document only if you have selected GIF in the Image conversion format field. Interlaced rendering is enabled by default. When enabled, Domino delivers GIFs interlaced—that is, it delivers every eighth line, then every fourth line, then every second line, then the remaining lines. The effect is that the receiver is able to discern what the image *will* look like before it is entirely rendered on-screen. This cuts down on the user's frustration factor.

▶ *Progressive rendering*—This field appears in the server document only if you have selected JPEG in the Image conversion format field. Progressive rendering is enabled by default. When enabled, the image is rendered at first blurry, then, with each pass, more clearly. Like interlaced GIF rendering, this enables the user to tell how the image *will* look before it is fully rendered.

▶ *JPEG image quality*—This field appears in the server document only if you have selected JPEG in the Image conversion format field. JPEG files are compressed in a way that causes them to lose fidelity with the original copy when decompressed. This is known as *lossy compression*; the other kind, used by GIF among other formats, is *lossless compression*, in which, when decompressed, the image retains 100 percent fidelity with the original. The benefit of using lossy compression is that you can obtain higher compression ratios and thus use less disk space when storing files and less time when transmitting them.

In this field, you can specify just how tightly JPEGs will compress or, to put it the other way, just how much fidelity they will lose when decompressed. A high number in this field means less compression, more fidelity. The default is 75; the range is zero to 100.

▶ Default lines per view—If a Notes view has more than the number of rows set in this field (default is 30), then Domino divides up the view into multiple view pages for delivery to the requester. Each view page has the number of rows dictated by this field. Every database is affected by this setting.

GIF versus JPEG

You have to decide whether to use GIF or JPEG when converting embedded images in Notes documents into graphics files that Web users will be able to see in their browsers. The factors are these:

▶ GIF (Graphics Interchange Format) files:

Are compressed by using a lossless compression scheme, meaning that the decompressed image is identical to the original.

Can display a maximum of 256 colors.

Are better than JPEG for computer-generated art.

▶ JPEG (Joint Photographic Experts Group) files:

Are compressed by using a lossy compression scheme. This means that, when decompressed, the resulting image loses some of the detail that the original image had. The trade-off is higher compression ratios. With JPEG compression, you can also specify ahead of time just how much compression/loss you will get. That is, at compression time you can specify 100 percent fidelity with no compression or progressively less fidelity with correspondingly greater compression. You may wonder why anyone would want to lose fidelity with the original image. Well, it turns out that, with photographic images, the losses aren't particularly noticeable to the human eye. By sacrificing a little, barely noticeable detail, you may be able to reclaim lots of disk space and transmission time. Considering that most video monitors are going to degrade a photographic image anyway, the trade-off may be well worthwhile.

▶ Can display upward of 16 million colors

▶ Cannot be displayed by some older browsers

▶ Are better than GIF for photographic art

So, which one should you choose? It depends on what types of images you are storing in your Notes databases—photographs or computer-generated art. If your Notes databases include predominantly photographs, choose JPEG; if computer-generated art, choose GIF. Sorry, you can't choose database-by-database. You could, however, alter the way you store images in a given database if you want to give viewers the benefits of both image types. For example, if your databases store mostly computer art, but one database stores photographs, you can choose GIF as the default graphics conversion format, but then store JPEG copies of embedded photographs as attachments to the documents in which the photographs appear.

▶ Default character set group and the Character Set Mapping fields—The Default character set group field defines what fields appear in the Character Set Mapping subsection of the HTTP Server section of the Server document. Together, the settings of this field and the field(s) that appear(s) in the Character Set Mapping subsection determine what character set is used to produce Web pages.

The Default character set group field defaults to Western, which only has one character set, Latin 1 (ISO-8859-1). As a result, the field named Western appears in the Character Set Mapping section, and its value evaluates automatically to Latin 1 (ISO-8859-1). Most of the other character set groups have more than one available character set. If you chose one of those character set groups in the Default character set group, the corresponding field in the Character Set Mapping subsection would permit you to choose which character set the server should use. Experiment with the settings of the Default character set group field to see how it affects the fields that appear in the Character Set Mapping subsection of the Server document.

Logging

Domino optionally maintains Web access and error logs. Domino can maintain these logs in the form of a Notes database, domlog.nsf, or as text files, or in both formats if you prefer. Lotus recommends logging to text files if your site is large or busy, because logging to text files is faster than logging to the Domino Log database. Also, if you use non-Lotus HTTP server reporting and management tools, you may find it easier to transfer Domino logging data to the other program via text files than via a Notes database. Logging to a Notes database is useful if you want to obtain reports based on Notes views or if you want to trigger workflows based on logged events. For example, you may want to receive mail notification upon the occurrence of certain types of errors.

Enable logging to a Domino Web Server Log database by creating a Web server log database in the Domino server's root data directory. Domino will automatically begin logging information to it. The file name of the database must be domlog.nsf. It must be based on the Domino Web Server Log design template, domlog.ntf. Be sure to stop and restart the HTTP server task (with *tell http quit* and *load http*) after creating the database, to kickstart Domino into using it.

Enable logging to text files by entering into the Access log and Error log fields the path names of the directories where access and error logs will be stored. Then stop the HTTP server task if it was running and restart it. On restart, Domino creates the directories you specified, then the files.

Caution

Experience in testing the process of setting up text file logging has shown that it does not generally work the way you would expect. For example, if you enter *domino\logs\access* in the Access log field and *domino\logs\error* in the Error log field, you would expect Domino to create a *logs* directory in the *domino* directory, and *access* and *error* directories in the *logs* directory, then place the access and error logs in the appropriate directories. Experience has shown, however, that Domino will create only the *logs* directory and place all of the logs there, or it will not create or use any subdirectories; instead, it will name *one* of the log files *logs.mmmddyy*. Our tests were inconclusive in that sometimes the server created a *logs* subdirectory in the *domino* subdirectory, and sometimes it did not create any directory, and we were never able to discover the variable that made it work intermittently. Our tests were conclusive in that we were never able to convince the server to create or use a subdirectory within the *logs* subdirectory. As a general rule, it appeared that plain, vanilla Domino would create and use either the *domino* directory or the *domino\logs* subdirectory, but no other directory. That is, if you told Domino to put the log files in the *domino\logs* directory, it would, but if you told it to put the log files in the *domino\logs\xyz* directory, it would still put them in the *domino\logs* directory. But, after further testing with virtual servers and Domino Advanced Services, Domino would no longer put the files anywhere but in the domino directory, and would use any subdirectory name that had been specified as the file name instead. So, be forewarned.

The log files increase in size fast. Each day at midnight Domino closes the previous day's text log files and creates new files for the new day. Don't enable logging without good reason; the log files will gradually take over your disk space. If you do enable logging, delete old log files when you no longer need them and delete old records in the log database when you no longer need them.

If you enable text file access logging, Domino creates two log files, named `agent_log.`*mmmddyy*, and `referer_log.`*mmmddyy*, where *mmmddyy* is the month, day, and year of the file. Domino records an entry into the current copy of each log whenever it receives a request for a document from a Web user. It enters the identity of the browser program in the agent log and either the IP address or the host name of the requesting computer in the referer log. It enters host names *only if you have enabled DNS lookup.* Otherwise, it enters IP addresses. See HTTP Server Basics, earlier in this chapter, for the details about DNS lookup.

> ⚛ **Tip**
>
> Because Domino appends *mmmddyy* to log file names, it becomes a little awkward to read the files in a text editor. If you try to double-click the log file, Windows reports that it does not recognize the extension. If you open your text editor, the log files do not appear in any Open File dialog boxes unless you tell it to display all types of files.
>
> A good way to open the file in Notepad under Windows NT 3.5*x* is to select the log file in File Manager, choose <u>F</u>ile, <u>R</u>un in the menu, then insert Notepad in front of the name of the file, and click OK.
>
> In Windows 95 or Windows NT 4.*x*, select the file in Windows Explorer (My Computer, Network Neighborhood), then, in the menu, choose <u>F</u>ile, Op<u>e</u>n with, and choose Notepad from the list of files that appears. Better yet, add Notepad to the Send To fly-out menu that appears in Explorer's File menu. Then select the file and choose <u>F</u>ile, Se<u>n</u>d To, Notepad.

> To add Notepad to the Send To menu, add a shortcut to it to the Send To folder, which appears either in the Windows folder or in your personal folder under the Profiles folder in the Windows folder. (Inhale!) Got that? If not, look it up in Explorer Help by searching for the word *send*.

If you enable error logging, Domino creates three log files: access.*mmmddyy*, errors.*mmmddyy*, and cgi_error.*mmmddyy*. Domino records internal errors in the first two log files and CGI errors in the last. When an internal error occurs, Domino records the identity of the requesting computer and the text of the request in the access log, and it records the Domino-generated error message in the errors log. See Figure 16.5, for a screen shot of the Logging section of the Server document.

Fig. 16.5

These fields define Web server logging characteristics.

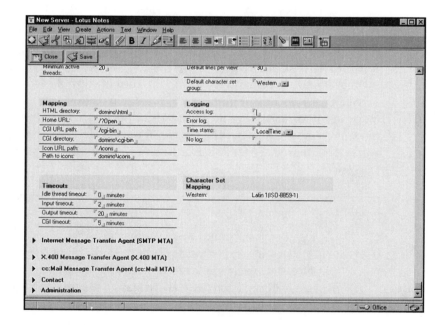

The actual field descriptions follow:

- ▶ *Access log*—Leave this blank to disable access logging. Enter a directory path name to enable access logging. Restart the HTTP server task after changing this entry.

- ▶ *Error log*—Leave this blank to disable error logging. Enter a directory path name to enable access logging. Restart the HTTP server task after changing this entry.

- ▶ *Time stamp*—This defaults to using Domino's local time when making entries in the logs. You can change it so that it uses Greenwich Mean Time.

> *No log*—Use this field to filter entries into the access logs. Enter here templates of either IP addresses or host/domain names. By templates, I mean you can use wildcards. For example, you can enter 192.192.*.*, or *.chestnet.com. Accesses to your server would not be logged if the accessing host has an IP address that begins with 192.192, or has a host name ending in chestnet.com. Separate entries in this field with spaces. You can use host names in this field *only if you have enabled DNS lookup*. Otherwise, you can only use IP addresses. See HTTP Server Basics, earlier in this chapter, for the details about DNS lookup.

Setting up Multi-Database Search Capabilities

When you conduct searches in Lotus Notes, you normally search within individual databases. When you conduct a search on the World Wide Web, you normally search an entire Web site. You can set up Notes to emulate standard Web site searches by having Notes search multiple databases with a single search query.

Notes' site search capability is actually more powerful, in a way, than that of a standard Web server, because you can configure it so that different subsets of databases get searched in different circumstances. For example, a search conducted from a site home page might involve every site-related database on the server, but a search conducted from within a product information page might only search product-related databases.

To set up site search capability, complete the following process:

1. Enable the *Include in multi-database indexing* option for the databases to be included in site searches.

   Do this one of two ways. Select each database, open its Database Properties InfoBox, go to the Design panel, and enable the option. Or, if you want to enable the option for many databases, do it from the Server Administrations screen. There you can open the Tools to Manage Notes Databases dialog box either by choosing Administration, Database Tools in the menu, or by clicking the Database Tools icon. In the dialog box, you can choose the Web site server in the Server field, choose one or more databases in the Databases field, choose Multi-Database Indexing in the Tool field, then select the Enable radio button and click the Update button. Domino will report either that it successfully updated the selected databases or it will report any errors. For example, Domino will report an error if you try to enable Multi-Database Indexing on a database to which you do not have Manager access. After you have enabled multi-database indexing for all the databases you want, click Done.

Tip
You must have Manager access to a database to enable Multi-Database Indexing on it.

2. On the Web site server create a site search database, using the Web Site Search (srchsite.ntf) design template.

3. In each site search database that you create, define the scope of the search by creating one or more Search Scope Configuration documents. You will only be able to do this if you (or a group of which you are a member) occupy the Role of [SearchSiteAdmin] in the Access Control List of the database. All other users will not only not be able to create this document, but they will not see any of the views that display the existing Search Scope Configuration documents.

Tip
You must occupy the role of [SearchSiteAdmin] in the access control list of the search site database to create Search Scope Configuration documents.

The Search Scope Configuration document includes as many as four fields. The fields that appear depend on your choice in the first field. The fields are as follows:

Scope: Choose *Database*, *Directory*, *Server*, or *Domain*. For a Web site search you would normally choose Server. If your Web-accessible servers are in their own, external domain, you might choose Domain. For a partial site search you might choose Database or Directory.

Domain: This field only appears if you chose Domain in the Scope field. Enter the name of the Notes domain. Enter only one Notes domain name in this field.

Server: This field only appears if you chose Server, Directory, or Database in the Scope field. Enter the name of the Web site server. Enter the name of only one server. If you leave this field blank, the search takes place on the server conducting it. If you want the search to encompass multiple servers, create one Server scope document for each server.

Directory: This field only appears if you chose Directory in the Scope field. Enter the name of only one subdirectory in this field. This will cause to be indexed all Multi-Database Index-enabled databases in that directory, its subdirectory tree, and directories pointed to by directory pointer files in its subdirectory tree. If you want the search to encompass multiple subdirectory trees, create one Directory scope document for each subdirectory tree.

Filename: This field appears only if you chose Database in the Scope field. Enter the name of only one database. If you want the search to encompass multiple databases, create one Database scope document for each database.

Full Text Index options: Enter *No Index, Index Summary Data (not rich text fields), Index Full Document,* or *Index Full Document and Attachments.* Use this field to limit the types of data that will be included in the index. Choose *No Index* to remove a server, subdirectory tree, or database from the scope of a search. Use *Index Summary Data* to limit the scope to data in summary (that is, non-rich-text) fields only. Use *Index Full Document* to index all fields but not the contents of files attached to rich text fields. Use *Index Full Document and Attachments* to index all fields and the textual contents of attached files.

Tip

You can create more than one Search Site database. Create one for each multi-database search you want to define.

In each Search Site database, you can create more than one Search Scope Configuration document. The scope of searches performed on that database is defined by the combination of all Search Scope Configuration documents in the database. For example, to include the contents of, say, three Web servers in an index, you could define three Server scope documents. If you then wanted to exclude one database from the index, you could define a Database scope document and set the Full Text Index options field to *No Index.*

For each Search Scope Configuration document that you create, you can name only one domain, server, directory, or database. Create multiple Search Scope Configuration documents if you need to index multiple servers, directories, or databases.

4. Create a full-text index for the site search database that you created in step 2. The index will include all database defined by the scope documents. Do not index the individual databases (unless you want them to be individually searchable). Create the index in the usual way—either in the Full Text panel of the Database Properties box or in the Database Tools dialog box of the Server Administration screen.

After the database is indexed, go to the Database By Title view to see what databases are included in the index. Open each database document to see the extent to which the database was indexed. If databases were indexed that should not have been or if databases that should have been indexed were not, refine your scope documents, then re-index.

You should also set the index update frequency to Daily. It defaults to Immediate. But multi-database indexes tend to be so large and take so long to re-index that Lotus recommends you update them no more often than daily. Set the update frequency in the Full Text panel of the Database Properties box. You can only set this when working locally at the server. The field is grayed out when viewed from a workstation. Daily updates take place, by default, at 2 am.

5. Notes users will be able to search a Search Site database simply by opening the database and filling in a search form. Web users can search a Search Site database the same way. However, you will want to make the Search Site databases more accessible to Web users by adding hyperlinks to the forms in your Web-accessible databases. You may especially want to replace the Search icon in the default View form so that it points to a Search Site database. Do this by creating a $$ViewTemplate for *viewname* form or a $$ViewTemplateDefault form in each affected database. For more information, see "Creating View Templates" in Chapter 10, "Using Special $$ Web Fields and Forms."

The URLs that link to Search Site databases should be in the following format:

http://Host/SiteSearchDBName/$SearchForm?SearchSite

where *Host* is the Internet host.domain name, intranet host name, or IP address of your Web site server and *SiteSearchDBName* is the file name of the site search database to be queried.

The URL in step 5 retrieves a search form from the database named in the URL. The preceding query returns the Simple search form to the Web user. This form appears in Figure 16.6. The Web user can click a link in the form, which then returns the Advanced search form, shown in Figure 16.7.

Alternately, you could directly retrieve the Web Search Advanced form with a URL like the following:

http://host/SiteSearchDBName/Web+Search+Advanced?OpenForm

Or you can make the Site Search Advanced form the default, so that $SearchForm retrieves it instead of the Site Search Simple. Do this by deleting the alias $$Search from the name of the Site Search Simple form and adding it to the name of the Site Search Advanced form.

Fig. 16.6

By default, you start a site search with the Simple search form.

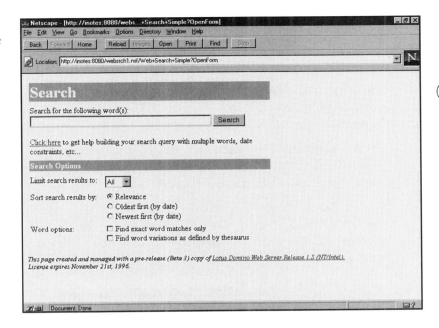

16

Fig. 16.7

You can then click a link to retrieve the Advanced search form.

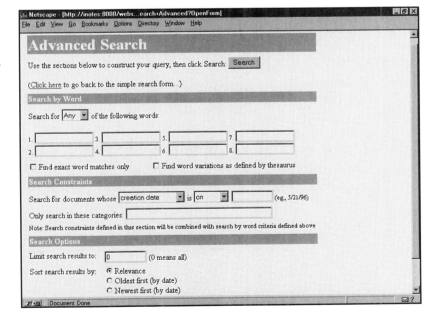

Finally, you can also query a site search site database directly by manually using an URL in the following form:

http:/HostSearchSiteDBName?SearchSite&Query=SearchString1+AND+SearchString2...

where the plus signs represent the space character and *SearchString1* and *SearchString2* are search strings separated by the logical AND. In other words, this query searches for all documents that include both *SearchString1* and *SearchString2*.

When a Web user fills in and submits one of the search forms, or when a user enters a manual search query like the one in the previous paragraph, Domino performs a search of the databases defined in the Databases By Title view of the site search database.

When Domino returns the results of a search, it uses the Results form from the site search database. This is a bare-bones form: Its title shows the query that produced it; it indicates the number of documents found by the search; and it lists the documents in the order specified in the search (see Figure 16.8).

Fig. 16.8

The Search Results form shows the search query, the number of documents found by the search query, and a list of links to the documents found.

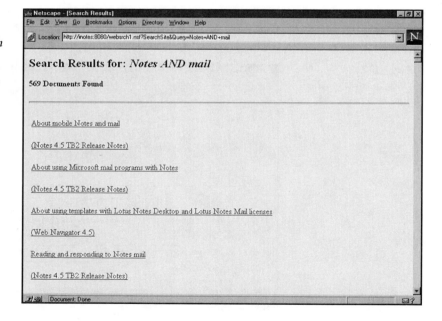

If you prefer, Domino will return the search results on a custom search results form, $$SearchSiteTemplate. For instructions on creating this form, see "Building Search Result Templates" in Chapter 10, "Using Special Web Fields and Forms."

Setting Up a Multi-Homed Site

Domino 4.5 is capable out-of-the-box of being configured as a multi-homed Web server. That is, you can run more than one virtual Web site on a single Domino server. For example, one of our servers runs both www.rockteam.com and www.planetnotes.com. If you look at either site, you may not be impressed by the vast differences between them. That's because we've been so busy writing and testing software that setting up planet notes as a separate site has taken a serious back seat—like all the way to the back of the bus—to the other projects. The point is, though, that www.rockteam.com and www.planetnotes.com are different Web sites—with entirely different host names and IP addresses—that just happen to reside on the same server.

Lotus added this capability to Domino in one of the later betas just before the release of Domino 4.5, in response to heavy demand for the feature from early adopters. The vision that popped into everyone's head, seemingly simultaneously, was, "Hey! If Domino was multi-homed, I could host my clients' Web sites on my server—and make lots of money!" And you can—set up a multi-homed Domino server, that is. It's easy to do. All you have to do is follow these instructions:

1. Assign multiple IP addresses to your Domino host, and corresponding host names—one IP address per virtual server

2. Create a Domino Configuration database

3. Create a Virtual Server document in the Domino Configuration database for each server after the first

4. Optionally, create a separate set of Domino data directories for your second and subsequent servers

The result will be a single Domino computer that appears to Web users to be more than one Web server. There are some limitations. For one, all Notes databases for all virtual servers continue to reside together in the Notes data directory tree. You will have to come up with some way of keeping the users of one virtual server out of databases intended for the exclusive use of users of another virtual server. Also, except for the Mapping section, which is duplicated in the Virtual Server document, all Domino HTTP settings apply to all virtual servers. For example, if you enable logging, you enable it for all virtual servers, all into one set of log files.

If either of these limitations upsets you, you should look at the option of using Domino Advanced Services to partition your server. With a partitioned Domino server, you can actually run entirely separated instances of Domino in separate partitions on the same computer. This way, you could maintain one set of data directories and log files for Server A and a different set for Server B. The only drawback here is cost. You have to pay about $1,000 for the Domino Advanced Services license—over and above the cost of the server license itself. A partitioned server requires more memory, more disk space, and more processing power than a plain old server configured as multiple Web servers.

Assigning Multiple IP Addresses to a Computer

Assigning multiple IP addresses to a computer is beyond the scope of this book (except, perhaps, for Appendix D, "Installing Windows NT Server 4.0"), but it is not very hard, either. Any network administrator with a little bit of TCP/IP experience should be able to figure out how to do it. Having made such a bold assertion, let's check behind the curtain and see how hard it would be to set up multiple IP addresses on a computer running Windows NT 4.0.

Click Start, Settings, Control Panel, then double-click the Network icon. The Network dialog box appears, where you click the Protocols tab to reveal the Protocols panel. There you select the TCP/IP protocol then click Properties. This opens the Microsoft TCP/IP Properties dialog box. There on the first panel, labeled IP Address, click the Advanced button. The Advanced IP Addressing dialog box opens. In the area marked IP Addresses, the Add button permits you to assign additional IP addresses to your computer.

Of course, if you are on a DNS-controlled network, you would also have to update your status on the DNS server. If you are accessing the Internet, you would have to use IP addresses that are properly registered with the InterNIC. But these issues really are beyond the scope of this book. The bottom line is that adding a second IP address to a computer is not much harder than adding the first one.

Creating the Domino Configuration Database

You create this database in the root data directory of the Domino Web server by using the Domino Configuration template, file name domcfg.ntf. The only other rule that you must follow is that the file name of the resulting Domino Configuration database must be domcfg.nsf. So, the steps are as follows:

1. Either have the right to create a new database on the Domino server or do your work at the Domino server computer. In the Notes menu, choose File, Database, New. The New Database dialog box opens.

2. In the Server field, enter either Local if you are working at the Domino server's console or the name of the Domino server if you are working at your workstation.

3. In the File Name field, enter domcfg.nsf.

4. In the Title field, enter Domino Configuration.

5. If you are not working at the Domino server's console, then click the Template Server button and change the template server from Local to the name of your Domino server.

6. In the list of database templates, choose Domino Configuration. When you have chosen correctly, the file name domcfg.ntf will appear to the right of the About button.

7. That's all. Click OK and the database will open up. Its About document, which is really not very helpful at all, being a blank screen, will appear. Close it and you will see that the database consists of five empty views: All Documents, Directory Mapping, URL Mapping, URL Redirections, and Virtual Servers.

Creating the Virtual Server Document

To create a virtual server, you will create a Virtual Server document. You can do this either at the server or at your workstation.

1. Open the Domino Configuration database. In the Notes menu, choose Create, Virtual Server. A new, Virtual Server form opens.

2. Enter the IP address of the virtual server. This is the only required field in this form.

3. Optionally, enter comments here that will help you, months from now, or your successor, years from now (you hope) to recall the purpose of this document when you created it. Be verbose here.

4. Optionally, change the file name of the default home page. You really only have to change this field if you will be using a non-Notes-generated home page, and even then you probably don't need to change this page.

5. Optionally, change the locations of the HTML, CGI, and Icons directories. You probably do *not* want to change the CGI URL path or the Icon URL path.

6. Optionally, change the Home URL. The default—/?Open—will cause a list of databases on the server to be displayed when a Web user sends the generic request (server name only) to this server. You probably want to change this so that this server's users see a real home page when they visit this site.

7. Close and save this Virtual Server document. Within 15 minutes, the Domino server will discover its existence and start fielding URLs for this virtual server.

Domino won't instantly recognize the existence of this new document. To force Domino to recognize it, bring down the HTTP server task, then restart it. Enter the following commands at the server console (or at the remote server console if you have that right):

```
tell http quit
load http
```

Alternatively, you can just type the abbreviated forms of these commands:

```
t http q
l http
```

Upon restart, the HTTP server task will look for the Domino Configuration database and read all the documents in it, including the new Virtual Server document you just saved.

Creating Separate Data Directories

If you specified a different set of data directories in a server's Virtual Server document, then you must create the data directories that you designated. That is, where your first Web server's data directories are the subdirectories of the data\domino directory, your second Web server's data directories, or any one of them, could be elsewhere on the server—in another subdirectory of the data directory, for example, or on another disk drive.

You don't have to create a complete set of Web data directories for each virtual Web server if you don't want to. For example, the data\domino\icons directory tends to have the same set of files in it on most servers, so your virtual servers might share a single instance of this directory. The Virtual Server document that you will create for each virtual Web server will default to the same set of directories that the original server uses. So, actually, keeping the same data directories for all of your virtual servers is the path of least resistance.

Creating a Scalable Web Site: Part 1

When you set up a Web site, you might initially assume that you will dedicate one computer to it. If you are ambitious you may, as in the previous section, intend to host more than one Web site on your one computer. But what happens if your Web site—or one of the Web sites on your computer—gets really popular, and you start getting thousands, even millions of hits per day. How will your one computer stand up? We're not talking about network bandwidth here, although that is going to be a whole problem in its own right if you become one of the top 10 sites on the Web. What we're getting at here is the notion that your processor just may not be able to handle all the demands made on it.

The fact may be that, instead of thinking grandiosely about running multiple Web sites on one computer, you should be thinking (even more grandiosely, perhaps) about running one Web site across multiple Domino servers. With Domino as your Web server and after all, Notes databases holding the bulk of your Web content, it is pretty easy, to scale up your Web site by simply moving certain databases onto other computers, then using the Domino Configuration database to automate the transfer of URL requests from one computer to another. If that doesn't meet your needs you can use Domino clustering along with third-party tools to build a very scalable site.

We will study these two approaches by studying two of Lotus's own Web sites— www.lotus.com and www.notes.net. In this section, we will examine www.lotus.com. Later, when we discuss Domino clustering, we will also examine www.notes.net.

The Lotus Web site was configured (on that day, at least) approximately as in Figure 16.9.

Fig. 16.9

Server1 serves the home page. Server2 serves downloads. Server3 serves the discussion database. They all replicate with Hub, which connects via null modem cable to the staging computer on the corporate LAN.

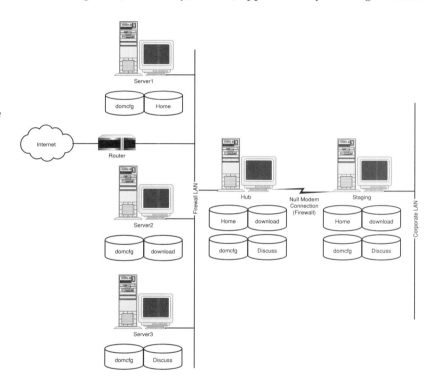

Server1 holds the home page database. Server2 holds the download database. Server3 holds the discussion database. All three replicate with a hub server which, in turn, replicates with a staging server. The first four are outside the corporate firewall, the fifth (the Stage) inside. The firewall remains intact despite the direct connection between the Hub and the Stage because the connection is a serial connection via null modem cable. Since no IP packets can cross the serial connection, no pirates can ride into the corporate LAN that way.

The Webmaster does all design work on the staging server. Content authors contribute all work to the staging server or to other servers inside the firewall. All that work then moves by replication first to the hub, then to the front-line servers, which have the HTTP server task running and which communicate directly with the Internet. If any input received from the Web results in the generation of a Notes document, that document can make its way back to the staging server either by replication or mail routing.

By setting up their Web site this way, the Webmasters at Lotus were able to distribute the load of Web visitors more or less evenly across three computers. When they first split the site into multiple computers, however, the Lotus Webmasters discovered that they had to re-link the databases to each other. Originally, they had used Notes Document, View, and Database links because, after all, those are self-sustaining. If a document pointed to by a Notes Link ever moves to a new location *on the same server*, Notes updates the link to reflect the new location.

However, by moving some of the databases to entirely new servers, they broke those links entirely and had to replace them. Initially, they replaced the links with URL links. However, they realized that, every time they made a move of a database, they would have to update all of the links in all of the other databases that pointed to that database. To ease that chore, they fell back on URL redirection.

URL redirection is a standard HTTP trick. When a Web server receives a URL from a browser, the server can either return the document that the URL refers to or it can return another URL. Normally, a server would return the document, but sometimes it cannot. For example, the Webmaster may, after learning his craft a little better, decide to reorganize the site. To avoid breaking all his users' bookmarks, the Webmaster uses URL redirection. When the server receives an URL to one of the old locations, the server returns the new URL to the browser. Upon receipt of the new URL, the browser automatically sends it out to the server named in it, and the server then (presumably) returns the document, from the *new* location, that the user was originally seeking.

The redirection process takes place entirely between the computers. The user who sent out the original URL may never even know that the redirection took place, except for one thing. If the redirecting computer sends a partial URL, say, just a different directory location in the same computer as the original URL, then the browser will reveal nothing about the change to the user. But if the redirecting computer sends a complete URL, including the protocol and host name of the responding computer, then the browser will report the new URL of the document when it finally receives it, and the user will be able to tell from looking at the Location field that the document arrived by redirection.

To accomplish redirection by Domino, you create a document in the Domino Configuration database. That is the same database in which we created Virtual Server documents to set up a multi-homed Web site in the previous section. This time you create a Redirection URL -> URL document, as in Figure 16.10.

Fig. 16.10

The first URL in this figure, /area/home, is the URL the browser sends to the server. The server returns the second URL to the browser, which sends it right back out in its own turn.

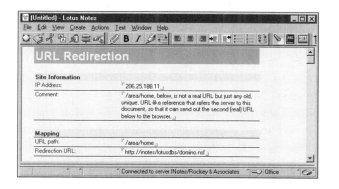

Three of the four fields in this document are required. You must enter the IP address of the server that will do the redirecting. Enter the URL that it receives in the URL path field, and the URL that it returns in the Redirection URL field. When creating these documents for your multi-server Web site, create one for every URL that refers to a location in another Notes database. Then, whenever you decide to move a database to another server, or simply to another directory on the same server, you can just update the Redirection documents that point to that database. Because many URLs in a database will be duplicates of each other, and because all the necessary changes can be seen and made at a glance in the Domino Configuration database, your life will be a lot easier if you use this method to link your databases to each other.

Caution

Remember that Domino won't act on your new URL Redirection document until after you shut down and restart the HTTP server task. At the Domino server console or the remote server console, enter *tell http quit* then *load http*. Upon restart, the HTTP server task will use the revised Domino Configuration database to set itself up, and it will recognize your new URL Redirection document.

Mirroring Web Sites with Domino

What if your overseas customers are crying the blues because accessing your site across the ocean is too slow and unreliable for them? Or what if you would just like to ease the pressure on your primary site by setting up a second site across the ocean/continent? You want the site to be essentially the same as your primary site, just closer to your most distant clients. Or maybe you just want a secondary site that will still be available should disaster strike your primary site. We're talking about setting up a "mirror" Web site. And Domino does it better than any other product.

A mirror Web site almost always must be identical or nearly identical to the primary site. Most Webmasters don't want to force users to go to two different sites, depending on what they are looking for; rather, they want to make the one site more conveniently available. With most Web products, this means having a primary, "active" site and one or more secondary, "inactive" sites. That is, the primary site receives all the user input, author updates, design changes, and the like. Then it forces those changes out to the secondary sites. The primary is the read/write site. The secondaries are, for the Web users, "read only" sites.

Most products set up mirror sites this way because they cannot perform true, two-way replication. All they can do is over-write the old information with the new. At best, they can update changed data only, but only in one direction. Domino, on the other hand, is the undisputed champion of two-way, changes-only replication. Because of Notes' replication prowess, setting up a mirror Web site—a true mirror, where both sites are read/write—is a no-brainer. You simply set up replicas of the databases on the mirror site, then set up a replication schedule between the sites. The sites can replicate across the Internet if you want; if you think you need a backup method of replication, you can set up a long-distance phone call as a secondary means of replication.

If one mirror site sustains substantially more volume than the other, you could spread the busy site across more computers than the other site. If, as described in the previous section, you use Redirection documents in the Domino Configuration database to maintain the links between the databases on each site, then it would be easy to maintain the links even though the two sites are configured differently. Just make sure that the Domino Configuration database used at the first site is not a replica copy of the Domino Configuration database used at the second site, so that you can maintain different redirections at the two sites.

The net result is that you now have two, identical Web sites. Both are active, read-write sites. All changes made to databases at one site will replicate eventually to the other site. If one site goes down for some reason, visitors can still get to the other site. If one site is in North America, the other in, say, Asia, then people can go to the local Web site, thereby avoiding low-bandwidth, high-traffic connections between the continents.

Scaling Up with Domino Server Clusters

Earlier in this chapter, you learned how Lotus Development built a scalable, multi-server Web site—www.lotus.com—using just the standard tools that are part of any Domino server. Here, you will see how Lotus used Domino Advanced Services to build an even more scalable Web site—www.notes.net. In this case, Lotus used Domino's server clustering capability, along with some non-Notes techniques, to build a site that could reliably deliver multi-megabyte files to large numbers of downloaders.

Before we can see how Lotus did this, however, we must learn a little bit about Domino Advanced Services, especially about Domino Server Clustering. So read on. The illustration of server scaling continues after the following section about Domino Advanced Services.

Understanding Domino Advanced Services

Domino Advanced Services is a package of Domino server enhancements that you can add to any Domino 4.5 server for a cost in the neighborhood of $1,000 over the price of the server license itself. The cost to you depends on your relationship to Lotus. Volume purchasers pay less; little guys pay more. Domino Advanced Services includes specifically three enhancements to the Domino server:

▶ Server Clustering—This permits configuring multiple Domino servers to replicate with each other in *real time* and to appear to the user as a single server. The benefits of server clustering include fault-tolerance, load balancing, and failover.

▶ Server Partitioning—This permits you to create multiple server partitions on one computer, which causes the computer to appear to users as multiple Domino servers. This is useful if you want to host multiple Web sites on one computer or if you want to host multiple Domino applications on one computer.

▶ Notes Billing—This permits you to track and compile system usage and use the information to bill users or to monitor trends.

Installing Advanced Services

You can install Domino Advanced Services from the standard Domino CD, using the standard installation process. The Lotus Notes Install program at some point offers you the choice of doing a "Standard" installation, a "Server" installation, or a "Customized" installation. "Standard" installs a Notes workstation. "Server" installs a plain vanilla Domino server. "Customized" gives you a choice of features to install. If you choose "Customized," the next screen shows the available features on two tabbed panels, and you can check off the ones you want. The second tabbed panel is labeled Advanced Services. There are either two or three choices on the panel—Domino Partitioned Server (2K), Advanced Services (182K), and Advanced Services Data (265K) (see Figure 16.11).

Fig. 16.11

To install clustering or usage tracking and billing services, check off the second and third boxes. To install the first partitioned server, check off all three boxes. To install later partitioned servers, check off the first and third boxes.

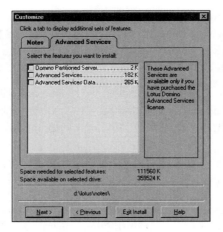

Domino partitions are available only for some versions of Domino, including the versions for Windows NT (Intel and Alpha) and the versions for UNIX. If you are running Domino over OS/2, NetWare, or Windows 95, partitions are not available to you.

If you want to install Clustering or Usage Tracking and Billing services, check off the last two boxes. If you want to install partitioned servers, then check off all three boxes for the first partitioned server, and just the first and third boxes for each additional partitioned server.

Understanding Server Clusters

Domino's server clustering feature permits the setup of up to six Domino servers in a named group called a *cluster*. The servers in the cluster work together as a unit to provide a series of benefits to Notes 4.*x* users:

▶ Failover—If one server in the cluster should go down, Notes 4.*x* users automatically fail over to another server in the cluster. Notes 3.*x* users and Web browser users do not fail over to another server automatically but rather would receive "server unavailable" error messages and would have to manually find another server.

▶ Workload balancing—If one server is a lot busier than others, it can automatically start passing off server requests to other members of the cluster to even the workload. You can set up any combination of Domino 4.5 servers in a cluster. They don't have to be identical in any other way. If one server happens to have a lot more or less processing power than others, you can adjust it to accept heavier or lighter loads than the others before passing off work to them.

▶ Cluster Replication—Within a cluster, Domino implements *event-based* replication. That is, whenever a change occurs in a database, the server immediately pushes the change to the other members of the cluster. That way, the servers in the cluster achieve near real-time replication of databases. Contrast this to standard Notes replication, which is schedule-based and always introduces some time delay into the replication process.

▶ Scalability—Because the servers in a cluster work together as a group to serve the needs of users, you can transparently scale them up or down by adding more servers to the cluster or removing servers from the cluster.

▶ High Database Availability—You can set up a given database to run on one, two, or more servers in the cluster, depending on the degree of availability that database should have to users. An especially mission-critical database might reside on every server in the cluster. The servers in the cluster know on which servers each database resides and they fail over and balance the workload according to that knowledge.

To establish a server cluster, you have to run down a long checklist of things to do. You have to do some careful planning about things like how the members of the cluster will relate to each other. You have to meet numerous prerequisites. Then in the Server-Servers view, you select one or more servers that will become members of the cluster and click the Add to Cluster button. Notes prompts you for the name of an existing cluster to add the servers to or for a new cluster name. Then the Administration Process takes over and performs a whole series of actions.

When the whole process is finished, you have from two to six servers that are aware that they are members of a cluster. They share a common Cluster ID number. They communicate with each other from time to time to keep each other up-to-date. They maintain a common database, the Cluster Database Directory (cldbdir.nsf) in which they track what databases each member maintains. They run a series of server tasks, including the Cluster Manager, the Cluster Database Directory Manager, which maintains the Cluster Database Directory, the Cluster Administration Process, and the Cluster Replicator, which manages event-driven replication among cluster managers.

You have to set a series of notes.ini variables on each cluster server and replicate various databases to chosen servers in the cluster, in order to set up load balancing, failover, and appropriate database availability. Then you have to monitor the performance of the servers in the cluster and make sure everything runs smoothly. To keep things running smoothly you can make use of server commands, the Notes log for each server, cluster statistics, event monitors, and the cluster analysis tool.

Clearly, setting up and maintaining server clusters is no trivial undertaking, but the benefits make the effort well worthwhile. When a user tries to open a database on one of the cluster servers, if the server in question is out of service or overworked, the user's Notes 4.*x* client software automatically fails over to a replica copy of the database on one of the other cluster servers, without the users even knowing about it. If you need to bring a server down for maintenance, the other servers just pick up the load, and the only reason users might know about it is if they try to access a database that resides only on the downed server. If over time the workload of the servers increases, due to heavier usage of Notes by existing users, or increased numbers of users, or the popularity of your Web site, you can just add more servers to the cluster.

Understanding Server Partitioning

Server partitioning is the inverse of server clusters. Where a server cluster is a group of servers running on separate computers but acting in concert, server partitioning is a series of unrelated servers sharing a single computer. You can install up to six server partitions on one computer. All six servers share the same program directory, but each has it own set of data directories. So, where a standalone Domino server might be located in the c:\notes directory and store its data in the c:\notes\data directory, the six servers on a partitioned server might all reside in c:\notes but have their data in c:\notes\ p1data, c:\notes\p2data, c:\notes\p3data, c:\notes\p4data, c:\notes\p5data, and c:\notes\p6data. Perhaps their data directories are on other drives.

When you start up each server, it runs in its own memory space. If you bring one server down or it crashes, the other servers continue to run unaffected. Also, if one server crashes, an automatic cleanup procedure makes it possible to restart the server without restarting the whole computer.

Each server also has its own notes.ini file. If the computer on which the servers run is not really powerful enough to support as many servers as you have running on it, you can set notes.ini variables that limit the number of concurrently logged-in users and the number of concurrent transactions the servers will allow.

The different servers can reside in the same or different Notes domains and Notes organizations. They can share or use different LAN adapters and IP addresses. A given server might participate in a server cluster if you need it to.

A possible beneficiary of server partitioning is the small organization—just a few people working together—who could not previously justify the expense of setting up a maintaining a computer dedicated as a Notes server. Now you can set them up in a separate partition of a server that they share with one or more organizations.

Understanding Notes Billing

The third feature of Domino Advanced Services is Notes Billing, which consists of a Domino server task called *Billing,* which collects information on as many as six classes of server usage and reports the information to a Notes billing database, a binary file, or both. Alternatively, you can write a program by using the Notes API that collects the information and delivers it to a third-party billing program.

16

The six classes of usage that Billing reports on are as follows:

> ▶ Session—Tracks the beginning and end of each user session and whenever certain types of activity take place, such as editing a document or replicating to a user workstation.

> ▶ Database—Tracks the opening and closing of all databases, by whom, and for how long they are kept open.

> ▶ Document—Tracks reads and writes of specified documents.

> ▶ Replication—Tracks replications initiated by the billing server.

> ▶ Mail—Tracks mail transfers from the billing server to other servers.

> ▶ Agent—Tracks the start and duration of agents run by users and other servers on the billing server.

You start the billing server task on a server by typing *load billing* at the server console. You specify which of the six classes of activity the task should track by listing the classes in a variable in notes.ini, as follows:

```
BillingClass=Session,Database,Document,Replication,Mail,Agent
```

The preceding line tells the billing task to track everything. Just remove from the line the words that represent classes you do not want to track.

Creating a Scalable Web Site: Part 2

Now we come to the description of www.notes.net. Earlier we saw how Lotus scaled www.lotus.com up by simply distributing the various databases to different servers. Now we will see how they achieved even greater scale with www.notes.net by setting up a server cluster.

With www.notes.net, Lotus' main goal was to set up a site where people could download software, retrieve information about Lotus Notes and Domino, and engage in discussions about Notes and Domino. Among other things, you can download a full copy of Notes/Domino—about 40M worth of software. Another goal was to demonstrate how easy it is to set up a large, robust, 24x7 available, easily maintained site on a modest budget.

Lotus used standard PCs running either Windows NT or OS/2. The computers had single 200 MHz Pentium Pro processors, 128M RAM, and three 3.2G hard drives. The three disks were configured in a RAID 5 array so that they had only 6.4G of disk capacity per computer. But the RAID 5 array gave them faster disk access as well as the ability, should any one disk fail, to keep operating without loss of data. They set up multiple computers in Domino server clusters. Their front line site was located at an ISP, and they had a duplicate administrative site at Iris, connected to the first site by T-1 line and kept up-to-date with it by Notes replication (see Figure 16.12).

Fig. 16.12

All servers in each cluster have every database on them.

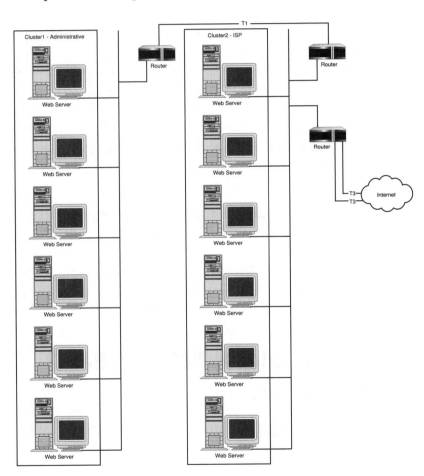

In the case of this site, Lotus maintained all Notes databases on every server in the cluster. Because Web browsers cannot take advantage of Domino cluster load balancing (only Notes 4.*x* clients can), Lotus used two third-party solutions to distribute Web requests evenly among the servers: rotating DNS and IBM Network Dispatcher.

Rotating or "round-robin" DNS is a standard feature of the DNS specification, by which each time a request comes in for a particular host name, DNS routes it first to one IP address, then to the next IP address, then to the next, and so on to all IP addresses supporting the host name. A weakness of rotating DNS is that Web browsers tend to cache addresses received from Web servers, then go back to those addresses again and again, bypassing the DNS after the first hit.

IBM Network Dispatcher is a load-balancing product that overcomes this weakness of rotating DNS by virtualizing the address of a requested host and sending a different address to the Web browser after each request, so that the browser can only come to Network Dispatcher each time it returns to the site. In this way, Network Dispatcher maintains greater control over the load balance than DNS can alone.

Another issue that arises in a high-volume site like notes.net, where they expect to receive a lot of registrations of users downloading software or participating in discussions, is the limitations of the Public Address Book. Group documents can accommodate 1,000 users each. At notes.net they have solved the group size limitation by writing their registration agent in such a way that it creates a new Group document when the one it has been using reaches a certain size, then including groups within groups. They also use a Master Address Book to break up the names of registered users into separate address books.

From Here...

In this chapter, you learned about several advanced Web server administration techniques as well as several features of Domino that are potentially useful when using Domino servers as Web servers. To learn more about the Domino administration, see *Special Edition Using Lotus Notes and Domino 4.5*, the full text of which is included in the CD-ROM that comes with this book.

Building a Domino Site

## chapter 17

Building a Domino Web Site in One Day with Domino Action

17

In this chapter

◆ **Set up Domino Action**
The Domino Action application consists of two databases. Here you learn which templates to select in creating the new databases needed for the application.

◆ **Set up the appearance, organization, and content-approval options for your site**
You decide how your Web site will look, which of the databases you'll want generated, and how you want them to look.

◆ **Configuring multiple areas using the site area databases such as Registration, About the Company, and Discussion**
Domino Action offers an assortment of database boilerplates, from which you select the site areas to be included in your Web site. Now you add your customized information to these site areas.

◆ **Generate the site using the SiteCreator**
Once you've supplied all of the information necessary to create your site, SiteCreator generates all of the necessary databases to complete your Web site.

I f you bought this book so you could learn how to design Notes applications for the World Wide Web, then this chapter is not for you, because frankly, with Domino Action you don't have to design anything. Domino Action has done all the design work and coding for you. All you have to do is fill in the blanks on a series of Notes documents, provide a few graphic images like company logo, product logos, photographs—whatever you think would look good on your Web site. Add some boilerplate text, such as copyright notices. Run an agent that generates a series of databases of your choosing. Then start generating content by creating Notes documents.

The idea here isn't to hand-tool a custom-designed site. Rather, you use Domino Action to establish a generic yet handsome, powerful, and sophisticated Web presence quickly and easily so you can meet your "yesterday" deadlines.

The purpose of this chapter is to familiarize you with the program prior to running it. Here, you can get a look at the databases and forms generated by using Domino Action.

What is Domino Action

Domino Action is a Lotus Notes application included with the Domino 4.5 server package. It creates and maintains a whole, Domino-based World Wide Web site. It simplifies the creation of a Web site by working from preset designs into which you plug your information and graphics. Domino Action leads you through the design process in a step-by-step manner in which you enter your company information and choose the functions your site will perform, how you want your site to look, and how you want your users to work with the site. Then Domino Action generates your Web site as a set of databases that can be used both in Notes and on the Web.

Domino Action lets you take advantage of Notes' workflow, security, and document-management features for your Web site. When you use Domino Action, you control who can author, edit, and approve Web pages for your site. You can selectively distribute the authoring, editing, and approval tasks so that, for example, one group of people is in charge of one database while another group handles a second database, and so on.

There is no real design, development, or code intervention here. This is simply a fill-out-the-forms-to-get-up-and-running-on-the-Web scenario.

Setting Up Domino Action

The Domino Action application consists of two database templates:

▶ *Domino Action SiteCreator (SiteAct.ntf)*. Configures and generates the databases that make up your site.

▶ *Domino Action Library (LibAct.ntf)*. Stores the design elements SiteCreator uses to build the site.

You may install these two templates locally (on your own computer) or on a server. However, once Domino Action generates the databases that make up your Web site, the generated databases must be located on the Domino server for the Web site to work.

The SiteCreator database lets you select and configure the elements of your site. You can decide where you want your site to be, how you want it to appear, and how you want visitors to interact with your site. Once you've supplied this information, SiteCreator generates your Web site as a set of Notes databases for use by both Notes clients and Web clients.

To create the SiteCreator database for your Web site:

1. Choose File, Database, New. The New Database dialog box appears (see Figure 17.1).
2. Specify the server (Local or the Domino server) in the Server box.
3. Enter a title for the database in the Title box. This is the title that appears on the database icon. You can choose SiteCreator if this is the only site you're going to make using the SiteCreator template, or make up a title that is specific to your Web site.
4. In the File Name box, enter the name of the database (with an .NSF file extension), or accept the name Notes generated.
5. From the list of templates, find and highlight the Domino Action SiteCreator template (SiteAct.ntf).
6. Leave Inherit Future Design Changes selected.
7. Click OK.

Fig. 17.1

The New Database dialog box uses the template Domino Action SiteCreator.

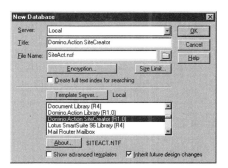

The second database you need is the Library, which includes forms, subforms, views, and other design elements that may be used to build your site. During the site generation process, the SiteCreator looks to the Library for the design elements you selected during your setup. When SiteCreator generates the site, several databases are created by marrying the information you supply in the Site Configuration document to the resources of the Domino Action Library.

To create the Library database:

1. Choose File, Database, New. The New Database dialog box appears as shown in Figure 17.1.

2. Specify the server (Local or the Domino server) in the Server box.

3. Enter a title for the database in the Title box. This is the title that appears on the database icon. You can choose Library if you're only making one Web site, or make up a title that is specific to your Web site.

4. In the File Name box, enter the name of the database (with an .NSF file extension), or accept the name Notes generated.

5. From the list of templates, find and highlight the Domino Action Library template (LibAct.ntf).

6. Leave Inherit Future Design Changes selected.

7. Click OK.

Open the SiteCreator database to begin building your Web site.

The Site Creation Process

When you open the SiteCreator database, the three pane view (see Figure 17.2) lists four categories:

▶ *Quickstart: Site Creator*. Contains five documents: the SiteCreator Overview document, one document for each of the three steps necessary to create a site, and one to Finish Your Site.

▶ *User's Guide*. Contains valuable information pertaining to Domino Action, including a section on Before You Begin.

▶ *Administrative Tasks*. Contains information on maintaining your site.

▶ *Release Notes*. Contains current Lotus Release Notes on this version of Domino Action.

The Preview pane (right side of the screen) displays the currently selected document in Preview mode. The first time you open the database in this view, the currently selected document is the SiteCreator Overview. This document explains how SiteCreator works, what happens during each phase of the site creation process, and what additional steps you must take at the end of the process. You can read the document when it's in Preview mode, but you must double-click the name of the document in the view to open the document.

At the bottom of the SiteCreator Overview document is a hotspot labeled LAUNCH STEP 1 (see Figure 17.3).

Fig. 17.2

The opening screen of the SiteCreator database provides an overview of Domino Action in the preview pane and the list of views in the navigator pane includes the User's Guide.

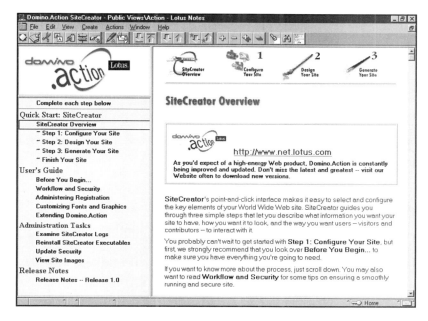

Fig. 17.3

Click the Launch hotspot to begin Step 1 of creating your Web site.

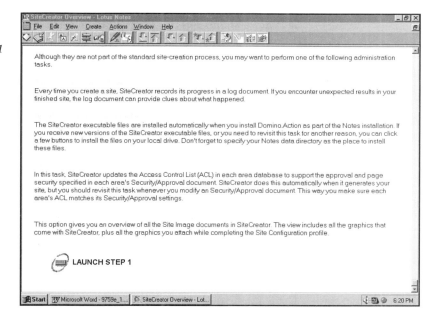

As you work through the steps in creating your site, SiteCreator offers you suggestions on the appearance and operation of your site. However, you should collect any information or graphics you want to include on your Web pages before starting this process and know the location of your graphics files.

The site creation process steps you through the following:

▶ *Step 1: Configure Your Site*. Here you supply information about your company, as well as where the Domino Action Library is located, the name and location of your Web site, who's in charge of your Web site, and so on. You'll also select the areas you want to have for your site. An *area* is a portion of the site containing related information, such as descriptions of your services or products. An area becomes a separate database when SiteCreator generates the site.

▶ *Step 2: Design Your Site*. You'll work with a series of documents that control the appearance, organization, and approval settings for each of the areas you've selected for your site. This is where you set the page layout, select background colors or images, choose categories, and specify who is authorized to compose, approve, and read the pages in the area. A Quick Design option lets you reduce your design time by using default settings. You can always go back later if you change your mind.

▶ *Step 3: Generate Your Site*. By using the design decisions you made and the data you included in the configuration information, SiteCreator retrieves the needed design elements from the Library database and creates a new database for each site area you specified in the site configuration.

▶ *Step 4: Finish Your Site*. Once you've completed the three important steps toward building your site, including building all the site areas, you refresh all the documents and establish all the links between the site areas.

Completing the Site Configuration Document

You specify the "backbone" information for your Web site in the Site Configuration document. In this document, you enter data on the name and location of the Library database, the name of your site, who's in charge of the site, what types of information you want included in the site, and information about your company. Much of this information will appear on your home page, as well as in the area databases SiteCreator will create.

To open the Site Configuration document:

1. Open the SiteCreator database.

2. In the SiteCreator Overview document, click the Launch Step 1 hotspot. Alternatively, in the main view, double-click Step 1: Configure Your Site to open that document (see Figure 17.4). This document briefly explains what will happen in this first step of the process.

Fig. 17.4

Step 1: Configure your Site explains the beginning of the site configuration process. Click the Configure Your Site button to begin the process.

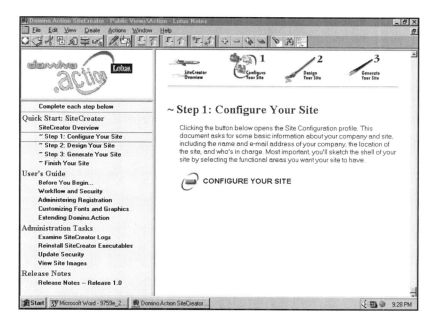

17

3. To continue the process, click the Configure Your Site button at the bottom of the document. This opens the Site Configuration view.

4. The Set Up Site Configuration document is automatically selected. Click the Edit hotspot on the Preview pane to change the default settings on the Site Configuration form (see Figure 17.5).

5. Complete the fields in the Site Configuration form using the following guidelines (fields marked by red stars are required fields). If you need more help as you're working through the fields, click QSG the "Help" light bulb symbol at the top or bottom of the form or the "Tell me more" light bulb symbol under the field.

> ▶ *Site Areas.* You can select up to 11 areas, each of which will become a database serving a particular purpose. The choices are explained in Table 17.1.

> ▶ *Site Manager(s).* The person or group who will have Manager access to all areas of your site and is the equivalent of the Webmaster for your site. SiteCreator assumes the person filling in this form will be the Site Manager, but you may enter the names of any person or group that appears in your Public Address Book (click the list button to open a browser that allows you to select people or groups from the Public Address Book). Because the databases you are creating can be accessed from both Notes and the Internet, all names must appear

in both hierarchical (Bob Dobbs/Planet Notes) and flat (Bob Dobbs) format. Separate multiple names with semicolons. In the group and person documents in the Public Address Book, be sure to enter the flat format name in each person document or for each participant in each group. This is a required field.

▶ *Company Name.* The name of the company which the site will serve. This is a required field.

▶ *Default Copyright Message.* A copyright notice that will appear throughout the site (make sure you enter the current year). You have the opportunity to change this message on specific pages later.

▶ *Company Contact Information.* The company postal address or any other contact information that you want, such as telephone or fax numbers. Don't include the company name as it already appears in the Company Name field.

▶ *Company Contact E-Mail Address.* Where you receive requests for information. This is a required field.

▶ *Site Image(s).* Click the Attach Image button to open the Site Design form, with which you can create an image library document. The .GIF and .JPEG images you attach will be available to use as you design your site. See the "Attaching a Site Image" section for more details.

▶ *Site Server.* The name of the Domino Web server. SiteCreator defaults to Local. Leave the select at Local if the Library database is located on the computer where you are working. *This is a required field.*

▶ *Site Directory.* Enter the directory where you want to create the site. It must be a subdirectory of \Notes\Data, so you need only enter the path relative to that directory. If the directory doesn't exist, SiteCreator creates it for you. The default setting is the \Action subdirectory. This is a required field.

▶ *Library Server Name.* The name of the server where the Library database is located. SiteCreator defaults to Local. Leave the selection at Local if the Library database is located on the computer where you are working. Otherwise, enter the name of the server where the Library database is located. This is a required field.

▶ *Library File Name.* The path and name of the Library database, relative to the Notes data directory. If you stored the Library file in c:\notes\data, enter just the file name of the Library database. If you stored the Library database in a subdirectory of the Notes data directory, list both the subdirectory in which the Library database is located and the file name of the Library database (for example, **\Website\ourWeb.nsf**). This field defaults to LibAct.nsf, so make sure you enter *your* Library file name. This is a required field.

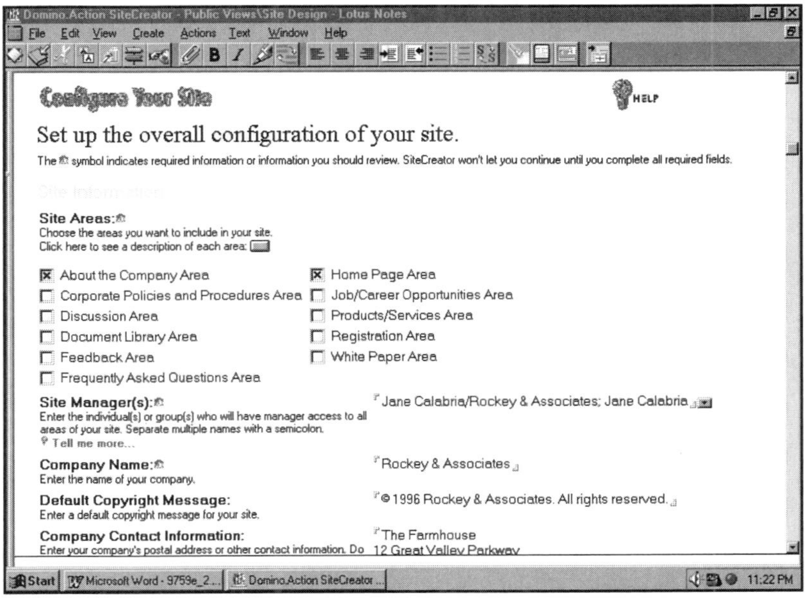

Fig. 17.5

The top portion of the Site Configuration form contains the site area choices. A separate database is created for each of the site areas you select.

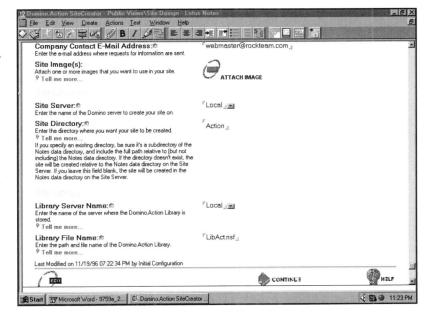

6. Save the form and close it. A check mark appears in front of Step 1 in the Main view to indicate that this step is complete.

Fig. 17.6

The Site Configuration form contains some required fields (marked by red stars); scroll down the page to see the entire form.

Table 17.1   Site Areas and Their Purpose

Area	Purpose
About the Company	General information about the company and its products and services.
Corporate Policies and Procedures	Policy and procedure guides, employee manuals, and human resources information. This area would be appropriate for a company's internal site.
Discussion	Visitors to this area can exchange information and ideas with each other and with company personnel who moderate the discussion.
Document Library	Store reference documents and important files in this area.
Feedback	Provides a questionnaire that visitors to your site can complete. You define the questions and answer choices that appear in the questionnaire.
Frequently Asked Questions	List the questions and answers most often handled by customer service, marketing, corporate communications, or technical support personnel.
Home Page	The site home page. The starting point from which users can reach all other areas of the site. This area is automatically selected for you.
Job/Career Opportunities	List of current employment opportunities in your company. This area would be appropriate for a company's internal site.
Product/Services	Descriptions of your products and services and pricing information.
Registration	Visitors to the site can register here.
White Paper	Store white papers in this area.

Attaching a Site Image

A *site image* could be your company logo, a photograph of your building, the map showing directions to your store, or a picture of the president of the company or of your product that you have created in a graphics program or scanned. For each image that you want to include in your site, you have to create a Site Image document (see Figure 17.7). Here you name the image, describe it, categorize it, and attach a copy of the image file.

A new Site Design document appears when you click the Attach Image button in the Site Image(s) field of the Site Configuration document. Images must be in .GIF or .JPEG format.

Caution

When you create or scan an image, you must save it in a .GIF or .JPEG file format. Be certain your image is saved in the same size you want it to appear on the Web page. You cannot resize it.

17

Fig. 17.7

You can attach a graphic file in the Site Design form. The file must be a .GIF or .JPEG format.

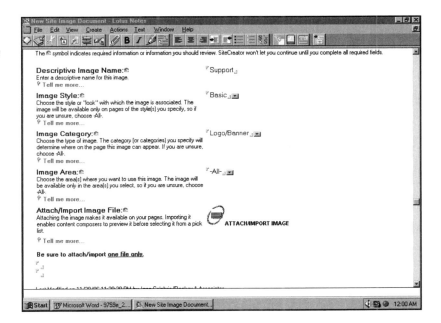

Complete the fields of the Site Design document as follows:

▶ *Descriptive Image Name.* Enter a brief name to identify the image. This name appears on the drop-down lists when you select images for your pages.

▶ *Image Style.* Select a "look" with which to associate the image. The choices include All, Basic, Corporate, and Contemporary. If you are not going to mix and match looks in your site, select All.

▶ *Image Category.* Select a category from the keyword list which appears when you click in the Image Category field. The category determines where the SiteCreator will place the image on your Web pages. The available categories are:

▶ *All*. An image that can fit in any of the following categories, or not quite in any one of them.

▶ *Logo/Banner*. Your company logo is an important image for your site. Lotus suggests that you capture your logo in more than one size or have differently colored logos for use on different types of pages. A banner image stretches across the top of a page. Both the Discussion and Feedback pages have banners on them so visitors can easily identify them. Domino Action provides banner options for those pages, but you can substitute your own graphics by customizing the pages.

▶ *Background*. A background image fills the entire background of a Web page. If your image is not large enough to fill that space, it will be repeated or *tiled* to fill the page. Background images should be light in color with a simple pattern so the text on top can be easily read by a visitor to the site. Typically, backgrounds have a textured look.

▶ *Product Image*. If you've included a product/services area, you may want to include pictures of your products.

▶ *Person Image*. If you want to display photos of employees or company officials in your About Company area or of authors in the White Paper area, place the photos in this category.

▶ *Image Area*. If you want to use an image only in a specific site area, select that area. Otherwise, specify All.

▶ *Attach/Import Image*. Click the Attach/Import Image button. In the Create Attachment dialog box, select the file you want to attach and then click Create. When the Import dialog box appears, select the same file and then click Import. Below the Attach/Import Image button, the attachment icon appears in the first available field, and then the picture of the image appears in the second available field.

To return to the Site Configuration page, click the Continue arrow or Back arrow at the bottom of the form. You will be prompted to save the file.

Click the Attach/Import Image button on the Site Configuration form and fill in a Site Design form for each image you need to store for your site.

Once you've completed the Site Configuration document, click the Exit or Continue hotspot at the bottom of the page. Click Exit if you do not intend to continue at this time with site configuration. Click Continue if you want to go to Step 2 now. This will return you to the navigator and place a check mark in front of Step 1.

Starting the Site Design

When you click the Continue hotspot at the bottom of the completed Site Configuration document, the SiteCreator returns you to the Main view. Click Step 2: Design Your Site in the Main view pane (lower-left of screen). This displays the Step 2: Design Your Site document in the Preview pane (right side of screen).

As the Design Your Site document explains, this step of the site creation process leads you through setting the appearance, organization, and content approvals for your pages.

You have two options at this point:

▶ Click the Quick Design hotspot at the bottom of the document to accept the Domino Action defaults for fast site setup.

▶ Click the Custom Design hotspot if you want to review each document as you go along.

If you choose the Quick Design method, you should still review the documents that have a star in front of them.

If you choose the Custom Design option, the Site Design view appears (see Figure 17.8), where you see listed all the site areas that you selected in the Site Configuration form. For each site area, there are several documents listed that you must complete to build your site.

Fig. 17.8

The Site Design view displays all of the documents you need to complete to configure your site, based upon selections you made in the Site Configuration document.

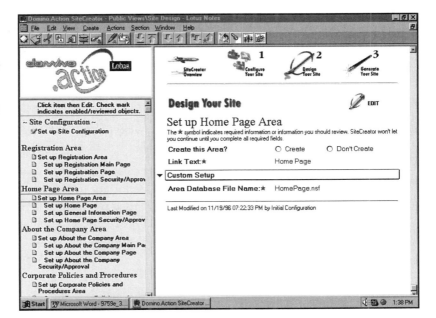

The most logical procedure is to start with the home page area and then work through the other site areas from the top and going down the list.

There are four documents listed under the Home Page Area category. The first document is Set Up Home Page Area. Double-click this document to open it. Then click the Edit hotspot.

The first field on the form is Create this Area?. Select Create so that the SiteCreator will later create a home page area for your site.

Caution

The Create radio button must be selected for every page type you want to use in your site.

The second field is Link Text. As visitors to your site view different pages, they may want to return to your home page so they can start in a different direction. On each page, you'll want to include a link that visitors may click to return automatically to the home page. Enter the text for the Home Page link in the Link Text field. Alternatively, accept the default text.

Click the Custom Setup section head to expand the section if you want to enter a name for the database that contains your home page area in the Area Database File Name field, such as OurHome.nsf. You can also accept the default name given here (HomePage.nsf).

When the Set Up Home Page Area form is complete, click the Continue hotspot at the bottom of the page to return to the Site Design view.

Setting Up the Home Page

From the Site Design view, double-click the Set Up Home Page document to open it (see Figure 17.9). Move the View pane border to display the form in full-screen size.

In this document, you will provide information about page layout, background color, background image, and copyright information for the home page. Remember that the home page is the page all visitors to your Web site will see first, so it is important to establish the "look" for your site here. This document actually prepares a home page form in the Home Page database that you will later use to add your own information for site visitors.

Fig. 17.9

The Set Up Home Page form creates a template for your home page. After you are finished with the SiteCreator process, you return to the Home Page form in your Home Page database to complete the text you want to appear on your home page.

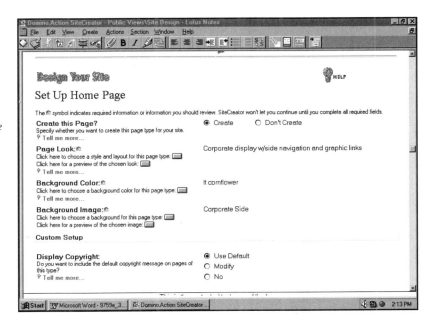

To complete this form:

1. To have the SiteCreator create this page (not now—during Step 3), select the Create radio button in the Create this Page? field.

2. Click the button next to the Page Look field to select one of the available layouts from the dialog list. This includes Basic, Contemporary, and Corporate layouts, with navigation information in different positions on the page. You can preview the selection before choosing it.

To preview a selection, click the button labeled Click Here for a Preview of the Chosen Layout. A screen similar to Figure 17.10 appears.

Fig. 17.10

You can preview the layout selection for basic Web pages. This allows you to deter-mine your preferences for your Web page appearances.

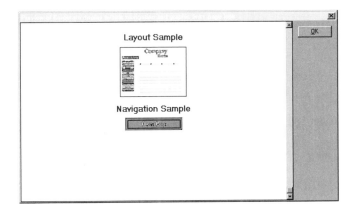

3. Click the Background Color button to choose a color for your page. Even if you are planning to use a background image, you should still select a color, because quite a few Web browsers offer their users the option to turn off backgrounds.

4. If you plan to use an image in the background (you should attach the file in the Site Configuration document), click the Background Image button and select the image from the dialog list. You can preview your images by clicking the preview button.

5. Click the Custom Setup section to expand it if you want to change the copyright settings you made in the Site Configuration form. There are three choices: None, Use Default (which uses the one you already specified), or Modify (which lets you change the copyright text just for this page).

6. Click the Continue hotspot. This returns you to the Site Design view.

Setting Up General Information Pages

You use General Information pages for documents that apply to your entire site, such as extended copyrights, licenses, and legal information. A By Title link on the home page gives you access to these documents.

To set up a General Information page:

1. Click Set Up General Information Page in Site Design view.

2. Click the Edit hotspot to modify the existing document.

3. Choose the Create option under Create This Page?.

4. Select a style and look for the page from the dialog list that appears when you click the Page Look button. To see what you choice looks like, click the preview button.

5. Click the Background Color button to choose a color for your page.

6. If you plan to use an image in the background, click the Background Image button and select the image name from the dialog list. To see what your selection looks like, click the preview button.

7. Click the Custom Setup section to expand it if you want to change the copyright settings you made in the Site Configuration form. There are three choices: None, Use Default (which uses the one you already specified), or Modify (which lets you change the copyright text just for this page).

8. Click the Continue hotspot. This returns you to Site Design view.

Setting Up the Home Page Approval Process

The next step is to setup your home page security/approval process. Double-click Set Up Home Page Approval Process in the navigator (if you didn't click Continue from the previous form). It is on this page that you specify who will be authorized to compose pages in the Home Page area, who will be authorized to approve the pages before they become available on the site, and who will be authorized to read pages in this area of the site (see Figure 17.11).

Fig. 17.11

The Home Page Approval Process form is a long form; be certain to scroll down to view the rest of the document.

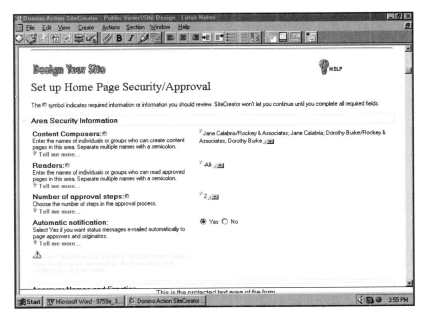

To complete this document, follow these steps:

1. In the Content Composers field, enter or select the names of the people or groups who may compose pages in this site area. If you click the down arrow, a browser opens that lets you choose names from the Public Address Book. If you leave the field empty, anyone will be able to compose pages. Multiple names must be separated by semicolons. For each person, both the hierarchical (Jim Harkin/Hamilton-Beaks) and the common name (Jim Harkin) must appear.

2. In the Readers field, specify the people or groups who may read the pages in this site area. The default is All, which means everyone will be able to read the pages. You would not ordinarily limit the readers of your home page, but you may very well limit the readers of pages in other site areas.

3. If you want to establish an approval process where people or groups approve the contents of the page, enter the number of steps (up to 5) you want in the Number of Approval Steps field. Otherwise, enter **0** for none.

4. If you entered a number of approval steps greater than zero, the Automatic Notification field appears. When you select Yes, e-mail is automatically sent to the approver alerting him or her that a page needs approval. Likewise, the composer of the page and the Webmaster are alerted when the page is accepted or rejected.

5. If you entered a number of approval steps greater than zero, the Approver Names and Functions section appears (see Figure 17.12). Under Approver Names, you see fields for Step 1 Approvers, Step 2 Approvers, and so on, depending on the number of steps you specified. In each of these fields, enter or select the names of people or groups who will be involved in that level of approval. Then under Approver Function, you may optionally enter a brief description of what an approver at that level must do.

Fig. 17.12

The Approver Names and Functions section of the Set Up Home Page Approval Process only appears if you have entered a number greater than 0 in the Number of Approval Steps field.

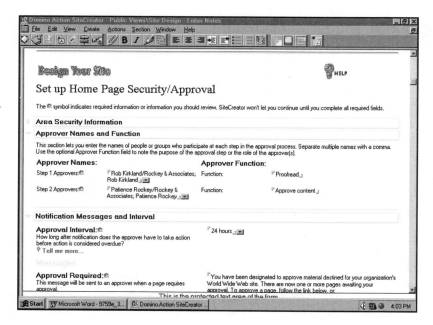

6. If you set Notification to Yes, the Notification Messages and Interval section appears (see Figure 17.13). You need to enter a time limit in the Approval Interval field to indicate how long after receiving notification the Approver will have to approve or reject. If the Approver does not reply within that time interval, the system sends out an overdue alert to the tardy approver.

Fig. 17.13
The Notification Messages and Interval section determines the workflow process and routing for approvals.

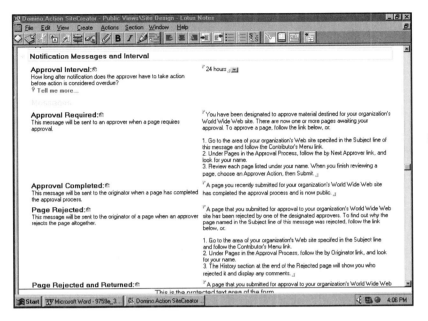

7. Also in the Notification Messages and Interval section, there are four fields in which appear the text of the messages that will go out to people during the approval process. You may edit the messages. The four fields are Approval Required Message, Approval Completed Message, Page Rejected, and the Page Rejected and Returned.

8. When you have completed this form, click the Continue hotspot to return to Site Design view.

Setting Up a Site Area

For each of the areas you selected on the Site Configuration document, you'll be setting up a Site Design document. You created a Site Design document for the home page area in the previous lesson. The Site Design document (see Figure 17.14) asks if you want to create the site, what link text you want to use to bring visitors to this area of the site, and what name you want to give to the database that SiteCreator will generate for this area.

Fig. 17.14

Each site area has a basic Site Design document. This figure displays the Site Design document for the About the Company area.

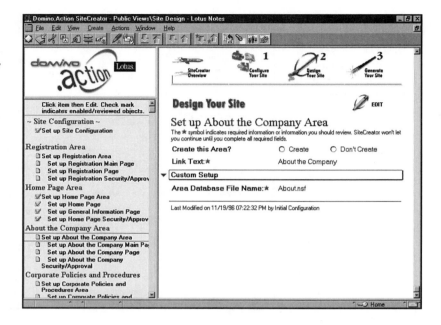

To complete the Site Design document:

1. In Site Design view, select the first document under the category heading for that area. For example, if you chose to create an About the Company area, the document is called Set Up About the Company Area.

2. Click the Edit hotspot in the Preview pane to modify the document. In the Create field, select Create to have the SiteCreator create the site area.

3. When visitors come to your Web site and want to learn about your company, they click a hyperlink to go immediately to that area of your site. In the Link Text field, enter the text the visitors click to go to this area. For example, to send a visitor to the About the Company area, you might enter **Learn more about our company**.

4. If you want to set the name of the database for this site area, click the Custom Setup section head and enter the file name in the Area Database File Name field.

5. Click the Continue hotspot to save the document and return to Site Design view.

Creating the Area Main Page

Once you set up an area, you need to create an area main page. This is the introductory page users see when they jump to a site area. Normally, this page contains information about the site area plus links to other pages in the area.

To create an area main page:

1. From Site Design view, select the Set Up Main Page document. For example, in the About the Company area this document is called Set Up About the Company Main Page (see Figure 17.15).

Fig. 17.15

Every area site has a main page that acts as an opening page for that database. This figure shows the About the Company Main Page document.

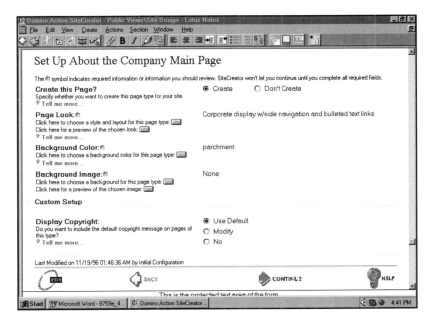

2. To have the SiteCreator create the page, select Create in the Create this Page? field.

3. Click the Page Look button and select one of the available page layouts (click the preview button to see what the layout looks like).

> **Tip**
>
> To gain some idea what any one of these layouts looks like, you can choose it from the list, then click the button labeled Click Here for a Preview of the Chosen Layout (see Figure 17.16).

4. Click the Background Color button and select a color for the background of the page from the list of colors.

5. If you want to use a background image, select the name of the background image you attached when you created the Site Configuration document.

Fig. 17.16

You can preview the layout of main pages in the same way you can preview the layout of a home page.

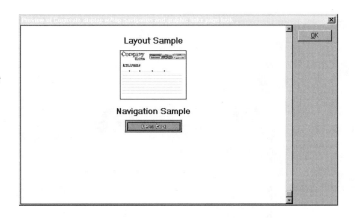

6. Click the Custom Setup section head if you want to change the copyright or not use one on this page. From the Display Copyright field, choose No, Use Default (the one you set in the Site Configuration document), or Modify (which gives you the ability to enter new text or correct the existing copyright).

7. Click the Continue hotspot to save the document and return to Site Design view.

Setting Up a Page

The next step is to set up pages for your site area. These pages can contain a variety of information, but the setup document lets you establish categories for the types of pages you make for that particular site area.

To set up pages for the site area:

1. From Site Design view, select the page set up document to display it in the Preview pane. For the About the Company area, this document is called Set Up About the Company Page (see Figure 17.17).

2. To have the SiteCreator create the page, select Create in the Create this Page? field.

3. In the Page Look field, click the button and select one of the available page looks from the dialog list.

4. Click the Background Color button to select a color for the background of the page from the list of colors.

5. If you want to use a background image, select the name of the background image you attached when you created the Site Configuration document. You can also use one of the predesigned background images provided by Domino Action.

6. To set up the categories for your pages, click the Content Index section head (see Figure 17.18). Your can sort your pages into five categories that you specify. For each category, enter a Label (descriptive title) for the category and Choices (set the

options a user can select). Then click Yes or No in the Choices field. If you select No, users will only be able to select from the categories listed in the Choices field. If you select Yes, users will be able to add categories other than those in the Choices field.

Fig. 17.17

Every area site has one or more page templates. The Set up About the Company Page document helps you create the About Database document for this site area that will tell your users what this area offers and provides links to other documents.

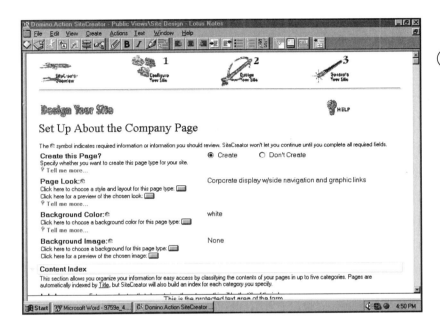

Fig. 17.18

Once you have provided information in the Content Index section, users who are authorized to provide content to your Web site will use the categories when they are creating new Web pages.

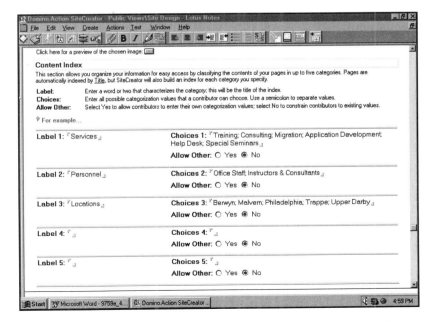

7. Click the Custom Setup section head if you want to eliminate or change the default copyright notice on this page. From the Display Copyright field, choose No, Use Default (the one you set in the Site Configuration document), or Modify (which gives you the ability to enter new text or correct the existing copyright).

8. Click the Continue hotspot to save the document and return to Site Design view.

Specifying the Approval Process

On the Security/Approval page, you specify who will be authorized to compose pages in the area, who will be authorized to approve the pages before they become available on the site, and who will be authorized to read pages in this area of the site. If you enable an approval process, you have to specify the details of how it will work.

To complete the Set Up Security/Approval process document:

1. Click the Set Up Security/Approval document to display it in the Preview pane. For example, in the About the Company site are, the document is called Set Up About the Company Security/Approval (see Figure 17.9).

Fig. 17.19

The Approval Process for the site area works like the approval process for the home page.

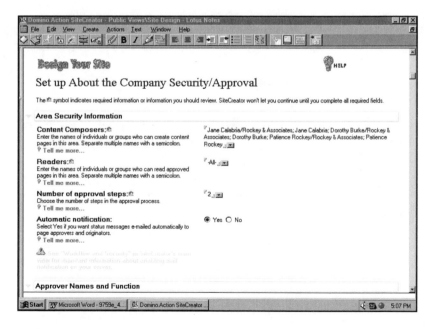

2. For the Content Composers field, enter or select the names of the people or groups who may compose pages in this site area. If you click the down arrow button to the right of the field, a browser opens that lets you choose names from the Public

Address Book. Use semicolons to separate multiple names, and be sure to use both the hierarchical (Joan Blossom/Blossom Fragrance) and common (Joan Blossom) names.

3. In the Readers field, specify the people or groups who may read the pages in this site area. Leave it set to All if you want everyone to read the pages.

4. If you want to establish an approval process where people or groups approve the contents of newly composed pages before they become available to readers, enter the number of steps (between 1 and 5) you want in the Number of Approval Steps field. To disable the approval process, enter **0** for no steps.

5. If you entered a number of approval steps greater than zero, the Automatic Notification field appears. When you select Yes, e-mail is automatically sent to the approver alerting him or her that a page needs approval. Likewise, the composer of the page and the Webmaster are alerted when the page is accepted or rejected.

6. If you set up approval steps, the Approver Names and Functions section appears Under Approver Names. You see fields for Step 1 Approvers, Step 2 Approvers, and so on, depending on the number of steps you specified. In each of these fields, enter or select the names of people or groups who will be involved in that level of approval. Then under Approver Function, you may optionally enter a brief description of what that level approver must do.

7. If you set Notification to Yes, the Notification Messages and Interval section appears. You need to enter a time limit in the Approval Interval field to indicate how long after receiving notification the Approver has to reply. If the Approver does not reply within that time interval, an overdue alert is sent.

8. Also in the Notification Messages and Interval section, there are four fields in which appear the text of the messages that will go out to people during the approval process. You may optionally edit the messages. The four fields are Approval Required Message, Approval Completed Message, Page Rejected, and Page Rejected and Returned.

9. Once you have completed the form, click the Continue hotspot to return to Site Design view.

Working with Site Areas

Most site area setup follows the procedures outlined in the section "Setting Up a Site Area." However, there may be some customization involved in certain site areas. For example, the Registration area requires that you work with agents.

In this section, each of the site areas is described and if customization is appropriate, it is defined.

About the Company

This is a very straightforward site to set up using the procedures outlined in the section "Setting Up a Site Area." It provides the visitor to your site with information about the company, its goals, products and services, officers, locations, and so on.

Corporate Policies and Procedures

This site area is geared more towards an intranet site rather than an Internet site. It is where users would find an employee manual, benefits information, vacation and sick leave policies, office procedures, and so on. You can easily set it up using the procedures outlined in the section "Setting Up a Site Area."

Discussion

The Discussion area is where users can comment on your company and services, ask questions, make suggestions, complain, and share information with each other. It is a Notes discussion database, but is available to Web users.

Banners

To make the Discussion area more inviting and identifiable, Domino Action adds a design feature to this site area main page. In the Set Up Discussion Main Topic Page document, there is an additional field called Banner where you may specify the banner you want to use on the page by clicking the Banner button and selecting one from the dialog list. A *banner* is a graphic that usually goes across the top of the page from left margin to right margin. Domino Action has several graphics available for you to use (see the list in Figure 17.20), but if you attached an image file as a banner in the Site Configuration document, you may specify the name of that file in the Banner field.

Fig. 17.20

The Banner selection dialog box lists prebuilt banners. To preview the banners, click the preview button located under Banner on the Site Design form.

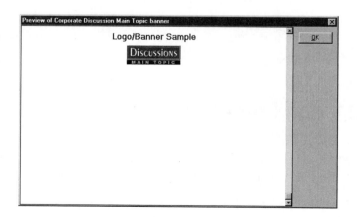

Domino Action also adds a banner to the Response pages in the Discussion site area. Pick a Response banner in the Banners field of the setup document for Response pages.

Categorization

Making the discussion area easy to use is important, and one way to do it is to index the pages. Each page in a discussion area is automatically indexed by author, date, and title. The Set Up Discussion Main Topic document has a Content Index collapsible section (see Figure 17.21) that allows you to further index discussions by category.

Fig. 17.21

The Content Index section of a discussion site differs from the content index in the About the Company form. These categories are made available to Web browsers who participate in the Web discussion database to categorize their main topics in the database.

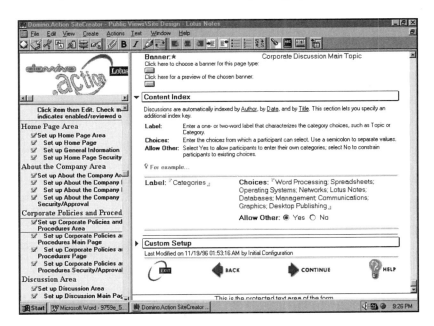

In the Label field, accept the default label of Categories, or enter a label that better defines the categorization choices. Enter the categorization choices in the Choices field if you want to narrow the categories to a select few. Select Yes under Allow Other if you want the users to be able to add new categories on their own, in which case any categories you entered in Choices are just to get the ball rolling. Don't allow other categories if you want to narrow the areas of discussion.

Discussion Response Page

The discussion site area provides an additional page type for users to respond to questions or comments posted by others. This page type also features a banner in its design. In all other ways, it sets up in the same way as other page types. In usage, as a response document, it inherits information from the document to which it responds.

Security/Approval

There are two additional fields in the Security/Approval page for the Discussion area. If you select Yes in the Allow Anonymous Access field, you are permitting any visitor to view the pages in this area without entering a user name or password. Selecting No restricts visitors to registered users or specified names or groups.

Selecting Yes in the Allow Anyone to Author field permits any visitor to author documents in this area. However, they will not be able to edit documents, not even the ones they created. Choosing No restricts authoring of documents to the individuals and groups specified in the Content Composers field.

Document Library

The Document Library provides an area where you can store documents for shared use or files for download. On the Set Up Document Library page, there is a Content Index section similar to the one in the Discussion site area (see Figure 17.22). Although the pages are automatically categorized by title, you may specify five additional categories.

In the Label field, enter a label that better defines the categorization choices (such as **Class Manuals**). Enter the categorization choices in the Choices field if you want to narrow the categories to a select few (**Introductory**, **Intermediate**, **Advanced**, and so on). Select Yes under Allow Other if you want the users to be able to add categories in addition to the ones you entered in the Choices field.

Fig. 17.22

The Content Index section of the Set Up Document Library Page document allows for additional categories.

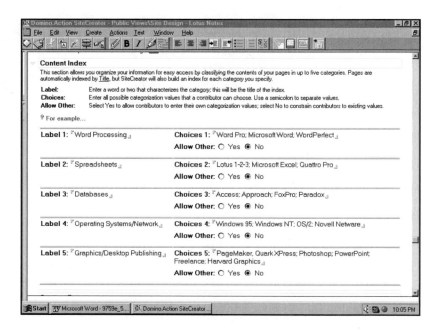

Feedback

The Feedback site area provides users with a feedback form to fill out and submit. The Banner choices allow you to set up either a user feedback (for your site) or a customer feedback page, although you can use a banner you attached to the Site Configuration document or no banner to create a different type of feedback page. The unique portion of setting up this site area is the Feedback Custom Questions section of the Set Up Feedback Page document. In this section (see Figure 17.23), you can specify up to five feedback questions to include on the feedback form.

Fig. 17.23

The Feedback Custom Questions section allows you to receive feedback from Web browsers.

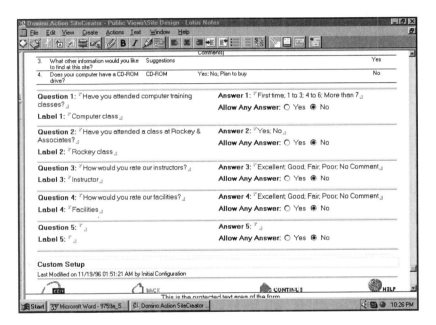

In the Question field, enter the question you want users to answer (such as **Did you find this site helpful?**).

Enter a brief label that characterizes the question in the Label field to help index the database information (such as **Rating**). You don't need to use date, author, or title because Feedback is automatically indexed by those categories (author information is automatically collected, so Feedback pages don't need an author field).

In the Answer field, enter all the possible answers to the question (such as **Extremely**, **Somewhat**, **Not much**, or **Not at all**). Separate multiple entries with a comma or semicolon. Leave the field blank if you want the users to supply their own answers, or choose Yes under Allow Any Answer to encourage user comments.

Frequently Asked Questions

You can publish frequently asked questions and their answers in this area of your Web site and save yourself the trouble of answering the same, repetitive questions over and over again, while providing useful information to visitors to your site.

Like several of the other site areas, the pages in the Frequently Asked Questions area are automatically indexed by title. You may specify additional indexing categories in the Content Index section of the Set Up FAQs Page document (see Figure 17.24).

Fig. 17.24

Categorization Questions section of Set Up FAQs Page document. The pages for this site area do not display a banner area, but you do have a full range of page layout choices.

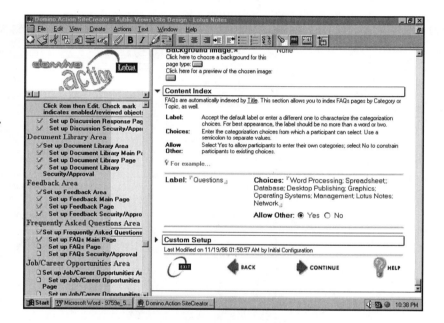

Specify an indexing category in the Label field (such as **Company**) and then enter possible options in the Choices field (**Directions**, **Experience**, and so on). If you want users to add their own categories, select Yes in the Allow Other field.

Job/Career Opportunities

Whether you're running an intranet or an Internet site, offering job opportunities will attract many users looking to improve their current positions, make career advancements, or start new jobs.

Pages in this site area are automatically indexed by title, but you can specify up to five categories in the Content Index section of the Set Up Job Posting Page document (see Figure 17.25).

Fig. 17.25

The Content Index section of Set Up Job/ Career Opportunities page provides an inexpensive way to widely advertise your job openings.

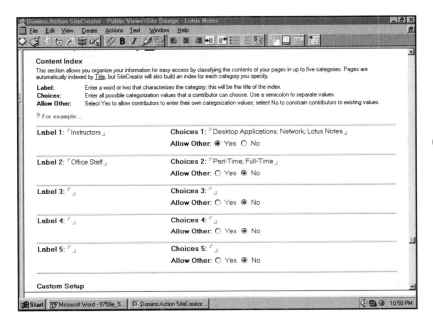

Specify an indexing category in the Label field (such as **Administrative Support**) and then enter possible options in the Choices field (**Secretary**, **Data Entry**, and so on). If you want users to add their own categories, select Yes in the Allow Other field.

Product/Services

The Product/Services area gives you a chance to sell, either by displaying your products or explaining your services. This site involves three types of pages: Product Information, Product Review, and Product Specification.

Product Information pages are automatically indexed by title, but you may specify five additional categories in the Content Index section of the Set Up Product Information Pages document.

Because the Product Review pages are responses to the Product Information documents, setting up these pages is straightforward and without categorization. Instead, these pages inherit the categories from their parent documents (the Product Information pages).

The Product Specification pages only have the standard fields and no categorization questions, as they inherit their category from their parent documents (the Product Information pages).

Registration

The Registration site area lets you collect information about visitors to your site and store it in a database. Once a visitor is registered, you can let him have greater privileges in your Web site. The registration process automatically adds newly registered users to a registered users group (defaults to DominoActionSiteUsers). By adding this group to database access control lists, you can give registered users rights different from those accorded to anonymous (non-registered) visitors to your site.

The Set Up Registration Page has some unique fields for you to complete. There are two collapsible sections on this document. The first one is called Registration (see Figure 17.26) and contains the administrative information for collecting and storing information on users.

Fig. 17.26

In the Registration section, you specify the name of the registered users group, what address book database you're using, and your Internet gateway address.

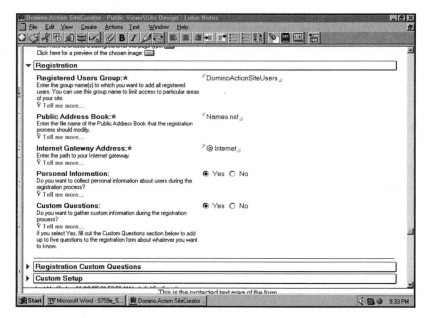

Complete these fields in this section:

▶ *Registered Users Group.* Enter the name of the group or groups in the Public Address Book to which you want to add all the registered users.

▶ *Public Address Book.* Enter the file name of the address book to which the registration information will be added. Names.nsf is the name of your company's Public Address Book, but you may want to create a new address book for testing purposes. The Public Address Book must reside on the Domino server and must be located in the Domino data directory. Always include the path in the file name if the file is located in a subdirectory.

> *Gateway Address.* Enter the address of your Internet mail gateway here. By default, @ Internet appears in this field. If your Domino server has direct access to the Internet gateway domain, use the SMTP gateway domain name. If not, enter all the mail routing hops necessary to get e-mail to your company's Internet gateway domain.

> *Personal Information.* Select Yes if you want to collect personal information about your users during the registration process, such as company name, address, and phone number.

> *Custom Questions.* Select Yes to ask up to five custom questions during the registration process and then fill out the Registration Custom Questions section of the Set Up Registration Pages document.

In the Registration Custom Questions section (see Figure 17.27), you can add up to five specific questions you want users to answer. Enter each question in the Question field, and then add a selection of possible answers in the Answer field. If you want users to add their own answers, select Yes in the Allow Other field.

Fig. 17.27

In the Registration Custom Questions section, you can enter up to five questions that you want to ask users who are registering at your site.

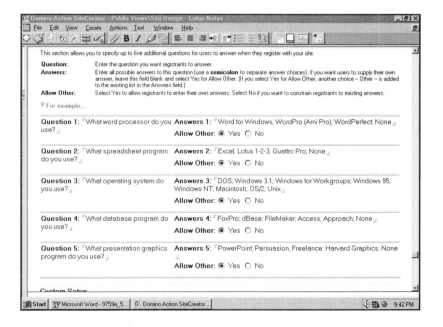

Once you have created the Registration Site Area database, be sure that the default access in the access control list is Author with the ability to create documents only. Make roles for Readers, Approvers, Composers, and WebMaster. Composer and Reader roles should also be given default access. Add the name of the Domino server to the access control list and assign it Manager access.

In the creation process, SiteCreator makes two agents for the Registration site area. The *Handle Requests agent* processes registration requests and password-change requests submitted by site visitors. Every time a visitor to your site submits a registration request, this agent creates a Person record in the Public Address Book on the server, then adds the person to the registered users group you specified in the Set Up Registration Page document (the default group name is DominoActionSiteUsers). When a password change is requested, the agent replaces the old password with the new password in the existing Person document.

The Handle Requests agent must be enabled and set up to run on the Domino server, or registration won't work. To set the agent up to run on the Domino server, click the Schedule button and select the Domino server's name from the Run Only On list box.

You must also enable the *Send Mail agent*. This agent automatically sends e-mail to users when:

▶ A registration request has been processed. A thank you message is sent saying:

```
Thank you for registering with http://siteURL. Your user name is username. Please
remember that your password is case-sensitive.
```

▶ A password change request is received. The agent sends the message:

```
Your password has successfully been changed. Your user name is username. You may
now log in with your new password. Please remember that your password is case-
sensitive.
```

▶ A registration or password-change request cannot be processed. The following message is sent:

```
There was a problem with your registration request. The error returned was: error.
Try resubmitting your request. If you get another error notification, contact the
Webmaster. Include the text of this message and describe the problems you are
experiencing.
```

Although the two agents operate automatically, you must enable them by opening the Notes client on the Domino server (using the server ID) and adding the Registration database (Registra.nsf, by default) to the workspace.

White Paper

The White Paper site area lets you store white papers for user reference. The pages are indexed by title, but as with many of the other site areas, you can add up to five categories in the Content Index section of the Set Up White Paper Page document. You could skip setting up the White Paper area entirely and include white papers as a category of document in the Document Library area of your site.

Generating Your Site

The generation process begins with the *AppAssembler*, which combines information you entered in SiteCreator with templates and other design elements from the library to generate the components of your site. These components are Lotus Notes databases that can be used in Notes or published to the Web for viewing from a Web browser. Follow these steps to generate your site:

1. Go to Step 3: Generate Your Site (see Figure 17.28).

Fig. 17.28

Step 3: Generate Your Site document begins the generation process for the site.

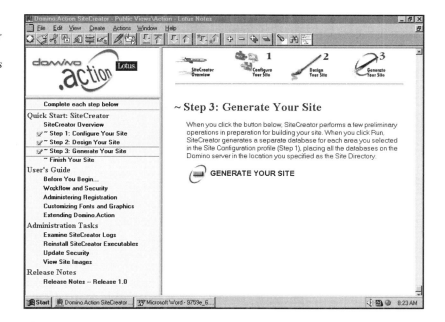

2. Click the Generate Your Site hotspot to begin the generation process.

3. Once the processing of documents is complete, the Run AppAssembler document appears in the preview pane (see Figure 17.29).

4. Click the Run button to begin assembling the application. The process may pause for you to enter your password before it completes the task. While the AppAssembler is running, you may run Notes or other applications in the background, but do not change any of the SiteCreator documents.

5. When the process is complete, click the Return to Main View button.

Fig. 17.29

Notice the message at the bottom of the page. AppAssembler could take up to 60 minutes to generate all of the databases in your Web site.

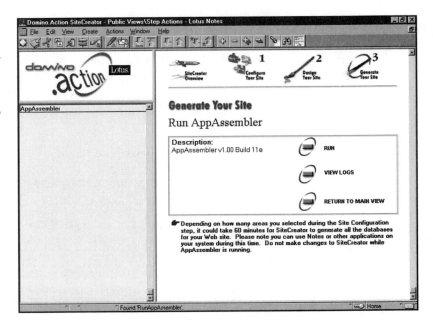

Finishing Your Site

The Finish Your Site step in the site creation process refreshes your database documents and establishes all the links between the documents. To finish your site:

1. From the Main view, select the Finish Your Site document (see Figure 17.30).

2. Click the Finish Your Site button. SiteCreator resets all the access control lists for each of the databases you created and updates them.

3. You may want to review the access control lists manually once this operation is complete and make sure that the names defined as Content Composer, Site Manager, and Approver are in the Public Address Book and in the same format as in the Security/Approval documents of each database.

Fig. 17.30

The process of finishing a site can take 15 minutes or so to complete.

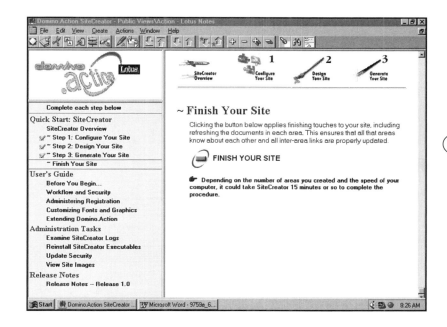

17

Getting Your Site Up and Running

The area databases now exist in the \Notes\Data\Action directory. You can open these databases or add their icons to your workspace. However, before your site can be up and running, there are a few finishing touches you must make.

Replicate any local databases to your Domino server, making certain that you change the Site Configuration document to specify the location of your databases as being on your Domino server instead of your "Local" computer.

Specify your home page database as the default home page (or have the Notes Administrator do this for you) by opening the Server document in the Public Address Book. Under the HTTP section, enter the file name of your home page database (unless you changed it, the file name is Homepage.nsf) in the Default Home Page field.

To add content to your pages (or have the Content Composer do it if you are not the designated Content Composer), start your Web browser, go to the specific area to which you want to add content, and click Edit/Approve This Page. Then, add a title and other content to the page, and select Process and Submit. If the Security/Approval profile for the area calls for one or more approval steps, each Approver must accept the content.

To approve pages if you are in the approval cycle, go to the main page for the site menu. From the Contributor's menu, select one of the Approval Process views and find the pages that need approval. Click Edit/Approve This Page, review the document, and select an Approver Action. Submit the form.

Remember to Full Text Index each area database. Now your site should be fully functional.

Updating the Site

To change the design of your area databases, make your changes to the area's Site Design documents in SiteCreator and then regenerate the site:

1. Disable any areas you are not changing. Select all the Site Design documents in all the unaffected areas by highlighting each one and then pressing the space bar. Once the unaffected documents are all selected, choose Actions, Public, Disable Creation.

2. Regenerate the site. Run Step 3: Generate Your Site again. Once the generation process is complete, click Finish Your Site.

3. Refresh updated documents. From the workspace, select each database with changes and then choose Actions, Update Existing Documents.

Replacing Graphics

To replace the graphic from the Web (you must use a Web browser that supports file upload, such as Netscape Navigator):

1. Go to the main page of the area where you want to replace the graphic.

2. Click the link to the Contributor's menu.

3. Click the File Library's By Category link to see a list of all the .GIF files.

4. Click Edit Page next to the graphic you want to replace.

5. A File Upload document opens. Scroll down the page and click Edit This Page.

6. Check Mark attachments for deletion.

7. Click Submit.

8. Once you see the `You successfully submitted this page` message, click the Go To link for the page you just submitted.

9. Click Edit This Page. Use the Browse button to locate the new .GIF file.

10. Click Submit.

You must follow these steps for each .GIF file you want to replace, and you must upload a file in each area in which it will be used.

To replace the graphic from Notes, you need to edit the Site Image documents:

1. From the main view of the SiteCreator, open the View Site Images document and click the button.
2. Select the image you want to replace, click the Edit icon.
3. Delete the existing .GIF file and image.
4. Click the Attach/Import Image button.
5. Use the Browser to locate the new .GIF file and then click Create.
6. Locate the image file and then click Import.
7. Save and close the document.

From Here...

Domino Action is the first of numerous Web development applications to be offered by Lotus for the Domino 4.5 server. The next scheduled application will be Domino. Merchant designed to support Internet-based sales of your company product line. Visit the Lotus Web site at **www.Lotus.com** often to keep abreast of new offerings. You might want to use the Page Minder feature of the Notes Web Navigator to automate the process of retrieving the latest updates from the Lotus Web site.

Without the aide of Domino Action, you can create all of your Web databases from scratch, or modify your Notes databases for Web clients. For more information, see the following chapters:

▶ Chapter 13, "Examining Special Function Databases for the Web," discusses databases like some of those used in Domino Action, and the design considerations for each.

▶ Chapter 18, "Building a Domino Site from Scratch," studies the ground up development of a Domino site without the intervention of Domino Action.

Building a Domino Web Site from Scratch

18

In this chapter

◆ **The planning of a Web site**
The planning stage of the Web site is the most critical stage. Learn considerations that you need to include in your planning process.

◆ **The evolution of a Web site**
Learn the details of the planning phase, the implementation and the future plans for a real Web site, www.planetdomino.com.

Building a Web Site with Domino involves more than application development skills. Systems knowledge, business knowledge, purpose, scope, and marketing ideas are just some of the tools needed to bring up and continue to run a successful Web site. Even with those tools, the success of a Web site can mean many different things to different people and organizations. As authors and Domino enthusiasts, we wanted to present you with a true case history of a Domino Web site. Working in conjunction with another Lotus Premium Business Partner, InterFusion, Inc. we helped to plan and design www. planetdomino.com, a real Web site developed during the writing of this book. We encourage you to visit "the planet" as we call it, to see the results and evolution of the site as it has changed and continues to change from the time we have documented its "birth" here, in this chapter.

Establish the Purpose of a Site

Information System professionals would likely tell you that the single most important part of *any* technology project is planning. Well, as can be imagined, a Web site is no different. Careful planning and thought, done in the beginning, is the single most important factor in achieving success.

In planning a Web site, you should first establish the purpose, or mission of the site. What is it that you expect to accomplish with this site? How will you meet this accomplishment? How will others locate your site? Will you advertise your site and where? How will you measure the success of your site? Who will be your visitors? What kinds of information will you provide for visitors? What is your ultimate goal?

Once you've answered these questions, you should develop a plan that includes the cost of the site design, installation, and maintenance. Throughout the development stage, do not lose site of your purpose and the method in which you determine that you have met your goal.

Know Your Audience

Not only is it important to know what you plan to do with a site, it is important to know your audience. There is potentially large exposure when you "go public" with a Web site, versus the limited exposure your site will have on a corporate intranet. Know who you want to visit your site, and find ways to attract those visitors through advertising, links from other sites, and association and links from search engines.

Use graphics, words, phrases, and language on your Web pages to which your audience can relate. Remember that a Web site is international, and certain kinds of humor (such as sarcasm) do not translate well. Even if your target audience is very narrow and focused, there is always the possibility that uninvited people will visit your site, be careful and considerate of cultural differences. You may want certain parts of your site to be available only to those who register—in which case, you should also consider what you will do with the registration information provided by the registrants. Can registration information become potential advertising addresses?

In the case of Planet Domino (the case study found in this chapter), we knew that the site would be experimental, and would be identified as such to its audience. Our goal was to provide a service, however, the service was completely free of charge and no direct selling was to be done at the site. Therefore, we felt we had limited exposure and hopefully, much forgiveness from our audience should something at the site fail. If your site is designed to sell a service, or market an organization, your audience might not be as forgiving or as understanding. When you know who your audience is and you know what they will tolerate, you'll also know how much "test" work you can put into a production environment (if any) and how much and what kind of content you will provide to all visitors, versus registered visitors.

Remember that a Web site is a reflection and an image of the company who sponsors it, and it is the visiting audience who conceives that image. Know as much about the audience you intend to attract as you do about the company you are developing for.

Choose and Prepare your Content Carefully

18

If you are building an internal Web site that will be seen by employees only, the rules for content may be different than those on the Web. Web content can be seen by limitless people of limitless education, age, cultures, languages and interests. Every page, every graphic and image and every word is important on a Web page.

In planning your content, be certain to consult with as many potential prospects and audience members as you can. For example, if the mission of the site is marketing and sales, then marketing and sales people should be involved during the planning cycle. If the mission is customer service, then your customer service people should be consulted during the planning cycle. If you can, also involve some customers or prospects during your planning cycle, and when your content is complete, have these people review the content, and encourage their remarks and feedback.

Your Web site is a business tool like other business tools used within an organization, such as brochures, mailers, and telephone solicitation. A successful site usually involves more staff than the Technical staff alone. Use this tool as you would other tools, for example, if your mission is marketing, then the Web becomes another medium, like print, radio,
or TV.

The rules of marketing are not any different on the Web then they are with these other mediums except for those rules that a medium-centric. Just like ways of using print advertising is different than the ways of using TV advertising, the ways to use the Web are different too; the goal is the same: To market your products.

Don't let yourself get overwhelmed by the mystique of the Web. It's not a special or scary place. Recognize that it is just a new way of doing what you are already doing. The Web is a new tool to help you run your business and help your business to be successful.

Grasp New Skills — or Hire Consultants

Using the Web as a business tool may require a set of skills that are new to you. If you aren't familiar with HTML, Web design, Web marketing, and services, seek out people who have expertise in using the Web medium to its fullest. Many of the technical skills required to build a Web site with Domino can be acquired here in this book. But if you're a consultant about to build a site for a client, you'll need more than application development and systems skills. Consult with your clients marketing and sales staff and all people associated with the client who will be contributing to the content at the site. Also, consult with those who may be receiving information from visitors at the site. Consider taking a class in Web marketing and design, or working with another consultant or group who bring design and marketing skills to your project. Present the ideas that the client has expressed for his site, and question them about content they'd like to see, or the manner in which they'd like the content presented. Should sound and videos be incorporated at this site? What keywords or buzz words would the content providers and audience like to see? Has the client (and have you) designed a process that will work well for both content providers and audience? Do you have the necessary skills on your team to assure a successful design and implementation process?

The best Web sites team combines marketing, advertising, technical, design, and graphic arts or illustration skills. If you don't possess all of these skills, consult with those who can bring these talents to your Web site project.

Determinine the Site's Requirements

The purpose, or mission of a site drives the functional requirements and the functional requirements drive the technical requirements.

The Functional Requirements of a Web site describe specifically what the Web site will be used for and who will use it, which will determine what information and features you will need on the Web site.

The Technical Requirements of a Web site include the development requirements, hardware, software networking, and Internet connectivity. Establish and document these requirements for your client or your employer. This is part of good planning. Will you utilize an existing server or Internet connection? What are the costs and delivery time for new equipment or services? What is the ongoing cost of operation and maintenance?

This information, documented, is a necessary part of the Web site planning process. Once you have defined your purpose or mission, identified your audience, established content for the site, determined the technical requirements, and documented this information, you have the start of a good plan for building a Web site.

The Planet Domino Web Site: A Case Study

Planet Domino began as two separate ideas. One of those ideas was to create a Web site for this book, to act as a case study and a way to provide additional information about Lotus Notes and Domino. The second idea was to combine support and information resources scattered all over the Internet into one Web site and provide users with a easy way to find this information.

The ideas were turned into reality by the authors of this book in collaboration with a Lotus Premium Business Partner, InterFusion, Inc., who has been working with Lotus Notes and Internet technologies for over two years.

The result is Planet Domino (see Figure 18.1), which can be found at:

www.planetdomino.net

Fig. 18.1

Planet Domino's Opening Page is changed and updated frequently to demonstrate to Web visitors that the site contains current information. A good Web site is tended to and updated often and it's important to indicate that to visitors by changing graphics, links or text at the very first page they see when visiting your site.

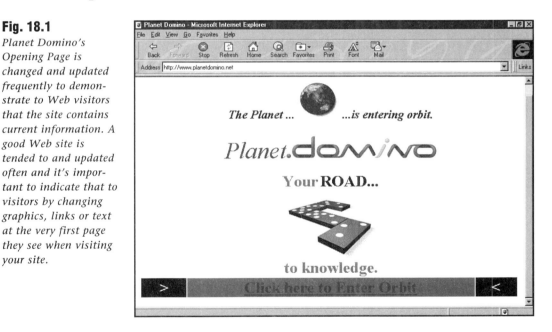

Some of the concepts behind Planet Domino had been under consideration for over a year. The initial concept was developed by Kenneth Adams, founder of InterFusion Inc. InterFusion is a Lotus Premium Business Partner located in Philadelphia, offering business solutions through Lotus Notes and Domino. InterFusion focuses its software development and consulting around Notes and Domino and is the host and primary designer of planetdomino.com.

This Web site began as a twinkle in the eye of Kenneth Adams in the fall of 1995. Ken felt there was a need to improve the process of gathering Lotus Notes technical information by locating the information at one Web site.

Much of the Notes information that was available at that time, existed in the form of Notes databases and Internet newsgroups, scattered throughout many databases, and over many sites. Ken thought it would be most helpful to have a single site in which Notes technical knowledge could be collected. Although he identified this need, he could not dedicate the time necessary to build the site. So, he waited and hoped that some improvements would be made at some Web site, making Notes technical information easier to locate.

Early in 1996, Ken saw some improvement in locating Notes documentation at various Lotus Web sites. But, on the whole, he felt that there was still a need to simplify the process for locating the information. He felt that technical information continued to be fragmented over too many sites and databases, requiring a search at each site or database.

In the fall of 1996, we ran into Ken at a trade show and discovered that we were also feeling frustrations when attempting to track information on Notes. We agreed that in conjunction with InterFusion Inc., we would build a site to act as a testing ground for supplying and linking Web visitors to important Notes and Domino information. We determined that we could use the site as a case history for this book, and as a potential solution to the information tracking dilemma. That site became www.planetdomino. com and it still operates today.

The Planet Domino Mission Statement

The purpose of this site, or the "mission" was envisioned in two parts: the ultimate, and the immediate. The ultimate purpose for the site is defined as:

1. Create a Web site that can provide Lotus Notes/Domino users with a comprehensive set of information resources.
2. Establish a production Web site that can be used to experiment with the newest, hottest Domino and Web technologies and ideas.
3. Provide the Internet and Notes/Domino communities with a non-Lotus, neutral source of information on Notes/Domino.

The immediate purpose of the site included the following:

1. Provide a good case study using the history of this Web site as an example for this chapter. The Web site should be one which manages large amounts of information.

2. Provide a single site on the Internet where visitors could find many of the public Notes databases with support information and discussion databases.

3. Provide a single search engine that could search all of the databases with one query.

4. Create a Web site that could act as an on-line extension of this book.

5. Create a Web site that could generate a lot of traffic and interest.

6. Provide a place to experiment with new Domino technologies and ideas.

7. Provide a place on the Web where the readers of this book and other Notes/Domino users could communicate with each other.

8. Create a Web site with a name that could develop into a brand name in the Notes/Domino community.

9. Provide a Web site that could act as a neutral place where Lotus Business Partners could partner with each other.

Identifying Our Audience

The $64,000 question became "who will visit this site?" Remembering that someone once said, "If you build it, they will come," we knew that those words would not hold true for an Internet site. You have to be very clear in defining the audience of your Web site. You must design the features and the information around your audience's needs and you must find ways to let your audience know that your site exists.

We designed Planet Domino for:

▶ Developers and Webmasters of Domino Web sites

▶ Lotus Business Partners

▶ Technology professionals using Lotus products

Planet Domino's audience is primarily technical—the people who have to make Lotus products work for their companies, and the companies that provide services to organizations that use Lotus products.

Defining the audience of the Web site helps to define the expectations, mission or purpose of the site. Knowing who the audience is will allow the builders of the site to develop a profile of their audience. In the case of Planet Domino, we felt that a good percentage of the audience would be the readers of this book.

We developed a User Profile which describes the audience we hope to draw to Planet Domino. We then used the User Profile as a tool during development, to assist us when we were developing content, hoping to remain focused and consistent in the type of information and the method of presenting information at our site. The following list outlines our thoughts about our prospective visitors.

▶ People with basic to moderately advanced skills with Lotus products are prospective visitors. The very advanced people will probably have already figured out clever ways to get the information they need. As Planet Domino develops, we hope the advanced Notes and Domino developers and systems people will find information at our site to be useful.

▶ We anticipate that technical people will be fairly "Web savvy," and will have high expectations of a Web site calling itself "Planet Domino." We should strive to meet those expectations by utilizing the most current design, content, and search technologies.

Planet Domino System Requirements

Now we can get into the good stuff! Here, we will cover the system requirements of our Web site. This includes both hardware and software, and connectivity and reliability requirements.

Internet Connection Considerations

All Web sites require a dedicated, full time connection. In order for people to reach a Web site, any time of the day or night, you must have a connection that is up 24 hours a day, 7 days a week. A dial-up connection is not adequate. Even ISDN may not be sufficient for the smallest of Web sites.

We felt we needed a T1 connection for Planet Domino. A T1 is a fully digital connection. You can get this service from all major Internet Access Providers.

Choosing an access provider is the most critical part of the system requirements, because your Internet connection will become your connection to the world. A Web site that is down has the same effect as a telephone or electrical system that is down. When no one is home, no new business will arrive, and the potential exists for losing existing customers. A reliable and experienced access provider with a good track record is critical.

We suggest choosing one of the handful of major access companies. All of them have some amount of national coverage in the US, and several have international service as well. These are the companies that are the backbone of the Internet. If you use a major provider, you are only one router hop away. If you use someone who is regional, or local, you are two or, usually, several hops away from the Internet backbone.

The T1 Internet service is a combination of the access service from the Internet provider, and a T1 line from your telephone company. Your monthly bill is actually a combination of a monthly charge from the Internet access provider and telephone company. The telephone company charge will vary depending on how far your office is located from the Internet access provider's nearest POP (Point Of Presence). However, the charge from your Internet access provider will usually be the same, regardless of where you are located.

Connection speed costs money. If you are not certain how fast of a connection you will need, you can start with a slower connection and easily increase its speed as your needs grow. To allow you to increase your speed you must start with a fractional T1, which typically start at speeds of 128Kbps.

A full T1 runs at a speed of 1.5Mbps. T1 lines are broken down into 24 channels of 64K or 56K each (depending on your Bell company). A fractional T1 is an allocation of only a certain number of channels. Purchasing your Internet access as a number of fractional T1 channels is a cost effective way to get connected, and provides room to grow.

18

Fractional T1 Internet access usually works like this, your Bell line to your provider's POP is actually capable of supporting full T1 speeds. However, your provider configures your connection to the speed that you have purchased. The equipment you purchase is also capable of supporting full T1 speeds. So, when you need to increase your speed, you simply contact your provider and order a speed increase. It can usually be processed in a few days. All that needs to be done to increase the speed is for the provider to reconfigure their equipment to the new speed, and you to reconfigure the equipment at your end. This usually involves changing a menu option on the equipment's configuration menu to the new speed.

An Internet access provider can usually manage the installation of the telephone line for you, as well as sell and configure the equipment that you will need. The equipment that you will need to purchase or lease includes a router and a T1 Data Service Unit or Channel Service Unit (DSU/CSU). The Data Service Unit connects data terminal equipment to digital communication lines, and the CSU is an electrical buffer between your equipment and the carrier's wide area network. The router connects to your internal network and to the T1 DSU/CSU. The T1 DSU/CSU connects to the T1 line from the telephone company. The telephone company may also provide you with additional on-site equipment to support the T1 line.

A good Internet access provider can make the installation relatively painless for you. They can do everything for you including plugging in the equipment and configuring your server if you wish to spend the money for those services.

You should consider using your existing systems integrator, provided they have sufficient experience with Internet connections. You could use a Lotus Business Partner who specializes in Internet connections. But, whomever you decide to use, or if you do it yourself, make absolutely certain that person has experience. When an individual or company is learning at your expense, you're paying a premium for those services. You may find that paying a seemingly more expensive rate for experienced professionals is less expensive in the long run when compared to the hours charged to you by those who are getting their experience at your expense.

If you are new to Internet connections, you can easily be overwhelmed by the myriad of service options that your Internet access provider can offer. A wise thing to do is to take the full service options. Don't try to save money by taking a basic service package, because you will be in way over your head. Specifically, services like Domain Name Service (DNS), remote management, and security/firewall services are things better left to the access provider. The rule of thumb is, "If you are not already doing it yourself, and have a lot of experience doing it, don't do it!" For more information on DNS, see "The Internet—What it is," in Chapter 1, "An Introduction to Domino 4.5 and the Internet."

With Planet Domino, our Internet connection was an easy process because InterFusion had an existing T1 Internet connection and Web servers. InterFusion's offices are located in the Greater Philadelphia area—a region covered by Bell Atlantic. The area is well wired with fiber optic cable. So, InterFusion was able to get a completely fiber optic connection to the Internet.

In fact, InterFusion has enough fiber optic cable and T1 line equipment to support 8 T1 lines. Bell Atlantic (our carrier) provided all of the T1 equipment as part of the installation. It includes fiber optic couplers, patch panels, T1 signal equipment, and a UPS that take up about 15 square feet of wall space (5' high by 3' wide). All of this equipment provides an automatic failover, in the event of a cable or T1 equipment failure. If some component breaks, automatic failover assures that another will pick up where the broken one has failed without interruption in service.

Server Hardware

Servers are the most critical hardware to your Web site, and you should not skimp when it comes to planning their cost and capabilities. Our experience shows that most of the performance and reliability problems of Web sites come from the servers themselves. Certainly, your Internet connection's speed will affect performance. But, if your connection is planned correctly, your speed can be easily increased when needed.

Server hardware has more impact on Web site performance than speed alone. On a sophisticated, interactive, secure Web site the server usually does a great deal of work to process Web pages. The *dynamic* nature of Domino requires the server to work harder than other, more traditional, Web servers, which essentially perform like file servers.

Our rule of thumb for Domino servers is:, "Spend as much money on the server as you can."

The server hardware and software configuration used with Planet Domino is as follows:

▶ HP Vectra XU

▶ Dual 120 Mhz Pentium processors

▶ 144Mb RAM

▶ 18Gb of disk drive space using disk mirroring and RAID 5 (13Gb total usable storage)
  - System drive is two 1Gb drives, mirrored
  - Data drive is four 4Gb drives, RAID 5

▶ Windows NT Server v4.0, Service Pack 2

▶ Lotus Domino server R4.5a

Fault Tolerance

What happens when (not if) your hardware or software fails? Do you have a recovery plan? Do you have redundant hardware installed so the system is tolerant to faults?

Fault tolerance is not just for the rich, it is essential for any Web site. If planned currently, fault tolerance doesn't have to cost a fortune.

There are several areas that must be protected against failures. In order of importance they are:

▶ Electric power failures

▶ Disk drive failures

▶ Whole server failures

▶ LAN failures

▶ Internet connection failures

▶ Building failures

The first three items on this list are very common and can be protected against fairly inexpensively. The last three fault tolerance items can be very expensive.

Electric Power Failures

The quality of electric power is on a continual downward slide as the population grows and power demand increases. Every time a new gadget is sold, it seems as if the quality of power goes down.

Quality problems can range from blackouts and brownouts to power surges, spikes, and noise. Blackouts and brownouts are pretty obvious (hopefully, you'll know you're in the dark) and for most of us, infrequent.

Power surges, spikes, and electrical noise happen all of the time, all day long, and are the most insidious types of power problems. They damage electronic equipment, prematurely age circuitry, and can cause unexplained lockups and crashes. We have seen, several times, people who have system lockups and crashes that looked like software bugs, but were actually caused by power quality problems. You can confirm surges, spikes, and noise by installing smart UPS's (Uninterruptible Power Supplies) that provide clean power and monitor and log the power problems.

We recommend using UPS systems that have monitoring and logging capabilities. It is the cheapest insurance you can buy.

InterFusion uses several American Power Conversion Smart UPS units to protect all of their servers and workstations. As authors of computer books and as Notes consultants, our equipment is very important to us and we have also installed American Power Conversion Smart UPS units on our servers and workstations at home.

Disk Drive Failures

Disk drive failures are more common than we like to admit, or even think about. If you have never experienced a drive failure, consider your days numbered. Time will soon catch up to you.

The two most often used techniques to protect against drive failures are drive mirroring and drive arrays, or RAID 5 (Redundant Array of Inexpensive Drives).

Drive mirroring, as the name implies, is when you use two drives when you need one, and the system mirrors or copies the same data to both drives.

RAID 5 is a technique that spreads the data evenly across all of the drives in the array, and generates parity information that can be used to reconstruct data, if there is a drive failure. Arrays require at least three drives.

Mirroring is usually faster writing information to the drives than RAID 5, but RAID 5 is usually faster than mirroring when reading. Depending on the drive controller hardware you use, RAID 5 can be faster at writing as well. RAID 5's speed can also increase as more drives are added, and less usable drive space is lost.

On the server running Planet Domino, we are using mirroring and RAID 5. The Windows NT system drive uses two 1Gb drives that are mirrored to provide faster virtual memory or paging performance. The drive used to run Domino and store all data is a RAID 5 array composed of four 4Gb drives, for a total of 16Gb of usable disk space. The array uses Windows NT's built-in RAID 5 software.

Wholes Server Failures

Whole server failures include power supply or motherboard failures and software failures such as protection faults and bugs. Software failures are more likely to rear their ugly heads and are worth trying to protect against.

Techniques to protect against whole server failures have not been widely used in the past because of their complexity and cost. Server clustering is a new technology that is cost effective and quickly becoming popular.

Clustering, unlike other techniques, does not require special and expensive hardware. Clustering allows you to group several servers in a cluster, and allows users to access the cluster as a whole, instead of depending on individual servers. As a result, the servers are all working together to balance the load for user, and, if a server fails, another server in the cluster automatically takes over. This eliminates the need to have expensive server hardware sitting idle, waiting for a server failure.

With server clustering, you can use workstation or even desktop class hardware, with redundant drives. Put several inexpensive machines in a cluster and they all balance the load, and provide fault tolerance for each other.

Clustering support is built into Domino R4.5. To use it you must purchase a Domino Advanced Services license. Today, Domino clustering provides load balancing and failover for Notes clients only. Web client support is not built into R4.5, but can be configured using a separate TCP/IP address management product, such as IBM's Site Manager. In future versions of Domino, IBM, and Lotus intend to build this support for Web server clusters into Domino.

With Planet Domino we have not yet implemented server clustering, but intend to in the future, as soon as we can get a Windows NT version of IBM's Site Manager, which, as we write this, is only available on IBM AIX. IBM Site Manager may be available for Windows NT by the time you read this. Check out the Web site at **www. planetdomino.net** for the latest.

LAN Failures

LAN failures mean failure of the LAN hardware, such as hubs and switches. These types of failures are fairly rare and can be very expensive, depending on the technique and equipment used. We currently have no automatic recovery for LAN failures installed for Planet Domino. If it were really important to us that our LAN not fail (if this site were more mission critical), we would install redundant equipment: hot spare servers, dual LAN adapters, and backup LANs.

Internet Connection Failures

There are many ways to design for automatic recovery for Internet connection failures such as a redundant Internet connection. You could go as far as having a different Internet access provider with a POP in a different city, with a different T1 connection to that POP.

Protecting against this type of failure can get very expensive. If this level of redundancy is required for your Web site, you may find it much less costly to host your Web site with a large Domino Web hosting provider, such as IBM's InterConnect service, Interliant, US West, Netcom, or other Domino hosting service. We currently have no plans to implement this level of redundancy for Planet Domino.

Building Failures

Protecting against fires, floods, and the like is another very expensive level of redundancy. To protect against this kind of disaster, you set up a second site, located distant from the first. All of the previous levels of redundancy would be included at this level. Using a Domino hosting service may be a much more cost effective way of providing this level of redundancy for your Web site. We currently have no plans to implement this for Planet Domino.

Designing the Site

Designing the site includes defining the information that will be found at the site, identifying the site's features, such as search capabilities, structuring the organization of the site, laying out the site's home page, and designing the user interface.

Start at the bottom. You will provide at the site the smallest details of the information. Work your way up, to the organization of the site. The content will drive the organization. For the Planet Notes Web site, we started with content.

Information on the Site

Identifying the information to be provided at the Web site is done first. This is driven by the mission and functional requirements. Later, we will take this detail and organize it into a structure and set of features for users.

Start this step by gathering information from all of the people involved in the Web site and be certain to include the groups within your organization and the audience of the Web site. Ask customers and partners what information they want the Web site to provide them.

With Planet Domino we had a large amount of information to choose from that, for the most part, existed somewhere on the Internet in some form or another. We also had a lot of book material from which to choose, from our publisher. Here is a list of some of the information we decided to include on the initial version of Planet Domino.

> ▶ InterFusion's Domino Discussion
> ▶ Lotus' Domino Discussion
> ▶ Lotus' Weblicator Discussion
> ▶ Lotus' Notes KnowledgeBase
> ▶ Lotus' cc:Mail KnowledgeBase
> ▶ Lotus' SmartSuite KnowledgeBase
> ▶ US Lotus Business Partner Catalog
> ▶ Worldwide Lotus Business Partner Catalog
> ▶ Mobile Survivor's Guide
> ▶ A sample Web site created with Domino.Action
> ▶ Lotus Notes/Domino R4.5 Help
> ▶ Lotus Notes/Domino R4.5 Administrator Help
> ▶ Lotus Domino R1.5 User's Guide
> ▶ Lotus Notes R4.5 Migration Guide
> ▶ Web versions of Internet newsgroups on Lotus products
> ▶ A catalog of books on Lotus products

All of these databases are available in Notes database format and on the Web on various Lotus Web sites. But they are not available in one place.

Features of the Site

Now that we have a list of information that we want to put on the Web site and we know what we want the Web site to do and who our audience is, we can design features that will help users find what they need.

One of the main goals of Planet Domino is to allow people to quickly get the information they need without having to surf all over the Internet. Therefore a site wide search capability was absolutely essential. Easy navigation between the huge amounts of data was also critical as is the ability to order books on-line.

Special features of Planet Domino:

▶ Site Search for all databases

▶ Easy navigation

▶ On-line book ordering

Setting up Site Search

Domino R4.5 has a great new feature called Site Search. It allows you to search several databases at once, and can be used from a Notes client and a Web browser.

Site Search works by using a Notes database to collect full text index information from the databases that you want to search. You set this up by enabling the databases that you want to include in the Site Search database for Multi-Database Searching, then defining the search scope in the Site Search database. For additional information on the Site Search database, refer to "Setting Up Multi-database Search Capabilities" in Chapter 16, "Using Advanced Administration Techniques."

The only thing that we changed in the Site Search for Planet Domino was the look of the search forms (see Figure 18.2). We wanted the forms to have the same background color as most of the other frequently used documents at the site. So, we did the following:

1. Opened the Design view of the Search Site database

2. Opened each of the Web specific forms in Design mode

3. Changed the Background Color for each form to White

Fig. 18.2

You can customize the Site Search database, changing the look of the search forms. At Planet Domino, we changed the background color of the search forms.

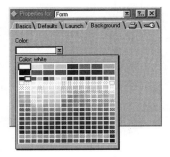

4. Turned off the "Inherit Design from Template" in Database Properties - Design so our design changes would not be overwritten (see Figure 18.3).

Fig. 18.3

Turn off "Inherit Design from Template" in the Web forms of the Search Site database to protect your changes from being overwritten.

Organizing the Site

Next, we needed to organize the information on the site. We felt the best organization for our information was by information *source* and information *type*. n. We wanted the discussion databases grouped together, the knowledgebases grouped together, and so on (see Figure 18.4).

Fig. 18.4

Organization of the information on Planet Domino.

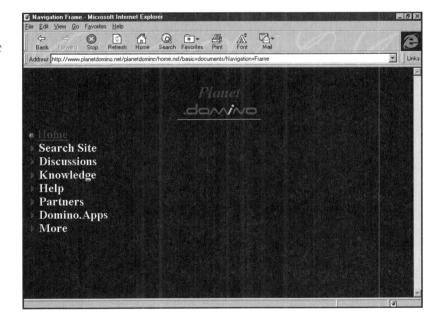

Search Site

In this section the links to the Search Site features, Simple Search and Advanced Search are added. Both of these search options are built into the Search Site database and required no extra work. There is also a link within the search forms for help. The Search Site database can provide your Web site with some very sophisticated features.

Discussions

All of the discussion databases are located in this section. This includes InterFusion's Domino Discussion started on June 3, 1996, and Lotus' Domino and Weblicator discussions. The Domino discussion is only an archive, and is not a live version of what Lotus has on their own domino.lotus.com Web site. Lotus uses their Domino Web site as a way to test alpha and beta version of Domino, and the traffic generated by the discussion is a great way for them to do that. This is why the version on Planet Domino is an archive.

Knowledge

All of the KnowledgeBases are located here. This includes the Notes, cc:Mail, and SmartSuite KnowledgeBases. Having all of them here allows Planet Domino users to include them in a site search, as well as browse the KnowledgeBase documents sorted in many ways.

Help

The major Lotus Help databases are found here. These databases are great examples of how good a Notes database can look on the Web, without any Web specific modifications.

Partners

Both the US and Worldwide Lotus Business Partner Catalogs are found at this location of the site. The many sorted views on these databases, as well as the database search feature, will allow visitors to find information on Business Partners fast.

Domino.Apps

This section is intended to contain information on the suite of Domino.Applications. As we write this book, this section of the site contains only one link to a sample Domino.Action created Web site. This Domino.Action sample site will allow you to see what Domino.Action can do. It has all of the Domino.Action areas enabled, with no security so you can browse all of the areas.

Two areas in the Domino.Action site that are being used in a production capacity by Planet Domino, are the User Registration and Feedback areas. The Feedback area is used to get feedback for the users of the site on ways we can improve Planet Domino. The User Registration area will be used to allow users to access future restricted areas, and participated in discussions that are not anonymous.

The "More" Section of the Site

This section is a catch all for anything that doesn't fall cleanly into the other categories. Right now the Mobile Survivor's Guide is located here. This guide contains up to the minute information on using Notes as a mobile user, including the latest modem command files.

Designing the Home Page

A Web site's home page (see Figure 18.5) is the most important page of the site, as it is the most frequently visited page and is the starting point and first impression of the site.

We developed our initial home page as a simple greeting to visitors. In the future, the home page will be used to interactively communicate the latest information about Planet Domino and Lotus technology.

Fig. 18.5

Planet Domino's Home Page.

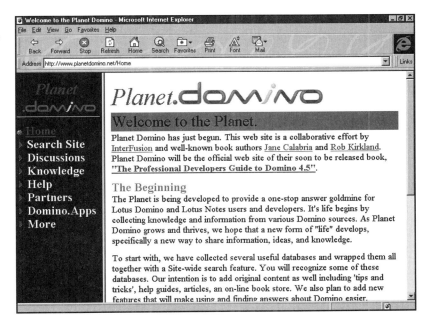

The User Interface

The user interface of a Web site should be consistent across the entire site. In order for users to be able to find what they need quickly and not get frustrated, the user interface should be direct and to the point.

Our main goal with the user interface was to keep it simple. We wanted to provide a navigation frame that would be visible at all time since every database on the site has a different way of organizing information.

The navigation frame allows the user to quickly go anywhere on the site (see Figure 18.6), and it is visible all of the time. It also acts as a reminder that they are on Planet Domino as the logo is always visible in the navigation frame.

Fig. 18.6

Domino Web site in the Simple Site Search area.

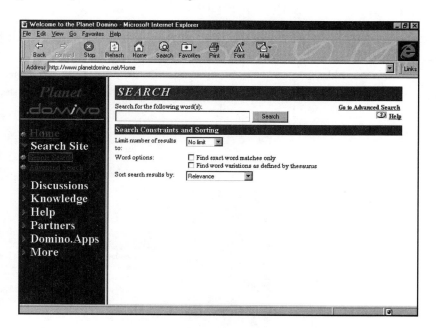

Creating the Site Database

The actual number of pages we had to create for Planet Domino was pretty small. Many of the databases found at the site were previously created and populated, so our content work was limited.

Our goal was simple and only one database was used to present the user interface and main pages. In the database we created only one simple form design and called it "Basic Document." (see Figure 18.7 and Figure 18.8) We also created a copy of this design with a black background and called it "Basic Black Document."

Fig. 18.7

A Basic Document containing Planet Domino's opening screen.

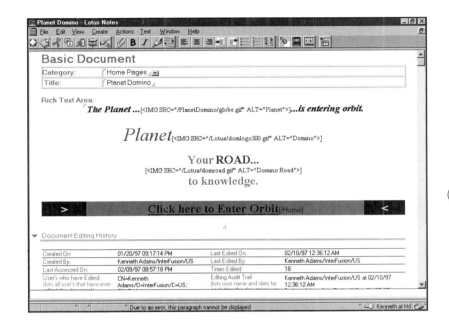

The Basic Document's design is pretty simple. The main part of the form contains only three fields: Category, Title, and the Rich Text Area, which contains the page that gets displayed on the Web. At the bottom of the form is a Document Editing History section (see Figure 18.9) that contains information about the document's history.

Fig. 18.8

The Basic Document form design.

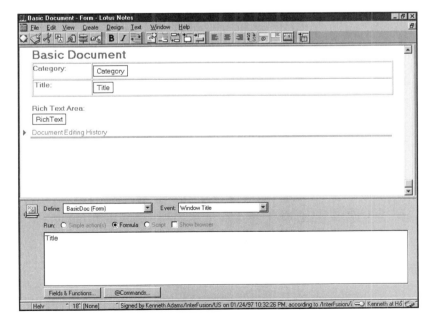

Category Field

The Category field is simply used to categorize the documents for the Webmaster. It is used in a Basic Documents By Category view to group the documents together.

Title Field

The Title field is used to provide a title that Domino can translate into a title for the Web browser and the Notes client.

RichText Field

The RichText field contains the document that is served to the Web browser. None of the other fields are visible to Web browsers, which are hidden using Hide When formulas. This field allows any information to be entered including font colors and sizes, tables, links, and more. Domino turns this into HTML for the Web browser.

Document Editing History Subform

This subform is used to keep track of useful information about the document. We use this subform in many of the Notes applications that we create. It includes information like the name of the person who created the document and who last edited it, the date it was created, last edited and last accessed, the number of times the document has been edited, and a audit trail of who and when the document was edited.

Fig. 18.9

The Document Editing History subform.

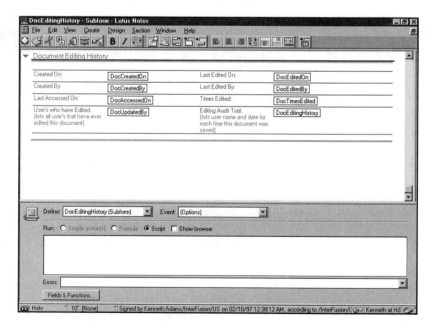

Setting up the Opening Page

The opening page of Planet Domino, is a document stored within the database. The opening page is setup to open automatically when a user accesses the URL www.planetdomino.net. Here's how it works:

1. The URL is redirected by Domino to the home.nsf database.

2. The home.nsf database is set to automatically launch a doclink in the About Database document. This is set using the Database Properties - Launch tab, and setting the Launch On Database Open to "Launch 1st doclink in About Database doc." (see Figure 18.10).

3. The doclink opens to the opening page document.

Fig. 18.10
Setting Launch option in Database Properties.

The Home Page

The Home page of Planet Domino is a combination of three documents. One document defines the frame interface, another is the navigator frame, and the last is the document that is displayed in the view frame.

Designing the Frames Interface

Frames are a very useful feature of Web browsers. They allow you to separate the browser window into multiple windows that can all display different pages.

Frames are actually very easy to set up. They just require the proper HTML tag syntax and a little testing. For more information on using frames with Domino, see Chapter 23 "Using the Personal Web Navigator."

On the Planet Domino Web site (see Figure 18.11), we just had to set them and forget them. Frames were used to provide a consistent user interface that allows the user to quickly jump to any part of the Web site, from any other part. This was accomplished using a frame that always displays navigation controls. The navigation frame displays links to all areas of the Web site, and is always visible.

Fig. 18.11

Planet Domino's Home Page.

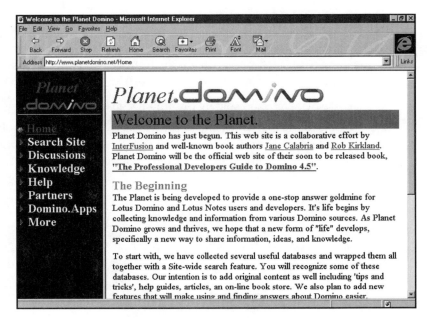

This was especially important because we were using databases from many sources, each with their own user interface. We couldn't create our own user interface for the databases, with links to other areas, because we needed to allow the design to be updated from its own source. Frames allowed us to provide a common user interface for the entire site, and still allowed the databases to have their designs change at any time.

The Frames Code

The frames are defined using HTML tags and attributes. The HTML code is:

```
<html>
<head>
   <title>Welcome to the Planet Domino</title>
</head>

<frameset cols="175,*">
     <frame name ="navframe" src="
/planetdomino/home.nsf/basic+documents/Navigation+Frame" noresize marginheight=0
marginwidth=0>
     <frame name ="viewframe"
src="/planetdomino/home.nsf/basic+documents/Planet+Domino+Home+Page">
</frameset>
</html>a
```

Table 18.1 breaks down of each of the HTML components used in this file.

Table 18.1 HTML Frame Code

Tag	Function
<html>	Starts the HTML file.
<head> <title>Welcome to Planet Domino</title> </head>	Defines the document header section. Includes the title of the page that will display in the window's title of the Web browser.
<frameset cols="175,*">	Starts the frame definition and specifics the width of the frame columns. There are two columns. The first is 175 pixels in width. The second column is set to "*" which is a wildcard that represents the remainder of the window.
<frame	Begins the definition of the first frame.
Name ="navframe"	Assigns a name to the first frame, so it can be referenced in links using the TARGET attribute.
Src="/planetdomino/home.nsf /basic+documents/Navigation+Frame"	Specifies the initial content of this frame.
Noresize	Prevents the user from resizing the frame.
Marginheight=0	Set the margin height for the frame.
Marginwidth=0>	Set the margin width for the frame. The greater than symbol ends the first frame definition.
<frame	Begins the definition of the second frame.
Name ="viewframe"	Assigns a name to the first frame.
Src="/planetdomino/home.nsf /basic+documents/Planet+Domino +Home+Page">	Specifies the initial content of this frame. The greater than symbol ends the second frame definition.
</frameset>	Ends the frame definition.
</html>	Ends the HTML file.

18

Storing HTML Code

The frames definition is stored in a separate HTML file. The tags could not just be typed into a Notes document, and served using HTML passthrough, because Domino adds some HTML when it translates the Notes document, even if you use HTML passthrough. The HTML that Domino would add can prevent the frames from working correctly.

We kept the frames definition in a physically separate file stored in the file system of the server, instead of storing it as an attached file in a document. Although storing it as an attached file would have worked correctly, we wanted to, to avoid any possibility of performance degradation by Domino having to translate the URL. Domino caches attached files, but because this was the home page and would be the first file downloaded, we wanted it to be as fast as possible to download.

How to Reference a File

If we wanted to store the HTML frames file in a Notes document, we would reference the file using a syntax similar to this:

```
/PlanetDomino/home.nsf/Basic+Documents/HTML+Files/$FILE/frames.htm
```

An URL like the one above will work fine with Domino and can be used to directly access any attached file in a Notes document. We use this syntax to reference GIF files that are stored in Notes documents. The exact syntax to reference a GIF file is:

```
[<IMG SRC="/PlanetDomino/home.nsf/Basic+Documents/GIFs/$FILE/DomServerTech.gif"
ALT="Domino Server">]
```

Table 18.2 breaks down this statement:

Table 18.2   HTML Code for Image Referencing

Code	Function
[<	The square bracket followed by a less than symbol, indicates HTML passthrough. The less than symbol is passed through, but the square bracket is removed.
IMG SRC="	This is the HTML tag for an image file. The filename would appear between the double quotes.
/PlanetDomino	This is the directory on the Domino server in which the database is located, under the server's data directory.
/home.nsf	This is the filename of the Notes database.
/Basic+Documents	This is the name of the view in the database that contains the document where the file is stored. The plus symbol is used instead of a space.

Code	Function
/GIFs	The view is sorted on the title of the documents, and it is the first column of the view. This is the key that Domino will search for, in other words the title of the document.
/$FILE	This references an attached file.
/DomServerTech.gif"	This is the filename of the attached file, with a closing double quote to close the IMG SRC tag.
ALT="Domino Server"	This is an HTML tag that defines the text that will be displayed before the image is downloaded to the Web browser, or displayed in place of the image if the browser has been set to not download images, or the transfer is stopped by the user before it is complete.
>]	This ends the HTML passthrough. The greater than symbol is passed through.

Referencing a Notes Document as HTML

In the frames file, we used an SRC attribute to specify the initial content to be displayed in the frame. The reference looked like the following:

/planetdomino/home.nsf/basic+documents/Planet+Domino+Home+Page

This is a reference to a Notes document stored in the database. The syntax is similar to a reference to an attached file, as illustrated above except that the URL reference ends with the title of the document. This is a powerful and easy to use way to reference Notes documents using HTML.

Setting Up the Databases

Only minor changes to the various databases were required to get them ready for the Web site. The two areas that needed to be changed were the Access Control List and the Database Launch options

All of the databases need to have their access for Default set to Reader. This would allow Web users to access the databases without a user account. For more information on the Access Control List, see "Database Access Control Lists" in Chapter 14, "Securing the Domino Web Server." Some of the databases needed to have their Database Launch option changed to a view or navigator that would be usable via a Web browser.

Redirecting Traffic from www.lotus.com

On Lotus' main Web site located at www.lotus.com, there is a link to InterFusion's Domino discussion database found at InterFusions corporate site. This link is located just one link away from the home page of www.lotus.com. This link has been generating a fair amount of traffic, and we wanted to take advantage of it.

The link on Lotus' Web site leads directly to the database filename, so we would need to put a new file in its place, with the same filename. We would move the discussion database file to a new location, and link to it from Planet Domino (see Figure 18.12).

The database that displays the moved page is based on the same design used for Planet Domino's main pages. The database is set to launch to a document that displays the moved page.

Fig. 18.12

We decided the best way to take advantage of the traffic was to redirect the traffic by replacing the discussion database with a page the notifies people that the discussion has moved to Planet Domino, and provides a link to Planet Domino.

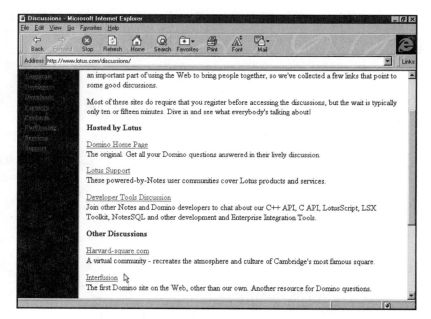

Linking It All Together

The links to the databases from the navigation frame, open the databases in the larger frame to the right. To accomplish this requires special HTML syntax in the navigation frame document.

The HTML attribute TARGET is used to direct the output from links to databases, to the other frame. In a HTML frame file we named the frame on the right "viewframe." So, the

HTML used in the document that makes up the navigation frame, uses HTML with the TARGET attribute set to "viewframe" as shown in Figure 18.13.

Fig. 18.13
Planet Domino's Navigation frame document, showing links using TARGET attribute.

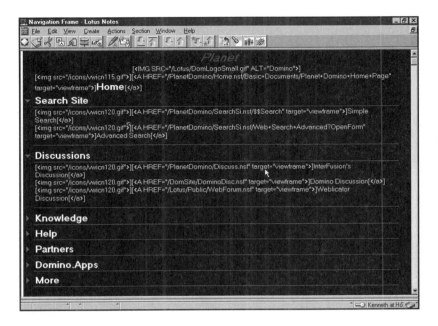

Going On-Line

To bring the Web site online, we needed our domain name and we needed to configure the server to point our new host name www.planetdomino.net to the right place.

Registering the Domain

Internet domain names ending in .COM or .NET are currently managed by an organization called the InterNIC, which stands for Internet Network Information Center. The process of registering a domain name can be mostly automatic, as long as the electronic forms are filled out correctly. You must be very careful to fill out these forms correctly, or it may require time consuming phone calls, e-mails, and faxes.

The InterNIC's Web site is located at www.internic.net and is shown in Figure 18.14.

From the InterNIC home page, select Registration Services. From there you should use the Template Guide. There you will be able to use Web-based templates that will guide you through the process of filling out the forms.

Fig. 18.14

InterNIC's Home Page.

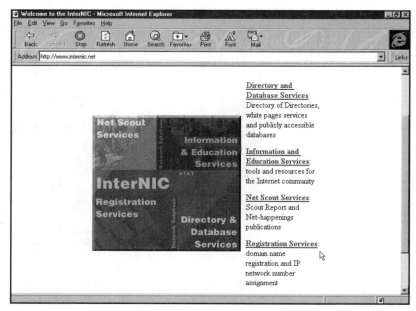

Setting Up the Host Name

The host name is the full address of the Web site, such as www.planetdomino.net. The domain name is the right portion (planetdomino.net) of the host name. This host name must be set up in the DNS servers that is assigned to your domain. If your Internet access provider is managing your DNS services, then they can usually handle registering your domain and setting up the host name in DNS.

Configuring the OS

The host name will be set up in DNS to point to a specific IP address. You must set up your server's operating system to receive requests at that IP address.

In Windows NT, this is a fairly simple process. It is done using Control Panel in the Network applet. In Windows NT v4.0, you would go to the Protocols tab, and display the Properties of TCP/IP. Additional IP addresses are set by clicking the Advanced button.

Windows NT can support many IP addresses on one server; therefore, one server can support many Web sites.

Configuring Domino

The Domino Web Server must be configured to direct a Web request on a specific IP address, to a Domino URL. Many Web sites can be configured on one Domino server. This is done in the Domino Web Server Configuration database (Domcfg.nsf).

Planet Domino uses two configuration documents in the Configuration database. The first is the Virtual Server document used (see Figure 18.15) to configure the host name www.planetdomino.net.

Fig. 18.15

Domino Configuration database, Virtual Server document for Planet Domino.

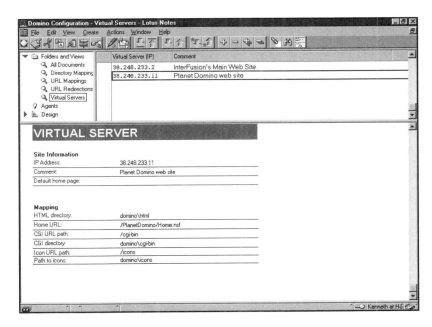

We used the second configuration document (see Figure 18.16) for the home page. This enables visitors to skip the opening page and allows the designer the flexibility of using an alias to point to the actual URL.

Fig. 18.16

Domino Configuration database, URL Mapping document for Planet Domino's home page.

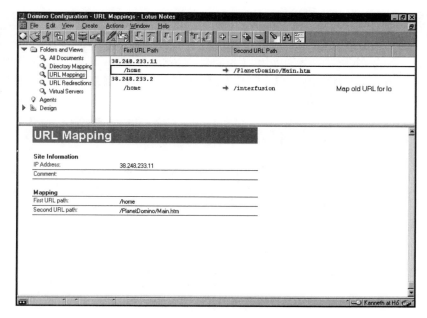

From Here...

As you have read in this chapter, the planning and implemention of a Web site is every bit as involved as the design process. For related information see the following chapters:

▶ Chapter 4, "Understanding Web Fundamentals," provides a basic understanding of HTML, Java applets, plug ins, and Active X.

▶ Chapter 12, "Applying a 'Web Look' to Notes Applications," shows how to incorporate frames into Domino applications.

▶ Chapter 19, "Migrating R3 Notes Applications to Domino," discusses how you can retrofit your Notes applications for optimum performance on the Web.

Migrating R3 Notes Applications to Domino

19

by Susan Trost

In this chapter

◆ **Reasons for migrating an application to Domino**
Here, we discuss the basis for upgrading R3 applications to Notes 4.5 and Domino and the advantages of extending your applications to non-Notes users.

◆ **How to plan a successful migration**
An important part of migration is the planning stage. The requirements survey for migration is discussed in this chapter.

◆ **Tips for a successful migration**
Recording techniques and testing the applications are some of the processes used by the professionals when migrating applications. Here, we reveal some "insider" tips.

◆ **Migration techniques**
Not all migrations are equal. Learn some considerations and techniques used when dealing with Notes versus Web clients.

In an ideal world, application developers would exploit every new feature in a development environment as it becomes available. However, there are consequences to enhancing any application environment or user interface, and many can be slow to implement changes due to the dynamics working in a large organization. Windows 95 migration is a good example. Windows 95 has been commercially available since August 1995, and widely available in beta form prior to then, yet today there are still many companies working with earlier versions of Windows. There are many reasons why organizations elect to slowly upgrade their hardware and software environments. Some common reasons include:

- ▶ cost
- ▶ training requirements
- ▶ support issues
- ▶ corporate IT strategy conflict
- ▶ logistic complexities
- ▶ lack of business justification

How many times have you witnessed users demanding environment upgrades because their home PC is a better specification and more updated than their office PC? This happens all too often! So, while you are anxious to implement those new capabilities of Lotus Notes R4.5 and Domino in your organization—your organization may not be ready or capable of accepting changes without compromising productivity or existing investment. Training and maintenance of applications represents a significant portion of the cost of ownership for PCs, so think twice before you get moving on deploying those new features; you may have a political battlefield to navigate through and it makes sense to work within your practical constraints.

This chapter explores the opportunity to take advantage of Domino features without compromising the existing application interface. The tips and techniques described in this chapter have been implemented in an organization that had a requirement to convert 12 complex and highly customized linked Lotus Notes databases that, in turn, connect to over 200 R3 Lotus Notes databases used by over 1,500 users in 16 countries.

The existing Lotus Notes environment and interface had evolved over a period of 12 months and, as with many large organizations, making changes to the behavior and application front end required a bevy of approvals. Our challenge was to implement as many Domino and R4.5 features as possible and create a corporate intranet without upgrading the existing R3 clients or changing the user interface and experience. In addition, we were asked to support access to these applications using a variety of Web clients. Our project window was eight weeks.

Why Migrate?

There are overwhelming technical reasons to upgrade to Lotus Notes R4.5 and Domino. For our project we could take advantage of many new security, administration, access, and Internet capabilities Lotus Notes R4.5 and Domino offered. Following are specific benefits we would realize from migrating our Lotus Notes R3 applications to a Domino server while preserving the existing interface and use of the Lotus Notes R3 client.

Extend Applications' Reach Beyond Notes Users

The potent capability of extending the reach of our applications to serve the budding intranet community and the many, many megabytes of information contained within the existing applications was the most overwhelming reason to move forward with a migration to Domino servers. In fact, a separate intranet team had been formed in another part of the organization and tasked with creating a corporate intranet. Domino was not a tool they were considering and, at first, we were working in an internally competitive environment. However, once the benefits of converting the first R3 application to Domino were demonstrated, Domino soon became a vital part of the corporate intranet strategy!

Preserve Existing Training Investment

User training represented a large portion of the cost to implement our existing system because of the organizational effect of implementing a workgroup environment in a traditional "pocket knowledge" environment. Team-working and collaboration techniques had to be taught in order to make the system valuable. For some time, during initial rollout, many users were very interested in accessing the contributions made by others but were very reticent when faced with having to make their own contributions. The user interface required many changes while in development (even to the exact size and color of button symbols) and the change approval process was difficult, at best, to navigate. Customized training for the existing system had already been developed and new users were being added daily; we could not compromise the existing investment made in training.

Leverage Domino Server Security with Web Clients

An extensive security model, in addition to the normal security capabilities contained within Lotus Notes, had been developed to monitor and control document author approval, editor, and access facilities. Using a Domino server enabled us to continue to support this extended security model when applications are accessed by a Web client. For more information on Domino security, see Chapter 14, "Securing the Domino Web Server," and Chapter 15, "Using Secure Sockets Layer (SSL) with Domino."

Use of the Full-Text Search Engine

By using a Domino server to host our intranet applications, we are able to let Web clients take advantage of using the full-text search engine with automatic indexing across the internal intranet and extend search capabilities to the Internet without having to set up direct Internet access from individual workstations.

19

Use of Native Notes Capabilities

Another power benefit of using a Domino server to host our intranet was the ability to take advantage of features like expanding and collapsing views and other navigational facilities. In addition, we could use sub-forms, sections, hide-when formulas, and other familiar Lotus Notes features when using a Domino server.

Create and Serve Files in HTML Format

The Domino server is an HTTP server that supports communication with Web clients. Web clients (and Notes clients) can make URL requests against the Domino server that are processed to determine if the request is for an item in a Lotus Notes database or an HTML document. For more information on the Domino HTTP server task, see Chapter 1, "An Introduction to Domino 4.5 and the Internet."

If the request is for an HTML file, Domino acts just like any other HTTP server and serves the file to the Web client. When the request is for something in a Notes database, Domino interacts with the Notes database to serve the information to the Web client or to put information from the Web client into the Notes database.

Domino supports extensions that enable URLs to expose Notes functionality to the Web client. For example, this URL opens the main database on the Domino site: **http://domino.lotus.com/domino.nsf?OpenDatabase.** To learn more about Domino URLs, see Chapter 3, "Working with Your Domino Web Site."

Domino also automatically translates Notes constructs such as navigators, , documents, and links into HTML for display in the Web client. For example, Notes links and action buttons become URLs in the Web client. You simply develop your Web application in Notes, and the Domino server handles the rest.

Run CGI Scripts

The Domino server supports the execution of CGI scripts. Remember, the Domino server does not provide file system access control here so you need to take steps to control access to ensure only authorized script execution occurs. Place CGI programs in the default cgi-bin directory or in a directory that has execute access.

Upgraded Notes Public Address Book

Web client passwords, password storage, and database access control are maintained in the Notes Public Name and Address Book. Web client authentication succeeds if the user name and password supplied by the user match the appropriate fields in the Person document of the Public Address Book on the Domino Web server and if the user is listed individually or as part of a group in the database access control list.

Although basic Web authentication is not considered as secure as Notes public key certificate-based authentication (because it doesn't involve certifiers that validate the client's identity), it does allow the Domino server to serve users through the Internet who are not running Notes workstation software.

In addition, access to Notes databases can be given to anonymous Web client users. Any Web user who doesn't supply a name and password is known by the name "anonymous." The server administrator and individual database managers decide what level of database access anonymous users have. To make a database available to anonymous Web users, create an "Anonymous" entry in the access control list and assign it the appropriate access: Reader access for an information database or Author for an interactive database unless there is a specific security concern. If the access control list for a database does not contain an "Anonymous" entry, all anonymous users receive the Default access. Administrators can also bar anonymous Web client access to Notes databases by selecting "No" for "Allow anonymous HTTP connections" in the Security section of the Server document. All anonymous Web users are prompted for a name and password when they access the server and receive an "authorization failure" message if they cannot supply ones that the server recognizes. This setting overrides individual database access controls for anonymous users.

Including Web Users in ACL Lists

Registered Web users whose names and passwords are stored in the Public Address Book can be listed in the ACL along with registered Notes users. Database access levels for Web users is limited by the "Maximum Internet browser access" option in the Advanced section of the ACL. Even if Web users are listed explicitly in the ACL with higher access, they never have an access level greater than the browser access option.

To ensure all Web users are granted access to a database, set "Maximum Internet browser access" to Reader or higher (the default is Editor access). To prevent Web user access to databases, set "Maximum Internet browser access" to "No access."For more information on access control, see Chapter 14 "Securing the Domino Web Server."

Use Domino URLs

The Domino server uses URLs to access servers, databases, and other components of a Web site and display them to Web users. There are a number of Domino URL commands that you can use to design links or enter commands directly into a browser to navigate a Domino site or reach specific components quickly.

Support for Creating and Launching File Attachments

Whether you work from a Web browser or Notes, you can attach any type of file to a document, including binary files, compressed files, executable files, and Notes database (.NSF) files. You can upload and download attachments from the Web or from Notes. See Chapter 13, "Examining Special Function Databases for the Web," for a closer look at a Web "download" database.

 Note
At the time of writing, Internet Explorer 3.0 did not support attaching files to documents in Domino databases.

Progressive Rendering of Text and Graphics

This feature allows documents (in both HTML and Notes document format) to render significantly faster.

Migration Planning

One of the major factors in ensuring a successful migration is executing a thorough migration plan. Even as we faced tight migration completion deadlines, we still spent a significant amount of time working on our migration plan. We created a migration requirements survey to aid us in identifying issues, tasks, and potential obstacles we could encounter from both technical and organizational perspectives.

Migration Requirements Survey

▶ List all server and client operating systems in use including version numbers

▶ List all Notes and Web client types in use and version numbers

▶ List the types of Internet access used and percentage of organization's PC user base with Internet access

▶ Describe typical project and project management techniques used in your organization

▶ Identify recent projects that have been successful in your organization and include key success factors

▶ Identify past projects that did not meet objectives and list reasons why

▶ Determine whether phased migration is an option for this project

▶ Describe your organization's IT training guidelines or department

▶ State your organization's IT strategy if there is one

▶ Describe the PC literacy and skill sets of your user base

▶ Identify applications currently in use that are mission-critical

▶ Identify business owner for each application considered for migration

▶ Determine if business owners have change control procedures for user interface or functionality upgrades

▶ Identify opportunities for bundling application upgrades with other software or hardware upgrades

▶ Describe your organization's application support structure and its effectiveness

▶ Describe user training techniques and methods used;

> ▶ one-to-one
>
> ▶ peer
>
> ▶ formal classroom
>
> ▶ computer-based training
>
> ▶ training videos

▶ Describe the geographical composition of your user population

> ▶ centralized
>
> ▶ dispersed
>
> ▶ mixed

▶ Describe your Lotus Notes administrative support structure

▶ Describe the overall acceptance and opinion of existing Lotus Notes applications

The results of the survey yielded information used to help develop our migration plan. In summary, our main objectives were to upgrade applications to the Domino server as quickly as possible without compromising anything but small cosmetic and unavoidable changes to the user interface as experienced by current Notes clients. In addition, we identified testing all Web clients against the applications on the Domino server as a high priority.

Next, we'll look at some tips used during our migration that aided us in achieving our objectives.

Tips for a Successful Migration

Upon completion of our migration, we were able to evaluate our success and attribute credit to the most useful elements of the project. In this section, we'll cover some of the factors we found critical to meeting the objectives of our migration.

The areas we'll cover include:

▶ creating a plan for your migration

▶ generalizing techniques to work in global situations

▶ using subforms

▶ recording techniques discovered

▶ testing your Domino applications with all Web clients used

Create a Plan for Your Migration

We have already covered migration planning and presented a survey checklist to assist in identifying requirements for your migration. Ensure your migration plan is comprehensive and thorough. Key elements to the migration plan include stating your objectives, specifying features that will be supported, outlining the migration scope, and delivery time-scales. A well-planned migration will run much more smoothly because you will have invested energy in identifying and eliminating as many obstacles and potential problems as possible prior to migration.

Generalize Techniques to Work in Global Situations

As you think about solutions for problems, try to develop solutions that will work across all your applications. For example, we always looked to use script libraries, subforms, and clever code instead of the quickest solution to implement (usually hard-coding). We know this will reduce the maintenance effort required and enable us to focus more on future application improvements.

Use Subforms

A subform is a great tool for streamlining repeating elements in forms. Subforms contain groups of fields and form elements that are stored as a single design element. We use subforms extensively in our applications and think of them as libraries of reusable fields.

Tip

Just as a form formula attached to a view changes how a whole document is displayed, a subform formula can be attached to a form to change how a portion of the document is displayed under different circumstances.

Record Techniques Discovered

Be effective at recording techniques and making them available for the development team to use in other areas. This is a common and useful technique that many developers don't take the time to use. Again, we know it's difficult to take the time to document techniques when working under tight deadlines but you'll reap benefits from it. Imagine your life as a Lotus Notes developer without having access to tools like Knowledge Base for Lotus Notes. We treat our internal effort to record techniques very seriously. A Lotus Notes database is ideal for creating and storing your techniques!

 Note

Knowledge Base for Lotus Notes is a repository of information collated, maintained, and published by Lotus in .NSF format. If you are a Lotus Notes developer or administrator, you will find Knowledge Base invaluable for its wealth of information on bugs, bug fixes, work-around solutions, technotes, and common Lotus Notes questions.

Test Your Domino Applications with All Web Clients Used

In addition to testing all your Domino applications with a Notes client, thoroughly test your applications using not only each Web client that you want to support but each version of the Web client. Due to the difference in Web clients, there is no guarantee that functions that work with one Web client will work using another. Even application presentation and layout varies with each Web client. We identified a number of issues to resolve when testing our migrated applications using different Web clients. There is limited documentation regarding functions supported and functions not supported among various Web clients in the help documentation, but it is not comprehensive, to say the least!

For example, the Domino server supports attaching files to Notes documents using a Web client. However, Microsoft's Internet Explorer R3.0 does not support the type of field required.

In addition, test graphics rendering for your applications on each Web client and table text, in particular, for inconsistencies.

Migration Techniques

As we already discussed, in an ideal world we'd be able to use all of the latest features of a product, we'd have as much time as we wanted in which to develop our applications, and we'd have no installed base of users to consider when we made our changes.

Unfortunately, in our experience the world is far from ideal! For example, consider our situation where we have an existing user base of several thousand Notes users, all still using Notes R3 clients. We also have an existing set of a couple of hundred Notes databases, all of which were designed for the R3 user interface. Sound familiar? Now the boss calls; he's heard that all he needs to do to make these databases available on the corporate intranet, winning fame and glory for the IT department, is to load them all on a Domino server and the job's done! Oh, and by the way, he wants the user interface on the intranet to be as close to that of the existing Notes database as possible and it's all to be done by the end of the month. As a result of the effort to migrate our R3 applications to a Domino server, we developed and used a number of techniques. Some of the more useful techniques we used to achieve our objectives are included in the next part of the chapter.

Fortunately, the servers had already been migrated to Domino 4.5, so our main task was to work out a way to reproduce an R3 style interface on a Web client. Domino does take care of much of the conversion for you, but there are a number of features of R3 databases that are either not supported by the Domino server or more usually by Web clients. For example, a common technique used in databases designed for Notes R3 clients is to use a form to display a set of push-buttons that implement a menu.

Unfortunately, when the Domino server translates such a form into HTML, it does not translate all of the buttons. The first button on the form is translated into a Submit button and the rest of the buttons are ignored. So, an unmodified "menu" form won't work with a Web client. The set of databases we were migrating contained many of this type of menu form and we experimented with a number of techniques. In the time available to us, we found the following technique to be useful.

Simulating an R3 Menu Form

So, how do you get that nice looking R3 menu form to display on a Web client? The answer is to design a second version of the menu form modified for use by Web clients. You then add a form formula to any views used to display the form. In the form formula, you select the appropriate form to use based on the type of client. Notes R3 users see the original R3-style menu form and Web client users see the modified version of the form. There are several tricks to this and we'll cover them in this section:

▶ How to use form aliases to distinguish between Notes and Web versions of a form.

▶ How to write a form formula that displays a different form depending on the type of client being used to view it.

▶ How to use a navigator within a form to simulate a set of buttons.

▶ How to use the Domino URL syntax to open views and display documents.

The first step in building a Web version of the R3-style menu form is to create a copy of it. This will become your new Web version of the form.

You're going to need some way of identifying which version of the form is for use by Notes R3 clients and which is designed for Web clients. An easy way to do this is to use the form alias. We always use "f " as the first letter of the form alias for Notes R3 versions of forms and "w" for Web client versions. For example, the Notes R3 version of the menu form would have an alias such as fHomePage and the Web version's alias would be wHomePage.

 Tip

It's a good idea to prefix the names of your 'Web only' versions of design elements with "Web" so that they are grouped together and easy to identify in design mode. For example, if the R3 version of a form is called Main Topic, call the Web version Web Main Topic.

Now that you have two versions of the menu form, you need a way of displaying the appropriate form based on the type of client being used to view it. You can use a form formula and the @UserRoles function to do this as shown in Figure 19.1. Simply add a form formula such as the following, to the view that is used to display the menu form:

```
@If(@Contains(@Implode("":@UserRoles); "$$Web"); "wHomePage"; "fHomePage")
```

19

Fig. 19.1

Use a form formula to display the appropriate version of a form.

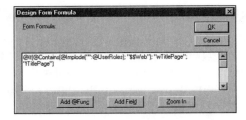

When the view is being displayed via a Web browser, the form formula ensures that all documents are displayed using the wHomePage form. If the view is accessed from a Notes client, the fHomePage form is used.

So far, all we've managed to do is display one of two identical forms depending on whether a Notes or Web client is being used. In itself, this hasn't helped us that much. The Web version of the form still doesn't display a set of buttons when viewed using a Web client. As with all other forms that contain buttons, only the first button on the form is displayed to the Web client. The rest of the buttons are ignored, and the one that is translated acts as a Submit button.

So the next step is to modify the Web version of the form so that all of the push-buttons are displayed. The way to do this is to make a bitmap that looks exactly the same as the set of R3 buttons and then include this bitmap as a navigator in the Web version of the form. When viewed via a Web client, the bitmap looks just the same as the original R3 form.

The steps involved are listed as follows:

1. Use a Notes client to open the database you are migrating and display the R3 style form

2. Take a screen shot of the R3 style form

3. Paste the screen shot into your favorite graphics program

4. Select the part of the screen shot that contains the push-buttons and copy it to the clipboard

5. Create a new navigator in the database you are migrating

6. Paste the copied part of the screen shot into the new navigator as a Graphic Background

7. Save the new navigator

You now have a navigator that looks like a set of push-buttons. You still need to include this navigator in the Web version of your form as follows:

1. Open the Web version of your form in design mode
2. Delete the push-buttons that you used to create the navigator bitmap and replace them with a computed field called $$NavigatorBody
3. Set the value of the $$NavigatorBody computed field to the name of the navigator you just created

Now when this form is displayed on a Web client, the navigator is displayed at the position of the $$NavigatorBody field. You should now have a form that looks the same on the Web as it does in Notes.

All you need to do now is to add hotspots to the navigator to make the "buttons" work. There are several options available for how to do this. One technique that we used extensively during the migration was the automatic generation and use of Domino URLs. With this technique, you add a hotspot around a button and then use a formula to create and open an URL. For example, the following code opens the view with alias vSearchResults in the database SEARCH.NSF in the WEB directory on the Domino server with IP address 199.199.199.1.

```
tmpServerAddress := "199.199.199.1";
tmpDBAddress := "/WEB/SEARCH.NSF";
tmpTargetView := "vSearchResults";
URL := "http://" + tmpServerAddress + tmpDBAddress + "/"+ tmpTargetView +
"?OpenView";
@URLOpen(URL)
```

We used variations on this technique where the various components of the URL were either looked up from views or stored directly on the forms so that they were not hard-coded into the hotspot formulas.

Using View Templates

Another technique that we used extensively to give the intranet site a common look and feel was the use of view templates to make sure that all of the views displayed in a similar format on the Web. A view template is simply a form that you use to specify how a view should look when viewed using a Web client. You can supply a default view template that specifies the layout of every view or you can override this for individual views by supplying a separate view template for each view.

The Notes system we were migrating consisted of many databases that had been developed over several years by different designers and included a number of off-the-shelf applications. We wanted to find a way of making the many different views within these databases have a common look and feel on our intranet site. View templates solved our problem. We added a standard default view template form, $$ViewTemplateDefault, to each database that was to be part of the intranet site. In this way, we standardized the background colors and actions that were available for each view. A simple view template is shown in Figure 19.2.

Fig. 19.2

Use view templates to give your views a common look and feel.

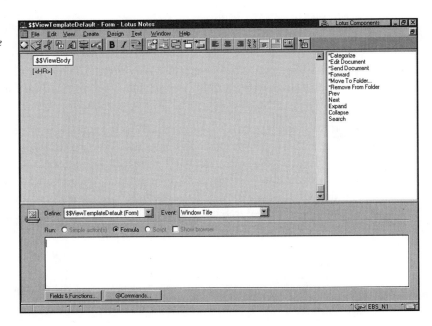

This is almost the world's simplest view template! It simply adds a horizontal rule below the view body and shows five standard action buttons at the top of the view. The $$ViewBody field indicates where the contents of the view should be displayed. The action buttons use a combination of standard @commands and special Domino commands to do their job. The view is expanded and collapsed using the standard [ViewExpandAll] and [ViewCollapseAll] @commands. To display different pages of the views, we used two of the new Domino @DBCommands. To display the previous view page, we used the following command:

```
@DbCommand("Domino";"ViewPreviousPage")
```

The next page is displayed using the following:

```
@DbCommand("Domino";"ViewNextPage")
```

It's easy to expand this technique to give your views a more "Web" feel such as including view background images and using tables to change the position of the view body. For example, if you put the $$ViewBody field inside a table, you can indent the view within a

Web page. This is useful if you want to show a graphic bar down the left side of your Web page and have the view start to the right of the bar.

By including graphics and common layout elements in the view template, you can make databases that look very different in Notes look very similar when viewed via a Web client. Again, remember that we didn't have the luxury of being able to redesign the R3 style user interfaces on our databases so this technique helped us to make our many different databases look more uniform and helped our intranet users by presenting them with a more common user interface.

Simulating a List Box

Several of the databases we migrated used prompt boxes to display lists of choices for the user. For example, one database contained a push-button that looked up a list of database names and locations (the server and file name for the database) and then presented the user with a prompt box containing the database names. When the user selected a database name, the appropriate database was located and opened. Our problem in trying to reproduce this for our intranet users was that Domino doesn't translate formulas containing the @Prompt function. To be fair, this is hardly surprising as Web clients don't natively support the display of prompt boxes. To get around the problem in the time available to us, we used the list of database names and locations to build a page of HTML on-the-fly. The HTML page displayed the list of database names and we used the list of locations to generate Domino URLs for each database. So as far as our intranet users were concerned, they clicked a button and got a list of database names; then when they clicked a database name, the appropriate database was opened. This works pretty much the way a prompt box works!

This is how it worked. We used the technique of using a navigator and a hotspot that we looked at earlier to find and display a document within the database. The form used to display this document contained a computed for display field with the following formula:

```
tmpServerAddress := "199.199.199.1";
tmpDBCategory := "Newswires";
tmpDBTitles := @DbLookup(""; ReferenceDBReplicaID; "vLookupKeywordsByCategory";
tmpDBCategory; 7);
tmpDBViews := @DbLookup(""; ReferenceDBReplicaID; "vLookupKeywordsByCategory";
tmpDBCategory; 6);
tmpDBNames := @DbLookup(""; ReferenceDBReplicaID; "vLookupKeywordsByCategory";
tmpDBCategory; 5);
tmpViews := @Implode(tmpDBViews; "#");
tmpViews2 := @ReplaceSubstring(tmpViews; " "; "+");
tmpViews3 := @Explode(tmpViews2; "#");
tmpURLs := "[<A HREF=http://" + tmpServerAddress + "/" + tmpDBNames + "/" +
tmpViews3 + "?OpenView>" + tmpDBTitles + "</A>]";
tmpURLs
```

19

The first line of the formula initializes the IP address of the Domino server. Line 2 specifies the category of database to include in the list of databases. The original Notes application grouped databases into several categories that the user could select. For the purposes of this example, we've hard-coded "Newswires" as a sample category. Lines 3, 4, and 5 of the formula use the category to look up the title, default view name, and file name of each database in the "Newswires" category from a reference database. Essentially what you get back are three lists: tmpDBTitles containing the list of the titles of the databases, tmpDBViews containing a list of the names or aliases of the views at which these databases should be opened, and tmpDBNames containing the full file names of each database. Lines 6, 7, and 8 convert the view names into the format required so that they can be used in a Domino URL. When you use a view name in a Domino URL, you have to replace any spaces in the view name with "+" characters. These three lines do this for you. Line 9 takes the three lists and converts the information in them into a set of URLs. For example, suppose there were two databases in the Newswire category, the first called Daily News, with file name DAILY.NSF to be opened at the view Hot Stories and the second called Company News, file name COMPANY.NSF to be opened at the All Documents view. Line 9 stores the following HTML in the tmpURLs variable:

```
[<A HREF=http://199.199.199.1/DAILY.NSF/Hot+Stories?OpenView>Daily News</A>]
[<A HREF=http://199.199.199.1/COMPANY.NSF/All+Documents?OpenView>Company News</A>]
```

Line 10 returns this HTML as the value of the computed field. When a document is displayed using this form via a Web client, the computed field is evaluated and the list of URLs is displayed. Clicking an URL opens the appropriate database at the specified view.

There is an extension to this technique that you may want to consider. Assuming that you have something similar to the reference database discussed earlier, you could include a graphic image in the reference information for each database. You could then modify the way that the list of URLs is built to include a reference to this graphic so your generated HTML page shows a set of graphic hotspots instead of text hotspots.

Customizing the Submit Message

In several of the Notes databases we were migrating, there were forms that contained a button that the user could click to save and close a document. In Notes, when the Save button was clicked, a prompt box was displayed thanking the users for their new document or their updates to an existing document. The users could click OK on the prompt box to close the document and return to the view from which the document was originally displayed. How do you reproduce this behavior for Web clients?

Well, Domino provides you with the $$Return field that you can customize to provide this behavior. When using a Web client to submit a form, if the form contains a $$Return field, its contents are evaluated and used to generate a page of HTML that is sent back to the Web client and displayed. If the form doesn't contain a $$Return field, you get Domino's standard "Form Processed" message. We used the $$Return field (and our extensive knowledge of writing one line JavaScript programs!) to simulate the way the R3 Notes user interface worked. We added a hidden computed $$Return field to those forms that needed to display the "thank you" message and set its formula to the following:

```
FirstName := @Left(@ProperCase(@Name([CN];@UserName));" ");
JavaProgram := "<SCRIPT LANGUAGE=\"JavaScript\">function GoBack(numpages){history.go(-
numpages);}</SCRIPT>";
Thanks:="";
REM;
REM "Message if user has created a new document";
REM "=====================================";
REM;
@If(@IsNewDoc;@Set("Thanks";"<TITLE>Contribution Submitted</TITLE><BODY
TEXT=\"000000\" BGCOLOR=\"80ff80\"><H2>Thank you for your contribution, "+
FirstName + "! </H2><HR><FORM><INPUT Type=Button Name=\"OK\" Value=\"OK\"
Onclick=\"GoBack(2);\">");"");
REM;
REM "Message if user has been editing an existing document and is allowed to edit
it.";
REM "==================================================================";
REM;
@If(!@IsNewDoc;@Set("Thanks"; "<TITLE>Contribution Submitted</TITLE><BODY
TEXT=\"000000\" BGCOLOR=\"80ff80\"><H2>Your edits have been submitted, "+
FirstName + "! </H2><HR><FORM><INPUT Type=Button Name=\"OK\" Value=\"OK\"
Onclick=\"GoBack(3);\">");"");
JavaProgram + Thanks
```

This generates the following HTML when new documents are submitted via a Web client:

```
<SCRIPT LANGUAGE="JavaScript">function GoBack(numpages){history.go(-
numpages);}</SCRIPT>
<TITLE>Contribution Submitted</TITLE>
<BODY TEXT="000000" BGCOLOR="80ff80">
<H2>Thank you for your contribution, Tim! </H2>
<HR>
<FORM>
<INPUT Type=Button Name="OK" Value="OK" Onclick="GoBack(2);">
```

and this HTML when existing documents are submitted:

```
<SCRIPT LANGUAGE="JavaScript">function GoBack(numpages){history.go(-
numpages);}</SCRIPT>
<TITLE>Contribution Submitted</TITLE>
<BODY TEXT="000000" BGCOLOR="80ff80">
<H2>Your edits have been submited, Tim! </H2>
<HR>
<FORM>
<INPUT Type=Button Name="OK" Value="OK" Onclick="GoBack(3);">
```

An example of the resulting Web page is shown in Figure 19.3.

19

Fig. 19.3

An example of using
$$Return to customize a
Web page.

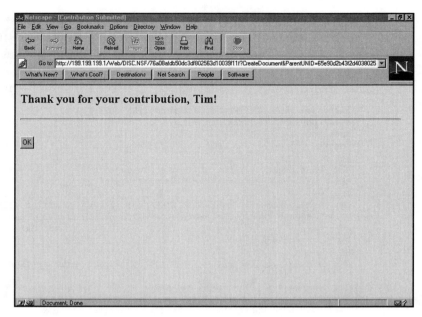

When the user clicks the OK button, the tiny JavaScript program is executed and this returns the user to the page displaying the view or document from which the document was originally opened. The JavaScript program does this using the Web client's history list to go back to the required number of pages. We used the <BGCOLOR> attribute of the <BODY> tag to change the color of the page that gets displayed to match the colors used throughout the rest of the site.

Customizing $$Return is a very powerful technique. For example, you could return a page of HTML that contains a navigation bar that the user can use to navigate to other parts of your site. Alternatively, you could use $$Return to automatically route a user to a specific page after they have submitted their form. The possibilities, if not endless, are sufficiently large to keep most Web developers happy!

Displaying Error Messages

In the Notes R3 client, when a user makes a data entry error, a nice friendly (well, usually friendly!) error message pops up in a prompt box. How do you reproduce this for Web clients? The answer is to use a similar technique to the $$Return field. In this case, you customize the Input Validation formula for the field you want to validate so that if an error occurs, a customized Web page is returned to the Web client. An example of the kind of code you may want to use follows:

```
PageHeader := "<TITLE>Input Validation Failed</TITLE><BODY TEXT=\"000000\"
BGCOLOR=\"80ff80\">";
JavaProgram := "<SCRIPT LANGUAGE=\"JavaScript\">function
GoBack(numpages){history.go(-numpages);}</SCRIPT>";
PageFooter := "<HR>";
Msg := "";
@If(Title = ""; @Failure(PageHeader + JavaProgram + "<H2>Please enter a
title<H2><FORM><INPUT Type=Button Name=\"OK\" Value=\"OK\"
Onclick=\"GoBack(1);\">" + PageFooter); @Success)
```

This code is similar to that used for the $$Return field in that it includes a tiny JavaScript program. The program displays an OK button that the user can click to confirm the error message and return to editing the document.

Using Subforms to Ensure a Consistent Look and Feel

As we began to migrate databases, we realized that we could use subforms in the Web versions of our forms to give them all a common look and feel. For example, to apply a common logo, background image, and layout to all of the Web versions of our forms, we created a simple subform that contained the required HTML. We then included this subform in all of the Web versions of our forms. In a similar way, we included a subform that provided a standard navigation bar that the Web client users could use to navigate around the intranet site. Whenever we needed to make changes to the navigation bar, we could simply update the subform and all of our Web pages would be automatically updated.

Using the Domino Configuration Database

You can keep HTML files, CGI scripts, and other related Web files in multiple locations or move them to new locations without breaking URL links or changing Server or Virtual Server documents.

Use the Mapping and Redirection forms in the Domino Configuration database to:

▶ Disguise the actual location of a directory and specify, read, or execute access to its files

▶ Map collections of URLs to a new location

▶ Redirect an URL to another URL

If you don't already have a Domino Web Server Configuration database, create one using the Domino Web Server Configuration template (domcfg.ntf). The database must be named domcfg.nsf.

Summary

In this chapter, we have described reasons to migrate Lotus Notes R3 applications to a Domino server, discussed migration planning, and covered various tips and techniques to help ensure a successful migration.

The migration project we described was a broad success, with minimal disruption and maximum impact. We achieved our goal of migrating the 12 complex linked front-end applications that in turn link to over 200 more applications used in 16 countries by 1,500 users. A content-rich corporate intranet was delivered in less than two months using two developers. The applications are now accessible by the growing population of Web clients and further initiatives are underway to extend these applications to the Internet and to develop potent intelligence-focused application on the Domino server platform.

The Lotus Notes development team was pleasantly surprised at how powerful the Domino server is and the impact it made within the organization. We were able to define, plan, and deliver a populated corporate intranet that serves the international Lotus Notes client and Web client population before the "official" intranet team was completely formed!

From Here...

Now that you are fired up and already dreaming of the glory you'll receive for solving your organization's intranet/Internet problems, you may want to take a closer look at the capabilities of Domino 4.5 application development.

For related information, see:

▶ Chapter 1, "An Introduction to Domino 4.5 and the Internet," for additional information on the Internet/intranet role of Domino.

▶ Chapter 3, "Working with Your Domino Web Site," to learn about the Domino directory structure, and about navigating with Domino URLs.

▶ Chapter 5, "Building a Web Database," for information on building a Web database from scratch.

▶ Chapter 20, "Preparing Existing Applications for the Web," for information on preparing Notes R4 applications for the Web.

Preparing Existing Applications for the Web

In this chapter

◆ **How various Notes elements respond when Domino converts Notes applications to Web applications**
We set forth which Notes elements, features, and functions won't translate well to the Web.

◆ **Which form and view properties are not supported on the Web**
We explain the changes needed in your Notes applications so that Web clients can use your databases.

◆ **How to hide information from Web or Notes clients**
Here, we examine a Hide-when formula, which determines whether a user is a Notes client or a Web client, and displays or hides information based on that determination.

◆ **How to handle the Launch options of the About Database document if you intend to use it as a site or home page on the Web**
Web databases may have different launch requirements than Notes databases. If you want to use the same database for both Web and Notes clients, we'll show you how to work around the launch options and we'll list those that won't work in Web databases.

What happens to Notes databases on the Web? In brief, Domino converts Notes views, forms and documents into HTML pages, which it then delivers to the Web client. If a Web client submits a form or query, the HTTP server task converts it to Notes format then submits it to the Notes database server, which processes it appropriately.

But not all design features, properties, elements, and functions of Notes databases apply to Web users; others, though applicable, do not translate to HTML. For example, HTML does not embody the concept of views, as Notes does. Web browsers don't have a Create menu populated with Notes forms, as Notes does. Therefore, to get Notes applications to work for a browser-based user the way they work for Notes-based users may require some re-design of the application.

You might think of Domino applications as falling into three categories: those that were designed for use only by Notes users, those that are designed only for use by Web users, and hybrids, intended for use by both Notes and Web users. Each type of application has its own design considerations. Our concern here is how to turn applications from type one to type two; that is, how to modify applications designed for Notes users so that they can be used by Web users as well.

First we will examine the Notes design elements that will either not convert to HTML at all or will function differently for a Web user than for a Notes user. Then we'll walk you through the steps you need to take for each existing Notes application that Domino will serve to Web clients.

Understanding Notes Databases and the Domino Conversion

Before you can determine how best (if at all) to modify your current applications or how to plan new applications, you must know what Notes database features will work on the Web and which will not.

Table 20.1 lists how Notes elements are handled by the HTTP server.

Table 20.1   How Notes Elements are Handled by the HTTP Server

Notes Element	Remarks
@Commands	Some are supported. Used to allow Web clients to create, edit, and delete documents, access views, and so forth. Most @Commands permit programmatic manipulation of the Notes menu interface and therefore are not relevant to a browser environment and are not translated when Domino translates a document containing them to HTML.
@Functions	Supported with exceptions.
Forms	Notes forms and HTML forms are not analogous to each

Notes Element	Remarks
	other. Notes forms are the templates that define what data appears or can be entered and how it looks when you create, edit, or read a Notes document. HTML forms are data input sections of HTML documents. Notes forms do get translated into HTML forms when you open them in a browser. Either the Web user must open a Notes form by entering its name in a URL or the Notes application developer must provide access to forms through Form or View Actions or through hotspot links in Notes forms.
Actions	Both view and form actions that use @functions and @commands are supported. Default actions, simple actions, and actions that use LotusScript are not supported.
Attachments	Supported. Attachments appearing in Notes documents appear and function fully in the HTML versions of those documents without any intervention on the part of the developer. A special field is required to allow attaching documents *from* Web clients.
Graphics	Supported. Domino converts graphics that appear in Notes documents to GIF or JPEG format so that Web users can view them.
Buttons	Not supported. The first button that appears on a form becomes the Submit button on the Web and can be customized. Subsequently appearing buttons disappear entirely from the translated Web form.
Database, View, and Document Links	Supported.
Hotspots	Supported, except for Pop-Up Hotspots.
Layout Regions	Not supported. Use tables to align form elements
Tables	Supported with some limitations imposed by HTML. Use tables to align form elements.
Collapsible sections	Supported.
OLE and OCX Objects	Supported for Windows NT and Windows 95. Savings edits to objects is not supported.
ActiveX objects	Supported for Windows NT and Windows 95. Note: Saving

20

continues

Table 20.1   Continued

Notes Element	Remarks
	edits to objects is not supported.
Hide When attributes	Supported.
Subforms and shared	Supported. They do, however, slow down the conversion of fields documents into HTML format.
Views	Supported. Views become HTML documents in which each document listed in the original view is listed in the HTML view document, along with a link to the Notes document.
Folders	Supported. However, Web clients cannot move documents to folders.
Collapsible Views	Supported.
Searches	Supported, but databases must be full-text indexed to be searchable. Domino also supports multi-database searches with the Site Search feature.
Calendar Views	Supported. They become HTML tables and are subject to the limitations of HTML tables.
Calendar and Time Controls	The Calendar Control in a Calendar view in Calendar Views translates to the Web version of the view, but Layout Regions do not function the same there as in Notes. Calendar and Time controls in Layout Regions are not supported, because Layout Regions themselves do not translate to HTML.
Graphical Navigators	Domino converts Graphical Navigators to image maps. Only graphic backgrounds, rectangular hotspots, and polygon hotspots translate to HTML. All other elements of Graphical Navigators are discarded on translation to HTML.
Agents	Agents that run on the Domino server are supported. Agents with the run option "If Document Has Been Pasted" or document selection option "Selected Documents" are not supported. Web users can activate agents that are activated by an action.
About Database document	Can be designated as a site or database home page.

Understanding Document Conversion

Lotus Notes and HTML arose from two unrelated groups of developers who had somewhat different goals in mind. As a result, there are fundamental incompatibilities between them that affect the way Notes documents will translate to HTML. Notes is a closed, proprietary system. Lotus has full control over the features that each version of Notes will support. HTML, on the other hand, is an open standard. Its creators had no control over who would use it, how, or on what platforms, and they never intended to exert such control.

Because of this fact, HTML cannot dictate how documents would appear on your computer in the same way that Notes or other proprietary systems can. For example, one person might want to view an HTML document on a computer that can display thousands of colors, hundreds of typefaces, text in any size, and formatting of all kinds. Another user might want to view that same HTML document on a monochrome dumb terminal that displays only one font in one size with choices of bold and underlining for emphasis.

Lotus can simply dictate that Notes won't run in such an environment and be done with it. HTML is expected to work in both these environments and on any hardware platform that you can cobble up. As a result, HTML documents typically don't do things like dictate typeface, type size, or methods of displaying emphasis.

Here are some of the principal ways your Notes documents may change when translated to HTML:

> ▶ **Font size.** Because the creator of an HTML document probably doesn't know what size fonts a given reader's computer can display, HTML doesn't normally dictate font size. Rather, it dictates that text can be of heading type <H1>, <H2>, and so on. The reader's browser can then treat the designated text however it can. One browser might make <H1> 8 points in size and <H2> 10 points in size, where another browser might not differentiate between them at all. Notes maps text sizes to HTML heading tags according to this table:
>
> | Point size in Notes | HTTP Heading Tag |
> | --- | --- |
> | 8 or less | <H1> |
> | 10 or less | <H2> |
> | 12 or less | <H3> |
> | 14 or less | <H4> |
> | 18 or less | <H5> |
> | 24 or less | <H6> |
> | over 24 | <H7> |

20

▶ **Typeface.** Standard (non-proprietary) HTML recognizes one proportional font and one non-proportional font. The browser determines which typeface will actually be used for each purpose. All Notes fonts get translated to HTML's proportional font except one. The default non-proportional font for the system on which Notes runs gets translated to HTML's non-proportional font (the HTML tag is <TT>). In Windows and OS/2 systems, that would be the Courier typeface.

▶ **Horizontal spacing.** Due to limitations in the way HTML formats text, white space inserted into a line of text either with tab characters or extra space characters will usually be closed up so that only one space character remains. As a result, any documents in which the elements (fields, graphics, hotspots, and so forth) are aligned on the screen with inserted tabs or spaces will lose their alignment when converted to HTML. Also, paragraph with indentation inserted either with tabs or by moving the markers on the Notes ruler, will translate to HTML as left-aligned paragraphs. The only exception to this behavior is text formatted with the system default monospace font (Courier on Windows systems). Text created in this font retains extra space characters inserted between words, but not tab characters. To align elements on a page in such a way that they retain their alignment when translated to HTML, either use tables to align the elements or use Courier and space characters.

▶ **Interline spacing**. All interline spacing gets converted in HTML to single spacing. Inter-paragraph spacing, on the other hand, is preserved in translation.

▶ **Tables**. Table borders are uniform in HTML. That is, all borders of all cells are the same. No variation allowed. The border style of the top left cell of a Notes table is the style used in the resulting HTML table.

▶ **Buttons**. Buttons in documents disappear entirely from HTML documents in read mode. A document in edit mode displays only the first button on the form, and HTML ignores the button's original programming but uses it instead as the trigger that submits a completed form back to the server.

Understanding Notes Forms versus Web Forms

Notes Forms provide the structure in Notes applications for entering and displaying data. They are the windows through which Notes users see the fields of a document in order to view the data in the database. They are also the document templates, which determine how documents will look when viewed. Notes Forms determine which fields will appear to the user. Notes Forms can contain fields, shared fields, static text, graphics, hotspots, buttons, layout regions, and subforms. Not all of these elements, of course, are supported in translation to HTML.

Web forms are not analogous to Notes forms. A Web form is a portion of an HTML document, set off by <FORM>...</FORM> tags, in which appear data input tags (<INPUT>, <TEXTAREA>, and <SELECT>) that appear as data input fields in a Web browser. Web forms always have an associated button—the Submit button—that, when you click it, sends the entered data back to the Web server that sent the HTML document. There may be more than one <FORM>...</FORM> section in a given HTML document. Each one would have its own associated Submit button and is effectively a separate input form from the other <FORM>...</FORM> sections. Clicking the Submit button for a given <FORM>...</FORM> section would submit only the data entered into its own data input fields.

When Domino sends a Notes form to a Web client, Domino translates the Notes form into a <FORM>...</FORM> section in an HTML document. However, not all characteristics or properties of Notes forms apply to Web users and some are not supported on the Web. Such properties will disappear from the Web version of the form. Table 20.2 lists those form properties that are not supported on the Web. The column labeled *Tabbed Page Title* refers to the tabbed pages in the properties box. Figure 20.1 shows a Form Properties box with its tabbed pages.

Fig. 20.1

Not all Form Properties will convert to or function properly on the Web. In retrofitting existing Notes apps, check the properties box for items in Table 20.1. You may want to make changes.

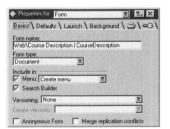

Table 20.2   Form Properties Not Supported On the Web

Tabbed Page Title	Item Not Supported	Remarks
Basics	Merge replication conflicts	Not applicable. Database replication does not take place between Domino and Web clients.
Basics	Version Control	
Basics	Anonymous forms	

continues

Table 20.2   Continued

Tabbed Page Title	Item Not Supported	Remarks
Defaults	Automatically refresh fields	
Defaults	Disable field exchange	
Defaults	On Create: Formulas inherit values from selected documents	HTML provides no way to select a document in a view, because HTML really doesn't support views at all. Therefore, field inheritance only works in a Web browser if you create a new document while the document to be inherited from is open.
Defaults	On Create: Inherit entire document into rich text field	
Defaults	On Open: Show context pane	
Defaults	Store form in document This is supported	Caution: do not store forms in documents that will be created *in read mode only* or edited on the Web.
Defaults	On Close: Present mail send dialog	Not supported.
Launch	Autolaunch options	Not supported.
Security	Default encryption keys	Doesn't apply to Web clients. The contents of encrypted fields are displayed unencrypted to Web clients.
Security	Disable printing, forwarding, and copying from clipboard	

Understanding Fields

Fields store data and determine what information is contained on a document. A field is defined by five elements: its name, its data type, an attribute that defines whether it is computed or editable, its display options, and formulas or scripts that determine its value or contents and appearance.

Not all field properties apply to Web clients and users. Those that do not are not ignored by Domino when translating to HTML. Table 20.3 lists field properties not supported on the Web.

Table 20.3   Field Properties Not Supported On the Web

Tabbed Page Title	Item Not Supported	Remarks
Basics	Compute after validation	
Options	Field Help	
Options	Security Options: Field Level encryption	Does not apply to Web clients.
Options	Give this field default focus	
Options	Signed fields	A pretty funny sitcom, but does not apply to Web clients.

For more information on fields, see Chapter 6, "Designing Forms To Display Documents on the Web."

Understanding Views and Folders

Views and folders are lists of Notes documents. They provide a method for accessing documents in a database. Views use selection formulas to determine what documents will appear in them. Their contents are, in other words, predetermined by the designer of the view. Folders work like views in every way except one—their contents are not determined by selection formulas but rather by the user (or by agents) on an ad hoc basis. The user (or agent) moves or copies documents into folders.

HTML supports nothing analogous to Notes views or the Notes notion of selecting documents in views. Domino therefore converts each Notes view to an HTML document consisting of a list of links to the documents in the view.

View and Folder properties that are *not* supported or are not applicable to Web users include:

▶ *On Open* options. These options are an outgrowth of Notes's ability to select a document in a view, which is not supported by HTML.

▶ *On Refresh* options.

▶ *Show in View menu.* Neither Notes menus nor their entries export to browsers.

▶ Style options for Unread rows, Show Selection margin, Alternate row colors.

▶ Beveled column headings.

▶ Moving or adding documents to folders. Web users cannot do it.

View columns and rows perform the same for Web clients as for Notes clients with a few exceptions. You need to tweak the setting for multi-line column headings and multi-line rows. Some HTML intervention is needed to prevent or allow word wrap. This is accomplished by specifying "1" in the View Properties box, under *Lines per heading* or *Lines per row*, to prevent word wrap. Domino translates and converts this to a NOWRAP HTML attribute. Any number greater than "1" causes lines to wrap on the Web.

Column properties that are *not* supported in views designed for Web clients are:

▶ Click column header to sort

▶ Resizable column

▶ "Show Twisties" when row is expandable. Twisties can't be hidden on the Web.

The default "home page" for a new, unconfigured Domino Web server is no home page at all—that is, just a list of all databases on the server at the time the Web browser hits your site. This list contains all databases whose properties include the selection *List in 'Open Database' dialog* on the Design tab of the Database Properties box. The list is the equivalent of what a Notes client would see when choosing File, Database, Open from the menu. The instructions provided for Domino to generate this view are located in the Server Document in the Default Home Page field of the Basics section located under HTTP Server. Figure 20.2 shows the default view.

When you select a database from this list, Domino typically serves up a list of available views and folders in the database. This would not include any views or folders from which Anonymous users have been excluded in the security panel of the View Properties box. See the example in Figure 20.3.

You will undoubtedly want browser clients to see a more inviting Home page when visiting your site, and changing the value of the Default Home page field to the file name of a home page HTML file or to a Notes database that contains an About page or a graphical navigator designed to work as a home page would give you the desired results.

Fig. 20.2

The default "home page" of a Web site as generated by Domino. This list contains all databases whose properties include the selection "List in 'Open Database' dialog."

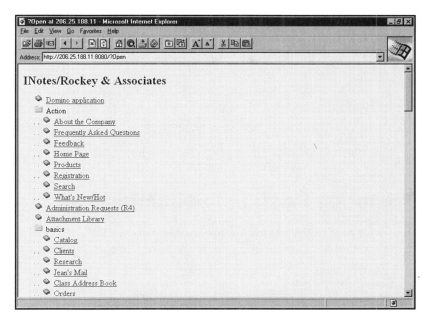

Fig. 20.3

By default, Domino delivers a list of all available views in a database, complete with hypertext links to each view.

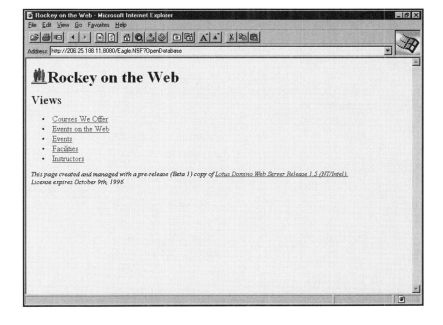

However, Web clients can still access a list of databases on your Domino server by using the Domino URL command ?open. There are two ways that you can limit Web users' access to the list of database on your server. First, you can hide an individual database from the list by deselecting "List in 'Open Database' dialog" on the properties box of that database. Second, you can prevent Web users entirely from retrieving a list of databases on your server by setting to "No" the field *Allow HTTP clients to browse databases* in the Security section of the Server document.

Refer to Chapter 14, "Securing the Domino Server," for information on securing your site.

Preparing Existing Applications

If your Notes application is free of any of the design features or elements that we've pointed out as potential problems on the Web, there is still work for you to do before you make it available to Web users.

Use the following checklist to ensure that Web Clients can:

▶ Access your database

▶ Navigate through your database

▶ Create, edit and delete documents (optional)

▶ Search your database

Table 20.4   Web Compatibility Check List

Item	Considerations	Actions
ACL	What degree of access to you want anonymous Web users to have? What degree do you want registered Web users to have?	Add Anonymous to the ACL and set its access rights. See Chapter 14, "Securing the Domino Web Server." Add WebClients to the ACL and set its access rights.
Database Properties	How are the Launch options set? Do they serve the Web client?	

Item	Considerations	Actions
Views	Are there icons in a column formula? Are all views applicable to Web clients?	Replace icons with GIFs. See Chapter 8. Create new views for web clients and/or restrict views through access control. See Chapter 8.
Forms	Should fields or areas of forms be hidden? Are form elements built inside of tables?	Use hide when formulas or computed subforms. Convert the form to tables to retain horizontal placement of elements when converted to HTML. See Chapter 6.
	Will you want Web clients to be able to fill out a form? How will they access it?	Use Actions and Action Hotspots to provide links to forms, views, and home page on your forms. See Chapters 6 and 8.
Navigators	Are Navigators created using graphic backgrounds?	Only graphic backgrounds, hotspot rectangles, and hotspot polygons will become part of the resulting HTML image map. If any other types of objects appear in your Navigator, redesign the Navigator to eliminate them.
Links	Do all Doc Links, view links and database links point to databases stored on the Domino Web server?	Change to launch options, consider launching About database document.
Index	Do Web clients need to search this database?	Full Text Index the database. Domino will take care of adding a search bar for the Web client.
Replication	Will the entire database reside on the Domino Web server, or just a replication subset?	

20

Examining the Database ACL

Make sure that the Default setting in the database Access Control List is appropriate for the database. As a general rule of thumb, default access should be No Access, unless you have a reason for setting it higher. If nobody ever paid attention to the ACL of a given database, Default access might be as high as Designer. You probably do not want to leave it that high.

Add an Anonymous setting if it doesn't already appear in the ACL. If Anonymous appears in the ACL, then all unauthenticated Web users will have the degree of database access set for Anonymous. If Anonymous does not appear in the ACL, then all unauthenticated Web users will have Default access to the database. The rule of thumb here is that, for databases in which Web users will not be adding, editing, or deleting documents, Anonymous should have Reader access to the database. For databases in which they *will* be adding, editing, or deleting documents, Anonymous should have Author access. Your circumstances might warrant higher access for a given database.

If you will be registering Web users and therefore allowing them to authenticate, so that the Domino server knows their identities, you should make sure the database ACL accommodates authenticated Web users in some way. Anonymous will no longer cover a Web user after he/she authenticates. The best way to handle authenticated Web users is to include their names in one or more Public Address Book groups, and to include the groups in the database ACL, assigned the appropriate level of database access.

Remember that, in the Advanced panel of the database Access Control List, Maximum Internet browser access is set to Editor. This means that under no circumstances will a Web user have higher access than that to the database in question, even if the user is personally identified with higher access in the database ACL. This is not really much of an issue, because there is not much in the nature of database design or access control that one can do from a Web browser. Nonetheless, you need to be aware of this limitation and the necessity to change it should you desire to give a Web user higher than Editor access, or should you wish to set the maximum possible browser access lower than Editor.

Using Database Launch Options

Notes provides many design options that trigger events when users open or access a database. Those options are found in the database Properties box, in the Launch panel in the dropdown list located under "On Database Open." Figure 20.4 displays the Launch options upon opening a database.

Fig. 20.4

Here are the Launch Options for database open. The About Database document can serve as the site or database "Home Page."

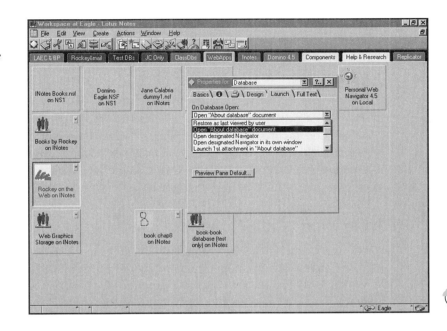

In Notes databases intended for Notes clients, the About Database document tells the user the purpose of the database, who to contact for support, and might even include a little about how to use the database (unless the instructions are long, in which case the *Using this Database* document is utilized). The database properties are usually set to launch this document the first time that a Notes client accesses the database. Thereafter, the About Database document is accessed through the Help menu and hardly anyone ever looks at it again.

In Notes databases intended for Web clients, the About Database document can be utilized as the database home page or site home page. Because it is virtually one large rich text field, the About Database Document can contain graphics, formatted text, HTML tags, URLs, links, Java applets, and anything else that can be placed in a rich text field. No fields can be placed on the About Database Document (it's not a form) but pointers can direct Web clients to views, documents, databases, or even other Web sites. If you decide to use the About Database document as a site or database home page, you must set the database Launch property to Launch "About Database" document. (Alternatively, you can set the Launch property to Launch 1st doclink in "About Database," then embed a doclink to any document on the same server. In this way you could use a document other than an About Database document as your home page.) Thereafter, both Notes and Web clients will always see this document first when opening the database.

To assign the About Database Document as the site home page, you need to identify it as such in the Server Document. Open the Domino server document and enter the file name of the database in the Home URL field. For more information on the Server Document, and configuring the Domino Web site, see Chapter 14, "Securing a Domino Server."

In Notes databases intended for both Notes and Web clients you don't want the About Database document to Launch on opening the database. Notes users will become quite unhappy if they have to view an About Database document littered with HTML tags every time they open the database. Create a new database for the sole (or at least primary) purpose of hosting the site home page for Web clients.

Applying Hide When Formulas

You control which fields and paragraphs are accessible to Notes users through form design and Hide when formulas. The same theory and practice applies to Notes databases intended for Web clients. In databases intended for both Notes and Web clients, you can hide information based on a formula that uses @Userroles to tell whether a user is a Notes user or a Web user. Some fields or information will apply to Web clients, others to Notes clients.

Hide-when formulas, which identify the User roles occupied by the current user, allow you to display information to Web or Notes clients only. The following Hide-when formulas can be used for paragraphs and fields:

```
!@Contains ( UserRoles ; "$$WebClient" )
```

resolves to true if the current user is not a Web client. Therefore, Notes clients cannot see the field or paragraph. Conversely,

```
@Contains ( UserRoles ; "$$WebClient" )
```

resolves to true if the current client *is* a Web client. Therefore, Web clients cannot see the field or paragraph.

Place these Hide-when formulas in the field or text properties box. Figure 20.5 displays the text properties box with a hide-when formula.For more information on forms, see Chapter 6, "Designing Forms to Display Documents on the Web."

Fig. 20.5

The text properties box. This formula hides information from Web clients. Place this formula in the field properties box to hide only the paragraph containing the field, or in a text properties box to hide one or more paragraphs at a time.

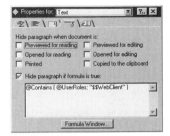

Providing Links to Forms and Views

The vast majority of links on a Domino server are created automatically. You only have to create a few of them yourself. If you replace the default home page, you have to add links to your home page by hand. You may also want to add links to other Web sites. You may want to put links in documents that shortcut you back to a view or a home page. Occasionally, you might want to set up a special relationship between two otherwise unlinked documents.

Most of the links you have to create by hand you will do with Notes linking techniques. Some—mostly to pages at other Web sites—you will do with HTML linking techniques. The linking techniques that Domino recognizes include the following:

▶ Notes document, view, and database links

▶ Link hotspots

▶ URL Link hotspots

▶ Action hotspots

▶ Actions on action bars

▶ Passthru HTML

The question arises: When should you choose one type of link instead of another? Here are some rules of thumb:

▶ Use links that Notes maintains whenever possible. These include document, view, and database links, and link hotspots. When you use URL Link hotspots, Passthru HTML, or an action bar action or action hotspot with @URLOpen, you enter a static URL. Notes cannot automatically update the URL if the address of the resource that it points to changes; you have to change it manually.

▶ Use link hotspots, URL link hotspots, and action hotspots when you want static text or a pasted graphic to appear as a link.

▶ Use action bar buttons when you want a link to appear as a "button" at the top of a document or view.

▶ You can only use Actions in forms and views. You can only use Action Hotspots in forms. You can use links of all kinds on forms and in rich text fields of documents. You can use pass-through HTML as static text in forms or in text fields or rich text fields in documents. For more on links, see Chapter 5, "Building a Web Database."

Implementing Selective Replication

You may have databases that Notes users use and which you would like to share only partially with Web users. For example, we have a database that includes information about computer classes that we offer, and we would like to make that information public by putting it on our Web site. However, the database in question also includes information that we don't want to publicize, such as the identities of people who have already signed up for the classes. (Wouldn't our competitors just love to get a hold of that information! "Hi, this is Acme Computer Training. We have a special on Notes training this week and you can sign up *now* for only [x amount, less 10%]. How about it?" "Duh, okay.")

You could deal with this situation in a couple different ways. One way would be to copy or mail (probably by agent) only the relevant documents from the in-house database to another, Web-accessible database. Another way would be to replicate only the relevant documents to the Web-accessible Domino server.

The problem with the first solution is that, every time someone edits an existing document in the in-house database, a new copy gets pasted/mailed to the Web database. That database, over time, accumulates near-duplicate copies of documents that describe the same class. To keep Web users from going nutty trying to figure out what classes are really being offered and when and where, you have to delete the older versions of the documents as the newer ones arrive. You could write an agent to take care of this, and if you have a little time on your hands and you are looking for excuses to write interesting agents, this would be a nice opportunity.

But the second way—replicating a subset of documents to the Web server—would be a lot easier to implement up front and wouldn't require any ongoing maintenance. What you do is set up a replication formula in the Web server's copy of the database. You can do this as follows:

1. If it doesn't already exist there, make a new replica copy of the database in question on the Web server. You can do this while sitting at either server or, if you have

Designer access to the database, user access to both servers, and the right to create replica databases on the destination server, while sitting at your own workstation. Make sure the destination server has at least Reader access to the database and the source server has at least Designer access to the database. Select the icon of the source database on the Notes desktop. Then choose File, Replication, New Replica in the Notes menu. The New Replica dialog box appears. Fill it in and click OK. While filling in the New Replica dialog box, you can click the Replication settings button to complete step two, if you want.

2. On the Web server, either during or after the process of creating the new replica (but preferably during), open the Replication Settings dialog box for the database in question. If you are in the process of making the new replica (Step 1, above), you can click the Replication settings button in the New Replica dialog box. If you have already created the new replica, you can open the Replication Settings dialog box in several ways, including:

   ▶ Right-click the new replica database's icon on the desktop to pop-up its menu, then choose Replication Settings.

   ▶ In the Notes menu, choose File, Replication, Settings.

   ▶ In the Database Properties box, on the Basics panel, click the Replication Settings button.

3. In the Replication Settings dialog box, put a checkmark in the Replicate a subset of documents checkbox. You can do this in either the Space Savers panel or the Advanced panel.

4. Choose a subset of documents to replicate. Use one of the two following methods:

   ▶ If the database is designed such that one or more views or folders holds all the documents that you want to replicate and, at the same time, none of the documents you do not want to replicate, then you can simply select the appropriate view(s) and/or folder(s) in the list that appears below the Replicate a subset of documents checkbox (see Figure 20.6).

   If you cannot select an appropriate subset of documents by choosing views and/or folders, then put another checkmark, this time in the Select by formula checkbox, and write a formula that describes exactly which documents you want to replicate (see Figure 20.7).

   In Figure 20.7, we have used a selection formula that selects only documents in which the Form field is set equal to Class and the ClassType field is set equal to Open Class. We did this because there were no views or folders that held this set of documents and no others.

5. When finished defining a replication subset, click OK and run a test replication to

20

Fig. 20.6

Here we have limited replication so only documents that appear in the Events\By Week view will be accepted by the Web server.

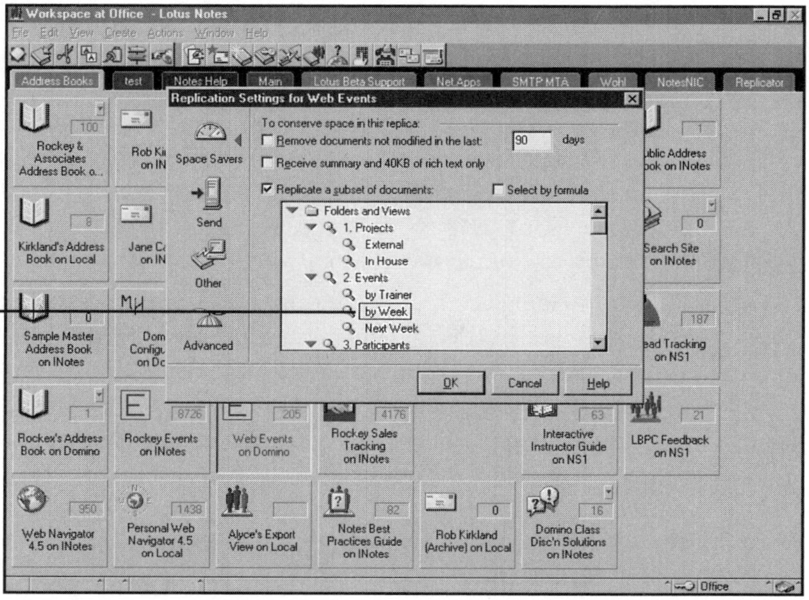

Selected view has box around it

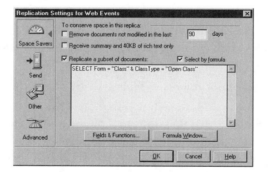

Fig. 20.7

Here we have used a selection formula to identify the documents to replicate. All selection formulas begin with the keyword SELECT.

ensure that you really do replicate only the documents that you want.

From this point forward, only the documents that you want Web users to see will appear in the Web server's copy of this database. Whenever anyone in the office adds, edits, or deletes one of these documents from the office's Domino server, replication will automatically update the copy on the Web-accessible server. If Web users have only Reader access to this database, you might define the Web server itself as having only Reader access. That way, no changes in the database can work their way from the Web server to the Office server.

If Web users have Author access to the database—say, for example, to submit inquiries about a class offering—you could design the input forms so that they mail into a database on the Office server instead of being saved into the class offerings database and replicating back to the Office server. That way you could still set up the Web server to have only Reader access to the office server's replica of the database.

From Here...

You might want to apply more features and formatting to your database to give it less of a "Notes" look, more of a "Web look." You can add HTML code, create a Home page for each database using the About Database document or a Navigator, or design subforms that act as site Navigators.

For related information, see the following chapters:

▶ Chapter 2, "Setting Up the Domino Server," discusses the default settings for the HTTP server, and explains what a Web client will see upon visiting your site should you accept the default HTTP Server settings.

▶ Chapter 5, "Building a Web Database," demonstrates the creation of a Home page and details information on linking the Web site. In this chapter, you learn about using Navigators as image maps.

▶ Chapter 6, "Designing Forms to Display Documents on the Web," describes the use of subforms, how to place attachments in forms, and how to create form backgrounds.

▶ Chapter 7, "Designing Forms for an Interactive Web Site," details the creation of use of input forms for Web users.

▶ Chapter 10, "Using Special Web Fields and Forms," shows how to customize the look of templates used by Domino.

20

Implementing and Using Domino's Other Internet Services

## chapter 21

Domino Server Internet Mail Features

In this chapter

◆ **How Internet Mail works**
Here, we offer a short history of Internet mail and how it works.

◆ **How the Notes and Internet mail systems interface with each other**
Here we describe how the SMTP/MIME MTA transports Notes and Internet mail.

◆ **About the Lotus SMTP/MIME MTA**
An SMTP/MIME MTA comes with Domino 4.5, enabling you to send and receive Internet mail through your Domino server. In this chapter, we show you how to configure this gateway.

◆ **About the Lotus POP3 mail server**
Learn how the POP3 server works and how to set up and configure Domino server as a POP3 mail server.

D omino 4.5 is all about connectivity. It is about connectivity among Notes users, of course. But more than any previous version of Notes, Domino 4.5 is about connectivity between Notes users and the Internet. The main thrust has been the integration of HTTP services into the Domino server. Another important thrust has been the incorporation of HTTP browser services into the Notes client. Yet a third thrust, and the subject of this chapter, has been the incorporation of Internet mail connectivity into the Domino server.

While for years Notes users have had Internet mail gateways available to them, Notes itself has always been a completely insular, proprietary mail system, internally unaware of other mail systems. With the release of Notes 4.0, this began to change as Notes began to support Internet-style addressing.

That is, if you address a Notes message to joe_doaks@xyz.com, Notes will recognize this as an Internet address and, if you have set up a Lotus SMTP/MIME MTA on one or more of your Domino servers, the Domino Router will attempt to send this message to the addressee named.

Prior to Release 4.0, Notes would not have recognized such an address. You would have had to set up a Foreign Domain (perhaps called Internet) to which to route all Internet mail, and you would have had to address all Internet mail to route via that domain, by addressing it like this: **joe_doaks@xyz.com@Internet**. This was a potentially awkward barrier to the use of any Internet gateway, either by Notes users or by Internet mail users, as our own experience illustrates. For several years we have had a gateway between our Notes domain and the Internet, provided to us by CompuServe. However, many of my colleagues either can't effectively use it or refuse to try to use it. Part of the problem is that they can't remember how to address mail to get it out the gateway, because the address is so long:

jdoaks@xyz.com@internet@compuserve

Now, that's not so long, but it is four parts, and some people have a hard time remembering it, or remembering the proper order of the parts. Another aspect of the problem is that, if my colleagues have to recite their Internet e-mail address to a correspondent, they get embarrassed about halfway through the recitation, and the person they are reciting it to begins to giggle:

jdoaks.rockey_&_associates@notesgw.compuserve.com

That's how you address Internet mail to our fictitious colleague, Joe Doaks. To fit this on our business cards, we had to print it so small that only our youngest clients can read it without a magnifying glass.

The point is that, with Notes Release 3.x, we could set up an Internet mail gateway, but it was sort of painful to use, because the addresses were sort of tortured. Domino 4.5 gives us a much less painful way to connect to the Internet. Beginning with Domino 4.5, Lotus now includes the SMTP/MIME MTA as part of every Domino server that ships, and includes as well a POP3 mail server. As a result, now you can set up any Domino server to transfer mail back and forth between Notes mail users and Internet mail users, using standard, two-part Internet addresses. Domino servers can now also transfer Notes mail across the Internet, transfer Internet mail across Notes domains, and act as mail drops for Internet mail users.

Overview of the Internet Mail Landscape

E-mail was one of the earliest features of the Internet. The standard of Internet mail by which we all now live, the Simple Mail Transfer Protocol or, more commonly, SMTP, came into being in 1982, and is set forth in two Requests for Comment: RFC821 and RFC822. RFC821 describes the transport method. RFC822 describes the internal structure of SMTP messages.

As originally constituted and as still constituted today (because SMTP has never been redefined or extended), SMTP provides only for the transfer of ASCII text messages. That is, each character must be no more than 7-bits wide and each line can be no longer than 1,000 characters. Of course, modern e-mail systems allow us to transfer not just ASCII text but formatted text, attached files, and all sorts of goodies. If you want to transfer anything other than ASCII text as part of your SMTP message, you have to convert it to ASCII text, transfer it, then convert it back to its original format. Over the years, correspondents have come up with a variety of ways of transferring non-ASCII information to one another in their SMTP correspondence.

One widely accepted and de facto standard way of accomplishing this is with a pair of programs called uuencode/uudecode. "uu" here stands for "user-to-user." uuencode takes non-ASCII data and converts it to ASCII. uudecode reconverts the data from ASCII back to its original format. So if I want to send you a graphics image, say, or a word processed file, I convert it to ASCII with uuencode, then send it to you via SMTP. Upon receipt, you uudecode it, converting it back to its original format, then open it in whatever program can interpret the particular file format it's in.

21

In 1993, the Internet community adopted a new and standard way of transporting non-ASCII material within the SMTP message format. Known as the Multipurpose Internet Mail Extensions, or just MIME, the standard has been widely adopted. It is described in RFC1521 and RFC1522 (as well as in several earlier RFCs). The MIME protocol is an extension of the SMTP protocol and basically describes standard methods of ordering information in the bodies of RFC822 messages. That is, RFC822 didn't bother to specify a standard way of formatting the body of an e-mail message, other than to require that messages be transmittable as 7-bit ASCII. MIME provides standard procedures for accomplishing several standard sorts of things:

▸ Formatting multipart messages.

▸ Formatting messages in non-ASCII character sets, including double-byte character sets such as Japanese, Chinese, and Korean.

▸ Converting files from any format to ASCII, attaching the ASCII version, along with header information describing the original format of the file, to an SMTP message, then reconverting the information back into its original format.

Among other things, MIME describes a series of header fields that must appear preceding a block of information in a message file. The first header field, the MIME-version header field, looks like this:

```
MIME-version: 1.0
```

It tells the reader that the message complies with RFC1521 and RFC1522.

MIME also describes the content-type header field, which would follow the MIME-version header field. The Content-type header field describes which of seven standard "content-types," and for each content-type, which of numerous possible subtypes, the block of data is that follows the content-type header field in question. The seven content-types and some of their principal subtypes, as defined in RFC1521, are as follows:

▶ **Text**—primarily textual data. Standard subtypes include *plain* and *richtext*.

▶ **Multipart**—data consisting of multiple parts, each of independent data type. Subtypes include *mixed, alternative, parallel,* and *digest*.

▶ **Message**—an encapsulated e-mail message. The primary subtype is *rfc822*.

▶ **Image**—pictures. Initial subtypes are *GIF* and *JPEG*.

▶ **Audio**—sound files. Initial subtype is *basic*.

▶ **Video**—moving pictures, with or without sound. Initial subtype is *MPEG*.

▶ **Application**—any other kind of data, typically uninterpreted binary data, which includes compiled programs. The primary subtype, *octet-stream*, is uninterpreted binary data. Another familiar subtype is *PostScript*.

Subtypes can be further differentiated with "parameters." For example, data of type text/plain might use the US-ASCII character set. A Content-type parameter sets forth that fact.

The Content-type header field is formatted as follows: Type/Subtype. For example, "Content-type: Text/plain; charset=us-ascii" is the standard designation of a standard RFC822 e-mail message.

MIME also describes the Content-Transfer-Encoding Header field. This field tells the reader how the following block of data is encoded (if at all). The field appears in the format:

```
Content-Transfer-Encoding: mechanism
```

Where *mechanism* is one of five defined methods of representing the data or a sixth, undefined method known as x-token. The six mechanisms are:

▶ **7-bit**—short lines of US-ASCII data.

▶ **8-bit**— short lines of non-ASCII characters.

▶ **binary**—not only are non-ASCII characters present, but the lines themselves are not necessarily short enough for SMTP transport.

▶ **quoted-printable**—converts 8-bit text streams into 7-bit, but readable text streams by converting all the non-text characters to two-digit hexadecimal numbers representing their byte value. The goal here is to convert text to a format that will cause the text not to be reformatted when it passes through gateways.

▶ **base64**—converts 24-bit groups of input bits into output strings of four encoded characters. Each character is made up of 6 bits from the original 24-bit string. Six bits permit the definition of a total of 64 characters, which in this case include the letters of the alphabet, upper case then lower case, the numbers 0 through 9, and a couple of non-alpha characters. In general, the data encoded this way translates reliably back into its original form no matter what happened to it in transport.

▶ **x-token**—Two people communicating with each other can agree between themselves on any other content-transfer-encoding that they want to use. To remain in compliance with MIME, they must identify their method in the content-transfer-encoding field beginning with the characters x and hyphen, so that, for example, their method might be called x-our-private-method.

Finally, MIME describes two optional fields, the Content-ID Header field and the Content-Description header field. You can see examples of the MIME header fields in Figure 21.1. The e-mail message in the figure has a plain text part and a uuencoded part. Note that the message is multipart/mixed, of which the two parts are text/plain and application/zip. Note also that, because uuencoding is not one of the standard content-transfer-encoding methods, the application/zip part is identified in the Content-Transfer-Encoding header field as x-uuencode.

Fig. 21.1

This multipart/mixed message has two sets of MIME headers.

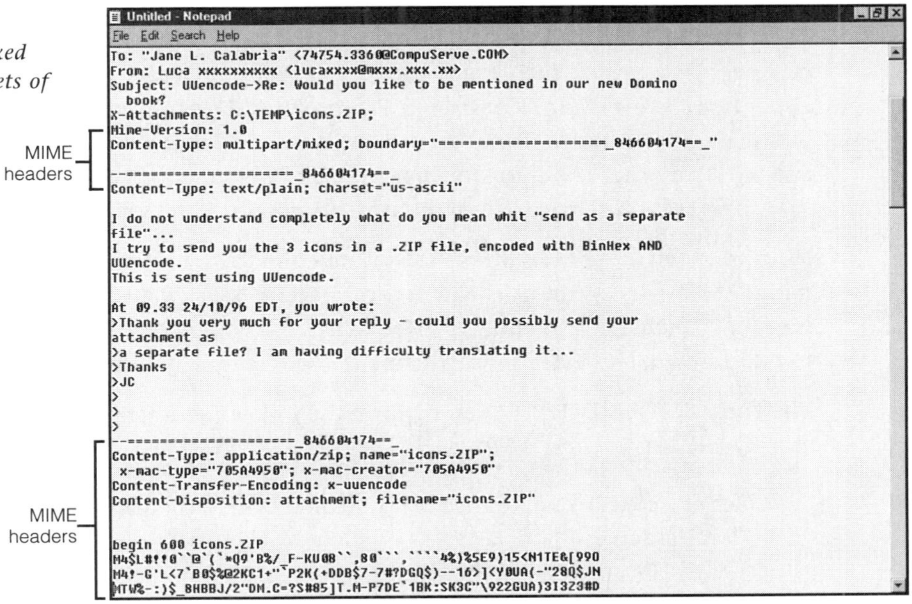

MIME has come to be used in many contexts, not just in connection with SMTP messages. For example, Web servers typically transfer files to browsers in the form of MIME extensions appended to HTML files.

Internet mail transfer typically begins with a User Agent (UA), continues through one or more Message Transfer Agents (MTAs), and ends with another User Agent. To put that in English, a sender composes and sends a message using an SMTP-compliant mail program, the User Agent. The sender delivers the message to a program (the first MTA) whose sole purpose in life is to take that message and deliver it to some other entity— either another MTA, one step closer to the recipient, or to the recipient itself. If the MTA delivers to the recipient, it is delivering to another UA.

Of course, if the final MTA cannot deliver the message directly to the intended recipient, it may drop the message off at a POP3 or IMAP4 mail server. As SMTP mail was originally conceived, users had mail accounts on mainframe computers, which were online all the time. When mail arrived for a user, the final MTA just held the message for the user until the user logged in and read the mail. Nowadays users may not have an account on a mainframe computer. POP3 and IMAP4 mail servers were designed to accommodate such users. POP3 and IMAP4 mail servers maintain mail drops for users, so that if a user is unable to retrieve mail from the MTA, the message will have a place to sit until the recipient user is able to retrieve the mail.

Lotus SMTP/MIME MTA

Notes does not format or deliver messages internally in compliance with SMTP or MIME. Therefore, when you address a message to someone who has only Internet mail or receives a message from such a one, the message must go through a translation process, either from Notes to SMTP or from SMTP to Notes. This translation is what a mail gateway does, and there are several mail gateways around that will translate between Notes and SMTP or other mail formats. In fact, one of the functions of the Lotus SMTP/MIME MTA is to act as a gateway—to translate between the Notes and SMTP mail formats.

However, the Lotus SMTP/MIME MTA is much more than just a mail gateway—it is a native SMTP message transfer agent. It can receive SMTP mail from one SMTP MTA and transfer it unchanged to another SMTP MTA. You could use the Lotus SMTP/MIME MTA to build a complete SMTP infrastructure on your company intranet, if you wanted to.

The Lotus SMTP/MIME MTA can perform the following functions:

▶ Receive, store, and forward either SMTP mail or Notes mail, without translation

▶ Received SMTP mail, translate it to Notes format, then forward to another Domino server

▶ Receive Notes mail, translate it to SMTP format, then forward to another SMTP MTA

The first listed function is what defines the Lotus SMTP/MIME MTA as more than just a gateway. The second and third functions are what any gateway between Notes and SMTP mail would do.

To put this another way, ask: What if you wanted to transfer a Notes message from your Notes domain, across the Internet, to my Notes domain? We could actually do it three different ways.

First, we could cross-certify our respective Internet-connected Domino servers and have them establish a pan-Internet Notes session whenever either one had a Notes message to deliver to the other. The problem here is that we would have to make the effort to cross-certify our servers. You and I are mere developers; to set up cross-certification we would have to go to some server administrator on our knees and beg. In some organizations, we would be turned down summarily. There must be another way.

Second, if we each were using, say, the SMTP gateway for Notes R3 servers, the first one would translate the message to SMTP/MIME format, then transfer it to an MTA on the Internet. When it arrived at my gateway, it would re-translate the message back into Notes format, then deliver it to a Notes server. In the translation, re-translation process, there is a good chance that the original message would have lost fidelity to its original form. It may very well look different on my screen, reading it, than it looked to you when you created it.

Third, we could use the Lotus SMTP/MIME MTA on each end. If it knew that the recipient was another Notes user, the one on your end would encapsulate your Notes-formatted message in an SMTP message, then send it out to the next MTA, somewhere on the Internet. Eventually, the message would arrive at my Lotus SMTP/MIME MTA, which would retrieve the original Notes message from encapsulation. It would arrive at my screen unchanged from your original (see Figure 21.2).

Or ask: What if one of your Lotus SMTP/MIME MTAs, connected to the Internet, received from the Internet an SMTP/MIME message addressed to an SMTP mail user on your company's intranet? The MTA could transfer the message, unchanged, to your other Lotus SMTP/MIME MTA, the one charged with receiving deliveries for your intranet SMTP mail users (see Figure 21.3).

The Lotus SMTP/MIME MTA can do these two things—transfer encapsulated Notes mail from Notes domain to Notes domain across the Internet and transfer SMTP mail unchanged across a Notes domain—because the Lotus SMTP/MIME MTA is a full-fledged SMTP/MIME MTA, not merely a Notes/SMTP gateway.

Fig. 21.2

*The first Lotus SMTP/
MIME MTA wraps the
Notes message in an
SMTP message. The
second one unwraps the
message. The message
never undergoes transla-
tion from another format.*

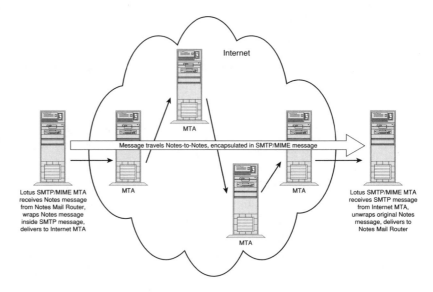

Fig. 21.3

*The first Lotus SMTP/
MIME MTA delivers the
SMTP message unaltered
to the second Lotus
SMTP/MIME MTA.*

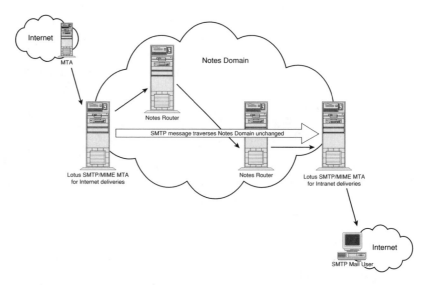

The Lotus SMTP/MIME MTA provides yet another benefit. Remember the long, multi-part e-mail address that we had to use when we were transferring mail to and from the Internet through a gateway? The Lotus SMTP/MIME MTA does away with that. Correspondents can now address mail to our colleagues at **jdoaks@rockteam.com**. We can address mail to our correspondents at **jdoaks@xyz.com**. The Lotus SMTP/MIME MTA automatically recognizes rockteam.com as the Internet domain for Notes users in Notes domain Rockey & Associates, and automatically translates the message to the correct addressing format. All Notes routers version 4.0 and later automatically recognize that mail addressed in the format **username@xyz.com** is intended for delivery to an Internet user and will deliver it to a Lotus SMTP/MIME MTA if one is set up in the Domain.

Furthermore, the Lotus SMTP/MIME MTA is very flexible in the way that it translates between Internet and Notes addresses for your Notes users. If your organization is not small, like ours, and **jdoaks@xyz.com** is not enough information to differentiate among all of your Notes users, the Lotus SMTP/MIME MTA will work with you to map Notes organizational unit names and Notes domain names into your users' Internet names. Thus, Joe Doaks/Sales/XYZCorp might map to this: **jdoaks.sales@xyz.com.** Or this: **jdoaks@sales.xyz.com**.

Also, instead of addressing to a user's short name, you could address to his full Notes name in one of these formats:

> **joseph_x_doaks@xyz.com**
>
> **joseph.x.doaks@xyz.com**
>
> **joseph%x%doaks@xyz.com**

So now my colleagues can have their short Internet address: jdoaks@rockteam.com. Or they can continue to have a long name like before: **jdoaks. rockey_&_associates@rockteam.com**

Installation and Configuration

To install the Lotus SMTP/MIME MTA is pretty easy, but it is a separate process from installing the Domino server. Lotus added it in as sort of a last-minute idea, so it is not included on the Domino CD-ROM or in the Domino installation program. It comes on a separate CD-ROM. You insert the CD-ROM in the drive, then find the Lotus SMTP/MIME MTA setup program (setup.exe) and run it (see Figure 21.4).

Fig. 21.4

The Lotus SMTP/ MIME MTA cdrom includes the setup.exe program. Setup.exe sets up an InstallShield Wizard, which in turn copies a series of files into your Notes program and data directories.

The setup program copies a series of executable programs and support files into your Notes program directory. It copies some Notes databases and database design templates into the Domino data directory. It also adds a couple of subforms to the design template for your Public Address Book, then updates the design of the Public Address Book with the design template.

After the setup program finishes, you have to complete five steps to properly configure and run the MTA. The steps are as follows:

1. Create a Global Domain document in the Public Address Book
2. Create a Foreign SMTP Domain document in the Public Address Book
3. Create an SMTP Connection document in the Public Address Book
4. Update the Server document in the Public Address Book
5. Run the MTA at the server console screen

Creating a Global Domain Document

The Global Domain document defines a global domain name, the member Notes domains of the global domain, and, most importantly, how Notes user names will map to Internet names, and vice versa (see Figure 21.5). You create the Global Domain document as follows:

1. Open the Public Address Book. Go to the Server-Domains view. Click the Add Domain button in the Action Bar. A new Domain document appears.
2. In the Domain Type field, choose Global Domain. The remaining fields change to reflect this Domain type.
3. Fill in the rest of the document, then save it. The fields are described as follows.

The fields in the Global Domain document are divided into four sections: Basics, Members, SMTP Address Conversion, and X.400 Address Conversion. You only have to enter information in a few fields; for most of the fields you can accept the default values. The fields that are relevant to the configuration of an SMTP MTA are as follows:

The Basics Section

Global domain name—Required. Enter any descriptive name here. Other documents in the Public Address Book will refer to this document by the name you enter in this field. Also, it will appear in the Servers-Domains view listed under this name.

Global domain role—Required. Choose SMTP MTA from the list of key words. This field identifies the MTA(s) that will rely on this document. Note that the information in the Administration Guide database is a little stale and refers to this field as the Global domain tasks field.

The Members Section

Notes domains and aliases—Enter the names of the Notes domains that will be served by the global domain defined in this document. If any of the Notes domains uses non-ASCII characters, you must define an ASCII alias for it, separating the Notes domain name from its alias with the separator character defined in the following field.

Alias separator character—Defaults to equals (=).

The SMTP Address Conversion Section

Note that the Administration Guide database that comes with the Lotus SMTP/MIME MTA version 1.05 is not up to date in its description of this section. Note also that, as you change the entries in some of the fields in this section, the Address example at the end of the section changes to display an example of how the settings in those fields will make return addresses look.

> **Tip**
>
> If any of our following explanations following of the field entries in this section don't seem clear at first, open a Global Domain document in edit mode, play with the fields in this section, and watch how your changes affect the Address example. The purpose of each field will seem much more clear after you see how changes in it affect the look of the Address example. Try it. It's cool.

21

Fig. 21.5

You must fill out a Global Domain document before the Lotus SMTP/ MIME MTA will work properly.

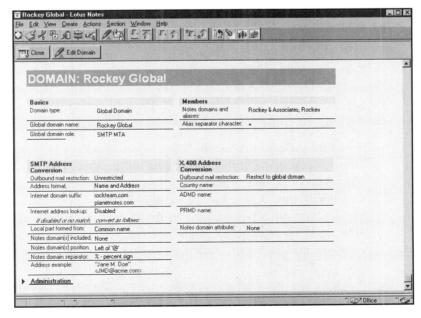

Outbound mail restriction—The default is *Unrestricted*. The other choice is *Restrict to global domain*. By default, the SMTP MTA will transfer all outbound mail without checking its origin. You can restrict it to transferring only mail that originated in one of the domains named in the *Notes domains and aliases* field.

Address format—Defaults to Address only, which would format the return address of the sender of outbound mail to the form **jdoaks@xyz.com**. Choosing Name and Address in this field would cause the sender's return address to be formatted in the form **"Joe Doaks"**<**jdoaks@xyz.com**>, where **"Joe Doaks"** is the sender's Notes common name, and <**jdoaks@xyz.com**> is the standard Internet address. This format is a little more informative to the recipient than the default format.

Internet domain suffix—Enter at least one and, optionally, up to 32 domain suffixes, that is, Internet domain names, in this field. The MTA will accept inbound mail for all Internet domains listed in this field. It will list only the first named Internet domain in the return address of any mail sent from this MTA.

Internet address lookup—Default is disabled. What used to be the Short name field of the Person document is now the Short name and Internet address field. The field may optionally include an Internet address. If you Enable Internet address lookup in this field, then, when processing outbound mail, the MTA will always first try to obtain the sender's return Internet address from the sender's Person document. If it fails to find an Internet address for the sender there, or if lookup is disabled, then the MTA uses the rules in the following fields to cobble up a return address. If you have not bothered to enter Internet addresses into your person documents, keep this field Disabled. If you have added Internet addresses to your Person documents, then Enabling this field can make for less work for the MTA and a speedier processing of outbound mail.

Local part formed from—Default is Full name. Other choices are Common name and Short name. Use the full name if you have to in order to differentiate among your Notes users. Use the short name only if you are sure that none of your Notes users share the same short name. Use the common name to keep the return address short.

Notes domain(s) included—The choices are All, One, or None. Default is All. What it means is how many of the Notes domain components that appear in a Notes user's address become part of the user's return Internet address. If a user in Domain A has to send e-mail via Domain B to get to the SMTP MTA in Domain C, that Notes user's return address from the MTA is **user @ Domain A @ Domain B**. If you leave this field set to All, then the user's Internet return address will look something like this: **user%domaina%domainb@xyz.com**. The benefit of doing this is that, when inbound mail arrives addressed to this user, the MTA will know from the return address that it should address the converted message to **user @ Domain A @ Domain B**. If you set the user's return address to include only One or None of the user's domain names, then the MTA will have to use other means (for example, cascading address books) to determine the user's correct address on the return mail. To keep return addresses short and sweet, choose None in this field, cascade on this server the public address books of all domains that will use this MTA, and include the names of all domains that will use this MTA in the Notes domains and aliases field in the Members section of this form.

Notes domain(s) position—In this field, you specify whether the appended Notes domain names in the previous field appear on the left or right side of the @ sign in the Internet return address. The default is the left side. If you don't have an overriding reason for putting the domains on the right side, leave them on the left side.

Notes domain separator—Defaults to the % sign. You may choose the period (.) instead. If you chose in the previous field to move the domains to the right of the @ sign, you must choose periods in this field.

Creating a Foreign SMTP Domain Document

Whenever you want to route mail between a Notes domain and a non-Notes domain, you must create a Foreign Domain document. When routing mail via a Lotus SMTP/MIME MTA, the Foreign Domain document must be a Foreign SMTP Domain document. See Figure 21.6. If you have multiple domains, you should create one of these for each domain. For example, if you have an internal company domain, where all your users reside, and an external, firewall domain, where your MTA resides, you must create a

Fig. 21.6

The top form is a Foreign SMTP Domain document for our internal domain, saying route all Internet mail to our external domain Rockex. The bottom form is the Foreign SMTP Domain document for the external domain.

Routes from internal Notes domain to External Notes Domain

Routes from external Notes Domain to the internet

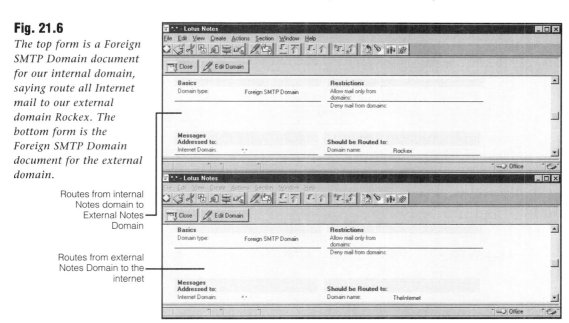

Foreign SMTP Domain document in each domain's Public Address Book.

Follow these steps to create a Foreign SMTP Domain document:

1. Open the Public Address Book. Go to the Server-Domains view. Click the Add Domain button in the Action Bar. A new Domain document appears.

2. In the Domain Type field, choose Foreign SMTP Domain. The remaining fields change to reflect this Domain type.

3. Fill in the rest of the document, then save it.

We really care about only two fields in this document: Internet domain and Domain name. In this document, you are telling the Domino server that, to route mail to Internet domain A, it should route mail to Notes domain X. So, if we have an internal domain, AcmeInternal, and an external domain, AcmeExternal, we would create two of these documents.

For the AcmeInternal domain, the Internet Domain field would be *.*—all Internet domains, and the Domain name field would be set to AcmeExternal. In other words, to route mail to all Internet domains, route it first to AcmeExternal.

For the AcmeExternal domain, the Internet Domain field would also be *.*—all Internet domains. But the Domain name field would by something descriptive, like Internet or The Internet, which we will later use to connect this document with the Connection document we will create in the next section. So, we are saying that, to route mail to all Internet domains, route it first to Internet or The Internet, whatever we entered in that field. When you say it like this, it doesn't make much sense; it sounds circular. But don't get all worked up; just do it; it works.

The other fields in this document, in the Restrictions section, allow you to specify which Notes domains can route mail to the Internet via this domain or, in other words, via this MTA. They are optional fields which you can ignore for now or use to block people, say, from other companies' Notes domains from using your MTA.

If you will be setting up multiple Lotus SMTP/MIME MTAs in your company, you can set them up so that they specialize. That is, you can set one up to deliver mail to one set of Internet domains, a second to deliver mail to another set of Internet domains, and yet a third to deliver mail to, say, all remaining Internet domains. You would do this by entering in the Internet Domain field, instead of *.*, either named Internet domains or some group of Internet domains less than *.* (all of them). For example, you might dedicate one MTA to the job of delivering mail to all Japanese domains by entering *.jp in the Internet Domains field.

Creating an SMTP Connection Document

Along with the Foreign SMTP Domain document that we created in the previous section, we must also create an SMTP Connection document (see Figure 21.7). In this case, however, you need to create only one—describing the connection between your Lotus SMTP/MIME MTA and the Internet. This document works together with the Foreign SMTP Domain document that we created in the previous section to define the MTA's connection to the Internet.

Follow these steps to create a Foreign SMTP Domain document:

1. Open the Public Address Book. Go to the Server-Connections view. Click the Add Connection button in the Action Bar. A new Connection document appears.

2. In the Connection Type field, choose SMTP. The remaining fields change to reflect this Connection type.

3. Fill in the rest of the document, then save it.

Fig. 21.7

You must fill out an SMTP Connection document before the Lotus SMTP/MIME MTA will work properly.

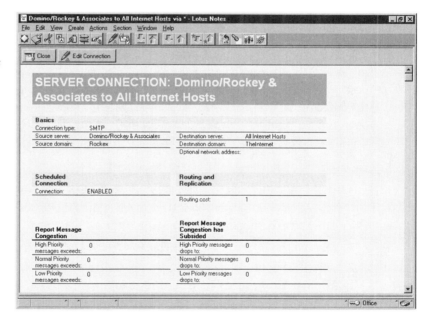

The SMTP Connection document five sections, though, to look at it, you may not realize it. The fourth and fifth sections, named Report Message Congestion and Report Message Congestion has Subsided, are part of a subform that somehow escaped from the overall redesign that the Public Address Book got for Release 4.5. The two sections in question don't have the nice gray background behind their titles, like most sections have. The fields in this document are as follows:

Source server—

Source domain—

Destination server—

Destination domain—

Optional network address—

Connection—

Routing cost—

High, Normal, and Low Priority messages exceeds—

High, Normal, and Low Priority messages drops to—

Updating the Server Document

The Server document is the last document we must address before we can finally start up our MTA. When we installed the Lotus SMTP/MIME MTA, one of the things the installation program did was add the Internet Message Transfer Agent (SMTP MTA) subform to the database, so that all Server documents, when we open them and expand that section, open to a full subform where we can fine-tune many of the details of the way the MTA on that server works. See Figure 21.8.

Follow these steps to edit the Server document:

1. Open the Public Address Book. Go to the Server-Servers view. Select the server on which you have set up the MTA. Click the Edit Server button in the Action Bar. The Server document opens in Edit Mode.

2. Expand the Internet Message Transfer Agent (SMTP MTA) section.

3. Fill in the appropriate fields, then save and close the Server document. The significant fields are described as follows.

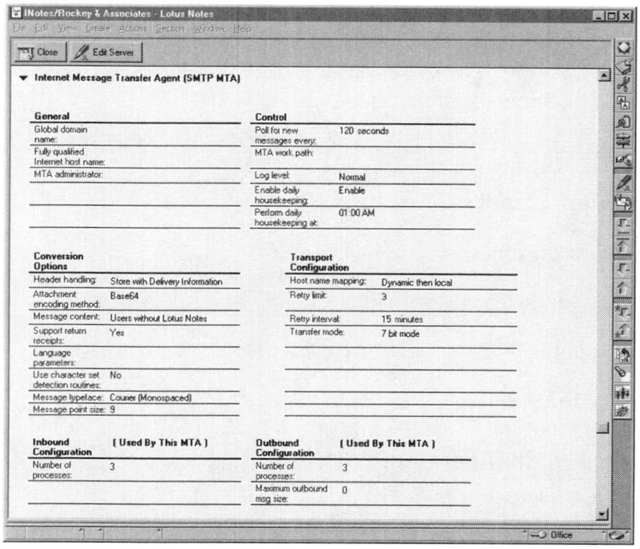

Fig. 21.8

You must edit the Internet Message Transfer Agent section of the Server Domain document before the Lotus SMTP/MIME MTA will work properly.

The fields in the Global Domain document are divided into six sections: General, Control, Conversion Options, Transport Configuration, Inbound Configuration, and Outbound Configuration. You only have to enter information in a few fields; for most of the fields you can accept the default values.

The General Section
Global domain name—

Fully qualified Internet host name—

MTA Administrator—

The Control Section
Poll for new messages every—

MTA work path—

Log level—

Enable daily housekeeping—

Perform daily housekeeping at—

The Conversion Options Section
Header handling—

Attachment encoding method—

Message content—

Support return receipts—

Language parameters—

Use character set detection routines—

Message typeface—

Message point size—

The Transport Configuration Section
Host name mapping—

Retry limit—

Retry interval—

Transfer mode—

The Inbound Configuration Section
Number of processes—

The Outbound Configuration Section
Number of processes—

Maximum outbound message size—

Starting and Stopping the Lotus SMTP/MIME MTA

Having installed the MTA, you can now run it and stop it at any time by entering the following commands at the server console:

```
load smtpmta
tell smtpmta quit
```

You can also start the MTA automatically whenever the Domino server starts up by adding smtpmta to the ServerTasks variable in the server's notes.ini file. The variable would end up looking something like this:

```
SERVERTASKS=Replica,Router,Update,Stats,AMgr,Adminp,HTTP,SMTPMTA
```

How the Lotus SMTP/MIME MTA Works

The Lotus SMTP/MIME MTA consists actually of a series of server tasks that perform different aspects of the MTA's responsibilities. It also sets up a series of Notes databases that it uses during conversion and transfer of messages. The server tasks include the following:

SMTPMTA	The Add-in Controller
SMTPMTA OMSGCNV	Outbound Message Conversion
SMTPMTA OSESCTL	Outbound Session Controller
SMTPMTA OSESHLR n	Outbound Session Handlers
SMTPMTA IMSGCNV	Inbound Message Conversion
SMTPMTA ISESCTL	Inbound Session Controller
SMTPMTA ISESHLR n	Inbound Message Conversion
SMTPMTA DRT	Delivery Report Task

The Add-in Controller (SMTPMTA) is the task that you load onto the Domino server. It is the controller of all the other tasks.

The Outbound Message Conversion (SMTPMTA OMSGCNV) task does the actual conversion of messages from Notes format to SMTP/MIME format.

The Outbound Session Controller (SMTPMTA OSESCTL) task controls the process of transporting messages to their destinations. It controls the session handlers which perform the actual, individual tasks involved in transporting the messages.

The Outbound Session Handlers (SMTPMTA OSESHLR n) perform the tasks of connecting to another MTA, delivering messages, and handling errors. They are child tasks of the Outbound Session Controller.

The Inbound Message Conversion (SMTPMTA IMSGCNV) task does the actual conversion of messages from SMTP/MIME format to Notes format. If the message is not convertible or deliverable, this task will generate a non-delivery report. If the message is not addressed to a Notes user, it will put the message into the Outbound Transport work queue.

The Inbound Session Controller (SMTPMTA ISESCTL) task receives listens on port 25 for incoming SMTP messages, accepts the connection when a message arrives on that port, then launches an Inbound Session Handler to take the connection. It also controls the session handlers which perform the actual, individual tasks involved in receiving the messages.

21

The Inbound Session Handlers (SMTPMTA ISESHLR n) perform the tasks of handshaking with a sending MTA and receiving and writing the incoming messages to the inbound work queue. They are child tasks of the Inbound Session Controller.

Finally, the Delivery Report Task (SMTPMTA DRT) manages the messages in the work queues, depending on the status of each message as reported by the other tasks. The DRT deletes messages from the queues when they are reported as successfully sent or received. It generates non-delivery reports for messages that have generated error status messages. It notifies the administrator if dead mail appears in the outgoing mailbox.

The databases associated with the Lotus SMTP/MIME MTA include the following:

SMTP Mail Box (smtp.box)—The Notes Router places all SMTP-bound messages into this database. The Outbound Message Conversion task polls this database from time to time for messages to be converted and sent out. The Delivery Report Task removes messages from this database after they have been successfully converted and transferred out or after it has generated a non-delivery report for an undeliverable message. The install program creates this database at installation time from the smtpbox.ntf design template.

SMTP Outbound Work Queue (smtpobwq.nsf)—After the Outbound Message Conversion Task converts a message, it drops the converted message in this database, where the message will sit until delivered or until otherwise processed by the Delivery Report Task.

SMTP Inbound Work Queue (smtpibwq.nsf)—The Inbound Session Handler drops newly received messages into this database, where they sit until converted and delivered. Both the Outbound Work Queue and Inbound Word Queue are generated and maintained by the MTA itself. They are both generated from the smtpwq.ntf design template.

MTA Tables database (mtatables.nsf)—This is a lookup table for both the Lotus SMTP/MIME MTA and the Lotus X.400 MTA. It holds data about character sets and MIME Type/Subtypes.

SMTP/MIME MTA System Administrator's Guide (smtpag.nsf)—This is the primary documentation supplied with the Lotus SMTP/MIME MTA. It contains all instructions for setting up, configuring, administering, and troubleshooting the Lotus SMTP/MIME MTA.

Release Notes for SMTP MTA 1.xx (rn_smtp.nsf)—This contains all the information about the MTA not published elsewhere at the time the product was released.

Figure 21.9 diagrams the flow of messages through the SMTP/MIME MTA.

Fig. 21.9
This diagram shows the flow of messages through the SMTP/MIME MTA.

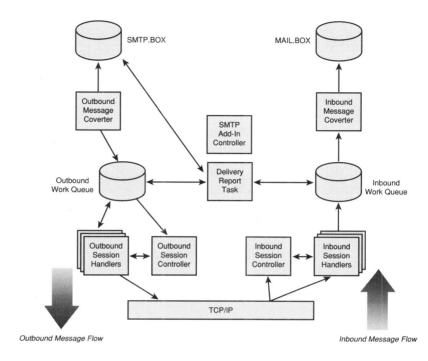

Lotus POP3 Mail Server

The Lotus POP3 mail server is an add-in task to the standard Domino 4.5 server. It enables the Domino server to become a mail server to POP3-compliant mail clients. These include such programs as Eudora Pro, Netscape Navigator, and Microsoft Internet Explorer. When a Domino server acts as a POP3 mail server, its POP3 clients all have Person documents and standard Notes mail databases assigned for their use. When mail arrives for such a client, the Notes mail router deposits the mail into the POP3 client's mail database just the same as it would deposit mail into the mail database of a standard Notes mail client.

The difference arises in the way that the POP3 mail client accesses its mail. Notes mail clients request the Domino database server for access to their mail databases. POP3 clients, on the other hand, connect to the POP3 server on IP port 110. The Lotus POP3 Mail Server constantly listens on the port for connections. When a POP3 client does connect, the client authenticates with the server. The client authenticates by identifying itself by account name and password. If authentication is successful, the server permits the client access to its mail file. The client can read and delete mail in the file, but the client does not directly save new mail to the file the way a Notes mail client does. Rather, the POP3 mail client must send mail to itself if it wants to retain copies of its mail in its Domino-based mail file.

To set POP3 running on a Domino server, all you do is enter the following command at the Domino server console:

```
load pop3
```

To stop the POP3 server, enter the following command:

```
tell pop3 quit
```

You can cause the POP3 server to start automatically when the Domino server starts by adding the pop3 parameter to the `ServerTasks` variable in notes.ini. The variable would end up looking something like this:

```
SERVERTASKS=Replica,Router,Update,Stats,AMgr,Adminp,POP3
```

To set up a POP3 client on a POP3-enabled server, you must do three things:

1. Purchase from Lotus a Server Mail Access license for the POP3 client. Lotus charges about $35 per Server Mail Access license, more or less, depending on your quantity discounts.

2. Create a mail database for the client using the standard Notes mail template as the design template.

3. Create a Person document for the POP3 mail client.

The Person document for the POP3 client must have the following fields filled in:

▶ `First name`, `Middle initial`, and `Last name` fields

▶ `Full name` field

▶ `Short name` field. This is the name the user enters when authenticating.

▶ `HTTP Password` field. This is the password the user enters when authenticating.

▶ `Mail system` field. Enter POP3.

▶ `Domain` field. Enter the domain of the POP3 server.

▶ `Mail server` field. Enter the fully distinguished name of the POP3 server.

▶ `Mail file` field. Enter the path name of the database created in step 2.

One last thing you must do. You must set up some server in the POP3 server's domain as an SMTP/MIME MTA using the Lotus SMTP/MIME MTA software. It does not have to be the same server as the POP3 server, though it could be. It does have to be a server that can route mail to the POP3 server.

Without this MTA, POP3 users would never receive any mail, for all mail delivered to POP3 users goes first to the MTA, then to the POP3 server for delivery to the POP3 user's mail database. The reason for this is that all POP3 mail users have delivery addresses in the form user@xyz.com. Domino mail routers interpret addresses in this form as Internet addresses and therefore automatically deliver all such mail to the SMTP MTA, which translates the message and address to Notes format so that the Domino mail router can properly interpret the address and deliver the mail to the POP3 user's mail database.

To set up the POP3 client software to use the Domino POP3 mail server, provide it the following information:

> ▶ The IP host names of the computers running the Lotus SMTP/MIME MTA and the POP3 server software. If the two programs are running on the same computer, the host names will be the same.

> ▶ The POP3 client's user name, which is identical to the short name in the Person document.

Also set up the POP3 client software to order the POP3 server to automatically delete mail after the POP3 client makes a local copy of it. Finally, set up the POP3 client to check for new mail no more often than every five minutes, so as not to impact server performance.

From Here...

21

Domino's support of the SMTP protocol and POP3 protocols are pretty complete. However, it appears that POP3 is becoming obsolete as a new mail protocol, the Internet Mail Access Protocol (IMAP4) is likely to replace it. The latest browser from Netscape already supports IMAP4 and we can expect other browsers and Internet mail programs to follow. We can also expect Lotus to add support for IMAP4 to a future release of Notes/Domino, since Lotus has pledged to incorporate support for all relevant Internet protocols into Note and Domino.

> ▶ For more information on the Lotus SMTP/MIME MTA, see the Sys Admin and Release Notes databases that come with the SMTP/MIME MTA. The SMTP/MIME MTA installation program decompresses them.

> ▶ For more information on the Lotus POP3 server, see the Administration Guide database that installs automatically on every Domino server when you install the server.

> ▶ For more information on the SMTP Internet standard, see RFC821 and RFC822.

> ▶ For more information on the MIME Internet standard, see RFC2045 through RFC2049.

▶ For more information on the POP3 Internet standard, see RFC1939.

▶ For information on the proposed successor to POP3, Internet Mail Access Protocol (IMAP4), see RFC2060.

You can access the RFCs (Requests for Comment) at the InterNIC by entering URLs in the following format:

ds.internic.net/rfc/rfcxxxx.txt

where xxxx is the number of the RFC.

## chapter 22

Using the Server Web Navigator

22

In this chapter

◆ **How the Server Web Navigator works**
What happens behind the scenes when you tell Notes to get a Web page?

◆ **How to set up the Server Web Navigator**
We walk through all of the steps. We look at all of the configuration options.

◆ **How to search the Web with the Server Web Navigator**
We step through all the different ways to locate Web documents in both versions of the Web Navigator.

◆ **How to customize the Server Web Navigator**
We show you how to change the links on the Home navigator and how to create your own Home navigator.

With the huge rise in popularity of the Internet over the past couple of years, Lotus realized that it had to incorporate Internet connectivity into Notes. With the release of Notes 4.0 in January 1996, Lotus incorporated a World Wide Web browser into Notes called InterNotes Web Navigator. This Web browser in Notes 4.0 worked through the Notes server, and you had to be connected to the Notes server to browse the Web. The Notes server had to be running the Web retrieval task, and when running this task was then referred to as the "InterNotes server."

In Domino 4.5, Lotus has enhanced Web Navigator so that now you can browse through the Domino server, as before, or directly from your Notes workstation. It has provided two browsers: the *Server Web Navigator*, which is used to browse the

Web through the Domino server (not much changed since the InterNotes version of this browser) and the *Personal Web Navigator* from which you can browse without a connection to the Domino server.

Understanding the Server Web Navigator

We'd like to define some of Domino 4.5's new terminology so that our references throughout the next two chapters are clear to previous users of the InterNotes Web Navigator. With the release of Domino 4.5, Lotus has dropped the word "InterNotes" and replaced it with "Server" when referring to the Web Navigator. In effect, the InterNotes Web Navigator has changed little since Notes 4.1, except for its name. In fact, "InterNotes" is still displayed across the home navigator of the Server Web Navigator although all through beta releases and testing, we were told by various and reliable sources at Lotus Development and Iris that the word "InterNotes" was going to disappear in version 4.5 of Domino.

The term "InterNotes" has not entirely disappeared. In addition to remaining on the home navigator of the Web Navigator database, the word "InterNotes" also continues to appear in the server and location documents when referring to the server running the Web retrieval process. So, if we understand this correctly, the old Notes server has become the new Domino 4.5 server. The old "Domino" has become the new HTTP server, unless of course it is also running the Web retrieval process, in which case it is the InterNotes server. In truth, a Domino 4.5 Web site that also provides Internet access to users would be referred to as a "Domino 4.5 HTTP/InterNotes server." Now that we've totally confused the issue, let's address the fact that we no longer have one browser, and that the two browsers have different system requirements, and very different looks.

The Server Web Navigator is a Web browser built into Notes, along with a companion Notes database that stores the Web pages retrieved by the browser. In the server version of the Web Navigator, the browser and the database, named Web Navigator, both reside on a Domino server (although you can put a replica copy of the database on your workstation, if you want). In the personal version, the browser and the database (this one is named Personal Web Navigator) both reside on the Notes client.For more information about the Personal Web Navigator, see Chapter 23, "Using the Personal Web Navigator" on p. xx

The user can browse the World Wide Web, or the corporate intranet, by either entering an URL into a dialog box or clicking an URL in a Notes document. Whether the server or client does the actual browsing—and whether browsing occurs at all—depends on a setting in the user's current Location document. This allows the user to use the server version sometimes, the personal version other times, and no browser at still other times.

For example, Jane, an ace account representative, works all morning at her New York City office, preparing for tomorrow's meeting with her client in San Francisco. She flies there during the afternoon and spends the night in a hotel. While in the office, her Office Location document specifies that she use the server version of Server Web Navigator. On the plane, she has no Internet connection and so cannot browse—not online at least. However, if she has a Personal Web Navigator database or a replica copy of the Server Web Navigator database on her laptop, she can browse within the database. Her Island Location document specifies No Retrievals in the Retrieve/Open pages field, so if she clicks the URL of a document not in the database, Notes displays an error message. In the hotel, she switches to a Travel Location document, which specifies From Notes Workstation in the Retrieve/Open pages field. She dials out to the Internet with her modem and, when she opens a URL, Notes automatically uses the Personal Web Navigator to browse.

Working with InterNotes Web Navigator

When you enter an URL in Notes, or click one in a Notes or Web document in Notes, exactly what happens depends on what choices you have made in your current Location document. There you can choose to browse indirectly through a Notes server, directly from your Notes client, from a third-party Web browser, or not at all.

If you have chosen to browse with the Server Web Navigator, then your copy of Notes forwards the URL to your designated InterNotes server. A server task called Web Retriever forwards the URL to the destination server. If the destination server returns a page, Web Retriever converts it to Notes format. Then the Database Server task stores it in the Server Web Navigator database and forwards a copy to you, which your copy of Notes displays on your screen (see Figure 22.1).

22

Actually, when you enter or click an URL, Notes may not forward the URL to another computer at all. If you ask for a page that InterNotes Web Navigator has retrieved recently, it may simply return to you the copy sitting in its database. This is one of the advantages of using Notes to browse the Web.

 Tip
You can quickly download a whole series of Web pages into your Web Navigator database without spending much time in them. Then you can disconnect and read the pages more carefully offline, at your leisure, without accumulating connect charges.

Fig. 22.1

*When you use the
Server Web Navigator,
your InterNotes server
retrieves pages for you.*

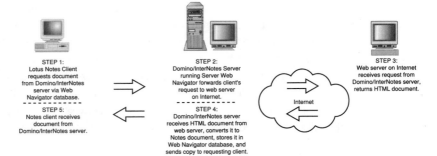

STEP 1:
Lotus Notes Client
requests document
from Domino/InterNotes
server via Web
Navigator database.

STEP 2:
Domino/InterNotes Server
running Server Web
Navigator forwards client's
request to web server
on Internet.

STEP 3:
Web server on Internet
receives request from
Domino/InterNotes server,
returns HTML document.

STEP 5:
Notes client receives
document from
Domino/InterNotes server.

STEP 4:
Domino/InterNotes server
receives HTML document from
web server, converts it to
Notes document, stores it in
Web Navigator database, and
sends copy to requesting client.

Internet

Notes works a little different when you browse the Web than it works when you explore
non-Web-related Notes databases. When you open standard Notes documents, each
document appears in its own window. However, when you browse with Web Navigator,
your Web pages all appear in the same window. They designed Notes to browse this way
because Notes can only open nine sub-windows at most. When you browse the Web,
you tend to open so many Web documents so quickly that, if Notes opened a window
for each one, you would quickly reach the maximum number of windows and then
would have to stop and close a window every time you want to jump to a new one.

As you browse, Notes maintains a history of the pages you viewed. You can see the pages
listed in the History dialog box. You can open this by clicking the History button that
appears whenever you view a Web page. You can jump directly to any listed page by
double-clicking its title in the History dialog box.

Configuring the Server Web Navigator

You don't have to *install* the Server Web Navigator. It is part of Domino 4.5 and was
installed along with the server software. To use it, however, you have to do a bit of setup.
Please note that the setup requirements are not the same for Personal Web Navigator and
Server Web Navigator.

Before you can use Server Web Navigator, take the following steps to set it up:

1. Meet system and network requirements and those for running the Domino 4.5
   server. For more information on setting up the Domino Server, see Chapter 2, "Setting Up the Domino Server."

2. On the Domino 4.5 server, load the Web Retriever into memory (making it now
   the "InterNotes server").

3. In the Server documents of the Home/Mail servers of the users who will be using a given InterNotes server, enter the InterNotes server's fully distinguished name in the InterNotes server field.

4. Notify and train your users.

System Requirements for Server Web Navigator

System requirements for the server running Server Web Navigator, over and above those for a standard Domino 4.5 server, include the following:

▶ Potential additional memory and disk space requirements

▶ Specific network requirements necessary to connect the InterNotes server to the Internet or company intranet

Whether you need additional RAM or disk space on the InterNotes server depends on how much demand your users will make on Web Navigator. You can assume that the Web Navigator database will grow very large; you should reserve at least 500M of disk space for it; that is the default maximum size.

Beyond that, the general rule is that, for each additional Web Retriever process (over the default number of 25) that you add in the Concurrent Retrievers field of the InterNotes server's Server document, you should add:

▶ 2M RAM to the base RAM requirements for your server platform

▶ 10M disk space to the default page file size for your server platform

22

Second, you must have access to some sort to the Internet or a company intranet; otherwise, there is no Web to browse. You obtain access to the Internet through an Internet Service Provider (ISP). ISPs are connected to the Internet and they are in the business of extending their Internet connections to "the rest of us."

There are several ways to classify connection to the Internet. One distinction is between direct and indirect connections. You have a direct connection if your computer has an IP address issued by the InterNIC and can communicate directly with all the other direct-connected computers on the Net. You have an indirect connection if, IP address or no, you can only communicate with the computers on the Internet through a proxy server. That is, you send an URL to the proxy server and it sends the URL to the Web server on your behalf. The proxy server receives the page back from the Web server and forwards it to you.

In this case, the Server Web Navigator is a proxy server. It, in turn, may be using yet another proxy server. You may have the capacity to connect directly to the Internet. But when you are using Server Web Navigator, you are connecting indirectly. In fact, one of the most attractive features of Server Web Navigator is that you don't have to connect everyone in the office to the Internet; you can connect just the InterNotes server and let all the users connect indirectly through it.

You may very well have both direct and indirect connections. You may have a direct connection when you are dialing in from home and an indirect connection when you are in the office. The Internet is an infamously insecure and lawless place. Network administrators are notoriously skittish about the security of their data. So it is not at all uncommon for company local area networks (LANs) to be insulated from the Internet by firewalls and proxy servers.

Another distinction is between LAN-based connections and dial-up connections. Your computer may be connected to a LAN that is, in turn, connected to the Internet through a Router. Or, you may have to dial in to the Internet using your computer's modem or maybe a shared modem on the LAN.

LAN-based computers typically have more or less permanent access to the Internet. They also may have very high-speed access to the Internet. Say you are sitting in your office, reading your Notes mail, and a message arrives with an URL in it. You click the URL and the page arrives in your computer in about three finger-snaps. Either the page was in the Server Web Navigator database already or you have a LAN-based connection to the Internet. Except, if the page was already in the Server Web Publisher database, then it would have arrived in *one* finger-snap. Having the page already in the database is unquestionably the fastest way to retrieve it to your screen.

With dial-up access, you click the URL, then a message appears asking if you want to dial a certain phone number. You answer yes, then you wait while the computer dials and handshakes with the other computer (unless you have ISDN phone service, in which case dialing and handshaking are almost instantaneous). Then you play a little Solitaire, read your snail mail, get a cup of coffee—or you watch the numbers climb slowly as the page arrives, bit-by-bit, over the phone line. Modem access to the Internet is not fast.

 Tip

Get the fastest modem available. If ISDN isn't too prohibitively expensive in your area, and if you can find an Internet Service Provider (ISP) that provides it, get ISDN. It is four to eight times faster than the fastest analog modem.

If your computer is connected to a LAN and you are not connecting to the Internet through a proxy server, then you probably have a permanently assigned IP address. If you dial in to an ISP, your IP address is probably assigned to you at the beginning of the call and reassigned to another caller after you hang up.

If you actually have to set up all this stuff yourself, and you don't already have a pretty good idea how to do it, you may want to hire an ISP or a network/communications consultant to help you out. Meanwhile, refer to the documentation and help databases that come with the Notes server, especially the Web Navigator Administrator's Guide, which is available as both a printed book and a Notes database located in the *doc* subdirectory of the Notes data directory. See also several databases available on Lotus's Web site, including *The Internet Cookbook* and *Domino 4.5 and the Internet*. Lotus's Web site is located at **http://www.lotus.com**.

Starting and Stopping the Web Retriever

Notes servers all come with InterNotes Web Navigator installed. But they don't run it automatically. The Notes administrator must decide whether a Domino server will also be an InterNotes server, then he must set it up. To turn a Domino server into an InterNotes server, you connect it to the Internet/intranet (see preceding section) and you run the Web Retriever server task. To run the Web Retriever manually, you enter the following command at the server console or remote server console:

```
load web
```

To unload the Web Retriever, you enter the following command:

```
tell web quit
```

To set up a server so that the Web Retriever starts automatically whenever the server starts, edit the server's NOTES.INI file by adding the word Web to the ServerTasks variable. When you finish, the ServerTasks variable looks something like this:

```
ServerTasks=Replica,Router,Update,Stats,AMgr,Adminp,Sched,CalConn,Web
```

If the server is running when you edit NOTES.INI, you must bring the server down and restart it before it recognizes the change. Instead of doing that, however, you simply load the Web Retriever manually with the load web command.

Filling in the Location Document

The one thing you have to do to enable the Server Web Navigator, other than start it up, is tell the users about it. By that, we mean not only that you should inform your users, but also that you tell their copies of Notes that this is the server they should go to when the user requests a Web page. When that happens, the Notes client program is going to look around for the identity of the designated InterNotes server.

First, the Notes client looks in the current location document at the InterNotes server field. If a server is identified there, the Notes client tries to send the URL there. If that server is unavailable or refuses for any reason to play, or if the InterNotes server field in the Location document is empty, then the Notes client looks to the Server document of the user's Home/Mail server, and looks in the InterNotes server field there. If that field is empty, or the server named there won't play, then the request for the page fails.

So, the administrator's first job is to enter the name of the InterNotes server in one or both of those fields. Because it is a whole lot easier to fill in one field on one or a few server documents than it is to fill them in on, say, hundreds of Location documents scattered all over creation, the administrator adds the InterNotes server's fully distinguished name to the Server documents of the Home/Mail servers of the users who should use that InterNotes server. You don't really have to worry about the Location documents after that, except to override the Home server document. An example of when you would do that is the traveling employee. She spends most of her time in the New York City office. Her Home server is in that office. But when she is visiting clients in L.A., San Francisco, and Seattle, she switches to Location documents for each of those cities. Among other things, those Location documents name InterNotes servers in those cities, so that she doesn't have to reach all the way back to New York to surf the Net.

The administrator *can* predefine the entries to key fields in the Location documents for people he/she registers in the future as Notes users. That is, the administrator can create one or more User Setup Profile documents in the Public Address Book. User Setup Profile documents set forth a series of default entries that Notes can use when it sets up a new user workstation. At that time, Notes creates a Personal Address Book for the user and generates and adds to it several Location and Connection documents. Notes uses the settings in the User Setup Profile document to set up the Location and Connection documents properly.

The User Setup Profile Document Settings

Several settings in the User Setup Profile document are relevant to the Server Web Navigator. These settings are as follows:

▶ *Internet browser*—The default is Notes, but the user can specify another browser instead. Here, the administrator can define the default browser.

▶ *Retrieve/open pages*—The default is From the Notes Workstation. In other words, by default, when people want to retrieve Web pages, they use their Personal Web Navigator to do it. If the administrator wants users to use the Server Web Navigator instead, or wants to disable Web browsing, he should change this field to either From InterNotes Server or No Retrievals.

▶ *The Default Java Applet Security fields*—These are three fields that define how the Notes client handles pages that have Java applets embedded in them. Because Java applets are actual programs that the Notes client can run, the potential exists that they could damage the software and data on the computer or open network connections to other computers, thereby exposing your computer's and network's resources to outsiders. These fields let you define what computers Notes accepts or does not accept Java applets from and how it handles them when it does. See the section "Setting Up a Location Document for Personal Web Navigator," earlier in this chapter, for more information about these fields and their settings.

▶ *The Default Proxy Configuration fields*—These fields let the administrator define the URL of any proxy servers the users will be using. For more information regarding the use of User Setup Profile documents, see the section "Setting Up a Location Document for Personal Web Navigator," in Chapter 17, "Building a Domino Web Site in One Day with Domino Action."

The server document also governs how the Web Retriever runs. This time it is the InterNotes server's Server document that governs. The following fields are located in the Web Retriever Administration section of the Server document:

▶ **Web Navigator database**—This is the file name of the Server Web Navigator database. If you want to change the name of the actual database, you have to change it here as well.

▶ **Services**—InterNotes Web Navigator supports five Internet services, including HTTP, HTTPS, FTP, Gopher, and Finger. Here, you control which ones are available to users. By default, only HTTP, FTP, and Gopher are available.

▶ **Concurrent retrievers**—The default is 25, meaning the server services up to 25 simultaneous requests for documents. If the server sees heavy Web usage and slow responses to Web retrieval requests, increase this number. But remember to increase the amount of server RAM by 2M and the size of the page file by 10M for every retriever added.

▶ **Retriever log level**—The default is None; there is no logging of Web Retriever activity. If you want to log this activity to the server console and the LOG.NSF file, change this to Terse or Verbose.

▶ **Update cache**—The default is Never. The first time the Web Navigator receives a request for a page, it gets it from the designated Web server. It stores the page in the Web Navigator database and sends a copy to the requesting user. Thereafter, whenever someone requests that page again, the Web Navigator delivers the cached copy of the page instead of retrieving it anew from the Web server. By the

22

default of this field, Web Navigator never checks with the Web server to discover if the page has been updated since first retrieved. You can change this to Once Per Session or Every Time. If you choose Once Per Session, the Web Retriever does not check with the Web server if you ask for the same page again in the same browsing session, but it does check with the Web server if you ask for the page again in a future browsing session, or if some other user asks for it. If you choose Every Time, then every time anyone asks for a cached page, before the Web Retriever delivers the cached copy of the page, it queries the Web server to see if a new version of the document is on the server.

▸ **SMTP Domain**—When a user clicks a mailto URL on a Web page, Notes composes a new mail message addressed to the person named in the URL. The person's address looks like *personsname@domainname.xxx*. If your organization uses the Lotus SMTP Mail Gateway to route mail to the Internet, you must append to that your gateway's foreign domain name. Let's say you always mail to the Internet by addressing to *personsname@domainname.xxx@internet*, where *internet* is the gateway's foreign domain name. Notes appends *@internet* to the mailto address if you enter *internet* into this field.

▸ **Allow access to these Internet sites**—By default, you can access all Internet sites. If you enter site domain names or IP addresses into this field, you are, in effect, saying, "Allow access to only the listed sites *and no others*." Administrators can use this field to severely restrict the number of Web sites users can visit when using the Server Web Navigator.

▸ **Deny access to these Internet sites**—By default, no sites are denied to the user. If you enter site domain names or IP addresses into this field, you are saying, "Allow access to all sites *except those listed here*." Administrators can use this field to block users out of a relatively small number of sites.

The Web Navigator Administration Document Settings

Finally, the Web Navigator database itself has a configuration document called Administration that further governs the way Web Navigator works. The trick here is to figure out how to find the Administration document. You won't find it in any views. The only way to open it is as follows:

1. Open the Web Navigator database. The Home Navigator appears.

2. In the menu, choose File, Database, Access Control. If your name appears in the list, select it. If not, but a group appears that you are a member of, select that group. If you are not named individually and you do not belong to any groups that are listed here, then select Default. In the lower-right, note whether a check mark

appears next to the Role called [WebMaster]. If no check mark appears, then you do not occupy that Role and you are not able to open the Administration document.

3. Click Database Views in the lower-left corner of the Navigator. The Database Views Navigator appears.

4. Choose All Documents, then open the <u>A</u>ctions menu. If you are a member of the [WebMaster] role, then Administration should appear there. Click it. The Administration document opens at last.

In the Web Navigator Administration document, the following fields appear.

Server Basics

This section includes basic information about the InterNotes server. It includes four fields:

▶ **InterNotes server name**—This is the fully distinguished, canonical name of the InterNotes server that populates this database. The database could be replicated onto other servers, but only the server named in this field adds documents to it.

▶ **Maximum database size**—This is the maximum size this database is permitted to reach. The default is 500M.

▶ **Save author information**—By default, the server does not save the identity of the user who originally retrieved a page from the Internet. Add a check mark to the box to cause the server to start saving that information in a field called Save_Author. If you do save author information, then you must create a view to see the information.

▶ **Save HTML in Notes**—Notes converts HTML documents to Notes format, then saves them in this database. By default, Notes discards the HTML source code. Checking the box in this field causes the server to save the HTML source code in a field called HTMLSource.

Purge Agent Settings

The Web Navigator database has a built-in agent, called the Purge agent, intended to help the administrator manage the size of the database. The Purge agent purges old and large documents from the database. You can configure how it works by setting the following variables:

22

▶ **Purge agent action**—By default, it purges by reducing a document, which means it throws out the document but keeps the URL. As a result, the page continues to appear in views and, if anyone chooses to open it in the view, Web Retriever goes and gets a fresh copy of it. You can change this field to Delete page, which deletes the page from the database entirely.

▶ **Purge to what % of maximum database size**—When the purge agent runs, it purges enough documents to reduce the database to, by default, 80 percent of its maximum size as set in the Maximum database size field. At 500M, by default, in that field, 80 percent reduces to 400M. Because the purge agent runs nightly, the defaults give the Web Navigator database 100M of leeway for new documents in any one day.

▶ **Purge documents older than**—The purge agent purges oldest documents first, and, by default, looks for documents older than 30 days.

▶ **Purge documents larger than**—The purge agent also purges largest documents first, looking, by default, at documents larger than 256K.

▶ **Purge Private documents**—When a user retrieves pages from a Web site that requires authentication, the retrieved pages are not placed in the general views of the database for all to see. Rather, they are encrypted with the requester's public key, so that only the requester can open them, and they are placed in a folder that is private to the requester, so that other users don't even know the pages are in the database. This field allows the administrator to tell the purge agent to delete these private documents, which the purge agent would not do by default.

Caution

Authentication with Internet servers requires that user public keys are stored within the user documents of the Domino server domain Public Address Book. If the Domino server is in the same domain as the users, this happens automatically. If the Domino server resides in a different domain, say, for example, a firewall domain, then you have to copy the person documents of the users of that Domino server from the users' Public Address Book to the Domino server's Public Address Book.

HTML Preferences

These are the same preferences that appear in the Internet Options document in the Personal Web Navigator database. They were described earlier in the section "Presentation Preferences."

Browsing with the Server Web Navigator

Server Web Navigator has been around since Notes 4.0 arrived in January 1996. It was designed with the goals of introducing the World Wide Web to groups of people who may not previously have experienced it, of extracting synergies from the Web surfing experiences of groups of people, so that individual members of the group might benefit from the collective experiences of the whole group, and of letting employers limit the amount and kind of surfing employees do on company time. Server Web Navigator has a Navigator front end that invites the novice user to explore the unknown terrain of the Web by clicking hotspots and discovering where they lead. Also, Server Web Navigator has tools that allow you to share good and bad Web surfing experiences with each other. Finally, because the InterNotes server actually does the Web browsing for you, you can only surf where and when the server is willing.

The first time you open the Server Web Navigator, you will probably see the Home Navigator, as shown in Figure 22.2. It consists of a bunch of hotspots that, when you click them, load a Web page, open another Navigator, or open a dialog box.

Fig. 22.2

With Server Web Navigator, you get a flashy Navigator. Click one of the icons and see where it takes you.

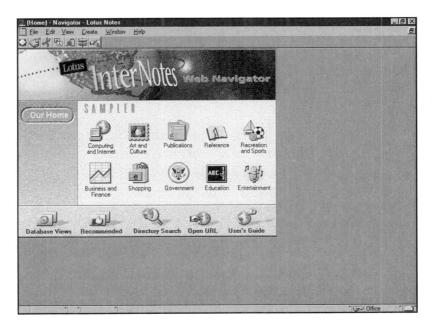

The hotspots in the Sampler section of the Home Navigator take you to another Navigator. The name of the Navigator varies, depending on which hotspot you click. They all look alike, though, showing you hotspots that open three of the more popular Web search engines. Alongside this Navigator, you see a View that displays the documents in the Web Navigator database that fall in the chosen category. Thus, you can browse the database for documents of the chosen type, or you can search the Web for more such documents. In Figure 22.3, the Entertainment appears.

Fig. 22.3

The Entertainment Navigator appears when you click the Entertainment Hotspot in the Sampler section of the Home Navigator.

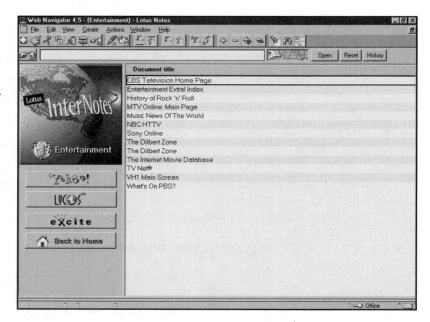

The icons along the bottom of the Home Navigator have the following functions:

▶ **Database Views**—Opens the View Navigator, which lists various Views of the Web pages already stored in the database

▶ **Recommended**—Opens the Recommended Navigator where you can see the Rated documents

▶ **Directory Search**—Displays a search form that lets you perform searches with Internet search engines

▶ **Open URL**—Displays a dialog box in which you enter the URL of a Web page in order to open it

▶ **User's Guide**—Opens the online Web Navigator User's Guide database

When you click Database Views in the Home Navigator, the View Navigator opens. Here, each hotspot opens a particular View of the contents of the Web Navigator database. Table 22.1 describes each button in the View Navigator.

Table 22.1   The View Navigator Buttons

Button	Click This Button to
My Bookmarks	Open pages you saved in your Bookmarks folder. To add a page to the Bookmarks folder, drag and drop the page onto this button. You add pages to the Bookmarks folder from the Web by clicking Bookmarks, selecting My Bookmarks in the Move to Folder dialog box, and clicking Add.
Folders	Opens a standard Folders Navigator.
All Documents	Displays all the Web pages stored in this database.
By Host	Displays all Web pages sorted by their host site.
File Archive	Displays all file attachments and their sizes.
Web Tours	Displays all the saved Web Tours.
Recommended	Opens the Recommended Navigator.
Back to Home	Returns to the Home Navigator.

The Server Web Navigator Action Bar

When you open a document stored in the Web Navigator database, an Action Bar appears. It is unlike the Action Bars in other Notes databases (except the Personal Web Navigator database). Rather, it emulates the Action Bars that you see in Web browsers such as Mosaic, Netscape Navigator, and Microsoft's Internet Explorer. This Action Bar helps you browse the Web (see Figure 22.4).

The buttons in the Action Bar serve the functions listed in Table 22.2.

Table 22.2   Action Buttons

Button	Button Name	Click to
Home	Home	Go back to the Home Page Navigator
Open	Open	Open the Open URL dialog box
Previous	Previous	Go to the previous page in the History file
Next	Next	Go to the next page in the History file

continues

Table 22.2   Continued

Button	Button Name	Click to
History	History	Open the History dialog box to save pages to the History or go to other pages listed in the History
	Reload	Reload the current Web page from the Internet server
	Recommend	Open the dialog box to enter your rating of the current Web page
Forward	Forward	Forward the Web page to someone by e-mail
Bookmarks	Bookmarks	Store the current Web page in the Bookmarks folder

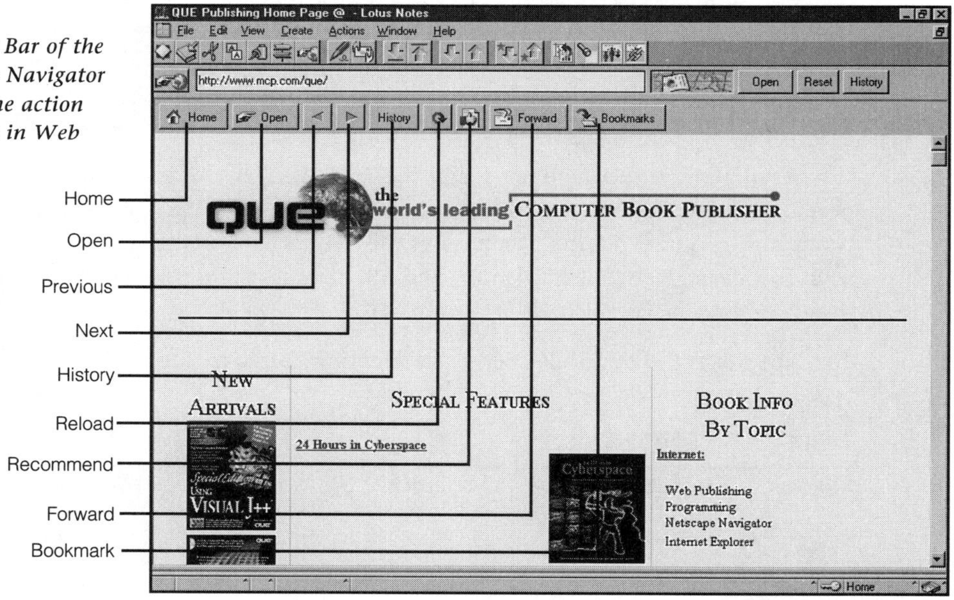

Fig. 22.4
The Action Bar of the Server Web Navigator emulates the action bar you see in Web browsers.

The Server Web Navigator Search Bar

The Search Bar in Domino 4.5 is actually a dual purpose tool. You can use it to enter an URL and retrieve a Web page, or you can search the Web Navigator database for text you enter in the Search Bar. You toggle between the two modes by clicking the icon at the left end of the Search Bar.

In the Web Navigator databases, the Search Bar appears when you are in a View or when a Web document is open; however, when a document is open you can only use the Search Bar to retrieve Web pages. In other databases, the Search Bar only appears when you are in a View, not when a document is open. The Search Bar appears by default only in databases that have been full-text indexed. If you don't see the Search Bar, select View, Search Bar.

The two versions of the Search Bar are potentially confusing. Make sure the proper icon is showing for the type of search you want to perform (see Figures 22.5 and 22.6). When you want to retrieve a Web page, you may need to click the Search icon to switch to Open URL mode. When you want to search for text within the pages of the database, you may need to click the Open URL icon to switch to Search mode.

Fig. 22.5
Here, the Search Bar is in Web retrieval mode. Note which icon appears on the left. Note what words appear in the buttons on the right. Compare to Figure 22.6.

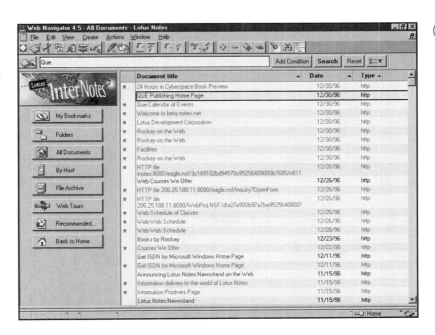

Fig. 22.6
Here, the Search Bar is in full-text search mode. Note which icon appears on the left. Note what words appear in the buttons on the right. Compare to Figure 22.5.

The buttons on the Open URL Search Bar are described in Table 22.3. The buttons in the Full Text Search Bar are described in Table 22.4.

Table 22.3   The Buttons on the Open URL Search Bar

Button	Description
	Sets which type of Search Bar you're using
http://www.mcp.com/que/	Enter the URL you want here
	Grayed out because not applicable when opening URLs
Open	Click to open the specified URL
Reset	Click to clear the URL name
History	If you are connected to the Internet/Intranet when you click this button, Notes displays the History dialog box, from where you can go directly to any page you have visited during the current session. If you are not connected to the Web, nothing happens when you click this box.

Table 22.4   The Buttons on the Text Search Bar

Button	Description
	Sets the Search Bar to search for text in the database.
Que	Enter the word or phrase you're looking for.
Create Index	This button only appears if the database is not indexed. Click it to start the index creation process.
Add Condition	The Create Index button becomes the Add Condition button after you create the index. Use it to display the Search Builder dialog box, where Notes does most of the work of building your search query.

Button	Description
Search	Click here to activate the search.
Reset	Click here to clear the search results from the View pane. The query that produced the search remains in the Search Bar for you to edit.
⌗▾	Drops down a menu of search options. The programmers couldn't think of a short description (like, say, "menu") for the button, so, in the spirit of "one word is worth 1000 pictures," they used an inscrutable diagram instead.

To search for text, your database must be full-text indexed. If it is not, the first button in the Search Bar is Create Index. Click it to open the Properties for Database InfoBox to the Full Text panel. There you can set options, then begin the index creation process. If you create an index for a Local database, you may have to wait around while Notes creates it. If you have not enabled local background indexing in User Preferences, you will have to wait around. If you have enabled local background indexing, you will still have to wait for Notes to create the index, but you can read your mail or something while waiting because Notes will create the index in the background. If it is a large database and Notes is making you wait, go get a cup of coffee or something.

22

Creating Web Tours and Recommendations

A Web tour is a record of your visit to a site, and you record this history by creating a Web tour document. When you create a Web tour, it is available to other users of the Server Web Navigator. To create a Web tour, click on the History button on the action bar. Click on the save button in the History dialog box. A Web Tour Document (see Figure 22.7) opens showing a list of the URLS in your history (the first line of each entry is the title of the URL and the second line is the actual URL).

Enter the title of your tour. If you want to change the order of the pages, or delete pages, edit the contents of the document. Enter a description of the tour in the Comments field. Save the document.

To load a Web Tour, select the Database Views icon on the Server Navigator Home page. Click on Web Tours, select the Web Tour you want to see and open the document. Click on the Load Tour button.

Fig. 22.7

A Web Tour Document lists your recent history. The first line of each entry is the title of the page and the second line is the actual URL.

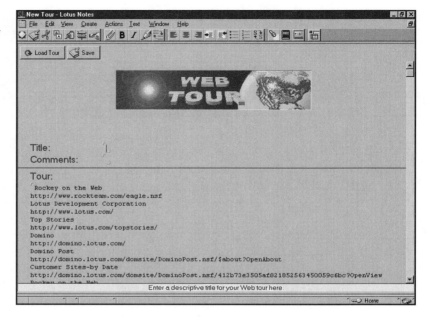

The Serve Web Navigator provides a method of rating or recommending Web pages. You might find some interesting business information on the Web that you want to bring to the attention of others. To recommend a page, open the page you wish to recommend, and click on the Recommend button in the Action bar. The recommend dialog box appears (see Figure 22.8). Select a rating from 1 to 5 for this page (5 is the highest rating), add your comments and select a category.

Fig. 22.8

The Recommend dialog box. Once Recommended pages are saved, they can be accessed by selecting the Recommend icon located on the Home Navigator of the Server Web Navigator.

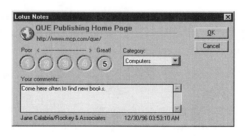

Programming and Customizing the Server Web Navigator

The Server Web Navigator template is customizable. You can program new functions or replace it with your own navigator. Both the Notes programming language and LotusScript can be used when customizing the database. You can change the Home navigator, change the graphics, or change URLs. Like any other Notes database, you can add or modify views, create smarticons, write agents, or create new action bar buttons.

Before you start to make design changes, make a backup of the database template (pubweb45.ntf) in addition to its documents. Backing up the documents assures that you will have a copy of the Administration document. As is the case for all database design in Notes, be certain to make your changes to the template (webpub45.ntf) as opposed to the database (webput45.nsf) to prevent your changes from being overwritten or erased by the template.

Modifying the Existing Home Navigator

To modify the Home navigator, open it in design mode. Use <u>V</u>iew, <u>S</u>how, <u>F</u>olders to access the folder view. If "Design" is not listed in the view pane, select <u>V</u>iew, <u>S</u>how, Design to access the design view. The name of the Home navigator is *Home* (works for us) and is found, of course in the Navigator view. Note that the navigator name appears in parenthesis to hide the navigator from appearing in any menus.

Figure 22.9 shows the Navigator in design mode. Also displayed is the properties box, with the Launch tab of the database properties showing. Modifying this navigator is a pretty straight-forward application design. You can see that the navigator is the selected launch option for the database, set to view in it's own window.

Domino converts navigators to image maps. Web users can see that image maps have areas that, when clicked, link to other Web pages or sites.

Caution
For Domino to convert navigators to image maps, they must be created as *Graphic Backgrounds*. Use the command <u>C</u>reate <u>G</u>raphic Background to assure conversion of your navigator. To learn more about navigators and image maps, see Chapter 12, "Applying a 'Web Look' to Notes Applications."

22

You can see in Figure 22.9 that the navigator contains hotspots. The hotspots are created by choosing Create Hotspot Rectangle or Create Hotspot Polygon and drawing polygons or rectangles around the regions of the bitmap which will act as links. Properties for the hotspots are set in the properties box,(*Auto adjust panes at runtime* does not apply to Web browsers) and actions for the hotspots are specified in the design pane. You can change the hotspots to point to different URLs, or to open a view or a form within the database. Simply modify the action in the design pane.

Fig. 22.9

The Home navigator in design mode. Database launch options set for this database (see the properties box) will display this navigator in its own window when users open the database.

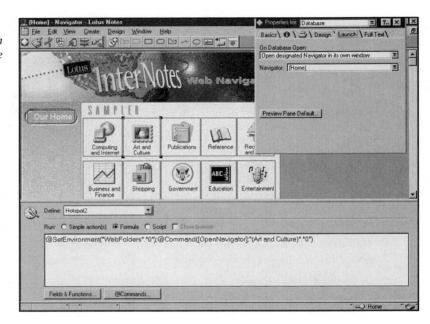

Caution
Use only Hotspot Rectangles or Polygons to create image map hotspots. Text boxes, graphics buttons and others are not supported.

Designing Your Own Home Navigator

Designing your own Home navigator is a two step process. First, you must create the navigator and specify it in the database properties box as the launch option. Second, you must change the formula in the HTML form and the $All view of the database.

Create the new navigator by opening the Web Navigator template (pubweb45.ntf).in design mode. Choose Create, Design, Navigator in the design view. Copy your bitmap to the Windows clipboard and paste it into the navigator, remembering to paste it as a *Graphic Background*. Create Hotspot Rectangles or Polygons, specifying the action for each in the design pane. Name and save the navigator and make it the default *On Database Open* by specifying the navigator name in the database properties box.

Once you've created the navigator, you need to make some changes in the HTML form and the $All view of the database. The HTML form is the form in use when Notes clients are viewing a web page. The Action bar of this form contains an action to return to the "Home" navigator (see Figure 22.10). Edit this action by specifying your new navigator name in the design pane.

Fig. 22.10

The Action Bar of the HTML form contains an action for returning "Home." You must specify your new navigator name in the action. Replace "Home" with "YourNavigatorName."

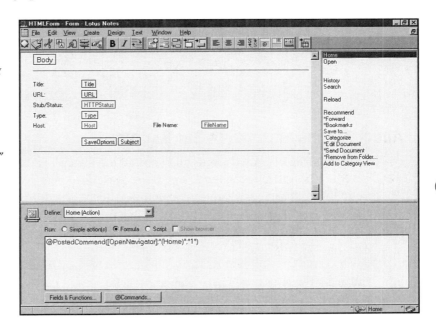

The $All view is the default view of the Server Web Navigator and contains an action to return "Back to Home." Edit this action and specify your new navigator name (see Figure 22.11).

Fig. 22.11

The default view of the Home navigator contains an action to return "Back to Home." You must specify your new navigator name in the action. Replace "Home" with "YourNavigatorName."

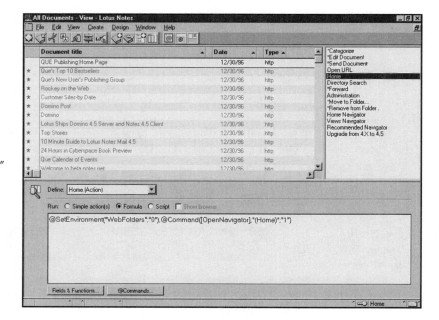

About Agents and Action Bar Buttons

You can create your own agents and you can use the agents that come with the Web Navigator, specifically the Purge and Refresh agents to help you manage the database (see "The Web Navigator Administration Document Settings" in this Chapter). Don't use the @URLOpen or @URLGetHeader function to create agents that will run manually from the menu. For more information on agents, see Chapter 11, "Automating Web Applications with Agents." Also refer to "Lotus Notes and the Internet" (internet.nsf) on your Domino server. There you will find agents to create Smarticons that display navigation history and agents to refresh web pages, among others.

Several Action Bar buttons are built into the Server Web Navigator, such as those that return to the Home navigator, open an URL, and open the History dialog box. You can add Actions by opening the Web Navigator template in design mode and selecting and opening the form to which you want to add your action.

 Tip
If you want your Action Button to appear on the each Web page, place it in the HTML form.

Choose Create, Action and enter a title (label) for the Button in the Action Properties box. Select an icon and a position for your button. Enter the formula in the design page and save your action. For more on actions, see Chapter 10, "Using Special Web Fields and Forms."

From Here...

The Server Web Navigator is a powerful adjunct to the overall functionality of Domino. By allowing you to extend Notes' reach to the far corners of the Internet, The Server Web Navigator truly enhances Notes' role as a repository for information of all kinds.

For related information, see the following chapters:

- ▶ Chapter 1, "An Introduction to Domino 4.5 and the Internet," describes URLs and their use.

- ▶ Chapter 3, "Working with Your Domino Web Site," defines Domino URLs used for searching a Domino Web site.

- ▶ Chapter 23, "Using the Personal Web Navigator," provides information on configuring and using the Personal Web Navigator and describes the agents available to make Web browsing faster and more efficient.

22

Using the Personal Web Navigator

In this chapter

◆ **How the Personal Web Navigator works**
What happens behind the scenes when you tell Notes to get a Web page.

◆ **How to set up the Personal Web Navigator**
We walk through all of the steps. We look at all of the configuration options.

◆ **How to search the Web with the Personal Web Navigator**
We step through all the different ways to locate Web documents using the Navigator and show you how to share and mail Web pages.

◆ **How to use agents to speed your browsing**
We examine Web Ahead and Page Minder, tools that automate the Web retrievals.

A new feature of the Notes 4.5 client is the Personal Web Navigator, a Web browser built into the client software, along with a companion Notes database that stores the Web pages retrieved by the browser. Every Web page you view is converted to a Notes document and stored in the Personal Web Navigator database, located on the Notes Workstation along with the browser.

Yes, this is a book about developing applications for Domino 4.5, but we feel we'd be remiss if we didn't provide information about all of the Internet features of Domino. After all, if you build it, they will come and if you build it in Domino, they just might come via the Personal Web Navigator. Besides, the feature is on your workstation, is an Internet tool, and you can use it (given Internet access) at will, as your default web browser if you wish. You may even decide to create applications that take advantage of the captured web pages in your personal web navigator database or write agents for your personal use in accessing the data you personally retrieve (DL).

Understanding the Personal Web Navigator

Unlike the Server Web Navigator (see Chapter 22, "Using the Server Web Navigator") both the Personal Web Navigator browser and database reside on the Notes client. This allows Notes users to browse the Web without connection to the Domino server.

When you request an URL from the Notes client, Notes sends the URL to the computer named in it. If the other computer responds by sending a Web page back to you, Notes converts that Web page to Notes format, stores it in the Personal Web Navigator database, and displays it to you on-screen (see Figure. 23.1).

Fig. 23.1

When you use the Personal Web Navigator, your own computer retrieves Web pages directly, without intervention by an InterNotes server.

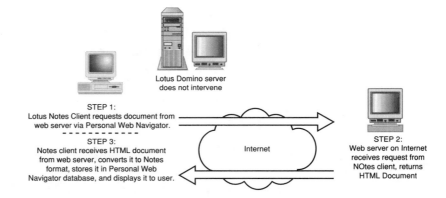

Lotus Domino server does not intervene

STEP 1:
Lotus Notes Client requests document from web server via Personal Web Navigator.

STEP 3:
Notes client receives HTML document from web server, converts it to Notes format, stores it in Personal Web Navigator database, and displays it to user.

Internet

STEP 2:
Web server on Internet receives request from NOtes client, returns HTML Document

Configuring the Personal Web Navigator

To use Personal Web Navigator, you have to take the following steps to set it up:

1. Meet system requirements for running Notes on your system. See the Notes Workstation Install Guide, the Domino 4.5 Release Notes, and Chapter 16 of this book for more information on Notes system requirements.

2. Use a Location document that specifies From Notes Workstation in the Retrieve/open pages field. All of the Location documents that come with a plain vanilla installation of Notes default to From InterNotes Server, so you must change the field before you can use Personal Web Navigator.

3. Open an URL, either from the menu by choosing File, Open URL, or from a Notes document by clicking an embedded URL, which appears underlined in green. This causes Notes to create the Personal Web Navigator database. The database receives the default name of perweb45.nsf, is based on the perweb45.ntf design template, and receives and stores all pages retrieved by the Personal Web Navigator.

System Requirements for Personal Web Navigator

The system requirements for Personal Web Navigator, over and above those for the Notes client itself, are the following:

▶ A connection to the Internet or intranet

▶ TCP/IP running on your workstation

▶ 500 megabytes free hard disk space

The last one isn't really a requirement, but a recommendation by Lotus. Lotus knows that you tend to accumulate Web pages fast when you surf the Web, and your Personal Web Navigator database is likely to get big. There is no specific minimum amount of disk space necessary to run Personal Web Navigator. But remember the axiom: You can never have too much disk space (or RAM or processing power or video resolution or network bandwidth or, well, you get the picture).

If you are connecting to the Internet, there are three possible ways:

▶ A direct connection, via your Local Area Network (LAN) or leased telephone line, to an Internet Service Provider (ISP)

▶ A direct connection, via modem, to an ISP

▶ An indirect connection to an ISP, via a proxy server, to which you will probably connect by LAN

When you are connected to your company's LAN, you probably connect to the Internet across the LAN, either directly to an ISP or indirectly through a proxy server. If you are at home or in a hotel room, you connect directly to an ISP using your modem.

If you are connecting to your company's intranet, you either connect directly across the LAN or, if you are out of the office, directly by modem or indirectly by proxy server. Because proxy servers protect your LAN from unauthorized access by outsiders, there is no need for you to use a proxy server when you are on the LAN. But going through a proxy server may be the only way to get to your intranet when you are on the outside.

In any event, you must have the TCP/IP protocol stack in your computer's memory to use the Personal Web Navigator. The TCP/IP protocol stack is the hallmark of the Internet and intranets. Without it, you are not on the Internet/intranet.

Setting Up a Location Document for Personal Web Navigator

To browse with Personal Web Navigator, you must be using a Location document that specifies From Notes Workstation in the Retrieve/open pages field. All of the Location documents that come with a plain vanilla installation of Notes default to "from InterNotes server." Notes interprets this to mean it should use the Server Web Navigator, so someone must change the field before you can use Personal Web Navigator. The Notes administrator can set this up before or after installing Notes or the user can set it up before using Personal Web Navigator for the first time.

If you are a Notes administrator and you intend for your users to use Personal Web Navigator rather than Server Web Navigator, the most efficient way to set them up is to create and assign a Profile document to new users when you register them. In the Profile document, you can specify "from Notes workstation" in the Retrieve/open pages field. When you set up the user's workstation, the Location documents inherit that setting (see Figure 23.2).

Fig. 23.2

Both Location documents and User Setup Profile documents have a Retrieve/ Open pages field. Clicking the button in the field opens the displayed dialog box.

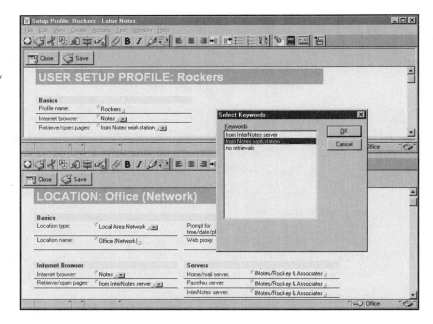

If users will use a proxy server to reach the Internet, you can also enter the proxy server addresses into the Profile document. The user Location documents will inherit those settings, too.

Finally, you can set forth in the Profile document what actions Notes will take when it receives a Web page that includes a Java applet. A Java applet is a program, and can potentially damage your software and data. Or it can make network connections to other hosts and give them access to your system and data. Notes allows you to list trusted hosts—computers from which you are reasonably sure you will never receive damaging Java applets—and specify what degree of access to your computer's resources are permitted to Java applets from either trusted or untrusted hosts (see Figure 23.3).

Fig. 23.3

Here are the Default Proxy Configuration and Default Java Applet Security sections of a User Setup Profile form. The dialog box shows the choices available in the Network access for trusted hosts field.

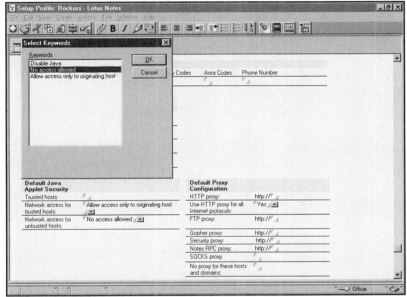

The choices for the Network access for trusted hosts field include the following five choices. The choices for the Network access for untrusted hosts field include the first three of the following choices:

▶ *Disable Java*—Notes does not run Java applets.

▶ *No access allowed*—Notes does not permit a Java applet to expose your computer's resources to any computer.

▶ *Allow access only to originating host*—Notes permits the Java applet to expose your computer's resources only to the computer from which it obtained the Java applet.

▶ *Allow access to any trusted host*—Notes permits the Java applet to expose your computer's resources to any computer in your list of trusted hosts. This is the default setting.

▶ *Allow access to any host*—Notes permits the Java applet to expose your computer's resources to any other computer.

If the Notes administrator did not have the opportunity or foresight to set up the location document using a User Setup Profile document, then either the administrator or the user will have to make changes to the appropriate Location documents themselves. In addition to the Retrieve/open pages field, the proxy server fields, and the Java security fields that were duplicated in the User Profile Setup document, the following are some other fields that may affect your Web browsing:

▸ *Internet browser*—Choose your Web browser here. Defaults to Notes but you can choose to have Notes display Web pages in another Web browser whenever you open an URL.

▸ *Web Retriever Configuration Section*—In this section of the Location document, you control several aspects of the behavior of the Personal Web Navigator. They include the following five fields:

  ▸ *Web Navigator database*—Holds the file name of the Personal Web Navigator database. If you ever decide to rename or change the location of the database, enter its new path name here.

  ▸ *Concurrent retrievers*—This is the number of retriever processes that can reside in memory concurrently. If you want to browse more intensively than you can with four retrievers, increase this number. Be sure to increase your RAM as well, by 2M for each additional retriever.

  ▸ *Retriever log level*—Notes logs retrieval activity to your Notes log by default. You can reduce the logging or turn it off entirely here.

  ▸ *Update cache*—The default is Never. The first time the Web Navigator receives a request for a page, it gets it from the designated Web server. It stores the page in the Web Navigator database and displays a copy to you. Thereafter, when you request that page again, the Web Navigator delivers the cached copy of the page instead of retrieving it anew from the Web server. By the default of this field, Web Navigator never checks with the Web server to discover if the page has been updated since first retrieved. You can change this to Once per Session or Every Time. If you choose Once per Session, the Web Retriever does not check with the Web server if you ask for the same page again in the same browsing session, but it does check with the Web server if you ask for the page again in a future browsing session. If you choose Every Time, then every time you ask for a cached page, before the Web Retriever delivers the cached copy of the page, it queries the originating Web server to see if a new version of the document is on the server.

  ▸ *Accept SSL site certificates*—The default is No. Change it to Yes to accept Secure Sockets Layer (SSL) certificates from computers with which you do not otherwise share a certificate issued by a third-party Certification Authority (CA). Then, if you do accept a certificate from a computer, you have to take it on faith that the computer you are talking to is really the computer it claims to be, because by accepting a certificate from the computer, you have no way of knowing who issued its public and private keys. However, you still get the other two benefits of SSL security—encryption of data transmissions between the two computers and assurance that no tampering with any secured message has occurred en route. See chapter 15, "Using Secure Sockets Layer (SSL) with Domino," for more information about SSL.

▶ *Java Applet Security Section*—In this section of the Location document, you control the way Personal Web Navigator handles incoming Java applets. The first three fields in this section are the same as the ones in the User Setup Profile document described earlier. If a certifier assigns a User Profile Document to a user at registration time, the entries in those fields in this Location document are inherited from the User Setup Profile when the new user's workstation is set up. This section has one additional field, Trust HTTP Proxy, that was not in the Java security section of the User Setup Profile. It is described in the next paragraph.

▶ *Trust HTTP proxy*—This field is only relevant if you access the Internet through an HTTP proxy server. The default is No, meaning that your computer makes its own determination of whether the host from which a Java applet is received is a trusted host. If you cannot run a Java applet, it may be because your computer cannot resolve the Web server's host name to its IP address. Changing this field to Yes tells your computer to assume that the HTTP proxy server successfully resolved the host name with the IP address, and to go ahead and run the applet according to the Trusted host/Untrusted host settings of the other fields in this section.

Creating the Personal Web Navigator Database

23

The last step of setting up the Personal Web Navigator is to create the Personal Web Navigator database. You don't have to do this yourself. All you have to do is retrieve a Web document. Do this any of several ways:Choose File, Open URL in the menu and enter an URL; click the Open URL SmartIcon and enter an URL; or click an URL embedded in any Notes document. You will recognize an embedded URL because it looks like an URL (for example, **http://www.lotus.com**) and it is underlined in green.

Tip
If URLs in your Notes documents are not underlined in green and Notes doesn't try to retrieve the document when you click the URL, it is probably because you have not enabled automatic conversion of URLs to Notes hotspots. To enable automatic conversion, follow these steps:

1. Choose File, Tools, User Preferences in the Notes menu. The User Preferences dialog box appears.

> **2.** In the Advanced Options field of the User Preferences dialog box, add a check mark to the list next to Make Internet URLs (**http://...**) into Hotspots.
>
> **3.** Click OK to accept the change.
>
> Next time you see an URL in a Notes document, it should appear and act as a Notes hotspot.

When you retrieve that first Web document, Personal Web Navigator creates the Personal Web Navigator database in the Notes data directory on your computer, then tries to retrieve the Web page. If it retrieves it successfully, it puts the page into the new database.

At this time, the Personal Web Navigator database also sets up a configuration document called Internet Options that you can use to fine-tune the way the database works. The Internet Options document has generally acceptable default settings, and you may never have to change it. However, the first time you open the Personal Web Navigator database, a dialog box will appear presenting you with the opportunity to review the Internet Options document and make any changes in it that you want. Except for that last step, the setup of Personal Web Navigator is now complete, and you can retrieve Web documents to your heart's content.

Setting Internet Options in the Personal Web Navigator Database

Any time you want to review or change the Internet Options document, you can do so by opening the Personal Web Navigator database and choosing Actions, Internet Options in the menu. The Internet Options document consists of eight fields, which are covered in the following sections.

Startup Options

Here, you can specify what happens when you open the Personal Web Navigator database. By default, it opens to a standard Notes three-pane interface in which you see a list of views in the upper-left corner, the documents in the currently selected view in the lower-left corner, and the currently selected document previewed on the right. You can instead open to a home page. To do so, you edit the following two fields:

> ▶ Put a check mark in the box labeled Open Home Page on Database Open.
>
> ▶ Optionally, enter the URL of the home page to which you want to open in the Home Page field. It defaults to **www.notes.net**, which is the home page of Lotus's InterNIC Web site.

Search Options

A preferred method to locate information on the Web is to use a search engine to search indexes of documents. This field permits you to choose a default search engine from several popular ones. It defaults to Yahoo!, but you can choose Alta Vista, Excite, Lycos, or enter the name of any other search engine you prefer. Whichever search engine you choose, it is not the one you will use to search your Web Navigator database; for that you will use Notes' own search engine.

Web Ahead Agent Preferences

In the Preload Web pages field, you can choose to retrieve pages one, two, three, or four levels ahead of the current page. If you have not enabled Web Ahead, a button labeled Enable Web Ahead also appears in this section. If the button does not appear, Web Ahead has been enabled. For more information on the Web Ahead feature, see *Using the Web Ahead Agent in Personal Web Navigator to Retrieve Multiple Related Pages* later in this chapter.

Page Minder Agent Preferences

Page Minder is an agent that watches for updates to chosen Web pages and notifies you when it finds them. It only runs when your Notes workstation is running, and it can only function when you are connected to the Internet, but it can keep you up-to-date on important events effortlessly.

Following are the fields in Page Minder agent preferences:

▸ **Search for updates every**—You can choose to search every hour, every four hours, every day, or every week. The default is every day.

▸ **When updates are found**—By default, the agent mails you a summary notifying you that the page has changed. In this field, you can change that to Send Me the Actual Page and receive the updated page in your mail.

▸ **Send to**—This automatically lists you as the addressee for change notices. You can add or substitute other addressees if you want.

Database Purge Options

With all these agents (not to mention enthusiastic humans) gathering pages from all over the Net and dropping them conveniently into your Personal Web Navigator database, you can imagine how quickly it takes over your hard disk. To combat this cancer, you can set up automatic purging of old files in the database. By default, this is enabled.

23

But you can change this to Reduce Full Pages to Links If Not Read Within, or Remove Pages from Database If Not Read Within, and then set a time limit. The time limit defaults to 30 days. You can change that to 60 or 90 days. Reduce Full Pages to Links means that the pages are purged from the database but their URLs are retained. You will still see the purged pages in the Personal Web Navigator database and, if you click one, Personal Web Navigator retrieves it anew for you.

You can also have Notes warn you when the Personal Web Navigator database exceeds 5, 10, 25, or 50 megabytes in size.

Presentation Preferences

Web documents are made up of plain text and embedded codes. The codes are part of the Internet protocol known as HyperText Markup Language (HTML) and they define the formatting of the document. Web browsers interpret the codes and replace them with formatting, so that you and I see a formatted document, not a bunch of inscrutable codes. You can affect how Web Navigator interprets the codes by altering the contents of the following fields:

▸ **Anchors**—These are the URL links that appear on HTML pages. They appear, by default, underlined and in blue. You can change this.

▸ **Body Text**—This defaults to 11pt Times. You can change it to 10 or 12pt and to Helvetica or Courier.

▸ **Fixed**—This is the typeface (defaulting to Courier) used within code pairs that begin with <CODE>, <KBD>, <SAMPLE>, and <TT>.

▸ **Plain**—This is the typeface (defaulting to Courier) used within code pairs that begin with <PLAINTEXT>, <PRE>, and <EXAMPLE>.

▸ **Address**—This is the typeface (defaulting to Times) used within the <ADDRESS> code pair.

▸ **Listing**—This is the typeface (defaulting to Courier) used within the <LISTING> code pair.

▸ **Save HTML in Note**—Notes converts HTML documents to Notes format, then saves them in this database. By default, Notes discards the HTML source code. Checking the box in this field causes the server to save the HTML source code in a field called HTMLSource.

Network Preferences

This last section of the Internet Options document includes a button that, when you click it, loads the current Location document so you can edit it and change your network preferences.

Using the Personal Web Navigator

The Personal Web Navigator was introduced with Notes 4.5 in response to the need of people to surf at times when they might not have an InterNotes server handy. It is intended primarily to meet the needs of individuals, not groups. Therefore it does not have a fancy front end like Server Web Navigator. It opens to the standard Notes split-screen—except that, in this case, the preview pane is open by default and it takes up most of the screen when it is open, so that we see a three-pane screen (see Figure 23.4). Personal Web Navigator has tools to enable the individual Notes user to gather information on the Web and keep up with changes in it; and it lacks the restrictive features included in the Server Web Navigator, which makes sense.

Fig. 23.4

Unlike Server Web Navigator, Personal Web Navigator opens up to the standard Notes three-pane window.

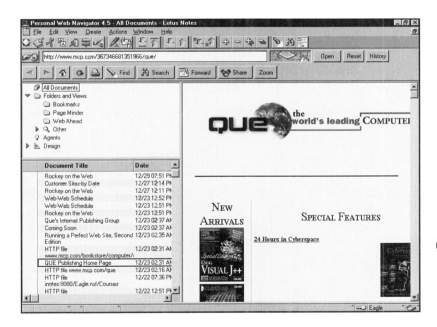

The default list of views and folders includes the following:

- ▶ **All Documents**—Shows all the Web pages in the database.

- ▶ **Bookmarks**—Use this folder to save your favorite Web pages for quick access later. To add a page to the Bookmarks folder, drag and drop the page onto this folder. When you're on the Web, add pages to the Bookmarks folder by clicking the Move to Folder action button, select Bookmarks as the folder, and choose Add.

- ▶ **Page Minder**—When you put a page in this folder, the Page Minder agent (if it is enabled) periodically checks its original site for updates. If it has been updated since you downloaded it, the agent notifies you. See Page Minder Agent Preferences earlier and Using the Page Minder Agent in the Personal Web Navigator later in this chapter for more details.

▶ **Web Ahead**—When you put a page in this folder, the Web Ahead agent (if it is enabled) retrieves in the background all the pages that it points to. Depending on how you have configured the agent, it may also retrieve all the pages pointed to by those pages, all by those, and all by those—that is, up to four levels of pages. A really good way to fill up a hard disk fast. See Web Ahead Agent Preferences in this chapter for more details.

▶ **File Archive**—Displays all file attachments and their sizes.

▶ **House Cleaning**—Displays Web pages sorted by size so you know which ones to reduce to their URLs.

▶ **Web Tours**—Displays all the Web Tour documents you've made.

The Personal Web Navigator Action Bar

The Personal Web Navigator has both View and Form Action Bars. They are nearly identical to each other, but they are different from the Action Bar that appears in the Server Web Navigator (see Figure 23.5). As with the Server Web Navigator, these Action Bars emulate those you see in Web browsers. They help you browse the Web. The Actions in the Action Bar are described in Table 23.1.

Fig. 23.5

The Action Bar of the Personal Web Navigator emulates those in Web browsers.

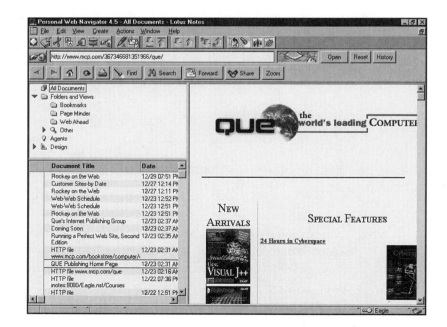

Table 23.1   Action Buttons

Button	Click to
◁	Goes to the previous page in the History list.
▷	Goes to the next page in the History list.
🏠	Goes to the page you defined in Internet Options as your home Web page.
↻	Reloads the current Web page from the Internet server.
🖨	Prints the current page.
🔍 Find	Finds pages from any of the views or finds text in any of the documents in the Personal Web Navigator database.
Search	Searches for pages on the Web using the Internet search engine you specified in Internet Options.
Forward	Forwards the Web page to someone via e-mail.
Share	Shares the Web page according to the specifications you made in Internet Options. This opens a dialog box in which you can choose to forward the page to someone, copy it to the Server Web Navigator database, or rate it and copy it and your rating to the Server Web Navigator database.
Zoom	Opens the Web page. This Action appears in the View Action Bar only.

Move to Folder Displays the Move to Folder dialog box, where you can choose a folder for the page. This Action appears in the Form Action Bar only.

The Personal Web Navigator Search Bar

The Search Bar works the same way in the Personal Web Navigator database as it does in the Server Web Navigator database. See details about its use in The Server Web Navigator Search Bar, earlier.

Using Internet Search Engines

Up until now, you worked your way around the Web by typing in an URL to go to a specific site. But what if you don't know the URL of a site you want to visit? Or what if you don't know what site would have information of the type you need? For example, what if you want to search for information about The King? You know, Elvis. You could try typing www.elvis.com. Is this a real Web site? Well, type it and find out. Of course, even if you get lucky and guess right on the name of a site, how do you know what other sites might also have valuable information about Elvis in them?

A more efficient way to locate information on the Web, when you don't know where to look, is to use an Internet search engine. With an Internet search engine you can type in a search term, such as *Elvis*, and the search engine searches one or more Web indexes for entries that contain the word *Elvis*; then it returns a list of links to the sites that it found. Most search engines will list the sites with the most *hits* at the top of the list.

Searching for *Elvis* might return an awful lot of hits—perhaps thousands, certainly hundreds, and probably more than you need. So, to narrow your search and find a better match, you can supply additional information to the search engine. For example, Elvis AND Sands AND Las Vegas AND October 1966 is bound to return a few less hits.

Different search engines maintain different lists of Web pages and after working with a few, you'll find one you like best. Or, if you need to do a really exhaustive search, you might run the same search with different search engines. When you select a search engine to use, InterNotes Web Publisher takes you to the home page of that search engine where you can type your search criteria. Although you can use any search engine, InterNotes makes it easy for you to choose Yahoo!, Lycos, Alta Vista, or Excite.

Searching the Web

The Personal Web Navigator allows you to select your preferred search engine, but using a search engine isn't quite as intuitive as it is in the Server Web Navigator. To access a search engine, you can either type in the search engine's URL, or you can set a preferred search engine in your Internet Options document. To set a preferred search engine, follow these steps:

1. From the workspace, select the Personal Web Navigator and choose <u>A</u>ctions, <u>I</u>nternet Options from the menu.

2. In the Search Options section, select the search engine you prefer in the Preferred Search Engine field. If you select Alta Vista, Excite, Lycos, or Yahoo!, save and close this document. If you choose Other, a new field appears and you must provide an URL in the new text field, as shown in Figure 23.6. Then save and close this document.

Fig. 23.6

Choose a preferred search engine in the Search Options section of the Internet Options document.

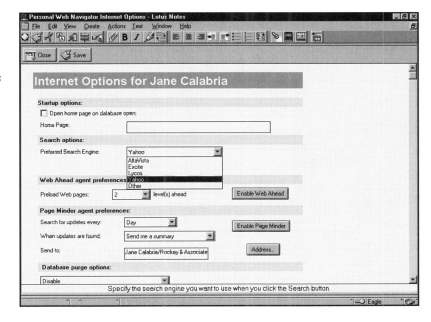

To use the search engine you just selected, follow these steps:

1. Open the Personal Web Navigator.
2. Click the Search icon on the Action Bar.
3. The Web Navigator retrieves the search engine Web page. Enter your search.

 Tip

You can perform searches on some Web pages. If a Web page is indexed, InterNotes Web Navigator displays a search button on the Action Bar. Often a Web page that is indexed indicates that it is indexed. Visit **http://www.sec.gov/cgi-bin/srch-edgar** to see an example of an indexed Web page.

Using Bookmarks

Have you had this frustrating experience? You initiate a search and drill deeper and deeper down through layer after layer of information. The address of the page you have reached is:

http:\\www.bongo.biz\technotes\dir_423\idea\ohno\iamlost\littlefeat

The phone rings, the system goes down, you get distracted, and did not make note of the address of this very important document. How do you ever find it again?

You could have saved the page in the Bookmarks folder. Both the Personal Web Navigator and the Server Web Navigator have them. The My Bookmarks folder in the Server Web Navigator is a private folder, stored on the Notes server; its contents are accessible only by you. If your Notes administrator has elected to periodically purge the Server Web Navigator database, the contents of the My Bookmarks folder and any subfolders you create under it are not, by default, deleted during the purge (although the Database Manager can override the default).

Saving Bookmarks

To add an open page to the Bookmarks folder while using the Personal Web Navigator, click the Move to Folder button in the Action Bar. The Move to Folder dialog box appears. Select the Bookmarks folder and choose Add.

To add a page to the My Bookmarks folder from the view pane of the database, drag and drop the page into the My Bookmarks Navigator button or folder icon.

Downloading Files from the Web

Some Web pages may have one or more files attached to them. The attached files sometimes appear as embedded icons with file names beneath them (see Figure 23.7). To retrieve such a file from a Web page, do the following:

1. Double-click the file name listed in the Web page, click the Download option on the Web page, or follow the instructions for downloading that appear on the page. The Attachment Properties box will appear, as shown in Figure 23.7. The Attachment Properties box displays details about the file and offers three options: View, Launch, and Detach.

2. Select Detach. The Save Attachment dialog box will appear, as in Figure 23.8, which follows.

3. Select a drive, directory, and file name under which to save the file. Click Detach. Notes will save the file. It doesn't actually detach the file but just detaches a copy. You could detach another copy later if you want.

Fig. 23.7

The Attachment Properties box shows the file name, size, and date and time of last modification of a file. You can view, launch, or detach a file.

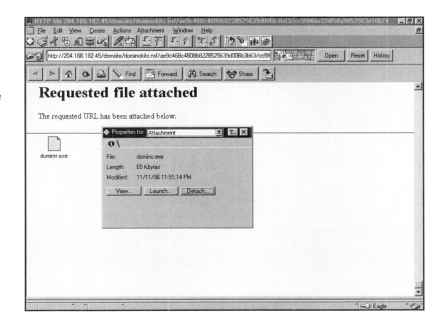

Fig. 23.8

Choose a drive, directory, and file name under which to save your file in the Save Attachment dialog box. Notes will offer to save under the file's original name.

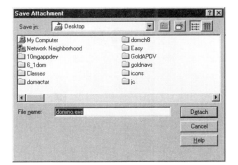

Sharing Information

You can share Web pages with others by e-mailing them or by making recommendations in the Server Web Navigator. *How* you share is slightly different in the Personal Web Navigator versus the Server Web Navigator.

Recommending or Sharing a Document in the Personal Web Navigator

You can share Web Pages with others by e-mailing them, sharing or recommending a page. Because the Personal Web Navigator database is your own personal database, not shared with others, it takes a little more effort than with the Server Web Navigator to share the fruits of your labors with others.

To recommend a Web page using the Personal Web Navigator, you first need to supply the name of your Notes server in your Internet Options document as explained in Setting Internet Options in the Personal Web Navigator Database, above, in this chapter. Then you must either forward the page's URL to people by mail or you must copy the page to the Server Web Navigator database. Notes automates both of these procedures, as follows:

1. Open the Personal Web Navigator.
2. Click a document in the Navigator pane, or open a document.
3. Click the Share button in the Action Bar.
4. A dialog box appears, as shown in Figure 23.9. This dialog box is different from the one the Server Web Navigator displays, and gives you three options:

Fig. 23.9

In this dialog box, you can forward a document's URL to someone, copy the document to the Server Web Navigator database, or copy it and recommend it.

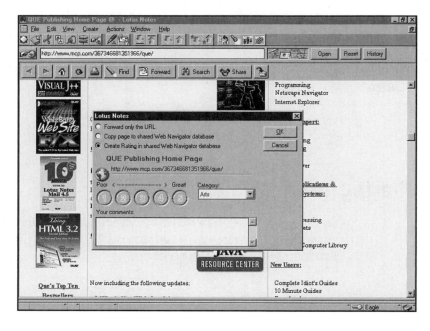

▶ **Forward only the URL**—Forwards the URL to others via e-mail. When you select this option, you are prompted for addressee names. You can fill in the name or click the address icon to select a name from your Personal Address Book. When you click OK, Notes sends a message to your addressee(s) in which the subject of the message is the title of the Web page as it appears in your database, and the body of the message is the URL of the database. If you are not connected to an InterNotes server, this is the only option you can choose.

▶ **Copy page to shared Web Navigator Database**—This copies the page to the All Documents view of the Server Web Navigator. You must be connected to the InterNotes server to choose this option.

▶ **Create Rating in shared Web Navigator Database**—This prompts you to create a rating as you would in the Server Web Navigator database and sends the page with its rating to the Recommended views of the Server Web Navigator. You must be connected to the InterNotes server to choose this option.

5. Click OK to send the document (or its URL) and close the dialog box.

Viewing Recommended Web Pages

To view the Web pages you and others have recommended in the Server Web Navigator, follow these steps:

1. Open the Server Web Navigator.

2. Click the Recommended button in the Navigator home page.

3. The Recommended Navigator appears on the left of the screen. It allows you to view the contents of the recommended Web pages in the following three ways:

▶ **By Category**—A list of classifications chosen when Web page ratings were created. A good view for finding pages by topics.

▶ **By Reviewer**—Sorted by the person who rated the Web page.

▶ **Top Ten**—Shows the top ten pages with the highest cumulative ratings.

Forwarding Web Pages to Other Users

You can e-mail a Web page to other Notes users from any view or any open document in the Web Navigator databases. Choose Actions, Forward in the menu, click the Actions Forward SmartIcon, or, if a document is open, click the Forward action in the Action Bar.

Notes will open a mail memo. The Web page appears in the body of the memo, and the subject line is automatically filled in with the title of the Web page. Figure 23.10 shows a Web page ready to be forwarded. Address the memo, add your comments, and click Send.

Fig. 23.10

You can Forward a Web page just like any other document. When the recipient opens the forwarded page, the links in it will be live.

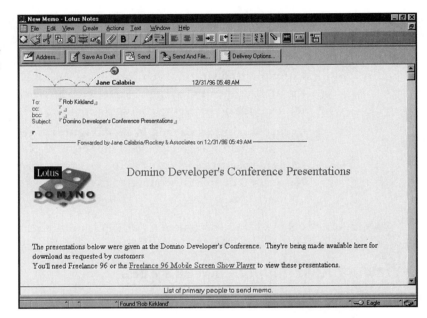

Viewing Java Applets

Java is a programming language that allows you to build small, cross-platform programs called "applets." You can embed an Applet in a Web page by including its URL in an HTML code with the <APPLET> tag. When Notes encounters the <APPLET> tag during interpretation of the page, it retrieves the applet itself from its location on the Web and copies it into memory. Then the Java interpreter that comes with Notes runs the Java applet.

Allowing Java applets to run on your computer raises questions of security. Because these applets are actual programs, they can harm your PC. Worse, they can expose your PC's resources and, by extension, the rest of your network to an outside computer. They pose a real security threat.

Lotus Notes allows you to decide if you want to enable Java applets and from whom (which hosts) you will allow Java applets to be received. Additionally, you can instruct Notes not to permit any outside host access to any of your system resources (files, environment variables, password files, and so on). For example, you may feel confident that

Lotus corporation isn't going to send you any viruses, and you can decide to trust the Lotus host. On the other hand, Elvis from Bulgaria may not be as trustworthy and you can decide to put him on your untrusted list, either not allowing him to send you applets or disabling some of the functionality of the ones you receive from him. If you don't enable applets, you still see the Web pages minus the applets.

In Chapters 4 and 12, we discussed most of the parameters that affect the performance of Java applets in Notes. However, here is a short recap:

▶ Enable Java applets on each computer by checking the Enable Java applets option under Advanced options in User Preferences. In the menu, choose File, Tools, User Preferences.

▶ Configure Java performance by filling in the fields in the Java Applet Security section of the Location document you will be using when browsing the Web. If you are a Notes administrator setting up new users, you can set most of these fields in a User Setup Profile document, which will then apply the settings to new users automatically.

Viewing HTML Code

If you ever do any HTML programming, then you might occasionally visit a Web page and say to yourself "How did they do that?" Really cool colors, formatting, and graphics help entice people to your site. Throughout this book you learn about building Notes applications and optimizing those applications for publication to the Web, and you learn about HTML code (see Chapter 8, "Building Views for Domino Web Applications").

Here, you can learn how to view the HTML code behind Web pages. So, if you see a cool Web page and you want to know more about the design of the page, you can view the HTML code on that page and get ideas for your own Web site.

To see the code underlying the HTML documents Notes retrieves, you must enable the *Save HTML in Note* option for the Web Navigator database. In Server Web Navigator, do this in the Administration document, which you open from the Actions menu when the All Documents view appears. In Personal Web Navigator, do it in the Internet Options page, also reachable in the Action menu.

By default, when Domino converts a retrieved HTML page to Notes format, it discards the HTML source code. After you enable the *Save HTML in Note* option (see Figure 23.11), Notes will save the HTML source code of newly retrieved pages in a hidden field called HTMLSource. You can view the HTML source code only in the Document Properties box of a Web page. It is a little difficult to read in that confined space, however. To ease the pain, copy the HTML source code from the Document Properties box to a text editor or a text field in a Notes document.

23

Viewing HTML Source Code in Notes documents in a Useable Form

You might think Lotus would provide a form which displays the HTML source code in a field. But Lotus has not yet done so and you cannot create such a form. The HTMLSource field is of data type HTML, which is not a data type you can choose when you create a field in a form. So, even if you create a form with a field in it called HTMLSource, and switch to that form when viewing a document, the HTML source code will not appear in that field.

What you *can* do is select the contents of the HTMLSource field in the Document Properties box, copy the selected text to the clipboard, and paste it into a text editor or a text field in a Notes document.

Fig. 23.11

If you check off the Save HTML in Note field, Notes will store the HTML code of a Web page in a hidden field called HTMLSource.

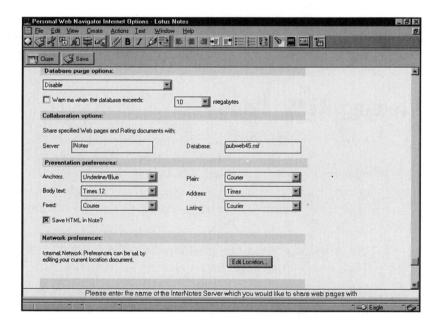

To view HTML code, follow these steps:

1. Select the Web page in either the Server or Personal Web Navigator.

2. Choose File, Document Properties from the menu.

3. Go to the Fields tab.

4. Select the HTMLSource field in the left column to see the HTML code in the right column.

5. Select the HTML code in the right column with your mouse, then copy it to the clipboard.

6. Paste the HTML code into a text editor or a text field in any Notes document. Print a copy if you like. Read it at your leisure.

Streamlining Web Page Retrieval

In general, Web Navigator is a slower Web browser than the mainstream standalone Web browsers, such as Netscape Navigator and Microsoft Internet Explorer. However, what Web Navigator offers that those browsers do not is delivery of Web pages into the Web Navigator databases. What this allows you to do is collect pages in these databases, then bring the power of Notes to bear on them. For example, you could retrieve a mass of pages, then go off-line (say, because you are getting on a plane to fly to a client site) and read the retrieved documents at your leisure.

If you do want to collect a lot of information from the Web in a hurry, there are two ways to do it. First, you can initiate retrieval of several Web pages at the same time. That is, you don't have to wait for one page to finish downloading before you start downloading a second, third, or fourth. Second, you can use the Web Ahead agent to retrieve whole groups of pages from the Web while you do something else.

Multiple, Simultaneous Web Retrievals

The Personal Web Navigator allows you to retrieve up to six pages simultaneously. To allow multiple Web retrievals, follow these steps:

23

1. Edit your Location Document by clicking the Location on the status bar and selecting Edit Current.

2. In the Concurrent Retrievers field, select the number of pages you want to be able to retrieve simultaneously. You can choose from two to six.

3. Save your changes and close the document.

After you have edited your Location Document, you can retrieve multiple Web pages at one time. For each Web page you want to open, choose File, Open URL from the menu, complete the fields in the Open URL dialog box, and click OK. Or enter successive URLs into the Open URL Search Bar. Personal Web Navigator opens a new Window for each Open URL command and retrieves the requested pages into the separate windows simultaneously. To see the pages, select Window from the menu and move from page to page from the Window menu, or choose Window, Cascade or Window, Tile to see all of your Web pages.

Using the Web Ahead Agent to Retrieve Multiple Related Pages

Web Ahead is a Notes agent that automatically retrieves into the Personal Web Navigator database all the pages pointed to by URLs on a given page. You can configure Web Ahead to retrieve up to four levels of pages. That is, you can pull in just the pages pointed to by URLs on the current page, or all of those plus all of the pages pointed to by the second level of pages, or plus the third level, or plus the fourth level. Warning: You better have a lot of free disk space if you plan to choose level four.

The idea here is that, instead of manually (and tediously) retrieving all the pages and having to wait around while they arrive, you can start the agent running, go off and do something else, then come back and browse at *your* pace (not the Web's) through the copies of the pages waiting in your database.

To use the Web Ahead agent, you must first enable it. To do so, follow these steps:

1. Choose File, Tools, User Preferences to open the User Preferences dialog box.

2. In User Preferences, place a check mark in the box labeled Enable Scheduled Local Agents. Then click OK to close User Preferences.

3. Open the Internet Options document in the Personal Web Navigator database. Click the Enable Web Ahead button, which appears in the Web Ahead Agent Preferences section. If asked what server to run it on, choose Local. Click OK. If the Enable Web Ahead button does not appear in the Internet Options document, it is because Web Ahead has already been enabled. You can verify that by checking the Agents view of the Web Navigator database. A checkmark should appear in the checkbox next to the Web Ahead listing.

4. Set the number of levels ahead that you want Web Ahead to retrieve. Set this in the Preload Web Pages field of the Web Ahead Agent Preferences section of the Internet Options document in the Personal Web Navigator database.

5. To use the Web Ahead agent, just drag a page into the Web Ahead folder. The agent does the rest automatically. You do, of course, have to have an active connection to the Internet for Web Ahead to be able to do its job.

Viewing the Most Current Version of a Web Page

Web pages are updated constantly. When you visit a Web site, you want current information, not last week's news. So, there is a chance that a Web page stored in your database could be out-of-date a day later. On the other hand, opening a Web page from the Notes database is a lot faster than opening a Web page on the Web. So, how can you balance between opening pages from the Web or the database?

There are three ways you can make sure you are looking at a relatively recent version of a Web page:

> First, you can manually refresh any page when you are looking at it by clicking the Re-load button on the Action Bar. (The Re-load button is the circular blue arrow.) This causes the Web Retriever to get a new copy of the page from the original source on the Web. It displays the new copy and overwrites the old copy in the Web Navigator database with the new copy. Also, when you retrieve a page in the Open URL dialog box, you can force Web Navigator to ignore any copy of the page that might already be in the Web Navigator database, and to overwrite that page, if it does exist, with a new copy from the Web, by selecting the *Reload from Internet Server* option before clicking OK.

> Second, you can set the Web Retriever cache options so that, under certain circumstances, the Web Retriever will retrieve a fresh copy of a page when you open it, even though a copy of the page already resides in the Web Navigator database. The drawback of this method is it updates all pages indiscriminately, even pages that are strictly archival and unchanging by nature.

> Third, and best of all, in the Personal Web Navigator database, you can activate the Page Minder agent, which will refresh pages that you designate on a scheduled basis. The really nice thing about this method is that the Page Minder will *tell you* when it has updated a page in the Web Navigator database. You don't have to affirmatively remember to check for updates.

Setting Web Retriever Cache Options

You set Web Retriever cache options for the Personal Web Navigator by changing the settings of the Update Cache field. The field is located in the *Web Retriever Configuration* section of the appropriate Location document in your *Personal Address Book*. The *appropriate* Location document is, of course, the one that is current whenever you browse with the Personal Web Navigator.

The choices in the Update Cache field are as follows:

> **Never**—This is the default setting. Select Never if you do not want your Web pages indiscriminately refreshed when you open them. With Never as your choice, you have to click the Reload button on the Action Bar to refresh your Web pages.

> **Once per session**—Select this option to refresh your Web page at the time you open it from the database, and not again during your current Notes session. If you are using the Server Web Navigator, Notes will give you a fresh re-load even if some other Notes user opened the same page one second before you did.

23

> ▶ **Everytime**—Select this option to refresh a Web page every time you open it from the database, even if the last time you (or anyone else) opened it was just a minute earlier during the same Notes session.

Using the Page Minder Agent in the Personal Web Navigator

To use the Page Minder agent in the Personal Web Navigator, do the following:

1. Enable background agents in User Preferences. Choose File, Tools, User Preferences in the menu. On the Basics page, under Startup Options, enter a checkmark next to *Enable scheduled local agents*. Click OK.

2. Enable the Page Minder agent in the Personal Web Navigator database. You can do this in one of two ways:

   ▶ In the *Page Minder agent preferences* section of the Internet Option document of the Personal Web Navigator database, click the Enable Page Minder button. (If the button doesn't appear there, you have already enabled the agent.)

   ▶ In the Agents view of the Personal Web Navigator database, put a checkmark in the check box next to the Page Minder agent listing.

3. Set Page Minder options in the *Page Minder agent preferences* section of the Internet Options document in the Personal Web Navigator database. You can set the frequency of updates to every hour, every four hours, every day, or every week. You can tell it whether to mail the updated page to you or to just mail you a notice that the page has been updated in the Web Navigator database. And you can designate the addressees of the new page or notice. See *Page Minder Agent Preferences* earlier in this chapter for more information about the Page Minder option fields in the Internet Options document.

4. Choose which Web pages should be updated by Page Minder. This is the easy part. If you want Page Minder to update a given page for you, just find the page in the Web Navigator database and put a copy of it in the Page Minder folder.

From Here...

The Personal Web Navigator is an exciting new feature of Domino 4.5, allowing you to expand Notes performance to the Internet. We have found Page Minder and Web Ahead invaluable tools in our research and Notes development.

For related information, see the following chapters:

> ▶ Chapter 1, "An Introduction to Domino 4.5 and the Internet," defines URLs and shows you how to use them.

▶ Chapter 3, "Working With Your Domino Web Site," defines Domino URLs used for searching a Domino Web site.

▶ Chapter 22, "Using the Server Web Navigator," provides information on configuring and using the Server Web Navigator as well as customization processes.

23

Using the InterNotes Web Publisher

24

InterNotes Web Publisher allows you to publish Notes databases on a scheduled basis to a set of HTML documents in the directory of your choice. It was originally intended to publish Notes databases to a Web server. However, Domino's built-in Web server has more or less eclipsed InterNotes Web Publisher as a tool for this purpose. Domino makes actual Notes databases available *in real time* to Web users.

However, we don't feel this tool is entirely obsolete. If you have a third-party (non-Domino) Web server in place and you don't want to replace it with a Domino Web server or add a Domino Web server to your mix of Web servers, then you can still make Notes databases available to Web users by using InterNotes Web Publisher to publish the Notes databases to your existing Web server(s). In addition, if you need a handy tool for converting Notes documents into HTML documents—for whatever reason—InterNotes Web Publisher is just the tool for you. Although its documentation tells you to name an HTML data directory of a Web server as the target directory for converted Notes documents, in fact you can name any directory, then do as you please with the converted document.

Understanding InterNotes Web Publisher

InterNotes Web Publisher is an add-in product to Lotus Notes. It publishes Notes databases as linked HTML pages to any Web (HTTP) server. It also publishes Notes forms, then accepts data entered into the forms in a Web browser, converting the data into documents in the underlying Notes database. It distributes Web page authorship to anyone who can create a Notes document. InterNotes Web Publisher maintains your HTML document-base because every time a Notes document changes, InterNotes Web Publisher republishes it, refreshing its links in the process.

You can download InterNotes Web Publisher free of charge from the Lotus Web site (**http://www.internotes.lotus.com**). Version 2.1 works with Notes Release 3.x servers. Version 4.0 works with Notes Release 4.x servers. We will concern ourselves with InterNotes Web Publisher version 4.0 only.

Since Lotus' successor to InterNotes Web Publisher, Domino Web Server, is incorporated into the Notes 4.5 server, and because Domino is generally more capable and easier to use than InterNotes Web Publisher, most people will prefer to use Domino over InterNotes Web Publisher.

However, InterNotes Web Publisher does a couple things better than Domino, and it does one thing that Domino does not do at all—it publishes Notes databases to third-party Web servers. If you already have a third-party Web server in production, and you don't want to replace it with a Domino Web server or set up a Domino server as a second Web server, and you want to publish Notes databases to the Web, then InterNotes Web Publisher is just the product for you.

InterNotes Web Publisher features:

▶ *HTML publishing.* InterNotes Web Publisher publishes Notes databases as HTML pages on HTTP servers.

▶ *Document conversion.* InterNotes Web Publisher converts Notes documents and views into HTML pages, and it converts data entered into HTML forms into Notes documents.

▶ *HTML maintenance.* InterNotes Web Publisher maintains the Notes-originated HTML pages and their links by updating them whenever the underlying Notes database is updated.

▶ *Search engine.* InterNotes Web Publisher extends Notes' full-text search capability to Web users. They enter a query into a field in a search form. InterNotes Web Publisher conveys the query to Notes, which conducts the search. InterNotes Web Publisher then conveys the results of the search to the user as a list of links to the HTML pages that meet the search criteria.

▶ *Information retrieval.* InterNotes Web Publisher publishes Notes forms as HTML forms, fillable in Web browsers. When a Web user submits a form, InterNotes Web Publisher conveys it to the underlying Notes database as a standard Notes document. That document can then become a part of a standard Notes workflow application, or it can in turn be republished by InterNotes Web Publisher as an HTML document.

▶ *Discussion site.* Because InterNotes Web Publisher permits the republishing of forms completed by Web users as HTML documents, your Web site can be used as a discussion database. You can effectively extend the utility of Notes' discussion databases to your Web users.

Understanding System Requirements

Since InterNotes Web Publisher resides on the Lotus Notes server, the system requirements are the same as for the Lotus Notes server, except that additional memory is required. There are versions of InterNotes Web Publisher for the Windows NT/95, OS/2, Sun Solaris (SPARC and X86), IBM AIX, and HP UX versions of the Lotus Notes server.

InterNotes Web Publisher runs on whatever hardware platform the underlying Notes server and operating system run on. The only special consideration is that you may want to add more RAM and more drive capacity than the server might otherwise require. Lotus suggests you add between 16M and 32M more RAM than the Notes server would otherwise require.

InterNotes Web Publisher works with all standard Web servers and browsers. If you will be running the Web server on the same computer as InterNotes Web Publisher, as Lotus recommends, then the computer should have enough RAM and disk space to accommodate both products. That is, RAM and disk space should be sufficient to accommodate the underlying operating system, the Lotus Notes server, InterNotes Web Publisher, the Web server, and the library of published documents as well as some (though not necessarily all) of the Notes databases to be published.

24

Configuring Your Site

Lotus InterNotes Web Publisher resides on a Lotus Notes server and publishes to an HTTP server. You can run both servers on the same computer or on separate computers. If they run on separate computers, the two computers must be able to communicate with each other via TCP/IP.

You lose the interactivity features (form inputs and full-text searches) if both servers are not on the same computer. Therefore, we recommend that you run your Notes server, InterNotes Web Publisher, and your HTTP server all on one computer, as illustrated in Figure 24.1.

Fig. 24.1

You can configure InterNotes Web Publisher so that it and the Notes server run on the same computer as your Web server, or on a different computer.

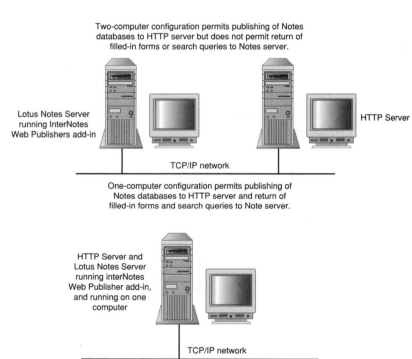

Two-computer configuration permits publishing of Notes databases to HTTP server but does not permit return of filled-in forms or search queries to Notes server.

Lotus Notes Server running InterNotes Web Publishers add-in

HTTP Server

TCP/IP network

One-computer configuration permits publishing of Notes databases to HTTP server and return of filled-in forms and search queries to Note server.

HTTP Server and Lotus Notes Server running interNotes Web Publisher add-in, and running on one computer

TCP/IP network

The Lotus Notes server is actually a group of programs that share memory space on the computer and work cooperatively with one another. The mix of programs that constitute a given Notes server varies according to the tasks it must perform. For example, one Notes server may act as a gateway to other mail systems and would run mail gateway software that other Notes servers would have no need to run. The other Notes servers, when they have mail to deliver outside of Notes mail system, would simply deliver it to the gateway server.

A Lotus InterNotes server is itself a gateway server. It transfers information back and forth between the Notes domain and the Web server with which it is paired. The InterNotes Web Publisher program runs on the Notes server as a Notes server add-in program. InterNotes Web Publisher consists of a publishing module, an interactivity module, a CGI script, a configuration database, a log database, and miscellaneous supporting files and databases.

The two modules are executable programs. Along with the CGI script, they do the actual work of converting and passing information back and forth between Notes and HTTP servers. They refer to documents in the configuration database to determine precisely how to do their jobs. All of their activities are recorded in the log database.

The publishing and interactivity modules reside on disk in the Notes program directory and in memory with the other Notes server modules. The CGI script resides in the HTTP server's designated CGI script directory, and the HTTP server pulls it into memory as needed. The actual names of these files vary to conform with the underlying operating system, and are set forth in Table 24.1.

Table 24.1   InterNotes Files by Operating System

File Type	OS/2	Windows NT/95	Solaris, AIX, HP UX
Publishing module	iwebpub.exe	nwebpub.exe	webpub
Interactivity module	iinotes.exe	ninotes.exe	inotes
CGI script	inotes.exe	inotes.exe	iwpcgi
Miscellaneous DLLs	in2h.dll webpubrs.dll	nn2h.dll webpubrs.dll	
Documentation	webguide.nsf	webguide.nsf	webguide.nsf
Configuration database	webcfg.nsf	webcfg.nsf	webcfg.nsf
Log database	weblog.nsf	weblog.nsf	weblog.nsf
Sample databases	mercury.nsf webkit.nsf	mercury.nsf webkit.nsf	mercury.nsf webkit.nsf

24

The publishing module is the main server add-in program that actually converts Notes databases to HTML files and puts them in the HTTP server's output directory. The interactivity module works with the CGI script to convert information entered into search fields and forms by Web surfers into queries of and documents in Notes databases (see Figure 24.2).

Fig. 24.2

Webpub converts Notes data to HTML and delivers it to the HTTP server. The HTTP server uses the inotes CGI script to deliver user input to the Notes server, where inotes converts it back into Notes format.

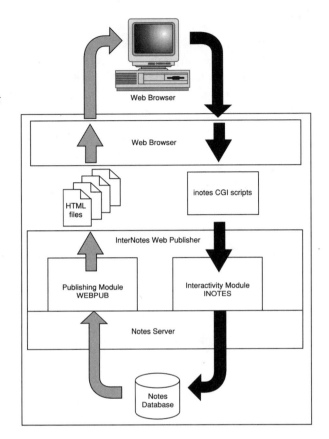

You configure these programs in a Notes database called the Web Publisher Configuration database. One of the documents in this database is the WebMaster Options document. Here, you set global variables that affect all your published databases. For each published database there is also a Database Publishing Record document that defines the "local" variables of the publication of that database.

Installing InterNotes Web Publisher

The precise details of installing InterNotes Web Publisher vary depending on the underlying operating system. Lotus provides detailed installation instructions with the software. In all cases, you perform the following steps:

1. Run the install program, which prompts you for information. The program then installs the InterNotes Web Publisher program files and CGI script in the Notes program directory, and the InterNotes Web Publisher databases in the Notes data directory. You may have to tell the install program the names of these directories.

2. If the HTTP server resides on the same computer as the Notes server, copy the InterNotes CGI script from the Notes program directory to your HTTP server's designated script directory. The Windows install process does this for you. (On other platforms, you will have to do this yourself.)

3. Add the InterNotes Web Publisher databases to the workspaces of the Notes clients from which you administer the Notes server.

4. Modify the WebMaster Options document in the Web Publisher Configuration database. For details on how to do this, see the section, "Completing the WebMaster Options Document," later in this chapter.

Starting InterNotes Web Publisher

To start InterNotes Web Publisher manually, enter commands at the Notes server console. To start the publishing module, type

```
load webpub
```

To start the interactivity module, type

```
load inotes
```

To cause InterNotes Web Publisher to start automatically whenever you start the Notes server, edit the SERVERTASKS variable in the Notes initialization file, NOTES.INI. You can either edit the file directly or use the SET CONFIGURATION command at the Notes server console. In either case, you want to add the variables *webpub* and *inotes* to the list of variables already there. For example, if the line currently reads

```
SERVERTASKS=Replica,Router,Update,Stats,Amgr,Adminp
```

you will edit it to read

```
SERVERTASKS=Replica,Router,Update,Stats,Amgr,Adminp,Webpub,Inotes
```

You may want to load multiple instances of the interactivity module into memory. Each instance of it can handle only one request at a time. If you anticipate heavy usage of the search or form fill-in features of InterNotes Web Publisher, loading multiple copies of the interactivity module in memory will allow your site to process multiple requests simultaneously. To load multiple copies manually, just enter the load inotes command once for each instance of the interactivity module. To set up Notes to load multiple instances automatically whenever the server starts up, edit the SERVERTASKS variable so that it looks something like this:

```
SERVERTASKS=Replica,Router,Update,Stats,Amgr,Adminp,Webpub,Inotes,Inotes,Inotes
```

Each instance of the interactivity module occupies about 2.5M of RAM.

When the publishing module starts, it looks in the root Notes data directory for the Web Publisher Configuration database. It looks for it under the default file name of webcfg.nsf. If you want to store the file in another data directory or you want to give it a different file name, you must add a variable to the NOTES.INI file, such as follows:

```
webpubcfg=path\filename
```

where `path` is the partial path, starting at the root Notes data directory, to the sub-directory in which the database will reside, and `filename` is the alternative file name of the Web Publisher Configuration database.

Stopping InterNotes Web Publisher

To stop InterNotes Web Publisher manually, enter commands at the server console. To stop the publishing module:

```
tell webpub quit
```

To stop the interactivity module:

```
tell inotes quit
```

One instance of the `tell inotes quit` command stops all instances of the interactivity module currently in memory.

To stop InterNotes Web Publisher from starting automatically when the Notes server starts, remove the variables `webpub` and `inotes` from the SERVERTASKS variable in NOTES.INI.

You can also disable publishing of databases without stopping InterNotes Web Publisher. To disable publishing of all databases, set the Publishing Enabled field to *Disabled* in the WebMaster Options document in the Web Publisher Configuration database. To disable publishing of any one database, set the Publishing Status field to *Disable* in the Database Publishing Record for that database in the Web Publisher Configuration database.

Organizing Your HTML Files

Notes doesn't do all of your Web site management for you. You still have to do a little site maintenance manually (but only a little). For example, if you publish multiple Notes databases, you have to link them to one another manually.

Also, we presume you want to integrate Notes-published pages into a preexisting Web site, already occupied by non-Notes-generated pages. Otherwise, you would be using Domino, not InterNotes Web Publisher, and you wouldn't even be reading this. You are going to have to make sure that the Notes-generated pages don't overwrite the non-Notes pages, especially the site home page. (What a bummer *that* would be!) You also need to manually link your non-Notes site home page to your Notes database home pages.

Setting Your Web Server's Directory Structure

When you configure your Web server, you typically specify a directory as the root directory of your Web site. The name of this directory depends on which brand of Web server you are running. We have seen it called \HTML, \HTTP, and \WWWROOT, among other names. (This was on computers using Microsoft operating systems. UNIX computers would use directory names like /html, /http, and /wwwroot. Notice that UNIX uses the forward slash instead of the backslash, and the directory names are typically all lowercase.)

Your site home page resides here, and it has a file name that your Web server looks for whenever Web users enter your site URL without specifying what page they want to retrieve. That is, if someone enters **http://www.lotus.com** in their browser, the server at that site serves up the site home page. The file may be called INDEX.HTM or DEFAULT.HTM or something equally as clever and original. (On a UNIX computer, the file name might be index.html.)

Your site home page will have links embedded in it that will lead eventually to every other publicly available page in your site, as well as to pages at other sites. Some of the pages on your site will typically reside in subdirectories of the site root directory. Thus, the structure of your site might look something like what's shown in Figure 24.3.

Fig. 24.3

This is the data directory structure of an HTTP server in which all HTML pages are generated manually, and an InterNotes Web Publisher is not yet involved.

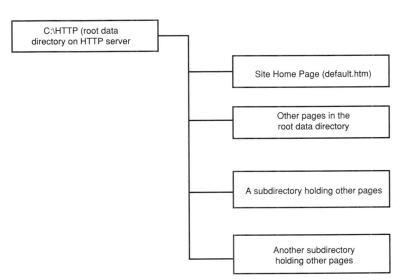

24

When you configure your InterNotes server, you have to go through the same exercise. That is, you have to tell InterNotes Web Publisher into which output directory on the Web server to place its HTML files, and you have to specify a file name for your Notes home pages, that is, for each published Notes database's home page. You do these things in the WebMaster Options document, in the Web Publisher Configuration database, which is located on the InterNotes server. For details, see the section, "Completing the WebMaster Options Document," later in this chapter.

When InterNotes Web Publisher publishes a Notes database, it always creates a subdirectory for that database beneath the output directory designated in the WebMaster Options document, and in all but one case it puts every generated page in that subdirectory. That way you have a nice, clean Web server, and it is obvious which pages belong to which Notes database.

The one case in which Notes does not put every page of a database in that database's subdirectory is when you designate the single database (in the Database Publishing Record) as the Notes Home Page database. In that case, Notes puts the database's home page in the root output directory and all other pages in the subdirectory.

Because you will be adding Notes-generated pages to an established Web server, you will want to set up InterNotes Web Publisher as follows:

1. Designate a subdirectory of your root HTML output directory as the root output directory for Notes-generated pages. You may do this in both your Web server configuration screens and in the Notes WebMaster Options document.

2. Designate one Notes database as the Home Page database. This database might have no other purpose than to be the Home Page database, or it could be a general-purpose database. Its home page would reside in the root Notes output directory and would hold the pointers to all the other Notes-generated pages, which would reside in subdirectories of the root Notes output directory.

3. Add a pointer to your site home page that points to the Notes Home Page database's home page in the root Notes output directory.

4. Add pointers to the Notes Home Page database's home page, one pointer to the home page of each other Notes database that you publish.

This scenario is illustrated in Figure 24.4.

Fig. 24.4

Here, all Notes-generated pages are in subdirectories off a special Notes root subdirectory.

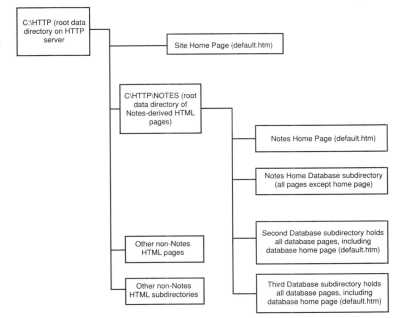

Data directory structure of HTTP server in which only some HTML pages are derived from Lotus Notes databases Notes-derived pages occupy directories branching off from the "NOTES" directory in this diagram

Completing the WebMaster Options Document

The WebMaster Options document sets "global" variables for InterNotes Web Publisher. It sets the locations of the directory into which InterNotes Web Publisher will publish Notes databases and the directory where CGI scripts are located. It sets the file name InterNotes Web Publisher should use for home pages and the extension it should use for all HTML files it creates. You also use it to enable/disable database publishing entirely, and to set purging and server console options. An example WebMaster Options document appears in Figure 24.5.

Note the following about the WebMaster Options document that appears in Figure 24.5:

▶ It came from a computer running Windows NT.

▶ The Web server software occupies a subdirectory called c:\inetsrv.

▶ The Web server stores its HTML files in c:\inetsrv\wwwroot.

Fig. 24.5

The WebMaster Options document tells Notes where to put its HTML output, how to name its HTML output files, and where to look for the inotes CGI script.

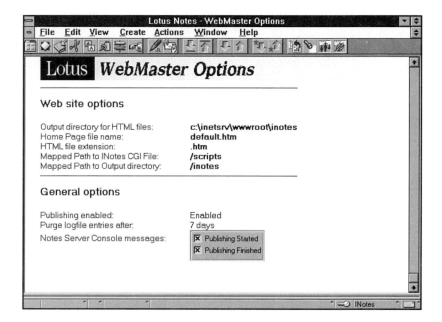

▶ InterNotes Web Publisher stores its output files in c:\inetsrv\wwwroot\inotes.

▶ Script files are stored in c:\inetsrv\scripts.

In the Web server, the following "mapped path names" have been assigned:

▶ c:\inetsrv\wwwroot is / (forward slash), which means "root."

▶ c:\inetsrv\scripts is /scripts.

▶ c:\inetsrv\wwwroot\inotes is /inotes.

The idea behind the mapped path names is to give the Web user and CGI programmer short names to use when referring to the locations of files. Mapped path names always use forward slashes because URLs (Uniform Resource Locators) use forward slashes (example: **http://www.internotes.lotus.com/default.htm**). You set mapped path names in your Web server, so you need to be familiar with the configuration options of your Web server or you need to consult with your Webmaster when completing these fields.

A default WebMaster Options document already exists in the Web Publisher Configuration database. There should be *only one* WebMaster Options document, so do not create a new one. Rather, edit the existing one. To do so, follow these steps:

1. Open the Web Publisher Configuration database. If it does not appear on the Notes workspace, choose File, Database, Open, choose or enter the name of the

InterNotes server in the Server field, click Open, then choose the Web Publisher Configuration database from the list that appears.

2. The WebMaster Options document appears in the All Documents by Form Name view. Open it in Edit mode by selecting it and clicking the Edit action button or by selecting it and choosing Actions, Edit Document.

3. Output Directory for HTML Files. Enter the name of the directory to which InterNotes Web Publisher should publish Notes databases. InterNotes Web Publisher actually only publishes the Notes site home page to that directory; it publishes all other documents to subdirectories under it.

4. Home Page File Name. Optionally, change the name InterNotes Web Publisher gives to the home page of each published database. Or simply accept the default.

5. HTML File Extension. Optionally, change the extension Notes assigns to each HTML file it creates. Or simply accept the default.

6. Mapped Path to inotes CGI File. Enter the mapped name of the directory where your Web server looks for CGI scripts. You need to do this only if you will be running your InterNotes server and Web servers together on one computer and if you will be permitting Web users to return information to Notes using interactive forms and search queries.

7. Mapped Path to Output Directory. Enter the mapped name of the directory where InterNotes Web Publisher should put its HTML files. You only need to fill in this field if InterNotes Web Publisher will be using a field other than the Web server's root data directory. This might be the case where you are adding Notes output to a preexisting Web server.

8. Publishing Enabled. Set it to Enabled by pressing the space bar or the letter E.

9. Close and save the WebMaster Options document.

Making Hypertext References in Notes

24

You have to add a pointer from your site home page to the home page of the Notes Home Page database. Your Webmaster should already know how to do this. You have to add pointers from the Notes Home Page database's home page that point to the home pages of all your other Notes home pages.

There are several ways to do this. Some of them use Notes native links—document, view, and database links, and link hotspots—which InterNotes Web Publisher converts to HTML hypertext links. These links work both in the original Notes databases and the published HTML pages. You should use them whenever you can because Notes will automatically update them for you if the target documents change their locations within the Notes databases. With the other methods, you enter the URL of the target document. If the target later moves and changes its URL, you will have to update the URL manually.

All of the methods for inserting links are illustrated in Figures 24.6 and 24.7.

Fig. 24.6

This figure shows a form in Notes in Design mode. It includes four examples of the same URL: a document Link, a text URL, a graphic URL, and a link hotspot URL.

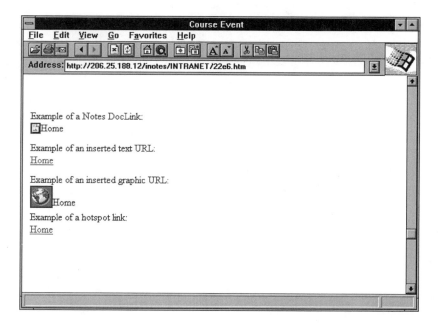

All the examples in Figure 24.6 include the word "Home," which is descriptive, intended to tell the reader what document this URL will return. The notation "[/]" is the URL. It points to the home page of the current Web server. The Properties box in Figure 24.6 shows the URL for the hotspot link. Figure 24.7 shows how each of these references appears from within a Web browser.

Fig. 24.7

This figure shows how the examples in Figure 24.6 appear in a Web browser.

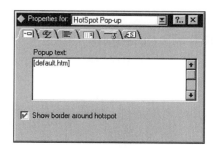

Document, View, and Database Links

You can link Notes documents to other Notes documents with document links, to Notes views with view links, or to other Notes databases with database links. You create Notes links as follows:

1. Navigate to the document, view, or database icon that you want to link to and select or open it.

2. With the target selected, choose Edit, Copy as Link, then Document Link, View Link, or Database Link.

3. Navigate back to the document that contains the link, and place the insertion point where you want the link to appear.

4. Choose Edit, Paste. A link icon appears.

Link Hotspots

Link hotspots act like document, view, and database links but look like boxed text. You create Link hotspots the same as standard Notes links, except that in Step 4, instead of choosing Edit, Paste, you select a block of text, then choose Create, Hotspot, Link Hotspot. The selected text appears to be outlined by a box.

Text Links, Graphics Links, and Hotspot Pop-Ups

You can insert URL references directly into Notes documents or forms. These can link to any page in your site, to a Notes view, or to another Web site. You can do this as a text link, a graphic link, or a hotspot pop-up. To create a text link:

1. Underline a block of text, then move the insertion point to the immediate right of the last underlined character.

2. Insert the URL reference, enclosed in square brackets. There should be no spaces or other intervening characters between the underlined text and the bracketed URL.

To create a graphic link:

1. Embed a graphic image in your Notes document, then move the insertion point to the immediate right of the graphic image.

2. Insert the URL reference, enclosed in square brackets. There should be no spaces or other intervening characters between the graphic image and the bracketed URL.

Figure 24.6 shows how text links and graphic links appear in a Notes form in Design mode. Figure 24.7 shows how they appear in a Web browser. These two types of links will appear a little strange to your Notes users, so you might want to hide them from Notes users' view.

You can create a hotspot pop-up in a Notes document or form. It looks just like a link hotspot, except you enter an URL into it, and it acts like a text pop-up in a Notes database, and shows the URL when you pop it up.

24

1. Select a block of text in a rich text field or in a form in Design mode.

2. Choose Create, Hotspot, Text Popup Hotspot. The selected text appears to be outlined by a box, and the Hotspot Properties Box appears.

3. On the first tabbed page of the Properties box, in the Popup text field, enter the URL surrounded by square brackets (refer to Figure 24.6).

The benefit of using these last three linking methods is that you can link to pages that do not originate in one of your Notes databases. You can link to the non-Notes pages at your own Web site and to pages on other Web sites. In the case of a text link, you can enter it into a non-rich text field in a Notes document.

Publishing Notes Databases to Your Web Server

You can publish Notes databases to the Web in one of two ways: You can quickly publish a database "as is," using the InterNotes Web Publisher default settings; or you can redesign the database to take advantage of special features of InterNotes Web Publisher and HTML. The first way is quick and easy, and the second way takes time and effort but will result in a nicer-looking, more useful product.

Publishing a Notes Database Using the Default Settings

To publish a Notes database using the InterNotes Web Publisher defaults is easy. You perform two steps, the first of which is optional:

1. Edit the contents of the About This Database document, since the About This Database document becomes the published database's home page. (This step is optional.)

2. Complete and save a Database Publishing Record in the Web Publisher Configuration database on the InterNotes server. Complete the fields that specify the location of the database being published, and how and when it should be published.

When you publish a Notes database using InterNotes Web Publisher's default settings, the following happen:

1. The About This Database document becomes the home page of the database. InterNotes Web Publisher appends a list of all the views in the database to the bottom of the home page, with links to each view.

2. Each view becomes an HTML page or, if the view has a lot of documents in it, a series of linked HTML pages. Each view page consists of a list of the documents in the view, along with links to the documents.

3. Each Notes document in the database becomes an HTML page.

4. Any links that were embedded in the Notes database become hypertext links.

Each time Notes republishes the database, any changes that have occurred in the database are republished. New documents added to the Notes database become new HTML pages. Edited documents become updated HTML pages. InterNotes Web Publisher removes HTML pages representing deleted Notes documents, and the home page and view pages are all updated.

Editing the About This Database Document

Since the About This Database document becomes home page of each database, you may want to edit it. You may want to enter explanatory or welcoming text, graphic elements, or pointers to other pages on your Web site or other Web sites. See, for example, Figures 24.8 and 24.9, which show, respectively, an About This Database document in Design mode, and the same document as a published home page, viewed from a browser.

Fig. 24.8

An About This Database document, in Design mode, being prepared to become a database home page.

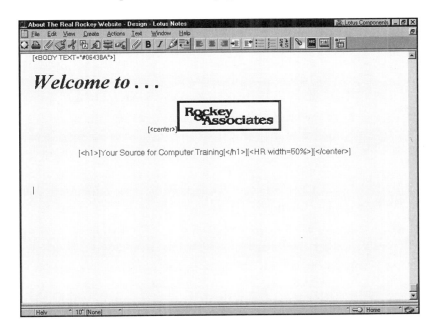

To edit an About This Database document, you must have designer access to the subject database, and you should follow these steps:

1. Open the subject database in Notes by double-clicking its icon on the Notes workspace. If it does not appear on the workspace, choose File, Database, Open to locate the database.

Fig. 24.9

The same document as it appears after publication as the database home page.

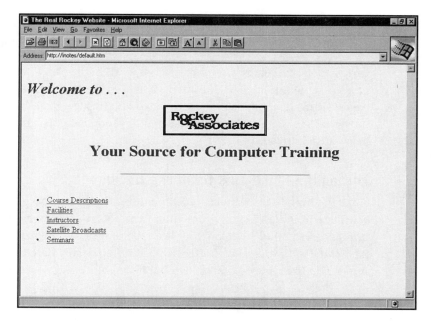

2. If a graphical navigator (one or more pictures) appears in the Navigator pane (left side of screen), instead of a list of views and folders, then, in the menu, choose View, Show, Folders. The graphical navigator is replaced by the folders navigator.

3. In the Navigator pane, click Design to see the design elements. If Design does not appear in the Navigator pane, then, in the menu, choose View, Show, Design; the word Design should then appear at the bottom of the list in the Navigator pane. Click it to expand it.

4. Click Other in the Navigator pane. A list of design elements appears in the Views pane (right side of screen).

5. Double-click "About Database" Document in the Views pane to open the About This Database document in Design mode.

6. In Design mode, the About This Database document is one big rich text field. This means it is effectively a word processor document and you can put almost anything you want on it: formatted text, tables, pictures, hypertext links, or Java applets.

7. When finished, close and save the document by pressing Esc or Ctrl+W, or by choosing File, Close from the menu.

Completing a Database Publishing Record

To publish a database to the Web server, you must complete a Database Publishing Record for it in the Web Publisher Configuration database. In this document, you specify the name and location of the database being published, the publishing mode and schedule, and logging and publishing options.

You may find the Database Publishing Record a formidable-looking document. Not to worry! You have to deal with only a few of the fields. In fact, you may never, ever have to deal with most of the fields on the document, which are set to generally acceptable defaults (see Figures 24.10 and 24.11).

Fig. 24.10

The top half of a Database Publishing Record in Edit mode.

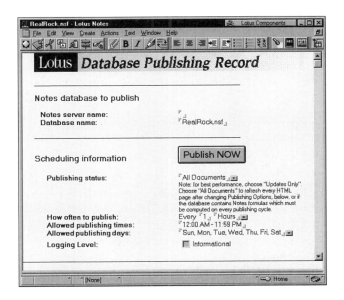

Fig. 24.11

The bottom half of a Database Publishing Record in Edit mode.

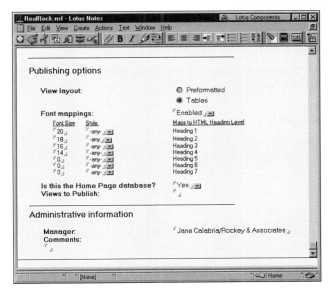

24

To create a Database Publishing Record for a new database, follow the steps in the list. However, note that the fields are listed in order of overall importance, not in the order in which you encounter them in the form.

1. Open the Web Publisher Configuration database.

2. In the menu, choose Create, Database Publishing Record. A new Database Publishing Record appears. You must fill in fields in the first two sections, Notes Database to Publish and Scheduling Information. (Optionally, you can fill in fields in the last two sections, Publishing Options and Administrative Information.)

3. Notes Server Name (Optional): If the database to be published is located on the InterNotes server, you can leave this field blank. Otherwise, enter the fully distinguished name (**servername/OrgUnitname/Orgname**) of the host server in this field.

4. Database Name (Required): Enter the file name of the database. If the database is located in a directory other than the root Notes data directory, enter the relative path name of the database.

   For example, if the root Notes data directory is c:\notes\data, and the database's complete file name is c:\notes\data\fn.nsf, then enter just the filename: **fn.nsf**. If the database resides in a subdirectory of the root Notes data directory, for example, c:\notes\data\sub1\fn.nsf, then enter **sub1\fn.nsf** in the field. If the database resides outside the Notes data directories, then enter the full path name of the database file.

5. Publishing Status (Required): If you are publishing the database, choose either Updates Only or All Documents. If you want to temporarily stop publishing a database, choose Disable. If you want to remove a database from the Web site, choose Remove from Web Site.

6. Is This a Home Page Database? (Optional): Defaults to No. Leave it that way for all databases except the *one database* that will be your Home Page database. If you name more than one Home Page database, the home page of one will overwrite the home page of the other whenever InterNotes Web Publisher publishes. It will be an ugly mess. Don't do it.

7. Views to Publish (Optional): Leave this field blank to publish every view in the database, including views hidden to Notes users. Otherwise, enter the names of only the views that you want to publish. Enter the view names exactly as they appear in the View Properties Boxes, including case and spacing. You can use the alias/synonym view names, rather than the full view names.

8. Publishing Status (Optional): You can publish as often as every one second, as seldom as once every couple weeks, or anything in between.

9. Allowed Publishing Times and Allowed Publishing Days (Optional): By default, InterNotes Web Publisher publishes 24 hours a day, seven days a week. You can limit publishing times and days.

10. At this point, you have reviewed/edited the fields that are most relevant to publishing a new database, and you could save and close the document (or press the Publish NOW! button to publish the database immediately, then save and close the document).

The other fields in the Database Publishing Record, and their purposes, are as follows:

▸ Logging level (Optional): You can turn on detailed logging if you want.

▸ View layout (Optional): If you anticipate that users will be using old, text-based browsers, change this to Preformatted. InterNotes Web Publisher publishes using a fixed pitch font, and preserves spacing and line breaks. Otherwise, leave this field set to Tables.

▸ Font mappings (Optional): In general, you do not need to change anything in this set of fields. Web browsers use HTML heading tags (from Heading 1, the largest, to Heading 7, the smallest) to define displayed font sizes in HTML documents. Some browsers permit you to assign styles to the heading tags; others do not. If you know your users will be using browsers that do not permit the assignment of styles to heading tags, you can disable font mapping.

▸ Manager (Optional): Enter the fully distinguished name of the Database Manager.

▸ Comments (Optional): Enter any descriptive information about the database that you think might be useful to someone who comes upon this document years in the future, and who must make heads or tails of it.

Enhancing a Database

The set of pages that results from a default publication of a database, as described in the previous section, is perfectly serviceable. If your purpose is to make a Notes reference or broadcast database more widely available, it is all you really need to do. But if you want to add some flash or additional functionality to your Web pages, or if you want to get data from Web users back into your Notes workflows, then you need to use some of the following techniques to customize your databases.

24

Among the ways you might want to enhance your database are:

▸ Customize a home page and view pages with image maps.

▸ Add a search bar to the home page, any view page, or any document page.

▸ Add HTML codes to enhance the look of your published output.

▶ Create fielded forms fillable by Web users, which then get pulled back into the Notes database and become part of any Notes application.

Creating a Custom Home Page and Custom View Pages

When you use the default settings, your home page and view pages have a plain, generic look. Your home page can have formatted text, tables, graphics, links, and, at the bottom, a linked list of all published views. Your view pages have a title and a linked list of documents, and that's about it.

If that is not enough for you, you can enhance both the home page and view pages by creating special forms. In addition to formatted text, tables, graphics, and links, a form can include fields and HTML codes. In addition to the standard fields you would include in any form, Notes provides several special fields that are designed specifically to enhance the home page and view pages when they are published to the Web. The fields are listed in Table 24.2.

The forms you create in order to customize home and view pages are different from standard Notes forms. For one thing, you will never actually create any documents based on these forms. Rather, InterNotes Web Publisher will create HTML documents based on them. So don't bother to list the forms in the Create menu. Second, these forms have special names, and third, they incorporate the special fields mentioned in the previous paragraph.

To design a custom home or view page, create a form and, when you name it, give it a special alias—$$Home for the home page, $$ViewTemplate or $$*viewname* (where *viewname* is the name of the desired view) for the view pages. Design the form using the usual Notes form design elements—formatted static text, graphics, fields, links—but also add the special fields listed in Table 24.2.

Table 24.2   Special Fields for Home and View Page Forms

Field	What It Does
$$AboutDatabase	Inserts the contents of the About This Database document into the home or view page.
$$ViewList	Inserts a list of all database views into the home or view page, and creates links to each view in the list.
$$ViewBody	Inserts a specific view into the home or view page, and creates a link to each document listed in the view.
$$ImageMapBody	Inserts a specific image map into the home or view page.

The steps for creating a custom home or view page are as follows:

1. In Notes, open the database.

2. Choose Create, Design, Form from the menu. A new, blank form appears. You enter elements onto the form in the top half of the screen (the Design pane) and enter formulas in the bottom half of the screen (the Formula pane).

3. Choose Design, Form Properties (or press Alt+Enter) to open the Form Properties box. If it appears as Properties for Text, Field, Database or anything but Properties for Form, click the Properties For field and pick Form from the list that appears.

4. Enter the name and alias of the form in the Form Name field. See the section "How to Name the Home Page and View Page Forms," for the naming rules.

5. While in the Form Properties Box, select any other form attributes that you want. Do not include the form in the menu; you will never actually create any documents with this form.

6. Switch to the Database Properties Box by choosing Database in the Properties For field of the Properties box. In the Design pane, make sure Inherit Design from Template is not selected. (Otherwise, the form may be deleted the next time the server refreshes the design of the database, which servers do by default every night at 1:00 A.M.)

7. Add static text, tables, and graphics to the form. See "Special Text Formatting Considerations for Web Pages," for tips on formatting text for best display in a Web browser.

8. Add fields to the form by choosing Create, Field from the menu. An untitled field appears at the position of the insertion point. The Field Properties Box appears. See "The $$AboutDatabase and $$ViewList Fields" and "The $$ViewBody and $$ImageMapBody Fields," for special consideration regarding the special fields listed in Table 24.2. For all other fields, define them as you would in any Notes form, except be sure they are of type Computed for Display; no other type is functional.

9. Add links to the form using the techniques described in the earlier section, "Making Hypertext References in Notes."

10. Save and close the form.

How to Name the Home Page and View Page Forms

The home and view page forms must be named in a certain way, the general form being: Window Title | Alias. The first part, Window Title, appears in the window title bar when the home or view page is viewed in a browser. The second part, Alias, tells InterNotes Web Publisher to use this form when publishing the home and view page HTML documents. Use the following aliases in Table 24.3.

Table 24.3   Home and View Page Aliases

Alias	Usage	Example
$$Home	Designates the home page.	Welcome \| $$Home
$$ViewTemplate	Designates a view page form that will be the template for all published views.	Discussion \| $$ViewTemplate
$$viewname	Designates a view page that will be the template only for the view called *viewname*. Substitute the actual view name or alias for *viewname*. The name is case-sensitive.	Location View Form \| $$OurLocations

In the table, the example home page name would cause the word "Welcome" to appear in the title bar when the home page appears in a browser. The word "Discussion" would appear in the second example. The words "Location View Form" would appear in the third example. You would use $$ViewTemplate in a database that includes only one view, such as a discussion database, or where you don't care to customize each view. See Figure 24.12.

Fig. 24.12

The Form Properties Box, showing the format of the form name for a form that will become a view page. Note the $$ViewBody field to the left.

Special Text Formatting Considerations for Web Pages

Notes text formatting does not translate well to HTML. The primary problem is that all HTML text formats to left alignment, no matter how it was aligned or tabbed in Notes. Centered or right-aligned paragraphs become left-aligned. Tabbed columns all crowd over to the left, with a single space between your original columns.

To preserve centered paragraphs, you will have to embed special HTML formatting codes in your Notes forms and documents. However, the formatting will look a little strange to anyone viewing the form or document in Notes. At the beginning of a paragraph to be centered, add [<CENTER>]; at the end add [</CENTER>]. Standard HTML code syntax surrounds HTML codes with angle brackets (<) and (>). When you add HTML codes to Notes documents, you further surround them with square brackets, ([) and (]).

Forget about preserving right alignment. There is no HTML code that right aligns text. You can pad text with spaces, then use the [<PRE>] and [</PRE>] ("preformatted text") codes to force browsers to accept the padding, but this works only if you use a mono-space font like Courier, and the browser *will* use a monospace font when displaying such a paragraph, whether you like it or not.

To preserve column alignment (but not column widths), you have to use tables in Notes. Of course, if you haven't discovered Notes tables yet, you are in for a pleasant surprise anyway, so don't feel bad. To create a table in Notes, do the following:

1. Place the text insertion point where you want the table to appear. If you are in design mode, you can put the table anywhere. If you are composing a document, you can place tables only in rich text fields.

2. Choose Create, Table from the menu. The Create Table dialog box appears.

3. In the Create Table dialog box, enter the number of rows and columns for your table. If you are not sure how many rows or columns you will need, you can add or remove rows or columns later. Click OK. The table appears in your form or document.

4. Enter text, pictures, or fields in the cells of the table. Text wraps within the confines of each cell. Each row automatically grows vertically to accommodate the amount of text you enter into each cell. You can adjust the width of each column manually, but many browsers cannot preserve column width, so you may decide not to sweat column width until after you see how the table will look in a browser.

Also, recall that InterNotes Web Publisher will map your text to HTML heading tags according to the settings in the Database Publishing Record for this database. For example (if you did not change the settings in the Database Publishing Record), text using 20-point type will map to HTML tag Heading 1.

You can override these mappings by assigning paragraph styles to the Notes paragraphs. Creating and assigning a Notes paragraph style named Heading 1 causes the HTML tag <H1> to be applied to that paragraph no matter what the font size of the text in the paragraph. To create a paragraph style in Notes, follow these steps:

1. In Notes, place the text insertion point either in a rich text field or in the Design pane of a form in Design mode. This causes the Text menu to appear in the Notes menu bar. A quick way to get to a rich text field is to compose a mail memo, and put the insertion point into the Body field, which is a rich text field.

2. Format a paragraph of text (any text will do, including nonsense text) the way you want the style to be defined. If you are creating a "Heading n" style, you don't much care about the Notes formatting, since the purpose of this style is to assign an HTML paragraph style to the HTML version of the paragraph. But you should

24

format the paragraph so that it at least approximates the look of the corresponding HTML style.

3. Choose Text, Text Properties from the menu. The Text Properties Box appears.

4. Click the last tab in the Text Properties Box. The tab looks like a tag with the letter S in it. The paragraph style panel appears.

5. Click the Create Style button. The Create Named Style dialog box appears.

6. Enter a name for the style in the Style Name field. Call it **Heading *n***, where *n* is the number corresponding to the HTML heading style number this style should translate to. The available HTML heading style numbers are 1 through 7.

7. Check the boxes in the other three fields according to your own preferences. For most styles, I prefer to check all three boxes. Click the Help button to learn more about each field. Click OK when finished.

The new style appears in the list of available styles in the Text Properties Box and in the status bar at the bottom of the Notes program window. Apply a style to a paragraph by placing the insertion point anywhere in the paragraph, then selecting the desired style in either style list (the one in the Text Properties Box or the one in the status bar). Or assign the style by cycling to it with repeated presses of the Cycle (F11) key. While the goal here is to control text formatting in HTML documents published by InterNotes Web Publisher, take note that paragraph styles are also a great, fast, easy way to apply formatting to any Notes document.

The $$AboutDatabase and $$ViewList Fields

Placing the $$AboutDatabase field into a home or view page form causes the contents of the About This Database document to appear in the field's position in the published home or view page. Placing the $$ViewList field into a home or view page form causes a linked list of the names of all published views to appear in this field's position in the published home or view page.

If you add either of these fields to the form, you will need only to enter the field name into the Fields Properties box. InterNotes Web Publisher ignores all other settings. Easy, no?

The $$ViewBody and $$ImageMapBody Fields

Placing the $$ViewBody field into a home or view page form causes the actual contents of a named view to appear in the field's position in the published home or view page. Placing the $$ImageMapBody field into a home or view page form causes a named graphical navigator to appear in this field's position in the published home or view page.

The graphical navigator functions as an image map in the resulting HTML document. See the section, "Adding Image Maps," for more information on image maps.

If you add a $$ViewBody or $$ImageMapBody field to the form, you must complete two fields in the Field Properties box. Enter the field name into the Name field. Enter the name of the view or navigator to be displayed into the Help Description field. InterNotes Web Publisher ignores all other settings. Make sure you enter the view or navigator name exactly as it appears in the View/Navigator Properties box; this is case- and space-sensitive. You can use an alias name rather than the full name of the view or navigator.

If you want to add more than one $$ViewBody or $$ImageMapBody field to a form, name them $$ViewBody_1, $$ViewBody_2, $$ImageMapBody_1, $$ImageMapBody_2, and so on.

Adding HTML Codes

You can enhance the appearance of any document, view, or home page as it appears in a browser by inserting HTML tags right into the Notes document that defines the page. As we saw in the section, "Special Text Formatting Considerations for Web Pages," you can enter individual tags anywhere on a form in Design mode or into any field when creating or editing a document. You can also define a paragraph style called HTML, and you can define a rich text field called HTML. Both of these capabilities give you even more versatility.

As mentioned earlier, when you want to intermix an HTML tag with the other contents of a field, you enclose the HTML tag first in angle brackets (<) and (>), which is the standard HTML syntax, then in square brackets ([) and (]), which is Notes' own delimiter for HTML tags. Thus, for example, if you want a horizontal rule to appear on a published page, you could enter [<HR>] into the Notes document or form. If you enter it on a form, the rule will appear on every document created with that form. If you enter it into a field when creating a document, the rule will appear only on the published version of that document.

The HTML Paragraph Style

You can also create a paragraph style called HTML. When you assign the style to a paragraph of text, Notes assumes that paragraph consists of HTML tags. By using the HTML paragraph style in this way, you eliminate the need to enclose HTML tags in square brackets. You only need to enclose them in HTML's own angle brackets. So, a horizontal rule code could be entered as <HR>, rather than [<HR>].

Hiding HTML Codes from Notes Users

These codes convert to formatting when viewed in a Web browser, but in Notes they appear to the reader as *codes*. To hide the codes from Notes users, you can apply Hide When attributes to the paragraphs in which the codes appear. (Remember, however, that if a code appears in the same paragraph as regular text, hiding the paragraph will hide both the code and the text.)

To apply Hide When attributes to a paragraph, put the insertion point anywhere in the text, then choose Text, Text Properties in the menu. In the Text Properties box, go to the Hide When panel by clicking the "window shade" tab. In the Hide When panel, choose to hide the paragraph when Previewed for Reading, Opened for Reading, and Printed. That will hide the codes from readers but not from editors of a document.

The HTML Field

If you have preexisting HTML documents, you can store them in Notes databases and publish them via InterNotes Web Publisher. When you publish them, only the preexisting HTML document publishes.

To set this up, create a new form. Name it whatever you like. Include it in the menu, so you can choose it when you want to create new documents. Add a rich text field to it and name the field HTML. Add to the form any other fields or static text that you like. Then save the form.

Then, create documents with the new form. Copy your HTML documents into the field named HTML, then save the document. When you publish the document, only the field called HTML will be published. Nothing else on the form will be published; not static text, not pictures, not other fields.

The key here is the rich text field named HTML. As soon as InterNotes Web Publisher encounters such a field in a document, it disregards all other fields and publishes only that field. In effect, HTML is a reserved field name, and you should avoid naming a field HTML unless you intend to use the field in this way.

Adding Image Maps

An image map is a graphic image, included in an HTML document that has hotspot links associated with different parts of it. If you click *this* portion of the image, you are requesting one document; if you click *that* portion of the image, you are requesting another document. InterNotes Web Publisher permits you to create and incorporate image maps into your published databases. To create an image map, you create a graphical navigator and apply to it hotspots that link to other HTML pages. Then you incorporate the image map into a form—a home page form, a view page form, or a form with which publishable documents will be created. Incorporate the image map into the form by naming the image map in an $$ImageMapBody field that you place anywhere in the form. To create a navigator, follow these steps:

1. Create or open in a paint or drawing program the graphic image that will become the image map.

2. Copy the image (or the portion of it that you want) to the Clipboard. Most programs allow you to do this by selecting the image (or part of it) and then choosing Edit, Copy. You can also select the image, then press Ctrl+C.

3. Return to Notes. Open the database in which you intend to create the navigator.

4. Create a new navigator by choosing Create, Design, Navigator. A new navigator design window appears.

5. Choose Design, Navigator Properties. The Navigator Properties box appears.

6. Enter a name for the navigator in the Name field of the Properties box. You can give it an alias as well as a name by naming it in the format "Navigator Name | Alias."

7. Paste the Clipboard image into the navigator by choosing Create, Graphic Background. Important: Do not paste the image using Edit, Paste because it doesn't work that way.

8. Assign URL links to different portions of the image. To do this, define an URL link in a graphical navigator, create a hotspot rectangle or hotspot polygon and assign the @URLOpen ("*URLname*") @function to it (see Figure 24.13).

9. Save and close the navigator.

Fig. 24.13

A navigator in Design mode. Note the @URLOpen @function in the Formula pane.

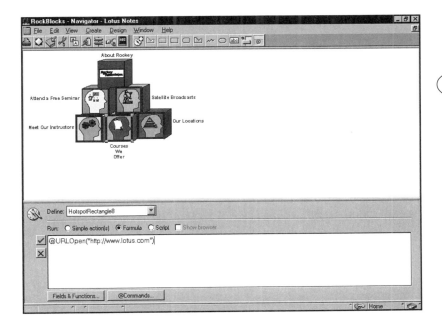

24

Creating a Hotspot Rectangle

To create a hotspot rectangle, choose Create, Hotspot Rectangle. Or click the red rectangle icon in the toolbar. Your mouse pointer becomes a crosshair. Place the crosshair at one corner of the area to be covered by the rectangle, then, holding the mouse button down, drag the crosshair to the opposite corner. You see a black rectangle appear as you draw. When you release the mouse button, it becomes a red rectangle.

If you are not happy with the resulting rectangle, you can resize it by dragging on the corner handles. If no corner handles appear, click anywhere on the rectangle to make them appear.

Creating a Hotspot Polygon

Use the hotspot polygon to define a non-rectangular portion of the graphic image. To create a hotspot polygon, choose Create, Hotspot Polygon. Or choose the red polygon icon in the toolbar. Your mouse pointer becomes a crosshair.

Place the crosshair at one apex of the area to be defined. Click the mouse button to anchor a line at that point. Move the mouse pointer to an adjacent apex. A line connects the first apex to your mouse pointer.

At the second apex, click the mouse again to anchor the other end of the first line and create an anchor for your next line. Move the mouse pointer to the third apex. Click to create the third line.

Continue until you have reached the last unconnected apex. There you will double-click, which will create the second-to-last line and the last line between the last apex and the first apex. The secret to using the hotspot polygon tool is to remember to double-click the last apex to close the polygon.

When you finish creating the hotspot polygon, the lines will turn red, and corner handles will appear when the hotspot polygon is selected. If you want to adjust the shape of the polygon, drag the handles.

Defining Hotspot Properties

After you have created a hotspot rectangle or polygon, you can define its properties in the HotspotRectangle/HotspotPolygon Properties box. You can rename it in the Name field. You can lock or unlock its size and position. You can define whether the outline of the hotspot appears either when you touch it with the mouse pointer or when you click it. Finally, you can define the weight and color of the outline.

Assigning an URL to a Hotspot Rectangle or Polygon

To assign an URL to a hotspot rectangle or hotspot polygon in a graphic navigator, select the rectangle or polygon while in Design mode. Handles will appear at the corners of the object when it is selected. Or you can select the name of the hotspot from the list in the Define field in the Formula pane of the window. Then, in the Run field, choose Formula. In the Formula pane, enter **@URLOpen("*URLname*")**, where *URLname* is the URL of the page that this hotspot should point to.

For example, if the hotspot should point to the Lotus InterNotes Web site, the formula should read:

@URLOpen("www.internotes.lotus.com")

To point to the home page of your own site, the formula could read:

@URLOpen("/")

Interactivity: Returning Information to Notes

One of the things that sets Notes apart from other groupware products is its capability to automate the workflows that take place in an enterprise. The real power of InterNotes Web Publisher rests in its capability to bring Web users into Notes workflows. That is, InterNotes Web Publisher makes it easy for the Web server to return information submitted by Web users back to the InterNotes server, which can then process the information in the same ways it can process any information.

InterNotes Web Publisher provides two tools for returning information from Web users to the Notes server. One is the *search bar*, which enables Web users to perform Boolean searches of Notes databases. The second is the *interactive form*, which is a standard Notes form that Web users can fill in and submit, and which the Notes server can treat like any form saved by a Notes user.

To enable the interactivity features of InterNotes Web Publisher, you must set it up to meet two conditions. First, your Web server and InterNotes server must both be on the same computer. Second, a copy of any interactive database must reside on the InterNotes server.

24

Making a Database Searchable

Just as Web users can use Web-based search engines, such as Yahoo!, WebCrawler, and AltaVista, to conduct Boolean searches of Web sites, they can also search Notes databases. That is, you can insert a search bar into a Notes home page or view page. The only limitation is that Web users will only be able to search one database at a time, rather than all databases on the Notes server. (For that capability, look to Domino Web server.)

To set up search capability, you must set up both servers on the same computer, put a replica copy of the database to be searched on the InterNotes server, full-text index the database on the InterNotes server, and add a search bar to the home page or one or more views in the database.

The result of setting up a search capability is that Web users can enter Boolean search terms into the search bar. The Web server returns the search term to the Notes server. The Notes server performs the search, then publishes the results of the search as a linked list of documents. The Web server then transmits the list to the Web user, who can open any document in the list by clicking it in the list.

Full-Text Indexing a Database

To make a full-text index of a database, follow these steps:

1. Select the icon of the database to be full-text indexed. Or open the database. Be sure to select/open the copy of the database on the InterNotes server.

2. Choose File, Database, Properties to open the Database Properties box.

3. Click the Full Text tab to go to the Full Text panel.

4. If the message appears in the Full Text panel that the Database Is Not Full Text Indexed, click the Create Index button. The Full Text Create Index dialog box appears.

5. Choose the options you want in the Full Text Create Index dialog box, then click OK. The server creates the index, which may take a few seconds, a few minutes, or longer, depending on the size of the database and the amount of text in it.

When selecting options in the Full Text Create Index dialog box, keep in mind that most of the options will tend to increase the size on disk of the index. The ones that will not increase the size of the index are Exclude Words in Stop Word File and Word Breaks Only.

Adding a $$ViewSearchBar Field to a Home or View Page Form

Add a search bar to a form by creating a field called $$ViewSearchBar. The steps are as follows:

1. Open the home page form or any view page form in Design mode.

2. Place the insertion point where you want the search bar to appear, then create a new field by choosing Create, Field. A new, untitled field appears, along with the Field Properties box.

3. Enter the name **$$ViewSearchBar** in the Name field in the Properties box.

4. If you are adding the $$ViewSearchBar field to the home page form, you must also specify a view for InterNotes Web Publisher to use when publishing the results of a search. Do this by entering the name of an appropriate view into the Help Description field on the Options panel of the Field Properties box. (This step is unnecessary when adding the $$ViewSearchBar field to a view page form, because Notes automatically uses the same view it uses to display documents in the view page itself.) See Figures 24.14 and 24.15.

5. Do not enter any other information about this field. (InterNotes Web Publisher will ignore it, so don't waste your time.) Save and close the form.

Fig. 24.14

This is a home page form in Design mode. Note the $$ViewSearchBar field. It also includes HTML tags and a $$ViewList field, side-by-side in a table.

Fig. 24.15

The same home page as seen in a browser. Note the search bar, and note the size of the title, resulting from the HTML tags, and the list of views to the right of the title.

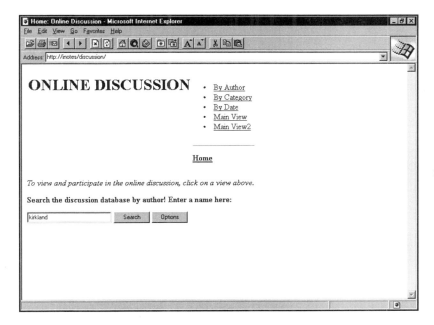

Creating Interactive Forms

Search queries are not the only information the Web server can return to the InterNotes server. You can create specialized forms of which the sole function is to be filled in and returned by Web users. Not only can these forms return information entered manually by the Web user, they can also return information gathered by the Web server automatically, in the form of CGI variables.

To set up interactive forms, you need to take three steps: Create an interactive form in Notes; use the alias of $$Web when naming the form; and create links from the home page, views, or documents to the form, so that people can get to the form to fill it in.

When a Web user submits a form, the Web server runs the inotes CGI script, located in the Web server's script directory. The inotes CGI script formats and submits the form back to the Notes server, where the interactivity module (named ninotes.exe in NT, iinotes.exe in OS/2, and inotes in UNIX-based Notes servers) receives it and stores it in the Notes database as a standard Notes document.

To create an interactive form in Notes, follow these steps:

1. Open the Notes database.
2. Choose <u>C</u>reate, <u>D</u>esign, <u>F</u>orm in the menu. A new, untitled form design window opens.
3. Choose <u>D</u>esign, Form <u>P</u>roperties to open the Form Properties box.
4. Name the form. Give it an alias of **$$Web**. This tells InterNotes Web Publisher to publish the form when it publishes the rest of the database.

   When InterNotes Web Publisher does publish this form, it gives it a file name equal to the first part of the form name. That is, if you name the form Register | $$Web, InterNotes Web Publisher names the resulting HTML file:

   Register.htm (assuming you have not changed the default extension from .htm).

   If you name the file Registration Form | $$Web, InterNotes Web Publisher names the resulting HTML form:

   Registration+Form.htm, converting the space to a plus character. Therefore, you might want to keep the first part of the form name short and sweet.
5. If you intend that only Web users create documents with this form, deselect the Include in Menu option. Notes users will not then be able to create forms with it.
6. Add static text, graphics elements, links, and fields to this form in the usual fashion.
7. Save and Close the form.

When creating fields in an interactive form, you can use most of the programming features that you use when creating standard forms. For example, you can use computed and editable fields. You can use Default Value, Input Translation, and Input Validation formulas. You can create all variations of keyword fields—standard, radio buttons, and check boxes. You can use computed and named subforms.

You can also use HTML tags to control field input. For example, you can control the width and maximum characters in a text field by entering a code similar to the following into the Help Description field of a Field Properties box: [<SIZE=30 MAXLENGTH=50>]. This example would set the width of the field as displayed in a browser at 30 characters, and would permit entry of up to 50 characters into the field.

You can control how many keywords appear in the browser display of a keyword file by putting the following code into the Help Description field of the Field Properties box: [<SIZE=4>]. This would cause a scroll bar to appear in the field if more than four keywords were available.

You can control the size and wrap characteristics of a rich text field with the following code:

```
[<ROWS=12 COLS=75 WRAP=VIRTUAL>]
```

This would cause cause the rich text field to display in the browser as a 12-row by 75-column text entry area, and your text would wrap within the confines of this space but be transmitted as long, unbroken lines. WRAP=PHYSICAL would cause lines to wrap and be transmitted with breaks at wrap points. WRAP=OFF would (you guessed it) turn word wrap off, so that the typist would have to press Enter to force wrapping.

To make the new form usable, you have to place links to it into other forms. You can place links into the home page, other home pages, view pages, and forms from which documents will be created and published. For more information on creating links in Notes, see the section "Making Hypertext References in Notes."

24

The Submit Button

InterNotes Web Publisher automatically adds a Submit button to the bottom of any form intended to be filled in and returned by Web users. The default Submit button has the word "Submit" on it. If you want, you can create your own Submit button. By doing so, you can change the text on the button to something else, say, "Register," and you can control the placement of the "Submit" button on your form.

To add your own submit button, do the following:

1. Open the form in Design mode.
2. Move the insertion point where you want the button to appear.

3. Choose <u>C</u>reate, <u>H</u>otspot, <u>B</u>utton. A button appears on your form and the Button Properties box opens.

4. In the Button Properties box, enter the desired button text into the Button Label field.

5. Save and close the form.

Don't bother trying to program an action for the button. InterNotes Web Publisher will ignore your programming. The only button it recognizes is the Submit button.

Customizing Responses to User Submissions with the $$Return Field

When a Web user submits a form, InterNotes Web Publisher displays the following default response: "Form Submitted." You can customize this response with $$Return field. For example, you could cause InterNotes Web Publisher to respond: "Thank you, Rob. One of our representatives will reply to you within 48 hours."

You do this by adding a computed field to the form that users will submit, and naming the field $$Return. In the Formula pane, you would enter a formula defining the response message. The formula that responds with the "Thank you" message would look something like this:

```
@Return("<H2>Thank you, " + FirstName + ". One of our representatives will
reply to you within 48 hours.</H2>")
```

The following formula would say "Thank you, Rob," and display, on the line below, a hotspot back to the site home page:

```
@Return("<H2>Thank you, " + FirstName + ".</H2><BR><H4><a href=/</a>")
```

You could also use $$Return to run a CGI script or to display a selected HTML page.

Creating Response Forms with the $$Response Field

You can create Response and Response to Response forms, so that users can respond to documents they read in your databases. You can then republish users' responses and, in this way, set up a discussion database available to Web users. There is a good example of this at Lotus' InterNotes Web site (**http://www.internotes.lotus.com**).

To set this up, create a Response or Response to Response form. When you name the form, use the alias **$$Web**, so that it will publish. Then add a field called $$Response to the form to which the user wants to respond. When defining the $$Response field in the main document, enter the name of the Response form in the Help Description field of the Field Properties box.

When the user reads the main form, the $$Response field will appear as a text hotspot that says "Response." Therefore, on the main form, you might insert the field following the static text "Compose a," so that the reader would see the words "Compose a Response." When the reader clicks the word "Response," the response form opens. The reader fills it in and clicks the Submit button. InterNotes Web Publisher returns the form to the InterNotes server, where it becomes part of the database, appearing in views as a response to the main document. Then, of course, it gets published to the Web, where it also shows up in views as a response to the main document.

If you add the $$Response field to the Response form as well as the main form, referring in the Field Properties box to its own form name, then readers of the response can respond to it. Upon submission, that response will be republished, and a reader of it can respond to it, ad nauseam. Voilá! A discussion database!

Returning Information with CGI Variables

In addition to returning text entered by Web users into the fields in your forms, InterNotes Web Publisher can return information gathered automatically from the user by the Web server. This information is stored as CGI variables, and you can retrieve it by adding specially named fields to your submission forms. Specifically, you add text fields named for the specific CGI variables whose data you want to collect. See the section "Returning Information with CGI Variables" in Chapter 7, "Designing Forms for an Interactive Web Site."

Because the user submitting the form will not be filling in these fields manually, you should mark them hidden. To do so, open the Field Properties box for each such field. Go to Hide When panel by clicking the "window shade" tab. Mark the field Hide When Editing.

The CGI variable names that InterNotes Web Publisher recognizes include those in Table 24.4.

Table 24.4   CGI Environment Variables

Auth_Type	Content_Length	Content_Type	Gateway_Interface
HTTP_Accept	HTTP_Referer	HTTP_User_Agent	HTTPS
Path_Info	Path_Translated	Query_String	Remote_Addr
Remote_Ident	Remote_User	Request_Method	Script_Name
Server_Name	Server_Port	Server_Protocol	Server_Software
Server_URL			

Experiment with these to see what each one returns.

From Here...

See especially the User's Guide, Tips and Techniques, Technotes and Troubleshooting, and Web Publisher Samples pages at **http://www.internotes.lotus.com**. If you need a copy of InterNotes Web Publisher, you can download all versions of it from the Lotus InterNotes site at **http://www.internotes.lotus.com**. Also of interest at that Web site:

▶ User's Guide

▶ Tips and Techniques

▶ Technotes and Troubleshooting

▶ Web Publisher Samples

Appendixes

Domino URLs

Browsers use URLs to access the components of Web servers. Domino Web servers recognize a superset of the standard URL syntax that includes references to Notes objects, actions that one can perform on them, and arguments that qualify the actions.

Basic Syntax of a Domino URL

The basic syntax of a Domino URL is as follows:

http://Host/NotesObject[?Action[&Argument...]]

where:

Host is a Domino server, referred to by its DNS host name or its IP address.

NotesObject is a Notes object such as a database, a view, a form, a navigator, a document, and so on.

?Action is the action to be performed on the object. Examples include ?Open, ?OpenDatabase, ?OpenView, ?EditDocument.

&Argument... is one or more qualifiers of the action. Each argument is preceded by an ampersand. An example is **http://Host/Database/View?OpenView &Count=10**. This would open the view referred to by //Host/Database/View and limit it to 10 rows of objects per screen.

About the Host Parameter

Domino URLs never refer to a Domino server by its Notes server name, but always by either its DNS host name or its IP address.

About Notes Objects

You can refer to a Notes database by its file name or its Replica ID.

Example: **http://www.planetnotes.com/home.nsf**

You can refer to other Notes objects by their name, universal ID, or NoteID, or in some cases by special identifiers.

Example: **http://Host/names.nsf/people**

Example: **http://Host/names.nsf/PeopleViewUNID**

Example: **http://Host/names.nsf/PeopleViewNoteID**

Example: **http://Host/names.nsf/$defaultView**

A Notes object's name and universal ID do not change from one replica of a database to another. An object's NoteID is unique within a database but may change from one replica of the database to another. Therefore, under most circumstances, you would prefer to refer to an object by its name or universal ID, not by its NoteID.

An object's universal ID is a 32-digit, hexadecimal number. It is also known as a unique ID and a UNID. An object's NoteID identifies its location within a database.

Special identifiers of Notes objects include $defaultView, $defaultForm, $defaultNav, which retrieve the default object of each type. Another special identifier, $searchForm, retrieves the standard search form for use in initiating a full-text search on a database. Another, $file, retrieves a file from a Notes document. $icon retrieves the database icon. $help retrieves the Using Database document. $about retrieves the About Database document.

If an object name has spaces in it, replace them with plus signs (+). Spaces are illegal in URLs. Example: Refer to the By Date view in a database as: **http://Host/Database/ By+Date**.

If an object name uses a backslash, substitute a forward slash. This situation would arise if a database is in a subdirectory or a view or form is in a submenu.

Example: Refer to c:\notes\data\sub1\filename.nsf as http://Host/sub1/filename.nsf.

Example: Refer to the Public Address Book view Server\Connections as http://Host/ names.nsf/server/connections.

About Actions

Actions can be explicit or implicit. Examples of explicit actions include ?OpenDatabase, ?OpenView, ?EditDocument. Examples of implicit actions include ?Open, ?Edit, ?Delete. If an URL does not specify an action, Domino assumes defaults to ?Open.

About Arguments

Possible Notes Objects include:

Server—However, Domino URLs never refer to servers by their Notes server name, but rather by their DNS host name or their IP address.

Database—Refer to them either by their file name or their Replica ID.

View

Form

Navigator

Agent

Document

Field

Offset(within Field)

SubOffset (such as attachment name)

DatabaseIcon

DatabaseHelp

DatabaseAbout

IconNote

HelpNote

AboutNote

SearchForm

Examples of NotesObjectPath include the following:

Server

Server/**Database**

Server/Database/**DatabaseIcon**

Server/Database/**IconNote/Field/Offset**

Server/Database/**DatabaseAbout**

Server/Database/**AboutNote/Field/Offset**

Server/Database/**View**

Server/Database/View/**Document**

Server/Database/View/Document/**Field/Offset**

Server/Database/View/Document/Field/Offset/**SubOffset**

Server/Database/View/$searchForm

Server/Database/**Form**

Server/Database/Form/**Field/Offset**

Server/Database/Form/Field/Offset/**SubOffset**

Server/Database/**Navigator**

Server/Database/Navigator/**Field/Offset**

Server/Database/Agent

Ways to identify NotesObjects include:

Server=	**Nothing**
Database=	/directory/fileName.nsf
View=	NoteID|NoteUNID|Name|$defaultView
Form=	NoteID|NoteUNID|Name|$defaultForm
Navigator	NoteID|NoteUNID|Name|$defaultNav
Agent=	NoteID|NoteUNID|Name
Document=	NoteID|NoteUNID
Field=	Name
Offset=	x.y
SubOffset=	Name
DatabaseIcon=	$icon
DatabaseHelp=	$help

A

DatabaseAbout=	$about
IconNote=	NoteID
HelpNote=	NoteID
AboutNote=	NoteID
SearchForm=	$searchForm

Possible Actions include:

Nothing
ImplicitAction
ExplicitAction

ImplicitActions include:

Open
Create (documents only)
Edit (documents only)
Save (documents only)
Delete (documents only)
Search (views only)

Possible ExplicitActions include:

```
OpenServer
OpenDatabase
OpenView
OpenForm
OpenNavigator
OpenAgent
OpenDocument
OpenElement (such as attachments)
CreateDocument (Form Post Action only)
EditDocument
SaveDocument (Form Post Action only)
Delete Document
SearchView
```

Possible Arguments include:

Start(OpenView)
Count(OpenView)
Expand(OpenView)
ExpandView(OpenView)
Collapse(OpenView)
CollapseView(OpenView)
FieldElemType(OpenElement)
FieldElemFormat(OpenElement)
SearchForm(Open the search form)
Query(SearchView)
OldSearchQuery
SearchMax(SearchView)
SearchWV(SearchView)
SearchOrder
SearchThesaurus
ParentUNID

$$ Web Forms and Fields

B

The following are special Domino-reserved fields used in Web applications.

Field name	Value
$$ViewBody	"ViewName" or a formula that resolves to "ViewName"
$$ViewList	None
$$NavigatorBody	"NavigatorName" or a formula $$ that resolves to "NavigatorName"
$$Return	A text message or a formula that computes a message a user sees when he submits a form
$$HTMLHead	A formula that computes the Head tag information
$$QueryOpenAgent	"AgentName" or a formula that resolves to "AgentName"
$$QuerySaveAgent	"AgentName" or a formula that resolves to "AgentName"

The $$ Forms Used in Web Applications

For information on using some of these forms, see Chapter 10.

Form Name	Requires the Field	Remarks
$$ViewTemplateDefault	$$ViewBody	Acts as the default form (template) for views on the Web.
$$ViewTemplate for *viewname*	$$Viewbody	Where *viewname* is the alias (preferred) or view name, serves as the form (template) used to display that view.
$$NavigatorTemplateDefault	$$NavigatorBody	Serves as the default form (template) used to display navigators.
$$NavigatorTemplate for *navigatorname*	$$NavigatorBody	Where *navigatorname* is the navigator name, serves as the default form (template) used to display that navigator.
$$SearchTemplateDefault	$$ViewBody	Serves as the default form (template) for search results on the Web.
$$SearchTemplateDefault for *viewname*	$$ViewBody	Where *viewname* is the view name, serves as the default form (template) for search results for a view.
$$Search(alias)		If you create a form with the alias $$Search, Domino will use it whenever a Web user initiates a search on a Domino server. If you create no such form, Domino uses the file search.htm in the icons directory.

Domino Resources

Visit these Web sites for help and information on Domino:

http://www.domino.lotus.com

This is *the* Domino resource center, developed and supported by Lotus and by the Domino team. Here, you can find downloads, discussion databases, and FAQs. This is the first site you should go to when searching for information on Domino. Here you'll find the latest version news, lots of template and sample databases, and very active discussion databases. Most of what you need to know about Domino can be found here. If the information is not at this site, it probably doesn't exist. From this site, you can link to Domino sites around the world and experience what others are creating with their Domino servers.

http://www.lotus.com

This is the Lotus home page. You can find links here to the Domino site as well as the entire Lotus site. Services, important press releases, product information, partner information, support, and purchasing information are here, or can be reached from this site.

http://www.notes.net

Supported by Iris Associates, this is a great place for technical support and information.
A technical discussion database can be found here as well as FAQs about Notes and Domino.

http://lotus.com/devtools

This is the propeller-head section of the Lotus site. Here, you can find tools APIs, whitepapers, redbooks, and technical discussion databases.

http://www.support.lotus.com

The Lotus support information site, this site includes information about all Lotus products. Here you can find answers and phone numbers and you can search the KnowledgBase, which contains technical information on Lotus products.

http://lotus.com/partners

If you are thinking about becoming a Lotus Business Partner, visit the partner site to learn about qualifying. This is also a very good source for locating Business Partners to help you with your Domino site.

Installing Windows NT Server 4.0

With the release of Domino server powered by Notes, Lotus has made some significant advances to collaborating Microsoft's Windows NT with Lotus Notes. Just a couple of these new features include logging in to Windows NT and Notes simultaneously, and including Notes log statistics in the NT Event Viewer.

The focus of this appendix is to give you an easy step-by-step guide to installing the fastest growing server operating system today, Windows NT. You'll also learn how to integrate some of the new Notes features with Windows NT. But first, let's go through some initial planning steps before you actually install NT server.

Pre-Installation Steps

As with all installations of software, it's always a good idea to go through some initial planning and preparation before you get in over your head and have to reinstall something over and over again. Windows NT is no exception to this rule, it's a good idea to take a little extra time with Windows NT because it's a networked application. Accidentally dropping a user off your network is probably not a problem you want to deal with. The primary warm-up steps that you need to be concerned with are:

▶ **What are the hardware considerations to be aware of for the Windows NT server?**

Probably the most common mistake many administrators make is installing Windows NT on a system with not enough memory or too little hard drive space. In this section, you'll learn what the minimum requirements are for a successful install as well as what pitfalls to avoid when choosing hardware.

▶ **What file system do I use?**

Windows NT offers the use of three separate file systems; FAT (File Allocation Tables), HPFS (high-performance file system), NTFS (NT file system). You'll get a solid heads-up on choosing the right file system for your server and the differences between the three file systems.

Caution
The OS/2 HPFS (High Performance System) is no longer supported by Windows NT 4.0 server. However, you can still access HPFS files by a Windows NT 3.x server which may be connected to your network.

▶ **What will be the Security Role of the server?**

The Security Role the Windows NT Domain will play is an integral part of your server installation. You'll learn the difference between a PDC, BDC, and a plain server in your NT Domain.

▶ **What protocol do I use?**

Windows NT supports the use of three protocols; TCP/IP, NetBUI, NWLink. This appendix will focus on TCP/IP, since it's the most widely used protocol in the computer industry today. As you may know, the IP portion of TCP/IP stands for *Internet Protocol,* which has virtually become a standard in the computer industry.

Understanding Hardware Requirements for Windows NT Server

The great thing about Windows NT is that it can be installed on almost any type of system, with many different types of configurations. The three most widely used system architectures are the Intel x86, Power PC, and the DEC Alpha RISC processors. You could have a multitude of configurations with as much memory and hard drive space as you want. Unfortunately, that can get quite expensive so it's recommended to stay within reasonable limits. Table D.1 shows some typical hardware configurations for Windows NT servers.

Table D.1   Windows NT Hardware Configurations

Processor	Memory and Hard Disk Space
Intel x86	120MB RAM and 16GB hard disk.
Intel Pentium	64MB RAM and 8GB hard disk.
Power PC	240MB RAM and 32GB hard disk.
Alpha RISC	164MB RAM and 20GB hard disk.

The list can go on and on, but what's important is what's right for your situation. Obviously the more users that will access your system, the more memory and hard disk space will be required. There is no right or wrong hardware configuration, but a minimum configuration should include at least a 486 processor with 16MB of RAM or better. You should reserve at least 125MB of hard disk space for the operating system and any additional space to install your applications. The 386 processor was formerly an option but is currently not supported by Windows NT 4.0.

D

Choosing a File System

The file system selection portion of the install will require you to select one of two file systems. The choices will be:

▶ **FAT file system**

The FAT (File Allocation Tables) file system is the file system of choice for DOS. If you plan on using a good part of your hard disk space on DOS applications and you are not concerned about security on your files, then FAT is the file system for you.

▶ **NTFS (NT file system)**

The NT file system is the file system of choice when installing Windows NT. It provides full support for Windows NT security and supports the use of long filenames. The NT file system will also read any FAT or HPFS files, but the reverse is not true.

The focus of this appendix section will be on installing NTFS as the file system to encourage optimum security for your Notes databases as well keeping other important Notes files secure.

Choosing a Security Role for the Windows NT Server

Similar to Lotus Notes, Windows NT is organized into a Domain structure. The Windows NT Domain is basically a structure composed of other Windows NT servers, all sharing one administrative database. The NT Domain structure simplifies administration by allowing the use of one NT server to administer all the servers under a particular Domain. The three types of security roles in a Windows NT Domain are:

▶ **Primary Domain Controller (PDC)**

The PDC stores and maintains the main copy of the domain database. A PDC must be created when installing the first NT server in the domain.

▶ **Backup Domain Controller (BDC)**

Stores a backup copy of the domain account database. The BDC resides in a domain under a PDC.

▶ **Server**

A server in a Windows NT domain does not store a copy of the domain account database. It simply resides in a Windows NT domain as another server.

You might ask "Why do I need to know all this, this is going to be used as a Notes server, not a file server?" That's a good question, but it's still important to understand the differences in security roles since it can be quite cumbersome to go back and reinstall NT if you decide to manage files and login accounts in the future. A good choice here would be to install Windows NT on a partition using the FAT file system and create another partition for the Notes databases using NTFS. The main idea is to keep your Notes databases secure on the network and still have the ability to use a DOS based file system if needed.

Installing Windows NT

Now that you've got a good handle on what's required before you install Windows NT, let's jump right into the actual installation. The first step in the installation is to determine what media will be used to copy the files from.

 Note

Windows NT can be installed from a CD-ROM, a network server, or floppy disks. The CD-ROM installation is the most widely used and will be the focus of this appendix section.

If you purchased a Windows NT disk package, it should have come with a CD and three floppies. Most servers purchased today come with an internal CD-ROM drive already installed and probably the easiest to implement. Follow these steps to begin your Windows NT install from a CD-ROM:

1. Insert the floppy disk labeled "Setup Boot Disk" in drive A:. Also, insert the CD into your CD-ROM drive of your computer.

 Note

To create floppy disks in the installation, you can type `d:\i386\winnt /ox` from a DOS prompt. The CD-ROM drive letter may be different depending upon your hard disk partitions. You will also need a fair amount of extra hard disk space on your server since temporary files are copied on to the hard disk for use at install. See Figure D.1.

Fig. D.1

The dialog box for creating Windows NT setup disks requires the use of three formatted blank disks.

2. Reboot or turn on the computer.
3. Insert Disk #2 when prompted. You should at this point notice that Windows NT is loading all the drivers necessary for the installation.

The next screen is the Windows NT Server Setup screen. You will be prompted to make one of four choices:

▶ To learn more about Windows NT Setup before continuing, press F1.

▶ To set up Windows NT now, press ENTER.

▶ To repair a damaged Windows NT version 4.00 installation, press R.

▶ To quit setup without installing Windows NT, press F3.

It's a good idea to hit F1 to read more about the Windows NT installation if you are not too familiar with it. You also may need to continue your install at a later time, which will require you to hit the F3 key and exit the setup.

4. To continue with the installation, press <Enter>.

Next, Windows NT will prompt you to allow setup to detect any mass storage devices such as SCSI adapters or CD-ROM drives. The choices available are to hit <Enter> to allow Windows NT to detect any mass storage devices, or press S to skip the detection. Unless you're really short on time, it's usually a good idea to allow the setup to detect any mass storage devices.

5. Hit <Enter> to continue with the detection of mass storage devices. Insert Disk #3 when prompted. If you still want to skip this step, press S.

At this point, the Windows NT setup will detect any device drivers and show you a list of all the drivers that were found. You will also be prompted to specify any additional drivers with a device support disk or to continue with the setup.

6. Press <Enter> to continue with the setup.

Caution

If Windows NT setup fails in detecting your device drivers, it will be necessary to press S and supply a device driver diskette with the proper drivers to continue setup.

Once all of the device drivers have been properly loaded, the next step in the setup change or accept the hardware/software components which NT has found on your system. Typically, the type of information you'll see will be the type of computer, display, keyboard, and type of mouse.

7. If the hardware/software coincides with your computer, hit <Enter> to accept the list. If you need to make any changes to the selections, scroll up or down and make the change and then hit <Enter> to accept the list.

Anyone who has installed an operating system or almost any network application for that matter will be quite familiar with the next step. If you've made it this far, you'll know it's time to select partitioning information for Windows NT. Setup will show you the available drives and available space where Windows NT can be installed. Depending upon your pre-installation choices, you might see one or several hard disk partitions with varying amounts of free disk space. The Windows NT setup will give you three options for installing Windows NT on your hard disk:

▶ To install Windows NT on the highlighted partition or unpartitioned space, press ENTER.

▶ To create a partition in the unpartitioned space, press C.

▶ To delete the highlighted partition, press D.

8. Select one of the available options to create a new partition or to use an existing partition. Select the partition to install Windows NT and hit <Enter>.

Caution

It's important to partition enough hard disk space for Windows NT and for any applications you may want to install in the future. If not enough space is allocated for your applications you may have to reformat your hard drive and reinstall Windows NT.

Once you've selected the partition where Windows NT will be installed, you'll need to determine what type of file system you'd like to use (refer to pre-installation section earlier in this chapter).

D

Tip

Unless your Windows NT server will be a dual boot PC or security is not an issue, it's recommended to select NTFS as the file system choice.

9. Select the file system choice by hitting <Enter> over the highlighted option.

10. Now you'll need to type a directory where Windows NT will be installed. The default directory is \winnt. You may want to specify a different directory for Windows NT files, but it's recommended to leave the default directory since many applications will reference it in the future.

The final step before setup begins to copy files to your computer is the exhaustive examination of your hard disks. This is where your computer gets to work up a sweat. NT setup will give you a choice of whether to run the examination or to skip it.

11. To run the exhaustive examination hit the <Enter> key. You may also choose to skip the examination by hitting the <Esc> key (the examination may take a few minutes to complete).

12. Once the exhaustive examination of your hard disk(s) is completed, remove any floppy disk from your disk drive and press <Enter> to restart your computer.

Gathering Information About Your Computer

After the computer is restarted you'll be taken to the fun part of the Windows NT setup. If you've ever setup Windows 95, you'll see that these next steps will appear quite familiar. Even if you've never installed Windows, you should now be quite familiar with the graphical user interface of Windows. You'll be presented with the next three parts of the setup which are:

▶ Gathering information about your computer

▶ Installing Windows NT networking

▶ Finishing setup

The first step in installing Windows NT after copying files and restarting your computer is called gathering information about your computer. This portion of the setup requires you to input information such as your name and your company name, product ID, setting a security role, selecting a computer name for your server, and which applications you'd like to install.

1. In the Name and Organization window type in your name and company in the spaces provided. Click Next when finished.

Now you'll need to select what type of license mode will be used when running the server. The two types of licensing options are:

▶ Per Server

▶ Per Seat

The difference between the licensing modes is simple. Per Server mode is licensed by each concurrent connection to the server, whereas Per Client requires a license for each user. So depending upon your company's licensing plan you may have to purchase a license for each client or for each connection to your NT server. If this installation will be used primarily as a Notes server, you probably won't need to purchase many clients licenses.

Caution

It's imperative to properly license your Windows NT server before installation. It is a violation of the law to install Windows NT without a proper license agreement.

2. Select the licensing mode for your Windows NT server by clicking the appropriate radio button and selecting Next or hitting the <Enter> key. Also, if you choose per server, you will also need to indicate the amount of concurrent connections by typing in a number in the space provided.

3. In the Computer Name window, enter a computer name which will identify your server in your windows network.

Note
The Computer Name must be unique within your windows network. You will be prompted to enter a unique name if a duplicate Computer Name is entered.

4. In the Server Type window you'll need to select a security role for your NT server (see pre-installation steps). Select a server type by clicking on the appropriate radio button and hitting the Next button.

Caution
If Backup Domain Controller is selected, you will need to know the name of the Primary Domain Controller which it will connect to.

5. In the Emergency Repair Disk window click Yes or No to create a repair disk. It's usually a good idea to create a repair disk in case you'll need to repair Windows NT at a later date.

Tip
The Windows NT Emergency Repair Disk can be created by running RDISK from a regular DOS prompt or from the Start menu anytime after setup.

The final step in gathering information about your computer is selecting what components you'd like to install to use with Windows NT. The Select Components window will require you to select the components from the left window pane. Once you've checked off what applications to install, press the Next key to proceed to installing the network.

Installing Windows NT Networking

As you know, Windows NT is a networked operating system and will require you to make some decisions about your network cards and protocols. It will be helpful to know some key pieces of information about your network before you continue. Here's some questions you need to answer before you move on:

▶ What type of network will the NT server be connecting to?

▶ What type of Network card is installed in the server?

▶ How is the network configured?

▶ Is TCP/IP an available protocol on the network?

Ask your network administrator if you need help answering these questions.

1. The first step in connecting your Windows NT server to your network is to select the type of network connection you are using. The two check boxes relating to the network connection are: Wired to the network, and Remote Access to the Network. Click the appropriate check box with your mouse and then click Next.

Now Windows NT will do another search on the type(s) of network adapters installed on your system. If you want to skip the search you can click Select from list and manually select an adapter, otherwise click Start Search.

2. The list of network adapters will appear and you'll need to click the adapter to select it. Click Next when finished.

3. Click TCP/IP Protocol in the network protocols window. Click next to continue.

Now take a deep breath because you're getting close to the end of the setup. You're next decision will entail what type of network services you'd like to install. This part may require a little bit of research on your part. However, if you just want to install the basic services and worry about the others later, just leave the current default options checked and click Next to continue. If you know which services you want to install, click Select from list and choose which services to install. Click Next to complete your selections.

4. Finally it's time to begin copying your selections to the computer. Select Next to start copying the files.

Once all of the networking components are installed, you'll need to configure each of the network components separately.

5. From the Microsoft TCP/IP Properties window, type in an IP address for your server and any other pertinent information about your network. You may need to supply a DNS, WINS address, DHCP Relay, or Routing information (see Figure D.2).

6. Click ok when all the information has been supplied.

Windows NT setup will now inform you that it's ready to connect to the network. If all the information you supplied in step 5 is correct, click Next to connect to the network. Otherwise, click Back if you need to change any of the information.

7. If you selected Backup Domain Controller in step 4 of Gathering Information, then you'll now need to type in a Domain name to connect to as well as a user with

administrative rights to add backup domain controllers to the primary domain. If this is a Primary Domain Controller, type in the name of the domain to be used as the Primary Domain Controller. If this is a server, type in the name of the server and a password for the administrator account. Click Next when finished.

Fig. D.2

You will need to specify IP addresses specific to your network environment through the Microsoft TCP/IP Properties window.

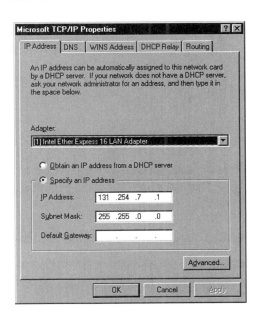

D

Now you're almost home free, the final screen on Finishing Setup will take you through the final steps of the Windows NT setup before you begin networking.

Finishing Setup

After completing gathering information and installing NT networking, you're finally ready to complete the final steps in the Windows NT setup. You should be at the Windows NT Setup window with the finishing setup option auto selected. To complete the setup, select the Finish button.

Setting the Time and Date

The next two steps in the setup will require you to select a time zone and the current date and time. Select your time zone by clicking the map of your location or by selecting the drop down arrow and clicking on your time zone (see Figure D.3). Hit <Enter> to accept your selections.

Fig. D.3

Use the map to set the time zone for your region and the Date/ Time tab to change the date and time of your computer.

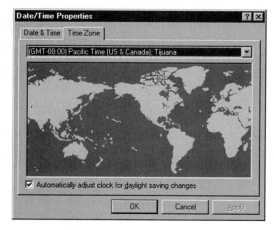

Display Settings

The last step in the setup is setting the display adapter and its settings. Windows NT will automatically detect your display adapter, your job is to select a color palette and desktop area if necessary. Depending upon the display adapter installed on your computer, you may have several options for a color palette (see Figure D.4). Select Test to make sure that your selected settings are displayed properly on your screen. The screen will momentarily switch to test mode and ask you if the bitmap was displayed properly. Select Yes or No depending upon whether your settings were displayed properly or not.

Fig. D.4

Use the Display Properties box to select the monitor display settings for your computer.

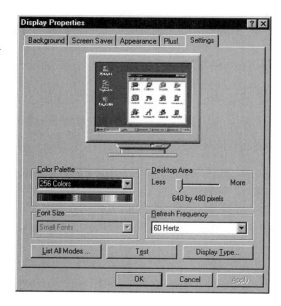

> **Tip**
>
> If the display adapter chosen by the NT setup is not compatible with your system or is not the correct driver, select the Display Type button and change the adapter type manually.

Once you've made all the necessary changes to your display, go ahead and hit Ok. Windows NT setup will accept your settings and save the configuration. The last step is to restart your computer to have the changes go into effect and log in to the server.

Integrating Windows NT with Lotus Notes 4.5

Now that you've got your Windows NT server up and running, let's take a look at some of the ways you can integrate your Notes server with your NT server. Here are some ways you can take advantage of Windows NT to help manage your Notes server:

▶ Install Lotus Notes as a Windows NT service.

▶ Use single password logon to log in to Notes and NT.

▶ Log Notes events into the NT event logger.

Let's see just how easy it is to set up each of these options separately.

Installing the Lotus Notes Server as an NT Service

To make administration easier for Notes gurus, Lotus gives us the option of running the Domino server as a Windows NT service. Why run Domino as an NT service? Well, for one, if the NT server is restarted it won't be necessary for you to also start the Domino server. Also, Windows NT services failures are logged in the NT Event Viewer which makes troubleshooting problems much easier. It's also easy for an administrator to stop and start an NT service from a remote workstation. Just follow these simple steps to install Notes as a Windows NT service:

1. From a \notes command prompt at the NT server, type ntsvinst -c.

2. Hit the <Enter> key.

Now, to enable Lotus Notes to startup automatically when Windows NT server is started, go to the Control Panel, Services program on your NT workspace.

3. Scroll down until you see Lotus Notes in the list of services and click the Startup button (see Figure D.5).

Fig. D.5

Starting the Lotus Notes service started automatically at NT server startup.

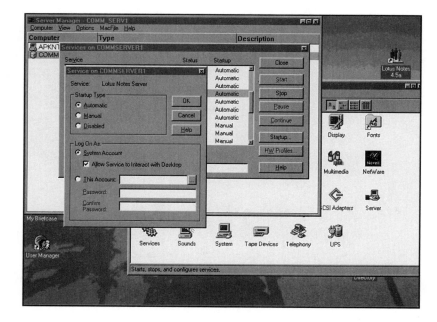

4. Select the Startup Type as automatic and Log on as to System account.
5. Click Ok to accept the settings.

If you want to test out your new Notes service, log out of NT and restart your server. When you log back in you should see that Notes started automatically.

Utilizing Single Password Logon with Notes and Windows NT

Lotus has gone to great lengths to help make the lives of NT and Notes users easier. Another convenient new feature in the new release of Domino server and Notes 4.5 is single logon for Notes and NT. Basically what occurs is when a user logs into their network through NT server or workstation, they are also consecutively logged into Lotus Notes as well. This eliminates the need to log into Notes again. Additionally, if you're like a lot of people, having to remember one less password is a nice advantage in itself.

What's an even a greater advantage to the Notes or NT administrator is that users only need to be created once. Notes gives the certifier the opportunity to create a Windows NT account for the Notes user and vice versa! That could save potentially hours of extra work for anyone who has to administer your network.

The nicest feature of single logon is that if you already setup Lotus Notes as an NT service, you've also setup single logon as well. Since the Notes/NT single logon feature runs as an NT service as does the Domino server, only one install is required to create both services. For a quick review on setting up Notes as an NT service, refer to the previous section on setting up Notes server as an NT service.

Logging Notes Events to the Windows NT Event Logger

To further simplify Notes administration, Lotus has given administrators the ability to log Notes server events to the NT Event Logger process. Then you can view your Notes statistics and NT statistics from the Windows NT Event Viewer. Here's what you need to do:

1. From Notes, open the Statistics and Events database. The database file name is events4.nsf.

2. Click the Event Monitors view and click the Add Event Monitor action button (see Figure D.6).

Fig. D.6

Add an event to log notes statistics to the NT Event viewer.

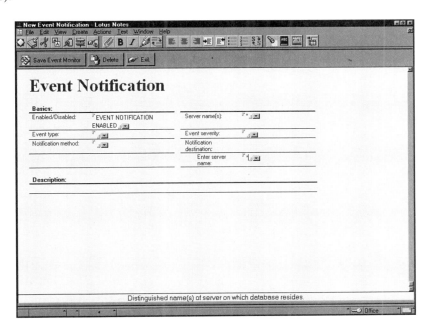

3. Fill in the Event type field with a selected event.

4. Click the drop-down arrow next to the Notification Method field. Select the keyword "Log to NT Event Viewer," (see Figure D.7).

5. Complete the Server Name and the Event severity fields and save the form.

Fig. D.7

*Select the Log to NT
Event Viewer keyword
to log Notes statistics
to the NT Event
Viewer.*

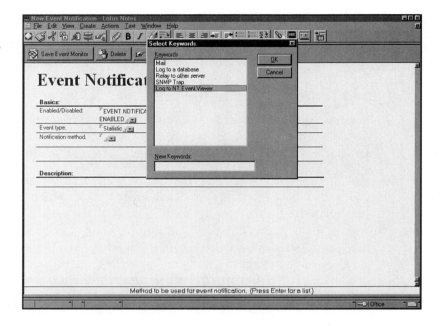

Lotus Add-In Products

L otus has developed NetApps, a series of templates from which you can, by filling in a series of forms, generate a whole, interactive Web application. You don't have to develop the applications or create the databases yourself. Just fill in the forms and NetApps does all the programming for you. The purpose of filling in the forms is so you can customize the resulting applications to your own needs, using your own names and vocabulary.

In essence, what Lotus is trying to accomplish here is to make Notes and the Domino server indispensable to anyone who wants to accomplish anything more elaborate on the Web than simple publishing. By marrying Notes technology to Web technology, Lotus gives you the tools to create powerful, interactive Internet applications with ease. Lotus makes it even easier by offering application generators that do all the work for you! All you have to do is set up Notes and Domino, connect the server to the Internet, and fill out a series of questionnaires. The application generator then creates all the Notes databases for you.

The templates available within the NetApps family include:

Domino.Action

Bundled with Domino server, Domino.Action brings up a full-service Web site, including home page, corporate information pages, user registration database, discussion/feedback, and more. With Domino.Action, you can essentially build an entire Web site in one day. Domino.Action is described in detail in Chapter 17, "Building a Domino Web Site in One Day with Domino Action".

Domino.Broadcast

Domino.Broadcast for PointCast combines the technology of the Domino application Web server with PointCast's I-Server™. The PointCast Network then delivers the enterprise information managed and stored by Domino.

PointCast is a news service. When you use PointCast over an intranet, it provides current news, stock prices, magazine articles, sports scores, weather information, and more to every user on the intranet. Depending on their levels of access and defined roles, users may personalize their news to receive only the types of information they need. Or, based on roles, the intranet can broadcast certain company-specific information to a particular group of users, such as data needed only by managers or supervisors.

Domino.Broadcast provides a framework that links headlines to detailed information, response forms, or document libraries for faster, more productive data gathering and decision making. Working over the foundation of Domino.Action, Domino.Broadcast can also disseminate information to the public via your Web site.

At the time of this printing, the list price for Domino.Broadcast was $1,295 ($1,995 if shipped with Domino Server software). For more information, check **http://domino.lotus.com** or **http://www.lotus.com**.

Domino.Connect

With Domino.Connect, you can incorporate information shared in databases, ERP systems and transaction systems into Domino Web sites and applications. Developers can create applications with either browser or Notes client-user interfaces to allow users to update databases or create complex transactions with the back-end system.

Developers can bring enterprises to the Internet in three ways:

▶ **Relational databases**. Domino.Connect includes NotesPump 2.0, a data distribution server that offers high volume data exchange and synchronization with DB2, Oracle, Lotus Notes, ASCII/Text, Sybase, and ODBC databases. LotusScript Data Object provides real-time data access via ODBC access to external databases. The Oracle plug-in provides real-time data access via Oracle's native protocols.

▶ **Transactional systems**. With Domino.Connect, developers can access more than 18 different platforms and systems via the MQSeries link plug-in from IBM (including CICS, IMS, HP-UX, Tandem, and Digital systems).

▶ **Applications systems**. Domino.Connect provides direct access to SAP's R/3 via the LotusScript BASIC plug-in, which allows bidirectional data exchange and is capable of both synchronous and asynchronous activity.

Sample applications packaged with Domino.Connect include a human resources task management application and a catalog for internal procurement or supply chain order management.

Projected list price for Domino.Connect was $7,995 (including maintenance) at the time of this printing. Check **http://www.lotus.com** for more current information.

Domino.Merchant

Domino.Merchant builds on the Domino.Action application to create a Web site geared for marketing and sales. Using the SiteCreator template, the application sets up a product catalog database, workflow documents, and site visitor registration.

SiteCreator generates a set of databases, each with a series of templates to create documents for that database. By supplying company information, providing graphics files, and selecting from preset designs, users get a fill-in-the-blanks application. They only have to provide specific information on the database pages. After the Notes databases are created, product and workflow information can be entered via the Web or through Notes.

To accept orders and process payments over the Web, Domino.Merchant incorporates third-party software. Taxware calculates sales taxes based on shipping and delivery points, and on taxable and non-taxable items. It also provides audit files for tax collection reporting purposes. To process credit card sales, Domino.Merchant works with CyberCash. Merchants set up CyberCash accounts through their banks, and users set up individual accounts with CyberCash where their credit card information is stored. User account information is encrypted. The merchants must provide a merchant ID to receive payment via CyberCash. This allows secure transactions via the Web.

At the time of this printing, the list price for Domino.Merchant was $1,295 ($1,995 if shipped with Domino Server software). More information is available at **http://www.lotus.com**. You can get more information about CyberCash at **http://www.cybercash.com**.

E

InterNotes News

nterNotes News is perhaps one of Lotus's earliest products connecting Notes to the Internet. Yet it is virtually a forgotten product. That is probably because the UseNet News Groups themselves, although hardly dying on the vine, have been largely overshadowed by the phenomenal growth of the World Wide Web. Certainly connecting Notes to the Web has been Lotus's primary focus, with the release first of InterNotes Web Publisher, then Domino Web Publisher and, now, Domino 4.5. Other Internet connectivity thrusts such as InterNotes News and the SMTP Mail Gateway and the SMTP/MIME MTA have been pale by comparison with the energy and attention Lotus has paid to Domino and the Web.

The UseNet News Groups are a series of Internet servers, known as News servers, that store databases of messages, known as "articles." News servers communicate with users and other news servers via a communications protocol known as NNTP or Network News Transfer Protocol. The articles in News databases are in reality just messages that members of the newsgroups compose offline and then submit to the servers. Other users can then "subscribe" to a newsgroup, which is meant that they can connect to a News server that hosts a particular newsgroup and receive a listing from the server of all the articles currently stored on the server for the particular newsgroup. The subscriber can then download the text of any articles that look interesting, read them, and then reply to them if they want.

If you haven't realized it yet, newsgroups are simply discussion groups. Users utilize a special type of program known as a news reader to list the available articles, read them, and reply to them.

Because newsgroups are discussion groups, they lend themselves to capture by Notes databases. In fact, that is exactly what InterNotes News does to them. It captures selected newsgroup discussions, then presents them to Notes users as Notes discussion databases. By reading them as Notes databases, Notes users can follow the discussion threads more easily than they might if they used standard news readers. Also, the Notes databases can be full-text indexed, so Notes users can find information in them more effectively than most subscribers can. Finally, Notes users can reply to News articles in Notes. The Notes news server will then convert and submit Notes users' replies back to the news servers.

InterNotes News consists of a server add-in called INNEWS, and database design templates that can be used as the basis for any subscribed newsgroups. The Notes administrator loads INNEWS on the News server and prepares several configuration forms, including:

▶ News Gateway form—which defines which Domino server will be the News Gateway server

▶ News Server form—which defines to which News server(s) the News Gateway server should connect

▶ News Connection form—which defines how often to connect to the News server

▶ News Database form—which defines which newsgroups should be retrieved into Notes databases

InterNotes News 1.0 was designed to work with Notes Release 3.x servers. InterNotes News 2.0 is designed to work with Notes 4.x servers and clients. InterNotes 2.0 was released into widespread beta in May 1996 but, as of February 1997, apparently has never been released from beta. There is a good chance it never will come out of beta, as, at Lotusphere 97, there was talk of incorporating the NNTP protocol directly into the Domino server. That would make sense, as it follows the same pattern Lotus has followed with all the other Internet protocols. If Lotus does do this, InterNotes News, which is essentially a gateway product, would go the way of the other Lotus gateways—the InterNotes Web Publisher and the SMTP Gateway. Domino with the NNTP protocol incorporated, along with all the other Internet protocols, would truly be an integrated Internet application server.

Domino Service Provider Applications

Lotus Notes has been a powerful, enabling tool for many organizations. However, organizations using it have always had to be able to support an infrastructure of servers, clients, and experts. This infrastructure represents a barrier to the flow of the benefits of Notes to small organizations and to small, short-term working groups within larger organizations. Domino Service Provider Applications (or, simply, Domino SPA) are intended to break through that barrier by making prebuilt but customizable Notes applications immediately available to groups of any size or composition for whatever periods of time necessary.

Lotus Notes is a tool to enable groups of people to work together more effectively. It
is a set of essential building blocks that people can apply to their specific organizing
problems. The building blocks include an object store technology, a set of tools for
developing applications that leverage this technology, and a set of tools for delivering the applications to users. The object store technology is the Notes storage facility, or .nsf file, and the programs that know how to put information into and extract it from the .nsf file. The application development tools include a whole array of tools for building useful applications based on the .nsf file. The delivery tools include the server back-end where the data is stored and the client front-ends where users access the data.

Lotus Notes can provide a whole infrastructure for managing communication, collaboration, and workflow within an organization and between organizations and it has, in fact, transformed the way whole organizations of people work. It has helped organizations to streamline the flow of work and information through the organization. It has helped to flatten the structure of the organization as work and information have flowed more effortlessly.

But Notes stores information in servers and someone must manage them. Users access Notes data via client software. Someone must install and maintain that software. Finally, someone must master the art of applying Notes to the needs of the people working with it; that is, someone must write and maintain Notes applications. For large organizations that already maintain staffs of people with this sort of expertise, adding Notes to the mix is a relatively straightforward problem and relatively inexpensive. For smaller organizations, supporting yet another server technology and yet another set of programmers can be a heavy expense to bear. For very small organizations, Notes becomes a prohibitively expensive addition, no matter how much benefit it may bring.

Domino SPA is a version of Notes intended to address this problem. Domino SPAs are "rentable" Notes applications. That is, they reside on Domino servers maintained by professional server maintenance organizations, that is, by Notes Public Network providers and Internet Service Providers. Anyone can write these applications, including especially the small army of Notes application developers represented by the Lotus Business Partner community. The applications are designed to be easy to set up by a particular group for their particular needs. They are intended to be easily accessible to the group because they reside on publicly available servers and can be used with a Web browser. And they are intended to be rented instead of bought.

So, for example, if I want to put together a small group of people to work on a short-term project, we can rent one or more Notes applications to help us work together on the project. We will access the applications on the World Wide Web using off-the-shelf browsers. We can set them up from our browsers to meet the particular needs of our group. Only the people working on the project will have access to the apps. The cost will be determined ahead of time and predictable. When we are finished, the service provider will close and archive everything.

The design of the applications and the system in which they reside is such that there is very little maintenance overhead. The customer can select, pay for, set up, configure, and begin using applications from within a Web browser with little or no interaction between the customer and the designer of the app or the people running the back-end system. Usage of the app is tracked and billed automatically, and payments received are automatically divvied up between the service provider and the owner of the application.

Domino SPA consists of several components:

▶ SPA.Host

▶ Domino SPA Developer Kit

▶ Some prebuilt applications, including Domino.Collaboration, Domino.Action SP, and Domino.Merchant SP.

First, there is a hosting environment called SPA.Host. It runs on Domino Server 4.5 and Domino Advanced Services. It provides the platform on which everything runs. It includes a "storefront" application where the service provider would display the applications available for rental. It includes tools for tying it to a service provider's back-end billing and management systems. It includes system management services so a service provider could monitor and balance the workload on the servers. And it includes the Domino SPA SP Integration Kit, which is an API and specifications for tying applications to service providers usage tracking and billing systems.

Second, the Domino SPA Developer Kit includes tools that allow developers to create Service Provider Applications. It includes an application programming interface (API), standard forms and subforms, sample code, and validation tools. For a Notes application to work as a service provider application, it must be instantiable, so that multiple end users can run multiple, unrelated instances of it; it must conform to the needs of SPA.Host, which is to say, for example, that it can be moved from server to server without breaking; and it must be billable within a service provider's billing models.

The API is intended to be language independent and to provide application access to SPA.Host functions. Release 1.0 will support LotusScript. Later releases will support Java and C++.

Third, Lotus is building three applications:

▶ Domino.Collaboration—Core group collaboration functions, including threaded discussions, file and document libraries, project calendars and project scheduling, project and task management applications

▶ Domino.Action SP—a tool for designing, creating, and maintaining a Web site, all from within a Web browser

▶ Domino.Merchant SP—a Web-based store or product catalog, with order tracking, payment processing, and customer record maintenance tools

Domino.Action SP and Domino.Merchant SP are service-provider versions of Domino.Action and Domino.Merchant. Where Domino.Action and Domino.Merchant are for stand-alone Domino servers and are licensed for one site per server, the SP versions of these programs are licensed so that service providers can rent sites to multiple customers and run them across an array of clustered servers.

Domino SPA benefits the end user in a variety of ways. First, it extends the power of Notes to small businesses that wouldn't otherwise be able to justify the overhead of Notes. Second, it makes Notes functionality available to any group that needs it quickly

G

or for a short period of time; say, over a weekend. Third, it represents a way for an organization considering Lotus Notes to get its toes wet before plunging in all the way. All in all, Domino SPA represents a very interesting direction for Notes to take, as well as an intriguing possibility for Web visibility for the small company that wants to provide a Web presence to a client base (or potential client base) with minimal effort.

Index

Symbols

X-Y-Z

Check out Que® Books on the World Wide Web
http://www.quecorp.com

As the biggest software release in computer history, Windows 95 continues to redefine the computer industry. Click here for the latest info on our Windows 95 books

Make computing quick and easy with these products designed exclusively for new and casual users

Examine the latest releases in word processing, spreadsheets, operating systems, and suites

The Internet, The World Wide Web, CompuServe®, America Online®, Prodigy® —it's a world of ever-changing information. Don't get left behind!

Find out about new additions to our site, new bestsellers and hot topics

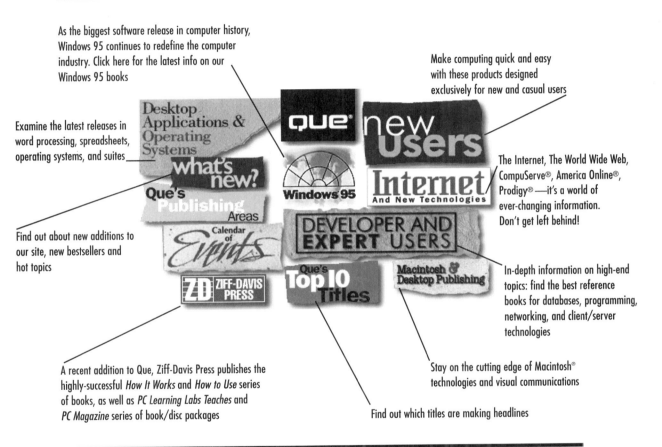

In-depth information on high-end topics: find the best reference books for databases, programming, networking, and client/server technologies

A recent addition to Que, Ziff-Davis Press publishes the highly-successful *How It Works* and *How to Use* series of books, as well as *PC Learning Labs Teaches* and *PC Magazine* series of book/disc packages

Stay on the cutting edge of Macintosh® technologies and visual communications

Find out which titles are making headlines

With 6 separate publishing groups, Que develops products for many specific market segments and areas of computer technology. Explore our Web Site and you'll find information on best-selling titles, newly published titles, upcoming products, authors, and much more.

- Stay informed on the latest industry trends and products available
- Visit our online bookstore for the latest information and editions
- Download software from Que's library of the best shareware and freeware

Before using any of the software on this disc, you need to install the software you plan to use. If you have problems with this CD-ROM, please contact Macmillan Technical Support at (317) 581-3833. We can be reached by e-mail at **support@mcp.com** or by CompuServe at GO QUEBOOKS.

Read this Before Opening Software

By opening this package, you are agreeing to be bound by the following:

This software is copyrighted and all rights are reserved by the publisher and its licensers. You are licensed to use this software on a single computer. You may copy the software for backup or archival purposes only. Making copies of the software for any other purpose is a violation of United States copyright laws. THIS SOFTWARE IS SOLD AS IS, WITHOUT WARRANTY OF ANY KIND, EITHER EXPRESSED OR IMPLIED, INCLUDING BUT NOT LIMITED TO THE IMPLIED WARRANTIES OF MERCHANTABILITY AND FITNESS FOR A PARTICULAR PURPOSE. Neither the publisher nor its dealers and distributors nor its licensers assume any liability for any alleged or actual damages arising from the use of this software. (Some states do not allow exclusion of implied warranties, so the exclusion may not apply to you.)

The entire contents of this disc and the compilation of the software are copyrighted and protected by United States copyright laws. The individual programs on the disc are copyrighted by the authors or owners of each program. Each program has its own use permissions and limitations. To use each program, you must follow the individual requirements and restrictions detailed for each. Do not use a program if you do not agree to follow its licensing agreement.

Planet.domino

Planet
.domino

- ♣**Home**
- ▼**Search Site**
- ●Simple Search
- ●Advanced Search
- ▼**Discussions**
- ●InterFusion's Discussion
- ●Domino Discussion
- ●Weblicator Discussion
- ▼**Knowledge**
- ●Notes Knowledge Base
- ●cc:Mail Knowledge Base
- ●SmartSuite Knowledge Base
- ▼**Help**
- ●Notes R4.5 Help
- ●Notes R4.5 Admin Help
- ●Domino R1.5 User Guide
- ●Notes R4.5 Migration
- ▼**Partners**
- ●US Partner Catalog
- ●World Wide Catalog
- ▼**Domino.Apps**
- ●Domino.Action
- ▼**More**
- ●Mobile Survivor's Guide

Planet.domino

Planet Domino is the
web site designed for this book,
**"The Professional Developers Guide
to Domino 4.5"**.

Planet Domino is a collaborative effort by **InterFusion** and the authors of this book, **Jane Calabria** and **Rob Kirkland**.

The Beginning

The Planet is being developed to provide a one-stop answer goldmine for Lotus Domino and Lotus Notes users and developers. It's life begins by collecting knowledge and information from various Domino sources. As Planet Domino grows and thrives, we hope that a new form of "life" develops, specifically a new way to share information, ideas, and knowledge.

To start with, we have collected several useful databases and wrapped them all together with a Site-wide search feature. You will recognize some of these databases. Our intention is to add original content as well including 'tips and tricks', help guides, articles, an on-line book store, and more. We also plan to add new features that will make using and finding answers about Domino easier.

Help us Grow

Our hope is that Planet Domino will grow into a place where individuals or organizations can go to gather and share information about Domino. To do that, however, we need your help. We are asking you - - both users and Business Partners - - to get involved by providing more content. We are looking for links, examples, success stories, questions, comments, products, technical information, resumes, job postings, etc. If it relates to Domino, it should be on the Planet.

Your ROAD to Knowledge

Inter Fusion

Domino and Notes
software development and consulting

InterFusion is a Lotus Premium Business Partner that specializes in Lotus Domino, Notes and Phone Notes software development and consulting.

- **Domino web site development**
  Develop a custom web site using Lotus Domino for the Internet or your InTRAnet.

- **Domino.Action**
  Custom template development and integration with Domino.Action.

- **Domino.Merchant**
  Deploy electronic commerce applications.

- **Domino.Broadcast**
  Broadcast corporate news via PointCast.

- **Notes development**
  Develop groupware applications for Notes clients.

- **Workflow**
  Develop Domino web and Notes based workflow applications.

- **Experience**

InterFusion has been working with Lotus Notes and Internet technology for over 2 years. We introduced the industry's first Notes based web hosting service in 1995, and put the first Domino web server on the Internet (other then Lotus) in June 1996.

- **Certified Professionals**
  We offer software development and consulting services provided by our staff of Certified Lotus Professionals, and certified network professionals.

InterFusion, Inc.
510 Third Avenue • Cherry Hill, NJ 08002
Voice: 1.609.663.7662 • Fax: 1.609.663.4485
Internet Web: www.interfusion.com
Internet E-mail: info@interfusion.com • Notes Net E-mail: info@interfusion@notes net